La Sylphide
Paris 1832 and beyond

La Sylphide

Paris 1832 and beyond

Marian Smith

DANCE
BOOKS

First published 2012
Dance Books Ltd,

Copyright © 2012 Marian Smith

ISBN 978-1-85-273156-4
A CIP catalogue record for this title
is available from the British Library

Printed in Great Britain

For Jack

Contents

Figures

4.1 Two Doodles from the Paris Opéra Violin Score. Mat. 19 [302 (26) p. 71 and 77. Bibliothèque nationale de France. By permission.
4.2 The Musical Form of Act One Scene ii. Form of opening scene. Note that t = transition.
4.3 Witch theme, 'à la Paganini', from Bartholomin violin rehearsal score, Act Two scene iv, page 146. Private collection.
4.4 Paris Opéra Violin Score Showing Re-use and Combination of Themes, Mat. 19 [302 (26), p. 52, Act I scene iv. Bibliothèque nationale de France. By permission.

6.1 August Malmström, *Älvalek* (*Elf-Play*, 1866), copyright the Nationalmuseum, Stockholm. By permission.
6.2 Nils Blommér, *Ängsälvor* (*Meadow Elves*, 1850), copyright the Nationalmuseum, Stockholm. By permission. Unfortunately for the distant observer on horseback, a few minutes spent watching an elf circle translated into the passage of many years in the human world.
6.3 Junker Ove surrounded by elf maidens in *Et Folkesagn*. Lithograph from the first published piano reduction of the ballet, ca. 1854.
6.4 Thomas Lund as James, surrounded by sylphs in Nikolaj Hübbe's 2003 Danish Royal Ballet production of *Sylphiden*. Photograph copyright Martin Mydtskov Rønne. By permission.

7.1 Herman Severin Løvenskiold (1815-1870). Drawing by L.A. Smith, 1843. The Museum of National History, Frederiksborg Castle, Hillerød. By permission.

8.1 Fanny Cerrito in *La Silfide* by Cortesi, colored lithograph by Roberto Focosi, Milan, ?1841. The New York Public Library for the Performing Arts / Jerome Robbins Dance Division, Cia Fornaroli Collection. By permission.
8.2 Flora Fabbri Bretin in *La Silfide* at the Ducale Teatro in Parma. Lithograph by Augusto Baritz, 1843. The New York Public Library for the Performing Arts / Jerome Robbins Dance Division, Cia Fornaroli Collection. By permission. (n.d.)
8.3 Drawing by C. Gallina of Sofia Fuoco in *La Silfide* at the Teatro alla Scala. (n.d.) Teatro alla Scala. By permission.
8.4 'Les Sylphides', Figurine Liebig, serie 866, ca 1895-1905. Collection of Ornella di Tondo.

9.1 Model of the original Act Two set by Ciceri for *La Sylphide*. Photo used by permission of Ivor Guest.

12.1 Information given in a programme from the first Russian Season,1909.

Musical examples

Notes on contributors

Erik Aschengreen created the first university dance education programme in Denmark at the University of Copenhagen, and directed it until his retirement in 2000. Between 1964-2005 he was dance critic at the daily newspaper *Berlingske Tidende*; has also served as lecturer at the Royal Danish Ballet School. Among the many volumes he has written or edited are *Etudes* (1970), *The Beautiful Danger* (1974), *Balletbogen (The Ballet Book*, 1982, re-vised edition 1992), *Jean Cocteau and the Dance* (1986), *Der går dans (The Dance is on: The Royal Danish Ballet 1948-1998*, 1998), *Harald Lander: His Life and Ballets* (2009), and *Forført af balletten (Seduced by the dance*, 2011). In 2002 he was presented with the Festschrift *Of Another World: Dancing between Dream and Reality* (ed. Monna Dithmer) and in 2010 was awarded the 'Life for Dance' Lifetime Achievement at the International Ballet Festival. He is currently at work on a book on John R. Johnsen's ballet photographs, to be published in 2012.

Alexander Bennett (1929-2003) left a career in the Foreign Office in 1951 to join Ballet Rambert – where his roles included that of James in *La Sylphide* – and later danced with the Sadler's Wells Theatre Ballet, where he played, for instance, Siegfried in *Swan Lake*, Florimund in *The Sleeping Beauty*, Franz in *Coppélia*, the Poet in Frederick Ashton's *Apparitions* and the Husband in Kenneth MacMillan's *The Invitation*. After his official retirement from the stage, he served as ballet master with companies in Brazil, South Africa, Scotland, and the United States. Returning to Scotland in 2001, he per-formed the role of Drosselmeyer in a touring production of *The Nutcracker* he staged for Ballet West in Argyll, and at the time of his death was preparing a production of *Swan Lake* for the same company. He was also writing books on Marie Rambert and on *La Sylphide* (the forerunner of the present volume).

Ornella Di Tondo holds degrees in ethnomusicology and history from the University of Rome ('La Sapienza'), and is a performer, teacher, historian, and director of historical and ethnic dances. She served as Vice-president of the Italian Association of Research in Dance (AIRDanza) from 2004-2010. Among the volumes she has written or edited are *Il linguaggio del corpo: Storia della danza (Body Language: The History of Dance*, 1990), *La censura sui balli teatrali nella Roma dell'Ottocento (Censorship of Theatrical Dance in Nineteenth-century Rome*, 2008), *Corpi danzanti. Culture, tradizioni, identità (Dancing Bodies: Culture, Traditions, Identity*, with Immacolata Giannuzzi and Sergio Torsello, 2009) and *La danza fuori dalla scena. Cultura, media, educazione (Dance outside the stage: Culture, media, education*, with Alessandro Pontremoli and Francesco Stoppa, 2010). She is a Researcher in Dance History and Italian folk dances at the Università G. d'Annunzio-Chieti.

Matilda Ann Butkas Ertz, who teaches at the University of Louisville, is a recent recipient of the John M. Ward Fellowship in Dance and Music for the Theatre for study at the Harvard Theatre Collection on the choreography and music of the ballets of Antonio Pallerini. She contributed a chapter on Balanchine to the *Cambridge Companion to Ballet* (2007), and her Ph.D. dissertation,' Nineteenth-Century Italian Ballet Music Before National Unification: Sources, Style, and Context', was completed in 2010 at the University of Oregon.

Ivor Guest, who studied law at Trinity College Cambridge and is a solicitor by profession, has published more than thirty books on ballet, including four on the history of the Paris Opéra, biographies of Fanny Cerrito, Fanny Elssler, Jules Perrrot, and Adeline Genée, and translations of writings of Théophile Gautier and Arthur St.-Léon. His archival work in Paris was instrumental in the Royal Ballet's 1960 revival of *La Fille mal gardée*. He also served as chairman of the Royal Academy of Dance from 1963 to 1993, and was secretary and then trustee of the Radcliffe Trust (about which he wrote *Dr. John Radcliffe and his Trust*, 1991). His publications are listed in his *Adventures of a Dance Historian: an Unfinished Memoir* (1982); a supplementary bibliography appears in an issue of *Dance Chronicle* (2001) in celebration of his 80th birthday. Mr. Guest was given the Queen Elizabeth II Coronation Award for services to ballet in 1997 and named a Chevalier of the Ordre des Arts et des Lettres in 2000.

Sandra Noll Hammond is a dance historian specialising in ballet technique and training of the early nineteenth century. Her career has included performing, choreographing, and teaching, and her publications include numerous articles in dance-history journals as well as a facsimile edition, *The extraordinary Dance book T B. 1826* (with Armand Russell and Elizabeth Aldrich, 2000), and the textbooks *Ballet Basics* (which has also been translated and published in South Korea and Finland) and *Ballet: Beyond the Basics*. She was co-founder and first director of the dance major program at the University of Arizona and Professor and Director of Dance at the University of Hawaii, and was given a Lifetime Achievement Award in 2009 by CORPS de Ballet International. Her current research focus is ballet technique as depicted by Degas.

Ole Nørlyng holds degrees in Art History and Music from the University of Copenhagen. Since 1983 he has served as art and dance critic of the daily

Berlingske Tidende; he has also made new revised editions of the scores for *La Sylphide* and *A Folk Tale*, and served as dramaturg for many ballets. His publications include *Balletbogen* (*The Ballet Book*, with Erik Ashengreen 1982, rev. ed. 1993), *Springkraft og danseglæde* (with Thomas Lund, 2007), *Apollons mange masker* (*Apollo's Many Masks*, 1998), *Silja* (2009), and, most recently, a volume on the churches of Copenhagen, *Gudsfrygt, bøn og omvendelse* (with Karin Kryger, 2010). He also edited the volume *Dance is an Art* (in Danish and English, 2005), with English translation by Gaye Kynoch.

Marian Smith holds a Ph.D. in musicology from Yale University, and is on the faculty of the University of Oregon. Her articles and reviews appear in both music and dance journals, and she is the author of *Ballet and Opera in the age of 'Giselle'*, which was given the de la Torre Bueno Prize in 2001. She has served on the editorial boards of the *Cambridge Opera Journal*, *Dance Chronicle*, and *Studies in Dance History*, and recently collaborated with Peter Boal and Doug Fullington on Pacific Northwest Ballet's new production of *Giselle* (2011). She is currently writing a study of processions on the stage of the Paris Opéra in the 1830s and 1840s.

Debra Hickenlooper Sowell holds a Ph.D. in Performance Studies from New York University. Her book *The Christensen Brothers* won the 1999 de la Torre Bueno Prize Special Citation. She is also the co-author of *Il Balletto Romantico* (2007) and her articles on the Romantic ballet have appeared in both *Dance Research Journal* and *Dance Chronicle*. She is the recipient of a research grant from the San Francisco Performing Arts Library and Museum as well as a John M. Ward Fellowship in Dance and Music for the Theatre from the Harvard Theatre Collection. She has served as a board member and national officer of the Society of Dance History Scholars, and is founder of that organisation's Nineteenth Century working group. She currently serves on the Advisory Board of *Dance Chronicle* and is Professor of Humanities and Theatre History at Southern Virginia University.

Helena Spencer holds performance degrees from the Cleveland Institute of Music and the University of Oregon, and is currently a Ph.D. candidate in musicology at the University of Oregon. Her dissertation (in progress) traces the image of Armide's enchanted garden in nineteenth-century French opera and ballet; other research interests include nineteenth-century art song and Scandinavian music. She has published on Ibsen song settings in the journal *Studia Musicologica Norvegica*, and she has presented papers at meetings of the International Grieg Society, American Musicological Society, and the International Conference on Nineteenth-Century Music.

Introduction

The ballet called *La Sylphide* – one of the most enduring of the Romantic ballets in today's repertory – has never before been the subject of a book in the English language, a vacuum that Alexander Bennett (1929-2003), the dancer, director, teacher, and British Intelligence officer, aimed to fill. At the time of his death, aside from preparing a production of *Swan Lake* for Ballet West in Argyll, Alex was hard at work on a book about *La Sylphide*, a ballet in which he had taken the role of James many times, and staged as well. 'Tallish, blond and handsome, he was an alluring performer', wrote Nadine Meisner in an obituary. 'His abilities, however, existed not just in his body, but in his brain. He was a talented linguist and he had an engaging personality that was friendly, persuasive and resourceful.'[1]

Friendly, persuasive, and resourceful indeed! Alex called me out of the blue one day – I had never met him – and very affably told me about a rare document in his possession: a copy of an 1835 manuscript used by the nineteenth-century ballet master Victor Bartholomin and full of instructions for performing *La Sylphide*, the earliest known such document for this canonic Romantic ballet. He shortly thereafter sent me a copy! A few years later, he persuaded me to help him finish his book, entitled (after Cyril W. Beaumont's influential monographs on *Giselle* and *Swan Lake*) *The Ballet Called 'La Sylphide'*. And as I read the book manuscript, I was amazed by his resourcefulness: even as he had worked as a British Intelligence officer, and later as a dancer and director, he managed to carry out archival research all over Europe, interview other dancers, translate texts from Danish, French, and Russian, and ponder and record his own impressions as he had formed them on the stage, behind the scenes, and in the house. He had also, it turns out, managed to salvage the Bartholomin score from oblivion, for after persuading his teacher Margery Middleton to give him a photocopy of it, the original eventually vanished. He had recognised both the historical and practical value of this rare document, which gives more insight into the French incarnation of this ballet than any other. He put it to good use, without fanfare making it the basis for his several stagings of the ballet. And because he had performed the role of James in the celebrated revival of the Danish version of the ballet staged by Elsa Marianne von Rosen for Ballet

Rambert in 1960, Alex was able to appreciate the double heritage of this ballet (both Danish and French) as few others could have done.

The present volume, I hope, reflects Alex's enthusiasm for *La Sylphide* in its multiple versions, his sensitivity to both the Schneitzhoeffer and Løvenskiold music, his fascination with the cultural settings in which the ballet first sprang to life in Paris and beyond, and his deep respect for the ballet's history – a respect that was far more than theoretical. As a reflection of his expansive reach, I am pleased to say, contributors to this project represent both the fields of dance history and musicology, and bring to bear their wide variety of specialities including technique, literature, history, folklore, iconography, dance reconstruction, historiography, and performance practice. Indeed, nothing less is required to do justice to an immensely popular musico-dramatic stage work inspired by literature, influenced by the visual arts and *la mode*, a work that made history with its choreography and its star performer, and cropped up in countless productions, usually delighting its audiences (but sometimes dismaying them, for interesting reasons).

We begin (Ch. 1) with the narration by Ivor Guest of *La Sylphide*'s genesis in Paris (with thanks to the author for allowing us to reproduce his graceful words here). Debra H. Sowell (Ch. 2) focuses on the little-studied *pas de schall*, and the choreographic, symbolic, and narrative role of the scarf in ballet of the era of *La Sylphide*, deepening our contextual understanding of the instrument of the title character's death. Next, Sandra Noll Hammond (Ch. 3) offers a clear-eyed appraisal of Marie Taglioni's technique and choreography, bringing rigour and specificity (and a set of precautions) to questions of how to interpret the lithographs of the period using archival documents and syllabi, and showing how Marie Taglioni's dancing was connected to the past. Then, after a detailed description of Schneitzhoeffer's music for *La Sylphide* (Ch. 4) by Matilda Ertz (who makes good use of Victor Bartholomin's previously unknown 1835 *répétiteur*, or rehearsal score, for *La Sylphide*), we then depart France for Copenhagen.

Once we are settled in the Danish capital, Erik Aschengreen (Chapter 5), in his inimitable fashion, tells the story of how August Bournonville's *Sylphiden* came into being, and surveys some of its latter-day incarnations. Helena Kopchick Spencer (Ch. 6) then asks why *Sylphiden* was officially named to Danish Cultural Canon by the Danish government in 2006, and demonstrates that the ballet can be can be interpreted as a staging of the pan-Nordic enchantment ballad. This is followed (Ch. 7) by Ole Nørlyng's account of Løvenskiold's enduring score for the ballet and some of the revisions that have been made thereto.

Next, we proceed southward, across the Alps. Ornella di Tondo (Ch. 8) asks: why did *La Silfide* receive such a stormy reception in Italy? Her richly detailed survey of the ballet's life there from 1837-1861 – which brings to light no fewer than twenty-seven productions of the ballet – illuminates crucial differences between French and Italian production practices, and shows how, despite the French tastes underpinning the ballet, *La Silfide* did find some notable success in Italy, in part because of modifications made to suit Italian audiences.

Alexander Bennett's writings (Ch. 9-10), as many readers will perceive, follow the model of Cyril W. Beaumont in offering highly useful observations about the characters, settings, and machinery of *La Sylphide*, and a simplified choreographic script as well.

Finally, in a historiographical critique (Ch. 11), the Editor attempts to point out the unwitting role of *La Sylphide* in the discrediting of the nineteenth-century *danseur*. And in the Epilogue, she describes *Les Sylphides* (plural) hoping not only to straighten out any lingering confusion about the differences between that modern ballet (and it *is* modern) and the earlier one that is the main subject of this volume, but to demonstrate that the Sylph has endured into our own repertory in varied guises.

Eugene, Oregon
October 2, 2011

'Obituary: Alexander Bennett, Linguist turned ballet dancer', *The Independent*, 27 March 2003.

Acknowledgements

The idea for this book came from Alexander Bennett, and I am most grateful to the authors who lent their considerable expertise to help me realize his vision. Without the generous help of several individuals and institutions, though, I could not have done so. My thanks in particular go to Marc Vanscheeuwijck, who answered countless questions about Italian and French – sometimes from cyber cafés on both sides of the Adriatic Sea. (It was from Croatia that he explained the French term for 'she-monkey'.) Olga Aynvarg kindly translated Yuri Slonimsky's *'Sil'fida' Balet* into English as I started the project; Lynn Kane and Heather Lanctot swooped in at the end to help with citation-checking and other thankless tasks. Matilda Ertz and Helena Spencer, themselves contributors, supplied much-appreciated assistance (respectively) securing copyright permissions and doing extremely valuable editorial work.

A term in residence at the University of Oregon Humanities Center, and the warm welcome given me there by Julia Heydon, allowed me a refreshing respite from my teaching duties; further, thanks are owed to Cambridge University Press and the University of Chicago Press for allowing me to include herein new versions of essays of mine that they had previously published. Finally, I offer my deep gratitude to the imperturbable Liz Morrell at Dance Books, to my family, for tolerating my too-frequent disappearances up the chimney, and to David Leonard, whose devotion to books on dance and whose kindness and patience with regard to this particular one have been inexhaustible.

Chapter 1

The genesis of *La Sylphide*

Ivor Guest

After reorganising the hierarchy of the ballet company by placing Marie Taglioni at its head, [the Opéra director Louis] Véron could hardly have hoped for a more suitable ballet to justify his policy than *La Sylphide*. The scenario was brought to him while *Robert le Diable* was in rehearsal by the tenor Adolphe Nourrit, who had conceived it with Taglioni in mind as the heroine. It had the obvious merits of a simple, straightforward action and a pathetic ending. In its Scottish setting it provided scope for the introduction of local colour. But most important, it captured that Romantic mood of mystery which was being so successfully created in *Robert le Diable*. Nourrit could not have been inspired by Taglioni's performance in the Ballet of the Nuns, since the scenario was read to the choreographer a week before she ever began to rehearse her role. But preparations for the scene may have been sufficiently advanced for its mood to have been perceived by Nourrit. After *Robert le Diable* was produced, Véron realised full well the commercial value of exploiting the ethereal side of Taglioni's talent, but no one could foresee the full implication this was to have in the development of ballet.

The plot of this new ballet was inspired by a fantasy which Charles Nodier had written after a visit to Scotland some ten years before, called *Trilby, ou le Lutin de Argaïl*, but it was no less original because of this derivation. Instead of the goblin Trilby luring a peasant girl from her fisherman husband, the central character was a Sylphide (Taglioni) who, at curtain rise, is discovered gazing lovingly at a young Scottish peasant, James Reuben (Mazilier), asleep in a chair. James is engaged to marry Effie (Noblet), who is also loved by Gurn (Elie). Waking at the touch of the Sylphide's kiss, James catches only a glimpse of her before she vanishes up the chimney. This memory haunts him even when he is in Effie's presence, and his secret is divined by Old Madge (Mme. Elie), the witch, who tells Effie that it is Gurn, not James, who loves her truly. When James is alone again, the Sylphide reappears on the window ledge. Gurn observes their tender exchanges, but when he goes to the chair and pulls aside the plaid beneath which the Sylphide has hidden, there is nothing there. The wedding ceremony then begins, but as James is about to place his ring on Effie's finger, the Sylphide glides out from the chimney and snatches it from his hand. James follows her as she flies out of the cottage.

The second act opens with Madge and some other witches casting an evil spell over a scarf. Dawn breaks and a forest glade comes into view. James arrives searching for the Sylphide, whom he finds with her fellow spirits. While he is wondering whether he is chasing a chimera, Madge gives him the scarf, telling him that it will make the Sylphide's wings drop so that she will be his for ever. Eagerly James places the scarf on the Sylphide's shoulders. Her wings fall, as Madge had promised, but to his horror she dies and is borne away through the treetops. While James is left alone in his grief, the bridal procession of Gurn and Effie passes in the background.

Filippo Taglioni thought the story charming when Nourrit read it over to him on 23 October 1831, and within a fortnight he was hard at work sketching out the instructions for the musician. The score was to be composed by Jean Schneitzhoeffer, who for once conquered his natural indolence and set to work so conscientiously that rehearsals began before November was out. On December 29th, having relinquished her role in *Robert le Diable*, Marie Taglioni began learning her part with Joseph Mazilier, who was to play the role of James.

While rehearsals were in progress, Charles Maurice continued his campaign against the Taglionis in the *Courrier des Théâtres*. Reporting the acceptance of the scenario, he announced that Marie Taglioni was to play the Sylphide 'notwithstanding her figure, which is completely lacking in etherealness'.[1] How he must have regretted this phrase later! Marie, however, was well able to hold her own against all the intrigues which were instigated in the interests of dancers who felt themselves sacrificed by Véron's policy. She counted a very large band of admirers, not only among the public but also within the Opéra itself. Old Vestris, who had no axe to grind, sometimes made a show of being present only to see her dance, to the disgust of a number of interested occupants of the orchestra stalls.

Filippo Taglioni set great store on the effects in the second act and was bitterly frustrated because he was unable to stage the witches scene as he wished. Duponchel, who was at the same time preparing the orgy scene for the new opera-ballet, *La Tentation*, kept filching dancers from Taglioni to swell his crowd of devils. Taglioni plagued Véron with tearful complaints about the miserly nature of his own '*diableries*', with so few witches at his disposal but, if he received little satisfaction in this direction, he had the consolation of knowing that the flights which were being devised for the forest scene were far more complex than any which had been attempted before at the Opéra. Among these were a circling flight and, at the end, a magnificent multiple flight when the body of the Sylphide is borne away through the trees. These effects caused Véron unbelievable anxiety, which was not lessened by the dress rehearsals. At the first of these, on 10 March 1832, nothing went right, and the next day there might have been a disastrous accident: Marie Taglioni fell as she was vanishing up the chimney, but fortunately without injuring herself. Véron was very concerned for the safety of the dozen or fifteen girls who were to make the flights, for which they were to be rewarded with a special bonus of 10 francs for each performance. Throughout his management, he was to make a personal inspection of the flying apparatus before every performance of *La Sylphide*, and not once was there an accident.

Véron passed a sleepless night before the first performance of *La Sylphide* on 12 March 1832, but its splendid triumph must have more than compensated for all the anxiety he had suffered. The names of the authors – with the exception of Nourrit, who remained anonymous – were announced from the stage to loud applause, and when Marie Taglioni appeared to take her call, tremendous cheers broke out from all parts of the house.

La Sylphide sealed the triumph of Romanticism in the field of ballet. The Ballet of the Nuns had indicated the supernatural as a new and promising source for choreographers, but *La Sylphide*, though inspired by it, was a much profounder manifestation of Romanticism. Its plot introduced to French ballet the situation of a spirit falling in love with a mortal, epitomising, with haunting effect, the quest of the Romantic artist for the infinite and the unattainable. The discovery of this situation, which was to recur with frequent regularity in future years, was a turning-point of the greatest significance in the history of ballet. It ushered in a golden age – an era of moonlight and ethereal sprites, and *La Sylphide* was to become the prototype of many other masterpieces which were to embellish this period of the Romantic ballet.

The importance of *La Sylphide*, however, resided not merely in the introduction of a new formula, but in its inspired application. Though Marie Taglioni appeared as an interpreter of her father's choreographic design, her part in the ballet's creations was a fundamental one. The role of the Sylphide had been constructed with the object of revealing in a perfect setting her poetic style which had been acclaimed for its Romantic, even revolutionary, touch. This style had inspired her father who himself had been instrumental in forming it, and the finished choreography, therefore, was a true collaboration which revealed the genius of Marie Taglioni in its fullest glory.

The triumph of Marie Taglioni was complete. If Charles Maurice grumbled that she exerted herself very little, that was only an indication of his failure to understand the meaning of her role, which was conveyed by the expressiveness in her movement and not by feats of difficulty. The audience was given, not the momentary thrills of *tours de force*, but the haunting memory of an impalpable vision, 'a shadow condensed into a mist'.[2] There was poetry in her dancing, and nowhere was this more apparent than in the second act when the Sylphide was seen dancing with her companions.

'There is a sequence of furtive, aerial steps', wrote *L'Entr'acte*, 'something ravishing beyond description, in which painting, music and dancing all vie with one another. The irresolute flight of a butterfly, those round tufts which the mild wind of April plucks like down from the cups of flowers and balances in the air, these are the only points of comparison with the timid graces, the mocking abandon, and the artful modesty of the Sylphide. Really Taglioni is no mortal. God could not have imagined the cherubim better.'[3]

She had rendered more obsolete than ever the classical style which expressed itself in the *danse noble*, with its mannered poses, its stiffness, its stereotyped smiles, and above all its applause-catching tricks such as the *bouffante*, the conventional conclusion of a *pas noble* with a *pirouette sur la pointe* performed so that the skirt flared out to the delight of the gentlemen seated near the stage. 'Imagine our joy one evening', wrote Jules Janin, who held the *danse noble* in abhorrence, 'when, unsuspecting and by pure chance, like finding a pearl by the roadside, we were presented not with the *danse noble*, but with a simple, easy, naturally graceful Taglioni, with a figure of unheard-of elegance, arms of serpentine suppleness and legs to match, and feet like those of an ordinary woman, even though she be a dancer! When we first saw her so much at ease and dancing so happily – she danced like a bird singing – we could not understand it. "Where is the *danse noble*?" asked the old men. The *danse noble* is as foreign to Taglioni's style as natural dancing is to that of her rivals. She uses her hands when she dances! See how she bends her body, how she walks, how she always keeps to the ground! Notice the absence of pirouettes, *entrechats* and other technical difficulties!... She has given us a new art, she has initiated us into a new pleasure, for she has completely reformed the ballet of her time. All the *danseuses nobles*, after seeing how she is applauded, have clipped off some of their nobility, just as their ancestors cast off their panniers. They have been using their arms and legs like ordinary mortals, they have even risked splitting their satin corsets by bending their bodies more, while they bend their arms much less since Taglioni. The great Taglioni revolution has been specially felt in the arm movements; there is a sensible improvement in the bust, and an improvement is now beginning to show in the legs. That is a step forward. While waiting for the revolution to be fully accomplished, Taglioni continues her triumphs, every day learning to become more of a woman and less of a dancer than ever. Thanks be for that! But what must have really astonished those ladies is that this newcomer... does not allow herself a single *bouffante*. Not one poor little *bouffante* for the poor adoring public!'[4] Marie Taglioni was uncompromising in her art: in that lay the secret of her greatness.

Her father's choreography was praised by Castil-Blaze for being as varied in conception as it was excellently performed. Its originality was most apparent in the second act, where it reflected the ethereal mood of the scenario to perfection. Nearly all the details have now been forgotten, but Castil-Blaze described one entrance, 'of an original effect', in which the sylphides advanced from the back of the stage in groups of four to form a delightful group in the very front.'[5]

Of course, there were some who, for one reason or another, refused to admit that Filippo Taglioni's success was deserved. Among these was Elise Henry, the sister of the choreographer Louis Henry, who had himself produced a ballet called *La Silfide* at the Scala, Milan, in 1828 for Therese Heberle. Taking up the cudgels on her brother's behalf, she wrote to the paper, *La Renommée*, in October 1832, accusing Filippo Taglioni of plagiarism.[6] Apparently unaware that Nourrit was the author of the scenario, she alleged that Taglioni received every ballet scenario which was published and that he had even stolen some of her brother's choreography. 'I will mention', she specified, 'the *pas de deux* which has been inserted, since his return from London, in the second act of *La Sylphide*, when [Marie Taglioni] makes a *tour en attitude sur la pointe* and Mazilier supports her so well. This movement is my brother's, and a great part of this *pas* is composed of movements from the same source.'[7] To this outburst Filippo Taglioni replied that his only knowledge of Henry's *La Silfide* was that Heberle had once told him she had danced in it.

Schneitzhoeffer's music met with a mixed reception. One critic considered it the weakest element in the work, lacking in descriptive power, particularly in the witches scene, where something like the infernal music of *Robert le Diable* was needed, and again in the forest scene, for which more descriptively celestial music would have been appropriate for the aerial dances of the sylphides. However, Castil-Blaze found the score 'excellent' and 'infinitely remarkable in a branch which could become important if a man of talent and intelligence should decide to take it up'.[8] He only regretted that the composer had not made greater use of borrowed melodies, of which he recognised no more than a fragment of the trio from Boïeldieu's opera *Le Calife de Bagdad* and a little air by Pauline Duchambge, apart from the major interpolation in the witches scene. This last passage was based on Paganini's variations, *Le Streghe*, the theme of which the great violinist had himself borrowed from an earlier ballet: it came from a melody by Süssmayer in the score for Viganò's ballet, *Il Noce di Benevento*.[9]

The scenery and costumes of *La Sylphide* played a very important part in evoking the local colour of the first act and the ethereal mood of the second. Ciceri's set for the first act might have been a little sombre, and the colours of the costumes could also have been brighter, but thanks to Duponchel's supervision the Scottish costumes were at least credibly authentic. The second act was to remain one of Ciceri's masterpieces, and a murmur of appreciation ran through the audience when the gauze curtain rose after the witches scene and the forest set was gradually touched by the light of day.

The costumes were mostly designed by Eugène Lami. That Taglioni's sylphide costume, which initiated the fashion of the bell-shaped skirt now popularly known as the Romantic tutu, was designed by him rests, however, solely upon tradition, unsupported, it seems, by any contemporary evidence.[10] It is even possible that Lami did not design this costume: the absence of any sketch for it in the admittedly incomplete series of costume designs preserved at the Opéra may indicate that it was not specially designed at all in the way the Scottish costumes were, but was made up by the costume department merely on instructions to produce a plain white costume. Even the claim that it was the first bell-shaped skirt worn in ballet cannot be maintained. At the first performance in 1832 it was not very full, and certainly not more so than costumes which had been worn in some earlier ballets: a lithograph of Pauline Montessu in the sleepwalking scene from *La Somnambule* shows her in a costume of a very similar form, though more elaborate and with an even fuller skirt. The sylphide costume caused no stir at the time apparently because there was nothing unusual in its cut or style. It was its absolute simplicity which was novel, and while this made it a model for the ethereal scenes which were to become so popular in ballet, its significance was not immediately apparent. The development of the bell-shaped skirt was gradual and accompanied the fashions of the day, its circumference continuing to grow, until it reached its maximum under the Second Empire, in the heyday of the crinoline.

— From Guest, *The Romantic Ballet in Paris* (London: Dance Books, 1980), 112-117.

Anon. [Un vieil abonné]. *Ces Demoiselles de L'opéra.* Paris: Tresse & Stock, 1887.
Castil-Blaze. *L'académie Impérial de Musique.* Vol. II. Paris: Castil-Blaze, 1855.
Fischer, Carlos. *Les Costumes de L'opéra.* Paris: Librarie de France, 1931.
Unsigned. *Courrier des Théâtres,* 20 November 1831.
———. *L'Entr'acte,* 13 March 1832.
———. *Journal des Débats,* 24 August 1832.

Notes

1. Unsigned, *Courrier des Théâtres*, 20 November 1831.
2. Anon. [Un vieil abonné], *Ces Demoiselles de l'Opéra* (Paris: Tresse & Stock, 1887), 140.
3. Unsigned, *L'Entr'acte*, 13 March 1832.
4. Unsigned, *Journal des Débats*, 24 August 1832.
5. Castil-Blaze, *L'Académie impérial de musique*, vol. II (Paris: Castil-Blaze, 1855), 234.
6. *La Silfide*, choreography by Louis Henry, music by Luigi Carlini and (for *pas*) Rossini, Pacini, Carafa, sets by Alessandro Sanquirico, f.p. Scala, Milan, 28 May 1828.

Briefly the plot was as follows: Ezelda, a sylphide, has fallen in love with a mortal, Azalide, whom she has transported to her side. When he wakes and sees her, he falls in love with her. Ezelda's uncle, Almanzor, reveals that the fates have ordained that they must undergo the ordeal of the barrier of love. A garland of flowers is laid on the ground between the lovers. Ezelda tries to warn Azalide that he must keep to his own side, but he leaps across and she is changed into a statue. Only Azalide himself can now break the spell, but at the expense of sacrificing himself. He does not hesitate to do so, but in the end Hymen and the amorets restore him to life again and the ballet ends happily with the lovers reunited.

Elise Henry pointed out the following four similarities with *La Sylphide*:
1) The hero in each is discovered asleep.
2) The heroine expresses her love before he awakes.
3) The scene in Almanzor's cave has its counterpart in the witches scene.
4) Spring comes during Act I of Henry's ballet, whereas day breaks during Act I of Taglioni's ballet.

The superficiality of these similarities will be obvious to the reader. What Henry's ballet lacked was the Romanticism which Taglioni's ballet expressed in all its elements.
7. The correspondence is to be found in *Courrier des Théâtres*, 14, 17, 19, 21 and 22 October 1832.
8. Castil-Blaze, *L'Académie impérial de musique*, II, 234.
9. *Il Noce di Benevento*, choreography by Salvatore Viganò, music by Süssmayer, f.p. Scala, Milan, 25 April 1812.
10. Carlos Fischer was unable to obtain any corroboration from Lami's family. 'In his family', he wrote, 'Eugène Lami — who used to talk freely of the past, his youth and the Opéra — never breathed a word, it appears, of this invention of the tutu, of which he had the right, however, to be proud and which he would not have dreamt of denying. None of his relations knows if he really designed and made with his own hands the first ballet skirt with several layers of gauze and tarlatan, but they agree, with a smile, that he was quite capable of it.' Carlos Fischer, *Les Costumes de l'Opéra* (Paris: Librarie de France, 1931), 210.

Chapter 2

Contextualising Madge's Scarf:
The *Pas de Schall* as Romantic Convention

Debra H. Sowell

The scene is familiar to balletomanes and dance scholars alike: at the climax of *La Sylphide*, the Scottish crofter James wraps an enchanted scarf around the shoulders of his adored sylph, having been promised by Madge the Witch that doing so will cause the sylph's wings to fall off. James hopes to prevent the sylph from escaping his reach, in order that he may possess her, but instead Madge's scarf – the instrument of James's desire – becomes the tool by which he unwittingly causes the sylph's death and thus loses her forever (Figure 2.1). The love-and-death motif so common in literature of the Romantic era is played out in *La Sylphide* through the instrumentality of a simple length of fabric.

Although *La Sylphide* is credited with being a landmark work, ushering in the era of full-blown Romanticism in French ballet, Filippo Taglioni's employment of Madge's scarf in this ballet was hardly novel. Rather, his use of scarves and shawls in both *La Sylphide* and *Le Dieu et la Bayadère*, as well as Jules Perrot's similar use of scarves and shawls in *Esmeralda* and *Lalla Rookh*, exemplifies a well-established tradition of shawl dancing within the balletic repertory – one going back at least to the late eighteenth century and continuing well beyond the apogee of the Romantic era. Strangely, to date this phenomenon has not received widespread recognition. A brief entry on 'Attitude and Shawl Dancing' in the *International Encyclopedia of Dance* states that 'The *pas de schall* has received little attention' and notes that 'shawl dances today survive only in literature'.[1] Indeed, Sarah Davies Cordova's insightful study *Paris Dances* includes literary records of shawl dancing in its analysis of dancing scenes in nineteenth-century French novels such as Madame de Stael's *Delphine* and Julienne de Krüdener's *Valérie*.[2] But this choreographic custom also reveals itself through non-literary sources, including souvenir prints and music scores, opening our eyes to a multifaceted tradition with which Romantic audiences were very familiar. That tradition was rooted in contemporary fashion trends, but it also reflected the exotic component of the Romantic imagination.

Broadly speaking, patterns of nineteenth-century shawl dancing may be

2.1. *Les Beautés de l'Opéra.* (Paris: Soulié, 1845) Courtesy of Madison and Debra Sowell Collection, Provo, Utah.

divided into three categories: (1) the use of the shawl as talisman, (2) the shawl as choreographic tool or visual structuring device, and (3) the shawl as a cultural marker with distinct antique or orientalist implications. In the era of *La Sylphide*, the nomenclature of this choreographic practice was not standardised; dances that used either scarves or shawls earned a variety of labels. Although 'shawl dance' and '*pas de schall*' are among the most common, variants include *pas de schal, pas de châle, pas du châle, pas des schals, danse des schals*, and *passo a sciallo.*

The Shawl as Talisman
On the most elementary level, the shawl as a prop or talisman served as a

marker, indicating identity and relationships not easily communicated in a nonverbal art. Printed plot summaries in ballet libretti – both before and after *La Sylphide* – indicate instances of scarves or shawls used in this fashion. For example, in Aumer's 1827 *La Somnambule*, Gertrude flees the unwanted attentions of Saint-Rambert, but the latter snatches her scarf.[3] That scarf, now a token of male desire, is later discovered on Saint-Rambert's bed, where it is taken as a sign that she has slept with him and is thus highly incriminating. The topos of the scarf as a symbol of sexual desire and intimate relationships also found expression in Perrot's 1844 *La Esmeralda*. The gypsy Esmeralda, taken with the soldier Phoebus's good looks, toys with the end of his scarf.[4] (Ends were often the mostly highly ornamented and thus most attractive parts of scarves.) Phoebus gives the scarf to her, and it becomes her reminder of him, a symbol of his former presence and a token of their interchange. In Act Two, Phoebus's fiancée Fleur de Lys notices that the scarf she has embroidered for him is missing; when Esmeralda appears with the scarf, Fleur de Lys snatches it back, foreshadowing her ultimate hold upon Phoebus's loyalties. Similarly, in Paul Taglioni's 1847 *Coralia, or the Inconstant Knight*, the knight Hildebrand, while a guest of a Duke, attracts the favour of the Duke's daughter Bertha, who presents Hildebrand with a magic scarf.[5] However, Hildebrand must enter the Enchanted Forest, where he falls in love with the water nymph Coralia, who is being raised as a human by a poor fisherman. In one scene, Hildebrand uses Bertha's scarf to draw Coralia from the middle of the lake to the bank. The scarf becomes a symbol of the knight's passions; although he marries Coralia, Bertha regains the scarf and Hildebrand eventually returns to her.

In *La Sylphide*, a variant of the shawl as identity token is found in Act One; the Parisian libretto contains an interchange between James and the sylph in which she begs him to go to the forest with her. To her plea, 'Come, come with me', James replies, 'Abandon Effie! No, I'd rather die. Go away! You are nothing but a vain shadow (*ombre vain*) who is trying to deceive my senses.'[6] According to the libretto, he pushes her away with scorn, following which the sylph wraps around herself the plaid shawl Effie has left on the chair; when James returns he finds her at his feet, wrapped in Effie's plaid, now a fetish reminding him of his fiancée. At this sight James's reason is troubled; he pulls up the sylph, presses her to his heart, and gives her a kiss. Effie's plaid wrap thus suggests an altered or double identity – one that leads James to express affection for the sylph. In Act Two, of course, Madge's scarf does more than suggest identity; it plays a major role in the working out of the plot. Imbued with malevolent power, it represents the demonic aspect of the ballet's supernatural element and contributes directly to the sylph's death. (The title page to the section of *La Sylphide* in *Les Beautés de l'Opera* shows the

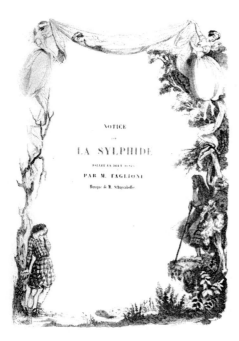

2.2. *Les Beautés de l'Opéra*. (Paris: Soulié, 1845) Courtesy of Madison and Debra Sowell Collection, Provo, Utah.

2.3. A lithograph plate showing a variety of ways of wearing shawls in early 19th-century France (ca. 1802-1814); re-drawn from various early 19th-century sources by Durin for Albert Charles Auguste Racinet's *Le Costume Historique* (1888).

deceased sylph being carried away on a long strip of fabric, presumably Madge's scarf; Figure 2.2.)

One reason the scarf entered balletic narratives so naturally was that scarves and shawls were prized fashion accessories in the late eighteenth century and throughout the nineteenth (with some variations between England and France). The protean quality of the shawl made it a versatile and useful accessory (Figure 2.3). In Britain the popularity of Kashmir shawls imported from India dovetailed with the Industrial Revolution, and weaving centers such as Norwich and Spitalfields mechanised the process that in India was completed by hand. In Scotland, major production centers were Edinburgh and Paisley, the latter so much so that the cone-based pattern produced in Paisley's factories became known by the city's name. In 1820 tulle shawls, sheer but often with a floral pattern, gained popularity.[7] In France, when shawls were introduced into fashion in 1790 they were described as 'an English fashion', albeit one stemming originally from India.[8] It was, somewhat ironically, Napoleon's Egyptian campaign in 1798 that catapulted the Indian Kashmir to popularity in France; the Empress Josephine developed a passion for shawls and had her portrait painted in them (Figure 2.4). Neoclassical artists such as Jacques-Louis David and Dominique Ingres

2.4. Pierre-Paul Prud'hon, *The Empress Josephine*, 1805. Photo: Gérard Blot. Réunion des Musées nationaux /Art Resource, NY. Musée du Louvre. By permission.

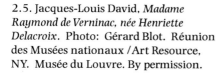

2.5. Jacques-Louis David, *Madame Raymond de Verninac, née Henriette Delacroix*. Photo: Gérard Blot. Réunion des Musées nationaux / Art Resource, NY. Musée du Louvre. By permission.

2.6. Jean Auguste Dominique Ingres, *Madame Rivière*. Réunion des Musées nationaux / Art Resource, NY. Musée du Louvre. By permission.

also incorporated shawls in their paintings of society women such as Madame Raymond de Verninac and Madame Rivière, respectively (Figures 2.5 and 2.6). Reflecting on this era in 1815, Pierre de la Mésangère, the editor of one of Paris's many fashion journals, recorded:

> Our beauties invented a thousand reasons why that taste 'for *kashmirs*' should be satisfied. The richest had only to pronounce those words, so omnipotent in their mouths: it is the fashion; women of the second rank insisted on the necessity of doing like everyone else; those further down the scale pleaded reasons of health and economy: a *kashmir*, said they, lasts for a very long time and dispenses with the need for a complete outfit. Finally, people who had no plausible reason for the purchase relied on that refrain, so powerful with the weak or amorous: 'if you don't give me a *kashmir* dress, it is because you don't love me.'[9]

In view of the overwhelming desirability of these fashion accessories, it would have been logical to *La Sylphide*'s audiences that the sylph would desire the scarf waved teasingly before her by James in Act Two.

2.7. E. A. Théleur, *Letters on Dancing* (London: Sherwood, 1831), plate 23. Courtesy of Madison and Debra Sowell Collection, Provo, Utah.

2.8. Romano A. Constantin pattern book sheet. Courtesy of Madison and Debra Sowell Collection, Provo, Utah.

The Shawl as Choreographic Tool and Visual Structuring Device

The *pas de schall* is not a ballet step in the sense that a *pas de bourée* or *pas de chat* is. One searches the treatises of Carlo Blasis, Léopold Adice, and E. A. Théleur in vain for any definition or description of the *pas de schall*, which may explain why this tradition has escaped scholarly scrutiny so long. But illustrations in both Blasis and Théleur include images of dancers with billowing strips of fabric, indicating at least an iconographic tradition[10] (Figure 2.7). Prints and pattern books in the Sowell Collection also feature dancers with scarves or lengths of fabrics which link the human figures and create groupings or specific shapes (Figure 2.8). Claudia Jeschke and Robert Atwood, in their discussion of the Opfermann *Tanz-Grüppen* 'pattern books' housed at the Derra de Moroda Dance Archives, explain the use of scarves and garlands in these formations of dancers as follows:

> Props are used to provide variations on and the intensification of the sculptural, architectural aspects of the female body. For example, the arrangement of scarves or the positioning of flower garlands forms and makes visible to the audience the space surrounding the bodies, thus making the kinesphere as significant as the bodies themselves.[11]

A series of groupings demonstrating this extended kinesphere may be found in line drawings for J. P. Aumer's 1823 *Aline, Reine de Golconde*, in which Aline's servants – Osmin, Zélie, and their child Nadir – execute a shawl dance whose groupings remind the queen of time spent with her former lover.[12]

Shawls and garlands may be comparable in their abilities to create lines in space, link dancers, create harmonious ensembles, and extend or elaborate upon the lines of the human figure. But these props differ significantly in the *quality* of their suggested movement: shawls are lighter and more flexible than garlands, as fabric floats and gives shape to currents of the air. Thus, shawls define the ineffable and suggest motion in a static image. This iconographic convention was in place well before *La Sylphide*; for example, a souvenir print of Mlle Parisot, who performed a shawl dance in James D'Egville's 1805 *La Belle Laitière*, shows her with a long, gauzy strip of fabric swelling out behind her figure. Romantic iconography adopted this apt convention, in which the shawl's airiness mimicked the ethereal qualities of the ballerina who danced on pointe. Prints of Marie Taglioni as the Bayadère, Fanny Cerrito in *Le Lac des Fees*, and Carolina Rosati in *Coralia* all feature billowing shawls – even though Coralia is a creature of the water rather than the air (Figures 2.9-2.11). Unlike the less flexible garland, the shawl reflects the ballerina's lightness and buoyancy. This would have been particularly true of the sheer tulle shawls that became popular in 1820. The French libretto of *La Sylphide* refers to Madge's enchanted scarf using both the terms *écharpe* and *gaze* (gauze), underscoring the lightness of its texture.

The practice of using scarves or shawls to link dancers visually or frame them *while creating specific shapes* is hinted at in several libretti and sometimes documented more fully in other sources. For example, the score for Aumer's 1830 opera ballet *Le Dieu et la Bayadère*, which had choreography by Filippo Taglioni, labels the Air de Danse in Act One a '*Pas de Schal*'. That term is not

2.9. Marie Taglioni as the Bayadère.
Lithograph by R. J. Lane after A. E.
Chalon, c. 1834-35. Courtesy of
Madison and Debra Sowell Collection,
Provo, Utah.

2.10. Fanny Cerrito in *Le Lac des Fées*.
Lithograph by J. S. Templeton after A. De
Valentini, c. 1840. Courtesy of Madison
and Debra Sowell Collection, Provo, Utah.

used in the libretto, but the latter's stage directions indicate which scene was
probably labelled the *pas de schall* in the score: Ninka says to her companions,
'See these precious fabrics', following which the bayadères fight over the
shawls, drape them around themselves, and, encircling Zoloé, create various
tableaux, while a stranger (the Mysterious Unknown, Zoloé's love interest)
looks on.[13] The brief description suggests that this *pas de schall*, which placed
the ballerina in a central position, surrounded by other dancers making tableaux or shapes with their fabrics, literally framed and presented the
ballerina for male gaze. That frame was so compelling that the male figure,
seeing the ballerina presented thus, was overcome by emotion and rose to
approach her.[14]   The libretto of the Paris 1857 production of Mazilier's
Marco Spada contains a scene with striking similarities.[15]   In Act Three, several young women appear carrying fabrics or veils while the Marchesa,
dressed in a simple gauze robe, stands before a mirror.   One young woman
hands her a veil, which she tries in different ways before the mirror.   She
strikes several poses, while the young women form varied groups around her.
Unbeknownst to her, her lover Pepinelli is hiding in the cupboard, and when

2.11. Carolina Rosati in *Coralia*. Lithograph by E. Desmaisons after A. De Valentini, 1847. Courtesy of Madison and Debra Sowell Collection, Provo, Utah.

he sees her 'arrayed in all her glory', he 'rushes towards the Marchesa and falls at her feet'.[16]

When descriptions such as these are combined with information from scores, libretti, and reviews, a recognisable pattern begins to emerge, indicating that the conventional *pas de schall* was a stock choreographic device both prior to and during the period of High Romanticism in ballet. It was part of a choreographer's bag of tricks, and it endured many decades. The Taglioni clan made good use of this device, and some evidence suggests that the shawl dance became closely identified with Marie herself. When appearing in *Flore et Zephyre* in London in June of 1830, the ballerina did a shawl dance with Coulon, in a performance highly lauded by the avid theatre-goer John Waldie in his journal.[17] A rare phenakistascope disk at the Harvard Theatre Collection contains nine images of Taglioni holding a shawl in various poses, so as to make a fluttering moving image when the disk is spun.[18] And as late as 1860, when Marie Taglioni created her one choreographic work *Le Papillon*, for Emma Livry, it included a '*pas de châle*', which Albéric Second, critic of *La*

2.12. Lady Emma Hamilton in a classical pose, dancing and poised on one foot. Engraving is by Thomas Piroli after Frederick Rehberg, copyright National Maritime Museum, Greenwich, UK. By permission.

Presse, announced that he 'did not particularly care for'.[19] (The '*pas de châle*' mentioned by Second most likely took place at a point in the libretto when an old fairy takes scarves out of an antique chest and drapes them about herself while posing in front of a mirror.)

The categories of talisman and choreographic tool are not meant to be mutually exclusive, as a shawl might easily fulfill both functions in the same work. Likewise, the boundary between these two functions and the third category is equally porous; a *pas de schall* using fabrics as visual building blocks of the choreography might also function as a cultural marker, contributing to the historical or geographical setting of the ballet.

The Shawl as Prop with Distinct Antique or Orientalist Implications

In a study devoted exclusively to scarves, shawls, and stoles, fashion historian Alice Mackrell explains that in England, shawls 'entered the wardrobes of fashionable ladies as part of neo-classical dress pioneered in the 1760s'.[20] The vogue for wearing imported Kashmir shawls, made from the wool of Tibetan sheep, began circa 1777, and within a decade was securely associated with the 'return to the Antique'.[21] Much credit for popularising Greek costume in Britain also goes to Lady Emma Hart Hamilton and her 'attitudes' performed in flowing draperies, first in Naples (where her husband Sir William Hamilton was the British Ambassador as well as an acknowledged authority on antiquities) and then in London (Figure 2.12). Goethe's description of Lady Hamilton's attitudes, recorded in his *Travels in Italy*, actually mentions her use of shawls as she enacted poses based on Greek statues and vase paintings:

> [Lord Hamilton] has had a Grecian costume made for her that suits her to perfection, and she lets down her hair, takes a few shawls, and varies her postures, gestures, expressions, etc. . . . Standing, kneeling, sitting, lying, grave, sad, roguish, wanton, penitent, enticing, menacing, fearful, etc., one follows upon the other and from the other. She knows how to choose and change the folds of her veil to set off each expression, and makes herself a hundred different headdresses with the same cloths.[22]

Although Cordova clarifies that Lady Hamilton's 'attitudes' were not dancing as such but rather a form of 'mimoplastics', Mackrell observes, 'It was Lady Hamilton's remarkable shawl dances which enthralled Goethe and a whole generation, and which first brought home the garment's protean qualities to the fashionable world at the end of the eighteenth century.'[23]

In France, in the era immediately preceding Romanticism, neoclassical styles and fashions were promoted by Napoleon, who borrowed imagery from antiquity to glorify his reign. Female figures manipulating fabric in frescoes at the Villa of the Mysteries at Pompeii are ancient examples of shawl dancing, suggesting that the nineteenth-century *pas de schall* had a possible classical connection (Figure 2.13). A late seventeenth-century, classically influenced costume plate by Jean Berain, *Dame en habit de ballet*, includes a long strip of billowing fabric, further illustrating the classical connection and suggesting a longstanding iconographic tradition (Figure 2.14). As a pivotal work signalling a thematic shift away from the anacreontic repertory, *La Sylphide* is usually seen as a *reaction against* rather than an *expression of* neoclassicism in ballet. However, there may be a connection between Madge's scarf and an incident in Ovid's *Metamorphoses*.[24] In Book IX, Ovid describes the events leading up to the death of Hercules, which is brought about by a poisoned garment. Hercules, travelling to Thebes with his bride Deianira, asks the passionate centaur Nessus to carry Deianira across the raging waters of the Evenus river, while Hercules himself swims across. On the other side, Hercules finds Nessus trying to rape Deianira and kills the centaur with an arrow whose tip has been dipped in Hydra's poison. The dying centaur, hoping for ultimate revenge, lets his tunic soak up his poisoned blood, and then deceitfully presents the tunic to Deianira as a magic charm, one that will 'induce a lost love to return'. Years later, when Deianira hears that Hercules is infatuated with Iole, she sends him the tunic in hopes it will restore his lost love for her. The unsuspecting Hercules drapes the tunic on his shoulders and suffers a painful death. While the instrument of death in Ovid is a tunic wrapped around the shoulders rather than a shawl, in both *The Metamorphoses* and *La Sylphide* a poisoned garment is employed to secure one's beloved and then unexpectedly causes the beloved's demise, as the result of a third party's spiteful trickery. It is possible that in an era in which the educated classes were expected to be familiar with Greek and Latin texts, the use of the shawl in *La Sylphide* might have constituted a recognisable echo of an Ovidian model.[25]

Parisians were introduced to Indian shawl dancing as early as 1768 through the performances of the Indian bayadère Bebaiourn.[26] In the popular tradition that ensued, shawl dancing combined 'steps from the bayadère's Indian dance with the poses and mimesis' inspired by Lady Hamilton's classically-inspired attitudes.[27] Thus, it may be more than coincidental that the two costume plates featuring shawls in Théleur's *Letters on Dancing* are Indian and Greek: number 7, 'Bayadère (with a Shawl)' and number 15, 'Grecian (Modern)' (Figures 2.15-2.16). However, Théleur's modern Greek plate represents the European interest in the *contemporary* Levant; its inspira-

2.13. Dancing figure from Villa of the Mysteries, Pompeii. From DVD 10.000 Mesiterwerke, The Yorck Project. By permission.

2.14. *Dame en habit de ballet.* Engraving by Jacques Le Pautre after Jean Bérain. Courtesy of Madison and Debra Sowell Collection, Provo, Utah.

2.15. E. A. Théleur, *Letters on Dancing* (London: Sherwood, 1831), plate 7, "Bayadère". Courtesy of Madison and Debra Sowell Collection, Provo, Utah.

2.16. E. A. Théleur, *Letters on Dancing* (London: Sherwood, 1831), plate 15, "Grecian, Modern". Courtesy of Madison and Debra Sowell Collection, Provo, Utah.

tion is the Orient viewed through a European lens, not Antiquity resuscitated.[28] By 1830 the shawl as prop signalling Oriental identity or culture was easily recognised by Romantic audiences and contributed to the 'local colour' of ballets set in such diverse locales as Egypt, Turkey, Syria, and (of course) the Indian sub-continent. Although frequently referred to as the Hindoostanee Shawl dance, dancing with shawls or similar lengths of exotic fabric established local colour for ballets set in Hindu and Muslim cultures alike. This undiscriminating practice reflects Edward Said's criticism that according to essentialist European thought of the early nineteenth century, 'Orientals were almost everywhere nearly the same.'[29]

Expanded from the level of individual dancer to that of group scene, the *pas de schall* contributed to the establishment of Oriental local colour in the first acts of three well-known Romantic works: *Le Dieu et la Bayadère*, *La Péri*, and *Lalla Rookh*. This practice corresponds to Said's description of the Romantics' penchant for creating 'Oriental genre tableaux' or the 'vision of the Orient as spectacle, or tableau vivant'.[30] The Oriental world constructed in Act One of *Le Dieu et la Bayadère* includes bayadères who drape themselves with precious fabrics they take from a chest of jewels the wealthy Olifour has sent to win Zoloé's favour. (One of the points at issue here is the richness of the fabric, which becomes the object of the women's materialistic desires.)

Likewise, sheet music for *La Péri* printed in London lists a '*Pas des schals*' first among its selections, most likely referring to the scene in the Parisian and London librettos in which as the curtain rises, Odalisques are occupied with their toilette.[31] Some braid strands of gold into their hair, some apply henna to their eyebrows, and some wave scarves over a vase of perfume to impregnate them with sweet-smelling vapours.[32] In both cases, the *pas de schall* forms part of the theatrical exposition locating these works in Oriental settings. Given that Goethe's poem *Der Gott und die Bajadere*, upon which the opera-ballet is based, includes no references to dancing with either shawls or scarves (Goethe's bayadère dances instead with a cymbal and has a nosegay), the insertion of the shawls in the opera-ballet's opening scene might be considered a kind of choreographic shorthand to help establish location quickly.

The *Pas Symbolique* in Perrot's *Lalla Rookh*, starring Fanny Cerrito, represents a high water mark in the *pas de schall* tradition, although by the ballet's première in 1846 that very tradition was considered dated and trite. This *pas de schall* also transpires near the beginning of the ballet; Lalla Rookh, the emperor's daughter, is leaving Lahore to be married, and women perform a shawl dance around her as a way of extolling her beauty.[33] According to the libretto, the *Pas Symbolique* presented twenty figures, including 'Hermes, the Shell, the Kiosks, the Cage, the Mirrors, the Harps, the framed Picture of the Morning Breeze, the Stars, the Pine Apples, the Car of the Rising Sun, the Butterflies, [and] the Sun's Rays', culminating in 'The Living Statue and its Pedestal'.[34] That the choreography created specific, recognisable images – as suggested by this series of titles – was confirmed by *The Morning Post*, which declared that 'every group was pictorial, as if it had stepped forth from the canvas of Boucher, or the still greater Guido'.[35] The critic of the London *Times* reported:

> The *Pas Symbolique* of Hindoo girls... may be pronounced one of the most elegant scarf dances ever yet contrived, and shows what new combinations are possible in a style apparently so hackneyed. The last figure in this *pas*, in which Cerrito stands as a statue on a pedestal and the girls with pink scarfs form a series of steps, is entirely novel in its effect, and admirably conceived.[36]

Here, as in *Le Dieu et la Bayadère*, the ballerina is framed and presented for an audience that includes a male love interest – in this case the poet Feramoz, who is Lalla Rookh's intended husband in disguise. Both instances recall Said's characterisation of the Orient as being '*contained* and *represented* by dominating frameworks', as the ballerinas are framed by shawls or scarves and presented before the male characters who will determine their ultimate destinies.[37]

2.17. Marie Taglioni as the Sylph. Lithograph by Thomas Herbert Maguire after A. E. Chalon. Courtesy of Madison and Debra Sowell Collection, Provo, Utah.

As Mackrell says in her confident summing up of the fashion situation, '[t]he nineteenth century was the Age of the Shawl, as the late eighteenth had been that of the scarf and neo-classical chemise.'[38] Certainly, visual records – as well as scores, libretti, and reviews – suggest that Madge's scarf was part of an ongoing tradition incorporating fabric of various shapes and sizes into choreography. During the period of the Romantic ballet, the nineteenth-century shawl maintained its pre-existing function as a prop that elucidated relationships or signalled plot developments, and it continued its role as a choreographic tool that defined or energised the kinesphere surrounding the dancer, sometimes into recognisable shapes. But during the heyday of Romanticism in ballet, the shawl or Kashmir was also used increasingly as a marker of the exoticism that was so prized by Romantics. That exoticism was sometimes tinged with eroticism, as the figures in a *pas de schall* literally framed celebrated ballerinas and presented them for the pleasure of male audiences on stage as well as in the theatre. Although largely forgotten today, the Romantic-era *pas de schall* was a meaningful tradition that deserves greater acknowledgment for the light it sheds on the repertory of the sylph and her companions (Figure 2.17).

Auber, D. F. E. *Le Dieu et la Bayadère.* Paris: Bezou, 1830.

Beaumont, Cyril, *Complete Book of Ballets: A Guide to the Principal Ballets of the Nineteenth and Twentieth Centuries.* New York: Grosset and Dunlap, 1938.

Bergmüller, Friedrich. *La Péri: Ballet in Two Acts.* London: R. Cocks, 1843.

Burwick, Frederick. *The Journal of John Waldie Theatre Commentaries.* University of California Los Angeles: Charles E. Young Research Library Department of Special Collections, 2008.

Coralli, Eugéne. *La Péri.* 2nd ed. Paris: Mme. Vve. Jonas, 1843.

Cordova, Sarah Davies. *Paris Dances: Textual Choreographies in the Nineteenth-Century French Novel.* Bethesda, MD: International Scholars Publications, 1999.

Day, David A. 'The Annotated Violon Repetiteur and Early Romantic Ballet at the Theatre Royal De Bruxelles (1815-1830)' Ph.D. diss., New York University, 2008.

Gautier, Théophile. *The Péri.* London: W. S. Johnson, 1843.

Goethe, Johann Wolfgang von. *Italian Journey.* Translated by Robert R. Heitner. Edited by Thomas P. Saine. New York: Suhrkamp Publishers, 1989.

Guest, Ivor. *Jules Perrot: Master of the Romantic Ballet.* New York: Dance Horizons, 1984.

Holmstrom, Kirsten Gram. 'Attitude and Shawl Dance', in *International Encyclopedia of Dance,* vol. 1. New York: Oxford University Press, 1998.

Jeschke, Claudia, and Robert Atwood. 'Expanding Horizons: Techniques of Choreo-Graphy in Nineteenth-Century Dance.' *Dance Chronicle* 29 (2006): 195-214.

Janin, Jules, Philarète Chasles, and Théophile Gautier. *Les beautés de l'Opéra; ou, Chefs-d'oeuvre lyriques: Illustrés par les premiers artistes de Paris et de Londres sous la direction de Giraldon.* Paris: Soulié, 1845.

Mackrell, Alice. *Shawls, Stoles, and Scarves.* The Costume Accessories Series. Edited by Aileen Ribeiro. London: B. T. Batsford, Ltd., 1986.

Mazilier, Joseph. *Marco Spada, ou, La Fille du Bandit.* Paris: Jonas, 1857.

Ovid. *Metamorphoses.* Translated by Charles Martin. New York: W. W. Norton and Company, 2004.

Perrot, Jules. *Lalla Rookh.* London: G. Stuart, 1846.

Racinet, A. *Le Costume Historique.* 6 vols. Vol. 6,1888.

Said, Edward W. *Orientalism.* 25th Anniversary Edition, 1994. New York: Random House Vintage Books, 1978.

Taglioni, Filippo. *La Sylphide.* Paris: J.-N. Barba, 1832.

Théleur, E. A. *Letters on Dancing.* ed. Sandra Noll Hammond. Studies in Dance History Vol. 2, Pennington, NJ: Society of Dance History Scholars, 1990.

Notes

1. Kirsten Gram Holmstrom, 'Attitude and Shawl Dance', in *International Encyclopedia of Dance* (New York: Oxford University Press, 1998), Vol I, 199.

2. Sarah Davies Cordova, *Paris Dances: Textual Choreographies in the Nineteenth-Century French Novel* (Bethesda, MD: International Scholars Publications, 1999), 22-23, 31-33.

3. Cyril Beaumont, *Complete Book of Ballets: A Guide to the Principal Ballets of the Nineteenth and Twentieth Centuries* (New York: Grosset and Dunlap, 1938), 68.

4. Ibid., 243.

5. Ibid., 297.

6. Filippo Taglioni, *La Sylphide* (Paris: J.-N. Barba, 1832), 30. All translations are my own.

7. Alice Mackrell, *Shawls, Stoles, and Scarves*, ed. Aileen Ribeiro, The Costume Accessories Series (London: B. T. Batsford, Ltd., 1986), 68.

8. Ibid., 38.

9. A. Racinet, *Le Costume Historique*, 6 vols., vol. 6 (1888), unpaginated. Quoted in Ibid.

10. Two Théleur examples include dancers in formations that include both a long scarf or shawl and floral garlands. E. A. Théleur *Letters on Dancing*, vol. 2, ed. Sandra Noll Hammond, Studies in Dance History (Pennington, NJ: Society of Dance History Scholars, 1990), after page 48.

11. Claudia Jeschke and Robert Atwood, 'Expanding Horizons: Techniques of Choreo-Graphy in Nineteenth-Century Dance', *Dance Chronicle* 29 (2006): 202.

12. David A. Day, 'The Annotated Violon Repetiteur and Early Romantic Ballet at the Theatre Royal de Bruxelles (1815-1830)' (Ph.D. diss., New York University, 2008), 160.

13. D. F. E. Auber, *Le Dieu et la Bayadère* (Paris: Bezou, 1830), 15.

14. The libretto states of the Unknown, 'Enfin, ne pouvant plus resister a "son emotion, il se lève en regardant Zoloe".' (At last, no longer able to resist his emotions, he rises while looking at Zoloe.) He is kept from going to her by the sound of trumpets and a group of people arriving.

15. Joseph Mazilier, *Marco Spada, ou, La Fille du Bandit* (Paris: Jonas, 1857), 40.

16. Beaumont, *Complete Book of Ballets*, 230.

17. Frederick Burwick, *The Journal of John Waldie Theatre Commentaries*, (University of California Los Angeles: Charles E. Young Research Library Department of Special Collections, 2008). 12 June 1830.

18. Binney object 47, uncatalogued, Harvard Theatre Collection, Harvard College Libraries.

19. *La Presse*, 2 December 1860, quoted in Beaumont, *Complete Book of Ballets*, 294.

20. Mackrell, *Shawls, Stoles, and Scarves*, 33.

21. Ibid.

22. Johann Wolfgang von Goethe, *Italian Journey*, ed. Thomas P. Saine, trans. Robert R. Heitner (New York: Suhrkamp Publishers, 1989), 171.

23. Cordova, *Paris Dances*, 17-18; Mackrell, *Shawls, Stoles, and Scarves*, 9.

24. I owe this insight to Madison Sowell. Ovid, *Metamorphoses*, trans. Charles Martin (New York: W. W. Norton and Company, 2004), 308.

25. The libretto of the earliest Italian production of *La Sylphide* – staged by Antonio Cortesi in Genova in 1837 – labelled the work not a *ballo romantico* but a *ballo mitologico*, a genre label I have pondered for years. Although such speculation is somewhat tangential to a discussion of the *pas de schal*, it is possible that Cortesi, whose libretti indicate that he was a man of learning and widespread interests, may have been aware of the Ovidian connection when he attached that label to the title of his ballet on the libretto. It is also possible he simply associated *La Sylphide*, with its flying characters and Act Two sylvan setting, with the anacreontic staple *Flore et Zéphyr*.

26. Holmstrom, 'Attitude and Shawl Dance', 199.

27. Cordova, *Paris Dances*, 17.

28. Théleur's illustrations clearly differentiate between the use of the shawl in the 'Bayadère (with a shawl)' and 'Grecian (Modern)' plates on one hand, and the presence of draped garland found with the more classically-influenced tunics and chemise dress of plates 2, 'Grecian, Zephyr', and 4, 'Grecian, Flora' on the other.

29. Edward W. Said, *Orientalism*, 25th Anniversary Edition, 1994 ed. (New York: Random House Vintage Books, 1978), 38.

30. Ibid., 118, 58.

31. Friedrich Bergmüller, *La Péri: Ballet in Two Acts* (London: R. Cocks, 1843).

32. Eugéne Coralli, *La Péri*, 2nd ed. (Paris: Mme. Vve. Jonas, 1843), 15; Théophile Gautier, *The Péri* (London: W. S. Johnson, 1843), 15.

33. Ivor Guest, *Jules Perrot: Master of the Romantic Ballet* (New York: Dance Horizons, 1984), 168.

34. Jules Perrot, *Lalla Rookh* (London: G. Stuart, 1846), 2.

35. Guest, *Jules Perrot: Master of the Romantic Ballet*, 169. The Guido in question may be the Italian baroque painter Guido Reni.

36. 12 June 1846. Quoted in Beaumont, *Complete Book of Ballets*, 265.

37. Said, *Orientalism*, 40.

38. Mackrell, *Shawls, Stoles, and Scarves*, 48.

Chapter 3

Dancing *La Sylphide* in 1832:
Something Old or Something New?

Sandra Noll Hammond

The Sylphide leans against the window frame, her right foot planted firmly on the window sill, her left leg crossed in front with its knee bent and well-turned out, the tip of her toes resting on the sill near her supporting foot. This familiar image of Marie Taglioni, her eyes downcast, her long arms crossed low in front and resting against her white bouffant skirt, is among six lithographs of the dancer in the role of the Sylphide drawn by the English artist Alfred E. Chalon in 1845 (Figure 3. 1).[1] A similar pose for the Sylphide appears in Act One of productions of the ballet, 'choreographed after Filippo Taglioni', by Pierre Lacotte, first in 1972 and later revised and then filmed in 2004, but it does not appear in the 1836 version by August Bournonville as it has survived in the repertory of the Royal Danish Ballet.

Does the image drawn in 1845 give an accurate rendering of a pose by Marie Taglioni in the original production of thirteen years before? Can it, or any iconography prior to the advent of photography and of moving pictures, provide truthful information about how and what dancers might have performed in the 1830s in ballets for which we have little, if any, primary choreographic documentation?[2] These questions are particularly challenging for those of us who are interested in the actual dancing – the steps, the poses, the dance technique – in ballets of the past. Is it even possible to speak with any specificity about the dancing of that first Sylphide, Marie Taglioni (1804-1884), who, to quote a twentieth-century ballet dictionary, 'assisted in creating a new style' and 'transformed the dance on points'?[3] Just how innovative was she? Was there any 'new' ballet technique revealed for the first time in *La Sylphide*? Are we seeing ballet technique and vocabulary typical of the 1830s in today's productions of *La Sylphide*? And where can we go for clues to answer to such questions?

For some answers to these questions, we can view dance images of the period as well as modern video recordings of performances of *La Sylphide*. To help in the analysis, we can look at writings by dancers who also were dance instructors in the period prior to, during, and shortly after the première of *La Sylphide*, as well as their choreographic notes and dance notations. In doing

3.1. Marie Taglioni in *La Sylphide*. Lithograph by J. S. Templeton after A. E. Chalon. The New York Public Library for the Performing Arts / Jerome Robbins Dance Division. By permission.

so, we can enlarge our understanding of a critical aspect of ballet history, its technical history.

Background of the choreographers

But first, a brief discussion is in order about the two choreographers responsible for the original French and Danish productions of *La Sylphide*, Filippo Taglioni (1777-1871) and August Bournonville (1805-1879).

Both men, born into 'ballet families', had fathers who were dancers and choreographers. Taglioni's father, Carlo, born in Torino circa 1750, performed in various Italian cities and in various styles. His choreographies were seen in Florence, Venice, and in Paris at the Gaîté and Porte-Saint-Martin theatres. Bournonville's father, Antoine (1760-1843), born in Lyon, studied with Jean-Georges Noverre (1727-1810), the prominent choreographer, ballet theorist, and early proponent of *ballet d'action*, the forerunner of pantomime-ballet. Antoine eventually settled in Copenhagen in 1792, first as a dancer and then as director of the Royal Danish Ballet from 1816-23.

Both sons eventually went to Paris to strengthen their technique and polish their style by taking lessons with the leading instructors of the time – Taglioni with Jean-François Coulon (1764-1836) beginning in 1799, and Bournonville in the 1820s with Auguste Vestris (1760-1842). Thus, to talk about dance technique at the time of *La Sylphide*, we must consider both the ballet traditions in Paris inherited from the previous century and the newer training methods that shaped these two great choreographers.

In the eighteenth century, it was customary, especially in France, to have three different genres of dances – the *noble*, the *demi-caractère*, and the *comique*, with the addition sometimes of a fourth category, the *grotesque*. Depending upon physical characteristics (height, muscularity, etc.) and movement aptitudes, a dancer was expected to excel in one of those styles. By the latter part of the eighteenth century, these separate genres were gradually disappearing, and by the time of *La Sylphide*, to the despair of some observers, there seemed to be only one category of dancer:

> Formerly we had (independent of the grotesque) three distinct styles of dances. First, the grand serious; this was used on all occasions where the intention was to personate grandeur, or majesty: secondly, the demi-character; this was used to personate all light, airy, or gay characters, such as zephyrs, pages, peasantry, etc.: thirdly the comic; this was used as a dance of country clowns, etc.: but of late the two first [styles] have been so blended with each other, that they now actually form but one, and the comic latterly has become almost obsolete.... Thus there remains at the present time (correctly speaking) only one style, in which all dancers strive to gain...the approbation of the public; thus it necessarily happens, that so few persons succeed in the attempt. How much better and more meritorious it would have been to have kept each style distinct....[4]

Perhaps the dancer most responsible for this merging of styles was Auguste Vestris. Indeed, Noverre wrote, not without some reservations, that Vestris 'eliminated the three well-known and distinct genres; he merged and amalgamated them...'[5]

Technical training

That amalgamated technique and style whereby greater and greater virtuosity, even including what had once seemed acrobatic elements, could appear effortless and elegant was to become the goal of a dancer's training in Paris, as it was also in Milan at La Scala in the classes of Carlo Blasis (1795-1878) and in Naples at the ballet school of the Teatro San Carlo, directed by Filippo's brother, Salvatore Taglioni (1789-1868). It was arduous work, as recalled by Giovanni Léopold Adice, whose training began in Italy[6] and whose association with the ballet at the Paris Opera as dancer and then instructor spanned a period from the early 1840s until his retirement in 1867. Barre work alone could include 128 *grands battements*, 96 *petits battements* (analogous to today's *battements tendus*), 64 slow *petits battements sur le cou de pied* and 120 rapid ones, as well as some 256 *ronds de jambes* of various kinds and speeds.[7] These exercises were merely the warm-up, as many were repeated in centre floor before going on to lengthy series of set combinations designed to develop 'aplomb', the ability to sustain movements of balance in a variety of poses. The combinations would progress into turning variations and finally light springs could be added, always keeping the classical ballet forms as established in the slower exercises. Following these were lengthy combinations of many different kinds of *pirouettes*. Finally, the class concluded with the '*tems terre à terre*', quick small steps woven into *enchaînements* (combinations) performed in different directions, and then the '*tems de vigueur*', the jumps which could be embellished with multiple beats, *ronds de jambe*, and turns.

The technical vocabulary and training were not too different for men than for women, even as they were expected to dance 'in a manner very different' from one another. The 'bold majestic execution' of the men should contrast with the 'lithesome and graceful motions' of the women.[8] Even so, they shared many of the same challenges. For example, pointe work, which now we associate only with female dancers, was, in the early nineteenth century, simply another level of elevation for anyone. Exercises to build strength in the feet for balancing on toe-tip were practised by most dancers, even ballroom dancers.[9] These exercises were practised and performed in the regular dancing slippers of the time. No new equipment was required. Gradually, darning around the sides provided some support and traction, but in 1832 there were no blocked, or reinforced, shoes as there are today.

Early evolutions of the choreographies of *La Sylphide*

Both Taglioni and Bournonville made alterations in later mountings of their versions of *La Sylphide*. For example, in 1839, seven years after its premier, Taglioni inserted the lengthy '*pas de l'Ombre*' or shadow dance in Act One, featuring James, Effie, and the elusive Sylphide, using additional music.[10]

Although Marie Taglioni retired from performing in 1847, the ballet most identified with her continued in the Paris Opera ballet repertory until 1858, when it was chosen for the debut performance of her 16-year-old protégée, Emma Livry (née Emarot). For the occasion, Joseph Mazilier, the *premier maître de ballet* (and the original James in the ballet), made some changes, including adding a new *pas de deux* for Act Two with music by Louis Clapisson.[11] What has variously been termed by Pierre Lacotte a 'reconstitution' of the ballet, a 'staging' of the ballet, and choreography 'after Taglioni', first appeared in 1972 as a made-for-television production and then, in a later staging at the Paris Opéra, it was filmed in 2004. Films from these productions are the principal sources of my comments on Lacotte's versions of the ballet.[12] However, to the frustration of dance historians, Lacotte has declined to reveal and document some of his crucial sources for the retrieval of Taglioni's original work.

In his memoirs, Bournonville states that he had seen 'the Parisian *Sylphide* but a single time' and came away 'filled with nought but admiration for Mlle. Taglioni's extraordinary bravura and amazement at the splendid machinery'. The idea of the ballet was 'most appealing', but the score was 'entirely too expensive, and those who could have taught me the roles (for they had to be taught) did not seem disposed to do so just then.' Desirous to present his talented student, Lucile Grahn, in the role of the Sylphide and being prompted to 'try a young musical talent' in Copenhagen, Herman Severin Løvenskjold, Bournonville retained the essence of the original story and characters, of prime importance at the time, but created new choreography to new music, not an unusual practice in those days, and expanded the role of James.[13]

According to the Danish dance historian Knud Arne Jürgensen, Bournonville did not make notations of his ballet until 1849, probably during or after rehearsals when he restaged it that year, which included additional music for a more extended divertissement for the sylphides in Act Two. Then in 1865, for still another production, Bournonville again rechoreographed the sylphides' divertissement, and interestingly, included 'notation...for steps performed on pointe', perhaps an indication that by this time more of the women's steps were being done on full pointe.[14] As will be discussed later, other changes have crept into the many productions of this, the oldest of Bournonville's ballets in the repertory of the Royal Danish Ballet; I base most of my comments about the current version of Bournonville's ballet on the 1988 film of a production by Hans Brenaa, as staged by Henning Kronstam and Arlette Weinrich for the Royal Danish Ballet.[15]

Analysing the choreography
Consider the following quite different views from eminent ballet historians about ballet art of the Romantic era:

> Our knowledge and understanding of ballet in the remote past would be immeasurably diminished were we to be deprived of the drawings and prints that enable us to see in our mind's eye how the dancers appeared to their contemporaries. The importance of pictorial material to the ballet historian can hardly be overstated. To begin with, it fires his imagination. This is of vital and indeed primary importance, for history is much more than a compilation of the facts gathered by research, for it is a literary art that carries the reader back in time with an insight into how things were and why....
>
> In ferreting out this material the ballet historian is blessed with an indispensable guide in the form of the iconographer. The period of the Romantic Ballet, which flourished so gloriously in the first half of the nineteenth century, has been specially well served by scholars of this nature, and most deservedly so, for it coincided with the golden age of the lithograph.[16]

> No lithographs of the Romantic era pretend to truth of representation. The exquisitely tapered feet, the delicate balance, the notions of flight and the prettily rounded but unmuscular limbs foster illusions about dancing and about womanhood. The Romantic ballerina was never truthfully represented save in the occasional portrait of her as a woman rather than as a dancing character.[17]

As we proceed in this discussion, we will see if our imaginations can be 'fired up' and if we can be 'ferreting out' some truths about how and what dancers were dancing. In such an endeavour, caution is advised. *Rule #1: Look for similarity of position or movement, not necessarily similarity of nomenclature, for ballet terminology can vary at different times and different locations.*[18]
Let us begin with that pose of Marie Taglioni, as the Sylphide leaning against the window frame, and the question raised at the beginning of this chapter: Does the image give an accurate rendering of a pose from the original production of the ballet? My answer would be yes, I think that it very well may. Was it something new for ballet? The answer is no, but, as will become clearer later on, it can serve as a link in ballet's technical history from the eighteenth to the present century. *Rule #2: beware of claiming that someone was 'the first to.....' or that this was 'the beginning of.....'*

Tracing the pose in the window

As documented by Edmund Fairfax, in his research of eighteenth-century theatrical dance technique, the term for the position of the legs in the pose in the window was '*la statue*', its introduction into ballet performance attributed to the famed danseur Gaëton (Gaetano) Vestris (1729-1808), father of Auguste Vestris. According to the *Journal des théâtres* in 1778, Vestris' stance conveyed nothing more than 'look how beautiful I am'.[19] Certainly Vestris was not the inventor of the pose; it appears frequently in male portraiture of the eighteenth century, and no doubt it had been seen in ballets prior to 1778. Nevertheless, the connection to Vestris prompts a speculation that the Sylphide's pose in the window can be read on at least two levels – the head and torso presumably express demure sadness for the impossibility of her infatuation for James, while the feet and legs suggest the strength and vanity once associated with the leading male danseur at the Opéra. The bi-gendered nature of the pose is evident in its many renderings in dance iconography of the nineteenth century, and, pertinent to this discussion, in the final pose of the male dancers in Lacotte's dance of the villagers in Act One.

Descriptions of the stance, as it typically appeared in academic ballet practice, are provided by two nineteenth-century dancer/authors. *Rule #3: by the time technique is written down, especially if published, it is already old enough to be considered part of the accepted tradition.*

In his instruction manual *Letters on Dancing* (London, 1831), the ballet dancer and dancing master Edward Allcock Théleur illustrates the pose, using a male figure and, in his idiosyncratic ballet nomenclature, designates it as one of his 'half aerial stations':

> The Second Half Aerial Station is when the weight of the body is on one foot, the other heel rose up, the toe slightly resting on the ground and close against the leg supporting the body. This may be done behind or before [the supporting leg] as circumstances may require.[20]

Fairfax has found a similar description of the pose by Franz Anton Roller, a professional dancer in the 1790s, in his book on dance technique published in Weimar in 1843. According to Roller, the stance was known as the *stée*:

> The *stée* is merely a position wherein one stands with one foot flat on the whole sole while the other, with the knee bent and well turned out to the side, is set firmly on the tip of the toe, enclosed in front or behind the other in fifth position.[21]

Here, then, is evidence that the Sylphide's pose in the window, as depicted by Chalon, is related to a venerable ballet position, one long in use, that logically

could have appeared in the original production of *La Sylphide* and that remained popular long afterward. And, when there appears a caricature of
Taglioni in the pose, albeit showing her as a rather tired sylphide leaning
sideways with her left elbow resting on a pedestal, the popular association of
the pose with the Sylphide is unmistakable.[22] Clearly the Chalon image and
the caricature of Taglioni show her raised foot further across her standing
leg than described above or shown in the illustration from Théleur, but such
augmentation of academic positions was so prevalent that Théleur even feels
the need to account for them by his new numbering system of what he pre-
fers to call 'stations'. As he explains:

> It may be remarked by some persons, that I am making the art more com-
> plicated, by introducing so many stations: let them observe carefully the
> present style of dancing, and they will perceive that the whole of the sta-
> tions I have mentioned are used in the art, and that the present system of
> the five positions is so far from being a sufficient guide, that we swerve
> considerably from it in almost every step we do, particularly when we go in
> an oblique direction.[23]

Both Théleur and Roller go on to 'fire the imagination' by their comments on
movements that can follow the position. Théleur's examples are for slow
movements, what today might be termed *adage* or *adagio*, while Roller suggests the opposite, what today might be termed *allegro*. By the time of *La
Sylphide*, it had long been customary for a solo entrée or *pas seul*, as well as
most *pas de deux*, to have two parts, beginning with a slow section followed by
a lively, quicker section.[24] Let us begin, then, with the slow movements from
Théleur's 'second half aerial station'.

It is, he says, used in the *pas grave* and sometimes as a preparation for the
coupés 'high or not, as circumstances require'.[25] In this instance, his *coupé*
was a leg extension, comparable to today's *développé*, and typically it was
preceded by a step forward, sideward, or backward or by a rise onto the balls
of the feet. 'High' would mean that the leg would unfold and extend to 'the
height of the hip'. As such, the *coupé/développé* could be performed in two
ways – by bringing the foot from the 'half aerial' position either up to the
knee, before the extension, or directly to a half-bent or *attitude* angle at hip
level, before the complete extension. In the nineteenth century, this latter
option seems to have been preferred when the extensions were performed
slowly, perhaps so that throughout the movement the foot would remain
visible below the dancers' skirts.[26]

When performing these movements, says Théleur, 'care should be taken,
while raising the leg, not to raise the knee above the line of the hip.' If the leg
is raised higher, which he does not recommend, then it 'must be performed

with the leg straight'.[27] Thus, one might unfold the leg to hip level, and then raise it higher, or, if one is executing a *grand battement*, it might go higher than hip level since the leg would be straight throughout the entire movement. Marie Taglioni was not known to have leg extensions higher than the norm, meaning hip level, which remained the standard practice throughout the century (beautifully rendered in late nineteenth-century drawings and paintings by Edgar Degas). Things were perhaps even stricter in the early 1900s, as stated in the section on *grands battements* in the 1922 Cecchetti manual, *Theory & Practice of Classical Theatrical Dancing*:

> On no account should the foot be raised higher than at right angles to the hip, for then the exercise tends to become an essay in acrobatics, which is opposed to the laws of the dance.[28]

It is doubtful that ballet audiences of 1832 and for the next hundred years or so would have seen many extensions above waist level, except by comic characters or acrobatic dancers, none of whom appeared in *La Sylphide*. In the present day, however, most dancers in the ballet often extend their legs far above the norm for extensions in the nineteenth and early twentieth centuries, and over-the-head extensions and 'six-o'clock' *arabesques penchées* are no strangers to the technique of a Sylphide.[29] Now, on to the *stée* as discussed by Roller:

> This position either precedes or ends a step, commonly in order to create a pause and to show a momentary rest of the whole body, whereupon, as a rule, quick or beaten steps follow by way of contrast.

What were the 'quick or beaten steps' that might have followed the *stée* in ballet choreography and how might the position relate to ballet allegro in *La Sylphide*? For some clues to these questions we can leap ahead to 1923, exactly eighty years after Roller's document, to a book entitled *The Art of Terpsichore* by Luigi Albertieri (c.1860-1930), a protégé of the famous teacher Enrico Cecchetti (1850-1928). In a 'Brief Dictionary of Dancing' at the back of his book, Albertieri lists the 'stay: A step in which you jump from one leg to the other, word without etymological origin [we now know better!], used commonly in the art of dance by the old masters.'[30] As explained by Albertieri, the 'stay' was a 'jump from one leg to the other', and as such differed from a '*jeté*' in which the 'body is thrown forward by a jump finishing on one leg'.[31]

In his six lessons of the week, loosely modelled on Cecchetti's, Albertieri includes numerous *enchaînements* with 'stays', such as '*petits* stays under the body, arms at the demi position, forward in an oblique line for sixteen counts'; 'stay, and *temps elevé*, eight times forward and eight times back-ward'; and many examples of 'stay, *petit battement*' which might very well be related to Roller's '*stée-battements*'. In the latter, beginning from a *stée*, one rises high onto the crossed foot and makes *battements* or beats in front and behind with the other foot.[32]

As these examples suggest, *la statue* is related to the *stée*, which was not only a pose that could precede or end a movement, but was also a position connected to lively steps, eventually becoming the 'stay', a movement or step on its own. In the Lacotte versions of *La Sylphide* as well as the traditional Royal Danish Ballet version, most of the characters provide many examples of what Albertieri might call '*petit* stays under the body, arms at the demi position', that is, small springs from one foot to the other, with the raised foot either in front or behind the other, and the arms held low. Indeed, today's Bournonville vocabulary includes '*petit jeté*', defined as 'a small jeté without a brush'.[33] So we have *petit jeté / petit stay / stée / statue* – a thread linking one ballet era to another and to the original Sylphide.

Rapidity and observing the *ballon*
Moving with speed and with lightness had long been a hallmark of the good dancer. In 1828, echoing his book of eight years earlier, Carlo Blasis wrote:

> Rapidity is also very pleasing in a dancer; lightness, still more so; the one imparts a brilliance to his performance, the other has in it something of an aerial appearance that charms the eye of the spectator. Observe the *ballon*; nothing can be more delightful than to see you bounding with graceful elasticity in your steps, scarcely touching the ground, and seeming at every moment on the point of flying in the air.[34]

This sounds like a description of the Sylphide, but she did not appear until several years later.

Certainly, any ballet from the period of *La Sylphide* contained dances rich with rapid and bounding allegro steps, augmented with beats and *ronds de jambe* and turns. A bountiful source of examples of classroom and theatrical *enchaînements* of steps can be found in the teaching notebooks compiled between 1829 and 1836 by Michel St. Léon (né Léon Michel),[35] father and first teacher of the famous dancer/choreographer Arthur Saint-Léon (1821-1870). *Brisés* of all kinds (either landing on one foot or on two; travelling upstage, downstage, sideways; turning; often with a third step as in *brisé à trois pas*), *entrechats* (*trois, quatre, cinq, six, sept* are common), *cabrioles* travelling forward and backward, and of course *pirouettes* of multiple spins (often with the raised leg changing from one position to another) are just some of the typical vocabulary for ballet allegro. *Enchaînements* were usually four to sixteen counts in length, usually performed to one side and then repeated to the other, or travelling forward and then in reverse, and sometimes repeated in the entirety.

The speed of ballet allegro in this period is an important factor in the staging of *La Sylphide*. Lacotte recalls that he was 'slightly perplexed because at one stage I could not reconcile steps and music'. So, he consulted one of his teachers, Lubov Egorova (1880-1972), who had knowledge of the ballet from her teacher, Christian Pehr Johansson (1817-1903), a student of Bournonville's who had been involved in the restaging of the ballet in St. Petersburg in 1892. Egorova told Lacotte that the steps 'correspond perfectly with the music....Only it is much quicker than what you are doing!'[36]

I have had this experience also when trying to reconstruct dances from the early 1800s. The sources reveal *enchaînements* with so many steps for, seemingly, so little music. The obvious solution is to reduce the size of the movements, but the not-so-obvious answer is to reduce the size of, or almost eliminate, the time-consuming *plié* when preparing for or landing from small allegro steps. Consider the advice from Théleur:

> In the jumping movement, the force should be taken principally with the feet, and under no circumstances assisted by the arms....Care should be taken in the descent to arrive on the points of the toes, and not allow the heels suddenly to reach the ground, but to take sufficient strength in the joints of the toes, and in the insteps, to support the body, permitting the heels to approach the ground gradually....With few exceptions, steps should terminate with the knees straight...thus making each step perfect in itself before the commencement of another.[37]

This did not mean that the legs were stiff or that they were straight all the time. For example, the 'commencement' of a step usually involved some bend of the supporting leg before the weight was taken onto the other leg or onto both legs, either by means of a rise or a spring. If the spring involved a higher jumping movement, then the landing would usually require some give or bend of the knees. However, the knees should quickly straighten, the 'few exceptions' being when another spring or jump was to immediately follow. Recalling her training, Marie Taglioni stated that springing must come from the heels, without any movement from the body, and the knees involved very little. Therefore, she said, one did not jump very high in these steps, but such '*élan*' gave her a delightful sense of vibrating in the air just above the ground.[38]

Examples of steps in the period of *La Sylphide*
As stated earlier, the step vocabulary at this time was vast and varied. And

one 'step' could have many parts. A good example is the *sissonne doublée*, a step with its genesis in the Baroque period, but which by the early 1800s consisted of an *assemblé*, a *sissonne*, a *coupé* (performed as a quick cut under the supporting foot) and another *assemblé* – all performed rapidly in the manner of a one-step unit. In the Bournonville *Sylphide* Act One, repeated *sissonnes doublées* are performed with great swiftness, and scarcely a hint of *plié*, in the Scottish dance of the wedding guests and James and Effie. This seems to be a typical execution of the step in the period of *La Sylphide*, for there are many similar examples in the notebooks of Michel St. Léon. As Bournonville pointed out, and notated in his *Études chorégraphiques*, the *sissonne doublée* was the new name of an old step, the *pas de rigaudon*.[39] Popular in brisk dances such as bourrées and rigaudons of the late seventeenth century and throughout much of the eighteenth, the *pas de rigaudon* consisted of the same basic movements as the 'new' *sissonne doublée*. *(Remember Rule #1.)*

Another fleet allegro series with a long history is one performed by James in the Bournonville Act One, a diagonal combination of *brisés sur un pied* (today sometimes termed *brisés volés*) performed three times and, with a final *assemblé* or *glissade*, completing one full revolution. This turning combination is repeated three times. The *enchaînement* itself is an embellishment on *passo di ciaccona*, as described by Gennaro Magri in 1779, in which the dancer performs a *jeté*, a *ballonné*, another *jeté*, and an *assemblé*, each movement done with a quarter of a turn, so a complete revolution is made by the end of the *enchaînement*.[40] And, Magri's *passo* was an embellishment on the old *pas de chaconne*, a complete turn made with a *jeté*, a hop, and a leap (*jeté contretemps ballonné*, in the vocabulary of the seventeenth and eighteenth centuries).

According to Jürgensen, changes have been made in the male solos of Act One. For example, it is possible that the variation originally for 'an unnamed Scottish peasant' was 'revised' by Gustave Carey (1812-1881) for Hans Beck 'sometime around 1878-1879.'[41] Beck (1861-1952) later took Bournonville *enchaînements* and turned them into formalised classroom combinations, thus preserving the technique and many repertoire excerpts in the 'Bournonville School' of daily classes. A variation from *La Sylphide*, possibly by Carey, is part of the Tuesday class, combination number 21 in the present Bournonville School. It is full of light, quick jumps, beats, changes of direction, and a step of some historical interest, the *chassé contretemps*. This was a name bestowed by Bournonville as better than the old term, *tems de cuisse*. For readers who are familiar with today's usual *temps de cuisse* (a quick *dégagé* to 5th *plié*, followed by a *sissonne*, that is, a spring off of two feet), they would know that it does not involve a 'beat' of the legs, no bringing one *cuisse*, the thigh, against the other. The explanation of *chassé contretemps* in contemporary Bournonville technique is a clear description of the 'old' *tems de cuisse*:

> Stand on the right [foot] with the left in tendu derrière, left coupé dessous, right posé en avant, and jump while simultaneously beating the left in 5th behind and then immediately passing left forward into croisé devant, transferring weight onto the left.[42]

The description goes on to say that the step should travel in a light, not high, manner with no rebounding quality of the leg after the beat, as occurs for instance in a *cabriole*. In his 1852 book on his system of dance notation, Arthur Saint-Léon shows this type of *tems de cuisse*, much as his father describes in two of his notebooks.[43]

Now, why would Bournonville prefer to call the step *chassé contretemps*? Perhaps he knew that the so-called *tems de cuisse* was an embellishment (the beat) on part of the old *contretemps de menuet*, with which he no doubt was familiar. Of course, the timing of the menuet contretemps step was different from the later 'versions', but the similarity of the movements is unmistakable. *(Remember Rule #1.)*

This brings up some interesting phenomena: changes in timing of steps and the use of the *plié*, both of which seem to have occurred somewhere after the 'baroque' and before the 'romantic' period of theatrical dance. A simple example is the *pas de bourrée*, a three-step sequence. As documented in the early decades of the eighteenth century, a preparatory bend happened on the 'and', or upbeat, before the musical measure, then the step (an up, up, down sequence) began on the first beat of the new measure. But in the nineteenth century, as clearly shown in Saint-Léon's notation system, the two up, up steps of the *pas de bourrée* happen before the measure, and the down step occurs on the first beat of the new measure. Thus, it is timed 'and-a-One', that is, step-step, *plié* – the accent now on the bend at the beginning of the measure, rather than on the rise as in the earlier form.[44] This 'new' timing seems to be preferred when the *pas de bourrée* is to be performed at a brisk tempo.

In the nineteenth century, even slow movements, such as the *grands coupés*, often began with a *plié* on the first beat of the measure, then a step or rise and a leg extension, whereas in the previous century the bend usually occurred before the measure and the rise or step occurred on the first beat of the new measure.[45] This 'new' timing occurs in the *divertissement* in the Bournonville version Act Two, when the sylphides close to fifth position on the first beat of the measure and then perform a *développé en avant*. This phrase is repeated several times. Changes in elevation (down versus up), in conjunction with changes in timing, add up to a new and different 'look' to

3.2. Fanny Cerrito in *Alma, London Illustrated News*, 17 August 1844, p. 112.

an old and similar movement. No doubt this was a gradual evolution. *(Remember Rule #2.)*

The *jeté battu, jeté tendu, jeté en attitude, jeté en tournant,* and *grand jeté* in *La Sylphide* were part of the vocabulary for both male and female dancers of the time, as much of the ballet vocabulary was shared by both sexes. Such rapid, complex, and aerial movements defy easy illustration by artists, and often we are left only with images of the Sylphide hovering barefoot (a great artistic license!) near the clouds. Sometimes nineteenth-century newspaper illustrations, such as the so-called 'gestural drawings' of the *Illustrated London News,* accompanying a performance review, allow a more honest view (Figure 3.2). Such sources, as well as the time-honoured method by which ballet step vocabulary has been handed down from teacher to student, suggest, for example, that *jetés en avant* in the period of *La Sylphide,* and long afterward, were not like the contemporary horizontal splits of the legs, but instead were arching leaps.

The rapidity of the allegro, the timing, as well as the phrase length and floor patterns of *enchaînements* of this period, as discussed above, are corroborated in the research by Jürgensen in his comparison of some of Bournonville's step phrases and those of Hans Beck, done to the same music. Beck was director of the Danish ballet from 1894-1915, and much of the surviving Bournonville repertory has been based on his later versions of the material. Jürgensen has found four distinct differences:

1. Bournonville had a step for almost every musical beat; Beck had fewer steps spread over many beats.

2. In Bournonville's steps and jumps, the accent goes down on the first beat of the measure; Beck's jumps are up on the first beat and land on the second or third beat.

3. Bournonville's floor patterns are smaller and more symmetrical than Beck's.

4. Bournonville uses smaller phrases and combinations of steps than Beck does.[46]

Scarcely touching the ground

A favourite 'scarcely touching the ground' image conveying 'an aerial appearance that charms the eye' seems to have been, and still is, that of a dancer poised high on the ball or tip of one foot while the other leg is raised behind. We know this pose today as *arabesque*, but at the time of *La Sylphide* the *attitude à la arabesque* could mean a pose in which one leg was raised either behind or in front. The arms could be arranged in a variety of ways, depending upon the character being portrayed. A common arrangement, used frequently in *La Sylphide*, was to have both arms extended forward of the body, elbows gently relaxed, the arm corresponding to the supporting leg raised slightly higher than the other arm. This became known as *arabesque à l'ange*, perhaps meant to convey flight associated with images of angels. Today's version, known also as *arabesque à deux bras* or third *arabesque*, often is performed with the arms farther apart and the elbows almost straight, rather than the gentle curve typically observed in the nineteenth century.

Another convention for the arms in an *arabesque*, observed throughout the nineteenth century and well into the twentieth, was for the forward arm (or the lower arm if both were raised) to be parallel to the floor from elbow to wrist.

At the time of *La Sylphide*, and throughout the rest of the century, female dancers wore corsets under their practice clothes and under their costumes, as was true for dancers in the previous century. Although the construction of corsets changed over time, corsets always restricted the height of an *arabesque*, because, at some level, the leg when raised to the back would cause the hip to hit the corset, and then the torso, by necessity, had to tilt forward, else the corset boning would pinch the flesh. The higher the leg, the more the torso must incline forward, requiring a change in balance. This is not an easy adjustment for a dancer today, who has been trained to keep her torso as upright as possible in an *arabesque*. Lacotte recalls that he 'went as far as asking the [Paris Opéra] dancers to wear their corsets during rehearsals.

They did so eventually, though only after threatening to strike...'.[47] Happily for the audience, this pragmatic adaptation created a greater image of lightness and lingering flight as the sylphs leaned forward, especially when the supporting foot was balanced on the 'tips of the toes'.

Dancing on the tips of the toes

Executing certain steps and poses on a higher and higher pointe of the foot was a well-established part of technical training by 1832. For at least twenty years prior, dance instruction manuals and notebooks had included specific information for how to rise onto the points of the toes and suggestions of exercises to build the strength for doing so.[48] (*Remember Rule #3.*) Choreographic notes during this period can be misleading, however, because of differences in terminology then and now. (*Remember Rule #1.*). A case in point (pardon the pun) is the phrase '*sur les pointes*' that by the latter part of the century as well as today implies on full pointe, but in the early nineteenth century could also mean on the balls of the feet. Blasis, for example, writes of 'on the toes', but his illustrations show only demi-pointes, high three-quarter pointes, and a higher position on the pads of the toes for ballet dancers as well as for social dancers. Only when an author illustrates or notates full pointe, or uses phrases such as 'on the tips of the toes' (as in Théleur) or '*sur les orteils*' (as in Arthur Saint-Léon and his father, Michel St. Léon), can we be reasonably certain that the use of full pointes is intended, and even then the implication may be for a rise to the pads of the toes. However, it is clear that more movements were performed higher and higher on the toes in later decades, when some reinforcement was added to the soft slippers.

Today's reinforced, blocked, pointe shoes were unimagined in 1832, with stronger shoes being the result of a very gradual development after mid-century. In the collection of the Paris Opéra, a pair of apparently unworn slippers attributed to Marie Taglioni appears to be rather delicate satin shoes with no structural reinforcement. Dancers in such soft slippers would need to either spring or press up from the heels, keeping their feet in a firm and compact unit, rather than roll up through the arches and toes onto the pointe position. Once there, they had to keep the toe joints straight and pressed together, maintaining a vertical line up through the insteps and ankles. No rolling over in these shoes! This endeavour required enormous strength and reflected hours of practice and refinement of correct alignment throughout the entire body (Figure 3.3).

Taglioni's daily practice, as she recalled, included *pliés* performed as gently and deeply as possible, in such a way that she could touch the floor with her hands, without bending her back, and then, she said, she rose smoothly and without effort to the extremities of the points of her toes.[49] She did have

3.3. Paul and Amalia Galster Taglioni in the first U.S. performance of the complete *La Sylphide* (1839, Park Theatre NYC). Lithograph by Napoleon Sarony. The New York Public Library for the Performing Arts / Jerome Robbins Dance Division, Cia Fornaroli Collection. By permission.

quite long arms, but this seems an unusual exercise in an era when typically *pliés* were practised without raising the heels from the floor. In his discussion of the lesson, Blasis firmly states that in the five positions of the feet 'the knees must be bent without raising the heels in the least from the ground', a sentiment echoed by Théleur.[50] There was no term 'grand' *plié*, although occasionally there were phrases like *plié bien bas*, or very low, in centre combinations of aplomb and pirouettes.

The 'exquisitely tapered feet' in shoes with pencil-point toes depicted in numerous lithographs of ballerinas in 'delicate' balances are neither truthful images of the slippers nor of the dancers. Some artists, Edgar Degas among them, occasionally reveal a more realistic view, one that shows the broad base of the end of the shoe and the wrinkled fabric as it crumpled under the pressure of the weight of the dancer.

Such realistic images of pointe technique are featured in *La Danse au Théâtre*, written in 1890 by Berthe Bernay, who had spent over two decades in ballet at the Paris Opéra, first as a student, then as dancer, and finally as teacher. During some of Bernay's student years, Marie Taglioni was an important member of the teaching faculty, bringing about certain reforms in the curriculum in the course of her tenure there from 1858 to 1870. By then, Taglioni was long-retired from her performing career, which ended in 1847, so Bernay would never have seen her on stage. Apparently, however, as reported by Bernay in her section on *pirouettes*, the accepted lore was that 'La Taglioni ne tournait pas *sur les pointes*' (La Taglioni did not turn *sur les pointes*).[51] If la Taglioni did not *pirouette* on full pointe, then it is fairly certain that no other dancer in *La Sylphide* did either. But, it is also fair to assume that all female dancers in the premier performance of *La Sylphide* were capable of performing the basic repertory of steps *sur les orteils* as documented in the manuals. Examples of these included steps *sur place* such as *tems de cou-de-pied* or rises in fifth position and from fifth position to second position; traveling steps such as a simple walks and rapid *emboités* forward, sideward, and backward; steps with slight springs such as *assemblés* and *changements de pieds*; and turns on two feet, *en dehors* and *en dedans*, rather like today's *soutenu* turn or *assemblé en tournant*.

Balances on one foot also are documented. A typical example from St. Léon is the following: after a rise *sur les orteils*, '*faites battement tendu devant de la jambe de devant de même derrière la jambe de derrière*'. In his notes of 1835 for a pas de deux, St. Léon includes a simple drawing of a dancer on full pointe in an '*attitude à l'arabesque*', her raised leg extended to the front, her balance sustained by her partner who holds her by the waist. This pose is at the conclusion of the opening andante section of the pas de deux.[52]

Granted a dancer could briefly sustain a pose on full pointe, but would she also have been able to slowly promenade on full pointe on one foot, even as she was steadied by her partner? Today's *Sylphide* productions suggest yes, but has the promenade been tried in soft, unblocked shoes?

It is doubtful that turns spinning across the floor, such as today's *déboulés* or *chaînés tours*, would have been performed on full pointe. Lacotte admits that his decision to 'introduce' such turns on full pointe, which he acknowledges were originally executed on demi-pointes, was simply a case of 'not disorienting the modern public'.[53]

Whether or not all female dancers *were* on full pointe in *La Sylphide* remains a question. Effie's friends in Act One are not on full pointe in the Bournonville version, which gives a meaningful contrast between those robust village girls and the ethereal forest sylphs of Act Two, who are on full pointe, a contrast missing in the Lacotte 'reconstitutions', where all female dancers, except the witches, are in pointe shoes.[54]

Something old or something new?

Perhaps, as this discussion has suggested, there may not have been much that was really new in 1832, or 1836, in the steps, poses, and *enchaînements*, or even in the technique used in performing those movements in *La Sylphide*, but changes have certainly crept in to the ballet's productions, beginning with additions and re-choreographed sections by Taglioni and Bournonville themselves. Through the years, the trend in performance has been toward more virtuosity – more steps, turns, and characters on full pointe; six-o'clock *arabesques*; split *grands jetés*; overhead lifts; arms higher and fingers spread wider, etc. This trend is not new; indeed it is really one of ballet's traditions. What at one time seems an acrobatic stunt often becomes, in succeeding generations of dancers, the accepted norm, as noted in 1754 by the dance historian Louis de Cahusac:

> Thus, for over a century, the same comments have been repeated concerning every single forward step which the Dance has made in our Theatres. What was universally revered as the Noble Dance was replaced by that characterised as worthy of Mountebanks. This exaggerated and extravagant dance in its turn became the only Noble Dance, for which a more animated dance was later substituted....[55]

However, novelties in ballet technique are never really 'new'; they are, as Lincoln Kirstein rightly observed,

> ...but the latest definition of some of the elements in the world of ideas, always ready for another assemblage. Their previous articulation, even in fragments, sows the soil for a new acceptance when that artist appears who will gather those that fit his uses, to stamp them with his mark.[56]

Put another way, innovations in ballet technique are based on technical developments that came before and that then, given the right artistic environment, suggest subsequent developments.[57]

For example, lifts of the danseuse. A danseuse was lifted by her partner in ballets long before 1832 (and even in the Renaissance *danse à deux*, the volta), but, as depicted in early nineteenth-century iconography, these seem to have continued to be the 'pick-her-up-briefly-in-front-of you' type, not the high overhead lifts or the lifts to the shoulder-sit, as seen repeatedly in Lacotte's productions, but missing in images and descriptions from the period. However, once lifts were connected to the image of the ephemeral Sylphide, higher lifts were understandable developments of a technique already in place.

What evidently appeared so 'new' about Marie Taglioni's performance in *La Sylphide*, at least for some of the audience of 1832, was that she seemed to eschew virtuosity. She did not follow the trend, outlined above. Instead, her movements appeared 'simple, easy, naturally graceful' while still presenting a 'figure of unheard of elegance'.[58] Technical change, that is, changes in how one dances, can be subtle, as in the changes of the timing of steps, the uses of *plié*, and the smoothness of the ascent to full pointe, as discussed earlier. Perhaps Marie Taglioni's mastery of such qualities helped give certain movements a gentler, softer, more delicate and 'natural' appearance than had been the custom, a vision that lingered in the memory. Such execution was hardly simple, however. Indeed, the strength and control necessary to make movements appear 'simple, easy, and naturally graceful' required regular practice of lengthy and difficult exercises, most with a long history. Taglioni was noted for her commitment to hours of rigorous daily practice throughout her career.

Arthur Saint-Léon wrote that Taglioni 'held her body more *en avant*, that is, more forward than the school at the time allowed'.[59] Judging by the drawings in technical manuals of the early nineteenth century, dancers' posture, when viewed in profile, appears slightly back of the centre line of the body, perhaps a compensation for the fact that the raked stages of European theatres sloped downward toward the audience. Therefore, Taglioni's 'more forward' posture, as well as the depth with which she bent her torso, was different and enough of a change to provoke criticism from the traditionalists, the 'fanatics', as Saint-Léon called them. Such observers also objected to 'her arms, which, unlike other dancers, she nearly always kept lowered', but others rhapsodised over her 'arms of serpentine suppleness'.[60] Even the way in which Taglioni used her hands caused comment, no doubt because, traditionally, there had been primarily just two positions, curved or open, for the hands in the noble dance genre. In most instances, the hands were rounded with the fingers slightly overlapping, and the thumb resting on the first knuckle of the first finger. For more 'voluptuous' poses and movements, such as *arabesques*, the hands could extend somewhat but the fingers still remained in close proximity to one another. Taglioni's more 'natural' uses of her hands while dancing was admired by those who had grown weary of the old 'conventional' style.

Did Marie Taglioni dance better than her predecessors, asked Arthur Saint-Léon? He then answered his own question: 'Certainly not, but her dancing differed from the style which then existed, and was specially remarkable for its mixture of poetry and simplicity, grace and gentleness....'[61] Bournonville had had similar reactions upon observing Taglioni's 'first triumphs in 1827-1829' and having danced with her a number of times: 'while fanatics tried to make people believe that this talent owed everything to nature, we connoisseurs had to admire the extraordinary technique she possessed and respectfully acknowledge her exemplary industry'. Even though Taglioni 'performed the very steps and attitudes that Parisian celebrities had long since rejected as Rococo'; they now 'appeared to be revived by the enlivening spirit of the Graces'. Taglioni remained for Bournonville 'the most charming Psyche, the most ethereal sylphide'.[62]

La Sylphide and its star, Marie Taglioni, have achieved an extraordinary high standing in the annals of ballet history, at least those published in the twentieth and twenty-first centuries. Her success, as seen in her own era, seems to embody the definition of 'Achievement, n. Something that has been accomplished successfully, esp. by means of exertion, skill, practice, or perseverance.' (*The American Heritage Dictionary*, 2nd edition.) By such means, Marie Taglioni took something old and made it seem new, with sincere appreciation, I hope, for the training from her father, his own ballet heritage, and for his choreography.

This discussion has not been an effort to diminish the effect of the initial productions of *La Sylphide* nor to try to determine what is or is not authentic in current productions of the ballet. Rather the effort has been to shed some light on ballet practices in the 1830s and how those practices might have been revealed in *La Sylphide*. In doing so, a particular history of ballet, some of its technical history, is revealed. Continuity exists in the training of dancers that proceeds from one period to the next. Changes do occur in the technique employed for steps, positions, poses, and movement dynamics but they are incremental and slow to be fully absorbed into the mainstream. In acknowledging this, we can better understand that ballet has a living history other than, but complementary to, a history of its theatrical productions.

An earlier version of this chapter was presented at the 2009 conference of the Council of Organized Researchers for Pedagogical Studies of Ballet (CORPS de Ballet International) at Texas Christian University, Ft. Worth.

La Sylphide. Directed by René Mathelin, music by J. M. Schneitzhoeffer, performed by the Paris Opéra Ballet. Le Service de la Musique. Sea Bright, NJ: Kultur Inc., 1971. Videocassette.

La Sylphide. Music by J. M. Schneitzhoeffer, Filmed live at the Opéra National de Paris, Palais Garnier in July 2004. Ratingen: TDK, 2005. DVD.

La Sylphide: Ballet in Two Acts. Production after Hans Brenaa, music by H. Løvenskiold, Royal Danish Ballet. West Long Branch, NJ: Kultur, 1988. DVD.

Adice, G. Léopold. *Théorie de la Gymnastique de la Danse Théâtrale* Paris: Chais, 1859.

Albertieri, Luigi. *The Art of Terpsichore - an Elementary, Theoretical, Physical, and Practical Treatise of Dancing*. New York: G. Ricordi, 1923.

Beaumont, Cyril W., and Stanislas Idzikowski. *A Manual of the Theory & Prac-*

tice of Classical Theatrical Dancing (Méthode Cecchetti). New York: Dover, 1975.

Bernay, Berthe. *La Danse au Théâtre*. Paris: Librairie de la Societé des Gens de Lettres, 1890.

Binney, Edwin. *Glories of the Romantic Ballet*. London: Dance Books, 1985.

Blasis, Carlo. *The Code of Terpsichore*. London: Edward Bull, 1828.

Bournonville, August. *My Theatre Life*. Translated by Patricia N. McAndrew. Middletown, CT: Wesleyan University Press, 1979.

Chapman, John. 'Auguste Vestris and the Expansion of Technique'. *Dance Research Journal* 19, no. 1 (Summer 1987): 11-18.

Clarke, Mary, and Clement Crisp. *Ballet Art from the Renaissance to the Present*. New York: Clarkson N. Potter, 1978.

de Cahusac, Louis. *La Danse Ancienne et Moderne ou Traité Historique de la Danse*. La Haye: Chez J. Neaulme, 1754.

Gottlieb, Robert, ed. *Reading Dance - a Gathering of Memoirs, Reportage, Criticism, Profiles, Interviews, and Some Uncategorizable Extras*. New York: Pantheon Books, 2008.

Guest, Ivor. *The Ballet of the Second Empire*.   London: Pitman Publishing, 1974.

————. *The Romantic Ballet in Paris*. London: Dance Books, 1980.

Hammond, Sandra Noll. 'Ballet's Technical Heritage: The Grammaire of Léopold Adice.' *Dance Research* 13 (1995): 35-58.

————. 'In the Dance Classroom with Edgar Degas: Historical Perspectives on Ballet Technique', in *Imaging Dance - Visual Representations of Dancers and Dancing*, Barbara Sparti and Judy Van Zile eds., with E. Ivancich Dunjn, N. G. Heller, and A. L. Kaeppler. Hildesheim: Georg Olms Verlag, 2011, 123-46.

————. 'A Nineteenth-Century Dancing Master at the Court of Württemberg: The Dance Notebooks of Michel St. Léon.' *Dance Chronicle* 15, no. 3 (1992): 291-315.

————. 'Searching for the Sylph: Documentation of Early Developments in Pointe Technique.' *Dance Research Journal* 19, no. 2 (1987-8): 27-31.

————. 'Steps through Time: Selected Dance Vocabulary of the Eighteenth and Nineteenth Centuries.' *Dance Research* 10, no. 2 (1992): 93-108.

————. 'Windows into Romantic Ballet, Part II: Content and Structure of Solo Entrées from the Early Nineteenth Century', in *Proceedings, Dance History Scholars*. Riverside, CA: Society of Dance History Scholars, 1998.

————. 'Windows into Romantic Ballet: Content and Structure of Four Early Nineteenth-Century Pas De Deux', in *Proceedings, Dance History Scholars*. Riverside, CA: Society of Dance History Scholars, 1997.

Hammond, Sandra Noll, and Phillip E. Hammond. 'Technique and Autonomy in the Development of Art: A Case Study in Ballet.' *Dance Research Journal* 21, no. 2 (1989): 15-24.

Jürgensen, Knud Arne. *The Bournonville Heritage: A Choreographic Record 1829-1875*. London: Dance Books, 1990.

Jürgensen, Knud Arne, and Francesca Falcone, eds. *Études Chorégraphiques (1848, 1855, 1861)*. Lucca: Libreria Musicale Italiana, 2005.

Jürgensen, Knud Arne, and Vivi Flindt. *Bournonville Ballet Technique - Fifty Enchaînements*. London: Dance Books, 1992.

Kirstein, Lincoln. *Dance: A Short History of Classic Theatrical Dancing*. New York: G. P. Putnam's Sons, 1935.

Koegler, Horst. *The Concise Oxford Dictionary of Ballet*. London: Oxford University Press, 1977.

Magri, Gennaro. *Trattato Teorico-Prattico Di Ballo*. Naples: Orsino, 1779.

McAndrew, Patricia. 'August Bournonville'. *International Encyclopedia of Dance*. New York: Oxford University Press, 1998. Vol. I, 503-514.

Moore, Lillian. *Images of the Dance: Historical Treasures of the Dance Collection 1581-1861*. New York: The New York Library, 1965.

Noverre, Jean-Georges. *Lettres sur la danse, et sur les ballets*. Stuttgart and Lyon. Delaroche, 1760.

Pastori, Jean-Pierre. *Pierre Lacotte: Tradition*. Paris: Favre, 1987.

Rameau, Pierre. *Abbregé de la nouvelle Methode dans l'art d'écrire ou de traçer toutes sortes de Danses de ville*. Paris: self-published, 1725.

Roller, Franz Anton. *Systematisches Lehrbuch der Bildenden Tanzkunst und Körperlichen Ausbildung*. Vienna: Bernh. Fr. Voigt, 1843.

Saint-Léon, Arthur. *De L'état Actuel de la Danse*. Lisbon: Typographie du Progresso, 1856.

———. *La Sténochorégraphie ou Art d'écrire promptement la Danse*. Paris: Chez l'Auteur et chez Brandus, 1852.

Schlüter, Anne Marie Vessel, project director. *The Bournonville School - the Dance Programme*. Copenhagen: the Royal Danish Theatre, 2005.

Sparti, Barbara and Judy Van Zile eds., with E. Ivancich Dunin, N. G. Heller, and A. L. Kaeppler. *Imaging Dance – Visual Representations of Dancers and Dancing*. Hildesheim: Georg Olms Verlag, 2011.

Théleur, E. A. *Letters on Dancing Reducing This Elegant and Healthful Exercise to Easy Scientific Principles*. London: Sherwood, 1831.

Vaillat, Léandre. *La Taglioni ou la Vie d'une Danseuse*. Paris: Albin Michel, 1942.

Winter, Marian Hannah. *The Pre-Romantic Ballet*. London: Pitman Publishing, 1974.

Notes

1. The entire portfolio of these Chalon prints is in the Dance Collection, Library of the Performing Arts, New York City. They are reproduced in, for example, Lillian Moore, *Images of the Dance - Historical Treasures of the Dance Collection 1581-1861* (New York: The New York Library, 1965), 48-49.
2. Questions such as these, about dance iconography from many centuries and many parts of the world, are the subjects of Barbara Sparti and Judy Van Zile eds., *Imaging Dance - Visual Representations of Dancers and Dancing* (Hildesheim: Georg Olms Verlag, 2011). On Degas and ballet technique, see in that volume Sandra Noll Hammond, 'In the Dance Classroom with Edgar Degas: Historical Perspectives on Ballet Technique', 123-46.
3. Horst Koegler, *The Concise Oxford Dictionary of Ballet* (London: Oxford University Press, 1977), 516.
4. E. A. Théleur, *Letters on Dancing reducing This elegant and healthful Exercise to Easy Scientific Principles* (London: Sherwood, 1831), 81. A second edition appeared the following year, 1832. A republication of the first edition, with an introductory essay by Hammond, was published in the *Studies in Dance History* series, by the Society of Dance History Scholars (Pennington, NJ: Princeton Periodicals, 1990).
5. Jean-Georges Noverre, *Lettres sur la danse, et sur les ballets.* (Stuttgart and Lyon: Delaroche, 1760, repr. Paris 1807) Vol. II, 126-127, as quoted in John Chapman, 'Auguste Vestris and the Expansion of Technique', *Dance Research Journal* 19, no. 1 (1987): 12.
6. Little is known of Adice's formative years, although in the Preface of his published book (see note below) he claims to have trained under Taglioni. His teacher was probably Salvatore, who along with Louis Henry founded the ballet school at Teatro San Carlo where Salvatore Taglioni also was ballet master. Filippo confined most of his teaching to his daughter, Marie.
7. G. Léopold Adice, *Théorie de la gymnastique de la danse théâtrale* (Paris: Chais, 1859), 74-75. See also Sandra Noll Hammond, 'Ballet's Technical Heritage: The Grammaire of Léopold Adice', *Dance Research* 13 (1995): 33-58.
8. Carlo Blasis, *Code of Terpsichore* (London: Edward Bull, 1828), 94-95.
9. See Sandra Noll Hammond, 'Searching for the Sylph: Documentation of Early Developments in Pointe Technique', *Dance Research Journal* 19, no. 2 (1987-8): 27-31.
10. Jean-Pierre Pastori, *Pierre Lacotte: Tradition* (Paris: Favre, 1987), 48. Lacotte attributes the music to 'a certain Bretelle'.
11. Ivor Guest, *The Ballet of the Second Empire* (London: Pitman Publishing, 1974), 131.
12. For the first version, see *La Sylphide*, Directed by René Mathelin, music by J.M. Schneitzhoeffer, performed by the Paris Opéra Ballet. Le Service de la Musique, Sea Bright, NJ: Kultur Inc., 1971, Videocassette. For the second, see *La Sylphide*, Music by J. M. Schneitzhoeffer, Filmed live at the Opéra National de Paris, Palais Garnier in July 2004, Ratingen: TDK, 2005, DVD.
13. August Bournonville, *My Theatre Life*, trans. Patricia N. McAndrew (Middletown, CT: Wesleyan University Press, 1979), 78-79.
14. Knud Arne Jürgensen, *The Bournonville Heritage: A choreographic record 1829-1875* (London: Dance Books, 1990), 4.
15. *La Sylphide: ballet in two acts*, Production after Hans Brenaa, music by H. Løvenskiold, Royal Danish Ballet, West Long Branch, NJ: Kultur, 1988, DVD.
16. From the Foreword by Ivor Guest in Edwin Binney, *Glories of the Romantic Ballet* (London: Dance Books, 1985).
17. Mary Clarke and Clement Crisp, *Ballet Art from the Renaissance to the Present* (New York: Clarkson N. Potter, 1978), 70.
18. For a discussion of this phenomenon, see Sandra Noll Hammond, 'Steps Through Time: Selected Dance Vocabulary of the Eighteenth and Nineteenth Centuries', *Dance Research* 10, no. 2 (1992): 93-108.
19. *Journal des théâtres*, 15 January, 1778. I gratefully acknowledge the information that Edmund Fairfax has shared with me, and I look forward to the publication of his much-needed, comprehensive second volume on eighteenth-century theatrical dance.
20. Théleur, *Letters on Dancing*, 16, plate 8. Recent personal communication from Théleur's great,

great-grandson, Kevin Taylor (Théleur), has provided much hitherto unknown information on E.A. Théleur and his theatrical family.

21. The quotations that Fairfax cites and translates from Roller come from Franz Anton Roller, *Systematisches Lehrbuch der bildenden Tanzkunst und körperlichen Ausbildung* (Vienna: Bernh. Fr. Voigt, 1843), 147.

22. From a private collection and reproduced as #47 in Clarke and Crisp, *Ballet Art from the Renaissance to the Present*, 46.

23. Théleur, *Letters on Dancing*, 8.

24. For discussions of early nineteenth-century *pas seul* and *pas de deux*, see Sandra Noll Hammond, 'Windows into Romantic Ballet: Content and Structure of Four Early Nineteenth-Century Pas de Deux', in *Proceedings, Dance History Scholars* (Riverside, CA: Society of Dance History Scholars, 1997), 137-44; and Sandra Noll Hammond, 'Windows into Romantic Ballet, Part II: Content and Structure of Solo Entrées from the Early Nineteenth Century', in *Proceedings, Dance History Scholars* (Riverside, CA: Society of Dance History Scholars, 1998), 47-53.

25. Théleur, *Letters on Dancing*, 16, 34.

26. See Arthur Saint-Léon, *La Sténochorégraphie ou Art d'écrire promptement la Danse* (Paris: Chez l'Auteur et chez Brandus, 1852), notation Examples 5-9.

27. Théleur, *Letters on Dancing*, 56.

28. Cyril W. Beaumont and Stanislas Idzikowski, *A Manual of the Theory & Practice of Classical Theatrical Dancing (Méthode Cecchetti)* (New York: Dover, 1975), 42; a republication of the London 1922 edition. Cecchetti was an Italian-trained dancer and a renowned teacher whose career included years at the Imperial Theatres in St. Petersburg and later with the Diaghilev Ballets Russes. Alexandra Danilova (1904 – 1997), ballerina and teacher, echoes Cecchetti's advice: 'When I was growing up in the Theatre School [St. Petersburg], a high extension was considered vulgar, and even Margot Fonteyn never raised her leg higher than her waist. It is only because of Balanchine, who wanted the leg higher that dancers have begun to develop their extensions, and I personally agree with Mr. B.' From Robert Gottlieb, ed., *Reading Dance – A Gathering of Memoirs, Reportage, Criticism, Profiles, Interviews, and Some Uncategorizable Extras* (New York: Pantheon Books, 2008), 1224.

29. See for example, the DVD cover photograph of Lis Jeppesen as the Sylphide in the Royal Danish Ballet version and the frontispiece photograph in Pastori (see endnote 10) of Ghislaine Thesmar in the same role in Lacotte's first production.

30. Albertieri, *The Art of Terpsichore - An Elementary, Theoretical, Physical, and Practical Treatise of Dancing* (New York: G. Ricordi, 1923), 134.

31. Ibid., 133.

32. Roller, *Systematisches Lehrbuch* 150-51.

33. Anne Marie Vessel Schlüter, project director, *The Bournonville School – the Dance Programme* (Copenhagen: the Royal Danish Theatre, 2005), 14.

34. Blasis, *Code of Terpsichore*, 52-53.

35. St. Léon's notebooks, compiled during his tenure as dancing master at the Court of Württemberg, include 'Cahier d'Exercices de 1829'; 'Cahier Exercices pour L.L.A.A. Royalles les Princesses de Wurtemberg 1830'; 2me Cahier Exercices de 1830' (containing material also dated 1831); and an untitled manuscript volume of *exercices, enchainements,* and theatrical dances dated 1833 - 1836. Bibliothèque de l'Opéra, Paris, Rés. 1137 and 1140. For discussion of this material, see Sandra Noll Hammond, 'A Nineteenth-Century Dancing Master at the Court of Württemberg: the Dance Notebooks of Michel St. Léon', *Dance Chronicle* 15 no. 3 (1992): 291-315.

36. Pastori, *Pierre Lacotte: Tradition*, 45.

37. Théleur, *Letters on Dancing*, 56-58.

38. 'La leçon de Marie Taglioni', cited by Léandre Vaillat, *La Taglioni ou la vie d'une danseuse* (Paris: Albin Michel, 1942), 76. 'Puis, on commence à sauter. L'élan ne doit partir que du talon, sans mouvement du corps. Il est évident qu'on ne sauté pas très haut d'abord. Les genoux doivent à peine ployer [...] J'adorais ces pas où j'avais des élans dans lesquels je ne sentais presque point la terre. Réellement, *je vibrais dans l'air.*'

39. For a discussion of the *pas de rigaudon/sissonne doublée* connection, see Hammond, 'Steps Through Time.' See also a study of Bournonvilles *Études chorégraphiques* in Knud Arne Jürgensen

and Francesca Falcone, eds, *Études chorégraphiques (1848, 1855, 1861)* (Lucca: Libreria Musicale Italiana, 2005).

40. Gennaro Magri, *Trattato teorico-prattico di ballo* (Naples: Orsino, 1779), Part I, 104. For even earlier versions of the step, see Hammond, 'Steps Through Time.'

41. Knud Arne Jürgensen and Vivi Flindt, *Bournonville Ballet Technique - Fifty Enchaînements* (London: Dance Books, 1992), 90-91.

42. From the section on Ballet Terminology by Kirsten Ralov, revised by Anne Marie Vessel Schlüter, in *The Bournonville School – the Dance Programme*, 13.

43. Saint-Léon, *La Sténochorégraphie*, Exemple 25. St. Léon, *Cahier 1829*, v. 9, and *2nd Cahier 1830*, r.6.

44. Ibid., Exemples 19 and 20. Landings from jumping movements tended to arrive on the first beat of a measure in most periods.

45. For eighteenth-century examples, see *Traité de la cadence*, in Pierre Rameau, *Abbregé de la nouvelle Methode dans l'art d'écrire ou de tracer toutes sortes de Danses de ville* (Paris: self-published, 1725). For examples from the next century, see Saint-Léon, *La Sténochorégraphie*, Exemples 9 and 10.

46. Knud Arne Jürgensen, information contained in the article on August Bournonville by Patricia McAndrew in *International Encyclopedia of Dance*, vol. 1 (New York: Oxford University Press, 1998), 512.

47. Pastori, *Pierre Lacotte: Tradition*, 46.

48. See Hammond, 'Searching for the Sylph', 27-31.

49. Taglioni as quoted by Vaillat in *La Taglioni*, 76. 'Ainsi, je pliais doucement et aussi profondément que possible, de façon à pouvoir toucher la terre avec les mains sans courber le dos, simplement pliant par les genoux et en me tenant très droite ensuite me relever doucement, sans secousse et sans effort, jusque sur l'extrémité de la pointe des pieds.'

50. Blasis, *Code of Terpsichore*, 99-100; Théleur, *Letters on Dancing*, 54.

51. Berthe Bernay, *La Danse au Théâtre* (Paris: Librairie de la Societé des Gens de Lettres, 1890), 174.

52. Michel St. Léon, untitled manuscript (see note 35 above), r 53, 'Pas de deux dansé par Arthur pour son second début à Munich le 12 août 1835.' For more on this *pas de deux*, see Hammond, 'Windows into Romantic Ballet: Content and Structure of Four Early Nineteenth-Century Pas De Deux.'

53. Pastori, *Pierre Lacotte: Tradition*, 54.

54. Bournonville states that among the changes he made in the plan of the original *La Sylphide* was that he 'gave the ballet a national colour that was not to be found in the Parisian version'. Bournonville, *My Theatre Life*, 79.

55. Louis de Cahusac, *La Danse ancienne et moderne ou Traité historique de la danse* (La Haye: Chez J. Neaulme, 1754). Translated and quoted in Marian Hannah Winter, *The Pre-Romantic Ballet* (London: Pitman Publishing, 1974), 189.

56. Lincoln Kirstein, *Dance: A Short History of Classic Theatrical Dancing* (New York: G. P. Putnam's Sons, 1935), 244.

57. For further analysis of this phenomenon in ballet's technical history, see Sandra Noll Hammond and Phillip E. Hammond, 'Technique and Autonomy in the Development of Art: A Case Study in Ballet', *Dance Research Journal* 21, no. 2 (1989): 15-24.

58. The dance critic Jules Janin, *Journal des Débats*, 24 August 1832. Translated and quoted in Ivor Guest, *The Romantic Ballet in Paris* (London: Dance Books, 1980), 115.

59. Arthur Saint-Léon, *De l'état actuel de la danse* (Lisbon: Typographie du Progresso, 1856), 16. Translated and quoted in Guest, *The Romantic Ballet in Paris*, 80.

60. Janin, *Journal des Débats*, 24 August 1842. Translated and quoted in Guest, *The Romantic Ballet in Paris*, 115.

61. Saint-Léon, *De l'état actuel de la danse*, 16. Translated and quoted in ibid., 79.

62. Bournonville, *My Theatre Life*, 48.

Chapter 4

Schneitzhoeffer's music for *La Sylphide*

Matilda Ann Butkas Ertz

The music for Filippo Taglioni's *La Sylphide*, composed by Jean-Madeleine Schneitzhoeffer (1785-1852), is far less known today than Løvenskjold's music for Bournonville's version of the ballet. This circumstance, of course, is owed to the fact that the Bournonville *Sylphide*, a standard of the repertory of the Royal Danish Ballet and a work widely presented by other companies, is much more often performed than any version employing the Schneitzhoeffer score.[1] Yet Schneitzhoeffer's version is highly effective, and well worth examining – indeed, since Taglioni's choreography has not survived into the present day, Schneitzhoeffer's music, and the annotations in early rehearsal scores, offer valuable information about the first production that is otherwise unavailable.

Jean-Madeleine Schneitzhoeffer

Before turning to the music, let us say a few words about the composer. Jean-Madeleine Schneitzhoeffer, who has been characterised by Fétis as 'too much a friend of pleasure' for his own good, was born in 1785, the son of an Opéra oboist. Showing considerable promise at a young age, Schneitzhoeffer studied harmony and composition at the Conservatoire with Charles-Simon Catel, and early in his career wrote several overtures and a symphony which were well received. His *oeuvre* also includes an unfinished opera, *Sardanapale*, and seven ballets: *Proserpine* (1818), *Le Séducteur de village* (1818), *L'Orgie*, with Carafa (1831), *Zémire et Azor* (1824), *Mars et Vénus* (1826), and *La Tempête* (1834). *La Sylphide* (1832), is considered his best work. Schneitzhoeffer (often called 'Chêneçerf' by Parisians, who had difficulty with his German surname) also served as tympanist in the Royal chapel and the orchestra of the Conservatoire, as *chef du chant* at the Opéra, and as professor in the choir school of the Conservatoire.[2]

Few details of Schneitzhoeffer's life are known. But it is clear from all accounts that he was admired in his own day as much for his musical abilities – he was said to be capable of playing all the instruments of the orchestra – as he was for his wit. His contemporaries were particularly amused by his calling cards: in response to the pianist Woets, whose card read

(Woetz, pronounced 'OUTS') Schneitzhoeffer printed his cards thus: 'Schneitzhoeffer, pronounced 'Bertrand'.[3] Friends also enjoyed telling the tale of his retirement from the post of tympanist at the Opéra. The conductor François-Antoine Habeneck, it seems, was reluctant to honour Schneitzhoeffer's requests to be relieved of his duties. So Schneitzhoeffer, during a ballet performance, at the most peaceful moment of a *pas de deux*, suddenly began to play a loud drum roll. He sustained it with full force for two or three minutes, to the great surprise of Habeneck, the dancers, and the audience. He then threw his drumsticks into the air and according to one account, 'caught them like a juggler'. Habeneck allowed him to leave the orchestra forthwith.[4]

In his own lifetime, his skills as a ballet composer were well appreciated. A critic for *La Revue Musicale*, making reference to Schneitzhoeffer's lack of ambition, remarked that '[t]he intervals between his ballets are too long. His talent deserves a wider reputation, his love of leisure has more dominion over him than a love of glory.'[5] He died in Montmartre in 1852 at the age of 67. His obituary in *La Revue et Gazette Musicale* called his ballet scores his 'true claim to fame', adding that 'one could fill volumes with accounts of jests of which Schneitzhoeffer was either the inventor or the perpetrator.'[6]

Schneitzhoeffer's *Sylphide* score – General comments

In *La Sylphide*, Schneitzhoeffer follows customs of the time for ballet composing: first, he provides music tailored for specific characters, moods, and situations; second, he uses themes that recur (sometimes in a transformed state); third, he uses borrowed music – though atypically, most of the music for this ballet is newly composed. The use of such borrowed music in ballet scores was an accepted practice in Paris well into the 1830s; as Castil-Blaze noted in his *Dictionnaire* under the entry for 'Ballet', ballet composers and arrangers made much use of excerpts from '... the beautiful symphonies of Haydn, overtures, ... concertos, violin duos, sonatas, romances, barcarolles...'[7] They also liked to borrow from opera, making good use of music ready-made for particular dramatic situations. Ferdinand Hérold, for example, used the storm music from Rossini's *La Cenerentola* for the thunderstorm scene in *La Fille mal gardée*, as well as the opening chorus from *Il Barbiere di Siviglia* ('Piano, pianissimo') for the heroine's tiptoe entrance.[8] (Among the music Schneitzhoeffer borrowed for *La Sylphide*, as we shall see below, were bits from Paganini's variations, *Le Streghe* Op. 8 on a theme by Süssmayr from the Viganò ballet *Il Noce di Benevento*, and Gluck's *Orphée et Euridice*.[9])

Schneitzhoeffer also follows the practice of writing music that meets the needs of the libretto by supplying music of two basic types: dance music and dramatic music (which followed and supported the action of the mime and action scenes). Schneitzhoeffer so seamlessly integrates the dance music and the dramatic music together, however – much more so than most ballet scores of the late 1820s and early 1830s, in which the two styles of music were more obviously different – that upon hearing the score for the first time, one may not recognise the distinction between them. (Indeed, one critic, perhaps reacting to this characteristic of Schneitzhoeffer's score for *La Sylphide*, called this music 'too uniform'.[10])

The primary sources
Music manuscripts. My descriptions of Schneitzhoeffer's music for *La Sylphide* depend upon the original libretto and three musical manuscripts:[11]

a) The full orchestral score at the Paris Opéra (A.501) (1832), in which the copyists have written many annotations matching the action to the music (for instance, 'The witches arrive in groups', 'Her wings beat faster', 'James is agitated').

b) A violin rehearsal score (répétiteur) at the Paris Opéra (Mat. 19 [302 (25-27) featuring two staves, sometimes three, apparently scored for violin and cello and featuring more annotations than the full orchestral score. This score is clearly a witness to many a rehearsal and performance, and contains scribblings, drawings (Figure 4.1), cross-outs, cuttings and pastings, and the names of specific dancers (such as Mazilier,[12] (Act One, p. 142), Dominique (Act Two p. 26) and Caroline, (Act Two, p. 34).

c) A violin rehearsal score for two violins (from the collection of the late

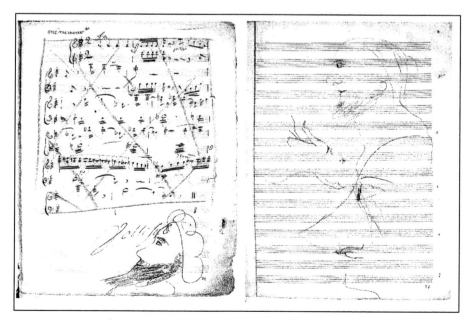

4.1. Two Doodles from the Paris Opéra Violin Score. Mat. 19 [302 (26) p. 71 and 77. Bibliothèque nationale de France. By permission.

Alexander Bennett) which was likely used by Victor Bartholomin (1799-1860) in 1835 for a staging of *La Sylphide* at the Théâtre de la Monnaie in Brussels. This score is the most fully annotated score for *La Sylphide* known today, and shows evidence of much use.[13] (See Appendix 5.) Many of its annotations match those of the full score, suggesting that it was prepared at the Paris Opéra's own copy shop; rehearsal scores were copied in Paris for sale to other opera houses and, probably, to private parties as well. Its instructions are far more plentiful than those in the Opéra's own scores, however – a typical feature of many such scores especially prepared for export[14] – and include information about how the stage for Act One was set (including mention of how the special effects were achieved).

Taken together, these manuscripts are very useful tools for helping one re-imagine the musical story of F. Taglioni's *La Sylphide*, despite the loss of the original choreography.

The printed libretto. La Sylphide's libretto was written by Adolphe Nourrit, who adapted it from Charles Nodier's story of 1822, *Trilby ou le lutin de l'Argail* (though, as Sally Banes and others point out, there are a great many disparities between the two.[15]) Bournonville, in turn, based his libretto on Nourrit's, and it is nearly identical to the French original. There are differences, however. For example, Madge the witch, in the 1832 French libretto, explains to James that 'she fears the storm' (a storm not found in the Danish version). In the next scene, the wind from this storm blows open the window to reveal the Sylphide; for this Schneitzhoeffer writes descriptive 'lightning and rain' music, and the word *'Orage'* (Storm) appears in the full score and Paris violin score. This rising modulatory passage has distinct octave pizzicato raindrops and a windy rush of strings.

Another difference in the libretti may be found in the scene immediately following James's first encounter with the Sylphide: in the French version, James awakens Gurn, who is fast asleep in a pile of hay and dreaming of Effie; in the Danish version, James awakens the other farmhands and then collides with Gurn, who is returning from a morning hunt. These two versions of the scene, of course, require different types of music.

Also, the French libretto contains much more written-out dialogue; for example:

Act One, scene iv
James asks [the Sylphide] what is the matter; she refuses to answer him, but gazes at him tenderly. He asks her again to confide her chagrin. — Oh! Can't you tell what is the matter with me? You are going to marry Effie! — What does it matter? — Alas, you can't understand my love. — What! You love me? That's not possible! You wish to play on my credulity.— The first

day when I saw you, my destiny was attached to yours. Visible or not, I am always near you. This foyer is my sanctuary; in the daytime, I accompany you to the depths of the forest, to the steep crags of our mountains. At night, I drive away the evil spirits from your cottage, and keep watch at your bedside, and your dreams of love: it is I who sends them to you.— James is deeply moved, and his heart is touched by the sylphide's love. She wishes to know if he is responding to her tenderness. — Duty prevents me; I have pledged myself to Effie, and I love no one but her. — (Libretto pp. 15-16.)

Such conversations were mimed on stage and given music to help bring them to life. (It is worth noting that Løvenskiold's music and the modern reproductions of Bournonville's choreography match up to these dialogue sections of the French libretto, even when they are not explicitly written out in the Danish libretto.)

Another major difference between the two libretti is found in the witches' scene that opens Act Two. The French version of this scene entails a long description of the spectacle of twenty witches, animals, a dazzling array of props to be used in the making of the brew, and a detailed description of the action; the Danish libretto offers a much shorter description, with far less detail. Omissions and crossouts in the Parisian scores, however, indicate that the long witches' scene described in the French libretto, for which Schneitzhoeffer composed about thirteen minutes' worth of music, was shortened at the Paris Opéra as well. The Parisian violin score lacks the Bach fugue and the *Grave* (approximately eighty measures of music) found in both the full score and the Bartholomin rehearsal score. Furthermore, an English libretto from the 1830s shortens the description of this scene while keeping the rest of the ballet's scenes intact.[16]

The Music
The following descriptions of selected scenes focuses on the music, with attention to the choreographic and narrative goals it served.

Act One, scene i: The Sylphide and James; his confusion
James sleeps, the Sylphide dances around him and kisses him; he pursues her, and she flies up the chimney. Then James ponders this strange apparition:

But Gurn was there — perhaps he saw the sylphide. He must be questioned. James awakens him and plies him with questions. Gurn was sleeping deeply, and all he saw, in a dream, was the lovely Effie, with whom he is desperately in love, despite her preference for James. This recollection soothes James's mind. He must forget this fantastic being who follows him everywhere, and think only of his love for Effie. In a few hours they will be married, and a happy future lies ahead of them. (Libretto, pp. 10-11.)

Schneitzhoeffer's music follows this scene closely, and one can discern three main sections in the music: a) curtain-up and the encounter of the Sylphide and James (ending with her flight up the chimney), b) James alone, and c) James and Gurn's dialogue (noted in the full score as the 'duet between James and Gurn', and annotated in all three manuscripts). Schneitzhoeffer writes a gently rocking lullaby *Adagio* to accompany the curtain rising, the Sylphide resting at James's feet and her first movements. (The Bartholomin score tells us that 'She passes before him several times.') Fluttering of the violins and pizzicato accompaniment provide the variation of this theme when, according to the conductor's and Bartholomin score annotations, she beats her wings near James and he stirs. Then begins an *Allegro* that features a bouncy violin solo in duple meter. For two phrases, she shows 'her joy at being close to the one she loves' as the libretto puts it. This short-lived solo melds into an agitated *tutti* with a prolonged flute cadenza that erupts into a *forte* dominant chord which is clearly marked with the annotation 'le baiser' – 'the kiss', in the full score and the Bartholomin rehearsal score.

The Sylphide, overcome with desire, kisses him. The agitated music then resumes, leading into a new theme in a new key as James awakens. Staccato triplets illustrate James's searching; ascending and descending flute scales show his pursuit and the Sylphide escaping his grasp, and finally, ascending scales accompany her up the chimney (these actions are annotated in the Bartholomin score). This music is so aptly illustrative that, having read the libretto, one may hear the details of the story as they unfold.[17]

The third and final part of this scene, the *Allegretto*, is ushered in with dotted rhythms and horns; James wakes up Gurn and the mood changes entirely. Their conversation is rendered as an aggressive back-and-forth. As the annotations in all of the scores tell us, 'Tom' (James) is represented by winds with prominent flute lines while 'Garne' (Gurn) is represented by low strings. James's 'persistent questioning' motive ends the entire scene vehemently in E-flat major.[18]

This opening scene, then, is a succession of many ideas, presented in small sections (usually eight to sixteen measures long). (Figure 4.2.) Some of these feature solid dance phrases, with clear periodicity, stable harmonies, and

Musical form: A - A¹ - B - C/t - D // E/t - F - A¹ // G - H
          Sylphide & James   // James alone // James & Gurn

Figure 4.2. Form of opening scene. Note that t = transition.

predictable cadences. Others are harmonically unstable, with odd phrase lengths. The music effectively matches the characters and their emotional shifts – James's bewilderment, the Sylphide's dangerous flirtatiousness and the aggressive tension between James and Gurn (who will soon get into an out-and-out scuffle).[19] Moreover, a motif from this argument music between James and Gurn recurs in Act Two just after James acquires the poisoned scarf, reminding us, perhaps, of James's competitive, aggressive side. (See below.)

Act One, scene ii: The young couple
Befitting the Scottish pastoral setting of the ballet, two overtly rustic themes open the second scene, in which, as the libretto explains:

> Effie enters, arm-in-arm with Mother Anne Reuben. Gurn rushes eagerly to the young Scots girl's side, greets her timidly, and offers as a decoration for her straw hat the feathers of a heron he has killed. Effie thanks him graciously, and approaches James, who, ever pre-occupied, didn't see his fiancée drawing near. (Libretto, p. 11.)

First, we hear Effie's entrance theme, which identifies her by its G-major 'country' sound: Schneitzhoeffer scores string accompaniment in rustic open fifths and a drone-like quality to imitate the sound of bagpipes; this serves as background to a simple folk-like pentatonic melody which sticks closely to the tonic. The action now shifts to an exchange between James and Effie in C major.

> [Effie] — What are you thinking about?— James comes back to her: 'I was thinking... I was thinking of you, my pretty cousin. — You're deceiving me. —No, I assure you. — You are sad, James, yet it is today that we will be betrothed! — Oh! I am happy, my dear Effie, because I love you and wish never to love anyone but you. — Very good. She gives him her hand to kiss. (Libretto p. 11.)

In this melody, which I have dubbed 'the James and Effie love theme', Effie is represented by the clarinet (which is often joined by the flute), with pizzicato accompaniment – all alluding to pastoral life (Example 4.1) – but whose lofty and soaring melodies will later be used when James experiences conflicting feelings of love for the Sylphide. This catchy and unassuming rendering of the theme has dotted rhythms and a conversational quality, but on the immediate repeat, the addition of a lush string sonority and fluttery violin embellishments remind us of the Sylphide. (See Figure 4.4 for the later combining of this theme with the Sylphide's love theme.)

Next there is a series of new ideas and themes, each with a specific purpose. (It is composed according to the principle of 'through-development' which, as Roland John Wiley has explained, is music that is 'continuously responsive to the narrative and to the emotional states of the characters.'[20]) First, Schneitzhoeffer supplies a new theme for James's anger at Gurn for trying to take Effie's hand, then a calm, resigned theme for Gurn's misery, then a series of solo instrumental gestures that accompany (as the libretto puts it): 'Mother Anne [places] Effie's hand in that of her cousin. The young couple kneel and receive Mother Anne's blessing.' The music matches the libretto closely, allowing for the development of Gurn's character by helping show his attempts to be noticed by Effie and his misery as the attempts fail.

Act One, scene iii: Rustic gathering, a witch appears
Now we are introduced to yet another rustic bagpipe theme in B-flat major as 'Effie's friends arrive, each of them carrying her wedding gift: a plaid, a belt, a crown, wedding veil, bouquet, etc.' (Libretto, p. 12). This theme – which will represent the village girls again later (see below, Example 4.8, No. 2) – is supported by a drone with drum-like pulsing while the strings outline triads in held notes with quick grace-note flourishes between.

Madge has crept onto the scene, unnoticed. Now James spies her by the hearth, and her theme is heard. Annotated '*à la Paganini*' in the full orchestral score, it is a quotation of *Le Streghe* (*The Witches*, also known as *The Witches' Dance*) by Franz Xaver Süssmayr – a work that had been popularized by Paganini, whose variations upon it are still well-known today (Examples 4.2 and 4.3).[21] In *La Sylphide* Schneitzhoeffer changes the mode of Paganini's variations set from mostly major (D major) to mostly minor (G minor). First introduced in the overture, the melody recurs several times as appropriate, including an instance late in Act Two just after Madge leaves her cavern (Figure 4.3).

Next, the triadic theme of the village girls returns as the girls intercede, asking that Madge be allowed to stay. Lively pizzicatos and staccatos accompany the jaunty palm-reading melody as the girls' fortunes are read (this music will re-appear in Act Two scene iv, when Madge deceives James in his moment of despair). This is followed by an emphatic G-minor melody marked *fortissimo*, which expresses James's anger (annotated in all three scores) at Madge. Next, the strings laugh and flutes twitter as the village girls make fun of Gurn ('the young girls mock Gurn', say both Parisian scores) – an annotation that calls attention to a detail that could be easily missed, as the laughing and mocking strings could be discerned merely as a little countermelody to the calming *Andante sostenuto* theme used as Effie seeks to calm James's anger (Example 4.4).

Example 4.1. Act One scene ii 'James and Effie Love Theme' first appearance

Example 4.2. 'Contradanza delle Streghe' from the Piano Score of *Il Noce di Benevento*
Süssmayr/Viganò 1822)

From: Franz Xaver Süssmayr, Salvatore Viganò, and Giulio Viganò, *Il Noce di Benevento: ballo allegorico*, John Milton and Ruth Neils Ward Collection (Harvard Theatre Collection), Biblioteca di musica, anno 3, classe 2, (Milano: Ricordi, 1822).

Example 4.3. Transcription of Theme from Paganini's 'Le Streghe' Op. 8 for Violin and Orchestra

From: Nicolò Paganini, *Le Streghe, Op. 8* (no. 3 delle opere postume), [for violin and piano], Milano: G. Ricordi, 1851. The *Tema* (theme) occurs after an *Introduzione* and *Larghetto*.

Example 4.4. The young girls mock Gurn, Reduced from the Paris Opera Full Score,
Only the instruments that play in this particular section are transcribed (the clarinets,
trumpets, etc. all have rests).

This mocking is illustrated through the laughing figures – short quick repeated gestures
– in the viola and bassoon lines.

Finally, a third pastoral theme is brought into play: open fifths accompany
a piccolo solo in the key of F major while 'the young girls bring in the wedding clothes so Effie can examine them' (an annotation found in all three
scores but not the libretto). (This theme, too, will recur at the beginning
of the *Divertissement* – the would-be wedding celebration – that closes Act
One.)

Act One, scene vi (Second Part): Visions of the Sylphide during the Divertissement

A celebration offers the perfect opportunity for long blocks of dancing (as
opposed to mime) in ballets of this period, and the celebration of James and
Effie's betrothal offers just such an opportunity.[22] This is not to say, however,
that dramatic action cannot transpire during a danced *Divertissement*, and
indeed, it does so here: James is distracted by the Sylphide, who flits in and
out, unnoticed by the rest of the crowd. Schneitzhoeffer handles this dramatic situation by writing mostly source music – that is, music originating

4.3. Witch theme, 'à la Paganini', from Bartholomin violin rehearsal score, Act Two scene iv, page 146. Private collection.

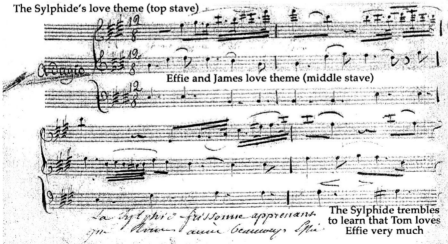

4.4. Paris Opéra Violin Score Showing Re-use and Combination of Themes, Mat. 19 [302 (26), p. 52, Act I scene iv. Bibliothèque nationale de France. By permission.

from within the ballet's world, and heard by the characters as music. (Such music is sometimes referred to as diegetic music.)

The scene consists of four discrete danced sections shown in Table 4.1.[23]

Table 4.1. Divertissement dances, Act One, scene vi

Divertissement dances	
Section 1: Country dances	Anglaise, allegretto poco Andante
	Ecossaise, Allegretto
	Anglaise prestissimo/Presto
Section 2: Pas de deux	Adagio - Allegretto - Andante - Plus vite
Section 3: Pas de trois	Andante - Allegro
Section 4: Finale	Anglaise

This is followed by an action and mime scene to close out the act. As the libretto tells us, there is disruption of the dancing when James sees the sylphide.

> In the middle of the groups formed by the dancers, the sylphide appears several times, visible only to James, who disrupts the contredanse by running after her. But she disappears at the moment when he believes he has caught her. (Libretto pp. 12-13.)

The Bartholomin score places one such appearance at measure 54 of the *Anglaise Prestissimo* (during the first section of country dancing). The whole orchestra is playing loudly with a strong rhythmic propulsion and drive appropriate for a country dance. The Sylphide's appearance comes during this dance, after a transitional section that extends beyond its expected boundaries; the music seems to lose footing and erupts into scales in the strings that bring to mind the title character's appearances earlier in the ballet.[24] She appears, according to the Bartholomin score, as the main *Anglaise* theme comes back.

Act Two, scene i: The Witches' Scene
In the witches' scene, as noted above, we find the most marked difference between the French and Danish libretti, and Schneitzhoeffer's score certainly matches the length and intricacy of what is described in the French libretto. (For details on how the libretto is matched to the music in this scene, see Table 4.2.) Schneitzhoeffer writes four large sections, the first of which could

Table 4.2. Libretto and Music for the Full Version of the Witch Scene, Act Two, scene i

Libretto	Music and Annotations*
I. Madge's preparations	
Libretto: Old Madge is occupied with preparing for the Sabbath. She traces a circle and places at its center a cauldron, which she turns upside down on a tripod; she arranges the utensils around it: bellows, a pan, the skimmer, two spheres, a skull, animal craniums, a transparent vase containing writhing reptiles, a bag filled with dried herbs, etc. She circles the cauldron three times, striking it with a ladle.	**(A)** A minor, duple, intro and variations (a,t,a^1,a^2) on a theme of piercing high string and wind motives with descending chromatic scales, pulsating bassoon octaves and flurries of string activity. It is night and 'Medje la sorciere fait une conjuration;' the music modulates to C major and F minor, cadences to C7 with annotation 'Elle frappe triois coups'
II. Witches arrive in groups	
Libretto: At this signal, there arrive twenty witches, riding broomsticks and each holding a glowing lantern. They ride in a circle three times; each witch is accompanied by a hideous animal: an ape, a tiger cat, a long-tailed monkey, a pig, an enormous owl, a crocodile, etc. At Madge's gesture, the animals place themselves around the cauldron; they turn it rightside up and poke at the fire while jumping grotesquely.	**(B)** J.S. Bach: Fugue in F Major from *The Well-tempered Clavier, Book II*, arranged and modified after the four subject entrances are complete, ends with a more homophonic section of dissonant chords, annotated at the opening 'Les Sorcières arrivent par groupes,' 'Cf. J.S. Bach – Clavecin bientempéré.' Each of the four groups is annotated at a subject entry of the fugue, each entry features varied instrumentation.
III. The witches help Madge plot revenge and add items to the cauldron	
Libretto: The witches leave their broomsticks and gather poisonous things to throw into the cauldron for the magic spell. One brings toads, the other a snake, this one brings lizards, that one brings an old howling cat, wolf's teeth, hemlock, the feet of a goat and the ears of a cat. Madge pours out some liquid; thick smoke rises from the cauldron. The long-tailed she-monkey is charged with	**(C)** *Grave*, in 4/4, E minor, this more sinister theme also starts imitatively, with the clarinets and high strings. Madge tells of James' affront and implores the others to help her get revenge. They promise to do so. There is more percussion here and the addition of the 'serpent' (a bassoon-like instrument with a snake-like curve). Tutti agitated chordal writing, colored by many

skimming the brew; the other animals blow air onto the fire with the bellows.

chromatic tones, swirling figures illustrate the swirling contents of the cauldron. Cadence to F-sharp major as dominant of the next part.

IV. *Danse des Sorcières*, completion of spell, departure

Libretto: Fantastic dance of the witches, which Madge brings to a halt after a short while.

(D) *The main Witch Dance theme*, annotated 'Danse des Sorcières,' B minor, march-like, pulsing bassoons with drums and cymbals, an orchestral melody climbs with eerie precision. Internal form of this section [aabaccdd¹] followed by a transition.

The cauldron is boiling; it overflows with foam. To work! To work! The witches mount their broomsticks and line up once again around the circle, each holding a glass. The animals crouch in front of the cauldron, forming a pulpit upon which Madge opens the large book of cabalistic signs. She casts the spell, and soaks various objects in the cauldron; these will become talismans. She distributes them to the witches, keeping a scarf for herself; she wraps herself up in it. After this procedure she again stirs the pot — a red flame leaps out, and with the ladle she fills the glasses, which the witches clink together while howling sharply; the animals answer. Glasses are emptied, the spell is cast; a new round. The witches set forth again on their broomsticks, just as they had arrived; the animals carry the utensils of the Sabbath, and all of them re-enter in the cave, in a chain formation. Towards the end of this scene the fog begins to dissipate, and one can see, little by little, a landscape which takes shape through the trees.

(E) A shift to 3/4 and a key signature shift to D minor begins a new section that builds in intensity through repeated patterns at higher pitch levels until erupting into *Allegro moderato* in full fledged D minor and transition in to 2/2 over a dominant pedal. The charm is created and the witches drink the potion here, according to the Bartholomin score.

(D) return of *the main theme* in D minor now (this is where the Paris violin score begins to match, but with different structure and many cross-outs). Madge takes the scarf and sends the other witches away. Internal structure of full score: [aa¹a¹ba²aca³a⁴closing]. (All themes except 'a' are new.) The (c) theme is swirling eighths with dynamic swells and woodwind screeches that must have accompanied the witches' howling. The closing theme begins a chromatic meltdown starting with the theme, then diminishing note values and relaxing the tempo for a final chromatic descent to cadence in D minor.

* Selected annotations and descriptions from the scores are included here; for annotations from all scores, see Appendix 6.

be regarded as a small entr'acte, setting the mood for the witches' Sabbath, with the curtain rising as early as the seventh measure, according to the Bartholomin score. The music is typical of 'witch' ballet music of that era, with overt dissonances, swirling motives and off-beat accents.[25] After Madge completes her initial preparations, which include arranging items she needs for the spell, such as 'a skull, animal craniums, a vase of writhing reptiles and a bag of dried herbs' (Libretto, pp. 21-22), she strikes the cauldron three times with the pot spoon (according to all three musical manuscripts). This is punctuated musically by three loud dominant chords which create a suspenseful half-cadence.

The next section begins with quotation of the four subject entries of Bach's Fugue in F major from *The Well-tempered Clavier, Book II*, as Madge calls her companions. (As noted above, however, this fugue is not included in the Paris rehearsal score, suggesting that it did not make it to the stage at the Opéra.) Each entry of the fugue was intended to bring out a group of witches (as the full-score annotations tell us), each group presumably being five in number, since the libretto calls for twenty witches riding broomsticks and holding lanterns.[26] Then, Schneitzhoeffer switches to dance music for the dance of the witches around the cauldron and its boiling contents. (Example 4.5 shows the main theme of the Witches' Dance.) Then the animals, ac-

Example 4.5. Witch Dance Main Theme, Act Two scene i

cording to the libretto, configure themselves in such a manner as to create a table for Madge's spell book. Following the casting of the spell, the poisonous scarf and other talismans are pulled out of the cauldron for the witches to take as party favours. The witches drink the potion as well. Madge pulls the scarf from the pot and at the close of this scene the participants leave, returning to the cave whence they came. An estimate of the total time for this spectacle is thirteen minutes (according to the music in the full score and the Bartholomin rehearsal score; however, the Paris violin score omits 80 measures of music from the witch spectacle, just before the danced segment, and cuts more music from the witches' dance) (see Table 4.2).

Act Two, scene ii: Sylphides dancing and flying

In stark contrast to the witches' night-time scene is the succeeding scene of the sylphides, which of course depicts an entirely different sort of supernatural creature, and occurs during the day. (In the Bartholomin score the words 'nuit' and 'jour' are written at the openings of scenes i and ii respectively, describing the lighting.) The daytime scene begins with a majestic and mysterious theme, with deceptive harmonies, as the day dawns. Adding two harps to the orchestra for this scene, Schneitzhoeffer employs shimmering string tremolos and birdsong in the flutes to evoke the woodland fantasy world. The two harps provide an undulating accompaniment to soaring violin melodies.

The first recognisable theme to appear out of the ether is the fluttering 'Sylph' theme (first heard in the overture), which accompanies the Sylphide and James at the beginning. A few other themes are prominent in this scene: the witch's music evokes a sense of danger (even though Madge is nowhere to be seen), the James vs. Gurn motive appears during James's solo section (indicated in the Paris violin score), and a third important theme is introduced when the *corps de ballet* enters to dance. This 'Sylph dance theme' is a peaceful swirling triadic melody in A major. We will learn to associate this theme with the sylphs and their world (and will recognise it later when it recurs). (Example 4.6.)

Example 4.6. Sylph Dance Theme, Act Two scene ii

Dramatically and musically, this extensive scene unfolds in three sections, with the large middle section dominated by dancing. In the first section, the Sylphide leads an anxious James along the rocks; he is unsure of the wisdom of breaking his vows to Effie. The second, and middle section consists of several danced numbers for the *corps de ballet*, a *pas de deux* (possibly for James and the Sylphide), and appearances by a trio of sylphides, as well as solos and other groupings.[27] James's spirit soars in this middle section: 'James is in ecstasy; these graceful pictures exalt his imagination; he is more charmed than ever with the Sylph' (Libretto, p. 25). (The A-major swirling 'Sylph dance theme' appears throughout the extended happy-sounding middle section.) The third section is similar to the first as James becomes anxious again, this time because the Sylphide has proven so elusive. He tries to seize her, but she, along with her sisters, escapes. James is left alone.

Act Two, scene iv: Unhappy James acquires the fatal scarf

James is now in despair, and an emphatic *Allegro agitato* theme in D minor reflects his state of unhappiness. As the sylphides take flight, *pianissimo* violin oscillations crescendo into large chords. These are interrupted by flute gestures that may have been intended to accompany the actual flight of the sylphides. Sustained lines in the flute and oboe over string triplets mark the sylphides' departure from the scene.

The troubled violin triplets are interrupted by a recurrence of the emphatic chords that opened this scene. Then trombones announce that the witch, Madge, is on hand. Her appearance is accompanied by her signature theme *Le Streghe* which is followed by music similar to her palm-reading music (from Act One) as she and James interact. After 'the witch reproaches James, who had chased her from the farm' (according to the annotations in both Parisian scores), a falling pattern in the strings illustrates his pleading as he begs; the music then modulates erratically as Madge feigns pity and gives him the scarf.

The culmination of this exchange, annotated in the full score as 'You will be happy [when you] envelop her in this scarf', is accompanied by a sorrowful B-minor melody in the violin, which does not at all seem to portend James's future happiness – in fact, it predicts what will really happen: the delicate wings will fall to the ground. James's happiness returns to the sound of a horn fanfare and the recurrence of 'James vs. Gurn' motives as he '... covers the scarf with kisses and thanks the witch'.[28] (As the libretto puts it, 'James kneels before the witch, he is overwhelmed with gratitude; he kisses a hundred times that marvelous talisman which will make him happy...'.) The music here is derived from the 'James versus Gurn' music in Act One, scene i (Example 4.7).

Example 4.7. Horn fanfare signalling James's happiness and triumph, Act Two scene iv

Little does James know that Madge has not told him the true powers of the scarf. But the music tells us of Madge's glee at fooling James and enacting her malicious plan. For the first time since the overture, *Le Streghe* is presented in a major key, closing out the scene.

Act Two, scene v (the final scene): Death of the Sylph, wedding procession of Effie, despair of James

Now Madge's machinations come to fruition: we see the capture and demise of the unfortunate Sylphide, the ruin of poor James, and the cheerful wedding of Effie and Gurn in the background. Schneitzhoeffer paints with vivid strokes, reusing themes in a meaningful way (the sylph dance theme, Effie's engagement theme), and neatly tying the drama together musically while reinforcing the notion that this outcome was determined by earlier events. Here I shall highlight Schneitzhoeffer's use of mime music, re-used themes and quotations.

Early in the scene:

The Sylph comes down and comes to offer him the nest which she holds in her hands in exchange for the scarf. — No, I do not want it; the poor little birds would die if they lost their freedom; you must give them back to their mother. —You are right. She goes and puts the nest back in the trunk of the tree... (Libretto p. 28.)

The analogy between the innocent birds in the nest and the Sylphide is reinforced by fluttering flutes and oboes for both images. Instrumental recitatives by violins alternating with flutes, punctuated by half-cadences in the strings spell out the conversation.

Later in the scene, after the Sylphide is captured and her wings fall off, the 'Sylph dance theme' from Act Two scene ii recurs briefly, only to halt suddenly as the Sylphide discovers she can no longer dance. Then, subdued string motives that sigh, and progress only haltingly, convey the final conversation:

What have you done? — I have attached you to me, and from now on you belong to me and we will never be apart. — You have made a mistake! All is finished for me.... in taking away my freedom you have robbed me of my life. —What are you saying? —You see the pallor of my brow: soon I shall be forever deprived your love. — Woe is me. (Libretto p. 29.)

To Théophile Gautier, this was one of the most moving mime sequences of the ballet; he wrote of Fanny Elssler's performance in 1838:

Her miming, when she is caught by her lover in the folds of the enchanted scarf, expresses with a very poetic regret and pardon the feeling of disaster and of error beyond repair, while her last long look at her wings which have fallen to the ground is full of great tragic beauty.[29]

Then Schneitzhoeffer briefly reuses the pastoral Effie and James engagement theme as a reminder of James's broken vows. This theme is soon diverted into a harmonically unstable *Allegro* in B minor with an urgent theme over swirling strings which itself morphs into tumultuous imitative passages erupting from different sections of the orchestra. This accompanies the Sylphide's death and the anguish of James. The full-score annotations read '*La Sylphide expire*' (the Sylphide expires), '*Désespoir de James*' (Despair of James) followed in the next measure by '*J'ai perdu mon Euridice*' ('I have lost my Euridice'), this latter referring to the well-known aria from Gluck's *Orphée et Euridice*, an aria sung by Orphée upon Euridice's death, and its main melody here played by the orchestra.[30] Soon thereafter, James hears the wedding bells.

To close out the entire ballet, Schneitzhoeffer brings back Effie's G-major engagement theme, this time to draw our attention to the distant celebration of her wedding to Gurn. Wedding-procession music is performed by a band on stage joined with the orchestra. Now, as the libretto reads, 'All at once, everything overwhelms poor James, who casts a last glance at the sylphide and falls to the ground in a faint.' We know from the libretto and the Bartholomin score that the dead sylphide is carried from the stage by the other sylphides.

Recurring themes

The use of recurring themes is integral to Schneitzhoeffer's approach to the ballet. I shall now discuss several of them briefly. Four of the recurring themes are overtly rustic and Scottish in character (Example 4.8). Three of these (Nos. 2, 3, and 4 from Example 4.8) resemble one another in their triadic gestures with quick flourishes between held notes in imitation of bagpipes.

Rustic theme 1: The Effie and James Love Theme is in C major and is catchy and sweet. It is first heard in Act One, scene ii. Distinctive clarinet and oboe melodies sing against a pizzicato background, accompanying a dialogue between Effie and James (quoted above). Here, James's public, realistic, and acceptable love for the attainable Effie is depicted by an easy tempo (*Allegretto grazioso*), the innocent key of C major and the light pizzicato background. The melody is uncomplicated and sweet (Example 4.8.1).

But when the theme returns in Act One scene iii as the Sylphide divulges her love to James and trembles at the notion that he loves Effie,[31] the tempo is

Example 4.8.1. Effie and James's love theme

Example 4.8.2. Village girls' triadic theme in B-flat major

Example 4.8.3. Village girls' pastoral theme in F major

Example 4.8.4. Effie and James's engagement theme in G major

slowed, the meter extended to 12/8, and the deeper timbre of the cello is brought forth, creating mystery and intimacy. Thus does the recurrence of this theme remind the audience aurally of Effie at the very moment the Sylphide attempts to undermine Effie's standing with James. Furthermore, the Sylphide's own love theme (introduced earlier in the scene) is added in as a countermelody to the now-transformed Effie/James love theme, and underneath these two melodies are shivers in the strings that illustrate the Sylphide's trembling (Figure 4.4.). This effective combination helps us aurally understand James's conflicting feelings of love for both Effie and the Sylphide.

Rustic Theme 2: The Village Girls' triadic theme in B-flat major, found in Act One, scene iii, is Scottish in character (more overtly so than the first one) with its open-fifths bass and quick, grace-note-like gestures between steadily held notes in the upper register (in the manner of bagpipe playing) (Example 4.8.2). Though this is dance music, it first accompanies a mimed sequence and refers to the village girls:

> Effie's friends arrive, each of them carrying her wedding gift: a plaid, a belt, a crown, wedding veil, bouquet, etc. The young girls congratulate James on his marriage, and laugh at the chagrin of Gurn, who would like to enlist them to speak in his favour. Effie kisses her companions and thanks them, and while she joyously adorns herself with the gifts she has received, James, ever distracted, drifts involuntarily toward the chimney. (Libretto, pp. 12-13.)

It recurs soon thereafter when the girls intercede on Madge's behalf. Then it comes back at the end of the first act as the second country dance in the *Divertissement*.

Rustic Theme 3: The Village-girls' Piccolo Theme in F major occurs late in Act One, scene iii, and calls for a piccolo solo and a drone-like accompaniment. In F major and in a duple meter, it is a simple, happy and playful melody, with hints of bagpipe as in the B-flat triadic theme (Example 4.8.3). It accompanies the action of the village girls bringing in the wedding clothes for Effie to see (as all scores tells us). It recurs later as the first country dance of the *Divertissement*, where it is used in conjunction with the aforementioned B-flat triadic theme.

Rustic Theme 4: the Effie and James engagement theme in G major, occurring in Act One scene ii, *Allegretto grazioso*, is reminiscent of Effie's G-major entrance theme and entails octave fifths accompanying an oboe solo that is then taken over by the strings (Example 4.8.4). It is the first music heard after the *Divertissement* as the following action takes place toward the end of Act One:

> The dancing ceases and they prepare for the betrothal ceremony; Effie's friends surround her. They place the bridal crown on her head, and hand her the bouquet, and she receives her engagement ring from old Mother Anne. All eyes are on Effie, and everyone congratulates her. (Libretto p. 19.)

It comes back twice at the end of Act Two (scene v), first when the Sylphide returns James's engagement ring to him shortly before her death. Here, perhaps, it is meant to reflect James's recollection of his engagement to Effie.

> [La Sylphide] — Don't weep, you whom I have loved so dearly! I could not belong to you.... I was blessed by your love; but I could not bring you happiness.... Adieu, I shall die.... Here, take your betrothal ring.... hasten away, you can marry the one you loved before you knew me.... Adieu, I die content, because I carry the hope that you will be happy. —No, if I must lose you, I wish to die too. (Libretto, p. 29.)

In this scene, Schneitzhoeffer has again mixed Effie's music into a crucial scene with the Sylphide, in a combination that is heard just at the moment when James takes the mysterious Sylphide and attempts to force her into the realm of realistic, living beings. The mixing of Effie's and the Sylphide's sonic identities throughout the ballet, indeed, portrays James's attempt to combine fantasy and reality in possessing the Sylphide and obtaining her in the way he would have obtained Effie had he married her.

Finally, as the witch shows James the wedding procession and wedding bells are heard from afar, the Effie and James engagement theme appears for a third time, this time representing Effie's marriage to Gurn. This rustic little G major theme thus brings the drama full circle and closes out the entire ballet.

Themes for James, the Sylphs, and Madge

Madge's Theme ('à la Paganini') Le Streghe has already been discussed at length above. First heard in the overture and last heard in the penultimate scene of the ballet, this theme is threaded into the score every time Madge interacts with the regular mortals, and is missing only when she celebrates the witches' Sabbath with her cohorts.

The *'James versus Gurn' theme* is first introduced in a conversation between the two rivals, but it expresses their antagonism and turns into an emphatic, manly sort of theme that reappears at other moments in the ballet and seems to represent James's more competitive, aggressive side (for he is, after all, someone who competes with and pushes away his rival). Specifically, this 'manly' theme comes into play when James feels that he is in control – for instance, just after James's solo during the sylph scene, and when James obtains the scarf from Madge and rejoices at his renewed sense of power. (See Example 4.7.)

The *Sylphides' theme*, on the other hand, is used primarily during their big scene in Act Two as a way to represent their idyllic airy existence (and from a technical standpoint, to tie together this lengthy scene). This swirling triadic theme in A major is lushly orchestrated, with the strings at the forefront. (See

Example 4.6.) It is a peaceful, happy and danceable theme, accompanying the sylphs in their supernatural world where a *grand jeté* may lead to flight in the woods. (The specific points at which the sylphs fly across the stage are identified in the scores.)

Thus the effect is poignant when the same music is brought back just as the Sylphide is about to die, after her wings have fallen off. The theme's brief recurrence (six measures followed by sudden silence) at this juncture seems to function as the symbol of an abruptly cut-off memory, or perhaps, a reminder of her lost freedom. At this point the Bartholomin score tells us that the sylphs reappear, dancing.

The *pas de deux* in *La Sylphide*

Act One. The first *pas de deux* in *La Sylphide*, according to all three musical sources, occurs during the *Divertissement* at the close of Act One during the celebration of James and Effie's union. The Paris violin score contains useful annotations indicating who danced when (Table 4.3).

The annotations in the Paris Opéra rehearsal score show that much of the time the male and female dancers were alternating (and it is likely that they were performing the same steps as well, a practice that Sandra Noll Hammond has explained[32]). This, then, is a *pas de deux* that does not fit the standard concept (held by some observers today) of the *pas de deux* as a showcase for the woman, in which the cavalier merely partners and supports, and then both partners dance a separate variation (a later nineteenth-century format). Here it appears that the male and female alternated sections of equal lengths, with the exception of the inner *Andante* danced by the woman. This alternation of phrases was a common feature of early nineteenth-century *pas de deux*, as Hammond has demonstrated. This musical form of this *pas de deux* is also similar to the multi-sectional slow-to-fast format found in Hammond's sources as well as contemporaneous Italian ballet *passo a due*.[33]

Of further note in this Act One *pas de deux* is its solo for keyed trumpet (*trompette à piston*), which did not go unnoticed by one period writer, who includes it amongst his examples of noteworthy instrumental solos used for dancing:

... concertos or *récits d'apparat*, played by one or several virtuosos of the orchestra, have been introduced, while the dancer arranges his *pas* to the brilliant flourishes of the violin, the mandoline, the cello, the flute, the clarinet, the oboe, the harp, and even the keyed trumpet....I will also cite the violin solo from *Les Pages du Duc de Vendôme*, the harp solo in *La Caravane*, the horn solo in *Hécube*, the flute solo in *Les Filets de Vulcain*, and the keyed-trumpet solo in *La Sylphide*.[34]

Table 4.3. Diagram of the *pas de deux* in the Act One *Divertissement*

Intro	A, A¹	B	A	C	D	E	F	transition	A	G	C¹	A/ close
Adagio 4/4 G major trumpet and horn fanfare	*Allegretto* 6/8 trumpet solo, flute, violin	light flute, violin 16th notes, move to V	*see A*	oboes with rocket melody, violin, flute, fuller texture	clarinets new harmony trumpet solo with winds – ends like E begins	D minor strings vs winds imitation flute and clarinet cadenza-like passage	*Andante* switch to 2/4 G minor oboe solo with strings	6/8 G major. A theme motives, trading flutes, violins, clarinets	*see A*	marked *plus vite* in violin score, A motives in trumpet accomp. triadic violin melody in G major	*see C*	clarinet transition (her), A theme (him), closing section (both)
- - - - -	dame, homme (8 each)	dame		homme	dame	homme	dame	homme	homme	dame	homme	dame, homme, then both
6.5 bars	8 + 8 16 bars	8 + 8 16 bars		17 bars	20 bars	15 bars	35 bars*	10 + 8 18 bars		16 bars	18 bars	4 + 8 + 7 19 bars

From the full score, Bibliothèque de l'Opéra, manuscript A. 501 and the violin score Mat. 19 [302 (25)]

*The full score matches the violin partitur exactly except for a later added set of repeat signs in the middle of this *Andante*.

The main trumpet theme (*Allegretto*), which is introduced after the opening fanfare (*Adagio*), is showy and buoyant but graceful against the lilting string accompaniment (Example 4.9).

Example 4.9. Main Trumpet Theme of the *Divertissement pas de deux*

Act Two. There were two *pas de deux* in the second act, one during the sylphs' scene in the woods (scene ii), which was primarily a danced scene,[35] and a number entitled (in the full score) '*Gavotte pas de deux avec sourdine*' (scene v). I shall focus now on this *Gavotte pas de deux*, because it is musically distinct and functions as a dramatic number rather than a purely danced number. Indeed, it culminates with the peak of the dramatic action: James wrapping the Sylphide with the scarf. It does not follow the same scheme as the first act *pas de deux* nor does it match the general outlines of *pas de deux* typical of the period.[36]

Schneitzhoeffer writes some of the most subtle and moving music of the entire ballet here, combining muted strings with flute, oboe, horn and bassoon. Rather than supplying mime music like that serving other dramatic sections of the ballet, Schneitzhoeffer chooses to encapsulate this dramatic climax in a gavotte. The music illustrates the action but does so subtly and within the confines of the predictable ternary musical form (ABA'), the peak of the action occurring during the transitional moments before the return of the A theme (see Table 4.4). The inevitability of the standard form seems to convey that both James and the Sylphide are oblivious to the actual consequences of their actions; too, they are propelled by the ceaseless and steady eighth notes of the Gavotte. They are ruled by desires – he wants to capture her, she wants the scarf – and have lost control of their destinies.[37]

A short comparison of Schneitzhoeffer's and Løvenskjold's scores for *La Sylphide*

Schneitzhoeffer's and Løvenskjold's scores for *La Sylphide* have much in common. Both composers – not surprisingly – make use of Scottish-sounding music for the village scenes, and provide source music for the *Divertissement*. Both composers depict Madge with dissonance, trombones, percussion, sudden jerky rhythms, pulsating pedal points, dances in duple, minor mode, and

Table 4.4. *Gavotte Pas de deux* **and Dramatic Action, Act Two scene v**

LIBRETTO	MUSIC and ANNOTATIONS* *Gavotte Pas de deux avec Sourdine*
...coming back to James, she tries to get hold of the scarf, which he refuses to give up. He is angry with her; she is always flying off and never lets herself get caught.	**(A)** E minor, 2/4, the muted strings have the melody with an unceasing stream of steady eighth notes as 'James calls to the Sylphide.' Phrases begin regularly and cadence at even intervals. The A theme repeats with an altered ending. The Bartholomin score has the Sylphide show James the nest at the beginning of this number. (16 measures)
The Sylph insists on having the scarf and promises never to fly away again.	**(B)** Several new musical ideas in succession, modulating while phrases grow increasingly irregular and cadences are avoided (just as the Sylph avoids being caught). The mood is lighter as the flutes trill, violins have light and quick swirling figures that suggest the Sylphide chasing the swirling scarf. The Bartholomin score states that the two make 'several passes together.' Tension builds throughout the section and crescendo to an accented *forte* and cadence in G major. (19 measures)
James pretends to refuse again. She approaches him to take it away; then he wraps it around her so she cannot draw up her arms. The Sylph is captured and she falls to her knees to ask for mercy; but James does not take the scarf away until he has seen her wings fall off. At the same moment, the sylphide has put her hand over her heart, as if struck by a fatal blow.	**(C / transition)** Similar to the opening material (A), but in G major (deceptively sweet), soon modulating to A minor and cadencing. (8 measures) **(false A)** A theme returns but in A minor decorated with a flute pedal note, but after one phrase, as the full score states 'Il l'enveloppe,' he wraps the scarf about the Sylphide; the cadence extends with a chromatic descent led by the flute down to the dominant as 'Les ailes se préparent' and her wings fall followed by horn and flute mini-solos. She pales during an instrumental lead-in to the true return of **(A)**. (17 measures)

James holds her in his arms, she re-pulses him; he throws himself at her feet ... mortal pallor covers the sylph's brow.	**(A)** True return of the opening theme this time with flute also on the melody and an altered ending, cadencing to E minor with a fermata and a double bar. During the last phrase, she falls. (17 measures)

Selected annotations and descriptions from the scores are included here; for annotations from all scores, see Appendix 6.

a general unpredictability. Both composers, too, represent the Sylphide with ethereal-sounding music using flute, harp and the solo violin as her solo voice. And both make use of recurring themes – for example, both composers identify Madge the witch with a theme and then bring it back just before the poison scene, when James obtains the scarf from her.

The two composers' approaches to structure differ in some ways. Schneitzhoeffer seamlessly melds successive ideas together according to the 'through-development' principle, avoiding full cadences; Løvenskjold often employs internal repetition schemes, such as the ABA or $AA^1 BA^2$ forms that occur in his opening scene, in which the B sections and transitions are used for mime. Løvenskjold favours clear eight-bar phrases and obvious cadences, even when mime is called for. Indeed, at many points in the ballet, instead of writing music that overtly illustrates or 'speaks', Løvenskjold continues to write evenly-phrased music that could work well for dance, even though it is intended for mime scenes. This is not to say that Løvenskjold fails to provide excellent mime music – there is plenty of it, including the evil orchestral cackling (complete with blasting trombones) that accompanies Madge's ap-pearances. But his frequent use of evenly-phrased danceable music during mimed action paints a general mood and leaves the burden of overt dramatic expression more to the dancers. It also imparts a smooth sound to the score, which features fewer irregular phrases and unpredictable musical outcomes than does Schneitzhoeffer's.

Reception

Schneitzhoeffer's music for *La Sylphide* was met with a mixed reception by the critics. A writer in the *Journal des Dames* states, 'The music is the weak link; it is too uniform'[38] – too uniform, perhaps, because of its generally seamless quality (as noted above). Another writes more extensively about Schneitzhoeffer's score, first praising him, then criticising his score quite pointedly for its lack of using '*airs connus*' – known melodies.

The music is by Mr. Schneitzhoeffer, to whom we already owe several other ballets, particularly *Les Filets de Vulcain*. Mr. Schneitzhoeffer is a talented musician who does not enjoy a reputation equal to his merit. Perhaps he has only himself to blame. The intervals between his ballets are too long. His talent deserves a wider reputation, his love of leisure has more dominion over him than a love of glory. At any rate, the music of *La Sylphide* is not just well made, it also shines with agreeable ideas and a scenic expression that is often felicitous. The instrumentation is vivid and the colour varied.

I will always vow that I do not approve of the system adopted by Mr. Schneitzhoeffer in the music of his ballets. The language of pantomime is quite imperfect; it leaves many things vague and uncertain, and music alone can supply what is lacking in clarity. But music is itself a vague art that needs the aid of the word in rendering positive ideas. Deprived of this help [i.e. the word] in ballets, it can at least recall situations or sentiments analogous to those which it must express by themes known to everyone. It is, in effect, by this procedure that several ballet music composers have known how to render mimic action intelligible; however, this is not at all how Mr. Schneitzhoeffer composes his own [ballet music]. Considering music as an art of expression, he seems to attribute to his means more power than [he should], disdaining, in general, known melodies, and methodically *composing ... all the music in his works*. From this, a fault of clarity has hurt him, perhaps more than he thinks, in his success. I offer this critique for his reflections.[39]

This commentator cites the accepted method of using a collage of familiar music to create a ballet score that helps explain the action; he does not approve of Schneitzhoeffer's predominately original score. The accepted practice of using borrowed music in ballet scores was soon to lose favour.[40] Schneitzhoeffer's score for *La Sylphide* was one of the last of the era of pastiche ballet scores and one of the first originally composed ones – it *did* make use of borrowed music, but not enough to satisfy all of the critics. Rather, Schneitzhoeffer employed his own *recurring* themes to jog the listener's memory. The nineteenth century would soon see the practice of composing original music for ballets become the norm, culminating in the great scores of Delibes and Tchaikovsky.

Schneitzhoeffer's score for *La Sylphide* has such vivid music that, for many sections of the score, one can simply follow along with the libretto in hand and hear the action unfold. And the three manuscript scores to which I have referred provide enough further detail to make it possible to line up the specific events and actions to the music and even, in some cases, to discern which character is dancing and at what time, and to better discern his or her mood and personality.

In turns happy, haunting, mysterious, foreboding, surprising, and tragic, Schneitzhoeffer's score speaks for its mute dancing characters with great variety and expressivity while holding together seamlessly. Also, it uses the relatively less common technique (for the 1830s) of recurring music for specific characters and topics in sophisticated ways that are more psychological than purely referential. Because of these musical-dramatic qualities, is it worth hearing in full and discovering again.

La Sylphide. Directed by René Mathelin, music by J.M. Schneitzhoeffer, performed by the Paris Opéra Ballet. Le Service de la Musique. Sea Bright, NJ: Kultur Inc., 1971. Videocassette. [Lacotte production]

La Sylphide. Music by J.M. Schneitzhoeffer, Filmed live at the Opéra National de Paris, Palais Garnier in July 2004. Ratingen: TDK, 2005. DVD. [Lacotte production]

Augustyn, Frank. 'Footnotes: The Classics of Ballet', vol. 1. West Long Branch, NJ: Kultur International Films, 1995.

Banes, Sally. *Dancing Women: Female Bodies on Stage*. London and New York: Routledge, 1998.

Berlioz, Hector. *Mozart, Weber and Wagner*. Translated by Edwin Evans. London: W. Reeves, n.d.

Castil-Blaze. 'Ballet', in *Dictionnaire De Musique Moderne*, vol. 1. Brussels: Académie de Musique, 1828.

———. *La Danse Et Les Ballets Depuis Bacchus Jusqu'à Mlle Taglioni*. Paris: Paulin, 1832.

Chazin-Bennahum, Judith. *The Lure of Perfection: Fashion and Ballet, 1780-1830*. New York: Routledge, 2005.

Collins, Willa. 'Adolphe Adam's Ballet *Le Corsaire* at the Paris Opéra, 1856-1868: A Source Study' Ph.D. diss., Cornell University, 2008.

Copeland, Roger, and Marshall Cohen. *What Is Dance? Readings in Theory and Criticism*. New York: Oxford University Press, 1983.

Day, David A. 'The Annotated Violon Repetiteur and Early Romantic Ballet at the Théâtre Royal de Bruxelles (1815-1830)' Ph.D. diss., New York University, 2008.

Delaforest, A. *Cours De Littérature Dramatique*. Paris: Allardin, 1836.

Ertz, Matilda Ann Butkas. 'Nineteenth-Century Italian Ballet Music before National Unification: Sources, Style and Context' Ph.D. diss., University of Oregon, 2010.

Fetis, Francois-Joseph. *Biographie universelle de musiciens*, 2nd ed. Paris: Firmin-Didot Frères, 1875.

Fléche, Alfred, L. W. Webb, and George Willig. *The Sylvia Waltz*. Baltimore: G. Willig Jr., 1840.

Guest, Ivor, and John Lanchberry. 'The Scores of *La Fille Mal Gardée*.' *Theatre Research* 3, no. 1 (1961): 32-42.

Hammond, Sandra Noll. 'Windows into Romantic Ballet, Part 2: Content and Structure of Solo Entrées from the Early Nineteenth Century', in *Proceedings, Dance History Scholars*. Riverside, CA: Society of Dance History Scholars, 1998.

———. 'Windows into Romantic Ballet: Content and Structure of Four Early Nineteenth-Century Pas De Deux', in *Proceedings, Dance History Scholars*. Riverside, CA: Society of Dance History Scholars, 1997.

Jarvis, Charles, Fanny Elssler, and Peter S. Duval. *Melle. Fanny Elssler's Quadrilles: Arranged for the Piano Forte*. Keffer Collection of Sheet Music. Philadelphia: A. Fiot, 1840.

Jordan, Stephanie. 'The Role of the Ballet Composer at the Paris Opera: 1820-1850', *Dance Chronicle* 4, no. 4 (1982): 374-88.

Løvenskiold, Herman Severin, and August Bournonville. *Les Sylphides: Contredances Françaises pour le pianoforte sur des motifs de la composition de Mr. H. de Løvenskjold*. Copenhagen: C.C. Lose and Olsen, 1837.

———. cond. David Garforth. *Music for the Bournonville Ballet La Sylphide*. Colchester, Essex, England: Chandos Records, 1986, reissued 1991, 2001, 2004.

Mayseder, Joseph. *La Sylphide as danced by Fanny Elssler*. New York: Atwill, 184?

———. *Souvenir de la Sylphide; Air de Mayseder arr. pour le piano seul par A. Thys*. Philadelphia: George Willig, 1840.

Meisner, Nadine. 'Pierre Lacotte and the Romantic Ballet', in *Preservation Politics: Dance Revived, Reconstructed, Remade (Proceedings of the Conference at the University of Surrey Roehampton, November, 8-9, 1997)*, ed. Stephanie Jordan. London: Dance Books, 1997.

Nectoux, Jean-Michel. 'Trois Orchestres Parisiens en 1830: L'académie Royal de Musique, le Théâtre-Italien et la Société des Concerts du Conservatoire', in *Music in Paris in the Eighteen-Thirties*, ed. Peter Bloom. Stuyvesant, NY: Pendragon Press, 1987.

Paganini, Nicolò, and Ricardo Tagliorozzo. *Le Streghe: variazioni per violino e pianoforte, op. 8* (no. 3 delle opere postume). Milan: G. Ricardi, 1918.

Schneitzhoeffer, J. M., and J. Tolbèque. *Trois Quatrilles: Sur Les Motifs de La Sylphide (for Flute and Piano)*. Paris: Aulagnier, 1832.

Schneitzhoeffer, Jean-Madeleine. *The Sylphid: A Ballet in Two Acts by M. Taglioni; the Music by M. Schneitzhoeffer*. London: W. Glindon, 183-?

Schneitzhoeffer, Jean Madeleine, and A. Aulagnier. *Rondino: Pour Le Piano, sur des motifs de La Sylphide: Op. 13* Paris: Aulagnier, 1832.

Schueneman, Bruce R., and William E. Studwell. *Minor Ballet Composers: Biographical Sketches of Sixty-Six Underappreciated yet Significant Contributors to the Body of Western Ballet Music.* New York: Haworth Press, 1997.

Séchan, Charles. *Souvenirs d'un homme de théatre, 1831-1855.* Paris: Calmann Lévy, 1883.

Second, Albéric. *Les Petits Mystères de l'opéra.* Paris: G. Kugelmann, 1844.

Smith, Marian. *Ballet and Opera in the Age of 'Giselle'.* Princeton: Princeton University Press, 2000.

————. 'Borrowings and Original Music: A Dilemma for the Ballet-Pantomime Composer.' *Dance Research* 6, no. 2 (1988): 3-29.

————. 'Music for the Ballet-Pantomime at the Paris Opéra, 1825-1850.' Ph.D. diss., Yale University, 1988.

Strakosch, Maurice. *La Sylphide, Fantasie Romantique.* New York: W. M. Hall and Son, 1849.

Süssmayr, Franz Xaver, Salvatore Viganò, and Giulio Viganò. *Il Noce Di Benevento: Ballo Al[l]egorico.* Biblioteca di Musica, Anno 3, Classe 2. Milan: Ricordi, 1822.

Wiley, Roland John. *Tchaikovsky's Ballets: Swan Lake, Sleeping Beauty, Nutcracker.* Oxford: Oxford University Press, 1985.

Notes

1. Pierre Lacotte's production of *La Sylphide*, which uses the Schneitzhoeffer score, may be seen in two video recordings: *La Sylphide*, Directed by René Mathelin, music by J.M. Schneitzhoeffer, performed by The Paris Opéra Ballet. Le Service de la Musique, Sea Bright, NJ: Kultur Inc., 1971, Videocassette; and *La Sylphide*, Music by J.M. Schneitzhoeffer, Filmed live at the Opéra National de Paris, Palais Garnier in July 2004, Ratingen: TDK, 2005, DVD. According to an interview with Nadine Meisner, Lacotte 'excised part of [the score for] *La Sylphide*, because people nowadays have shorter attention spans'. See Nadine Meisner, 'Pierre Lacotte and the Romantic Ballet', in *Preservation Politics: Dance Revived, Reconstructed, Remade (proceedings of the Conference at the University of Surrey Roehampton, November, 8-9, 1997)*, ed. Stephanie Jordan (London: Dance Books, 1997), 176.
2. François-Joseph Fétis, *Biographie universelle de musiciens*, 2nd ed. Paris: Firmin-Didot Frères, 1875. vol. 7, 495. The composer's name appears with various spellings in various publications, for example 'Schneitzoeffer' (*La Gazette musicale de Paris*, 21 September 1834), 'Schneitshoeffer' (*Le Ménestrel*, 21 September 21 1834,) 'Schneitzëffer' (*Le Constitutionnel*, 24 September 1838), 'Schneitzhofer' (Jean-Michel Nectoux, 'Trois Orchestres Parisiens en 1830: L'Académie Royal de Musique, Le Théâtre-Italien et la Société des Concerts du Conservatoire', in *Music in Paris in the Eighteen-Thirties*, ed. Peter Bloom (Stuyvesant, NY Pendragon Press, 1987, 505). *Le Figaro* (14 March 1832) and A. Delaforest, *Cours de Littérature Dramatique* (Paris: Allardin, 1836), entry of November 4, 1824, explain respectively that his name is pronounced 'Chènezefre'; 'Schnetcefre'.
3. *La Revue et Gazette Musicale de Paris*, 10 October 1852.
4. See Charles Séchan, *Souvenirs d'un homme de théatre, 1831-1855* (Paris: Calmann Lévy, 1883), 199-201; Hector Berlioz, *Mozart, Weber and Wagner*, trans. Edwin Evans, (London: W. Reeves, n.d.), 79; and Albéric Second, *Les Petits Mystères de l'Opéra* (Paris: G. Kugelmann, 1844), 42-44.

5. *La Revue Musicale*, 17 March 1832, 51.

6. *La Revue et Gazette Musicale de Paris*, 10 October 1852. The preceding three paragraphs on Schneitzhoeffer are from Marian Smith, 'Music for the ballet-pantomime at the Paris Opéra, 1825-1850' (Ph.D. diss., Yale University, 1988), 24-25. See also Bruce R. Schueneman and William E. Studwell, *Minor Ballet Composers: Biographical Sketches of Sixty-six Underappreciated Yet Significant Contributors to the Body of Western Ballet Music* (New York: Haworth Press, 1997), 80.

7. Castil-Blaze, 'Ballet', in *Dictionnaire de musique moderne* (Brussels: Académie de Musique, 1828), 44-46.

8. See Ivor Guest and John Lanchberry, 'The Scores of *La Fille Mal Gardée*', *Theatre Research* 3 (1961), no. 1: 32-42 and no. 2:121-134.

9. On practice of borrowing in ballet music See Marian Smith, *Ballet and opera in the Age of 'Giselle'* (Princeton: Princeton University Press, 2000), Chapter 4. See also Stephanie Jordan, 'The Role of the Ballet Composer at the Paris Opera: 1820-1850', *Dance Chronicle* 4, no. 4 (1982): 374-88. *Airs parlants* are 'short snippets of melodies from folksongs or opera arias, which could introduce actual explanatory words into the viewers' minds'. (Smith, *Ballet and opera in the Age of 'Giselle'*, 8.) Borrowings in *La Sylphide* identified in annotations in the score and in the card catalogue at the Bibliothèque de l'Opéra include excerpts from the trio of Boïeldieu's *Le Calife de Bagdad*, from the F major Fugue of J.S. Bach's Well-Tempered Clavier, Book II, and from Gluck's *Orphée et Euridice*; an air by Pauline Duchambge, and Paganini's variations, 'Le Streghe'. This ballet score, like many others, may have had even more quoted material from popular songs and operas no longer familiar to us.

10. *Journal des Dames*, 25 March 1832. Quoted in Judith Chazin-Bennahum, *The Lure of Perfection: Fashion and Ballet, 1780-1830* (New York: Routledge, 2005), 215.

11. Though I refer to scores of the complete ballet (in manuscript), it should be noted that printed excerpts from both the Danish and the French *Sylphide* scores were disseminated in arrangements for home use. The burgeoning market for home music making, especially at the keyboard, saw the publication for many pieces extracted from and inspired by ballets and operas, and *La Sylphide* was one of them. These products were often packaged with illustrations of the *Sylphide* herself, as danced by particular ballerinas, and their names and images were included as a selling point. See, for instance: Fanny Elssler, *La Sylphide* (New York: Atwill, 1834) (six pages of music with Elssler illustrated on the title page.); Joseph Mayseder, *Souvenir de La sylphide; air de Mayseder arr. pour le piano seul par A. Thys* (Philadelphia: George Willig, 1840) (nine pages of music, described on title page as 'dansé par Mlle. Taglioni'); Alfred Fléche, L. W. Webb, and George Willig, *The Sylvia waltz* (Baltimore: G. Willig Jr., 1840) (two pages of music, titles states 'Danced by Madlle. Fanny Ellster [sic] in *La Sylphide*'); Charles Jarvis, Fanny Elssler, and Peter S. Duval, *Melle. Fanny Elssler's quadrilles: arranged for the piano forte*, Keffer Collection of Sheet Music (Philadelphia: A. Fiot, 1840) (seven pages of music; No. 4 is titled 'La trènis: La sylphide'; the volume contains five portraits of Fanny Elssler in various dance poses and costumes, including that for *La Sylphide*); Jean Madeleine Schneitzhoeffer and A. Aulagnier, *Rondino: pour le piano, sur des motifs de La sylphide: op. 13* (Paris: Aulagnier, 1832); J. M. Schneitzhoeffer and J. Tolbèque, *Trois quatrilles: sur les motifs de La Sylphide (for flute and piano)* (Paris: Aulagnier, 1832); Herman Severin Løvenskiold and August Bournonville, *Les sylphides: contredances françaises pour le pianoforte sur des motifs de la composition de Mr. H. de Løvenskjold* (Copenhagen: C.C. Lose and Olsen, 1837). In addition numerous pieces were published in collections of salon pieces bearing the title 'La Sylphide' and some of these allude to events in the ballet. For example, Maurice Strakosch's *La Sylphide, Fantasie Romantique* (1849) contains sections entitled 'L'Orage' and 'Danse des Sylphides' (Maurice Strakosch, *La Sylphide, Fantasie Romantique* (New York: W. M. Hall and Son, 1849). The Sylphide was certainly part of the nineteenth-century popular imagery of woodland scenes and fairy-inspired tales, and composers partook fully in this trend.

12. Joseph Mazilier created the role of James in *La Sylphide* in 1832. His name appears after a number that appears in isolation after the conclusion of Act One in the Paris violin score and may have been inserted into the *Divertissement*. The music is marked *Moderato, Adagio, Moderato, Majeur* and *Coda*.

13. The name Ellsler [sic] appears in this score (on page 142), likely referring to Fanny Elssler.

14. See David A. Day, 'The Annotated Violon Repetiteur and Early Romantic Ballet at the Thèâtre

Royal de Bruxelles (1815-1830)' (Ph.D. diss., New York University, 2008).

15. Sally Banes, *Dancing Women: Female Bodies on Stage* (London and New York: Routledge, 1998), 14.

16. This English libretto which otherwise matches the French down to the minutest details does, however, shorten the witches' scene. Jean-Madeleine Schneitzhoeffer, *The Sylphid: a ballet in two acts by M. Taglioni; the music by M. Schneitzhoeffer* (London: W. Glindon, 183-?).

17. Lacotte's Paris Opéra productions, however, do not feature these elements as the annotations in the full score housed at the library of the Paris Opéra indicate. The Bartholomin rehearsal score has even greater detail. Were the choreography of this scene to follow the full score and Bartholomin score annotations, James's actions immediately following the Sylphide's disappearance would leave him on stage alone for a longer time and show that he goes through three emotional stages before awakening Gurn. The music and libretto clearly show that James is 1) 'disturbed by the mysterious appearance' with slow, chromatic downward modulations, 2) active and agitated, 'seeking to be convinced that is was a dream' and 3) calm as he resolves that 'his directions do not deceive him, he was awakened and his face still burns with the kiss' (accompanied by opening theme of the scene, reminding us and James of the Sylphide fluttering about him).

18. Smith also discusses this scene and provides musical examples of the Sylphide's fluttering wings, James summoning Gurn, their duet and conversation. See Smith, *Ballet and opera in the Age of 'Giselle'*, 8-9.

19. The rapidity of mood changes and shifts in action are intensified in Lacotte's productions by his cutting of repeated bits of musical material, including chunks of music intended to accompany James's questioning of Gurn. Schneitzhoeffer made frequent use of repeated material, perhaps to maximize the flexibility of the score.

20. Roland John Wiley, *Tchaikovsky's Ballets: Swan Lake, Sleeping Beauty, Nutcracker* (Oxford: Oxford University Press, 1985), 64.

21. The original Süssmayr number is a 'Contraddanza delle Streghe' [sic], which is preserved in a piano score from the Viganò ballet *Il Noce di Benevento* (1812) (a ballet about the legendary witches of Benevento). Franz Xaver Süssmayr, Salvatore Viganò, and Giulio Viganò, *Il noce di Benevento: ballo al[l]egorico*, Biblioteca di musica, anno 3, classe 2, (Milan: Ricordi, 1822).

22. See the table 'Rationales for Dancing in Operas and Ballet-Pantomimes' in Smith, *Ballet and opera in the Age of 'Giselle'*, 17.

23. Each of these four discrete sections may be divided into many musical subsections; the *Anglaise Finale*, for instance, was formed by regular chunks of music that are progressively repeated in a rondo-like form: aa-bb-a^{1}a^1-aa-cc-aa-bb-dd-d^{1}d^1-aa-bb-a^{1}a^1.

24. This music is not found in Lacotte's productions, from which extensive cuts have been made in the divertissement music.

25. For details on music for witches in Italian ballets from the same period see Matilda Ann Butkas Ertz, 'Nineteenth-century Italian Ballet Music before National Unification: Sources, Style and Context' (Ph.D. diss., University of Oregon, 2010), 265-79.

26. [Fugues in Parisian ballet scores of that era could signify villainy and evil-doing (as we may see in the examples of *Giselle* and *Le Corsaire* in which fugues accompany, respectively, the Wilis' attempts to kill Albrecht and the entrance of Birbanto and the other pirates into the corsairs' grotto. On *Le Corsaire*, see Willa Collins, 'Adolphe Adam's Ballet *Le Corsaire* at the Paris Opéra, 1856-1868: A Source Study' (Ph.D. diss., Cornell University, 2008). — Editor's Note.]

27. There are differences in this scene between the full score and Paris violin score, but they both indicate the presence of a *pas de deux*, sections intended for three sylphides and a part for James alone. The major difference appears to be a substitution in the Paris violin score of an alternative piece of music. This piece could have been a *pas de deux*. The Batholomin score offers a third variant: a different piece of music appears in the same spot but begins to match the full-score version midway through (see Appendix 6). It is typical for alternative versions of set pieces such as *pas de deux* to be substituted for existing pieces. In all three of the scores under scrutiny here, the set piece in this spot has the characteristics of a *pas de deux* of the period.

28. Paris Opéra full score, vol. III, 438-439.

29. Théophile Gautier, 'Revival of "La Sylphide".' Translated by Cyril Beaumont in Roger Copeland

and Marshall Cohen, *What Is Dance? Readings in Theory and Criticism* (New York: Oxford University Press, 1983), 436. See also Ivor Guest's translation of this passage in this volume, Chapter 10.

30. As Marian Smith notes, it was unusual for the text of an *air parlant* to be written down in the musical score. (Smith, *Ballet and Opera in the Age of 'Giselle'*, 110.)

31. This is indicated in both Parisian scores and the libretto.

32. Sandra Noll Hammond, 'Windows into Romantic Ballet: Content and Structure of Four Early Nineteenth-Century Pas de Deux', in *Proceedings, Dance History Scholars* (Riverside, CA: Society of Dance History Scholars, 1997), 137-44 and Sandra Noll Hammond, 'Windows into Romantic Ballet, Part 2: Content and Structure of Solo Entrées from the Early Nineteenth Century', in *Proceedings, Dance History Scholars* (Riverside, CA: Society of Dance History Scholars, 1998), 47-53.

33. Hammond's *pas de deux* examples (from Michel St. Leon, 1815-1835) were in two sections (such as Andante-Allegro), sometimes with a coda, while Italian *pas de deux* often had three or four sections, with the slow-to-fast tempi most common. Hammond, 'Windows into Romantic Ballet: Content and Structure of Four Early Nineteenth-Century Pas de Deux'. See also Ertz, 'Nineteenth-century Italian Ballet Music', 251-63.

34. Castil-Blaze, *La Danse et les Ballets depuis Bacchus jusqu'à Mlle Taglioni* (Paris: Paulin, 1832), 325. Translated and cited in Smith, *Ballet and Opera in the Age of 'Giselle'*, 248-49, n.25.

35. Each score offers different music for the Act Two *pas de deux* during the sylph scene, though they do agree on the location of the *pas de deux* within the scene. The only score to actually apply the label *pas de deux* to a specific piece is the Bartholomin score.

36. While we know that James and the Sylphide danced and mimed during this number, the Parisian scores do not tell us much (the full score indicates when the scarf is wrapped around the Sylphide and the wings fall, the Paris violin score is unmarked). It is the Bartholomin score that provides the most information.

37. The Bartholomin score contains more annotations than the other two scores but disagrees with the full score as to exactly when James wraps the scarf, placing this action just before the transition section. The placement in the full score seems more fitting, however.

38. *Le Journal des Dames*, 25 March 1832. Quoted in Chazin-Bennahum, *The Lure of Perfection*, 215.

39. *La Revue musicale*, 17 March 1832. Editor's emphasis.

40. Marian Smith, 'Borrowings and Original Music: A Dilemma for the Ballet-pantomime Composer', *Dance Research* 6, no. 2 (1988): 13.

Chapter 5

Bournonville's *La Sylphide* – a ballet about a dreamer and his longings

Erik Aschengreen

La Sylphide (1836) and *Napoli* (1842) are the two great Bournonville ballets. *Napoli* is the sunny ballet that tells the story of the fisherman and his bride who conquer all obstacles, both erotic and demonic, before arriving in the third act, which is the happiest tableau in the European ballet tradition. *Napoli* represents the lightness and optimism typical of Danish romanticism.[1]

August Bournonville believes in a world with meaning, order and beauty; his watchword is 'harmony' and it is up to his art to send this harmony over the footlights. For a moment his audience shall feel the lightness as if they were dancing themselves.

Napoli is the typical Bournonville ballet. *La Sylphide* is not. *La Sylphide* represents a strain of French Romanticism, and is a tragic ballet about a dreamer and his longings. For August Bournonville it was a very personal ballet, and so it has been for generations of Danish dancers and audiences over more than 170 years.

August Bournonville met the Sylphide in Paris. He was born in Copenhagen in 1805. His father was a French dancer – Antoine Bournonville – and his mother was Swedish, but Bournonville himself felt very Danish. He received his first dance training in the Ballet School of the Royal Danish Ballet, but later continued his studies in Paris. From 1824 to 1830 he studied in the French capital, where he made his debut at the Paris Opéra and was engaged as a dancer. But he returned home to Copenhagen to become Artistic Director for the Royal Danish Ballet in 1830.

He went back to his native city for several reasons. First of all, quite simply – as noted above – he felt Danish, and identified with Danish culture. Also, he wished to become both a choreographer and a director, and in Copenhagen he was given the opportunity to do so. Further, it was no doubt decisive that the male dancer was still an important figure in Denmark, while in much of the rest of Europe in the Romantic period the ballerinas were to reign.[2] In all of Bournonville's ballets, indeed, the male dancer is at the same level as the female. And this has been important for the whole tradition of prominent Danish male dancers to this very day.

In Denmark, where Bournonville served as Artistic Director of the Royal Danish Ballet until 1877 with two minor interruptions, he created his own style, the ideas and thoughts of his ballets closely following Danish Romanticism as we find it in literature and painting. But he started by introducing French Romanticism as he had met it in Paris in the 1820s, where Marie Taglioni was creating a great sensation at the Paris Opéra. In his memoirs *My Theatre Life* he wrote: 'I witnessed her first triumphs in 1827-1829 and danced with her a number of times. She lifted one up from this earth, and her divine dancing could make one weep; I saw Terpsichore realised in her person.'[3]

Marie Taglioni made her debut at the Paris Opéra in 1827 during the very summer that Victor Hugo wrote his historical closet drama *Cromwell*, with the preface that became the manifesto of the French Romantic movement. Romanticism had descended on Paris – in painting, in music, in literature, and in the theatre. In the ballet, however, it was to be some years before the decisive breakthrough took place.

The Romantic ballet first won recognition with the Ballet of the Nuns in the third act of Meyerbeer's 1831 opera *Robert le diable*.[4] This famous scene was originally to have taken place in conventional, mythological surroundings, but Henri Duponchel, who was in charge of the Opera's scenery department, conceived the idea of the moonlit cloister of St. Rosalie, and the famous designer Ciceri created a fantastic décor.[5] With its eerie nocturnal atmosphere and its strong emphasis on closely intertwined erotic and demonic elements, this scene struck a fundamental chord in Romantic ideology.

The Romantic era signalled a revitalisation of the ballet, which had been stagnating in the old mythological and allegorical subjects that had been popular in the late eighteenth and early nineteenth centuries. Without this revival, one could argue, ballet might have died as an art form, or at least as a serious art form that wished to do more than merely entertain with pretty dancing and delightful music. In the 1830s, ballet regained its strength, its vigour, and its popularity.

The changing of the course of ballet has something to do with the ballerina Marie Taglioni and her new way of dancing, but the revitalisation is hardly a question exclusively of Marie Taglioni's appearance on the French scene, even though she did happen to arrive at an extraordinarily fortuitous moment. The revival was concurrent with explosive developments in décor, lighting, and the art of the *mise en scène* that took place in the French theatre in the beginning of the 1800s. The melodramatic horror and exotic realism to be found on the boards of the boulevard theatres had anticipated the Romantic movement before the great writers of the 'high art' theatres emerged. The theatre had become new, exciting, and entertaining – not least because of the new popular audience that appeared after the French Revolution. For stylistically, the Romantic theatre – and also the ballet – owed a tremendous debt to the melodrama.[6]

For the ballet, the revival meant a new style with a new exploitation of classical technique. Marie Taglioni's approach to dancing played a major role in this revival, and struck many as something altogether new. As one eyewitness, Lady Blessington, described this style upon seeing her in *Le Sicilien* in 1827:

> Hers is a totally new style of dancing, graceful beyond all comparison, wonderful lightness, an absence of all violent effort, or at least the appearance of it, and a modesty as new as it is delightful to witness in her art. She seems to float and bound like a sylph across the stage, never executing those *tours de force* that we know to be difficult and wish were impossible, being always performed at the expense of decorum and grace, and requiring only activity for their achievement... There is a sentiment in the dancing of this charming votary of Terpsichore that elevates it far beyond the licentious style generally adopted by the ladies of her profession, and which bids fair to accomplish a reformation in it.[7]

This new style of dancing was one of the triumphs of *La Sylphide*, premiered at the Paris Opéra in 1832 with a libretto by Adolphe Nourrit, choreography by Filippo Taglioni and music by Jean-Madeleine Schneitzhoeffer. But the revitalisation went even further. It meant new costumes, an atmosphere redolent of night and moonlight, and the introduction of the grotesque, which was also a vital element of the Romantic drama.

That *La Sylphide* in 1832 went straight to the heart of Romantic ideology was due as much to Adolphe Nourrit, who created the libretto, as it was to Marie Taglioni, who walked off with the honour and the fame. The Paris Opéra's celebrated tenor understood from the depths of his soul the conflict and discord of Romanticism. He himself never succeeded in reconciling the many facets of existence into a harmonious whole; in 1839 he jumped out of a window of a hotel room in Naples, killing himself.

La Sylphide is the story of the young Scotsman, James, whose mind is divided and in a state of unrest. He does not feel truly at home in the snug, bourgeois world to which he is about to bind himself this very day by marrying the sweet Effy. He loves his Effy, but he also has dreams and longings that reach far beyond this mundane existence. He dreams of another world, and the Sylphide is the symbol of that world. She lures him away from his wedding and his beloved, out into the woods. In the libretto Nourrit lays out very plainly the very conflict that is James's problem and the passion to which he falls victim. *La Sylphide* is one of the most striking examples of the unrest and discord that came as a shock to the Romantic period. Passions were coming to be expressed more strongly and, at the same time, there was a vibrant longing for another, more pure and genuine world. The harmony inherited from the previous generation had been shattered. In France, unrest had been present ever since the Revolution of 1789 and had made the world insecure. When ideas came into conflict with reality, existence was no longer harmonious. *La Sylphide* expresses this conflict in an ingenious way.

The outcome of the story of James and the Sylphide is tragic. When he places the scarf about her shoulders in order to draw her down into the earthly sphere, she dies. This may represent James's inability to unite in his mind the two aspects of a dualistic worldview: reality and the realm of ideas. He is incapable of achieving balance and unity in his existence. The Sylphide's death is a symbolic expression of the fact that James cannot possibly achieve mental balance, and it is no accident that her death is bound up with direct erotic contact. James takes the Sylphide in his arms; at the same time her wings fall off. Something erotic, something sensuous, has come into play.

It is this erotic contact that is dangerous to the Sylphide. She is destined never to give happiness to the one she loves. Accordingly, throughout the second act in the forest she has avoided direct physical contact with James. Every time he reaches out for her, she eludes him, and when he finally takes her in his arms, she dies. Sylphides cannot become human beings; if they are captured, they die. This can be viewed as the fantasist's impossible attempt to turn his dream into reality, but is also an expression of the view that the harmony and happiness James has experienced in the woods are shattered the moment the sensuous and the sensual are admitted.

If we turn from this interpretation of *La Sylphide* to Victor Hugo's preface to *Cromwell*, we find striking agreement in the view of humanity and outlook on life. Hugo was fighting for a new drama as complex as life itself. Drama should portray actuality, he argued, reiterating the thesis that literature is a reflection of culture and society. Essential to the ideology of the Romantic period was the notion – which Hugo emphasises a number of times in his preface – that man is a dual being. This idea became a crucial point for Romanticism, which questioned whether the price of harmony was the exclusion of one side of man's nature, leaving only a half-complete human being.

These two sides of humankind are the material and spiritual, and *La Sylphide* is a picture of this duality. In this ballet the duality is manifested on several levels with many possibilities of interpretation. James is torn between

Effy and the Sylphide, between reality and the realm of ideas. The witch and the Sylphide each represent a strong force struggling to gain control of James; the constellation of the witch versus James represents the conflict between demonic forces and man, with the former emerging triumphant. It is Madge who gives James the scarf that kills the Sylphide and, with her, his striving for a higher world. Man is in the grip of dangerous forces – at least if he ventures outside the simple and known world. Also, the Sylphide and James represent the soul versus the body, the two sides of human nature, which according to the Romantic view were divided by the coming of Christianity.[8]

The concept of the witch is clearly related to Hugo's idea of the nature of a genuine work of art: he emphasises the necessary presence of the grotesque, and the witch and her entourage do indeed provide a background which throws the purity of the Sylphide into relief – if we choose to regard them as opposites and not as two incarnations of the demonic.[9]

La Sylphide was thus founded on Romanticism's fundamental idea of the duality of existence, and the sadness that pervades the whole ballet was not just an effect gathered from Scottish highlands or the German forests as a device for creating a theatrical impression. The sadness comes from within and results from the feeling that existence is no longer easy and harmonious.

The Ballet of the Nuns in *Robert le diable* shows us how the erotic and the demonic – often tightly interwoven – are fundamental features in the artistic physiognomy of the period. People then believed in swan-maidens, sylphs and naiads as little as we do today. These creatures were symbolic expressions, just as 'demonic' was the era's word for human nature's hidden and irresistible drives, which were now depicted with increasing audacity. Sexual anxiety, mental sterility, frigidity and the psychology of the seducer were bold new subjects of the time. They also 'infected' the world of ballet, and they are essential to Charles Nodier's *Trilby ou le Lutin d'Argail*, which was the inspiration behind Nourrit's libretto for *La Sylphide*.

Charles Nodier (1780-1844) was a writer, dreamer and one of the originators of the *conte fantastique*. He was also a botanist, philologist, bibliophile and entomologist. In civil life he had been librarian at the Bibliothèque de l'Arsenal since 1824, where he held a famous salon frequented by all the *coryphées* of Romanticism. In 1821 he visited Scotland and the following year he published *Trilby*, which was inspired by the Scottish landscape and by legends about brownies and other nature-beings. The writings of Walter Scott, too, stimulated Nodier's little story, which tells of the brownie Trilby's infatuation with and advances toward the young fisherman's wife Jeannie, who finally succumbs to her psychological conflicts and dies. To be sure, before this happens the brownie is driven out of the house with the help of the Church – a typical Romantic stroke, for only Christianity is able to overcome demonic power. But the demonic forces have got too strong a hold on Jeannie, and she cannot forget the dreams and longings that Trilby has aroused within her. She is divided between common earthly happiness with her husband, Dougal, and yearnings for another world, represented by Trilby. She cannot reconcile these two worlds and thus, like James in *La Sylphide*, becomes a victim of eroticism and the demonic. It is also typical of Romanticism that Trilby approaches Jeannie while she is sleeping in her chair – a parallel to the opening scene in *La Sylphide* – for it is in dreams that one makes contact with the subconscious.

It was in this Romantic atmosphere that Bournonville had lived in his youth in Paris. And from the bottom of his heart he knew the conflict between reality and dreams; between what his good judgment and upbringing dictated and the temptations of the senses that a young man could encounter in Paris. He was there to study dance and perfect his technique as far as possible. And so he did. But he was also a young man with senses and hot blood running in his veins. He had an affair with the sister of one of his dance comrades at the Opéra, and fathered a child with the young lady.[10] He did not tell anybody at home in Denmark about it. Neither his fiancée nor the managers of the Theatre would come to know what had happened. In those days, Bournonville would probably not have been given the post as Artistic Director in Copenhagen if theatre officials had discovered that he had been living such a life abroad. He tried to behave as a decent person: he followed and supported the daughter over the years and visited her as an uncle from the North. But in Denmark he kept silent on the matter. The conflict between body and soul was obvious and all too real for him, for he held a dark secret in his own life.

After having settled down in Copenhagen in 1830, August Bournonville kept in touch with the international ballet world, especially developments in Paris, the centre for ballet life at the time. In the spring of 1834 he went to Paris and on May 23rd, he saw Adolphe Nourrit's and Filippo Taglioni's *La Sylphide* at the Paris Opéra with Marie Taglioni, whom he knew from his Parisian years and admired. But in *My Theatre Life* he maintains that he originally had no intention of bringing *La Sylphide* to Copenhagen.

I saw the Parisian *Sylphide* but a single time and came away filled with nought but admiration for Mlle. Taglioni's extraordinary bravura and amazement at the splendid machinery. Both these things were equally unattainable at our theatre and, even though I found the main idea of the ballet most appealing, I felt that I would benefit most by drawing from my own fund of inspiration. Besides, the score was entirely too expensive and those who could have taught me the roles (for they had to be taught) did not seem disposed to do so just then.[11]

This seems fair enough. But the following two intertwining reasons also deserve our attention: Bournonville notes that he saw the position of the male dancer as under threat, and that the spotlight on the ballerina had the effect – he feared – of blurring the moral lesson in the story. Clearly, it was important for Bournonville to stress this moral. In *My Theatre Life* he writes:

> At that time there was in effect a system which was highly dangerous for male dancers; to wit, that of using them as props for their female partners. Hence, in *La Sylphide* James was simply a pedestal for the prima donna and the ingeniously poetic idea that man, in pursuing an imaginary happiness, neglects the true one and loses everything just when he thinks he is about to attain the object of his desire, was completely lost amid the wondrous virtuosity of the ballerina. I had consequently decided not to give *La Sylphide* at the Danish Theatre.[12]

But I don't believe him on this score, and never have. When he wrote these lines twelve years after the première in Copenhagen, it was important for him to emphasise that *La Sylphide* could be seen as a moral lecture. But probably it was not the morality of the story that struck him when he saw the ballet in Paris in 1834. Surely he was deeply touched by the dilemma in which James ends up, knowing the situation all too well from his own life. And it was James's unhappy situation and his emotional life that he put on the stage, with an understanding from inside, and not with a wagging finger of disapproval. Had *La Sylphide* been a moralistic ballet with a bourgeois outlook, it would not have lasted into the present day, in which we still feel sympathy for James and his unfortunate destiny.

Bournonville understood that this story was in some ways his own. He could relate to it, and the day before he returned to Denmark, he bought a copy of the libretto.

Officially he gave another explanation for deciding to produce *La Sylphide* after all:

> What prompted me, then, to change my mind? The desire to present a talented pupil [Lucile Grahn] who seemed made for the title role and whom I had trained entirely after the ideal of Taglioni, and also repeated requests that I try a young musical talent [Løvenskiold] well suited for this genre.[13]

Two years later, in 1836, he did produce *La Sylphide* in Copenhagen with Lucile Grahn in the title role, while he himself danced James.

Lucile Grahn (1819–1907) was Bournonville's favourite pupil and his first Sylphide. A few years later she flew out in the world to an international career. She even danced *La Sylphide* at the Paris Opéra. And she quarrelled with her old master. The theatre gossip has always given as explanation for the break that she rejected his amorous advances. It is possible, but we know absolutely nothing about that. What we do know is that she tried to change the choreography in his ballet, and he became furious. When she came back from Paris she intended – as it was quite common in the Parisian ballet world – to introduce steps of her own in which she could shine. But Bournonville did not want his ballerinas to change his choreography, and what we primarily see in their disagreement is a battle between dancer and choreographer.[14] Bournonville fought for the choreographer and his rights. He did not feel that the choreographer should be the servant of the ballerina. On the contrary.

Bournonville followed the French libretto closely, but made a few important changes: the witches' scene in the beginning of Act Two was calmed down a bit (fewer witches, fewer animals) and a new scene was added in Act Two, where James's rival Gurn finds James's hat. The witch Madge persuades Gurn not to tell anyone about the hat, and she pushes him into Effy's arms. Madge thus becomes an important figure in Bournonville's ballet, where the story never disappears to let the dance shine on its own. The drama is omnipresent. (That is the difference between Taglioni's and Bournonville's *La Sylphide*, at least as we know the former from Pierre Lacotte's 1971 production, wherein the dance takes over in the second act, and the story and the dramaturgy are blurred.)

Bournonville was well aware that he would be accused of plagiarism, even though copyright laws for dance did not exist at that time. So he defended himself, claiming that he had created an original work. And indeed he had.

Shortly after the première, he discussed the originality of his work in newspaper articles, and in *My Theatre Life* he admitted that the idea came from Nourrit and Filippo Taglioni. He asserts, however, that the choreography and the entire fashion in which he treated the story was his own.[15] In the first volume of *My Theatre Life*, he discusses his actions:

I made several changes in the plan, gave the ballet a national colour that was not to be found in the Parisian version, developed the character of James, and thought up new dances and groupings. Now, since the music was completely new, the gestures and *pas* also had to be new, inasmuch as the rhythms determine the makeup of the dances. The composition and staging therefore cost me as much industry and care as if I myself had invented the plan, and I have received testimony to the fact that not only is *my* ballet completely different from Taglioni's – it even wins the prize as far as dramatic merit and precision of execution are concerned.[16]

Bournonville is very keen to underscore how his *La Sylphide* is an original piece of art. But he cannot – nor does he wish to – run away from the fact that he did get the story with all its symbolic meanings from the French *La Sylphide*.[17]

Since 1836, Bournonville's *La Sylphide* has been performed in Copenhagen with little change. In the 1930s the balletmaster Harald Lander and Valborg Borchsenius, who had been a leading dancer around 1900, revised eight of the Bournonville ballets. In *La Sylphide* they took away some of the machinery – flying sylphs for instance – which had enchanted the audience in the Romantic period, but was regarded perhaps as a bit old-fashioned after the dawn of cinema. From photographs we can also see that they straightened lines and formations in the *divertissement* of the second act. The Lander-Borchsenius version has been the model ever since for the production of the Royal Danish Ballet — a dance for Effy has been added and minor passages have been taken out and have come back, but on the whole this production has been kept intact.

What *has* changed and what has kept our interest in this ballet is first of all the interpretation of the main characters. Despite the title *La Sylphide*, James is the central figure. With his melancholy and his unrest, James is the typical hero of the Romantic period. But his existential problem about how to live his life makes James quite modern. James is a mirror for young spectators of today.

The great Danish dancer Erik Bruhn, who danced James in the 1950s and 1960s, was the first to explore a psychological interpretation, looking for a personal approach to the figure of James. For Bruhn, James was a poet, a dreamer, and in some ways happy with his dream; a man running away from reality.[18] Peter Schaufuss's James, on the other hand, was a man who could not make his choice between two women; Nikolaj Hübbe was almost a schizophrenic in his interpretation, and so on. Every James is new, and takes his colour from the interpreter.

The Sylphide's timbre has changed as well. In the early part of the twentieth century, the Danish ballerinas who danced *La Sylphide*, such as Ulla Poulsen and Margrethe Schanne, were first of all beautiful and perhaps a little mysterious. But in the middle of the 1960s, the sylphides of the Danish productions were not entirely innocent. They were also 'the beautiful danger', luring men away from marriage and out into the woods. And Erik Bruhn's production of *La Sylphide* in Stockholm in 1968 actually suggested a relationship between the Sylphide and the witch Madge as two manifestations of the demonic, even as 'mirror images'. And he inserted a scene in which the witch and the sylphide pass each other and look at each other. This is surprising in that in all other productions the Sylphide and Madge never are on the stage at the same time. (Too, the sylphide in Bruhn's production had black hair, though in the Danish tradition she was normally blonde.)

The psychological viewpoint has also given new nuances to Madge. At the first performance of *La Sylphide* in 1836, Madge was performed by a man, Carl Fredstrup. Over the past 175 years we have seen both men and women playing the role of Madge. For about forty years (1956–1995), the principal interpreter in Copenhagen was the great mime Niels Bjørn Larsen, for whom Madge was wickedness personified – an impressive monster, whose gender identity was difficult to decide, even if he did wear a skirt. For Sorella Englund, who has now played the role for more than twenty-five years, Madge is definitely a woman. And even if she is ugly and vindictive, Madge as played by Englund makes us understand that the witch has a story and that her wickedness has come about for good reason. Perhaps she is a lost sylphide, a creature who has been hurt.[19]

August Bournonville's sunny ballet *Napoli* is the calling card of the Royal Danish Ballet with all its *joie de vivre*, while *La Sylphide* is the deep, serious ballet, where dancers – and audience – look at themselves as in a mirror. And the Danes took this beloved and disturbing ballet out in the world.

Bournonville's *La Sylphide* outside of Denmark

In 1953, the Danish version of *La Sylphide* became part of the international ballet repertoire when Harald Lander staged it for the Grand Ballet de Marquis de Cuevas in Paris, with Rosella Hightower as the ethereal Sylphide and Serge Golovine as James.[20] (See Appendix 1) Lander inserted new dances for Effy and Gurn, as well as flying sylphides as the French expected, because it was one of the things they could read about in descriptions of Filippo Taglioni's *La Sylphide* of 1832. With her airiness Rosella Hightower, as the critics reported, was marvellous in the title role; the notion of the Sylphide as a dangerous creature, too, lurked in the newspaper columns. Critics further, and not surprisingly, were astonished to see so much mime in this production. This discipline had been de-emphasised in French ballet training (compared to that in Copenhagen) and during rehearsals of *La Sylphide* Lander found himself obliged to work especially diligently on the mime element of the ballet.

In 1962 Lander staged *La Sylphide* for La Scala in Milan with Carla Fracci in the title role. And in 1964, for American Ballet Theatre, he created a new version, cutting out much of the mime and adding more dancing for the Sylphide and James. The major changes were made in the second act. Here, first of all, the witches' scene at the opening was expanded, and Lander had the witches fly away on broomsticks. He also added considerably more dancing – about fifteen minutes' worth. First, following the Sylphide's and James's solos in the divertissement, Lander added a long, newly choreographed *adagio pas de deux* – not difficult, but lovely with promenades and conveying the idea that the whole time it is as if she is disappearing from him. This *adagio* captures the feeling of yearning. It did fit nicely with the style of the ballet, even though we do not know other Bournonville *adagios* choreographed in this way. Second, towards the end of the ballet, he expanded the scarf number. Here was a new solo for James with big jumps and a solo for the Sylphide and the music became intensely dramatic. For this production, the Bulgarian composer Edgar Cosma created a new orchestration, which made the score sound fuller, and composed new music as well. Toni Lander and Royes Fernandez danced the leading parts, later alternating with Carla Fracci and Erik Bruhn.

The Danish-Swedish ballerina Elsa Marianne von Rosen has also made important contributions to the twentieth-century history of this ballet; she delved into the past of the living tradition in the Royal Theatre in Copenhagen and worked with the former Danish ballerina Ellen Price, who danced the Sylphide for the first time in 1903 and remembered details that had disappeared in the Royal Theatre's version, but now found their way back – for instance the beautiful the little mime scene in the first act, in which the Sylphide tells James that she has followed him since he was a child and protected him when he went hunting.

Twice in 1960 von Rosen staged *La Sylphide*, first for the Scandinavian Ballet (the company she founded with Allan Fridericia), and then for Ballet Rambert, where she also danced the title part with Flemming Flindt as James. Later von Rosen staged the Bournonville ballet with Carla Fracci and Rudolf Nureyev for the Ballet de Monte Carlo (1968), this time playing the role of Madge; she also staged *La Sylphide* for the National Ballet of Washington (1969) and the Maly Theatre Ballet (now Mikhailovsky Ballet) (1975).

For the London Festival Ballet (now known as the English National Ballet), Peter Schaufuss staged *La Sylphide* in 1979. He expanded the choreography, adding a solo for James in the first act, a beautiful dream *pas de trois* for Effy, the Sylphide and James in the middle of the Scottish reel, and expanding the existing numbers given to the sylphides in the second act in the wood. For all this new dancing Peter Schaufuss choreographed in the Bournonville style.[21]

In 2005, when Bournonville's 200th birthday was celebrated by the Royal Danish Ballet with the Third Bournonville Festival, *La Sylphide* was danced in Nikolaj Hübbe's traditional *mise en scène*, which he also staged for the National Ballet of Canada in Toronto, while Johan Kobborg and Sorella Englund the same year staged *La Sylphide* at Covent Garden in London, underlining the psychological aspect of the ballet and the idea of Madge as a fallen sylphide. Kobborg restored a lost scene to the first act in which the bewildered James asks Gurn and the farm-boys if they have seen what he has seen.[22] He also inserted a mime scene between Effy and James underlining her wish for marriage, and along the same lines he stressed the relationship between the Sylphide and James. She begs him not to touch her, but he insists on doing so and thus commits an offence against her.

A classic ballet is only interesting if every new generation can relate to its content. *La Sylphide* is deeply related to the Romantic period, in which it was created, but as a great work of art it is not isolated in its own time. *La Sylphide* also reaches our time and can still move us with its contrast between a quiet conventional world and a life where we reach for our dreams. Just as in the Romantic period, we feel it is both tempting and dangerous to run after the Sylphide into the forest.

Aasted, Elsebeth. *Sylfide Og Heks: Den Romantiske Balletdanserinde Lucile Grahn*. Danmarks Købstadsmuseums Skriftrække. Århus: Den Gamle By, 1996.

Aschengreen, Erik. *Harald Lander: His Life and Ballets*. Translated by Patricia N. McAndrew. Alton, Hampshire, UK: Dance Books, 2009.

Blessington, Marguerite. *The Idler in France*. 2 vols. London: H. Colburn, 1841.

Bournonville, August. *My Theatre Life*. Translated by Patricia N. McAndrew. Middletown, CT: Wesleyan University Press, 1979.

Brooks, Peter. *The Melodramatic Imagination - Balzac, Henry James, Melodrama, and the Mode of Excess*. New Haven, CT: Yale University Press, 1976.

Bruhn, Erik. 'Beyond Technique', *Dance Perspectives* 36 (1968).

Christensen, Anne Middelboe. 'Deadly Sylphs and Decent Mermaids: The Women in the Danish Romantic World of August Bournonville', in *The Cambridge Companion to Ballet*, ed. Marion Kant (Cambridge: Cambridge University Press, 2007).

———. *Sylfiden Findes: En Svævebog* [The Sylphide Exists: a Soaring Book]. Copenhagen: Schønberg, 2008.

Clark, Barrett Harper, ed. *European Theories of the Drama: An Anthology of Dramatic Theory* New York: D. Appleton and Company, 1929.

Crosten, William F. *French Grand Opera: An Art and a Business*. New York: King's Crown Press, 1948.

Guest, Ivor. *The Romantic Ballet in Paris*. 3rd ed. Alton, Hampshire, UK: Dance Books, 2008.

Hertel, Hans. 'P. L. Møller and Romanticism in Danish Literature.' *Scandinavica* 8 (1969): 35–48.

Hugo, Victor. *The Works of Victor Hugo*. Translated by George Burnham Ives. Vol. 3: Dramas, Boston: Little, Brown, & Company, 1909.

Jürgensen, Knud Arne. *The Bournonville Tradition: The First Fifty Years, 1829–1879*. 2 vols. Vol. I, London: Dance Books, 1997.

Meyerbeer, Giacomo. *Robert le diable*, Paris: Schlesinger, 183-, reprinted New York: Garland Publishing, 1980, 2 vols.

Nørlyng, Ole. 'Drøm eller virkelighed: om de musikalske kilders betydning i forbindelse med en idag forsvunden mimsk scene i *Sylphiden*', in *Bournonville: Tradition, Rekonstruktion*, ed. Ole Nørlyng and Henning Urup (Copenhagen: C.A. Reitzel, 1989).

Poesio, Giannandrea. 'Blasis, the Italian Ballo, and the Male Sylph', in *Rethinking the Sylph: New Perspectives on the Romantic Ballet*, ed. Lynn Garafola (Hanover, NH: Wesleyan University Press, 1997).

Rossel, Sven H. 'From Romanticism to Realism', in *A History of Danish Literature*, ed. Sven H. Rossel, *A History of Scandinavian Literatures* (Lincoln: University of Nebraska Press, 1992).

Scavenius, Bente, ed. *The Golden Age in Denmark: Art and Culture 1800–1850*. Copenhagen: Gyldendal, 1994.

Tobias, Tobi. 'The Royal Danish Ballet in New York', in *Seeing Things*. http://www.artsjournal.com/tobias/2011/06/the_royal_danish_ballet_in_new.html. Accessed 8 September 2011.

Véron, Louis. *Mémoires d'un Bourgeois de Paris*. Vol. 3, Paris: Librairie nouvelle, 1857.

Notes

1. On the suppression of Byronism and French *romantisme* in favour of a Biedermeier aesthetic in Danish national romanticism, see Hans Hertel, 'P.L. Møller and Romanticism in Danish Literature', *Scandinavica* 8 (1969): 40–42. For a survey of romanticism in nineteenth-century Danish literature, see Sven H. Rossel, 'From Romanticism to Realism', in *A History of Danish Literature*, ed. Sven H. Rossel, *A History of Scandinavian Literatures* (Lincoln: University of Nebraska Press, 1992). See also Bente Scavenius, ed. *The Golden Age in Denmark: Art and Culture 1800–1850* (Copenhagen: Gyldendal, 1994).

2. On the male dancer in Italy, see Giannandrea Poesio, 'Blasis, the Italian Ballo, and the Male Sylph', in *Rethinking the Sylph: New Perspectives on the Romantic Ballet*, ed. Lynn Garafola (Hanover, NH: Wesleyan University Press, 1997), 131–42. See also Chapter 11 of this volume.

3. August Bournonville, *My Theatre Life*, trans. Patricia N. McAndrew (Middletown, CT: Wesleyan University Press, 1979), 48.

4. In the score of *Robert le diable* published by Schlesinger in Paris [183-] and reprinted by Garland Publishing (New York: Garland, 1980, 2 vols), the scene is called 'Bacchanale', and includes three

airs de ballet: 'Séduction par l'ivresse', 'Séduction par le jeu', and 'Séduction par l'amour'.

5. As William F. Crosten describes it, quoting Louis Véron, Meyerbeer and Scribe 'suggested having the pantomime and dance unfold in the usual operatic Olympus, furnished on the standard pattern with a "superannuated apparatus of quivers, arrows, gauze and Cupids".' William F. Crosten, *French Grand Opera: An Art and a Business* (New York: King's Crown Press, 1948), 62. Quoting Louis Véron, *Mémoires d'un Bourgeois de Paris*, vol. 3 (Paris: Librairie nouvelle, 1857), 256–57.

6. See Peter Brooks, *The Melodramatic Imagination - Balzac, Henry James, melodrama, and the mode of excess* (New Haven, CT: Yale University Press, 1976).

7. Marguerite Blessington, *The Idler in France*, 2 vols. (London: H. Colburn, 1841), 83–4. Quoted in Ivor Guest, *The Romantic Ballet in Paris*, 3rd ed. (Alton, Hampshire, UK: Dance Books, 2008), 122.

8. 'On the day when Christianity said to man: "Thou art twofold, thou art made up of two beings, one perishable, the other immortal, one carnal, the other ethereal, one enslaved by appetites, cravings and passions, the other borne aloft on the wings of enthusiasm and reverie — in a word, the one always stooping toward the earth, its mother, the other always darting up toward heaven, its fatherland"— on that day the drama was created. Is it, in truth, anything other than that contrast of every day, that struggle of every moment, between two opposing principles which are ever face to face in life, and which dispute possession of man from the cradle to the tomb?' Preface to *Cromwell*, English translation in Barrett Harper Clark, ed. *European theories of the drama: an anthology of dramatic theory* (New York: D. Appleton and Company, 1929), 374.

9. *The Works of Victor Hugo*, trans. George Burnham Ives, vol. 3: Dramas (Boston: Little, Brown, & Company, 1909), 23. 'The fact is, then, that the grotesque is one of the supreme beauties of the drama. It is not simply an appropriate element of it, but is oftentimes a necessity.'

10. On Bournonville's first child, see Knud Arne Jürgensen, *The Bournonville Tradition: The First Fifty Years, 1829–1879*, 2 vols., vol. I (London: Dance Books, 1997), 20–21; and Anne Middelboe Christensen, 'Deadly sylphs and decent mermaids: the women in the Danish romantic world of August Bournonville', in *The Cambridge Companion to Ballet*, ed. Marion Kant (Cambridge: Cambridge University Press, 2007), 131.

11. Bournonville, *My Theatre Life*, 78.

12. Ibid.

13. Ibid.

14. The personal and professional relationship between Bournonville and Lucile Grahn is examined in Elsebeth Aasted, *Sylfide og Heks: den Romantiske Balletdanserinde Lucile Grahn*, Danmarks Købstadsmuseums Skriftrække (Århus: Den Gamle By, 1996).

15. 'It [*La Sylphide*] is therefore not of my own writing, but the Danish composition of the subject is mine, just as that of the French version is the work of Filippo Taglioni.' Bournonville, *My Theatre Life*, 78.

16. Ibid., 79.

17. A thorough examination of the criticism of *La Sylphide* from 1836 till 2008 may be found in Anne Middelboe Christensen, *Sylfiden findes: en svævebog* [The Sylphide Exists: a Soaring Book] (Copenhagen: Schønberg, 2008).

18. Erik Bruhn, 'Beyond Technique', *Dance Perspectives* 36 (1968).

19. Lis Jeppesen, famed for her interpretation of the Sylphide, has played the role of Madge since 2005. See Tobi Tobias, 'The Royal Danish Ballet in New York', *Seeing Things*, http://www.arts journal.com/tobias/2011/06/the_royal_danish_ballet_in_new.html [accessed 8 September 2011], including Mindy Aloff's comment of 24 June 2011. See also Tobi Tobias, project leader, *An Oral History of the Royal Danish Ballet and its Bournonville Tradition* Archival materials, Houghton Library, Harvard University.

20. See Erik Aschengreen, *Harald Lander: His Life and Ballets*, trans. Patricia N. McAndrew (Alton, Hampshire, UK: Dance Books, 2009), 155-157.

21. Many other dancers from the Royal Danish Ballet, including Hans Brenaa, Kirsten Ralov, Flemming Flindt, Peter Martins, Flemming Ryberg, Dinna Bjørn and Frank Andersen have staged Bournonville in various cities in Europe, the USA, Turkey, Japan and China.

22. See also Ole Nørlyng, 'Drøm eller virkelighed: om de musikalske kilders betydning i forbindelse med en idag forsvunden mimsk scene i *Sylphiden*', in *Bournonville: Tradition, Rekonstruktion*, ed. Ole Nørlyng and Henning Urup (Copenhagen: C.A. Reitzel, 1989), 146–66.

Chapter 6

Sylphiden and the Danish cultural canon

Helena Kopchick Spencer

On the 24th of January 2006, the Danish Ministry of Culture unveiled the *Dansk kulturkanon* (Danish Cultural Canon), a collection of 108 works said to epitomise Danish artistic achievement and serve as iconic expressions of Denmark's cultural heritage.[1] So it may initially seem strange that the only two nineteenth-century compositions chosen in the category of performing arts (*scenekunst*) were Adam Oehlenschläger's verse drama *Aladdin* (1805) and August Bournonville's ballet *Sylphiden* (1836). For, although Oehlenschläger is recognised as the poet laureate of Denmark and Bournonville's legacy in the Danish ballet tradition has been equally profound, *Aladdin* and *Sylphiden* are both French imports, set in foreign lands, with little obvious connection to native Danish culture: *Aladdin* was drawn from the French Orientalist Antoine Galland's translation of *The Arabian Nights* (*Les Mille et une Nuits*, 1704–17), and *Sylphiden* was based on *La Sylphide* (1832), a French ballet set in Scotland and featuring choreography by Filippo Taglioni, music by Jean-Madeleine Schneitzhoeffer, and a scenario by tenor Adolphe Nourrit of the Paris Opéra.

Why, then, did Bournonville's version of *La Sylphide* become a touchstone of nineteenth-century Danish dramaturgy? How did the Scottish farmer James and his woodland Sylph assume such important cultural currency in a period of national romanticism, when one might expect characters from Scandinavian folktales or Norse mythology to figure more prominently in defining Danish identity?[2] Indeed, it has been argued that *Sylphiden* is a product of French Romanticism and the least 'Danish' of Bournonville's ballets.[3] However, I would contend that *Sylphiden*'s longevity in the Danish theatre repertory might be explained by the same rationale offered by Elisabeth Oxfeldt for the canonical status of Oehlenschläger's *Aladdin*. In her monograph *Nordic Orientalism*, Oxfeldt has argued that the appropriation of French cultural trends – such as Orientalist imagery and topics in the case of *Aladdin* – was a means for Denmark, a peripheralised nation, to align itself with Parisian tastes and distance itself from German influence. In so doing, Denmark could shed the brutish and provincial reputation generally associated with Germanic countries in the early nineteenth century, instead clothing itself with the same attributes of elegance and refinement associated with Paris.[4]

Both Oehlenschläger and Bournonville even claimed to have improved on their source material. Thus, Denmark was not merely legitimised by the importation of French taste, but could even boast of having outdone the cultural capital of Europe. In the epilogue of *Aladdin*, the character Phantasia credits her son (that is, Oehlenschläger) with having repaired the damages promulgated by the 'Gaulish' bastardisation of the original Aladdin tale.[5] Similarly, Bournonville claimed to have penetrated his subject in a more authentic manner than the earlier French attempt, asserting in his memoirs *My Theatre Life* that Filippo Taglioni's *La Sylphide* had obscured the dramatic crux of the story by placing disproportionate emphasis on Marie Taglioni's 'wondrous virtuosity' in the role of the Sylph.[6]

Yet *Aladdin* and *Sylphiden* did not become emblematic of nineteenth-century Danish dramatic arts by sole virtue of having (ostensibly) eclipsed their French sources. After all, Bournonville had already discovered that not all ballets imported from France could be effectively 'transplanted onto Danish soil': for ballet to take root in Denmark, he noted, 'it would have to follow the same path as Heiberg's *vaudevilles*, that is, take advantage of the mood of the moment and play well-known themes and familiar tones.'[7] More than mere examples of Denmark's Parisian aspirations, *Aladdin* and *Sylphiden* both made use of these 'well-known themes and familiar tones', and thereby operated as constructions of the nineteenth-century Danish self. As literary theorist Wolfgang Iser has written, a basic condition of the human experience is the desire 'to be ourselves, and simultaneously outside ourselves.'[8] Even in seemingly distant theatrical realms such as the Persia of *Aladdin* or the Scotland of *Sylphiden*, the process of familiarisation was not far below the surface for nineteenth-century Danish audiences.

Oxfeldt asserts that Oehlenschläger's *Aladdin* resonated so deeply with Danish audiences for three reasons, all of which are also applicable to the reception of Bournonville's *Sylphiden*. First of all, many Danes had experienced Galland's *Arabian Nights* (first published in Danish in 1758) as childhood bedtime stories and therefore likely regarded the exotic Persian setting of *Aladdin* as nostalgically familiar.[9] Secondly, they perceived an ancient ethnic kinship with the characters that populated that setting, since the Nordic people were once believed to be of Asian descent (Snorri Sturluson, medieval historian and compiler of the *Prose Edda*, had thought that the Norse mythological gods were in fact Turkish kings, called Æsir because they had come from Asia).[10] Finally, Oehlenschläger's audience was able to identify their fellow Danes in the individual character types of *Aladdin*: according to Oxfeldt, '[...] Oriental props and clothing merely mask an unequivocally recognisable Danish/Nordic body. The drama unfolds in so-called Isphahan where some of the characters, despite their foreign names and customs, are so obviously Copenhageners that readers have been able to pinpoint their exact neighbourhood origins.'[11]

In a similar fashion, Bournonville's *Sylphiden* offered another mirror of the Danish self. Its rustic Scottish setting, infused with elements of the supernatural, was well known to Danish audiences familiar with the literary works and folktale collections of Sir Walter Scott. Moreover, the inhabitants of this romantic landscape were often viewed as brethren, owing to a mutual transculturation dating back to the Viking era. Finally, and most significantly for this study, the characters in *Sylphiden* (kilts and tartans notwithstanding) lent themselves to the familiar character types of the Scandinavian *tryllevise*, or enchantment ballad, an archetypal tale that warned against the dangerous allure of otherworldly creatures that inhabited the forest, water, or mountains. The ballad was long recognised as the central genre of expressive culture uniting Scotland and Scandinavia, and nineteenth-century ballad collectors often remarked on the similar narrative tropes found in the two regions.[12] In particular, the enchantment ballad type has been acknowledged in both the nineteenth and twentieth centuries as distinctive to Scotland and Scandinavia: for that reason, this collaborative *tryllevise* tradition can be considered 'pan-Nordic.'[13]

In this study, I posit that *Sylphiden's* triumph in Denmark was due in great part to its narrative resonance with the pan-Nordic enchantment ballad. Following an examination of Scotland's place in the nineteenth-century Danish imagination, including perceptions of kinship, I will detail characteristics of the enchantment ballad as found in nineteenth-century Danish ballad collections and realised in three musico-dramatic works: Johann Ludvig Heiberg's singspiel *Elverhøj* (*Elves' Hill*, 1828), Niels Gade's cantata *Elverskud* (*Elf-Struck*, 1854), and Bournonville's ballet *Et Folkesagn* (*A Folk Tale*, 1854). Finally, I will demonstrate how the narrative of Bournonville's *Sylphiden* can be interpreted as another staging of the pan-Nordic enchantment ballad.

Scotland in the nineteenth-century Danish imagination

Scotland was already a familiar destination in the Danish imagination long before Bournonville's Sylph graced the Danish stage, thanks to the wild popularity of Sir Walter Scott's novels. Scott's novels were available at Copenhagen bookstores from the early 1820s onward, not only in Danish translations, but also in German, French, and English.[14] The 1820s witnessed a veritable explosion of the Walter Scott vogue in Denmark, and this excitement was remarkable enough to be noted in Scotland itself, with a mention in the 5 January 1829 edition of the *Edinburgh Evening Courant*.[15] Scott's novels also provided fodder for theatrical adaptations on the Danish stage, although these various plays and operas never managed to achieve the same sensation as the original literary works.[16] Nevertheless, the impetus to produce these adaptations reflects the magnitude of the Scott craze, the recognition of the inherent pictorial qualities of Scott's writing, and the desire to recreate his vivid characters and scenic panoramas in the Copenhagen theatre.[17]

Scott's *The Heart of Midlothian* (1818), translated in 1822 by Caspar Johannes Boye under the title *Midlothians Hjerte eller Fængslet i Edinburgh* (*Midlothian's Heart, or the Prison in Edinburgh*), was particularly influential for the young Hans Christian Andersen, an enthusiastic admirer of Scott's novels who declared upon reading *Midlothians Hjerte* that he had looked into 'a new world', one which filled him with 'a holy shudder at the thought of the delight of being a poet'.[18] *Midlothians Hjerte* is also notable in another regard: it introduced Danish readers to the characters Effie Deans and Madge Wildfire. In Scott's novel, beautiful but wilful Effie Deans is falsely convicted of infanticide after she is seduced by dissolute nobleman George Staunton; in fact, Effie's son has been kidnapped by the conniving outlaw Meg Murdockson to exact revenge on Staunton, who had also fathered an illegitimate child with her daughter Magdalen, nicknamed 'Madge Wildfire'. Abandoned by Staunton, Madge descends into psychosis after her illegitimate child is murdered at the hands of her own mother, who sought to protect Madge from shame and allow her an advantageous marriage.

Danish readers of *Midlothians Hjerte* would therefore have associated the names Effie and Madge with wronged women: while Effie suffers silently, accepting her sentence rather than attempting escape from the Tollbooth Prison, Madge becomes a deranged pariah.[19] So when 'Effy' and 'Madge' appeared on the Copenhagen stage in *Sylphiden* as, respectively, James's blameless fiancée whom he leaves at the altar and the loathsome witch whom he attempts to banish from his hearth, Danish audiences would likely have recognised their names and general attributes from a well-known literary construction of Scotland.[20] Even if the Effy and Madge roles of *Sylphiden* were not precisely identical to their counterparts from *Midlothians Hjerte*, I would suggest that this name recognition created a sense of familiarity that welcomed Danish theatregoers into an imagined Scottish setting that encompassed both Scott's novels and Bournonville's ballet. Furthermore, since Scott's novels were praised in particular for their verisimilitude, it seems that the appearance of names from one of his novels would confer a certain authenticity of place in the mind of *Sylphiden* audiences.[21]

The early nineteenth-century Scottish craze was certainly not unique to Denmark. Yet unlike the rest of Europe, the attraction to Scottish literature and culture among Danes seems to have been less a fascination with the exotic than the cultivation of a perceived kinship. For example, Frederik

Schaldemose's 1826 Danish translation of 'Lochinvar' from Canto V of Sir Walter Scott's epic poem *Marmion* suggests an equivalence of Scotland and Denmark as fellow Nordic lands. Whereas Scott's young knight Lochinvar comes 'out of the west' in the original, he emerges from the north in the opening line of Schaldemose's translation: *Fra Norden kommer Lochinvar* (From the North comes Lochinvar). Scottish poet and literary scholar Tom Hubbard proposes the following intriguing possibility: 'Could it be that Schaldemose, as a Dane, the citizen of a northern country, is marking out Scotland as on that same latitude? It is as if there is a perception, conscious or otherwise, of a geocultural affinity.'[22] In addition, Schaldemose's translation heralds Lochinvar as 'the fair hero of the North' (*den fagre Nordlands Helt*). Perhaps Schaldemose was attempting to 'translate' – that is, move from one place to another – a Scottish hero into a Scandinavian hero for his Danish readers. It could even be that Schaldemose associated Scotland with other exotic Nordic countries like Norway and Iceland, thus repositioning Denmark as a European centre that looked northward for ancient legends and mythology. Or perhaps, as Hubbard has suggested, Schaldemose recognised a pan-Nordic cultural tradition that allowed him to claim the Scottish knight Lochinvar as *Nordlands Helt*.

Much of the Danish interest in Scotland stemmed from a fascination with its landscape: in particular, the heather-covered moors, coastal dunes, and sea inlets (*firths* in Scotland, *fjords* in Scandinavia) were seen as analogous to those of Denmark's own Jutland peninsula.[23] The Scottish terrain provided particular inspiration for the poet Steen Steensen-Blicher (1782–1848), who translated James Macpherson's *Poems of Ossian* into Danish between 1807 and 1809. Anna Harwell Celenza notes that despite the contested reception of Ossian in Denmark, Blicher nonetheless culled from Macpherson's so-called translations a poetic vocabulary for the stark, rough-hewn topographies that featured prominently in his own works.[24] Contemporary literary evidence supports this relationship between Blicher and Scotland even further. In the third chapter of Hans Christian Andersen's novel *O.T.* (1836), young Baron Vilhelm speaks to the recognised connection between Blicher's literary Jutland and the Scottish landscape, as well as the wistful feelings both inspired in the nineteenth-century Danish imagination:

'Jutland is certainly the most romantic part of Denmark! I have really taken an interest in that country since I read Steen-Blicher's [sic] novels. It seems to me that it must have much in common with the Scottish Lowlands! And aren't Gypsies there?'[25]

Danish archaeologist Jens Jakob Asmussen Worsaae's investigation of the perceived kinship between Scandinavia and Britain, *An Account of the Danes*

and Norwegians in England, Scotland, and Ireland (1852), affirmed the correspondence in geographic features of the two regions, and also attested to a
long history of intermarriage and immigration that had bound the Scots and
Danes together in familial relationships.[26] Based on his findings during a
yearlong expedition in Scotland, England, and Ireland, Worsaae hypoth-
esised that a large number of Danes had settled in Scotland after the Norman
invasion, asserting that just as Viking raids would have caused Anglo-Saxons to
flee England for Scotland, the Norman Conquest likely forced Danish and Norwegian settlers in northern England to migrate northward into the Scottish
Lowlands.[27] Worsaae also remarked that the Scandinavian presence in the
Scottish Lowlands could be discerned by the Lowlanders' physical appearance and the large number of linguistic borrowings:

> The same light-coloured hair and the same frame of body, which, in
> the north of England, remind us of the people's descent from the
> Scandinavians, indicate here also considerable immigrations of that peo-
> ple into the southern part of Scotland, and thence farther up along the
> east coast. According to a very common saying here, even the language of
> the Lowlands is so much like that of Scandinavia, that Lowland seamen
> wrecked on the coasts of Jutland and Norway have been able to converse
> without difficulty in their mother tongue with the common people there.
> This is undoubtedly a great exaggeration; but this much is certain, that
> the popular language in the Lowlands contains a still greater number of
> Scandinavian words and phrases than even the dialect of the north of
> England.[28]

In addition to similarities in landscape, physiognomy, and language, the
people of Scotland and Scandinavia also shared a rich ballad tradition. The
connection between Danish and Scottish ballads was given particular attention in the collection *Udvalgte Danske Viser fra Middelalderen* (*Selected Danish
Ballads from the Middle Ages*, 1812–14), published in five volumes by Werner
Hans Frederik Abrahamson, Knud Lyhne Rahbek and Rasmus Nyerup after
earlier ballad collections by Anders Sørensen Vedel (*Hundredvisebogen*, 1591)
and Peter Syv (*200 Viser om Konger, Kæmper og andre*, 1695). In his commentary to the fifth volume, dated 1 October 1813, Nyerup pointed out character
equivalencies and textual parallels between the ballads of *Udvalgte Danske
Viser* and those found in several prominent British collections: Thomas
Percy's *Reliques of Ancient English Poetry* (1765), Sir Walter Scott's *Minstrelsy
of the Scottish Border* (1802–03), and Robert Jamieson's *Popular Ballads and
Songs* (1806).[29] On the topic of this Dano-Scottish transculturation, Nyerup
deferred to Jamieson, who claimed that many of the ballads heard at that
time in the Scottish Lowlands and northern England dated from the first

'Cimbric' settlements in Britain, and that these ballads, despite having 'changed their dress and assumed some peculiar shades of complexion' as befitting the various stages of their transmission history, seemed not to have undergone significant modifications in 'general stamina' or distinguishing features.[30]

When discussing the origins of Scandinavian demonology, Nyerup also cited Sir Walter Scott's 'On the Fairies of Popular Superstition', an essay that appears in Scott's *Minstrelsy of the Scottish Border* as an introduction to 'The Young Tamlane', a ballad about a mortal man held captive by the Queen of the Fairies.[31] This essay provides further evidence of the recognised connection between Scandinavian and Scottish folklore in the early nineteenth century: in it, Scott writes that the fairies of British ballads were originally called elves, and 'the prototype of the English elf is to be sought chiefly in the *berg-elfen* [mountain elf], or *duergar* [dwarf], of the Scandinavians.'[32] According to Scott, the fairies of south Britain had been prettified with 'attractive and poetical embellishments', whereas the northern fairies of Scotland maintained a somewhat sinister aura that he considered a more 'ancient, and appropriate character'.[33] Indeed, Scott's description of Scottish fairies bears a strong resemblance to the elf maidens of Scandinavian lore, as we shall soon see. This is not surprising, given that Scott and Jamieson traced many plots and character types of British supernatural ballads to a centuries-old Nordic cultural influence.

As characterised by Scott, the Scottish fairies were 'of a mixed, or rather dubious nature, capricious in their dispositions, and mischievous in their resentment'.[34] They might live under the thresholds of human dwellings, but were most frequently found outside of human society, living underground or inside hills, on which they danced by moonlight. It was dangerous for a person to venture into one of these fairy rings after sunset, or to fall asleep on a fairy-hill, for the fairies were thought to abduct those unwitting humans who trespassed into their domain.[35] For those familiar with the *Sylphiden* plotline, Scott's description of the Scottish fairy is instantly reminiscent of the Sylph. She is certainly 'capricious in her disposition' and 'mischievous in her resentment': one need think only of her coy mannerisms, her stealing of the betrothal ring, and her sudden proclamations that she will die if James marries Effy. Furthermore, she can be found in thresholds of the Rubens farmhouse, but lives in the forest, where she and her sister sylphs revel in dancing. Most significantly, James's fateful entry into this enchanted space separates him forever from the human world.

In fact, in Bournonville's introduction to the published libretto of *Sylphiden*, dated 1 November 1836, he had even claimed that his subject was derived from a Scottish ballad.[36] Bournonville acknowledged that this supposed ballad tale was first realised as a ballet by Taglioni and set to music by

Schneitzhoeffer, but made no mention of Adolphe Nourrit's role in the genesis of the French *Sylphide*. Yet Bournonville was undoubtedly aware of Nourrit's authorship: during a two-month Parisian sojourn in the summer of 1834, Bournonville attended a performance of *La Sylphide* at the Opéra on 23 May, and purchased a copy of the libretto on the eve of his return to Copenhagen.[37] Indeed, he correctly attributed the original scenario to Nourrit on three separate occasions in *My Theatre Life*.[38]

By falsely identifying the source of *Sylphiden* as a Scottish ballad, however, Bournonville lent his ballet an imagined historicity that would have been especially appealing to Danes enamoured of the distant Scottish past as depicted in the novels of Sir Walter Scott, all of which had been translated into Danish by 1832 and many of which had been adapted for the Danish stage.[39] He also played to Danish readers, who held a particular interest in Scottish ballads because numerous folklorists (including Scott) had observed correspondences between British and Scandinavian balladry, especially in the supernatural types. Finally, by associating the story of *Sylphiden* with this collaborative, pan-Nordic ballad tradition, Bournonville could capitalise on the Danish appetite for stagings of national folklore subjects, an appetite already whetted by Heiberg's immensely popular singspiel *Elverhøj* and to which Bournonville would again appeal with his ballet *Et Folkesagn*. That *Sylphiden* was derived from a Scottish ballad would have been a believable fiction: its scenario follows the usual narrative trajectory of the pan-Nordic enchantment ballad, and the sylphs of *Sylphiden* are replicas of the supernatural forest women found in Danish folklore. To explore this connection, let us now examine the generic characteristics of the enchantment ballad.

An Overview of the Enchantment Ballad

In the typical enchantment ballad, a young person is seduced by a supernatural being and thereafter abandons the security of family, community, and often a virtuous (yet stiflingly ordinary) prospective spouse in order to join the bewitching creature in its native realm. In fact, the Scandinavian languages have specific words to describe this phenomenon: the missing person is said to be *bergtatt* or *haugtatt*, literally 'taken into the mountains' or 'taken into the hills' by the *huldrefolk* ('hidden people'), mostly unseen beings who conceal themselves in the landscape. Once the human protagonist has crossed the boundary from natural wilderness into supernatural dominion, he is not likely to return; if he does, he is forever transformed, a mere shell of his former self. Most often, he is punished for breaking the taboo of miscegenation through death, insanity, or permanent disappearance into the Otherworld. Enchantment ballad narratives, as anthropologist and folklorist James Moreira has observed, often focus on a human protagonist's attempts

6.1. August Malmström, *Älvalek* (*Elf-Play*, 1866), copyright the Nationalmuseum, Stockholm. By permission.

to escape these enclosed places of 'confinement, captivity, and death' or on the circumstances that led him across that brink.[40]

Since my intent is to explore how the characters and plot of Bournonville's *Sylphiden* align with the conventions of the enchantment ballad, I have restricted my focus to narratives involving encounters between a male human protagonist and a female supernatural; specifically a forest creature.[41] For though young men might also be threatened by demonic beings of the water and mountains, parallels are most evident between the Sylph and the forest sprites of Scandinavian folklore: the *hulder*, an exceptionally attractive girl whose supernatural Otherness is betrayed by her cow's tail; the *skogsrå* or *skogsfru* ('forest guardian' or 'lady of the forest'), a woodland nymph whose back is a rotten or hollowed-out tree trunk; and especially the *elvepige* or elf maiden, known for her ethereal dancing. The elf maiden emerges in the Danish tradition as the principal forest seductress, at times incorporating features of both the *hulder* and *skogsrå*. In fact, these forest creatures often shared names and traits: for example, a *skogsrå* might have a tail, an elf maiden might have a hollow back, and the term *hulder* is often used in a general sense to mean any preternatural woman with a deceptively beautiful appearance.[42]

Telltale features of Otherness mark these creatures as liminal beings that inhabit a spectral realm that lies in between humans and the surrounding landscape. In fact, these supernatural entities can be understood as ecomorphic: the *hulder*'s tail links her with the animals of the farm, the *skogsrå*'s bark-filled back indicates that she is an outgrowth of the trees, and the elf maiden is

6.2. Nils Blommér, *Ängsälvor* (*Meadow Elves*, 1850), copyright the Nationalmuseum, Stockholm. By permission. Unfortunately for the distant observer on horseback, a few minutes spent watching an elf circle translated into the passage of many years in the human world.

often portrayed as a personification of the air. In Scandinavian folklore, art, and literature, groups of elf maidens are found dancing in meadows, forests, and atop hills, arrayed in diaphanous gowns that give them the appearance of mist, fog, or other atmospheric phenomena. In Hans Christian Andersen's fairy tale 'Elverhøi' ('Elves' Hill', 1845), for example, elf maidens dance on their sacred mound with 'long shawls woven from haze and moonlight'.[43] Entwining elf maidens as a supernatural embodiment of mists 'dancing' across a woodland stream is perhaps best captured in the nineteenth-century Swedish painter August Malmström's (1829–1901) *Älvalek*, meaning 'elf-play' (Figure 6.1).

While the elf maidens of Andersen's 'Elverhøi' are benevolent, ethereal creatures, the forest sprites of Scandinavian legend were usually far more treacherous. As folklorist John Lindow reminds us, the presence of a tail on the otherwise beautiful female body of a *hulder* or *skogsrå* marks her animal-human hybridity and thus denotes her untamed sexuality, since control of one's passions was considered a human trait not shared by animals or super-natural beings.[44] Lindow has described the *skogsrå* as a 'would-be homewrecker' believed to lure men into sexual liaisons through such overtly libidinous tactics

6.3. Junker Ove surrounded by elf maidens in *Et Folkesagn*. Lithograph from the first published piano reduction of the ballet, ca. 1854.

as embracing them against her bosom or lifting her skirt. The wanton *skogsrå* might even trick a loyal husband into infidelity by disguising herself as his wife and bringing him little cakes in the forest.[45] Gunnar Grandberg's 1935 study of the *skogsrå* in folk belief includes the following two accounts of men who had the misfortune to encounter this creature:

> Anders Petter Svensson (b. 1855) from Eskilsäter, Värmland: 'The *skogsrå* had gotten power over a man. He went to the forest night after night. He was tormented and had lost weight. But then one night a bunch of men had gathered to hold on to him when the time arrived that he should be off. The *skogsrå* called out, but he did not come out. Then she approached more closely. And he went completely crazy, so that he was biting and foaming at the mouth. Someone went out and shot at her. But then immediately more *skogsrån* came out and dragged her back into the forest.'

> Pål Persson (b. 1835) from Silvåkra, Skåne: 'There was a coppersmith who lived at Torna Hällestad. And one day he had gone through the forest Prästaskogen down there, and he had met a lady and had some contact with her. But when they met him later, he had gone quite out of his mind and crazy, and he died a short time thereafter.'[46]

If the *skogsrå* seems to have used sexual intercourse to warp her victims' minds, drinking and dancing are the most common means of intoxication used by elf maidens to ensnare the young men who enter their domain. As

6.4. Thomas Lund as James, surrounded by sylphs in Nikolaj Hübbe's 2003 Danish Royal Ballet production of *Sylphiden*. Photograph copyright Martin Mydtskov Rønne. By permission.

choreographer and dance writer Janice LaPointe-Crump has observed, dancing elf maidens are traditionally depicted as 'encircling their [human] prey much as a spider does and enveloping him in a web of vaporous mist'.[47] In the Danish enchantment ballad 'Elvehøj' ('Elf Hill', *Danmarks gamle Folkeviser* [*DgF*] 46), a young man stumbles upon a circle of elf maidens, who encourage him to sing and dance with them. To quote Lanae H. Isaacson: 'The purpose of the dance, the magical, entrancing song, is [...] to link [him] physically, irrevocably with the elf-world, with *Elvehøj*.'[48] The man makes the imprudent decision to talk to one of the elf maidens and share a drink with her. He even asks to run away with her. Luckily for him, he is not lost forever among the elves: a cock's crow, heralding the dawn, breaks the spell. In his closing narration, the protagonist warns other men to avoid the hypnotic elfin dance.

Extraordinary skill in dance or music often betrays the identity of supernatural beings found in enchantment ballads and other folklore. After all, the average person could participate in popular social dances, or in the singing of church hymns and ballads, but exceptional ability in these performing arts was viewed as having unearthly origins, often the result of bargaining with demonic forces.[49] Graceful, mesmeric dancing is generally attributed to elf maidens, as illustrated in H.C. Andersen's fairy tale 'Elverhøi', the folk ballad 'Elvehøj', and Nils Blommér's painting *Ängsälvor* (Figure 6.2). Virtuosic music is primarily associated with the male water sprite known as the *nøkk*, although the female *hulder* might also use musical prowess to entice mortal men. The following legend, collected in the Telemark region of Norway, gives one such example of a *hulder*'s attempt to charm a young man through music:

> Once there was a man who was alone on a summer farm. One night he felt he had to go outside before he could go to bed. Suddenly a girl appeared, playing an instrument. The man had never heard anything so beautiful in all his life. He got scared and wanted to go inside, but the girl said: 'Wait a minute, let me talk to you for a little while.' They stood there talking, and in the end, the girl asked him to marry her. But he soon understood what kind of woman she was, and he plainly said no, it could never be. She had to leave then. Three nights in a row, she came back to tempt and court the man, but every time he said no, even though she was the most beautiful girl he had ever seen. He knew he had to send her away, and he finally got rid of her.[50]

Just as the supernatural beings of Scandinavian folk belief occupy an intermediary position between humans and the natural landscape, the human who encounters them is also placed in between these worlds, often living on the outskirts of society and working on a remote farm or in the forest. As a cautionary tale about the repercussions of violating sexual mores, the enchantment ballad reinforced appropriate behavioural conduct for farmhands, dairymaids, lumberjacks, and other individuals working in isolated rural areas.[51] Young unmarried men and women were considered especially prone to the enticements of unearthly interlopers because they stood on the cusp between adolescence and adulthood, ready to emerge into new frontiers of erotic love and sexuality. This was thought to be a dangerous time, during which one's virginity needed to be closely protected from the lure of supernatural Others. After all, these demonic beings were believed to have a certain *minkande kreft* or 'withering force.'[52] The same creatures blamed for crop failures and livestock illness could also be responsible for destroying the stability of domestic life by substituting changelings (*huldrebarn*) for stolen human infants, creating troll-human hybrid offspring, and interfering with betrothals or marriages. Folklorists have long asserted that magic takes on a greater role in events involving uncertainty and anxiety, and perhaps one sociological function of the enchantment ballad was the need to explain a fiancé's sudden change of heart, eccentric behaviour, or unexplained disappearance.

In many of these tales, the protagonist is engaged to be married, thus intensifying the transition from single youth to wedded adult. It is often on the eve of these impending nuptials, when liminal tension is strongest, that

the protagonist is most susceptible to the temptations of supernatural beings. Even if the protagonist resists these overtures, fidelity to one's human
fiancée could provoke the jealous retaliation of a supernatural enchantress.

In the Danish ballad 'Elveskud' ('Elf-Struck', *DgF* 47), Herr Oluf is riding
through the forest to meet his fiancée – and in some variants, he is on his way
to the wedding itself – when he encounters a coven of elf maidens. He is
invited to join in their dancing, but refuses, knowing the dance would bind
him to the elf world and wishing to remain faithful to his intended. The elf-
king's daughter repeatedly bids him dance with her, offering him various
treasures, yet he still refuses. Furious, the elf-king's daughter curses him,
allowing him to return home but promising that sickness and death will
follow him. Oluf dies the next day, and his fiancée and mother also die of
broken hearts.[53]

Remote parts of nature are not the only places for contact between humans and otherworldly creatures: these rendezvous might also take place in
locations that mark domestic boundaries, such as barns, storehouses, attics,
and cellars. Moreira theorises that these threshold areas are significant in
both British and Scandinavian balladry as spatial representations of the
young protagonist's liminality: poised to enter adulthood and 'the world of
romance and courtship', these characters are often situated in bower door-
ways or windows.[54] These thresholds take on an even greater metaphorical
significance in moments of human-*huldrefolk* relations, since a window or
doorway can act as a portal between the known domestic world on the inside
and the unknown spectral world on the outside. Another type of liminal
space in which humans might encounter supernatural Others is the dream
state, as in the Danish enchantment ballad 'Herr Bøsmer i Elvehjem' (Herr
Bosmer in the Home of the Elves, *DgF* 45). In this ballad, a beautiful elf
queen visits young Herr Bøsmer in a dream and urges him to meet her at the
river bridge (another type of threshold). Unable to resist this alluring vision,
he rides to the bridge early the next morning. His horse slips, and he falls into
the watery lair of the elf queen, who gives him wine that causes him to forget his
family and betrothed. Bøsmer has forsaken his earthly home for *Elvehjem*, a
place of no return.

The Enchantment Ballad in nineteenth-century Danish musico-dramatic Works

The mythos of the enchantment ballad provided fodder for a number of
nineteenth-century Danish musico-dramatic works, of which I will briefly
examine three: Johan Ludvig Heiberg's singspiel *Elverhøj* (1828) with music
by Friedrich Kuhlau; Niels W. Gade's cantata *Elverskud* (*Elf-Struck*, 1854);
and Bournonville's ballet *Et Folkesagn* (*A Folk Tale*, 1854) with music by Gade
and Johan Peter Emilius Hartmann. All three of these works feature the

motif of seductive, dancing elf maidens, an image that is also shared by Bournonville's *Sylphiden*.

Heiberg's *Elverhøj*, widely regarded as Denmark's first national play, borrowed from a deep repository of Danish elfin lore and even featured an arrangement of the ballad tune 'Jeg lagde mit hoved til Elverhøj' ([I laid my head down on Elves' Hill] 'Elvehøj', *Udvalgte danske Viser* 34B), sung by the peasant woman Karen at the beginning of the drama.[55] The plot of *Elverhøj* centres on Karen's adopted daughter Agnete who, like her namesake in the enchantment ballad 'Agnete og Havmanden' ('Agnete and the Merman', *DgF* 38), finds herself drawn to the supernatural realm. Act Four of the play is set on Elves' Hill at night, where Agnete slumbers and dreams of elf maidens dancing around her in the moonlit meadow. Friedrich Kuhlau's music for this ballet sequence is reminiscent of the fairies' theme from Mendelssohn's *Overture to A Midsummer Night's Dream* (1826): accented opening chords

Example 6.1. Kuhlau, *Elverhøj*, Act Four, No. 11: "Agnete's Dream" (ballet), mm. 40–57.

herald a scherzo in 3/8 time with *moto perpetuo* sixteenth notes in the strings, coloured by silvery triangle punctuations (Example 6.1).[56]

The nobleman Albert Ebbesen is also attracted to the mysterious Elves' Hill, where he is enthralled every night by Agnete's dancing. Ebbesen believes himself bewitched by an elf maiden; however, Agnete is ultimately discovered by a fictionalised King Christian IV (1588–1648) to be his goddaughter Elisabeth Munk, thus allowing her to marry his vassal Ebbeson. Though inspired by Danish folktales about elves and changelings, the supernatural forces in *Elverhøj* are proven innocuous, and Ebbesen's clandestine encounters with Agnete are made acceptable by King Christian IV's realisation of Agnete's true (human) identity.

Niels Gade's *Elverskud*, on the other hand, presents elf maidens as they traditionally appear in Danish balladry: dangerous, even life-threatening creatures who cajole human men into joining their dance. Gade dramatised the Danish ballad 'Elveskud' – the tale of Herr Oluf, struck down by the elf-king's daughter – as a cantata for soloists, choir, and orchestra. In Part II, No. 5 of the cantata, Herr Oluf first encounters the dancing elf maidens, who gambol through the forest while singing the refrain of the 'Elveskud' ballad: 'Dandsen gaaer saa let gjennem Lunden' (The dance goes so lightly through the grove).[57] Gade's music for the elf maidens' dance conveys the aerial essence of these creatures through string tremolos and ascending/descending arpeggio figures in the violins that imitate fluttering wings and mercurial flight (Example 6.2). Low-register flute lines evoke the wind's

Example 6.2. Gade, *Elverskud*, No. 5, mm. 1–12.

movement through the trees, while triangle strokes lend a shimmering aura of moonlight and enchantment to the scene.

Gade's elfin dance music is, like Kuhlau's, indebted to the 'fairy style' of Mendelssohn. However, when the elf-king's daughter appears and extends her hand to Oluf, she uses the soothing lilt of a barcarole to lull him into submission. She also displays her musical virtuosity by ending each of her entreaties with a melismatic incantation of Herr Oluf's name (Example 6.3). Her third and final bidding ascends to a supernal C flat, where she lingers, luxuriating in the glittering tone of her seraphic voice and encouraging Oluf to join her in this pleasure (Example 6.4). As in the original enchantment ballad, Oluf's rejection inflames her fury: she smites him with sickness and prophesies his death.

Around the same time that Gade was finishing *Elverskud*, he was commissioned by Bournonville to write the music to the first and third acts of the ballet *Et Folkesagn*. Bournonville declared *Et Folkesagn* to be his 'most perfect and finest choreographic work, especially as regards its Danish character',

Example 6.3.   Gade, *Elverskud*, No. 6, mm. 1–13.

and credited his inspiration to collections of Danish folksongs and tales by Nyerup, Berggreen, and Thiele.[58] *Et Folkesagn* is a composite of several stories, including a legend from Thiele's collection of *Danmarks Folkesagn* (1843) about young Svend Fælling's encounter with dancing elf maidens, one of whom offers him a goblet and bids him drink.[59] In Bournonville's scenario, the handsome Junker Ove is engaged to the temperamental Miss Birthe, heiress to a large manor. However, he dreads the marriage and retreats to the woods after dark, where he is approached by the beautiful and mysterious Hilda, who offers him a drink from her goblet. When Ove refuses to return the goblet, the witch Muri summons her elf maiden minions to trap him with their dizzying dance (Figure 6.3). As the elf maidens whirl about

Example 6.4. Gade, *Elverskud*, No. 6, mm. 48–55.

Example 6.5. Gade, *Et Folkesagn*, Act One, No. 5, mm. 1–13.

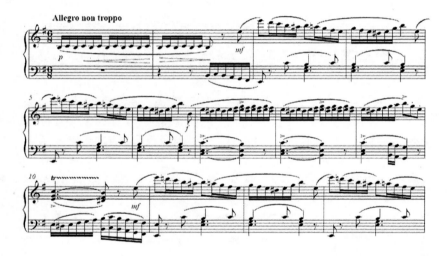

Ove with white veils, their diabolical mischief and Ove's frenzied bewilderment are communicated in Gade's score through a blistering *scherzo fantastique* (Example 6.5).

The influence of Heiberg's *Elverhøj* is apparent in *Et Folkesagn* in that both works resolve an impermissible relationship between a mortal man and a supernatural woman with the revelation that the supposed elf maiden is in fact human. As previously discussed, the supernatural Others of Scandinavian enchantment ballads were viewed as a threat to the sanctity of family life and the bonds of one's own community; moreover, as John Lindow has argued, these beings are often coded as ethnic Others, revealing cultural anxieties and prejudices linked to concepts of racial purity.[60] The young man who becomes involved with an elf maiden is usually punished for his transgression with lunacy, destruction, or death. However, Ove's attraction

Example 6.6. Løvenskiold, *Sylphiden*, Act One, No. 1, mm. 1–20.

to Hilda becomes socially acceptable once it is discovered that his fiancée Birthe is a *huldrebarn*, a changeling traded by the trolls for the human child Hilda. Birthe's troll identity is suggested by her irritability, clumsiness, and frizzy hair, and is ultimately confirmed when she is recognised by her troll brothers Diderik and Viderik. Once this deception is unravelled, Hilda assumes her rightful place as Ove's bride and heiress to the manor.

Sylphiden as an Enchantment Ballad

Given these examples of Danish *trylleviser* as recorded in ballad collections and represented in musico-dramatic works, how might the *Sylphiden* scenario – with its Scottish setting, character names, costumes, and traditional dances – be mapped onto the character types and narrative expectations of the enchantment ballad?

Like the title character of 'Herr Bøsmer i Elvehjem', James of *Sylphiden* is haunted by dreams of a beautiful supernatural woman whose charms he ultimately cannot resist, despite his better judgment. According to Bournonville's libretto, the Sylph 'has already enchanted him several times in dreams', and the ballet opens with the Sylph kneeling beside James while he sleeps in his armchair.[61] Much like the words 'once upon a time' invite the listener into a fairy tale, Løvenskiold's opening musical gesture of sustained woodwind chords and ascending harp flourishes draws the audience into the idyllic mood of James's daydream and establishes a mythopoetic setting in which sylphs and witches might coexist with human characters (Example 6.6).

In both her appearance and behaviour, the Sylph bears a close resemblance to the vaporous, gossamer-draped elf maidens of Danish folklore.[62] Like them, she, too is a creature of the air, signalled by her movement through apertures like windows and chimneys, her seemingly weightless dancing on pointe, the flowing white tulle of her Romantic tutu, and, of course, her wings (a trait not shared by elf maidens). And like her elfin kindred, the Sylph has a prodigious talent for dancing — and the use of pointe technique exclusively by the Sylph and her coterie, a tradition maintained in Danish productions of *Sylphiden*, is crucial in portraying the aerial, otherworldly nature of these beings. On pointe, the sylphs appear to float above their human counterparts, while Effy and her friends wear heeled shoes that reinforce their grounded human nature and normal dancing abilities.[63] Moreover, the Sylph's preternatural artistry is demonstrated through both Bournonville's choreography and Løvenskiold's score, resulting in a conflation of terpsichorean and musical virtuosity. In the Act One opening, the Sylph first begins to dance to the strains of a solo violin whose trills and roulades not only provide a pictorial representation of the Sylph's fluttering wings as she hovers around James, but also emphasise the Sylph's otherworldly faculties by borrowing trademark figures of the nineteenth-century instrumental showpiece (See again example 6.6).[64]

The Sylph's dance becomes livelier, and she gazes on James with delight. As she will reveal to James in Act One No. 4 (the Window Scene), she has long admired him and has followed him like a sort of guardian angel. This suggests an affinity between the Sylph and the elf queen of 'Herr Bøsmer i Elvehjem', who has languished in desire for 'fifteen winters and a year' before she finally claims Herr Bøsmer as her own.[65] Both of these 'fairy lovers' seem to have watched their chosen mortal men from childhood, waiting until these men have reached a marriageable age before making their presence known. The Sylph's kiss awakens James, who is beside himself with confusion and amazement, unsure whether his fantasy has in fact materialised or if he is merely hallucinating. Notably, he has not encountered the Sylph in the flesh until the day of his betrothal to Effy: like both Herr Oluf of 'Elveskud' and Herr Bøsmer, James is about to be married when he encounters physical temptation in the form of an otherworldly woman. Furthermore, it is at the very moment of James and Effy's betrothal ceremony when the Sylph's enticement proves too great and James abandons his human bride to join the Sylph in the forest.

The Sylph is coquettish and even manipulative, with no qualms about interfering with James's plans to marry a mortal girl. Bournonville himself recognised the latent danger of this seemingly gentle and guileless sprite, characterising the Sylph as 'a bad angel' with 'poisonous breath' who 'crushes and ruins' the men who encounter her.[66] When James resists her during the Window Scene (Act One No. 4) after remembering his commitment to Effy, the Sylph wraps herself in the scarf made from James's family tartan, indicating her desire to supplant Effy as James's intended spouse. The tartan scarf is, of course, also a presage of the cursed rose-coloured scarf of Act Two that James believes will bind the Sylph to him.[67] The Sylph next appears at James and Effy's wedding festivities, distracting James as he dances with his bride-to-be. She even steals the wedding ring intended for Effy, places it on her own finger, then runs off to the forest with James in pursuit. This propensity for destroying men's domestic welfare puts her in league with her Scandinavian sisters, the *hulder*, the *skogsrå*, and the *elvepige*. In particular, the elf maidens of the enchantment ballads 'Elveskud' and 'Herr Bøsmer i Elvehjem' show blatant disregard for human fiancées. In 'Elveskud', the elf-king's daughter mercilessly ignores Herr Oluf's plea: 'I dare not, I must not: tomorrow shall be my wedding.'[68] And when Herr Bøsmer tells the elf-queen that his betrothed – with whom he will both live and die – is in Denmark, the elf-queen orders her attendant to bring the wine that will cloud Bøsmer's memory. After drinking from the horn goblet, Bøsmer proclaims that here in *Elvehjem* is his betrothed (the elf-queen), with whom he will both live and die.[69]

As in the typical enchantment ballad, threshold spaces figure prominently in *Sylphiden* at the moments when James is most drawn to the Sylph's fantastic realm.[70] After James first sees the Sylph, he attempts to take her in his arms, but she eludes him and disappears up through the fireplace, a passage between the interior hearth and exterior chimney of the farmhouse. Her next visitation to James is at the casement, which opens to reveal a view of the mysterious, uncharted woodland that lies just past the windowpane. During James and Effy's betrothal festivities, the Sylph appears on the staircase: this might be interpreted as a symbolic invitation for James to travel with her to the supernatural wilderness that exists beyond his mundane country life. What James does not realise, however, is that the world of *huldrefolk* is an inversion of human society: within the farm community, James was pursued by the Sylph and had power over Madge; yet in the forest, James must pursue the evasive Sylph and surrender to Madge's authority.

Moreira remarks that the Scandinavian enchantment ballad often features a 'domestic interior of the Otherworld, which is a mirror image of the social world.'[71] This holds true in the dramatic structure of *Sylphiden*, as well: the celebratory folk dances of Effy and her friends at the farmhouse are mirrored by the round dances of the sylphs in their moonlit glade. By fleeing from his wedding with Effy and entering into the sylphs' dance, James – like the human protagonist of an enchantment ballad – rejects a hearth and home within his own community, uniting himself instead with the domestic interior world of these creatures. As James wanders through the sylphs' circle in the Act Two No. 4 *Divertissement*, his sense of both delight and disorientation is musically evoked in Løvenskiold's score by a hypnotic barcarole. At first blush, this may seem like an unusual musical choice: unlike the *scherzo fantastique* so often used in the mid-nineteenth century to portray fairies and elves, the barcarole does not illustrate the sylphs' otherworldly virtuosity, insect-like flight, or capricious temperament. Instead, this music demonstrates these creatures' ability to mesmerise humans through sounds and gestures of sublime, captivating beauty. In his categorisation of different barcarole types in nineteenth-century music, Rodney Stenning Edgecombe has designated the Act Two barcarole from Løvenskiold's *Sylphiden* as the 'supernal' type, through which the dichotomy between dream and reality is obscured. Edgecombe writes:

> Løvenskjold, like Schneitzhöffer before him, chose a barcarole to represent James's vision of the other world: a corps de ballet of sylphs rocking back and forth in *developpés devants* (unfolding the leg to the front) and *arabesques penchées* (unfolding the leg to the back) in a way that evokes the lapping of waves. Adolphe Adam similarly wrote a barcarole for the *ballabile* of the Wilis in act II of *Giselle* (1841), and Ludwig Minkus, many decades later, for the entrée of the phantasms in the Kingdom of the Shades (*La Bayadère*, 1877). The supernal barcarole, concerned with reverie and mental escape, can therefore be regarded as having a distinct subtype, namely, one that depicts a movement between mythologically demarcated worlds. This I shall call the psychopompic barcarole, eliding the space of life with the space of afterlife, and measuring the distance with an *incessus deificus* (godly motion): remember that Aeneas recognised Venus as a goddess by the way she walked.[72]

The nexus of water, women, and song is also strongly associated with male desire in nineteenth-century opera and ballet, as shown by the Act Two bathers' chorus 'Jeunes beautés, sous ce feuillage' from Meyerbeer's *Les Huguenots* (1836), the Elves' Song from Offenbach's opera *Die Rheinnixen* (1864) – better known as the Act 2 duet 'Belle nuit, ô nuit d'amour' from *Les contes d'Hoffmann* – and the Act 3 *Danse barcarolle* from Delibes's *Sylvia* (1876), to name only a few prominent examples. This phenomenon may be explained by what Lawrence Kramer has described as the 'liquefaction of desire', the developing nineteenth-century conception of sexuality as fluid. According to Kramer, 'the fire of classical desire [was] replaced by that endlessly circulating, endlessly rhythmic, medium – water.'[73] During the Act Two barcarole of *Sylphiden*, James searches in vain for his elusive Sylph among her sisters, lured by a lyrical melody that alternates between solo violin – the same instrument associated with the Sylph in her Act One opening solo – and solo flute, an instrument associated not only with the pastoral and celestial, but also with delusion and false idyll, as in Donizetti's *Lucia di Lammermoor* (1835). James's desire is envoiced by a solo cello countermelody that ardently strives to reach the same heights as the violin and flute, much like James aspires to be united with the Sylph. After he catches a fleeting glimpse of his beloved, the cello countermelody returns with even greater volume and intensity. A rippling harp accompaniment weaves through this musical texture, lending a magical timbre that heightens James's sense of wonderment. Yet despite the tranquillity and gracefulness of this tableau, Bournonville's typically welcoming and 'melodic' use of the arms make the sylphs seem akin to a colony of beautiful but predatory sea anemones whose undulating tentacles draw in their prey (Figure 6.4).

Due to *Sylphiden*'s tragic ending, coupled with its emphasis on erotic and demonic subject matter, Erik Aschengreen has argued that it is the least typically Danish of Bournonville's ballets, which otherwise cultivated the harmonious *biedermeier* aesthetic prized in Golden-Age Denmark.[74] As Aschengreen points out, this Danish *biedermeier* aesthetic is evident in Bournonville's *Napoli* (1842) and *Et Folkesagn* (1854), in which supernatural conflicts are resolved in happy endings: in *Napoli*, Gennaro and Teresina escape from the sea demon Golfo's Blue Grotto through Christian faith; and in *Et Folkesagn*, Ove's love for the elf maiden Hilda is made admissible by the discovery that she is not an elf maiden but a human, switched at birth with a troll child. Ironically, though, one could argue that *Sylphiden* actually surpasses *Et Folkesagn* in terms of fidelity to Danish folk literature. The punitive conclusion of *Sylphiden* closely aligns this ballet – supposedly an anomalous import of French Romanticism – with the narrative expectations of Scandinavian enchantment ballads, most of which ended badly for human protagonists who dared engage in relations with the *huldrefolk*.[75] Like both

Herr Oluf and Herr Bøsmer of Scandinavian balladry, James is lost forever to the human world after venturing into supernatural territory. Moreover, the siren who led him to that inescapable place is not an exotic *bayadère* or *péri*; rather, the Sylph is nearly identical to the elf maidens of Danish folklore in terms of her physical appearance, close association with the natural environment, preference for manifesting herself in threshold areas, extraordinary artistic abilities (especially in dance), and above all else, her disruption of domestic stability through her seduction of a young man engaged to be married.

Most importantly, Bournonville himself acknowledged the symmetry between *Sylphiden* and Scandinavian folk belief. Reflecting on his ballet *The Mountain Hut* (1859), in which villagers suspect a young girl of being a mountain-dwelling enchantress, Bournonville wrote: 'The legend of the *hulder* lies all too near the balletic domain for me not to have thought of using it in my compositions. It was merely a question of whether I should use the material in order to achieve a serious effect, as in *La Sylphide* and *A Folk Tale*, or treat it as an outright superstition having an influence on everyday life.'[76] (In the case of *The Mountain Hut*, Bournonville chose the latter: it turns out that the mountain girl's father is an exiled criminal, thus necessitating their reclusive lifestyle.) Bournonville's identification of the Sylph as a type of *hulder* demonstrates that he recognised the Sylph as a manifestation of the well-known sylvan temptress of Scandinavian folklore.

Danish National Character in *Sylphiden*

In his survey of the friendship between August Bournonville and Hans Christian Andersen, Ebbe Mørk makes the following enigmatic statement: 'The Emperor of China in Andersen's fairy-tale *The Nightingale* is as Danish as the Scot, James, in Bournonville's *La Sylphide*. The exotic demanded by Romanticism never betrayed 'national character' in either fairy-tale or ballet.'[77] Like Andersen's Chinese emperor, who rejects the grey-brown nightingale in favour of a bejewelled mechanical bird only to regret this choice on his deathbed, James also rejects the natural – his Scottish fiancée Effy – in favour of the Sylph, an idealised woman who is ephemeral and unattainable. Effy is attractive but common, dancing a peasant reel with her friends and wearing the character shoes of a 'real' person instead of the pointe shoes of the supernatural sylphs, thus solidifying her connection with the rural folk.[78] She also wears a tartan that marks her association with an earthly clan instead of the white gown and wings that visually designate the Sylph as a spirit of the air, the embodiment of an unseen element. James's pursuit of the Sylph is the fruitless desire for an artificial ideal, a concept that Bournonville grasped in his summation of *Sylphiden*'s fundamental poetic idea: 'that man, in pursuing an imaginary happiness, neglects the true one and loses everything just when he thinks he is about to attain the object of his desire.'[79] James laments his foolhardiness after witnessing the funeral procession of his beloved Sylph and the wedding procession of Effy and Gurn, but unfortunately, it is too late.

More importantly, however, James can be considered an emblem of Danish national character because he is essentially indistinguishable from the typical protagonist of the pan-Nordic enchantment ballad. His dilemma between remaining in his known human community and surrendering to the unknown supernatural realm is shared by the young men of the Danish ballads 'Elvehøi', 'Elveskud', and 'Herr Bøsmer i Elvehjem', the folklore-inspired musico-dramatic works *Elverhøj*, *Elverskud*, and *Et Folkesagn*, and numerous other legends and memorates. Consequently, Bournonville's *Sylphiden* is more than an infusion of French Romanticism within an otherwise light-hearted Danish theatre culture: rather, this ballet can be understood as an icon of Danish identity for its effective utilisation of what Bournonville described as 'well-known themes and familiar tones'.[80] Its Scottish setting was a *terra cognita* for nineteenth-century Danes, thanks to the novels of Sir Walter Scott, and this supposedly exotic locale was in fact viewed as a kindred Nordic country by many nineteenth-century Danish writers, folklorists, and other social scientists. Above all else, *Sylphiden* has a sympathetic resonance with the enchantment ballads that flourished in both Scotland and Scandinavia, thus revealing James and the Sylph beneath their purely Scottish trappings to be avatars of this pan-Nordic folk culture.

Abrahamson, Werner H., Rasmus Nyerup, and Knud Lyne Rahbek. *Udvalgte Danske Viser fra Middelalderen* [Selected Danish Ballads from the Middle Ages]. 5 vols. Copenhagen: J.F. Schultz, 1812–14.

Afzelius, Erik Gustaf Geijer and Arvid August. *Svenska Folk-Visor från Forntiden* [Swedish Folk Ballads from Ancient Times]. 3 vols. Stockholm: Strinnholm and Häggström, 1814–16.

Andersen, Hans Christian. *O.T.* Borgen: Det danske Sprog- og Litteraturselskab, 1987.

Arwidsson, Adolph Ivar. *Svenska Fornsånger* [Ancient Swedish Songs]. 3 vols. Stockholm: P.A. Norstedt, 1834–42.

Aschengreen, Erik. *The Beautiful Danger: Facets of the Romantic Ballet.* Translated by Patricia N. McAndrew. *Dance Perspectives*. Vol. 58, New York: Dance Perspectives Foundation, 1974.

———. 'The Beautiful Danger: Facets of the Romantic Ballet.' *Dance Perspectives* 58 (1974).

Banes, Sally. *Dancing Women: Female Bodies on Stage*. New York: Routledge, 1998.

Banes, Sally, and Noël Carroll. 'Marriage and the Inhuman: *La Sylphide*'s Narratives of Domesticity and Community', in *Rethinking the Sylph: New Perspectives on the Romantic Ballet*, ed. Lynn Garafola (Hanover, NH: Wesleyan University Press, 1997).

Borrow, George. *Romantic Ballads*. London: J. Taylor, 1826.

Bournonville, August. *My Theatre Life*. Translated by Patricia N. McAndrew. Middletown, CT: Wesleyan University Press, 1979.

———. *Sylphiden: Romantisk Ballet in to Akter*. Copenhagen: J.H. Schubothe, 1836.

Brittan, Francesca. 'Miniaturism, Nostalgia, and Musical Microscopy: The Fairy Fantastic in Nineteenth-Century France.' Paper presented at the American Musicological Society Annual Meeting, Nashville, November 2008.

———. 'On Microscopic Hearing: Fairy Magic, Natural Science, and the *Scherzo Fantastique*.' *Journal of the American Musicological Society* 64, no. 3 (2011): 527-600.

Bruzelius, Margaret, 'Women – Wild and Otherwise', in *Romancing the Novel: Adventure from Scott to Sebald* (Lewisburg, PA: Bucknell University Press, 2007).

Buchan, David. 'Ballads of Otherworld Beings', in *The Good People: New Fairylore Essays*, ed. Peter Narváez (New York: Garland, 1991).

———. 'Talerole Analysis and Child's Supernatural Ballads', in *The Ballad and Oral Literature*, ed. Joseph Harris (Cambridge, MA: Harvard University Press, 1991).

Celenza, Anna Harwell. '*Efterklange af Ossian*: The Reception of James Macpherson's *Poems of Ossian* in Denmark's Literature, Art, and Music.' *Scandinavian Studies* 70, no. 3 (1998): 359–96.

———. *Hans Christian Andersen and Music: The Nightingale Revealed*. Burlington, VT: Ashgate, 2005.

Child, Francis James. *English and Scottish Ballads*. 8 vols. Boston: Little, Brown, & Co., 1857–59.

Cooper, Suzanne Fagence. 'The Liquefaction of Desire: Music, Water and Femininity in Victorian Aestheticism.' *Women: A Cultural Review* 20, no. 2 (2009): 186–201.

Crowe, David M. 'The Roma Holocaust', in *The Holocaust's Ghost: Writings on*

Art, Politics, Law and Education, ed. F.C. DeCoste and Bernard Schwartz (Edmonton: University of Alberta Press, 2000).

Cunningham, Allan. *The Songs of Scotland*. 4 vols. London: J. Taylor, 1825.

Dal, Erik, ed. *H.C. Andersens Nye Eventyr og Historier*, H.C. Andersens Eventyr, vol. II. Copenhagen: Hans Reitzel, 1964.

Duelund, Peter. 'Denmark: Cultural Policy Profile', in *Compendium: Cultural Policies and Trends in Europe* (2011). http://www.culturalpolicies.net/web/denmark.php. Accessed 23 August 2011.

Edgecombe, Rodney Stenning. 'On the Limits of Genre: Some Nineteenth-Century Barcaroles.' *Nineteenth-Century Music* 24, no. 3 (2001): 252–67.

Finlay, John. *Scottish Historical and Romantic Ballads*. 2 vols. Edinburgh: J. Ballantyne, 1808.

Flom, George Tobias. *Scandinavian Influence on Southern Lowland Scotch: A Contribution to the Study of the Linguistic Relations of English and Scandinavian*. Columbia University Germanic Studies. New York: Columbia University Press, 1900.

Granberg, Gunnar. *Skogsrået i yngre nordisk folktradition*. Skrifter utgivna av Gustav Adolfs Akademien för Folklivsforskning. Uppsala: Lundequistska bokhandeln, 1935.

Greiling, R.O., and A.G. Smith. 'The Dalradian of Scotland: Missing Link between the Vendian of Northern and Southern Scandinavia?' *Physics and Chemistry of the Earth, Part A: Solid Earth and Geodesy* 25, no. 5 (2000): 495–98.

Grundtvig, Svend. *Engelske og Skotske Folkeviser* [English and Scottish Folk Ballads]. 4 vols. Copenhagen: Wahlske Boghandling, 1842–46.

Grundtvig, Svend, Axel Olrik, Hakon Grüner-Nielsen, Hjalmar Thuren, and Sven H. Rossel, eds. *Danmarks gamle Folkeviser*. 12 vols. Copenhagen: Samfundet til den danske Literaturs Fremme, 1853–1976.

Hall, Alaric. 'Getting Shot of Elves: Healing, Witchcraft and Fairies in the Scottish Witchcraft Trials.' *Folklore* 116 (2005): 19–36.

Howitt, William and Mary. *Literature and Romance of Northern Europe*. 2 vols. London: Colburn, 1852.

Hubbard, Tom, 'European Reception of Scott's Poetry: Translation as the Front Line', in *The Reception of Sir Walter Scott in Europe*, ed. Murray Pittock (London, New York: Continuum, 2006).

Hustvedt, Sigurd Bernhard. *Ballad Criticism in Scandinavia and Great Britain During the Eighteenth Century*. New York: American-Scandinavian Foundation, 1916.

Isaacson, Lanae H. 'Dramatic Discourse in the Scandinavian Ballad.' *Scandinavian Studies* 64, no. 1 (1992): 68–95.

Jamieson, Robert. *Popular Ballads and Songs*. 2 vols. Edinburgh: A. Constable, 1806.

Kawabata, Maiko. 'Virtuosity, the Violin, the Devil...What Really Made Paganini "Demonic"?' *Current Musicology* 83 (2007): 85–108.

Kramer, Lawrence. 'Musical Form and *Fin-De-Siècle* Sexuality', in *Music as Cultural Practice, 1800–1900* (Los Angeles: University of California Press, 1990).

Kværndrup, Sigurd. *Den Østnordiske Ballade – Oral Teori og Tekstanalyse: Studier i Danmarks gamle Folkeviser*. Copenhagen: Museum Tusculanum, 2006.

Kvideland, Reimund, and Henning K. Sehmsdorf, eds. *Scandinavian Folk Belief and Legend*. Minneapolis: University of Minnesota Press 1988.

Landstad, Magnus Brostrup. *Norske Folkeviser* [Norwegian Folk Ballads]. Christiania: Tönsberg, 1853.

LaPointe-Crump, Janice D. 'Birth of a Ballet: August Bournonville's *a Folk Tale*, 1854.' Ph.D. diss., Texas Woman's University, 1980.

Leeder, Paul Robert. 'Scott and Scandinavian Literature: The Influence of Bartholin and Others.' *Smith College Studies in Modern Languages* 2 (1920): 8–57.

Lindow, John. 'Supernatural Others and Ethnic Others: A Millennium of World View.' *Scandinavian Studies* 67, no. 1 (1995): 8–31.

Moreira, James H. 'Narrative Expectations and Domestic Space in the Telemark Ballads.' *Scandinavian Studies* 73, no. 3 (2001): 317–48.

Mørk, Ebbe. 'A Friendship: Andersen and Bournonville', in *The Royal Danish Ballet and Bournonville* (Copenhagen: Ministry of Foreign Affairs of Denmark, 1979).

Motherwell, William. *Minstrelsy, Ancient and Modern*. Glasgow: J. Wylie, 1827.

Nielsen, Jørgen Erik. '"His Pirates Had Foray'd on Scottish Hill": Scott in Denmark with an Overview of His Reception in Norway and Sweden', in *The Reception of Sir Walter Scott in Europe*, ed. Murray Pittock (New York, London: Continuum, 2006).

Olwig, Kenneth. 'Place, Society, and the Individual in the Authorship of St. St. Blicher', in *Omkring Blicher 1974*, ed. Felix Nørgaard (Copenhagen: Gyldendal, 1974).

Oxfeldt, Elisabeth. *Nordic Orientalism: Paris and the Cosmopolitan Imagination 1800–1900*. Copenhagen: Museum Tusculanum Press, 2005.

Pittock, Murray, 'Scott and the European Nationalities Question', in *The Reception of Sir Walter Scott in Europe*, ed. Murray Pittock (New York, London: Continuum, 2006).

Prior, R.C. Alexander. *Ancient Danish Ballads*. 3 vols. London, Edinburgh: Williams and Norgate, 1860.

Russell, Peter. *The Themes of the German Lied from Mozart to Strauss*. Studies in the History and Interpretation of Music. Vol. 84, Lewiston: Edwin Mellen, 2002.

Rygg, Kristin. 'Mystification through Musicalization and Demystification through Music: The Case of *Haugtussa*', in *Cultural Functions of Intermedial Exploration*, ed. Erik Hedling (New York: Rodopi, 2002).

Scott, Sir Walter. 'The Fairies of Popular Superstition', in *Minstrelsy of the Scottish Border*, vol. II (Kelso: J. Ballantyne, 1802).

———. *Minstrelsy of the Scottish Border*. 2 vols. Kelso: J. Ballantyne, 1802.

Shore, Dan. 'The Emergence of Danish National Opera, 1779–1846', dissertation, CUNY, 2008.

Tangherlini, Timothy R. 'From Trolls to Turks: Change and Continuity in Danish Legend Tradition.' *Scandinavian Studies* 67, no. 1 (1995): 32–62.

Thiele, J.M. *Danmarks Folkesagn*. 2 vols. Vol. II, Copenhagen: Reitzel, 1843.

Weber, Henry, Robert Jamieson, and Sir Walter Scott. *Illustrations of Northern Antiquities*. Edinburgh: J. Ballantyne, 1814.

Worsaae, Jens Jakob Asmussen. *An Account of the Danes and Norwegians in England, Scotland, and Ireland*. London: J. Murray, 1852.

Notes

1. Among the reasons cited by the Ministry for the creation of an official cultural canon are that these works 'serve as a compass showing the directions and milestones in Denmark's long and complex cultural history', 'give us reference points and awareness of what is special about Danes and Denmark in an ever more globalised world', and 'strengthen the sense of community by showing key parts of our common historical possessions'. Quoted in Chapter 4.1 of Peter Duelund, 'Denmark: Cultural Policy Profile', *Compendium: Cultural Policies and Trends in Europe* (2011), http://www.culturalpolicies.net/web/denmark.php [accessed 23 August 2011].

2. For example, among the nineteenth-century musical compositions selected for the Danish Cultural Canon is Niels W. Gade's cantata *Elverskud* (*Elf-Struck*, 1854), based on a Danish folk ballad about young Herr Oluf's ill-fated encounter with the Elf-King's daughter.

3. Erik Aschengreen, *The Beautiful Danger: Facets of the Romantic Ballet*, trans. Patricia N. McAndrew, vol. 58, Dance Perspectives (New York: Dance Perspectives Foundation, 1974), 44. See also Chapter 5 of the present volume.

4. Elisabeth Oxfeldt, *Nordic Orientalism: Paris and the Cosmopolitan Imagination 1800–1900* (Copenhagen: Museum Tusculanum Press, 2005), 12. Hans Christian Andersen's novel *O.T.: A Danish Romance* (1836), a critique of 1830s Danish society, illuminates the mixed feelings of admiration, envy, and rivalry that the Copenhagen bourgeoisie harboured toward Paris. In Chapter 28, Vilhelm's cousin Joachim has returned from Paris, and debates with his hosts the relative merits of the theatre in Paris versus that of Copenhagen. Joachim extols — among other things — the richness and splendour of the scenic designs in Parisian productions of *La Sylphide*, *Nathalie*, and other ballets, eventually declaring, 'Copenhagen should be the Paris of the North' (*Kjøbenhavn skulde være det nordiske Paris*). Hans Christian Andersen, *O.T.* (Borgen: Det danske Sprog- og Litteraturselskab, 1987), 159. The bleak realism of *O.T.* was unappealing to nineteenth-century Danish readers, yet Andersen wrote prophetically of his novel's enduring value: 'It is a description of our own time from 1829 to 1835 and is set in Denmark only. I think the fact that the writer describes what he knows, the environment where he lives, will be valuable and will give the work a particular interest. In future years, people will have a true picture of our time [...].' Quoted in Anna Harwell

Celenza, *Hans Christian Andersen and Music: The Nightingale Revealed* (Burlington, VT: Ashgate, 2005), 81.

5. Oxfeldt, *Nordic Orientalism*, 23.

6. August Bournonville, *My Theatre Life*, trans. Patricia N. McAndrew (Middletown, CT: Wesleyan University Press, 1979), 78–79.

7. Ibid., 68. Prior to rendering Taglioni's *La Sylphide* into the Danish *Sylphiden*, Bournonville had adapted other Parisian ballets, with mixed results: his *Søvngængersken* (1830) after Aumer's *La Somnambule* (1827) had enjoyed a resounding success, while his versions of *Les Pages du Duc de Vendôme* and *Paul et Virginie* had generated only a tepid response. The Danish poet Johan Ludvig Heiberg (1791–1860) had introduced the Parisian *vaudeville* to Copenhagen audiences in 1825, expertly balancing the French theatrical model with Danish language, popular songs, and subject matter.

8. Quoted in Tom Hubbard, 'European Reception of Scott's Poetry: Translation as the Front Line', in *The Reception of Sir Walter Scott in Europe*, ed. Murray Pittock (London, New York: Continuum, 2006), 269.

9. Oxfeldt, *Nordic Orientalism*, 28.

10. Ibid., 23.

11. Ibid., 25.

12. Sigurd Bernhard Hustvedt, *Ballad Criticism in Scandinavia and Great Britain during the Eighteenth Century* (New York: American-Scandinavian Foundation, 1916), 15–19. Among these folklorists, different theories were put forward regarding the precise origin of the shared ballads, despite general agreement on the clear connection between Scottish and Scandinavian traditions. See for example Sir Walter Scott, *Minstrelsy of the Scottish Border*, 2 vols. (Kelso: J. Ballantyne, 1802); Robert Jamieson, *Popular Ballads and Songs*, 2 vols. (Edinburgh: A. Constable, 1806); John Finlay, *Scottish Historical and Romantic Ballads*, 2 vols. (Edinburgh: J. Ballantyne, 1808); Werner H. Abrahamson, Rasmus Nyerup, and Knud Lyne Rahbek, *Udvalgte Danske Viser fra Middelalderen* [Selected Danish Ballads from the Middle Ages], 5 vols. (Copenhagen: J.F. Schultz, 1812–14); Henry Weber, Robert Jamieson, and Sir Walter Scott, *Illustrations of Northern Antiquities* (Edinburgh: J. Ballantyne, 1814); Erik Gustaf Geijer and Arvid August Afzelius, *Svenska Folk-Visor från Forntiden* [Swedish Folk Ballads from Ancient Times], 3 vols. (Stockholm: Strinnholm and Häggström, 1814–16); Allan Cunningham, *The Songs of Scotland*, 4 vols. (London: J. Taylor, 1825); George Borrow, *Romantic Ballads* (London: J. Taylor, 1826); William Motherwell, *Minstrelsy, Ancient and Modern* (Glasgow: J. Wylie, 1827); Adolph Ivar Arwidsson, *Svenska Fornsånger* [Ancient Swedish Songs], 3 vols. (Stockholm: P.A. Norstedt, 1834–42); Svend Grundtvig, *Engelske og Skotske Folkeviser* [English and Scottish Folk Ballads], 4 vols. (Copenhagen: Wahlske Boghandling, 1842–46); Svend Grundtvig et al., eds., *Danmarks gamle Folkeviser*, 12 vols. (Copenhagen: Samfundet til den danske Literaturs Fremme, 1853–1976); William and Mary Howitt, *Literature and Romance of Northern Europe*, 2 vols. (London: Colburn, 1852); Magnus Brostrup Landstad, *Norske Folkeviser* [Norwegian Folk Ballads] (Christiania: Tönsberg, 1853); Francis James Child, *English and Scottish Ballads*, 8 vols. (Boston: Little, Brown, & Co., 1857–59); R.C. Alexander Prior, *Ancient Danish Ballads*, 3 vols. (London, Edinburgh: Williams and Norgate, 1860).

13. The folklorist David Buchan gives particular attention to the connection between Scottish and Scandinavian supernatural enchantment ballads. See for example David Buchan, 'Talerole Analysis and Child's Supernatural Ballads', in *The Ballad and Oral Literature*, ed. Joseph Harris (Cambridge, MA: Harvard University Press, 1991), 60–77; David Buchan, 'Ballads of Otherworld Beings', in *The Good People: New Fairylore Essays*, ed. Peter Narváez (New York: Garland, 1991), 142–54.

14. Jørgen Erik Nielsen, '"His pirates had foray'd on Scottish hill": Scott in Denmark with an Overview of his Reception in Norway and Sweden', in *The Reception of Sir Walter Scott in Europe*, ed. Murray Pittock (New York, London: Continuum, 2006), 255. Even Scott's name was worth literary gold, as evinced by the case of the spurious *Lord Sydenham, Historisk Roman af Walter Scotts efterladte Papirer* (*Lord Sydenham, Historical novel from the posthumous papers of Walter Scott*, 1835), purportedly translated by an 'S.J. Bang'. In reality, *Lord Sydenham* was an 1831 translation of Lee Gibbons's novel *The Cavalier*. It can be inferred that four years later, following low sales of this translation, the publisher hoped to sell more copies by fabricating a new title and attributing the book to Scott and a

fictitious translator. Ibid., 254.

15. Murray Pittock, 'Scott and the European Nationalities Question', in *The Reception of Sir Walter Scott in Europe*, ed. Murray Pittock (New York, London: Continuum, 2006), 9.

16. Adaptations of *Ivanhoe* included the play *Tempelherre-Retten* (The Templars' Court, 1824) and the opera *Tempelherren og Jødinden* (The Templar and the Jewess, 1834), both German works translated into Danish. *Pigen ved Søen* (The Lady of the Lake, 1828), Heiberg's translation of Rossini's opera *La donna del lago* (1819), was mounted at the Royal Theatre in honour of the King's birthday on 29 January 1829. In addition, Hans Christian Andersen wrote libretti for two Scott operas: *Bruden fra Lammermoor* (The Bride of Lammermoor, 1832, with music by Bredal) and *Festen paa Kenilworth* (The Celebration at Kenilworth, 1836, with music by Weyse). Copenhagen audiences had another opportunity to see the tragedy of Scott's ill-fated bride in the 1842–43 season, when an Italian opera company performed Donizetti's *Lucia di Lammermoor* at the Court Theatre. Nielsen, 'Scott in Denmark', 264.

17. Regarding the Danish appreciation of Scott's picturesque writing, Nielsen notes that Adam Oehlenschläger described Scott's works as 'historical portraits' (*historiske Portrætter*) in his treatise 'Om det Musikalske, det Philophiske, det Maleriske og det Historiske i Poesien' (On the Musical, the Philosophical, the Picturesque, and the Historic in Poetry, 1833). Ibid., 257.

18. Quoted in ibid., 260.

19. On the 'wild women' in Scott's novels, see Margaret Bruzelius, 'Women – Wild and Otherwise', in *Romancing the Novel: Adventure from Scott to Sebald* (Lewisburg, PA: Bucknell University Press, 2007), 111–28. Bruzelius notes the following character traits shared by these women (traits that apply not only to Madge Wildfire of Scott's *The Heart of Midlothian*, but also to Madge of Bournonville's *Sylphiden*): 'These women are dispossessed members of the lower classes, frequently half-crazed or otherwise maimed, and are often felt to have supernatural powers, especially second sight. They figure as guides for the hero. It is their detailed knowledge of the exotic landscape that allows the hero access to the generative space whose secret he must learn.' Ibid., 117.

20. Since the name of James's fiancée is spelled 'Effy' rather than 'Effie' in Bournonville's 1836 libretto, I use the spelling 'Effy' to refer specifically to the Effy of the Danish *Sylphiden*, as opposed to the Effie of the French *La Sylphide* and of Scott's *The Heart of Midlothian*.

21. An example of Danish critical acclaim for Scott's realistic evocation of the historical past can be found in eight anonymous reviews that appeared from 1821 through 1827 in *Dansk Litteratur-Tidende*. Nielsen, 'Scott in Denmark', 256.

22. Hubbard, 'European Reception of Scott's Poetry', 275.

23. These intuitions of geographic similarities between Scotland and Scandinavia are in fact justified: geological evidence indicates that Scotland provides an offshore 'missing link' between upper and lower Scandinavian rock sequences. In other words, Scotland at one time lay in between southern and northern Scandinavia as part of the same landmass. See R.O. Greiling and A.G. Smith, 'The Dalradian of Scotland: Missing Link Between the Vendian of Northern and Southern Scandinavia?,' *Physics and Chemistry of the Earth, Part A: Solid Earth and Geodesy* 25, no. 5 (2000): 495–98.

24. 'A native of northern Jutland, a region which, like the heaths of Scotland, is known for its harsh and rugged terrain, Blicher was captivated by Ossian's bleak and barren landscapes. Indeed, the inspiration Blicher derived from Ossian was as much an identification with a panorama as with an ancient bard or culture. Blicher used Ossian's austere landscapes as fuel for his own work, and in so doing, developed a literary style which enabled him to create illustrative descriptions of Jutland's dark and untamed qualities.' Anna Harwell Celenza, '*Efterklange af Ossian*: The Reception of James Macpherson's *Poems of Ossian* in Denmark's Literature, Art, and Music', *Scandinavian Studies* 70, no. 3 (1998): 368. Kenneth Olwig has even suggested that Steensen-Blicher turned to Ossian for the scenic just as much as for the historic or lyric. See Kenneth Olwig, 'Place, Society, and the Individual in the Authorship of St. St. Blicher', in *Omkring Blicher 1974*, ed. Felix Nørgaard (Copenhagen: Gyldendal, 1974). The same might be argued for Blicher's subsequent affinity for the novels of Sir Walter Scott, though Blicher also shared Scott's interest in using local dialects, legends, and traditions to lend verisimilitude to his fictional works. Jørgen Erik Nielsen reminds us that the desire to explore regional folklore was 'in the air' in the nineteenth century, yet acknowledges that Blicher's short story 'Fjorten Dage i Jylland' (Fourteen Days in Jutland) shows the influence of Scott's novels.

with parallels to *The Antiquary* and *Guy Mannering*. Nielsen, 'Scott in Denmark', 259.

25. '*Jylland er dog den meest romantiske Deel af Danmark! Jeg har ret faaet Interesse for det Land, siden jeg læste Steen-Blichers Noveller. Jeg synes, det maa have meget tilfælles med de skotske Lavlande! og der er jo Zigeunere?*' Andersen, *O.T.*, 17. Vilhelm's association of Gypsies with Jutland is likely an attempt to characterise the region as wild, even dangerous, through stereotypes about the Roma people: earlier in the chapter, Vilhelm tells Otto, 'I should like to see the North Sea, but the devil might live there!' Persecution of Jutland's Roma was contemporaneous with the publication of *O.T.*: in November of 1835, there had been a 'Gypsy hunt' in Jutland that massacred over two hundred and sixty Roma. See David M. Crowe, 'The Roma Holocaust', in *The Holocaust's Ghost: Writings on Art, Politics, Law and Education*, ed. F.C. DeCoste and Bernard Schwartz (Edmonton: University of Alberta Press, 2000), 182.

26. 'Even from the oldest times, connections, both of a warlike and peaceful nature, had existed between Scotland and the opposite shores of Scandinavia. The old Sagas, for instance, bear witness that the Danish king Frode's daughter, Ulfhilde, was married to 'the founder of the Scottish kingdom'; and that the Danish prince Amleth (Hamlet) married the Scotch queen Hermuntrude. From Denmark, moreover, and particularly from Jutland, many colonists afterwards emigrated to the Scotch Lowlands, whose coasts were, besides, plundered by the Danish Vikings.' Jens Jakob Asmussen Worsaae, *An Account of the Danes and Norwegians in England, Scotland, and Ireland* (London: J. Murray, 1852), 196. Worsaae's *Account* was the result of his 1846–47 travels in Britain at the behest of King Christian VIII of Denmark. According to Worsaae, King Christian VIII had been convinced of the importance of this task by the efforts of two British noblemen, the Duke of Sutherland and his brother Lord Francis Egerton (later the Earl of Ellesmere), whose letters to the Royal Society of Northern Antiquities promised that a Danish archaeologist who visited Scotland would be welcomed with 'all possible assistance, especially in Sutherland, a district so rich in Scandinavian antiquities.' ibid., vii.

27. Ibid., 204–05.

28. Ibid., 201–02. See also George Tobias Flom, *Scandinavian Influence on Southern Lowland Scotch: A Contribution to the Study of the Linguistic Relations of English and Scandinavian*, Columbia University Germanic Studies (New York: Columbia University Press, 1900).

29. Abrahamson, Nyerup, and Rahbek, *Udvalgte Danske Viser*, V, 12–16. The previously described Danish interest in Sir Walter Scott might have stemmed in part from a perception of the author as a kindred spirit, due to his collection of folk ballads. Rahbek, a translator of several Scott works who was drawn to the history and folklore of both Scotland and Scandinavia, sent Scott a copy of *Udvalgte Danske Viser*; in his response of 30 June 1822, Scott informed Rahbek that he also had Peder Syv's 1695 edition of Danish ballads in his possession, but that he still needed to learn Danish to properly appreciate these collections. Although Scott apparently did not devote much time to this task, he did seem to have a genuine interest in Scandinavian history and folk culture. Nielsen, 'Scott in Denmark', 253–54. See also Paul Robert Leeder, 'Scott and Scandinavian Literature: the Influence of Bartholin and Others', *Smith College Studies in Modern Languages* 2 (1920): 8–57.

30. Robert Jamieson, *Popular Ballads and Songs*, vol. II (Edinburgh: A. Constable, 1806), 87. Quoted in Abrahamson, Nyerup, and Rahbek, *Udvalgte Danske Viser*, V, 12. Jamieson seems to have equated the Cimbri with the Jutes (identified in Bede's *Ecclesiastical History of the English People* as invading England along with the Saxons and Angles following the Roman withdrawal), or may have simply used the term 'Cimbric' for any people originating from the Jutland peninsula: 'The Cimbric adventurers, who possessed themselves of a great part of England soon after the departure of the Romans, brought with them all the appendages of royal and feudal state (if such a term may be allowed) in their own country. Among these, the Scald, or Bard, was not the least considerable. To the poetry introduced by them, much was probably added, and much, that was becoming obsolete, revived, by the various Scandinavian intruders, who infested Britain some centuries after. "The North Countrie", the cradle, nursery, and sanctuary of ballad poetry, was, from particular circumstances, more especially liable to this influence.' Jamieson, *Popular Ballads and Songs*, II, 88–89.

31. Abrahamson, Nyerup, and Rahbek, *Udvalgte Danske Viser*, V, 10.

32. Sir Walter Scott, 'The Fairies of Popular Superstition', in *Minstrelsy of the Scottish Border* (Kelso: J. Ballantyne, 1802), 168.

33. Ibid., 213. Scott attributes this variation in part to a difference in landscape: '[...] we should naturally attribute a less malicious disposition, and a less frightful appearance, to the fays who glide by moon-light, through the oaks of Windsor, than to those who haunt the solitary heaths and lofty mountains of the North.' Ibid.

34. Ibid., 214.

35. Ibid., 219.

36. August Bournonville, *Sylphiden: Romantisk Ballet in to Akter* (Copenhagen: J.H. Schubothe, 1836), 3. '*Emnet, taget af en Skotsk Ballade, er første Gang blevet behandlet som Ballet af Taglioni, til Musik af Schneitzhoëffer*' (The subject, taken from a Scottish ballad, was first treated as a ballet by Taglioni, to music by Schneitzhoeffer).

37. Erik Aschengreen, 'The Beautiful Danger: Facets of the Romantic Ballet', *Dance Perspectives* 58 (1974): 43.

38 'The singer Nourrit has written *La Sylphide* [...]'; 'He [Nourrit] wrote the libretto for *La Sylphide* [...]'; '[...] I must mention as one of my most successful compositions *La Sylphide*, whose original plan and libretto were conceived by the singer Adolphe Nourrit.' Bournonville, *My Theatre Life*, 20, 42, 78.

39. Nielsen, 'Scott in Denmark', 255.

40. James H. Moreira, 'Narrative Expectations and Domestic Space in the Telemark Ballads', *Scandinavian Studies* 73, no. 3 (2001): 331.

41. This pairing of human male-supernatural female does not by any means dominate the enchantment ballad tradition: human females were also susceptible to the temptations and perils of the Otherworld. Female protagonists could fall victim to water sprites, as in the ballad '*Nøkkens Svig*' ('The Nix's Deceit', *Danmarks gamle Folkeviser* [DgF] 39), mountain trolls, or dwarves, as in the ballad '*Jomfruen og Dværgekongen*' ('The Maiden and the Dwarf King', *DgF* 37). For synopses of these ballads, see Lanae H. Isaacson, 'Dramatic Discourse in the Scandinavian Ballad', *Scandinavian Studies* 64, no. 1 (1992): 76–77.

42. See for example Sections 45 ('The Dangerous Encounter') and 46 ('The Fairy Lover') of Reimund Kvideland and Henning K. Sehmsdorf, eds., *Scandinavian Folk Belief and Legend* (Minneapolis: University of Minnesota Press 1988), 207–22.

43. '*Elverpigerne dandsede allerede paa Elverhøi, og de dandsede med Langschawl vævet af Taage og Maaneskin, og det seer nydelig ud for dem, der synes om den Slags.*' (The elf maidens were already dancing on Elves' Hill, and they danced with long shawls woven from haze and moonlight, which looks pretty to those who like such things.) Erik Dal, ed. *H.C. Andersens Nye Eventyr og Historier*, H.C. Andersens Eventyr (Copenhagen: Hans Reitzel, 1964), 80.

44. John Lindow, 'Supernatural Others and Ethnic Others: A Millennium of World View', *Scandinavian Studies* 67, no. 1 (1995): 23–27. Markers of animal-human hybridity on supernatural women are not exclusive to Scandinavian folklore, but can also be found in legends such as the Melusine tales, among others.

45. Ibid., 26.

46. Gunnar Granberg, *Skogsrået i yngre nordisk folktradition*, Skrifter utgivna av Gustav Adolfs Akademien för Folklivsforskning (Uppsala: Lundequistska bokhandeln, 1935), 245. Translated and quoted in Lindow, 'Supernatural Others and Ethnic Others', 20. See also Kvideland and Sehmsdorf, *Scandinavian Folk Belief and Legend*, 215–16.

47. Janice D. LaPointe-Crump, 'Birth of a Ballet: August Bournonville's *A Folk Tale*, 1854' (Ph.D. diss., Texas Woman's University, 1980), 181.

48. Isaacson, 'Dramatic Discourse in the Scandinavian Ballad', 84.

49. Lindow, 'Supernatural Others and Ethnic Others', 27. Of course, this association between exceptional ability and the supernatural is found not only in Scandinavian folk belief, but in other traditions as well, pointing to a widespread, cross-cultural bias against the unusual. Suspicion of musical virtuosity is perhaps best exemplified by the mythos surrounding nineteenth-century violinist Niccolò Paganini, rumoured to have acquired his talent from the Devil. For an in-depth exploration of the Paganini myth, see Maiko Kawabata, 'Virtuosity, the Violin, the Devil...What Really Made Paganini "Demonic"?' *Current Musicology* 83 (2007): 85–108. Similarly, Norwegian violin virtuoso Ole Bull was associated with the *nøkk*, the fiddle- or harp-playing water sprite. H.C.

Andersen often compared Bull's playing to that of the *nøkk*, and it may have inspired Andersen's libretto for the opera *Nøkken* (*The Water Sprite*, 1853). Celenza, *Hans Christian Andersen and Music*, 172. The music of the *nøkk* was also closely linked to dancing: upon hearing it, villagers could be compelled to dance themselves to death, and even inanimate objects would join in the dance. Since the *nøkk* took on several qualities of the Devil, it is no coincidence that *nøkk* or 'nix' became an epithet for Satan in the English language ('Old Nick'). Kvideland and Sehmsdorf, *Scandinavian Folk Belief and Legend*, 253–55.

50. Quoted in Kvideland and Sehmsdorf, *Scandinavian Folk Belief and Legend*, 215. Originally collected by Olav Nordbø and published in Nordbø's *Segner og sogur frå Bøherad* (1945). The motif of *hulder*-song is prominent in Arne Garborg's poetic cycle *Haugtussa* (1895), eight selections of which were set as a song cycle by Edvard Grieg. See Kristin Rygg, 'Mystification through Musicalization and Demystification through Music: the Case of *Haugtussa*', in *Cultural Functions of Intermedial Exploration*, ed. Erik Hedling (New York: Rodopi, 2002), 87–102.

51. Kvideland and Sehmsdorf, *Scandinavian Folk Belief and Legend*, 214. Sally Banes has argued that *La Sylphide* is a ballet enmeshed in nineteenth-century bourgeois concerns, namely, issues of whom one should marry and even the institution of marriage itself. See Sally Banes, *Dancing Women: Female Bodies on Stage* (New York: Routledge, 1998), 12–23; Sally Banes and Noël Carroll, 'Marriage and the Inhuman: *La Sylphide*'s Narratives of Domesticity and Community', in *Rethinking the Sylph: New Perspectives on the Romantic Ballet*, ed. Lynn Garafola (Hanover, NH: Wesleyan University Press, 1997), 91–105. Yet these often xenophobic concerns with endogamy were shared by rural classes, as evinced by numerous folk ballads that warn against imprudent unions with supernatural Others — and, by extension, ethnic Others. See Timothy R. Tangherlini, 'From Trolls to Turks: Change and Continuity in Danish Legend Tradition', *Scandinavian Studies* 67, no. 1 (1995): 32–62; Lindow, 'Supernatural Others and Ethnic Others.'

52. Moreira, 'Narrative Expectations and Domestic Space', 326.

53. Nineteenth-century folklorist Frances James Child recognised 'Elveskud' as analogous to 'Clerk Colvill' (Child 42), a British ballad about a young man's fatal encounter with a seductive mermaid. See Child, *English and Scottish Ballads*, I, 310–12 and 403–06. Furthermore, the concept of being shot or struck by elves was shared by Danish and Scottish folk culture: the term 'elf-shot' had appeared in Scotland and northern England in the late sixteenth century to describe pain or disease inflicted by elves. See Alaric Hall, 'Getting Shot of Elves: Healing, Witchcraft and Fairies in the Scottish Witchcraft Trials', *Folklore* 116 (2005): 19–36; Scott, 'The Fairies of Popular Superstition', 214. The 'Elveskud' legend also appeared in Johann Gottfried von Herder's *Stimmen der Völker in Liedern* (1778–79) in the German translation 'Erlkönigs Tochter', which later served as the inspiration for Goethe's 'Der Erlkönig.' See Peter Russell, *The Themes of the German Lied from Mozart to Strauss*, vol. 84, Studies in the History and Interpretation of Music (Lewiston: Edwin Mellen, 2002), 240.

54. Moreira, 'Narrative Expectations and Domestic Space', 344–45.

55. See Chapter 5, 'Danish Ballad as Opera Libretto: Friedrich Kuhlau, *Elverhøj* (1828, J.L. Heiberg)' in Dan Shore, 'The Emergence of Danish National Opera, 1779–1846' (dissertation, CUNY, 2008), 119–58.

56. The significance of the *style féerique*, 'spectral' timbres, and the *scherzo fantastique* genre in nineteenth-century fairy music as a confluence between folklore and advances in natural science has recently been expounded in Francesca Brittan, 'Miniaturism, Nostalgia, and Musical Microscopy: the Fairy Fantastic in Nineteenth-Century France' (paper presented at the American Musicological Society Annual Meeting, Nashville, November 2008). See also Francesca Brittan, 'On Microscopic Hearing: Fairy Magic, Natural Science, and the *Scherzo fantastique*', *Journal of the American Musicological Society* 64, no.3 (2011): 527–600.

57. Abrahamson, Nyerup, and Rahbek, *Udvalgte Danske Viser*, I, 237–40; Grundtvig et al., *Danmarks gamle Folkeviser*, II, 444–45.

58. Bournonville, *My Theatre Life*, 210.

59. J.M. Thiele, *Danmarks Folkesagn*, 2 vols., vol. II (Copenhagen: Reitzel, 1843), 230–31.

60. Lindow, 'Supernatural Others and Ethnic Others'. 26. See also Tangherlini, 'From Trolls to Turks.' Drawing on the work of folklorists Carl Wilhelm von Sydow, Alan Dundes, Beverly Crane, and Donald Ward, Tangherlini examines how the dangers portrayed in the Scandinavian super-

natural ballads have been updated in the contemporary Danish urban legend. Troll women have become girls from Arab countries or Greenland, a country even more peripheralised than Denmark. Tangherlini writes, 'The perceptions of the Other, the object of conflict, reveals the cultural views of *where* the threat comes from. The actions of the Other in such conflict reveal the cultural views of *what* is threatened' (33).

61. See the original libretto, translated by Patricia N. McAndrew, Appendix 3 of this volume.

62. The visual parallel between the Sylph and the elf maiden is particularly noticeable in Per Morten Abrahamsen's recent photographic interpretation of *Sylphiden* for the Royal Danish Ballet's 2005 Bournonville calendar: January's photograph features a circle of eleven white-clad sylphs dancing by a pond in a misty, tree-framed meadow, an image instantly reminiscent of Blommér's *Meadow Elves*.

63. See Sandra Noll Hammond, Chapter 3 of this volume.

64. The violin is the instrument most closely associated with supernatural music in Scandinavian folklore, although the ubiquity of the violin as a solo instrumental voice in nineteenth-century opera and ballet scores makes this perhaps only a happy coincidence.

65. '*Den elle-kone boede sig ude ved aa. [...] Ude ved aa, vel femten vintre lagde hun det i traa, femten vintre og end et aar. [...] Og end et aar: alt hvor hun skulde Hr Bøsmer faa.*' (The elf-queen lived [settled herself] out by the river. Out by the river, indeed fifteen winters she laid in desire, fifteen winters and still a year. And still a year: ever [in the place] where she would get Herr Bøsmer.) Quoted in Sigurd Kværndrup, *Den Østnordiske Ballade – Oral Teori og Tekstanalyse: Studier i Danmarks gamle Folkeviser* (Copenhagen: Museum Tusculanum, 2006), 552.

66. Bournonville, *My Theatre Life*, 79. These comments were equally directed at the ballet *Sylphiden* itself, since Bournonville was dogged by accusations of plagiarism. Bournonville claimed that the Sylph, as described above, 'has been for me the same as she was for James'.

67. This dual symbolism of the tartan scarf has also been noted in Banes and Carroll, 'Marriage and the Inhuman', 100–01.

68. '*Jeg ikke tør, jeg ikke maa: i morgen skal mit brøllup staa.*' Version B in Grundtvig et al., *Danmarks gamle Folkeviser*, II, 114.

69. Ibid., 104.

70. Sally Banes has noted that both the Sylph and Madge are symbolically associated with thresholds: '[...] the Sylphide has a special relationship to the apertures of the house (the chimney, the window, the door), and [...] Madge, too, is first sighted at the hearth. Both are liminal figures, who straddle cultural boundaries — inside/outside, natural/supernatural.' Banes, *Dancing Women*, 19.

71. Moreira, 'Narrative Expectations and Domestic Space', 333.

72. Rodney Stenning Edgecombe, 'On the Limits of Genre: Some Nineteenth-Century Barcaroles', *Nineteenth-Century Music* 24, no. 3 (2001): 259.

73. Lawrence Kramer, 'Musical Form and *Fin-de-siècle* Sexuality', in *Music as Cultural Practice, 1800–1900* (Los Angeles: University of California Press, 1990), 142. Quoted in Suzanne Fagence Cooper, 'The Liquefaction of Desire: Music, Water and Femininity in Victorian Aestheticism' in *Women: A Cultural Review* 20, no. 2 (2009): 189.

74. Aschengreen, 'The Beautiful Danger', 44.

75. This seems to indicate a disconnect between theatrical stagings of folklore subjects and the original, often tragic narratives found in oral tradition and written records. The somewhat sterilised transmission of folklore through the nineteenth-century Danish theatre might be likened to present-day American animated feature films such as Disney's *The Little Mermaid* (1989) in which H.C. Andersen's mermaid is not dissolved into sea foam, but happily reunited with her prince and allowed to keep her human form.

76. Bournonville, *My Theatre Life*, 273. As mentioned previously, the term *hulder* can be used in a general sense to mean any supernatural woman with seductive powers; this is how Bournonville uses it here.

77. Ebbe Mørk, 'A Friendship: Andersen and Bournonville', in *The Royal Danish Ballet and Bournonville* (Copenhagen: Ministry of Foreign Affairs of Denmark, 1979), 32.

78. Sandra Noll Hammond, Chapter 3 in this volume.

79. Bournonville, *My Theatre Life*, 78.

80. Ibid., 68. See note 7 above.

Chapter 7

The Body that Sings

Ole Nørlyng

'The Dance can, with the aid of music, rise to the heights of poetry.'
— August Bournonville, Choreographic credo[1]

'The idea of dancing is inseparable from music, and in her nature Terpsichore embodies both rhythm and movement.'
— August Bournonville, *My Theatre Life*[2]

Given August Bournonville's great innate musicality, it seems likely that he could just as easily have become a musician as a ballet master. For his very understanding of dance depended on music, which – be it Dionysian or Apollonian – he regarded as the force that generates and governs the dance. Moreover, August Bournonville, as a Romantic artist, fully acknowledged music as a *følelsernes vidunderland*, a wonderland of feeling and sentiment, though which the inexpressible – emotional intensity, the power of sensuousness and the irrational nature of life – could be expressed. Music begins where words stop, a very important point for a choreographer. Bournonville himself put it this way in his first piece of writing, 'New Year's Gift for Dance Lovers' (Copenhagen, 1829): 'Music is the most excellent organ of imagination.'[3] He later echoed this sentiment in his memoirs, *My Theatre Life*: 'With the help of music, dance can rise to the heights of poetry.'[4] He noted, further, that dance is 'the body that sings'.[5]

Bournonville fully understood the vital role that music played in Romantic ballet: each score was created to fill the particular needs of a ballet, its music illustrating and supporting the drama. Given its importance, Bournonville chose to include a detailed discussion of ballet music – as well as the collaboration between choreographer and composer – in his memoir, *My Theatre Life*.[6] We can read, for instance, the following description:

When I have completed my libretto, I set it aside for a while. Then, if I read through it again with the same interest and every picture stands clear before me, I consider it ready for composition. I turn to the music composer, who receives a separate outline for each scene that makes up a musical number; he then comes to an agreement with me as to rhythm and character. Usually, by means of gestures and *pas*, I manage to give him a rough idea of what is to be performed; I improvise a melody to it; sometimes this melody contains a useful theme, which may be picked up, shaped, and modulated.[7]

Bournonville had seen the ballet *La Sylphide* in Paris, where he bought a copy of the libretto by Adolphe Nourrit and Filippo Taglioni. He encountered a problem, however, when he decided to produce his own version of the work: a lack of the funds necessary to buy Jean-Madeleine Schneitzhoeffer's score.[8] Thus he sought a suitable musical collaborator in Denmark who could not only furnish the necessary dance rhythms for the various *pas* and dramatic music to illustrate the extensive mime, but also create a musical universe that encompassed the floating poetry of the sylph, the grotesque eeriness of the witch, and the everyday reality of the happy Scotsman.

This was a demanding task, especially in the 1830s, a time when ballet music in Denmark was usually arranged and pieced together from pre-existing works.[9] This custom had been taken up in Denmark when the collaboration between the choreographer Vincenzo Galeotti and the composer/music director Claus Schall had ended with Galeotti's death in 1816.[10] Philip Ludwig Keck's arranged score for the ballet *Faust* (1832), Bournonville's first truly ambitious attempt at an original choreography, exemplifies this unoriginal – if practical – musical custom.[11] Far more newly composed music can be found in the scores of the idyllic ballet *Tyrolerne* (*The Tyroleans*, 1835) – which still, however, included three excerpts from Rossini's *Guillaume Tell* and *Le Comte Ory* – and the large-scale national-historical ballet *Waldemar* (1835), both composed by Johan F. Frohlich (1806-1860) the violinist, composer and conductor who served as Bournonville's house composer until 1845.[12]

These important collaborations with Frohlich, however, did not prevent Bournonville, an able talent scout, from seeking out other musical partners. For instance, during his tenure as ballet master in 1830 up to his departure from the dancing ranks in 1848, Bournonville worked with many different composers, including a total of eight on two ballets alone, *Fantasiens Ø eller Fra Kinas Kyst* (*The Isle of Fantasy or From the Shore of China*, 1838) and *Napoli* (1842) (see Table 7.1). Some of the important musical partnerships he began during these early years continued, notably those with Johan Peter Emilius Hartmann (1805–1900) and Niels W. Gade (1817–1890), the two most important Danish composers from about 1830 to 1890. Bournonville's partnership with Hartmann and Gade culminated in *Et Folkesagn* (*A Folk Tale*, 1854), for which Gade composed the first and third acts, and Hartmann the second. In addition, Bournonville's later collabora-

Table 7.1. Composers of two Bournonville ballets

Title	Composers
Fantasiens Ø eller Fra Kinas Kyst (*The Isle of Fantasy or From the Shore of China*, 1838)	I. F. Bredal J.P.E. Hartmann Edvard Helsted H. S. Løvenskiold H. S. Paulli L. Zinck
Napoli, 1842	Niels W. Gade Edvard Helsted Hans Christian Lumbye H. S. Paulli

tions with Hartmann resulted in several excellent scores, the most important of which are for the great Nordic mythological ballets *Valkyrien* (*The Valkyrie*, 1861) and *Trymsquiden* (*The Lay of Thrym*, 1868) and the historical ballet *Arcona* (1875). One could make the case that Bournonville was the most important musical employer in Denmark from 1830 to 1877.[13]

Sylphiden and Løvenskiold

The première of *Waldemar* was barely over before the thirty-year-old ballet master sought out a twenty-year-old nobleman, Herman Severin Løvenskiold (1815-1870), to discuss the music for his forthcoming ballet, *Sylphiden*. Løvenskiold had been born a baron in Holden, Norway. His father, heir to the Holden Ironworks, was a capable amateur musician, and his mother was not only a music lover but also a composer of some experience.[14] Visitors told of the lively artistic atmosphere that pervaded the Løvenskiold family's daily life, and of their passionate pursuit of music. The family's acquaintances included the north-German immigrant Friedrich Kuhlau (1786-1832), who had established himself as the most important composer of dramatic music for the Royal Theatre in Copenhagen. In 1827, Løvenskiold's first composition was published: a variation for piano in the style of Kuhlau based on a theme from Carl Maria von Weber's *Preciosa*.

In 1829, the family moved to Denmark, where the fourteen-year-old Løvenskiold was drawn to the theatre. A production of *Don Giovanni* was a revelation to him, and Løvenskiold started studying music seriously. His teachers included the composer Peter Caspar Krossing (1793–1838) and the bassoonist and organist Frantz Jacob August Keyper (1792–1859), a member of the orchestra of the Royal Theatre. In 1832, Løvenskiold enrolled in Giuseppe Siboni's music academy, where he studied music theory with J. P. E. Hartmann. Quickly winning a name for himself as a pianist, he played pri-

7.1. Herman Severin Løvenskiold (1815-1870). Drawing by L.A. Smith, 1843. The Museum of National History, Frederiksborg Castle, Hillerød. By permission.

vately for the King and Queen, and in 1835 published a set of *Hofbaldanse* (Court Ball Dances), which demonstrated both his feeling for dance music and his close connection with the court.

We do not know precisely how the contact between Bournonville and Løvenskiold was established, nor do we know details of their collaboration, but in *My Theatre Life*, Bournonville tells of 'repeated requests that I try a young musical talent well suited for this genre.'[15] And from Løvenskiold we know that in April 1836 he had nearly completed the composition of *Sylphiden* and that Bournonville was very satisfied with it.[16] We know, too, that Løvenskiold composed the music for *Sylphiden* over about a five-month period, carrying out the instrumentation of the score in the summer of 1836.

In the days leading up to *Sylphiden's* first performance, the orchestra was busy rehearsing the music for the ballet and its extensive overture. A letter from Løvenskiold to Hartmann, dated 26 November 1836 – two days before the première – tells us that Bournonville had found the harmonisation of a theme in the overture rather forced and unnatural; Løvenskiold (who was bedridden) asked Hartmann in the letter to correct and smooth out the harmony in question.[17] That Bournonville would take notice of a harmonic infelicity in this piece of instrumental music is a sign of his attention to detail and his dedication to the musical aspect of ballet.

From Bournonville's *Posthumous Writings*, collected and edited by his daughter Charlotte and published in 1891, we can gain a sense of how he viewed the collaboration between choreographer and composer. He stresses that the two must be well acquainted with each other's art forms, and explains his practice of analysing the libretto scene by scene and then making suggestions to the composer about character and how long each scene should be. After a musical number was sketched out, either in response to a dramatic scene in the libretto or to underscore a purely danced section, Bournonville would hear it played on the piano. Then, if he decided to keep it, the number would be written out for two violins (for the *répétiteur*, or rehearsal score). 'In this way,' wrote Bournonville, 'the music is composed for *a written libretto*, and the ballet [the choreography] is created to follow the rhythms and melodies of the music. Thus do the two art forms of music and dance meld together to common effect.'[18]

Løvenskiold's *Sylphiden* – Layout and general description

Løvenskiold's music for *Sylphiden* consists of a long overture followed by two acts. (See Table 7.2.) The first act (as it is usually performed today) is divided into seven musical numbers; the second act has eight.

This score, however, has been subjected to significant revisions through the years.[19] Mime scenes as well as dance segments have been expunged, and new additions have been made. The most essential modifications to the first act are the jettisoning of the mime scene at No. 1 after the opening, the shortening of Act One No. 5 (*Pas d'Ecossaise*), and the elimination of the *pas de deux* of James and Effie in No. 6. Moreover, the Witch Scene has been shortened and the original *pas de deux* for James and the Sylphide in the

Table 7.2.
Løvenskiold's *Sylphiden*
Summary of Numbers

The score requires a full orchestra not atypical of Løvenskiold's day: 2 flutes, 2 oboes, 2 clarinets, 2 bassoons, 4 horns, 2 trumpets, 3 trombones, percussion, harp and strings.

This summary reflects the recordings made of this score in 1986 (conductor David Garforth, Royal Danish Orchestra) and 2005 (conductor Peter Ernst Lassen, Aalborg Sympony Orchestra).

Overture
Grave maestoso energico/ Andante con molto espressivo/ Allegro vivace e con spirito/ Con fuoco assai

ACT ONE

No. 1
Introduzione
Andante/ Allegro non tanto e grazioso/ Allegro molto vivace/
Allegro agitato/ Moderato/ Allegro vivo
 A mime scene immediately succeeding the introduzione in the original version, opening with an *Allegro agitato* and featuring a dialogue between Gurn and James, was removed — probably incrementally — in the nineteenth century.

No. 2
Effy's entrée
Andantino
 Short mime passages with melodramatic middle section. The music is in a Scottish folk style

No. 3
James, Effy and the Witch
Allegro/ Andantino (Effy solo) / Allegro con fuoco assai/ Andantino/ (the prediction or the fortunetelling scene)/ Meno Allegro
 A complex number in several tempi. Quotation of "Auld lang syne", Effy´s solo, musical portrayal of the Witch, the Fortunetelling Scene, lyrical *attacca* to

No. 4
James and the Sylphide
Andantino doloroso / Allegro vivo / Allegretto grazioso (solo of the sylph) /
Andantion/ Allegro con fuoco assai/ Allegro molto vivace.
 The Window Scene, which is a lyrical mime scene interspersed with vivid dance sections for the Sylph, *attacca* to

No. 5 **Pas d'Ecossaise** ["Scottish dance"]
Allegro vivace / meno (first male solo, Gurn) / Tempo di Marcia, con spirito (second male solo, James) / L'istesso tempo (Effy solo) / piu mosso
  Arrival of the guests; series of dance numbers

No. 6 **Pas de deux and Reel**
Moderato / Andante siciliano / Reel: Allegro
  Short *pas de deux* for James and Effy followed by a reel for the corps de ballet (The original pas de deux has been excised.)

No. 7
Finale
Andante / Allegro molto agitato / Presto/ Piu stretto/ marcato assai
  Finale, with melodramatic ending

ACT TWO

No. 1
The Witch Scene
Grave / Poco piu mosso/ Moderato/ Allegro con fuoco / Poco meno Allegro/ Allegro con fuoco assai
  Mime and action scene, with musical description of the demonic and grotesque.
  This scene has been shortened. Today it is customary to perform:
  Grave/ Poco piu mosse/ Poco meno Allegro/ Allegro con fuoco

No. 2 **James and the Sylphide in the forest** (or **"The Forest Scene"**)
Andante / Andantino / Andante amoroso/ Allegretto grazioso / Piu mosso/ Andante

  Lyrical mime scene and shorter dance sections.

  In the first production of 1836, this scene led to an extensive *pas de deux* between James and the Sylph (no. 3 in the original score).[1] It was omitted at the end of the 1837-38 season, and later gradually re-introduced and developed in the Divertissement (No. 4) that we know today, though this divertissement does not have a *pas de deux*.

  Tempi of the *pas de deux*
  Adagio / Alla polacca / Allegro grazioso / Allegretto / Alla polacca/ Coda Piu animato

No. 3 **The Sylphide calls the sylphs**
Allegro

No. 4 **Divertissement**
Strictly dance music.
Andante con molto espressione (the sylphs)

Piu vivo e con grazia (The Sylphide solo 1)
Allegretto (molto tenuto) (James, solo 1)
Allegro vivo e grazioso (the sylphs)
Piu lento (The Sylphide, solo 2)
Piu mosso (James, solo 2)
Coda (ensemble)

No. 5 James pursues the Sylphide
Allegro ben agitato / Allegro con fuoco

No. 6 Gurn, Effy and the Witch
Moderato / Allegro con fuoco / Moderato / Moderato / Allegro vivo
  Mime scene with use of melodies re-played from earlier in the drama.

No. 7 James and the Witch, the scarf
Allegro / Maestoso / Allegro con fuoco assai
  Action and mime music. Some of this music was first heard in the coda of
  the overture, where it pre-figured this scene.

No. 8 Finale
Andante tranquillo / Allegro vivo e agitato /Allegro con spirito e con fuoco
assai / Lagrimoso / Adagio / Andante /Allegro Air Ecossais / Grave maestoso
/ Allegro furioso / Andante / Grave e lugubre
  Complex number in several tempi, much use of reminiscence motifs.

[1] This original *pas de deux* was recorded for the first time by the Royal Danish
Orchestra, conducted by David Garforth, Chandos 1986. This performance
was later re-issued in 1991, 2001, 2004 Chandos 6546. See also the record-
ing, *Music to the Bournonville Ballets*, Performed by the Aaloborg Symphony
orchestra, directed by Ernst Lassen, Copenhagen: Danacord, 2005, CD.

Forest Scene (Act Two No. 2) has been omitted (though it was brought back
for the Peter Schaufuss version in London in 1979). The Divertissement in
Act Two (No. 4) has over the years developed to the larger dimension we
know today. (Please note: the actual numbering of the different sections of
the score has been fluid, and varies from source to source.)

The Overture
Before the curtain goes up, the orchestra evokes the atmosphere of the
drama in its entirety, and introduces us to important melodic motifs associated with the protagonists of the ballet.

  In the slow, rather long and very dark-coloured opening, marked *Grave
maestoso energico*, a quartet of horns evokes the loneliness of the Scottish
forest. The sound of the horn is crucial throughout the score as an acoustic
symbol of melancholy 'forest-loneliness' *(skovensomhed)*. The introduction

builds up striking contrasts between lyrical cello solos, dramatic *fortissimo tutti* passages, and other strong sound effects, including a grotesque dotted-rhythm motif – almost hobbling – denoting the characteristics of the Witch.

In the *Andante con molto expressione* the first real melody is introduced (Example 7.1). This phrase, played by the horn quartet and accompanied by

Example 7.1. Løvenskiold, *Sylphiden*, Overture: first melody

harp, is later connected with the death of the Sylphide. A subsequent descending minor third is a kind of lamentation motif, symbolising the disappearance of life – a much-used motif in the Romantic period. Also noteworthy in this section are the strong harmonic tension, chromatic passages, and expressive dissonances.

The main part of the overture, the *Allegro vivace e con spirito*, is in a simple sonata form with a principal and a secondary theme, recapitulation, and a dashing coda. The principal theme, brought in by the strings and then repeated by the woodwinds in the manner of Scottish bagpipes, is cheerful and rhythmically springy, almost capricious (Example 7.2). This melody is linked

Example 7.2. Løvenskiold, *Sylphiden*, Overture: principal theme

to the Sylphide and her joy in flying; it recurs several times as a motif in connection with her exhilaration and ability to tempt James.

After a short development, there comes (in the dominant key) a secondary theme recognisable as the Scottish folk tune 'Auld Lang Syne'. Indeed, in order to create local colour Løvenskiold used not only this melody – famous through its connection to Robert Burns's text 'Should auld acquaintance be forgot' (Example 7.3) – but also several other Scottish (or Scottish-sounding) tunes elsewhere in his score. These include the *ecossaise* heard in Act One No. 5 and in the Act Two Finale, perhaps an original tune in the Scottish style by Løvenskiold, and the Reel of Act One No. 6, which is a rather free improvisation on motifs of several authentic Scottish Strathspey reels, such as 'Miss Weddersburn's Reel' and 'Miss Hope's Strathspey'.[20]

Example 7.3. Løvenskiold, *Sylphiden*, Overture: secondary theme, recognisable as 'Auld Lang Syne'

Before proceeding further, it must be noted that the Scottish setting of this ballet reflected a Romantic craving for the exotic and the Nordic, and that Scotland has long served as this type of imaginative setting in literature, theatre and music. (See also Chapter 6 of this volume.) In Denmark the Scottish fashion was introduced to the visual arts by the painter Nicolai Abildgaard (1743–1809) as early as in the 1780s.[21] It grew as a result of the popularity of the novels of Walter Scott, and reached its peak in the 1830s. Indeed, two of Scott's novels were produced as operas at the Royal Theatre in Copenhagen: *Bruden fra Lammermoor* (*The Bride of Lammermoor*, 1832; H.C. Andersen, libretto; I.F. Bredal, music) and *Festen paa Kenilworth* (*Festival at Kenilworth*, 1836) (H.C. Andersen, libretto; C.E.F. Weyse, music). So the Danish audience, including the young Løvenskiold, was familiar with at least a theatrical Scotland.[22]

To return to the overture: its energetic string passages and striking use of syncopation reveal both Løvenskiold's inventiveness and his knowledge of Weber, Rossini, and other theatre music of the time. Actual development is kept to a minimum here, and after a repetition of the principal and secondary themes, the overture ends with an effective coda (*con fuoco assai – Vivace*) (Example 7.4). In this rather brilliant coda Løvenskiold shows the influence of Weber's *Der Freischütz*, an opera in the repertoire of the Royal Theatre at

Example 7.4. Løvenskiold, *Sylphiden*, Overture: theme from coda

the time. (Because the coda is later repeated in the scene featuring James, the Witch and Sylphide in the second act, it seems that its motif was meant to be associated with the bewitched scarf.)

The overture is a long and quite mature piece of orchestral music, one very effective for the theatre, for it points directly to the drama and the unhappy ending of the ballet. Thus, it is regrettable that over the years this overture has been considerably shortened when played in the theatre.[23]

The music for the ballet itself follows the typical approach to ballet music of that time in that it is divided clearly into two distinct styles, one for mime passages, and the other for dancing. For the mime passages, Løvenskiold composed narrative, illustrative music in open form (also known as 'through-composed form'). For the dancing, he wrote lively and closed-form dance music, often including repetition.[24] The mime music sometimes sounds like music for silent movies, with, for example, sudden loud notes, pauses, drum rolls, short snatches of melodies, imitations of natural sounds (wind and thunder, for example), and other programmatic effects. Dance music, on the other hand, is usually in even phrases, with danceable rhythms, and lacking in pauses or sudden changes.

The music for the dramatic passages has been more or less neglected, however, because it does not follow the rules of absolute, autonomous music. Lincoln Kirstein, in an article entitled 'Ballet and Music' in *The International Cyclopedia of Music and Musicians*, wrote the following words about the role of music in ballet, and indeed music as part of any stage-related genre, noting how it helps to convey the action.[25]

> Music written for theatre, that is, to accompany dance or sung action, has certain limitations not shared by other music. [...] Theatre-music is 'impure' and dependent on many extra-musical or arbitrary features of style, mood, and expression. It is 'occasional' music in so much that in the greater part it is created for specific theatrical occasions; it is illustrative in so much that it accentuates or clarifies specific dramatic or visual activities.[26]

In his *Posthumous Writings*, Bournonville discussed the role of music composed for ballet, pointing out its essential value:

> Music [for ballet], which for the uninitiated may seem to serve the ballet in a complementary role, can on closer examination be recognised as its very essence. Its melody and harmony give rise to mood and character, the rhythms determine the gesture, and a piece of music is produced, which somehow carries the words forth and helps considerably to express the meaning – indeed, to paint the whole situation.[27]

Løvenskiold, working closely with Bournonville, understood quite well the need for these extra-musical elements in the music (that is, elements which referred to characters, action, etc.). And from that standpoint his ballet-pantomime music is truly excellent.

Act One
To set the scene for the poetic opening tableau, there is a powerful harmonic

shift from the E major of the Overture to the E-flat major of the tableau. This
immediately imparts a mistily poetic atmosphere, which is emphasised by the
use of the elegiac minor-subdominant soon thereafter. The solo violin – the
instrument of the Sylphide – is then heard in this *Andante con molto gusto ed
espressione* (Example 7.5). This is the first musical characterisation of the
Sylphide, whose melody is distinguished by three important elements:

Example 7.5. Løvenskiold, *Sylphiden*, Act One No.1: violin solo characterising the Sylphide

a) the ascending scale starting from the fifth, leading to
b) the third, after which the melody goes on to
c) the sixth (either above or below)

When studying the melodies connected with the world of the sylphs and
the Sylphide herself, one finds these three elements again and again: for instance, in the principal theme of the main section of the Overture (Example
7.2), and in the melody accompanying the joyful dancing of the Sylphide – a
melody that later recurs in the Act One Window Scene. (In this Window
Scene, too, is an *Allegro grazioso* solo for the Sylphide with the same characteristics.) These features are also found in the opening of the Forest Scene of
Act Two (this time played by the horn) and in the original *pas de deux* for
James and the Sylphide. These similarities in melodic structure show us how
painstakingly Løvenskiold worked to create musical characterisation for this
ballet.

The earliest printed source to this opening scene tell us that the Sylphide
fans James with cool air with her fluttering wings, whereupon the tempo
increases to a 'dancing' *Allegro non tanto e grazioso*.[28] The tight weaving
together of mime and dance within a single scene is typical of Bournonville,
who also sought to ensure that the mime, like the dancing, was closely and
carefully coordinated with the music. In this instance, dancing breaks forth
at the moment the Sylphide awakens James with a kiss. James's reaction is
spontaneous and intense, for which reason we are given an *Allegro vivace*,
with a crescendo building up to a *fortissimo marcatissimo*. Then, the Sylphide
vanishes through the chimney – musically illustrated by surprising octave
leaps, rests, and a long held note.

A lost mime scene in Act One: James and Gurn
The well-known opening tableau was originally followed by a rather long

mime scene in which James tells Gurn about the Sylph (causing Gurn to break out in laughter and declare it all had been a dream), and then comes to himself and remembers that it is the day of his wedding to Effy. In this scene Gurn complains about the injustice Effy shows him by rejecting him in favor of James – the *grillefænger* (dreamer who can get swept away by wild ideas).[29]

This mime scene was expunged, but its music survives (in part) in the original orchestral score and (in full) in Løvenskiold's piano arrangement of the Act One introduction (published as the second part of the *Musikalsk Trilogie* collection, 1859). This score also includes detailed interlinear descriptions of the action.[30] Also, a segment of it may be found in the original rehearsal score (or *répétiteur*) in the Royal Library in Copenhagen (a copy of which is held at the New York Public Library).[31] The scene is noteworthy from a dramaturgical standpoint in that it explicitly highlights the opposition of dream and reality, and plainly shows that Gurn cannot see the Sylphide (though of course later in the first act he *does* see her as James embraces her briefly).

This long-suppressed scene is also remarkable musically; two isolated passages shall be mentioned here. Note, first, that the scene consisted of three sections: *Allegro agitato* (148 bars), *Moderato* (29 bars) and *Allegro vivo* (37 bars). The *Allegro agitato* is comprised of a new motif that gradually grows louder as it is interwoven with the previously heard music describing the dialogue between Gurn and James. The musical tension accelerates when Gurn refuses to entertain the idea of a supernatural creature. As Gurn argues that it was only a dream, Løvenskiold introduces a series of chromatically descending fully-diminished seventh chords, culminating in an extraordinarily vivid *forzando* (suddenly accented, 'forceful') F half-diminished seventh chord in second inversion that, technically, is analysed as a borrowed $ii^{ø4}/_3$ in E-flat major (Example 7.6). This is one of the most suspense-filled chords in Romantic harmony, and the young Løvenskiold uses it exactly at the moment in the drama where fantasy and reality come directly into confrontation. (Once Gurn has given a rational explanation for James's vision of the Sylph, this unstable harmony resolves into an expected cadential pattern: $I^6/_4 - V^7 - I$.)

The subsequent *Moderato* section offers more charming motives, including among other things, a languishing 'bel canto' passage for woodwinds and solo oboe in parallel thirds exactly as we find it as an established ingredient in Bellini's love duets (Example 7.7). As the interlinear text tells us, this is the moment at which James first remembers that he is to be married today to the sweet Effy.

By studying the melodies and the harmonies in the score, we can see how carefully and precisely Løvenskiold crafted this music. The down-to-earth Effy is characterised in Act One No. 2 by a folk-like bagpipe melody (orches-

Example 7.6. *Allegro vivace* section of the excised mime scene: *Forzando* chord at the moment when the discussion turns to the fantastic. ('Some of the friends laugh at him, others become afraid, but Gurn believes that it is possible to explain as a fantastic [dream].)

Example 7.7. *Moderato* section of the excised mime scene: 'bel canto' passage when James remembers that it is his wedding day

trated in a way that makes its folk implications clear), and which recurs as a reminiscence motif in the Window Scene when James thinks of Effy (Example 7.8).

The characterisation of the witch begins in Act One No. 3 when James

Example 7.8. Løvenskiold, *Sylphiden*, Act One No.2: Effy's *entrée*

first sees her by the fireplace. This moment is marked by a tonal shift from E major to C major and is typical of Løvenkiold's use of harmony at the service of the drama. The ensuing Fortuneteller Scene employs a chatty tune, string tremolo, *sforzandi*, pauses, fierce *tutti* chords, and ascending chromatic movements which lead to chilling unisons – all typical elements of the melodramatic sound world of mime music.

In the Witch scene of Act Two No. 1, Løvenskiold makes much use of diminished seventh chords and other devices of the time – had the young composer been studying the Wolf's Glen Scene from Weber's *Der Freischütz*? – but he was not able to create anything of real interest; the musical substance is this scene, which has been considerably shortened though time, is rather thin. So, too, it must be said, is the musical depiction of the witch in Act One, though it is far better than that in Act Two.

But if Løvenskiold is found wanting in his musical portrayal of the grotesque, he is very inventive in his treatment of the encounter between James and the Sylphide in the Window Scene. Here, he succeeds fully in showing that, as Bournonville put it, music provides ballets with 'very essence' (literally, 'principle of life' or *Livsprincip*).[32] The music of this scene has recently been analysed by Jörg Rothkamm, who points out that the scene begins with James and his melancholy reflections, musically illustrated by a melodic E-minor cantilena in *bel canto* style (*Andante doloroso molto expressivo*), but the elegiac mood is disrupted when the Sylphide appears in the window.[33] This is the moment at which the supernatural enters into James's ordinary world. The need for a great shift in the music at this point is met by Løvenskiold with a melodramatic sound effect: a powerful harmonic colouring and the eerie timbre of *sul ponticello* strings tremolo paint James's response ('What do I hear?'), followed by a long fermata.

Precisely at the moment the music reaches its high point, the window opens, fusing music and magic (just as in a film, wherein music can persuade the spectator of the presence of the supernatural). Then, after the window has opened, James invites the Sylphide into his world. This calls for dialogue music, and the 'question-answer' music here adds a verbal quality to the wordless action. This music, indeed, has the capacity to illustrate action down into the smallest detail, not only bringing the dialogue to life, but acoustically depicting the Sylphide's weightless floating from the window

frame down to the floor, and then carefully illustrating the two dancers' hesi-
tating steps forward. Furthermore, this music (which sounds at this point
quite like silent-film music that closely hews to the action) is played *ad libitum*; that is, the orchestra conductor is instructed to follow the performers'
movements and gestures. A tighter symbiosis between sound, physical gesture movement, and emotional content would be difficult to imagine.

Next, the dialogue becomes more intense, and Løvenskiold correspond-
ingly intensifies the music with dissonances, a rising melodic line and stark
dynamic contrasts; to this he adds *accelerando* and *tremolo*. The result is a
psychological soundscape of despair.[34] If judged from a purely musical point
of view such music would seem absurd, but from a theatrical point of view, it
is quite effective.

All the sadness is then suddenly swept away and we hear and see the
Sylphide's happiness, and recognise the principal theme of the overture. This
joyful section is developed into a proper solo for the Sylphide, the *Allegro
grazioso*, which is even more joyful (Example 7.9).

Example 7.9. Løvenskiold, *Sylphiden*, Act One No. 4: (the Window Scene): the Sylphide's solo

Then, with a good sense of dramatic structure, Bournonville interrupts
the happy scene between James and the Sylphide with the arrival of Gurn,
who makes a noise at the door, then by Effy and her friends, who have heard
that James might have arrived, and finally by the wedding guests, whose
entrée is No. 5, the *Pas d'Ecossaise*. This ensemble dance contains several
solos that are now danced respectively by Gurn and James, though earlier in
the life of this ballet, there had been a solo for Effy as well, and in the subsequent No. 6 (*Pas de Deux* and Reel) there was originally a longer lullaby-like
movement (the *Andante siciliano*, marked *espressivo e dolce*), probably danced
by James and Effy (Example 7.10).

Next, in a striking contrast, the dancers break into a reel. Here,

Example 7.10. Løvenskiold, *Sylphiden, Andante siciliano*, Act One No.6

Løvenskiold has created a folk-like number with trumpet calls and orchestral instruments imitating bagpipes. Just as Bournonville developed a folk dance into a large work for *corps de ballet*, so Løvenskiold has developed the folk dance's simple musical structure into a large rondo-like whole with a sweeping finish.[35] Yet, while on the surface this is a cheerful ensemble dance (and Løvenskiold sustains the festive *Affekt* well), in the bustle of the moment Bournonville allows James to see the Sylphide twice, which leads James to abandon the ensemble dance. It is an effective dramatic touch for Løvenskiold to keep the reel going without interruption, for we hear what James and the revellers are hearing, even as we see him being tempted away from the scene by the Sylphide.

Act Two

In Act Two we first meet the Witch and her coven. Here, we find gloomy and often grotesque mime music with many sound effects but (as noted above) little substance. The noisiness of the trombones and percussion disappears as the rays of the sun reach the trees in the beautiful forest, and now the music changes completely. After the E-minor tonality of the Witches' Scene, the key of E-flat major is introduced as the Romantic, natural world of the sylphs unfolds before our eyes. It is a scene of pure beauty for which Løvenskiold gives us a graceful, dignified melody originally played by the horn (Example 7.11).

Example 7.11. Løvenskiold, *Sylphiden*, Act Two No.2: *Andante* horn solo

(Due to difficulties experienced by horn players, especially with the high notes, the phrase was later given to the cello – one of several such instances in this score. The young Løvenskiold was not yet experienced at instrumentation!)

At this point, more instruments are added: clarinets and the flute, playing light figurations. And it is the flute that introduces the *entreé* (Act Two No. 2) of the Sylphide with a cadenza *ad libitum*. In the Forest Scene (later in Act Two, No. 2), the solo violin dominates, followed by the flute – two instruments particularly able to convey the airy nature of the Sylphide and her world.

Originally Bournonville included a full *pas de deux* for James and the Sylphide. This *pas de deux*, traditionally enough, consisted of an introductory *Adagio* (with a melody typical of Løvenskiold in its romantic, emotional flavour, ascending direction, and use of the third and the lowered sixth

Example 7.12. Løvenskiold, *Sylphiden*, Act Two No.2: *Pas de deux* (excised from the original score), *Adagio* introduction

Example 7.13. Løvenskiold, *Sylphiden*, Act Two No.2: *Pas de deux* (excised from the original score), Polacca for solo violin and brass

(Example 7.12), followed by a buoyant, joyful Polacca for solo violin and brass (Example 7.13).

The *pas de deux* continues with a series of variations, each with its own characteristic solo instrument, and, following a repetition of the Polacca, it reaches its conclusion with a crescendo in the coda. This *pas de deux* was criticised because the two protagonists were in close physical contact as they performed it – something that contradicted the dramatic situation at hand, since James was actually frustrated in his attempts to become close to the Sylphide. Apparently Bournonville eliminated this *pas de deux* very early in the life of the ballet.[36]

Having given up the original *pas de deux*, Bournonville probably replaced the Løvenskiold music with *pas de deux* music by the Austrian violinist and composer Josef Mayseder (1789–1863), though we do not know the details of when and how this took place (the source material is not forthcoming in this regard). In any case, parts of the Mayseder *pas de deux* were interpolated in the Sylph Scene (Act Two No. 4) and probably at a very early date; then over the course of time it gradually developed into the *Divertissement* (also Act Two No. 4).[37] August Bournonville restaged *Sylphiden* five times in Copenhagen (in 1849, 1856, 1865, 1867 and 1871), and we presume that the development of the *Divertissement* unfolded over the course of these Bournonville restagings.

We do know that in 1849, Bournonville inserted a longer section from another Bournonville-Løvenskiold ballet, *Den nye Penelope eller Foraarsfesten i Athen* (*The New Penelope, or The Spring Festival in Athens*, 1847), into the *Divertissement* in question – that is, the then-shorter Sylph Scene. This section, originally composed for the Belt Dance in the second act of *The New Penelope*, was now placed in *Sylphiden* for the first three segments of Act Two, No. 4 for the sylphs of the *corps de ballet*, while the Mayseder music was used for the second solo for the Sylphide, the second solo for James, and the coda of the whole *Divertissement*.

In 1865, Bournonville undertook a new revision of *Sylphiden* based on the version that he had staged during his residency at the Royal Theatre in Stockholm (1861–64).[38] It was in this new 1865 production that the replacement of the *pas de deux* with the Act Two No. 4 *Divertissement* was finally settled. (That the change took place in 1865 is made evident in Bournonville's production notes for this version.[39])

Thus the *Divertissement* as it appears today was created over the course of several periods: the opening *barcarola* and the first Sylphide solo date from 1836. James's first solo is probably the last section to have been added (perhaps for the Hans Beck production of 1891); the identity of its composer is unknown (though it may be H.S. Paulli). The Belt Dance from *The New Penelope* was added in 1849 (as noted above). The Mayseder sections (i.e., the second solos for the Sylphide and James, respectively, and the Coda) had probably been added to *Sylphiden* very early on, most likely in 1842.

The Mayseder music, it should be noted, had been employed earlier by Bournonville in his ballet *Fantasiens Ø (The Isle of Fantasy*, 1838), and he had probably bought a copy of it in Paris or Berlin. It is from a *Divertissement* (op. 35 no. 1) of Mayseder, published in Vienna in 1823. This music has also been linked to the F. Taglioni *La Sylphide*: it was printed in New York in the 1840s with the words 'La Sylphide as danced by Mlle Fanny Elssler' (Elssler had first danced *La Sylphide* in 1838 at the Paris Opera, and then performed the role in the USA to much acclaim in 1840).[40]

The alteration (noted above) in the Forest Scene of Act Two (i.e., Act Two no. 2) changed the ballet considerably. Originally in 1836, the *pas de deux* and the far shorter Sylph Scene served as lyrical moments with dance that grew naturally from the dramatic context. Later (in the 1842, 1849, and 1865 productions) – probably in response to Act Two of *Giselle*, which Bournonville had seen in rehearsal in 1841, and because of general developments in the ballet in Europe — Bournonville created a greater concentration of pure dance, leaving the preceding scene (the Forest Scene) as a pantomimic prelude. The second act, as it existed in 1836, had rather a different sort of flow. Indeed, the original short version of the Sylph Scene did not end with a full conclusion at all, but continued *attacca* (without pause) into the succeeding number (*Allegro ben agitato*) in which James chases the Sylphide.

The music for the scene of Gurn, the Witch and Effy (Act Two No. 6) brings back the motif from the Fortunetelling Scene (in Act One No. 3), a very logical use of a reminiscence motif. In the subsequent scene between James and the Witch (Act Two No. 7), the coda motif from the overture is used as an illustration of the cursed scarf. In the Finale (Act Two No. 8), we return to the horn quartet first heard in the overture. (Indeed, the use of horn and horn quartet is typical for the whole score, and is especially noteworthy in the Forest Scene, Act Two No. 2.) When the horn quartet returns in the Finale, it recapitulates the atmosphere of forest-loneliness (*skovensomhed*) before the dramatic development finds its mournful climax in the capturing and death of the Sylphide.[41] In this sad moment, the horn introduces the melancholic melody from the slow section of the overture.

Let us have a closer look at this melody (see Example 7.1). From the opening scene of the ballet the melodic characterisation of the Sylphide was dominated by a progression from the fifth to the third and then to the sixth scale degrees. It seems at first blush that if this melody were truly related to the one used at the end to illustrate the death of the Sylphide, it would include the sixth scale degree as a kind of culmination – yet Løvenskiold did not introduce the sixth in this presentation of the melody in the overture. But when we move to the end of the ballet, we *do* get the sixth as a very

Example 7.14. Løvenskiold, *Sylphiden*, Act Two Finale, *Andante*

noticeable highpoint following the descending minor thirds that describe the end of the Sylphide's life (Example 7.14). This is the most powerful use of the sixth in the whole score – it is strongly emphasised by the forceful dissonances of the accompaniment, it coincides precisely with the woeful climax, and it is repeated right before the very end of the ballet.

In this typical Romantic drama, based on confrontation and catastrophe, the music follows and reinforces the unfolding of the action. Løvenskiold understood the drama and he created tension that culminates in the final resolution. He was able to transform his understanding into music, and he surprises the listener with the use of innovative harmonies and the deployment of reminiscence motifs – especially at the very end of the ballet when he finally gives us the sixth we have expected through the whole score.

The Reception of Løvenskiold's music for *La Sylphide*

Løvenskiold's music for *La Sylphide* received a mixed reception. The young composer was perfectly aware that as a nobleman he had many opponents amongst the liberal-thinking citizenry. Indeed, he had written to his cousin on December 2, 1836, only four days after the première of *La Sylphide* – while confined to his bed in Kulhuse – that '[t]his music has many detractors, and there are cabals determined to convince everyone that it is no good at all'.[42]

Here is Løvenskiold's account of the première:

Under these circumstances came the 28th [of November], the momentous day on which my fate should be decided. The king, queen and the whole court were in the theatre along with an enormous number of people; but instead of the fate that I had expected, the ballet was not shunned when the curtain fell at the end of the evening. Many places during the very performance itself were tumultuously applauded and my music was unanimously received with favour and astonishment despite the fact that people seem to have expected [a] terribly slovenly work.[43]

He goes on to say that on the second evening the overture – in a departure from normal custom – was also strongly applauded. The young composer was also aware that King Frederik VI was said to have objected to Løvenskiold's detractors.[44]

Løvenskiold's description of the première matches that of the theatre chronicler Thomas Overskou, who offers a sympathetic description of the event in his *Den Danske Skueplads* (1854–64).[45] After first commending the ballet and Lucile Grahn (who played the title role), he deems the music extremely successful, and writes:

They wanted to give his music a reception that would suffice to scare him away from any attempt to rival 'our brilliant composer'.[46] The fact that he was a baron could have been used to arouse prejudice against his artistic abilities: as a nobleman, the thinking went, he was of course a mere dilettante who should be patronised by the court ... [But] [h]is genius put the cabal to shame: the music's liveliness, its many singular and beautiful melodies, its characteristic expression and striking orchestration pleased the public very much, and the spitefulness of his detractors resulted in the composition receiving more praise than it would have otherwise.[47]

Thus did the delicacy of the situation concerning Løvenskiold's noble background bring much attention to the music. There were three contemporaneous reviews published, the most favourable of which appeared in *Dagen* (*The Daily*), opening with a paragraph about pre-performance intrigue and rumours that the music would be spitefully received. The reviewer acknowledged that the score was not perfect (especially in regard to the instrumentation), but stated that above all, the music's *Affekt* (*holdningen*) deserved recognition. Moreover, the reviewer noted that there was more than simply the *Affekt* to appreciate in Løvenskiold's score.[48] Two weeks after the première, *Kjøbenhavnsposten* (*The Copenhagen Post*), the mouthpiece of the liberal opposition, spoke its mind. First, they chided Bournonville for staging a work that was not original but copied from a French source.[49] Then, six days later, came a second article, long and severe, and devoted exclusively to the music. Its author maintains that Løvenskiold should not have undertaken the task in the first place, because as a composer he lacked both genius and technical training. This judgment is owed to

> the complete absence of anything that can be called sylph-like....Had Mr. Løvenskiold supplied us something like, for example, what can be found in Mendelssohn-Bartholdy's magnificent Overture to *A Midsummer Night's Dream*, we could have spoken of his genius.[50]

Concerning the lack of technical accomplishments, the reviewer cites the strange instrumentation that one finds, for example, in the *pas de deux* for James and the Sylphide in Act Two no. 2, in which a solo violin is accompanied by three trombones. He also notes that some of the notes in the horn parts were unplayable.

This time, Løvenskiold did not escape the dreaded critics, and, indeed, he seems to have taken their comments to heart. We know, for example, from a letter to the Royal Theatre's management from March 5, 1837, that he applied for permission to correct substantial shortcomings in the score.[51] Indeed, the original score bears many markings, for over the course of time it was altered not only by the composer himself, but also by many others (including J. P. E. Hartmann and V. C. Holm) to correct infelicities in the instrumentation.[52] (For example, many of the difficult passages for horn quartet and for solo horn were moved to the celli, as noted above.)

When considering the reception of Løvenskiold's *Sylphiden* score, we must of course include Bournonville's assessment. Even though Bournonville and Løvenskiold collaborated only a twice after *Sylphiden* – on *The Isle of Fantasy* (1838) and *The New Penelope* (1847) – there is nothing to suggest that Bournonville was not happy with the music for *Sylphiden*. On the contrary. Here is a letter of endorsement Bournonville provided the young composer after the première of *Sylphiden* as Løvenskiold set in motion his plans for an educational trip to Germany, Austria, and Italy:

> It is my happy duty and a true pleasure to give the young aspiring artist, H. S. v. Løvenskiold, this attestation that he has interpreted the character and the expression of the ballet *The Sylphide* with great adroitness, and furnished me a melodious and brilliant music, which gave me considerable assistance as I composed the dance and mime. I owe him, therefore, my great gratitude, along with the wish for his further studies that will allow the advancement of a growing genius with which Providence has endowed to this talented young man. August Bournonville, December 18, 1836.[53]

Despite the criticism, the music for *Sylphiden* represented a great success for the young composer, and indeed favourable opinions continued to be expressed for this score. Over a century after its première, the twentieth-century dance critic David Hunt, after having seen *Sylphiden*, *Napoli*, *The Conservatory* and *A Folk Tale*, wrote that of them all, *Sylphiden* was

> ... the most interesting musically. This music is far superior in every way to Jean Schneitzhoeffer's score of the original Paris production [....]. Herman Løvenskiold has obviously been greatly influenced by the music of Weber and by *Der Freischütz* in particular. But what better model for a composer existed in those early days of the Romantic movement than that magical score with its evocation of the supernatural?...[54]

After *Sylphiden*, Løvenskiold followed his original plan and set about obtaining money to finance his educational trip. In 1838 he departed, and stayed first in Berlin before visiting Mendelssohn in Leipzig. He was completely carried away by this luminary, so well respected as a composer, conductor, and pianist. Later he studied in Vienna and also travelled in Italy.

As for composing, the two-year tour produced a series of piano works including *Characterstücke* op. 12 and the collection *Sogni d'Italia* op. 17, as well as a concert overture based on Schiller's play *Die Jungfrau von Orleans* (*The Maid of Orleans*), which Løvenskiold dedicated to Mendelssohn.

Back in Copenhagen, life became more and more difficult for him. He had originally planned to find employment at the Court composing music for royal occasions, or serving as a choirmaster at the Royal Theatre. But the theatre job was given to someone else, and after the death of Court Composer Christoph Ernst Friedrich Weyse (1774–1842), Weyse's position was abolished. Løvenskiold supplied the theatre with music on several occasions but with little success, and his singspiel *Sara* was booed off the stage. The satirical press now set to work – for instance, one could read in the periodical *Corsaren (The Corsair)*:

> ... The music is by a baron and it is bad. Should it not be possible for a baron to possess a talent for composition? We would by no means deny this out of hand, a baron being, after all, human. The misfortune is that as a newly-born baron, gifted with a talent for composing, he imbibed with his mother's – or rather his baroness's – milk so many incorrect transitions, so many aristocratic fifths and eighths, so much chasing after tinsel and effect, that his talent was bound to be warped unless the little gentleman had been sent out immediately to live amongst the common folk. The little Baron was not sent out – *ergo* – *Sat Sapient!* [a word to the wise].[55]

Such critics effectively removed Løvenskiold from the musical life of Copenhagen. The changing political situation made success impossible for a nobleman who did not understand the social evolution that was taking place and was unable to adapt to the new democracy. In 1848, Denmark's last absolute monarch, King Christian VIII, died; with his successor Frederik VII, democracy was established. Løvenskiold was given the position of Court Organist in 1851 and he produced some works, including an opera, *Turandot*, a piano quartet, and a concert overture *Fra Skoven ved Furesø (From the Forest by Furesø Lake)*. But he never attained a position of any great significance, and in 1870 his death went unnoticed. Løvenskiold had been forgotten.

Today his name is only remembered because of *Sylphiden*, for which he created an important score that showed great understanding of the basic rules for ballet music at the time, and of dramatic narrative music in general. The score of *Sylphiden* has also meant that, today, he is one of the most performed Danish composers in the world. Thus he occupies a paradoxical position: largely forgotten, but often performed.

— Translated from the Danish by Holland Phillips

Appendix

Some Source Material for *La Sylphide*
Manuscripts
Det Kongelige Bibliotek (The Royal Library), Copenhagen:
Sylphiden Ballet i to Acter ved August Bournonville sat i Musik af H.S. Løvenskiold. Orchestral score. Ms Autograph H.S. Løvenskiold. (1836) C II, 117 d tv 2.
http://img.kb.dk/ma/teater/sylfiden_part-m.pdf

For information on the restoration of this score see
www.kb.dk/da/nb/nyheder/mta/breve2011/1102sylfiden.html

Sylphiden Ripiteur Partie til Balletten Sylphiden af Bournonville Musik af Herm. Løvenskiold. Ms unsigned and undated (1836) DKKk; MA ms 2970a (KTB 275)
http://img.kb.dk/ma/danmus/sylph_rep-m.pdf

In *The Bournonville Tradition* The *first fifty years 1829*-1879, Vol. II (Dance Books London 1997), pp. 35-38, Knud Arne Jürgensen provides a chronology of events, the performing history, and an annotated bibliography of sources for *Sylphiden*, including two fragments of orchestral scores which contain the music for sections omitted from the Løvenskiold score at a later restaging.

Musikaliska Akademiens Bibliotek (Library of the Music Academy), Stockholm:
Sylphiden, Copy of the orchestral score c. 1860

Printed music
La *Sylphide, Ouverture et Morceaux Choisis*, Copenhagen: Lose & Olsen, 1837.
I Musikalsk Trilogie, which includes the Introduction of Act I of Sylphiden arranged by the composer, Copenhagen: Wilhelm Hansen 1859-60.

Bournonville, August. *Efterladte Skrifter* [Posthumous Writings]. Edited by Charlotte Bournonville Copenhagen: Andr. Schous Forlag, 1891.
———. *My Theatre Life*. Translated by Patricia N. McAndrew. Middletown, CT: Wesleyan University Press, 1979.
Celenza, Anna Harwell. *The Early Works of Niels Gade: In Search of the Poetic*. Burlington, VT: Ashgate, 2001.
———. 'Efterklange Af Ossian: The Reception of James Macpherson's *Poems*

of Ossian in Denmark's Literature, Art, and Music.' *Scandinavian Studies* 70, no. 3 (1998): 359–96.

Christensen, Anne Middelboe. *Sylfiden Findes: En Svævebog* [The Sylphide Exists: a Soaring Book]. Copenhagen: Schønberg, 2008.

Christensen, Charlotte. 'Temaer fra Shakespeare og Ossian', in *Maleren Nicolai Abilgaard* (Copenhagen: Gyldendal, 1999).

Fog, Dan. *Musikhandel og Nodetryk i Danmark Efter 1750*. 2 vols. Copenhagen: Dan Fog, 1984.

Greskovic, Robert. *Ballet 101: A Complete Guide to Learning and Loving the Ballet*. Pompton Plains, NJ: Limelight Editions, 2005. New York: Hyperion, 1998.

Hunt, David. 'Ballet Music from Denmark', *Dance and Dancers* (October 1953): 9.

Jensen, Lisbeth Ahlgren. *Det Kvindelige Spillerum: Fem Kvindelige Komponister i Danmark i 1800-Tallet*. Copenhagen: Multivers, 2007.

Jürgensen, Knud Arne. *The Bournonville Tradition: The First Fifty Years, 1829-1879*. 2 vols. London: Dance Books, 1997.

Kirstein, Lincoln. 'Ballet and Music', in *The International Cyclopedia of Music and Musicians*, ed. Oscar Thompson and Bruce Bohle, 10th ed. New York: Dodd, Mead, 1975.

Løvenskiold, Herman Severin. *Contredanses Françaises sur des motifs de La Sylphide* [French Contradances on the Motives of *La Sylphide*]. Copenhagen: Lose & Olsen, 1837.

————. *Introduction af Første Act af Balletten Sylphiden arr. af Componisten* [Introduction to Act One of the Ballet *Sylphiden*]. *Musikalsk Trilogie* [Musical Trilogy]. Copenhagen: Wilhelm Hansen, 1859.

————. *La Sylphide, Ouverture et Morceaux choisis* [*La Sylphide*, Overture and Selected Pieces]. Copenhagen: Lose & Olsen, 1837.

————. 'To Herman Frederik Løvenskiold.' In Private Archive of Herman Frederik Løvenskiold. Copenhagen: Danish National Archives.

————. 'To J. P. E. Hartmann', in Manuscript Department. Copenhagen: The Royal Library.

————. 'To the Management of the Royal Danish Theatre', in Royal Danish Theatre Journalbog. Copenhagen: Danish National Archives.

Marx, Wolfgang, 'The Ballet as a "Genre": Initial Thoughts on the Genetic Identity of a Multimedia Art Form', in *Die Beziehung von Musik und Choreographie im Ballett*, ed. Michael Malkiewicz and Jörg Rothkamm. Berlin: Vorwerk 8, 2007.

Mayseder, Joseph. *La Sylphide as danced by Fanny Elssler*. New York: Atwill, 184?.

Mitchell, Jerome. *The Walter Scott Operas: An Analysis of Operas Based on the*

Works of Sir Walter Scott. Birmingham: University of Alabama Press, 1977.

Nørlyng, Ole. 'Bournonville og hans musikalske medarbejdere', [Bournonville and his musical collaborators] in *Perspektiv på Bournonville*, ed. Marianne Hallar Erik Aschengreen, and Jørgen Heiner. Copenhagen: Nyt nordisk forlag, 1980.

———. *The Composer Herman Severin Lövenskiold.* Liner Notes. Chandos ABRD-1200, 1986. LP [now CHAN 6546, CD].

———, 'Drøm eller virkelighed: om de musikalske kilders betydning i forbindelse med en idag forsvunden mimsk scene i *Sylphiden*', in *Bournonville: Tradition, Rekonstruktion*, ed. Ole Nørlyng and Henning Urup (Copenhagen: C.A. Reitzel, 1989).

———. *The Music for La Sylphide.* Liner Notes. Chandos ABRD-1200, 1986. LP [now CHAN 6546, CD].

———, 'Musikken Er Phantasiens skjønneste Organ', in *Salut for Bournonville*, ed. Ebbe Mørk. Copenhagen: Statens Museum for Kunst, 1979.

Overskou, Thomas. *Den danske Skueplads i dens Historie Fra De Første Spor af danske Skuespil indtil vor Tid.* 7 vols. Copenhagen: Thieles, 1864.

Rothkamm, Jörg. *Balletmusik im 19. und 20. Jahrhundert: Dramaturgie einer Gattung.* Mainz: Schott Music, 2011.

———. 'Dialogähnliche und acktionsbezogene Musik im Ballett *Sylphiden* von Herman Løvenskjold und August Bournonville (1836).' *Die Tonkunst* 2 (2008): 20–33.

Smith, Marian. *Ballet and Opera in the Age of Giselle.* Princeton: Princeton University Press, 2000.

Taruskin, Richard and Weiss, Piero, eds 'The "Music of the Future" Controversy', in *Music in the Western World: A History in Documents*, 2nd ed. Belmont, CA: Thomson/Schirmer, 2008, 380-385.

Notes

1. August Bournonville, *My Theatre Life*, trans. Patricia N. McAndrew (Middletown, CT; Wesleyan University Press, 1979), 133.
2. Ibid., 7. On Bournonville's musical aesthetic, see Ole Nørlyng, 'Bournonville og hans musikalske medarbejdere', in *Perspektiv på Bournonville*, ed. Marianne Hallar Erik Aschengreen and Jørgen Heiner (Copenhagen: Nyt nordisk forlag, 1980), 243–303, and Ole Nørlyng, 'Musikken er Phantasiens skjønneste Organ', in *Salut for Bournonville*, ed. Ebbe Mørk (Copenhagen: Statens Museum for Kunst, 1979), 51–61. See also Knud Arne Jürgensen, *The Bournonville Tradition: The First Fifty Years, 1829–1879*, 2 vols., vol. I (London: Dance Books, 1997); Anne Middelboe Christensen, *Sylfiden findes: en svævebog* [The Sylphide Exists: a Soaring Book] (Copenhagen: Schønberg, 2008).
3. Quoted in Nørlyng, 'Musikken er Phantasiens skjønneste Organ', 51.

4. Bournonville, *My Theatre Life*, 133.

5. Ibid., 7. Bournonville's concept of dance as a 'singing body' is linked to his account of divine Creation: 'This creation called forth praise and admiration. The word was not yet formed, but the voice sounded and the paean exultantly rang out. The listeners stood round about, filled with excitement. They wished to imitate these sounds, but for one thing they lacked the gift of melody, and for another they feared to disturb the magic. Then the hand followed the eye toward the admired regions of the body. It was as if the steps wished to accompany the undulations of the sounds. The body sang...'
   Much of the opening paragraph in this chapter quotes verbatim the translation by Gaye Kynoch of Ole Nørlyng, *The Composer Herman Severin Løvenskiold*, Liner Notes, Chandos ABRD-1200, 1986, LP [now CHAN 6546, CD].

6. Bournonville's writings are extensive and fall into several categories, including autobiography, translations, and essays on broader cultural and political matters and ballet theory. See 'Appendix B: The Literary Works' in Jürgensen, *The Bournonville Tradition*, I, 151–92.

7. Bournonville, *My Theatre Life*, 30. See also Jörg Rothkamm, 'Dialogähnliche und acktionsbezogene Musik im Ballett *Sylphiden* von Herman Løvenskjold und August Bournonville (1836)', *Die Tonkunst* 2 (2008): 20–33.

8. '[...] the score was entirely too expensive, and those who could have taught me the roles (for they had to be taught) did not seem disposed to do so just then.' Bournonville, *My Theatre Life*, 78.

9. [On pastiche ballet scores in France and Italy, see, respectively, Marian Smith, *Ballet and Opera in the Age of Giselle* (Princeton: Princeton University Press, 2000), 103-108, and this volume, Chapter 8. — Editor's note.]

10. Ballet music had undergone a considerable flowering with the composer Claus Schall during Vincenzo Galeotti's time as ballet master (1776–1816). In a fruitful collaboration, these artists created works such as the Nordic mythological ballet *Lagetha* (1801), the Romantic-horror ballet *Rolf Blaaskæg* (*Rolf Bluebeard*, 1808), and two Shakespeare ballets, *Romeo and Juliet* (1811) and *Macbeth* (1816). However, Claus Schall's musical language, just like Galeotti's choreographic work, was regarded as old-fashioned by Bournonville's time.

11. The score incorporates music by J.-M. Schneitzhoeffer, L. Carlini, F. Sor, G. Spontini, C.M. von Weber and G. Rossini.

12. The score of *Waldemar* in particular demonstrates Frohlich's skill as a ballet composer. However, this music is largely forgotten, due to *Waldemar*'s disappearance from the repertory of the Royal Danish Ballet after the 1920s. Note that the custom of making musical borrowings did not disappear with the advent of Frohlich's work; *Napoli* (1842), for example, includes music by Rossini as well as popular songs and folk tunes.

13. Bournonville served as balletmaster until 1877, excepting interludes in Vienna (1855-56) and Stockholm (1861-63). See Knud Arne Jürgensen, 'Bournonville Composers', *International Encyclopedia of Dance* (New York: Oxford University Press), vol. I, 514-516.

14. Lisbeth Ahlgren Jensen, *Det Kvindelige Spillerum: Fem Kvindelige Komponister i Danmark i 1800-tallet* (Copenhagen: Multivers, 2007), 49–70. For a sketch of Løvenskiold's life, see Nørlyng, *The Composer Herman Severin Løvenskiold*.

15. Bournonville, *My Theatre Life*, 78.

16. Herman Severin Løvenskiold, 'to Herman Frederik Løvenskiold', in Private Archive of Herman Frederik Løvenskiold (Copenhagen: Danish National Archives).

17. Herman Severin Løvenskiold, 'to J. P. E. Hartmann', in Manuscript Department (Copenhagen: The Royal Library).

18. August Bournonville, *Efterladte Skrifter* [Posthumous Writings], ed. Charlotte Bournonville (Copenhagen: Andr. Schous Forlag, 1891), 167. Concerning répétiteur scores for one or two violins, see Rothkamm, 'Dialogähnliche und acktionsbezogene Musik im Ballett *Sylphiden*', 21-23.

19. Music from Løvenskiold's score was also published under a variety of different arrangements after the première of *Sylphiden*. These include Herman Severin Løvenskiold, *La Sylphide, Ouverture et morceaux choisis* [*La Sylphide*, Overture and Selected Pieces] (Copenhagen: Lose & Olsen, 1837); Herman Severin Løvenskiold, *Introduction af Første Act af Balletten Sylphiden arr. af Componisten* [Introduction to Act One of the Ballet *Sylphiden*], *Musikalsk Trilogie* [Musical Trilogy] (Copenhagen:

Wilhelm Hansen, 1859); Herman Severin Løvenskiold, *Contredanses françaises sur des motifs de La Sylphide* [French Contradances on the Motives of *La Sylphide*] (Copenhagen: Lose & Olsen, 1837). See Dan Fog, *Musikhandel og nodetryk i Danmark efter 1750*, 2 vols. (Copenhagen: Dan Fog, 1984).

20. Knud Arne Jürgensen, *The Bournonville Tradition: The First Fifty Years, 1829–1879*, 2 vols., vol. II (London: Dance Books, 1997), 35.

21. Charlotte Christensen, 'Temaer fra Shakespeare og Ossian', in *Maleren Nicolai Abildgaard* (Copenhagen: Gyldendal, 1999), 69–91.

22. Løvenskiold also composed a *syngespil* (singspiel) *Sara* (1838) based on *Sarah, ou l'orpheline de Glencoe* by Mélesville (the pen name of Anne-Honoré-Joseph Duveyrier de Mélésville, 1787–1865), based on a story of Walter Scott. See also Jerome Mitchell, *The Walter Scott Operas: An Analysis of Operas Based on the Works of Sir Walter Scott* (Birmingham: University of Alabama Press, 1977). The culmination of this interest in Scotland, the Ossian poems, and Walter Scott was the composer Niels W. Gade's breakthrough composition *Efterklange af Ossian* (1840) (the original composition contest entry was titled *Gjenklange af Ossian/Nachklänge von Ossian*). [See also Anna Harwell Celenza, '*Efterklange af Ossian*: The Reception of James Macpherson's *Poems of Ossian* in Denmark's Literature, Art, and Music', *Scandinavian Studies* 70, no. 3 (1998); Anna Harwell Celenza, *The Early Works of Niels Gade: In Search of the Poetic* (Burlington, VT: Ashgate, 2001). Celenza argues that Danish interest in the Ossian poems was short-lived, due to their dubious authorship and portrayal of Scandinavians as cruel and barbaric. Celenza also contends that Gade's *Efterklange af Ossian* was written to cater to a German – not Danish – taste for Ossianic subject matter. — Editor's note.] Regarding Scott operas by both German and Italian composers heard in Danish translations, see this volume, Chapter 6, note 16.

23. Recordings of *Sylphiden* by David Garforth and the Royal Danish Orchestra (Chandos ABRD-1200, LP [now CHAN 6546, CD], 1986) and Peter Ernst Lassen and Aalborg Symphony Orchestra (DACOCD 631, CD, 2005) contain all the musical material of the overture.

24. On the two types of music found in ballet-pantomime scores of the 1830s and 1840s, see Marian Smith, *Ballet and Opera in the Age of Giselle* (Princeton: Princeton University Press, 2000), 6–18.

25. [Kirstein calls music written for ballet, or indeed any stage-related genre, 'impure' in keeping with the point of view (not atypical of twentieth-century scholarship, and derived in part from polemical exchanges in the late nineteenth-century German press) that non-theatrical music, lacking in extra-musical implications, was 'pure' or 'absolute.' See 'The "Music of the Future" Controversy', in *Music in the Western World: A History in Documents*, ed. Richard Taruskin and Piero Weiss (Belmont, CA: Thomson/Schirmer, 2008), 324–29. — Editor's note.]

26. Lincoln Kirstein, 'Ballet and Music', in *The International Cyclopedia of Music and Musicians*, ed. Oscar Thompson and Bruce Bohle (New York: Dodd, Mean, 1975), 123.

27. Bournonville, *Efterladte Skrifter*, 160. See also Wolfgang Marx, 'The Ballet as a "Genre": Initial Thoughts on the Genetic Identity of a Multimedia Art Form', in *Die Beziehung von Musik und Choreographie im Ballett*, ed. Michael Malkiewicz and Jörg Rothkamm (Berlin: Vorwerk 8, 2007), 15.

28. Løvenskiold, *Introduction af Første Act*, 3.

29. See the original libretto, translated by Patricia N. McAndrew, Appendix 3 of this volume. 'James comes to himself again and remembers that this very day he is to be betrothed to his cousin, the amiable Effy. Vexed, Gurn leaves him, bemoaning the injustice he must suffer because of the superiority that Effy bestows upon this daydreamer.' See also Ole Nørlyng, 'Drøm eller virkelighed: om de musikalske kilders betydning i forbindelse med en idag forsvunden mimsk scene i *Sylphiden*', in *Bournonville: Tradition, Rekonstruktion*, ed. Ole Nørlyng and Henning Urup (Copenhagen: C.A. Reitzel, 1989), 146–64.

30. Løvenskiold, *Introduction af Første Act*, 6–12.

31. This mime scene is also described in the original printed libretto. The scene was included in Johan Kobborg's production of *La Sylphide* for the Royal Ballet in London in 2005, though some of the segments had to be orchestrated because the music for the scene survived only in the piano arrangement.

32. (See the full quotation above.) Bournonville, *Efterladte Skrifter*, 160. See also Nørlyng, 'Bournonville og hans musikalske medarbejdere', 259.

33. Rothkamm, 'Dialogähnliche und acktionsbezogene Musik im Ballett *Sylphiden*', 23-28.

34. Jörg Rothkamm points out that this section might have been inspired by an instrumental recitative in Carl Maria von Weber's *Der Freischütz*: Agathe's scene 'Welch schöne Nacht', in which she opens the balcony door. Ibid., 28 and note 25.

35. Ibid., 29-32.

36. Jürgensen, *The Bournonville Tradition*, II, 36. The original *pas de deux* is recorded both by David Garforth (Chandos ABRD-1200, LP [now CHAN 6546, CD], 1986) and Peter Ernst Lassen (DACOCD 631, CD, 2005).   Anna Lærkesen used the music for a *pas de deux* entitled 'Hommage à Bournonville', created for Silja Schandorff and Henning Albrechtsen in 1989. Parts of the *pas de deux* have been interpolated into productions of *La Sylphide* by Peter Schaufuss (London Festival Ballet, later the English National Ballet, 1979) and Johan Kobborg (Royal Ballet, 2005).

37. See Robert Greskovic, *Ballet 101: A Complete Guide to Learning and Loving the Ballet* (Pompton Plains, NJ: Limelight Editions, 2005), 338–40. He writes that the Mayseder interpolations occur here within a seven-part divertissement as solos for James and the Sylph.

38. For further details see Jürgensen, *The Bournonville Tradition*, II, 273–74 and 306–07. Even though much of the written material about the different productions is still in existence today, it is difficult to establish an exact chronology for the changes, cuts and new additions that have been made over the years.

39. Repetiteur Partie til Balletten Sylphiden af Bournonville sat i Musik af. Herm. Løvenskiold, Royal Library, DK-Kk MA (Ktb 275 parti ms). A copy of this is preserved on microfilm in the Dance Collection at the New York Public Library.

40. *La Sylphide as danced by Fanny Elssler* (New York: Atwill, [184-?]).

41. The opening theme of the finale is now played by cellos instead of horn quartet at the Royal Danish Ballet, though in Peter Schaufuss's version and the recordings thereof this theme is played by the horn quartet.

42. Løvenskiold, 'to Herman Frederik Løvenskiold'.

43. Ibid.

44. Ibid.

45. Overskou was the godfather of Bournonville's daughter Augusta. See Jürgensen, *The Bournonville Tradition*, I, 128.

46. This was probably Henrik Rung.

47. Thomas Overskou, *Den danske Skueplads i dens Historie fra de første Spor af danske Skuespil indtil vor Tid*, 7 vols., vol. V (Copenhagen: Thieles, 1864), 300–01.

48. *Dagen*, 29 November 1836.

49. *Kjøbenhavnsposten* (Copenhagen), 12 December 1836.

50. Ibid., 18 December 1836.

51. Herman Severin Løvenskiold, 'to the Management of the Royal Danish Theatre', in *Royal Danish Theatre Journalbog* (Copenhagen: Danish National Archives).

52. Jürgensen, *The Bournonville Tradition*, II, 37. See also Gaye Kynoch's translation of Ole Nørlyng, *The Music for La Sylphide*, Liner Notes, Chandos ABRD-1200, 1986, LP [now CHAN 6546, CD].

53. Journal no. 1497-98-991836. The Royal Library, Copenhagen.

54. David Hunt, 'Ballet Music from Denmark', *Dance and Dancers* (October 1953): 9.

55. *Corsaren* (Copenhagen), 1846. Translated by Gaye Kynoch in Nørlyng, *The Composer Herman Severin Løvenskiold*.

Chapter 8

The Italian *Silfide* and the contentious reception

of ultramontane ballet

Ornella Di Tondo

'A sylphide has finally driven [. . .] all that melancholy choreography away. No more brawling amongst citizens, no more military camps, battles, massacres, deaths; no more wounded, no more agonising; but instead delicious woodland scenes in which love drips its "sweet anger, sweet disdain and sweet peace" into the hearts of graceful nymphs and lovestruck country folk.' (Anonymous critic, *Gazzetta di Genova*, 1837[1])

'It's a sort of Beauty that includes women hatching out of the ground like chicks from an egg, and calls for the unfledged to die, only to rise again with wings, as genies, sylphides or wilis, or what have you. [...] Truly, the French have invented a beautiful approach to the marvellous: the marvellous of the eye – utterly implausible, both physiologically and artistically – and the marvellous of the unpredictable.' (Tommaso Locatelli, *Gazzetta privilegiata di Venezia*, 1843[2])

These opinions – one each from opposing camps – are only two of the many critical reviews of ballet that appeared in Italy from the late 1830s to the late 1840s, the decade that witnessed the arrival of French romantic ballets of the fantastic type, such *La Sylphide* (which was followed by *Giselle*, *La Fille du Danube*, *La Jolie fille de Gand*, and *La Péri*). Such ballets rarely alighted on the peninsula in their original form, as scholars have long noted. Instead, they were presented in a wide array of versions, staged locally by various choreographers.[3]

Less known, however, is the fact that *oltremontano* ballet was met with heated debate in Italy – and robust resistance in some quarters. (The adjective *d'oltremonte*, meaning 'from the other side of the mountains', was not always complimentary, and was applied to every expression of romanticism of French or German provenance, whether literary, musical or choreographic.) The aim of this study is to discover what made *La Silfide's* Italian reception so contentious, and to do so by examining archival information about the Italian versions of the ballet *La Silfide* and their dissemination.

Such an undertaking inevitably brings into view the sharp differences between French and Italian approaches to ballet – its production, performance practices, aesthetics, and ways of representing identity and cultural traditions on stage. Moreover, the procedure of cultural transfer – how a work is converted, re-elaborated and re-invented in a new context (a subject with which historians and anthropologists are familiar) – must be borne in mind. Clearly, when it came to transplanting French choreographic subjects in Italy in the nineteenth century, nothing less than Italian identity itself was at stake, along with the defence of homeland traditions and values. The Italian people, after all, were in the midst of constructing a national image and striving for liberation from foreign oppression. Italian national identity, indeed, must be counted among the deep-seated reasons for the rough reception given to *La Silfide* upon its arrival in Italy. For both the aesthetic and the dramaturgy of this ballet were deemed thoroughly un-Italian in taste and character.

We must also bear in mind the crisis in Italian choreography that was taking place at the time – a crisis readily discernible in contemporary theatrical reviews. For, apparently, the momentum gained by the great coreodrammas of Salvatore Viganò (1769-1821) and Gaetano Gioia (1768-1826) had been exhausted, despite the best efforts of several highly regarded choreographers in the 1830s and 1840s. So until a mid-century revitalisation was brought about by Giuseppe Rota (1822-1865), the Italian choreographic tradition found itself particularly exposed to outside influences. Many critics did raise a spirited defence against French subject matter and the French approach to choreography, this latter being manifested not so much in the action of the ballet, which was entrusted to Italian mimes, as the danced segments, be they *assolo, passo a due, passo a tre*, etc. (solo, *pas de deux, pas de trois*, etc.). These danced segments were performed by *primi danzatori di rango francese* (first dancers of the French rank), who danced in the French style even though they were not necessarily of French nationality. Indeed, the circulation of *La Silfide* coincided exactly with the years in which the Italian peninsula was being criss-crossed by a good many dancers and choreographers who were French in origin or at least in training.

The public's desire for novelty, the advance of the new romantic sensibility across Europe, the necessity of continually offering new productions and responding to new trends – these were just some of the reasons many Italian choreographers began to experiment with the new style and the new subject matter of French romantic choreography. By no means, however, did they abandon the production of Italian-style *balli di carattere storico e drammatico* (ballets of historic and dramatic character), which still constituted the most important segment of the repertoire during this era. But at the same time, French-style ballets held the considerable advantage of requiring fewer performers and being less complicated (and therefore less expensive) to stage.

They also featured fewer long pantomime scenes than Italian ballets did, making the French ballets easier to understand. Further, French ballets, although considered *leggeri*, or light, and often trite in subject matter, were nevertheless seen as more immediately enjoyable and replete with *diletto*, or delight.

So, what exactly happened when Italian and French choreographic traditions encountered one another? Which elements of French ballet (choreographic, dramatic, stylistic, musical, and so forth) met with the warmest reception in Italy? And, on the other hand, which elements were deemed least pleasing? Pursuing answers to these questions will help illuminate the full panorama of Italian ballet in these years.

Of course, this investigation is complicated by the ephemeral nature of dance and the scarcity of documentation. In the case of *La Silfide*, the absence of choreographic notation has made it difficult to obtain specific information about the choreography and style of the many versions performed in Italy in the nineteenth century. Published ballet libretti, however, have made it possible to make worthwhile observations about the different versions of the story, and printed scores help show the diversity of musical versions. Reviews, critical writings and other primary documents (including memoirs, diaries, autobiographies), further, cast light on the nature of the reception of *La Silfide* in Italy and therefore on French romantic ballet in general.

Romanticism in Italy; the difficult reception of *La Silfide*
The spread of European romanticism in Italy, especially in the beginning, did not come easily. In the late 1810s through the 1820s, the literary community gathered on two opposing fronts: classicists defending the perfection of the illustrious Italian tradition, and romantics, whose ranks were drawn especially from the younger generations, and who were open to new influences from French romanticism as inspired by German models. The Italian romantic movement, strongly oriented towards liberalism and patriotic nationalism, had been characterised by civil and pedagogic goals – that is, literature and art had become means of educating the public, for they built a common language and helped to construct a civil consciousness in a nation divided into many states, cultures, and dialects.[4] Thus the Italian romantic movement had emphasised historical narratives and realistic modes. Its adherents disliked many aspects of German and English romanticism, such as fable and fantasy, dreams and illusion, the horrible and the nightmarish. (Such motifs, however, would slowly gain acceptance starting around mid century, and were, indeed, characteristic of the Scapigliatura movement's latter developments of the 1860s and 1870s. This artistic and literary movement – aside from bringing new words into the Italian language from the realms of symbolism

and realism – revisited romantic themes and genres still foreign to Italian culture and emulated such models as E. T. A. Hoffmann and Théophile Gautier.)

The Italian theatrical production system itself also contributed to the rough welcome given to French ballets in the 1830s and 1840s. This system was characterised in ballet by a plurality and polycentrism unknown in other European countries, a direct consequence of the particularism of Italy's geography and its politics. Also, the fundamental importance of the *balli drammatici e storici* with their complex plots, rich with spectacular and cata- strophic events, must be considered. These works often featured obscure events and figures alluding to Italy's past glories and to the liberation of the homeland. Further, one must note that Italian choreographers, starting in the 1830s, were typically quite well versed in Italian culture (history, music, painting, literature and so on). Also, Italian ballet had its own distinctive, original choreographic language, characterised by technical virtuosity and brilliance of style, a complex and varied pantomimic language, and a careful deployment of massed groups.[5]

Another roadblock to the simple importation of French ballet was that Italian choreographers were accustomed to having control of the entire creative process – everything from choosing the subject, writing the libretto (and at times even coming up with the music), as well as providing the pre- liminary design drafts of costumes, décor, machines and equipment (though all this was subject to the approval of directors, theatrical commissioners, and political and religious censors, all of whom could impose modifications and cuts).[6] The professionalism and the output of the choreographers was closely scrutinised by the specialised press and by a knowledgeable, impas- sioned public.

Also, choreographers were accustomed to dealing with a constant need for new works, a requirement of the production system that prevailed in most of the important Italian theatres. In these Italian theatres – quite un- like those in France – the concept of a 'repertory' of dance was practically non-existent until the last decades of the century. Indeed, until at least 1848, three or four ballets were produced for the main theatrical season, that of *Carnevale*. (The other theatrical seasons were *Autunno, Estate, Primavera*; that is, autumn, summer, and spring.) Of these three or four ballets, two would be serious and the other(s) demi-character, and they were composed, or at least newly re-worked, expressly for the city in question. Under the pressure of ever-tighter theatre schedules, choreographers were often obliged to re-use segments of pre-existing works for new productions. In the absence of effective copyright protection, these choreographers would borrow other choreographers' works and stage programmes,[7] making numerous dra- matic, choreographic and musical modifications.

Given the pervasiveness of this practice, it is not surprising that even the masterpieces of French romantic ballet, in order to be adapted to the Italian taste (or rather, to the local taste, which varied from Naples, to Rome, to Milan, and so forth), were subjected to many changes indeed, be they to the choreography, to the music or to the plot. Yet the Italian temperament, which was less inclined to the fantastic and dreamlike than that of northern Europe, did respond warmly to certain aspects of French ballet, including lively pantomimic ballets with adventure-based plots (which were often audacious and melodramatic in quality, and full of stage artifices) and exoticism and local colour. Less successful in Italy, however, were the plots of the *ballets blancs* or 'white ballets', so-called because the action transpired in a supernatural setting with female protagonists who wore airy tutus to represent ethereal spirits such as sylphides and fairies.

Let us pause for a moment to consider two important terms: *ballet blanc* and *romantic*. The term *ballet blanc* enjoyed a tenacious historiographical success when applied, in the twentieth century, to Italian ballet, despite the fact that it had nothing whatsoever to do with the Italian tradition of the period.[8] And the adjective 'romantic', in regard to ballet, did not hold a uniform meaning during the period in question, and did not even appear in Italian ballet libretti until the 1820s. Often used in its various formations – 'romantic-mythological', 'romantic-historic', 'romantic-allegoric', 'romantic-tragic', and with the exception of 'romantic-fantastic' – the term seemed to apply, at least in the first half of the century, to ballets enlivened by stage effects and a strong element of adventure. Even in the theoretical works of the Italian Carlo Blasis (1795-1878), the term does not appear until 1828, in his *Code of Terpsichore*. An important figure in the history of ballet, Blasis was a dancer, choreographer, teacher and dance theorist who was heavily influenced during his contact with French circles and by the example of Jean Aumer. Blasis was also an heir of Dauberval and the *ballet d'action*, and thus an artist whose choreographic compositions were more indebted to the great French school of the early nineteenth century than to the new romantic aesthetic.

In this early nineteenth-century French setting, we find the term used in the title of Blasis' libretto for *Zara* (1828), a ballet set in medieval Spain and chock-full of intrigue and exoticism.[9] *Zara* exemplifies the *style troubadour*, which dates to the end of the eighteenth century and may be found in various choreographic works, especially in the beginning of the nineteenth century. Such works attest to this commingling of old and new sensibilities typical of that era.

In the writings of Blasis, the term 'romantic' re-appeared much later in his *Studi sulle Arti imitatrici* (1844) in a highly noteworthy passage in which the author compares French and Italian opera in order to explain the differences in the two choreographic languages. The French favoured the *meraviglioso visibile* (visible marvelous), he writes, while the Italians preferred historical subjects, as well as tragic and comic works performed in a simple manner. As for the romantic genre, introduced about twenty years earlier in literature, Blasis refers to it as a 'confusing of all the genres' which made for a 'mixed genre', signalling therefore the commingling of diverse elements and the breakdown of rigorous traditional generic distinctions.[10]

Blasis's comparison of nineteenth-century opera to theatrical dance provides an important key for interpreting the contrasts between the specifics of the French and the Italian styles. French ballet, he explains, was closely related to the great theatrical tradition of the *tragédie lyrique* (seventeenth-century French tragic opera) and then, later, to grand opéra (of the nineteenth century); French ballet also adhered to the fabulous and marvellous (*meraviglioso*), inspired first by mythology and then by traditional Nordic legends with adventurous themes. In Italian ballet, on the other hand, the imagery as well as the dramatic and stylistic approach are closely linked to Italian opera and to Italian drama and painting. The plots for both Italian opera and ballet were taken almost entirely from either contemporary Italian and foreign literature and dramaturgy, from the great classics of the past, including Dante, Ariosto, Tasso and Shakespeare, from historical narratives, or from contemporary theatrical productions, including the French *mélodrame* and the Italian *commedia*. The exceptions to this rule included material drawn from supernatural and fantastic themes of French origin.

So there were mutual influences between Italian opera and ballet – for example in the use of opera music in ballet; in shared titles and approaches to set design and in dramatic *topoi*; in the gestural expressions of the protagonists (for opera singers imitated the gestures of mimes and actors and vice versa), and in the fact that a subject was often used first in a ballet and then in an opera. Common to both Italian opera and ballet, too, were a highly emotive temperament and the display of extreme passions and actions, from the most sublime (such as love beyond death, maternal, paternal or filial sacrifice, fraternal friendship, self sacrifice for the nation or for liberty) to the most base (sinister betrayal, implacable revenge, mad jealousy), all being a part of the vast popular and romantic *imaginaire* diffused also throughout France. (No wonder, then – given these extremes – that to some Italian audiences the frail vicissitudes of French choreography of the fantastic and supernatural type paled in comparison to Italian opera and dramatic ballets.)

Filippo Taglioni's *Sylphide* (1832) and its antecedents. Luigi Henry's *La Silfide ovvero il genio dell'aria* (1828).

Before beginning our discussion of the Italian *Silfide*, it would be useful to remember that the Parisian *Sylphide* of Filippo Taglioni, with music by Jean Schneitzhoeffer, was staged for the first time at the Théâtre de l'Académie

Royale de Musique (the Paris Opéra) on March 12, 1832. The lead roles were given to Maria Taglioni as the Sylphide and Joseph Mazilier as James.[11] The ballet was a great success, as confirmed by the numerous performances at the Opéra in the following years and by its diffusion in all of Europe and beyond. The role of the sylphide later became the signature piece for all the celebrated ballerinas of the era. And Filippo Taglioni's *La Sylphide* was recognised later (by Théophile Gautier, for example, in a famous passage review dating more than a decade after the first staging) as the vehicle of a new aesthetic and the beginning of a profound stylistic and dramatic renewal.[12]

La Sylphide's anonymous libretto is attributed to the tenor Adolphe Nourrit, who is said to have been inspired by the gothic-style tale by Charles Emmanuel Nodier entitled *Trilby ou le Lutin d'Argail* (first edition 1822, reprinted in 1832).[13] But the ballet plot, only loosely modelled on Nodier's story, was really woven around the character of the tender and charming sylphide, an air spirit who comes to trouble the sleep of the young James, with whom she has fallen in love. (The ballet libretto differed from Nodier's novel in many ways, starting with a gender reversal: Nourrit's supernatural being was a female seductress, and not a seducing spirit in the tradition of male sylphs in love with beautiful mortal women.)

Here is a plot summary: The Sylphide, appearing to James, lures him away on the day of his planned wedding to Effie, leading him into the forest, which represents the spirits' realm. The Sylphide, however, becomes a victim of an evil spell cast by Madge, who was offended earlier when James chased her away. James, for his part, becomes irritated when the sorceress reveals to Effie that he is not truly in love with her, and that Gurn, James's simpleton friend, shall be the one to become her bridegroom. An evil spell, cast by Madge and her fellow witches during a witches' Sabbath, results in the creation of a magic scarf which will cause the wings of the sylphide to fall off, an act which would guarantee James possession of the Sylphide. This spell is brought to completion. But instead of leading to the result James wishes, the spell causes the death of the sylphide, who is then carried away in flight by other sylphides. James also ends up losing Effie, and nearly his senses, as well. In the finale, he finds himself in despair, while Madge laughs triumphantly and points toward Effie's wedding cortege in the distance. For Effie has married the faithful Gurn, restoring her happy social and familial circle to wholeness after its being troubled by the supernatural disturbance.[14]

In the realm of the literature and the theatre, bewitchingly attractive sylphides who fall in love with mortals had certainly existed before the ballets of Taglioni. The character of the ethereal sylphide and her male counterpart, the *silfo*, has a long history. Starting with the sixteenth-century *Liber de Nymphis, Sylphis, Pygmaeis et Salamandris et coeteris spiritibus* of Paracelsus, the sylphs and sylphides crossed the centuries and gained new momentum in the hands of Nicolas Montfaucon de Villars in the seventeeth century and Alexander Pope in the eighteenth century, and finally arrived in the romantic era, especially Germany, where they appeared in the writings of Heine and Goethe.

In the 1730s, too, the figure of the male *silfo* (and less frequently of the female *silfide*) as a lover of mortals began to appear in various novels (some of them of the libertine sort) by such authors as Crébillon fils (1730), de Crouzenac (1730), le comte de Caylus (1734), Jean Galli de Bibiena (1744), Marmontel (1761), Jacques Cazotte (1772), Georgiana Cavendish, Duchess of Devonshire (1788) and Pierre-Jean-Bapstiste Nougaret (1800).[15] In these novels, impalpable mythological beings fall hopelessly in love with humans. At first invisible to the humans' eyes, the sylphs disturb their sleep; voluptuous, seductive, high-minded, they represent the perfect realisation of love that was often denied by the marriages of convenience that young women of noble birth were forced into in that era. In several cases, the *silfo* or *silfide* is far from being a mere chimera and is quite of the carnal world.

The subject was so in vogue that in the wake of the enthusiasm for writings like *Le comte de Gabalis ou Entretiens sur les sciences secretes* (Paris, 1670) by Montfaucon de Villars or opera-ballets like *Zélindor roi des Sylphes* (1745, see below), rejected young lovers or unsatisfied husbands created elaborate stagings,[16] taking the role of *silfos* or *silfides* acting out the conquest of mortals, in order to win over reluctant loved ones.

In the theatrical realm, further, one may find comedies, operas and ballets which used the theme of the sylph (male or female) who falls in love with a mortal; these appeared long before the Nourrit/Taglioni ballet, and it is possible that Nourrit or at least Nodier was familiar with such works.[17] Early examples include the French *comédie* entitled *La Sylphide*, attributed to Arlecchino Dominique Biancolelli and performed by the Comédiens Italiens Ordinaires du Roi in Paris on September 11, 1730. This work bears several similarities to Nourrit's version of *La Sylphide*, though the earlier version the story, unlike Nourrit's, is treated with an ironic and light tone.[18]

There also existed comedies about a male sylph who loves mortal women (with a flesh-and-blood lover and the libertine question of love between humans and elemental spirits lurking in the background). Examples include *Le Sylphe ou le mari comme il y en a peu* by Martin de Choisy (1778) and *L'amant sylphe* by the comte of Linières, François-Antoine Quétant (1783).[19]

In ballets, the theme of a human enamoured of a sylphide had appeared in *Zélindor, Roi des Sylphes* (Versailles, 1745) with music by François Rebel and François Francoeur, which was performed again in 1752 at Versailles[20] – and in Italy at the Teatro Real in Parma (Autumn 1757) (with choreography by Delisle)[21] – wherein the 'King of the Sylphs' Zélindor desires the mortal Zirphé, and attains love in the end. Sylphs and sylphides, together

with other winged spirits, thereafter joined the cortege of divinities in mythological ballets – for instance, in the *ballet-héroïque Le Jugement de Pâris* by
Jean-Georges Noverre (Marseille, 1751) – and for a long time could be found
among Noverre's storehouse of characters.[22]

In Italy, a ballet entitled *La Silfide* already existed several years before the
ballet of the same name by Taglioni: *La Silfide ovvero il genio dell'aria*,[23] a *ballo
magico mitologico* (magic mythological ballet) created by the French choreographer Louis (or Luigi) Henry, music by Luigi Carlini.[24] It was performed at
La Scala in the spring season of 1828, featuring famous Austrian ballerina
Teresa (Thérèse) Héberlé, and Antonio Guerra. The plot, according to the
libretto, was inspired by an unnamed eastern manuscript, and is about a
sylphide, Ezelda, who loves an Asian prince, Azalide, and wishes to make him
her bridegroom. Destiny, however, imposes an obstruction which cannot be
lifted unless the sylphide and her prince overcome an exacting trial: a garland of flowers is placed between them, a barrier Azalide must not cross. But
the sylphide Ezelda is not allowed to explain to her beloved why he must
restrain himself. The young man is unable to resist, and the sylphide is transformed into a statue. In order to break the spell, the prince Azalide agrees to be
transformed into a statue in Ezelda's stead. Thanks to the providential intervention of Amore and Imene, who break the spell, the two are able to crown
their dream of love in a finale that (as we shall see below) is quite like some of
the versions of the later Italian *Silfide*.

Despite the many differences between Henry's and Taglioni's *Sylphide* ballets, there are also affinities between the two, at least in the initial setup:
in both instances a sylphide loves, and is loved in return, by a mortal, but
is prevented by her supernatural nature from attaining him. While in
Taglioni's *La Sylphide* the protagonist beseeches in vain to be set free, in Henry's version, the sylphide desires on her own accord to burn her wings, which
symbolise her elusiveness and, in the eyes of her beloved, her inconstancy
and fickleness.[25]

Whatever the similarities and differences, Henry, provoked by the appearance of Taglioni's *La Sylphide* in March 1832, published a protest in a
Parisian newspaper in October of the same year (with the help of his sister
Elise), claiming that Taglioni had copied his ballet. But whether or not
Taglioni (or perhaps even Nourrit) knew, or copied, Henry's *Silfide*, Henry's
work received a lukewarm reception and was given only a limited circulation, perhaps because it smacked of the old anacreontic and mythological
taste, and was thus seen in a more classicist light than a romantic one.[26]
(This may be why no reference appears to Henry's earlier version in the reviews of the later Taglioni-inspired Italian *Silfide*.) Also in keeping with this
fantastico-mitologico trend is the later ballet *Nadan o l'orgoglio punito*, an *azione
fantastica* set in the Orient and choreographed by Salvatore Taglioni, per-

formed at the San Carlo in Naples in October 1839; its leading character is the handsome 'Persian Signore' Nadan, with whom the silfide Dinazarde falls vainly in love.[27]

Diffusion and circulation of the Italian *Silfide*

La Sylphide made its initial appearance in Italy about five years after the Paris première, and after its diffusion European capitals such as London and St Petersburg. After 1861 the ballet would not be restaged in Italy until several decades later.

Let us now ask: what was the extent of the diffusion and circulation of Taglioni's *Sylphide* in Italy? Where was it staged and in what versions? What sorts of modifications did Italian choreographers make to the drama, the choreography and the music? Are the various Italian performances of the Silfide best considered reproductions, re-creations or reinventions of Taglioni's ballet? What aspects made the greatest impressions on the Italian audience? What are the characteristics of the version of the ballet said to have been staged by Filippo Taglioni and performed by Maria Taglioni in Italy between 1841 and 1842?

One of the most important observations we can draw from the impressively long list of performances of *La Silfide* in Italy is that it circulated widely between 1837 and 1861 in numerous versions rendered by different choreographers, among whom (as noted above) is Taglioni himself (see Appendix A at the end of this chapter). Indeed, between 1837 and 1861, no fewer than twenty-seven productions of *La Silfide* appeared there. They were created by fourteen different choreographers, and appeared in twenty-two theatres in eighteen cities, large and small. There is evidence, too, that music was either arranged or composed especially for at least six of these productions (some of it later published in Milan by Giovanni Ricordi, a point that will be elaborated upon below).

Some of these twenty-seven productions, it is true, must be counted as restagings or reinterpretations. But, on the other hand, there are probably even more *Silfides* in Italy remaining to be re-discovered – for this ballet may have been produced in provincial cities with smaller-sized theatres, the evidence now lurking only in local publications.

Seventeen libretti have been located for this study. (Here it should be noted that libretti for demi-character ballets – of which *La Silfide* was an example – were not always printed; neither did theatres in smaller towns always print ballet libretti.) And it is the version 'composed and directed' by Antonio Cortesi that emerges as especially relevant – for it was the *only* version staged in Italy between the years 1837 and 1841, and it appeared the most important theatres of the peninsula (Carlo Felice in Genoa, La Pergola in Florence, La Fenice in Venice, Regio in Turin, La Scala in Milan), and in 1844 and

1845, respectively, in Bologna (Teatro Comunitativo) and Venice (Teatro Gallo a San Benedetto). This version appeared yet again in a 'reproduction' by Andrea Paladini and Agostino Panni,[28] perhaps authorised by Cortesi himself, between the years 1848 (at La Scala in Milan and the San Carlo in Naples) and 1851 (at the Teatro Borgognissanti in Florence), and also 1856 (at the Teatro Comunale in Modena).

The monopoly of the Cortesi version ended in 1841 with the appearance of Filippo Taglioni's 'original' *La Silfide* at La Scala and in 1842 in Vicenza at the Teatro Eretenio, with Maria Taglioni in the lead role. Thereafter, all over Italy, numerous versions of *La Silfide* appeared, by various choreographers. These included a version by Luigi Bretin, who had played the role of James in Cortesi's Turin production; this production was given in three different houses in 1843 (the Apollo theatre in Rome, the Ducale in Parma and the Grande in Trieste). An 1842 production, attributable to Ferdinando Rugali, was given at the Teatro Civico in Alessandria, and in 1846, three more *Silfides* appeared: Giuseppe Lasina's at the Teatro Civico in Cagliari, one by an anonymous choreographer (perhaps Nicola Libonati) at the Teatro Sociale in Voghera, and Giovanni Galzerani's at the Teatro Apollo in Rome. This was followed in 1847 by Raffaello Gambardella's production at the Teatro del Pavone in Perugia. In the years to come, aside from the versions by Cortesi noted above, there were other productions, including the version choreographed in 1854 by Antonio Giuliani (Civic Theatre of Cuneo), the other probably dating to 1856 (see below) by David Costa (Teatro Carolino, Palermo), as well as versions by Tommaso Ferranti in 1859-60 at the Teatro S. Ferdinando in Palermo and by Federico Massini in 1860-61 at the Teatro della Canobbiana in Milan and at the Regio in Turin.

A reading of these libretti and a study of their dissemination suggests that Cortesi's versions of *La Silfide* rather than Filippo Taglioni's Italian *Silfide* – which by dint of its lower number of performances and the more limited circulation of its libretto was harder to imitate – served as the more important model for other choreographers who staged the ballet.

This leads to the fact that one choreographer tended to rely upon another in creating new versions of the ballet. One must certainly not underestimate Italian choreographers' creative autonomy in this regard, however. Nor can one think that drawing upon other choreographers' ballets necessarily meant making a mere duplication of the original libretto or choreography. It is best to bear malleability in mind as a key feature in the dissemination of ballet in Italy.

This malleability, too, helps one understand the alterations that many of the principal leads were able to demand from the choreographer (according to the practice of the period) when it came to their own solo variations. Further, one must consider the variable availability of a large *corps de ballet* and stage machinery needed for the appearances and disappearances of the sylphides and other winged fairies, requirements not all theatres could meet. And when it comes to variants in the libretti, one might hypothesise that every choreographer – even in the case of those who re-produced or restaged material – gave the ballet his own bold personal stamp.

Bold personal stamps do mark the *Silfide* productions of the early 1860s – not surprisingly, considering the multiple musical versions of *La Silfide* that cropped up in Italy, and the plurality of the musical versions of the Italian *Silfide*. Such bold stamps were especially notable in the case of choreographers with the greatest experience and personality, such as Giovanni Galzerani, or from those belonging to a particular ballet tradition, such as the French choreographer Louis (Luigi) Bretin.

Variants in the plot. The libretto versions of Antonio Cortesi (1837-38, 1841-44) and of Filippo Taglioni (1841-42). The Venetian libretto of 1845.

Another point of interest is that many of the libretti examined for this study contain significant variants in the plot. (See Appendix C.) But before turning to these variants, it must be noted that an examination of the seventeen libretti I have found for this study shows that almost all the libretti produced between 1837 and 1841, and many of the later ones as well, copied the text of the libretto of Antonio Cortesi, the first producer of the ballet in Italy. Two exceptions to this trend are Filippo Taglioni and Giovanni Galzerani, whose libretti are inspired directly by Nourrit's original.

Antonio Cortesi (1796-1879) was born into a family of artists, became a performer in the ballets of Gioia, Galzerani and Antonio Montici, and taught at the school of dance at the Teatro Regio in Turin. Most importantly, Cortesi was a prolific choreographer who was active in a variety of European capitals such as London, Lisbon and Vienna and who, by the end of his life, had almost one hundred attributable productions to his name. He was especially famous for his wide-ranging *balli eroici, storici e drammatici* (heroic, historical and dramatic ballets) – for example *Ines di Castro, L'ultimo giorno di Missolungi, Marco Visconti, Il Pescatore di Brindisi* (i.e. the Masaniello story), *Gugliemo Tell* – which were inspired by the style of Salvatore Viganò and Giovanni Galzerani.[29] Aside from staging *La Silfide*, Cortesi was the first, or among the first, to stage *Gisella* (1843, with Fanny Cerrito), *La figlia del Danubio* ('in the footsteps of the programme of Mr. Filippo Taglioni', 1845, with Maria Taglioni) and *Beatrice di Gand* (also known as *La Bella fanciulla di Gand*, 'in the footsteps of the programme of Mr. de Saint-Georges', 1845, with Fanny Elssler[30]). His versions strike a successful compromise between French sensibility and Italian tradition, all while bearing his own personal stamp. In this regard, it is worth noting the preface to his 1843 Milan version of *Giselle*, in which he practically apologises for relying on a well-known subject. Here, Cortesi points out his own original contribution, which was necessitated by a need to satisfy both the 'Italian taste' and his own creative abilities.[31]

> If I return with a subject already performed in France, I have at the very least made an effort to alter it according to the Italian taste. I have expanded it and sought to render the action more interesting, and I have inserted new dances, all of my own invention.[32]

Cortesi's *Silfide* libretti. For the Florentine *Silfide* production of September 1837 (and again for the Venetian production of 1837-38) Cortesi prepared a libretto consisting of a condensed version of the Nourrit text. It is possible that Cortesi was aware of both the first Nourrit version of 1832 and the reprint of 1834, which were similar to one another. In any case, because of its greater brevity – in keeping with the Italian tradition – this Cortesi libretto is less poetic and descriptive than Nourrit's. Indeed, Italian ballet libretti in general did not have the same poetic or rhetorico-literary ambitions as in France, where ballet libretti were often written by professional literary figures and therefore tended to be too complex to suit the purpose for which they were created (at least according to some critics).[33] In Italy, as noted above, the libretto was instead written by the choreographer who, in some cases, did consult with literary professionals or men of the theatre,[34] since the audience was rather demanding in regard to verisimilitude and the treatment of the action. But the overall aim of the Italian ballet libretto was to provide the spectator with a source to leaf through before or during the performance, and which could serve as a quick reference for following the plot. Cortesi's version of the *La Silfide* libretto, for example (which is in two acts and without the typical French division into scenes), sacrifices many of the descriptions of the scenery, effects, and the dramatic and mimed actions present in the French text; even the direct quotations of the dialogues and monologues are absent.

In Cortesi's 1837 libretto, which presents the work as 'a mythological ballet composed and directed by Antonio Cortesi' the ballet's classification as 'mythological' is particularly notable. Probably prompted by the fantastic subject matter and the presence of supernatural beings, Cortesi used a genre name that was familiar to the audiences. The cast list of principal characters is practically the same as that found in the Nourrit libretto, except for the role of Anna who, instead of being James's mother, becomes Effie's mother. In Cortesi's version, too, Gurn is designated as 'James's friend (foolish)', which suggests a mime characterisation of the character already present in Nourrit's libretto, and which is connected to the figure of the awkward suitor typical in many eighteenth-century *ballets comiques*, including Dauverbal's *La Fille mal gardée* (1789).

Apart from its greater conciseness, the Cortesi libretto differentiates itself from Nourrit's especially by the absence of both the Sabbath and the evil spell cast by the witch Madge and her female cohorts. In Nourrit's version, this scene is described in great detail in Act Two, scene i, while the Cortesi libretto simply indicates: 'old Madge sets out to seek vengeance from James.' Thus the demonic, witch-like characterisation of Madge of the Nourrit libretto is considerably weakened. Another important modification is the transposition of the action from Scotland to Switzerland. The reason behind this change is not clear; perhaps suitably Scottish-looking props, sets, and costumes were unavailable. In any case, this instance confirms how one sort of 'exotic', 'characteristic', or 'local colour' could be easily interchanged with another.

In January of 1841, on the occasion of the performance of his *Silfide* at La Scala, Cortesi prepared a new version of the libretto. Probably in anticipation of the coming of Filippo Taglioni and his daughter Maria at the same theatre for the upcoming spring season, Cortesi's libretto was modified in several ways, some tending toward a greater fidelity to the French original. For example, Nourrit's name – absent from Cortesi's previous libretto – is mentioned in the frontispiece of this version: *'Ballo di mezzo carattere fantastico composto da Antonio Cortesi sul programma del Sig. Nourrit'* ('fantastic demi-character ballet created by Antonio Cortesi after the libretto of Signore Nourrit'). This seeming clarification could also be interpreted as a proud affirmation by Cortesi of his own creative autonomy in the making of the ballet, albeit one based on a non-original subject. Other new features include the number of acts (three instead of two) and a new genre designation: instead of a *'Ballo mitologico'* (mythological ballet), it was now a *'ballo di mezzo carattere fantastico'* (fantastic demi-character ballet). (In this case 'demi-character' seems to refer to the uncomplicated plot, which takes place in a bucolic setting and features character dances, as opposed to the term *serio* – serious – which was used in Italy to refer to the great dramatic, historic and spectacular ballets.) And the term *fantastico*, which became more and more popular between 1840 and 1850 for ballets featuring sylphides, willis, péris, ondines, etc., of course indicates the fabulous, magical and supernatural element. In keeping with the Nourrit libretto, the action is moved back to the original Scotland, while the second act takes place in the 'dwelling place of the witches.' In this version – perhaps because of the availability both of adequate scenery and a larger and better trained *corps de ballet* – the scene in which the enchanted scarf is concocted by Madge and her cohorts is included, though it is described very succinctly.[35] Unlike Cortesi's earlier versions (though similar to Henry's version), the ballet ends with a final apotheosis and the reunion of the two lovers atop Olympus, all thanks to the intervention of Love as *deus ex machina*.[36] (This ending would later be repeated in Cortesi's 1844 Bologna libretto, which was completely identical to his Milan libretto.)

Taglioni's *Silfide* libretti. In May of 1841 in Milan, only about five months after the appearance of Cortesi's *Silfide*, Filippo Taglioni presented his own version of the ballet. Despite the low number of performances – only three, because *La Gitana*, new to Milan, was Maria Taglioni's top choice for her debut[37] – a libretto was published (and reproduced without alteration in Vicenza in 1842). Far from being a literal translation of the Nourrit libretto as one might expect, this Italian version of the Nourrit/Taglioni ballet presents a text that is quite scaled down (even more so than the Cortesi version), probably because it was intended specifically for an Italian audience. In Taglioni's Italian *Silfide* (which is designated as *ballo fantastico* or 'fantastic ballet'), even the second act (which includes the Witches' Sabbath, carried out by witches and 'disgusting animals') is described rather briefly.[38] The account of the tragic ending, however, does follow the original libretto closely.

Especially noteworthy in the opening *Avvertimento* to Taglioni's Italian libretto is his claim of complete authority for the patrimony of the ballet and, at the same time, his expressed desire to reproduce this acclaimed ballet as he had revised it 'in other locations.'

> Having been invited to stage my ballet *La Silfide* in this theatre, I wanted to present it as I had done it in other locations. In presenting these modifications, I do not intend to improve upon an acclaimed work already favourably received by this perceptive and courteous audience, but rather, since this ballet is my own, I want to present it under the form that has already procured me favour. I hope in this instance, too, that my ballet will be warmly received.

The first act of the version Taglioni produced in Milan featured a *pas de trois* that he had originally choreographed for the November 1839 St Petersburg production of the ballet *l'Ombre*. In this number – which was also incorporated in the version of *La Sylphide* performed by his daughter Maria Taglioni, in July 1840 at the Paris Opéra – the jealous sylphide, invisible to Effie but not to James, intervenes in the relationship between these two mortals, demonstrating not only a psychological but also a stylistic and technical contrast with her rival, represented by the *terre-à-terre* style of Effie and the *aérien* style of the sylphide. (In Italy the *passo a tre* of the Sylphide, James and Effie was often performed as a separate number, as was the famous *passo a due* between the Sylphide and James in the Forest Act.) In the Taglionis' subsequent Vicenza production of 1842, moreover, Maria Taglioni inserted a *Passo dell'Ombra*, in which the Sylphide dances with her own shadow, believing it is a rival. This became a topos in the repertoire of many dancers.

A later *Silfide*, performed by Maria Taglioni in March 1845 at the Teatro Gallo a San Benedetto in Venice, raises many questions. For even though the frontispiece of its libretto clearly calls it a '*Ballo fantastico in tre atti composto dal signor Filippo Taglioni*' ('fantastic ballet in three acts composed by Signor Filippo Taglioni'), its text is not the same as the one Taglioni used in Milan and Vicenza. It bears far closer similarities to the one Cortesi had published in Milan, with only a few differences (the ending is tragic and the Sabbath scene is described even more briefly). Thus it is likely that the choreographer of this production was Cortesi himself, understandably sticking with his own libretto. (In the same season Cortesi did stage at least one other ballet featuring Maria Taglioni, namely *La Fille du Danube*.) In any case, whether Cortesi created this 1845 Venetian version of *Silfide* himself or not, the use of a libretto so similar to his confirms the success of his libretto, which was now considered canonic.

From this Venetian production, too, we may discern that the choreographer's influence was limited. Maria Taglioni, who had of course performed the original role of the sylphide in Paris, surely retained a certain amount of independence when she performed in this Venetian production. (Here, one must recall that in soloists in ballets of the eighteenth century and well into the nineteenth – just as in operas of the same era with its *aria di baule* or 'suitcase arias' – could alter the *pas* as they wished, or insert a successful and popular solo or *passo a due* created by another choreographer or by the dancer him- or herself.) In the case of Maria Taglioni dancing in a production of *La Silfide* other than her father's, it is likely that she danced her father's choreography in her own solos and in the *passi a due* with James, but did not concern herself with the overall choreography of the ballet, in particular the dancing of the other performers and the *corps de ballet*, whether it was Cortesi's or her father's original. As for the possibility of inserting one's own *pas*, a contract between Maria Taglioni and La Scala (dated May 17, 1840) for performances in spring 1841 stipulated that Maria Taglioni could indicate the repertoire in which she wished to perform. From amongst her usual favourite *pas* she could choose whichever one she wished, and in which ballets they would be inserted. Not only that, she could chose her own male partner, and select the soloists from the roster of dancers under contract to the theatre for the season. Such was the power of the stars of the romantic ballet.[39]

More variants in the plot. Libretti by Ferdinando Rugali (Alessandria, 1842), Giovanni Galzerani (Rome, 1846).

Amongst the other versions of the libretto, that of Ferdinand Rugali (Teatro Civico di Alessandria, Carnival 1842) follows Taglioni's quite closely except for the ending. Here, it is not just the Sylphide who dies, but also James, who expires at the end of Act Three, to be brought back to life in Act Four by Amore and transported along with the Sylphide to a 'Palace of Love'.[40]   In this version, the mortal lover liberates himself from his mortal body in order to be reunited with his non-human lover in the supernatural realm, a resolution that recalls the aforementioned *La Péri* of Jean Coralli and Théophile Gautier (1843).

Another important *Silfide* libretto, quite independent in some respects from the Nourrit and Cortesi versions, was prepared by the choreographer Giovanni Galzerani for a Roman production in March 1846, featuring Maria Taglioni and Francesco Penco in the lead roles. Galzerani was a choreographer of *balli storici e avventurosi* (historical and adventure ballets) in the 1820s and '30s whose work was characterised by movement *en masse* for large ensembles and long mime scenes. In the 1840s he competed with Cortesi (with less convincing results, however) in producing ballets inspired by the new French romantic style.

The three-act Galzerani *Silfide* libretto constitutes an original translation which in some ways is more careful to respect the Nourrit libretto than either the Cortesi or the Italian Taglioni versions. Among the elements taken from Nourrit is the genre designation *ballo* and a detailed description of the stage scenery. Specific details missing in other versions are included in Galzerani's libretto, such as the heron feather given to Effie by Gurn, and some written-out dialogues that correspond to mime scenes. (But it also includes a scene in Act Two in which the Sylph expresses her joy 'with cheerful gestures which are delightfully repeated by her own shadow in the moonlight' – this is actually a passage from *l'Ombre*, which Maria Taglioni also performed as a self-standing separate solo number during her stay in Rome.)

A notable difference between the Nourrit and Galzerani libretti is that in the spell-casting scene Galzerani's Madge is changed from 'old witch' to 'old gypsy', and 'held to be an enchantress by the entire village'. And the dramatic resolution conceived by Galzerani in Act Two was entirely original: here, Madge's vendetta against James is actually prompted by a request from Effie and Anna, both of whom, accompanied by Gurn, beseech the witch's help. Madge, promising to 'avenge herself on the one who led James astray', brings out the 'mysterious veil' without revealing its purpose, despite Effie's pleas for her to do so.[41] This innovation, even if seeming to lighten the moral profile of Madge, somewhat alters the original character of Effie, who in the Nourrit libretto was a simple and love-struck girl, wishing to marry and to create a family, a duty for which she has always been ready but one that James eludes. (This is an Effie who ends up fulfilling this vow with the simple-minded yet faithful Gurn.) What remains unclear, however, is the motivation behind this modification, which makes Effie at least partly responsible for the punishment meted out to disloyal characters such as James, and those who, like the Sylphide, seduce other people's spouses.

A plausible explanation is the intervention of Roman censors, who were particularly vigilant when it came to matters of morality and religion. Indeed, on more than one occasion they had opposed romantic-influenced ballet plots. In the name of a cultural politics founded on a polemical anti-romantic stance, and in the defence of classical erudition, romanticism's opponents viewed the new movement as excessive and dangerous from an ideological standpoint since it was so strongly associated with liberal and progressive ideas – ideas strongly disliked by the papal government.[42] Since in Rome cabalistic and witch scenes were quite out of favour (to put it mildly), it is not surprising that the Roman *Silfide* libretto of 1846 would omit the diabolical spell cast by Madge and her companion during the Witches' Sabbath, the very name of which was not even to be pronounced in the capital of the papal state. The Nourrit libretto, indeed, was utterly unacceptable in the milieu of papal Rome (not on the stage but in print as well) for it included such unholy things as magic circles traced by Madge, and a cauldron with a boiling brew in which the witches immersed the scarf and various magical instruments and objects (cabalistic books, spheres, skulls, poisonous herbs, reptiles and other wild and frightful animals, and so forth).

More variants in the plot. Libretti by Antonio Giuliani (Cuneo, 1854), David Costa (Palermo, 1856?), Tommaso Ferranti (Palermo, 1860) and Federico Massini (Milan, Turin, 1860-61).
Subsequent productions of *La Silfide*, which display notable divergences from the Cortesi libretti that inspired them, date from the mid 1850s. In the *Silfide* of Antonio Giuliani (Cuneo, 1854), whose libretto is otherwise quite similar to that of Taglioni, a previously unknown character appears: a 'Genius of the air' (a term used on the other libretti to designate the Silfide), who functions as a sort of *deus ex machina*. In Act One it is this Genius, profiting from the confusion of the wedding festival, who helps James slip away; shortly thereafter, the Genius appears to Effie (who is in tears) promising revenge, something that is promptly achieved, for it is the Genius again, in the following act, who orders Madge to fabricate the fatal scarf. In the last act it is again the Genius and not Amore (as it is in other versions) who restores the Silfide to life and grants her in marriage to James.

There is another notable post-1850 version, almost certainly from Palermo, though its libretto is missing a frontispiece, and thus silent as to when this *Silfide* was performed. According to an indirect reference to a *Silfide* given at the Teatro Carolino (now the Teatro Bellini) in Palermo in 1856 with Amina Boschetti, the famous ballerina, in the title role [43] the ballet may have been performed in this city and its choreography entrusted (as was often the case) to the premier danseur and interpreter of the role of James, that is, David Costa.

In any case, the libretto under discussion introduced a change that is far from trivial: it moves the setting of the story to China. It also changes the names of all the characters except for the Sylphide and Madge: James becomes 'Zabì', Effie 'Danina', Gurn 'Joffrè', and Anna (usually Effie's mother in Italian *Silfide* libretti) is replaced by 'Zolì', Effie's father. And, in the *corps de ballet*, in addition to the usual characters, i.e. 'sylphides', 'genies', 'witches', the villagers are not Swiss or Scottish, but Chinese. The unusual Eastern setting, which recalls Louis Henry's version in 1828 (with its Asian prince Azalide), probably played a role in the scenic design, the choreography (think especially in the dances of the 'villagers' during the engagement party), and perhaps in the music as well. The staging must have been tinged with exotic touches, too – not unreasonable, considering that it is a fairy-tale story, and certainly a far cry from the usual image of *La Sylphide* set in Nordic mists and enlivened by colourful 'national' Scottish dancing. This 'Chinese' approach had no successors, for the title character in the later ballet *Una Silfide a Pekino (A Sylphide in Beijing)* by Giuseppe Rota (1859-60), was actually the prima ballerina of Europe, Amina, in Beijing with a ballet company and bedevilled by a Mandarin.[44]

In the Palermo 'Chinese' libretto it is worth noting that, aside from the larger role given to Madge (in Act One, for example, it is she and not Gurn who warns of James's betrayal and leads the villagers to look for him), new characters are added to the witches' Sabbath: 'Fire', ''Vengeance, 'Poison', and 'Rage' and 'all who can bring about the revenge Madge desires' – and they also crop up in subsequent libretti of the late 1850s and early 1860s. Apart from that, the plot does not deviate substantially from the familiar version of the story, and it repeats extensive passages from the Cortesi libretto of 1840-41, with the same tragic ending.

Later versions are indebted to the allegorical and complex taste of the Italian *ballo grande* popular in those years (i.e., the late 1850s and early 1860s). (The *ballo grande* was a kind of grand spectacle emphasising mimed action and *ballabile*, lavish scenery and costumes, and deploying a large *corpo di ballo* in great mass scenes.) This taste accounts for the return of the genre designation *ballo mitologico* in *Silfide* libretti of the late 1850s and early 1860s. It also accounts for changes in the later scenes, including devils, repulsive animals and allegorical figures in the Sabbath scene, as well as the parade of mythological deities, genies, cupids, and angels in the final scene on Mt. Olympus. In Tomasso Ferranti's *Silfide* (Teatro S. Ferdinando di Palermo, 1859-60), for example, the presence of 'furies' and of the figures of 'Fire, Vengeance, Poison and Rage' in the ballet troupe are quite noteworthy. (All these figures surely appeared in the witches' Sabbath.) Also, the character of Anna, who is usually identified in the Italian libretti as the mother of Effie, is changed into 'Giovanni Keuber, father of Effie', a change which in some respects renders the young man's flight and broken promise even more disgraceful. In the finale, the Sylphide reappears upon Olympus, where she unites James and Effie in matrimony. In this case the sylphide herself ratifies the happy ending, celebrating the marriage of the two earthly newlyweds who are also placed upon the summit of Olympus.

An even more divergent finale is that of Federico Massimi's *Silfide* (Teatro della Canobbiana of Milan, Regio Teatro of Turin, *Carnevale* 1860-61). Here, the action also ends upon Olympus where various divinities (Latona, Minerva, Apollo, Diane, Mercury, Jove, Mars) as well as 'genies, cupids and little angels, etc.' welcome the Sylphide in a grand final tableau.

As for the other libretti of the *Silfide* cited in Appendix C, all the choreographers who took on the subject matter copied Cortesi's libretti of 1837-38 and 1841-44 (or less frequently, Taglioni's) rather faithfully, save for a few modifications and additions relating especially to Madge's magic scene – a scene which is at times entirely absent, at other times performed by Madge alone, and at times performed in the company of other witches. Finally, we find the addition of new characters (who do not, however, influence the plot). Examples include a 'Rosa' (perhaps a relative or a friend of Effie) in the Cortesi libretto of 1841, an 'Amalia, sister of Effie', and a 'Notary' – probably charged with writing up James and Effie's marriage contract – in the *Silfide* of Giuseppe Lasina (Cagliari, 1846).

The reason for these alterations is not always clear. When the Sabbath scene was eliminated, it may have been (aside from the objections on religious grounds in Rome) because it required additional lighting and other similar effects, props, and costumes, as well as dancers apart from those already assigned to sylph roles. Too, the scenery had the potential, especially if not well executed, of looking trite to a sophisticated Italian audience, or even superfluous to the action, and creating perhaps too stark a contrast to the sylphides' supernatural and intensely poetic world. (It was perhaps for these reasons that the Forest Act was often chosen when only a part of the ballet was presented.)

The *lieto fine* (happy ending) is easier to explain, since it followed a practice popular with Italian audiences and was quite in keeping with *La Silfide*'s status as a demi-character ballet, or at least not a tragic one. Since the ballet (especially in its early years in Italy) was perceived as belonging to the mythological and fantastic genre, too, the intervention of the *deus ex machina* and the final ascent to Olympus were fully justified. And the addition in the cast of mimes or dancers needing employment could explain the introduction of new characters.

In any case, the existence of multiple dramatic variations confirms how, from an Italian point of view, a ballet libretto was something that could be altered and supplemented at will, regardless of the original author's intentions. So even though Nourrit is cited in Cortesi's libretti – starting in 1841, at least – the appropriations made by other choreographers from Cortesi libretti is never noted, an omission fully in keeping with the customs of the period. In the case of Taglioni, however, one often finds in the frontispiece a phrase such as 'Ballet by Filippo Taglioni staged by ...'.

The reception of *La Silfide* in the theatrical and periodical press. The performances of Antonio Cortesi's and Filippo Taglioni's versions.

Useful information about the reception of the main Italian productions of *La Silfide* survives not only in the libretti but in other personal primary sources (diaries, letters, autobiographies, etc.), archival documents, critical writings, theatrical anecdotes, and reviews appearing in the local press and especially in the specialised arts press. Indeed, numerous Italian theatre and music journals devoted considerable attention to theatrical dance.[45] Such publications kept track of major Italian and foreign dance artists and their tours to various theatrical centres. They also reported news of ballets under rehearsal and of debuts and premiers, offering detailed reports.[46]

The critical attitude towards *La Silfide*, as already noted, was divided, starting with the arrival of the ballet in Italy in 1837. Those who spoke highly of the ballet, especially on the occasion of its very first performances, did so more to take a stand against the *ballo storico e drammatico* (historical and dramatic ballet), which was based on sieges, catastrophes, plots, homicides, etc., (as noted above) rather than to express a true liking for *La Silfide*. Their comments most often praise the 'pleasure' derived from viewing *La Silfide*. Indeed, critics writing for music and theatre periodicals had little appreciation for the *storico e drammatico* ballets, and had for some years bemoaned the staleness of Italian choreographers and the excessive gloominess of their works.[47]

But the reviews of the early 1840s reflected the fact that critics were now being 'won over' by ballet; these reviews reflected a new type of criticism that distanced itself decisively from that of the music critics who had been writing critiques of ballet. Now, literary scholars and passionate connoisseurs were turning their attention to ballet, and their judgments were based less on systematic analysis than on their own intuition; their own emotional responses to the performance. In this respect, these critics were closer to the public's attitude. Their reviews especially praised the interpretations of not only the great female romantic dancers (Fanny Cerrito, Maria Taglioni, Flora Fabbri Bretin), but also male dancers of the French school (including Francesco Merante, Louis Bretin, Arthur Saint-Léon), all of whom were appreciated in Italy for their technical ability and their mimic and expressive *brio*. Many critics particularly praised the grace, novelty and poetic qualities of the dancers who, in their eyes, conveyed an expression of sentiment and a transfiguration of the body – qualities that made the spectators feel as if they were transported into the fantastic domain of the spirit and the imagination.

Equally vocal in this period, however, were the critics who distanced themselves from an aesthetic and a dramaturgy that struck them as both implausible and contrary to Italian tastes. They emphasised the importance of rejecting foreign cultural traditions in favour of defending the immensely rich Italian dance tradition and the models of the great masters Salvatore Viganò and Gaetano Gioia.

Let us now take a closer look at these reviews. Cortesi's first Italian performance took place with great success in May of 1837 at the Teatro Carlo Felice in Genoa and featured Amalia Lumelli, the *prima ballerina italiana*, who was probably chosen because of the importance attributed by Cortesi to stage and gestural action, thus following the Italian tradition. (Subsequently, however, the role of the sylphide would be given to ballerinas of the *rango francese*, or French rank.) The role of James went to Francesco Rosati, *primo ballerino di scuola francese* (first ballerino of the French school) who was of the same rank as Fanny Rebel, who played Effie. The other roles were, on the other hand, given to the *primi ballerini per le parti*, the performers to whom the mime segments were customarily entrusted.[48] The performance had a positive resonance in the theatrical press, even beyond the local level; this may be seen, for example in the short review of the Milanese periodical *Glissons n'appuyons pas*, which commended the ballet, which, though different from the original version, the critic found very pleasing:

> Genova. [A performance of] . . . *La Silfide*, – even if it could not be quite the same as that in Paris – never ceased to be pleasing, because of the lightness and agility of signora Lumelli.[49]

Also interesting is the critique in the important periodical *Teatri Arti e Letteratura*:

> *La Silfide*, a new ballet by Cortesi of the mythological genre, has been met with much success; it would be appropriate to cast away now that melancholy choreography which calls for battles, the dead, wounded and agonising on the stage. Such things frighten, and do not delight! This

ballet *is* delightful, agreeable and is sure to please all. Lumelli, Rabel and
the excellent Rosati were the heroes of this triumph.[50]

The tone of this review is the same as in another review in the more widely
circulated *Gazzetta di Genova*. Similiarly opposed to the *ballo storico e tragico*
(historical and tragic ballet), its author praises the subject of *La Silfide* as
pleasing and 'delightful', and poised to drive 'all that melancholy choreography' away.[51] Of further interest are the critic's comments about the light and
seductive quality of Lumelli's character and the final flight of the sylphides,
something that had greatly worried the Genoese dancers. ('No wonder their
faces are white with fear and they cry out', wrote the critic for the *Gazetta*.[52])
One could not blame them for being concerned, considering the accidents
involved in the staging of *La Sylphide* in Paris.[53] But because such flights had
been a fundamental part of ballet since the sixteenth and seventeenth centuries when the 'marvellous' in Italian choreography consisted of flying cupids
and mythological beings,[54] they did not create much uproar in Italy in the
case of *La Silfide*, nor did they present the machinists with a difficult challenge.

A production in Florence was met with equal success; performed at the
Teatro la Pergola in September of 1837, it featured (again) Rosati as James
and Lumelli as the Sylphide. In subsequent performances, the title character
was interpreted by Amalia Brugnoli Samengo, a pioneer in Italian dance in
her use of pointe.[55] (In this particular production, Samengo's pointes may
have figured quite prominently: she was said to have 'described the notes
with her feet'.[56]) A production at the Teatro della Fenice in Venice on 30 January 1838 was viewed less favourably, however. The leads were Domenico
Matis and, once again, Amalia Brugnoli Samengo. A review in the *Gazzetta
Privilegiata di Venezia* expressed great distaste for this production of *La Silfide*,
which it claimed constituted a last-minute slapdash solution to the failure of
the season's first serious ballet (Cortesi's *Il ratto delle Venete donzelle*), and
moreover presented a 'world turned upside down, where the active is made
passive and the women pursue the men'.[57] The same ideas were expressed in
rather strong satirical verses that spread quickly through the city. An example reads:

Per dar Cortesi, un ballo all'improvviso
Fece andar le puttane in paradiso.[58]

To create a ballet quickly
Cortesi sent whores into paradise.

Indeed, the seduction of James by the Sylphide, which seemed to overturn

the natural order of things, was neither accepted nor approved of, even ironically. In Italian society women were expected to be discreet and refrain from
displaying their personal desires in public; for some observers, it was inconceivable to see any specimen of a female being on stage – even if winged and
transposed into a fantastic context – who ran after a man and distracted him
from his marital and procreative duties. Even in the performance following
those in Venice, at the Teatro Regio in Turin in December of 1839, the only
thing to be praised was the performance of the principal leads, Luigia Groll
and Luigi Bretin.[59]

Until 1840, then, *La Silfide*, or at least its subject matter, was not uniformly
appreciated. In 1841 the situation improved in Milan where Cortesi and
Taglioni staged *La Silfide* within only a few months of each other (as noted
above). In many aspects, in fact, 1841 represented a turning point in the
history of *La Silfide*'s reception in Italy, and this was surely owed in large part
to the important theatrical centre of Milan. For Milan was the scene of lively
artistic and cultural activities and moreover, boasted a theatre production
system well suited to ballet.

Specifically, the improvement in *La Silfide*'s reception (evidenced in the
attention of the critics and their near-unanimous laudatory acclaim) may be
attributed to the wider presence in Milan of the northern European romantic
aesthetic, and the fascination surrounding any artistic enterprise arriving
from Paris. Another reason for *La Silfide*'s warmer post-1840 reception may
be that audiences in Milan were now given the opportunity to compare the
Cortesi version (the only one previously known) with the Filippo Taglioni
version, and thereby see dancers who more likely played the roles with the
original choreography, in particular, the roles of the Sylphide (Maria
Taglioni) and James (Francesco Merante, one of la Taglioni's favourite partners in Italy).

First, the Cortesi version. The January 1841 staging of the ballet at the
Teatro alla Scala, with choreography by Cortesi and music by Gioacchino
Rossini, Saverio Mercadante, Antonio Mussi, was met with great success and
had a notable number of performances, twenty-seven to be exact. The principal leads were Fanny Cerrito, a dancer well-liked by Milanese audiences
(who apparently choreographed her own variations in the first and third
acts) and Francesco Merante, an Italo-French dancer with great elegance
who was well-liked in his role as James.[60] (He performed many times in Italy
with different partners, and in Paris with Maria Taglioni at the Opéra.) A
beautiful lithograph by Roberto Focosi depicting the Milan performance has
survived; it depicts Fanny Cerrito in one of the greatest moments of dance
lyricism, holding a dove's nest which she is about to offer to James (Figure
8.1).

8.1. Fanny Cerrito in *La Silfide* by Cortesi, colored lithograph by Roberto Focosi, Milan, ?1841. The New York Public Library for the Performing Arts / Jerome Robbins Dance Division, Cia Fornaroli Collection. By permission.

Cerrito took up the role of the sylphide again at the Teatro Comunitativo in Bologna, in 1844, still following Cortesi's choreography. Her performance there was an enormous success, as was that of her partner, the dancer and choreographer Arthur Saint-Léon. This performance met with resounding acclaim, as seen for example in the *Strenna Teatrale Europea*, in which a reviewer expressed great esteem for Cerrito, and praised Saint-Léon not only for his technical prowess (including 'a *quartina*, in which he leaped backwards with his legs, leaving everyone stupefied') but for his fine talent as a violinist as well. The same critic lauded Cortesi as the rightful heir to 'the divine art of Viganò and Gioia', which in the critic's view had fallen into a state of decadence, in part because of the presence of French ballets, which he deemed foolish and unworthy even of puppet theatres.[61] (This perspective confirms, again, how controversial it was to bring French choreographic tastes into Italy.) Abroad, Cerrito took up the role of the sylphide in London in May of 1841 (only four months after the Milan performance) and in Vienna, where she was admired for her youthful naturalness and the humanity pervading her role.

Regarding the Milan performance of Cortesi's version of the ballet in 1841, a long article by Lambertini, entitled 'La Cerrito nella *Silfide*' and published in *Teatri, arti e letteratura*, provides a wealth of revealing information.[62] For instance, in Lambertini's plot synopsis, he offers details not given in the libretti. He writes of Madge's predictions, for example, and of the sylphide 'who, as if balanced upon the air, flutters her wings naturally with the mechanism' referring to the device which enabled the dancer to move her wings. Lambertini also writes of the mythological quality of the final scene that depicted the reunion of the lovers with a staged scene change into the fiery Olympus 'among the celestial spheres and the golden circles of the stars and the ethereal court' where the 'long-awaited wedding' between the sylphide and James takes place.

Most importantly, we learn from this article that in Milan *La Silfide* (defined as a *balletto scherzoso* or humourous ballet, confirming that in Italy the subject was perceived as light) had triumphed despite 'the gloomy predictions, the discontent, the quarrels and the gossip which preceded and followed it.' These difficulties are never explained further, but they could be linked to the much-talked-about imminent arrival of Taglioni, or Cerrito's claim to have intervened in the choreography. 'This strange piece', writes Lambertini, 'in which Maria Taglioni has made a show of extraordinary virtuosity on several stages' was admired for the performance of Cerrito as well. In the Milan performance, in fact, Cerrito even reminded Lambertini of the paintings of Correggio (1489-1584), who was revered by neoclassicists (and often praised in Stendhal's writings on Italian stage settings for the tender and elegant grace, and the softness of his figures).

Several more of his comments are particularly noteworthy – for example one concerning the first act, in which there was

character dance performed to great effect, and so well done that applause was even given the choreographer Cortesi, who very quickly and gallantly made an appearance on the stage, happy to have reproduced the Taglioni work with additions and improvements.

Lambertini thus deems Cortesi's version as 'reproduced' from, but better than, Taglioni's ballet. Even if this opinion was not based on a direct comparison with the original choreographic version, it was in agreement with what was probably a commonly held viewpoint (at least until the appearance several months later of the Taglioni version), namely, that Cortesi's ballet was an improved version of Taglioni's original – at least in the first act.

The act involving the sorcery was not well-received, however, Lambertini reports: 'it is an act lacking innovation, so much so that the spells were almost dissolved by the public's disapproval.' The public's interest was concentrated on the 'new', poetic and enchanting dance of Cerrito and her partner, more so than on the 'mass of spells, flights, jokes and other bizarre happenings.'[63] Lambertini concluded by praising the production:

> ...we no longer wish to have mythology as a subject for books or the stage; we prefer interesting and graceful *diletto* (delight), even if it is superficial, to the horrible soul-scorching calamities usually presented as public entertainment.

This closing comment, of course, is quite in step with those offered by critics of *La Silfide* from the very first performance in Genoa, all centred on the distaste for tragic ballets and the contrasting 'delight' offered by the new ballets of French origin.

Public opinion surrounding the ballet and its performers was, however, destined to change, and the ballet began to find more approval for its inherent merits, in particular the poetry of the choreography and sublime grace of its female interpreters. In the spring of 1841, Filippo Taglioni was received for the first time in Milan as guest choreographer, together with his daughter Maria, still in the glow of her international success. After three performances of *La Gitana* performed with Francesco Merante, Maria Taglioni, on 29 May, began a series of the same number of performances of her signature role in *La Silfide*. She danced, once again, alongside Merante and the same cast as the Cortesi production, in a three-act version and which probably used the same scenery and costumes. As for the music, Giacomo Panizza composed well-applauded variations specifically for the *passo a due* between the sylphide and James in Act Three. The famous first clarinettist of La Scala, Ernesto Cavallini, performed these variations (and also appeared with the La Scala orchestra in a concert under Maria Taglioni's hotel windows the night of her departure from Milan).

The reaction of the Milanese audience to the Taglioni *Silfide* was enthusiastic, in particular because it provided an opportunity, as a writer for *La Corriere delle Dame* put it, to discover the ballet 'in its entirety as it was conceived, and without that final apotheosis that flew in the face of common sense',[64] referring to the finale of Cortesi's version, which featured fireworks atop Mount Olympus. The most enthusiastically received scene was the Sabbath scene in Act Two which had been disappointing in the Cortesi version, apparently because it did not assimilate well into the Italian choreographer's compositional vein.

Both Luigia Bussola (Effie) and Merante (James) were praised, but at the centre of all attention was Maria Taglioni as the Sylphide. Comparison with

Cerrito was inevitable, as one may see, for example, in the aforementioned *Corriere delle Dame* review, which praised the nimbleness, 'effortless abandon', extreme technical confidence and poetic qualities that characterised Taglioni's performance. This opinion therefore contrasted her with the more seductive and voluptuous Cerrito. The opposing physical characters of the two dancers, indeed, came to be repeatedly emphasised in the commentary of the period: Cerrito had a round, graceful and earthly aspect, while Taglioni had a more spiritual and ethereal quality. Thus Taglioni was widely considered more apt for performing the bodiless, de-materialised and airy being of the sylphide, which pulled spectators 'into a world of visions and illusions'.[65] Critiques of similar tone appeared in newspapers such as *La Gazzetta privilegiata di Milano*, in the periodicals *La Moda*, *Figaro*, and in the specialised reviews *Strenna teatrale europea* and *Il Pirata*. This last publication in particular emphasised Taglioni's sublime artistry, which permitted her to make everything seem 'natural, spontaneous, true, and inspired' and to make her being itself, as a sylphide, 'agile, quick, elegant, light and almost inconceivable'.[66] *Il Pirata* also alluded to the mysterious aura the character bestowed upon the performer, and vice versa.

It is not surprising, then, that the public and the newspapers soon were divided, and began to favour one or the other of the two dancers. The competition between the two opposing parties, the 'Taglionisti' and the 'Cerritisti', gave rise to countless satirical epigrams, sonnets (in general of little literary value and overflowing with classical metaphors), comments, anecdotes, commemorative medals, prints, figurines, etc. The rivalry was destined to resurface in Milan during Spring 1843 – when Maria Taglioni appeared with Francesco Merante in twelve performances, including the new ballet *Satanella*, as well as *La Gitana*, *La Ninfa Egea* and the *passo a due* of *La Silfide* – and above all in *Carnevale* of 1842-43 when Taglioni found herself dancing at La Scala in the same season as Cerrito. In this season Taglioni gave no fewer than thirty-seven performances, always appearing with Merante, in mixed-bill programmes including *passi a due* and *passi a sei* from the historical ballet *Luisa Strozzi* by Augusto Hus, and *passi a due*, *a tre* and *a se* from ballets of Filippo Taglioni, namely *La Silfide*, *La Gitana*, *Il chiaro di Luna*, *La caccia di Diana*, and a new ballet, *La Péri* (which, however, did not please the Milanese audience).[67] The rivalry between la Taglioni and la Cerrito arose every time these famous ballerinas performed during the same time – or nearly so – in the same city or the same theatre. But this 'competition' was actually instigated by agents and entrepreneurs who saw it as a way to bring in greater payments for the artists and bring larger audiences to the theatre. Tickets, in fact, were sold out despite double and triple prices. (Gino Monaldi plausibly argues that this rivalry was one of the fundamental reasons why French ballets, which otherwise have fallen flat because of their inconsistency, were kept alive at all.[68])

The next complete performance of Taglioni's *Silfide* took place in August of 1842 at the Teatro Eretenio in Vicenza, with Maria Taglioni and Domenico Matis in the leading roles. It was greatly successful, due as usual to the performance of Taglioni, whose mere presence enlivened the 'simple, yet highly acclaimed, subject matter' and who made the ballet a canvas upon which she sketched 'the newest graces of the art'. 'The air is her element' wrote J. Casabianca in *Teatri, arti e letteratura*, 'so much so that it seems she just brushes over the earth so she may draw close to the mortal whom she adores.'[69] Another performance of *La Silfide* – with music composed especially for the occasion by Giuseppe Alessandro Scaramelli – took place in Trieste at the Teatro Grande in March 1845. The performance featured the same leads as in Milan, Maria Taglioni and Francesco Merante. As Bottura writes, 'the thinness' of the ballet was amply compensated for by Maria Taglioni's presence, which was greeted with a crescendo of applause, flowers and crowns of laurel. (Indeed, the theatre took advantage of Maria Taglioni's celebrity status and raised the ticket prices considerably.[70])

Also in Venice, at the Teatro San Gallo a Benedetto in November 1845, the ballet was successful thanks to Taglioni, who despite being over forty, was still considered 'unstoppable.' Given the fact that Nathalie Fitzjames and Fanny Cerrito were also present in the city (at the Teatro de La Fenice), comparisons and comments on the three dancers and the dances they performed flowed freely. Also, various critics took advantage of the situation in order to make ironic comments about the implausibility of the subject matter of romantic ballets, rekindling the debate between the supporters of the Italian historical ballet and those who preferred the French fantastic ballet.[71]

Critical reviews. The performances of Luigi Bretin and Giovanni Galzerani. Other performances, 1848-61.

In 1843 the French dancer and choreographer Luigi Bretin, highly admired in Italy for his elegance and style,[72] staged his own version of the *Silfide* in which he subsequently performed in Rome, Parma and Trieste with his wife Flora Fabbri Bretin. Fabbri, daughter of an artistic family (who had trained with the couple Carlo Blasis and Annunziata Ramaccini at their school in Milan), was on the brink of an international career that would take her all over Europe, including the Paris Opéra where, in 1844, she would successfully perform the role of the Sylphide.

Luigi Bretin's *Silfide* was an enormous success in Rome – in the words of contemporary observers, a *'fece fanatismo'* (that is, it was made an object of fanaticism).[73] In 1843 at the Teatro Apollo (where Bretin may have been assisted by the illustrious choreographer of that season, Domenico Ronzani),

8.2. Flora Fabbri Bretin in *La Silfide* at the Ducale Teatro in Parma. Lithograph by Augusto Baritz, 1843. The New York Public Library for the Performing Arts / Jerome Robbins Dance Division, Cia Fornaroli Collection. By permission.

the ballet's favourable outcome was, for the most part, due to Flora Fabbri Bretin's interpretation. Sonnets, odes and commemorative prints were dedicated to Fabbri, including a beautiful lithograph that would later be reproduced exactly – except the name of the theatre – for a subsequent run of performances at the Ducale in Parma (Fig 8.2) where, however, *La Silfide* was performed in its entirety only five times, starting on 15 May. The reception was lukewarm, so much so that subsequently only the *passo a due* was performed.[74]

The problem in Parma was that the Bretin husband-and-wife team, who were presented as p*rimi ballerini assoluti seri francesi*, found themselves overshadowed by the success of the Italian *primi ballerini seri assoluti* Ginevra Viganò (from the lineage of Salvatore Viganò) and Donato Mazzei. These latter two were engaged as a dance couple in the first ballet of the season, *Giaffar il Barmecida*, choreographed by Michele Dell'Amore. Even though according to Alessandro Stocchi, the author of the *Diario del Teatro Ducale di Parma dell'anno 1843*, this ballet was 'stolen in its entirety' – perhaps from the ballet of the same name by Giovanni Briol – it nonetheless enjoyed a great success, as its forty performances from 17 April to 1 June attest.

During the course of the dance performances that season in Parma, the two dance couples developed new dance steps: the Bretin pair proved their prowess in the *styrienne* and in the *galoppe*. It was, however, Ginevra Viganò – and not Flora Fabbri Bretin – who won the victory laurel, with both ballerinas being supported by their respective factions, the 'Bretinisti' and the 'Viganisti'. This 'victory' was evidenced by the disparity in the precious objects publicly presented to each ballerina on the occasion of the last performance of the season: Flora Fabbri received only a gold bracelet while Ginevra Viganò was given a gold necklace, pendants and various trinkets. To understand the enormous success of these two dancers, one need only consider that the famous singer Giuseppina Strepponi, who performed in her future husband Verdi's *Nabucco* in Parma that season, received as a gift only a bouquet of flowers, albeit an enormous one.

As for the Trieste performance of *La Silfide*, there was no talk of it in the theatre press. From the libretto, one learns that the second act was staged 'in a forest with a lake', perhaps because of the influence of other French ballets, such as *Le lac des Fées* and *Giselle*. The figure of the ballerina who glides on water had by now entered the *imaginaire* and the iconography of the romantic ballet, unifying two elements often associated with this style: air and water. Also from the libretto, we learn that in Trieste the role of Gurn was carried out by a ballerina *en travesti*, most likely because of the lack of male dancers in several theatres. Madge, too, was played by a woman in this production (and probably for the same reason), though the role was performed in almost all the Italian productions from 1839 on by well respected male mimes such as Luigi Lorea, Francesco Magri, Agostino Panni, Antonio Cecchetti, and Augusto and Giovanni Poggiolesi, all of whom surely conferred on this role a heightened characterisation and dramatisation according to Italian custom.

For the Roman production of *La Silfide* of 1846, choreographed by Giovanni Galzerani, fuller information survives. The premier took place on 3 February 1846, with Maria Taglioni and Francesco Penco in the principal roles. It was rather favourably reviewed despite the malfunction at the première of the mechanism regulating the final flight of the sylphides. The third-act *passo a due* was especially appreciated; its music (surely the same piece composed by Panizza for the *passo a due* in the Milan version of 1841) featured a clarinet solo. In any case, Penco was well praised by the critics, though the appearance of Maria Taglioni was met with a lukewarm reception. In another ballet, *La Caccia di Diana*, her performance was more successful and, as the commentator remarks in a pointed reference to her no-longer-youthful age, she was more convincing in the role of a '*deità meno fanciulla della Silfide*' (deity less childlike than the *Silfide*).[75]

Even though she was impatiently anticipated and warmly applauded, Maria Taglioni was by now, in the opinion of many, approaching the decline of her artistic career, and inferior to Fanny Elssler. Elssler, indeed, had recently appeared in Rome and already replaced Fanny Cerrito in the hearts of the Romans, as evident in her overwhelming reception there in 1843, where she became the subject of portraits, and was showered with gifts, sonnets and laudatory odes.

The period in which praise, café discussion and salon gossip centring on these ballerinas ended, however, with the arrival of the Danish Lucile Grahn in 1845 and of Carlotta Grisi in 1847. And then, between 1847 and 1849, Rome became the stage for turmoil and unrest, and the city would be deeply unsettled. After the bloody epilogue of the Repubblica Romana, the city sank into the oppressive climate of restored papal power.

1848 was a watershed year. Beyond the political situation of the Italian peninsula, which was torn by turmoil of the Risorgimento and the first Austrian war of independence, the theatrical situation was also in disarray, with the closure of many theatres and the onset of a lingering economic crisis. All of this may account for the scarcity of records pertaining to Cortesi's *Silfide*, which was staged at La Scala in Milan by Agostino Panni in February of 1848 – a production hastily put together because of the failure of Jules Perrot's ballet *Faust* in the wake of the anti-Austrian resistance of the Cinque Giornate.[76] The *passo a due* performed by the leading couple was choreographed by Carlo Blasis (proving that such set pieces were considered independent and therefore could be entrusted to outside choreographers – although in this case the *passo a due* was clearly not a success). The role of the sylphide was performed by the American Augusta Maywood, who had fine-tuned her training in Milan, made her debut in Vienna, and now had come to La Scala for two seasons. Maywood performed, most likely, with her Russian-American partner Eraclito Nikitin and perhaps also with Perrot. It is improbable, however, that the Austrian Fanny Elssler participated, for she was strongly opposed by the Milanese. Maywood was well received in the role, even though outside of Italy her style was criticised as being too Italian.

Still more performances of *La Silfide* took place in April 1851 at the Teatro di Borgognissanti in Florence in a production by Agostino Panni, who 'riduceva in più piccole dimensioni codesto ballo del Cortesi' (scaled Cortesi's ballet down to smaller dimensions). The Florentine performance featured the principal dancers Virginia Lamanta, whose 'every step was fervently applauded', and Dario Fissi.[77] But the critic of *L'Italia musicale* declared that the whole enterprise was worth no more than the cheap price of admission and therefore left something to be desired, as did the orchestra.[78]

In April of the same year Cortesi's *La Silfide* was reproduced once again, this time by Andrea Paladino in Naples, in a version with well-received music by Giuseppe Giaquinto. The ballerina Luigia Zaccaria of Bologna and her partner Francesco Merante, whose 'greatness' was much admired, both enjoyed 'a resounding success'. The ballerina was praised for imitating 'marvellously well' Maria Taglioni's style, which was considered an ever-standing model.[79] There is practically no record, however, of the productions given in Cuneo in 1854 (with choreography by Antonio Giuliani; here the main interpreters were the little-known Carlotta Lazzeri and Carlo Bavassano) and in Modena for *Carnevale* of 1856 (with choreography by Antonio Cortesi, staged most likely at the Teatro Comunale). Probably because the subject was considered to be well-worn, no trace of it is found in the theatrical press. The same may be said of the 'Chinese' production of the Teatro Carolino in Palermo in 1856, played by the well-known Amalia Boschetti teamed with David Costa.

With regard to the performances of the years 1860-61, theatrical journals were silent, probably because the subject was considered old news. The names of the performers in Tommaso Ferranti's rendition of *La Silfide*, which took place at the Teatro S. Fernando di Palermo for *Carnevale* in 1860, remain unknown and are unfortunately not reported in the libretto. The two productions staged by Federico Massimi for *Carnevale* of 1860-61 at the Teatro della Canobbiana in Milan (with musical accompaniment by Basso, Boro and Carignani[80]) and at the Regio Teatro in Turin, featured (in Milan) Enrichetta Massini and Giovanni della Croce, and (in Turin) the famous Olimpia Priora and Eugenio Durand. (Priora had performed the role of the sylphide at the Paris Opéra in 1852 in Arthur Saint-Léon's revival but the reviews were not entirely positive.[81]) In the Turin production the role of Fire was executed by Raffaele Gambardella, who may have contributed to the choreography. (It seems likely, because he had choreographed a version of the ballet in 1847.) Also in the Turin production, the penultimate act is set upon a 'flowered hill, with a small lake', as inherited from the *locus amoenus* of the Italian tradition, which corresponds to the flowery and decorative taste of the period. This type of staging may also be related to *Giselle*.

Before drawing our survey of Italian *Silfide* performances to a close, it is important to note that beyond the documented stagings of the ballet in its entirety, a very good many first-rank dancers of the period sought to perform excerpts from the ballet. The was especially the case for the famous *passo a due*, the performance of which soon became a rite of passage for many a dancer, whether male or female. Among these dancers, for example, were Sofia Fuoco (the stage name of Maria Angiola Brambilla), already a brilliant student at La Scala during the 1841 performances. (Brambilla had also performed 1846 in the Milanese rendition of Jules Perrot's *Pas de quatre*, along with Maria Taglioni and two other pupils at La Scala, Carolina Rosati and Carolina Vente.) Brambilla was renowned for the vivacity of her temperament and interpretations, as well as her prodigious technique and steel pointe work.

Fuoco (that is, Brambilla) is shown in a life portrait, with an unknown

8.3. Drawing by C. Gallina of Sofia Fuoco in *La Silfide* at the Teatro alla Scala. (n.d.) Teatro alla Scala. By permission.

performer in the role of James, who is seated upon an armchair in a performance of *La Silfide* at La Scala. Unfortunately, this performance is not mentioned in official records (Figure 8.3).

Rarely did the dancers turn down the chance of being immortalised in costume as the winged Sylphide, whether in a lithograph or a photograph.[82] A depiction of one such ballerina, Angelina Fioretti, shows her suspended in mid-air; it dates from the 1866-67 season of the Teatro Verdi in Trieste. Her partner, Alessandro Brighenti Rossi, in a costume generically Renaissance in style and with his arms raised, appears to be trying to catch her, though in fact he is most likely attempting to help his dance partner maintain a difficult position in the air. Fioretti delicately places a finger upon her lips, a detail that would become typical in the iconography of the Sylphide. This iconic gesture most likely originates from a pose crystallised in lithographs of *La Sylphide* and *l'Ombre*, which portrayed Maria Taglioni with her finger lightly placed under her chin or her cheek. Taglioni's pose is probably the result of the extreme length of her arms and is to be likened to other positions such as the arms slightly crossed upon the breast, or held *en couronne* or *en lyre* – above the head. Taglioni's iconic pose denotes, according to antique iconography, a state of reflection or pensiveness and could be read as an allusion to the mystery shrouding the sylphide.

The music of the Italian *Silfide* productions.

There is no evidence that the original music by Jean Schneitzhoeffer was ever used for any productions in Italy of *La Silfide*. But the possibility – however remote – must not be dismissed, especially in the case of the 1841 Milan performance with choreography by Filippo Taglioni. For Taglioni's arrangement with La Scala did require him to provide both the choreography and the music. (And another ballet performed in the same season, *La Gitana*, was performed with its original music, by Schmidt.) This being said, however, it seems more likely that Taglioni – whose production only ran for three performances – used the music that had been played for Cortesi's production of *La Silfide* only a few months earlier. In any case, exorbitant costs generally made it impossible to acquire a ballet score from elsewhere, and it was far less expensive to commission a new score from amongst the numerous composers and arrangers of ballet music, or from a local musician already on the payroll of the theatre. (August Bournonville for example, for his 1836 Danish version of *La Silfide*, found it less expensive to commission an entirely new score in Copenhagen.) Further, local musicians offered the added benefit of being familiar with the taste of local theatregoers.

What, then, was the music for Italian *Silfide* like? To put it more metaphorically, what musical garment did the Sylphide wear in Italy? This question has no easy answer, in part because surviving libretti of the ballet offer no information about even who the composers were. In two exceptional cases, however, libretti do indicate the identity of the *primo violino per i balli* (first violinist for ballets), that is, the theatre's house musician who was charged with the conducting, instrumentation, and often even the composition, or at least the arrangement, of ballet music. (We don't know, however, in the case of these two productions if they were responsible for the creation of the ballet music.[83]) But the composer, or composers, of ballet scores were rarely named, even on the posters and in the press, and the composers were usually of little renown. (Even today their names appear only rarely in musical encyclopedias.)

Retrieving the ballet scores themselves, too, has been difficult since, according to a practice dating back to the eighteenth century, they were often considered the property of the choreographer, who used them (and perhaps discarded them) as he needed. It should also be remembered that there was no reason for ballet music to be preserved intact; as functional music, meant for use in the theatre but not bound to text, it was frequently subjected to cuts and accretions. These phenomena explain the disappearance of a large quantity of musical output, including most likely a good part of the music used in Italy for *La Silfide*.[84]

In some cases, if ballet music was at all successful, it was printed. The printed versions typically consisted of reductions of the most danceable segments for two-hand or four-hand piano, and were intended mostly for piano amateurs. The music from the mimed scenes – intended to illustrate and narrate the action, and in a certain sense, to 'translate' the gestures of the actors – was much less likely to be included in these published arrangements. This is indeed the case with the music of *La Silfide*, for which, as we will see, there exist only a few published and often incomplete scores (see Appendix C). All of these were published by Giovanni Ricordi in Milan, the most important music publishing house in Italy.

As mentioned above, original music was composed for Cortesi's 1841 Milan production of *La Sifide*. One number from this score, a *passo a due* composed by Antonio Mussi and performed by Fanny Cerrito and Francesco Merante, was arranged for four-hand piano by Luigi Truzzi. (Mussi was a former student at the Conservatorio di Milano and studied with the ballet music specialist Cesare Pugni; he was also a much-appreciated pianist who arranged and composed many ballets between the 1830s and 1860s, the great majority of which were performed at La Scala and many of which were published by Ricordi.) Shortly after the publication of this arrangement, a piano-solo reduction of the entire ballet appeared in an arrangement by Giovanni Toja, testifying to the public's interest in the ballet.

The Toja arrangement cites the names of three composers: Antonio Mussi (who is credited with most of it), Gioacchino Rossini and Saverio Mercadante. This score was analysed by Knud Arne Jürgensen,[85] who concludes that three of the ten pieces in Act One were borrowings from pre-existing works of Rossini. According to Jürgensen, the seven remaining pieces are previously unknown pieces composed by Rossini specifically for the ballet upon Cortesi's request. This commission would have been carried out, perhaps, during Rossini's brief stay in Milan at the close of 1840. Jürgensen's scenario, which lacks direct proof, is in any case improbable since any new music by Rossini would not have gone unnoticed in this period when his fame was widespread.

As for the music for the brief second act, which contains the diabolic Sabbath and is credited to Saverio Mercadante in the score, Jürgensen finds that it has no affinity with Mercadante's operas, nor with four of his ballets. Jürgensen thus hypothesises that the music for Act Two, a well-unified piece of music, was commissioned by Cortesi from Mercadante specifically for the

1837 Genova production of *La Silfide*. This would have transpired when the composer was *maestro di capella* of the Novara cathedral. But this supposition is not supported by existing documentation, nor is there any trace of it in either the press or in the libretti. The search for possible likenesses between the music of *La Silfide* and the musical production of Mercadante should, at the very least, be extended beyond the four ballets he wrote as a student at the Conservatorio di Napoli[86] to include his vast corpus of highly-regarded ballet music.

It is considerably more plausible that, in keeping with a widespread practice in Italy at the time, the music for this ballet is a collage made up of various pre-existing pieces. According to this theory, this music was not commissioned from Mercadante or Rossini but instead was drawn from among now-little-known ballet or chamber music compositions, some of them by Mercadante and Rossini, two of the most plagiarised composers of music for the ballet. Or, on the other hand, it was taken from the works of obscure second-rate composers not named in the score. Another possibility would be to attribute the work – at least some of it – to Cortesi himself. For in at least one earlier instance Cortesi is cited as a composer of the music of his own ballet: the libretto for his celebrated *Ines di Castro* (Venice, 1830) indicates that 'the music is by great *maestri di musica*, and is in part composed for this occasion by Cortesi himself'. Thus it is plausible that Cortesi composed some of the music for *La Silfide*, or at the very least arranged it.

As for the 1841 Milan performances of *La Silfide*, with choreography by F. Taglioni (featuring Maria Taglioni and Francesco Merante): the music for the *passo a due* between the two protagonists is extant. Composed by Giacomo Panizza, it was performed by the renowned Ernesto Cavallini, principal clarinettist at La Scala. (Panizza composed the music for roughly twenty ballets between 1855 and 1860, and was also the *maestro concertatore ed ispettore del musica dei balli alla Scala*, or master music coordinator and inspector of ballet music at La Scala.) The *passo a due* was published in two versions: a reduction for B-flat clarinet and piano, arranged by the author himself, and an arrangement by Luigi Truzzi for piano solo.[87] In the piano solo version (which consists of the Preludio, Variazione I, Variazione II, Variazione III and Coda), abbreviated stage directions are included: for instance, at mm. 11-12 the 'Sylphide's exit' is noted; at mm. 25-26 'the lovers meet'. Such brief stage indications – typical in published ballet music – were insufficient to reflect accurately or fully what happened on the stage; they were meant simply to recall significant moments of the ballet to the performer's memory.[88]

Some questions arise, then, concerning the circulation and function of published sheet music for *La Silfide*, and for that matter, the numerous reductions of music from other ballets put forth by such publishing houses as Ricordi and Bertuzzi in Milan, Ratti and Cencetti in Rome, Cottrau and

Girard in Naples, and Artaria in Florence. Were these scores meant for amateur pianists (as suggested by the lack of music for the mimed scenes), or were they also intended for choreographers who wished to stage the ballet? And if so, was the ballet score used in its entirety? And how important was the music; was it considered an essential part of a given production?

There are no records indicating that the above-cited scores for *La Silfide* (one by Mussi/Rossini/Mercadante, the other by Panizza) were used in subsequent *Silfide* performances in Italy. The only trace is connected to the aforementioned 1846 *Silfide* in Rome, in which it is known that the *passo a due* was performed to the music of a clarinet – most likely the music composed by Panizza for Ernesto Cavallini at La Scala in 1841.

Moreover, there were definitely instances in which a *newly*-produced musical score was preferred when a new production of *La Silfide* was mounted. It is certain, for example, that for the 1845 production in Trieste with Maria Taglioni the music was '*appositamente composta*' (expressly composed) by Giuseppe Alessandro Scaramelli (the orchestra director, violinist and composer who subsequently composed various other successful music scores for ballet). The music for the spring 1851 Naples performance, with choreography by Andrea Palladino (after Cortesi), was also '*appositamente composta*', this time by Giuseppe Giaquinto, a very prolific Italian ballet composer (and a composer of operas, too, which were mainly performed at the San Carlo in Naples). It is clear from press reviews that the music of this *Silfide* was a great success. The 'refinement' of the music was praised, in particular the 'Dawn scene' (surely toward the beginning of Act Two when the Sylphide and James meet in the forest), and the scene of the 'witches and evil spirits', i.e. the Witches' Sabbath.[89]

As for the *Silfide* set in China (Palermo, 1856), the libretto indicates that two specialists in dance music, the famous Luigi Alfano, '*Direttore e Maestro compositore per la musica de' balli*' at the Teatro Carolino in Palermo, and Agostino Auriemma, also a composer of ballet music for that theatre, expressly composed (respectively) a '*passo a due serio*' and the '*passo solo*' in Act One.[90]

No information has been found, however, about the composers of the 1860-61 Milan *Carnevale* performance with choreography by Federico Massini, aside from the fact that their names were Basso, Boro and Carignani. They were perhaps instrumentalists either at the Teatro alla Canobbiana, where the ballet was staged, or La Scala.

There is also no doubt that *La Silfide* inspired instrumental music, romances, songs, and dance music for piano amateurs in Italy (as well as in France, Germany and England) (see Appendix C). Among this music, we might note a waltz for piano entitled *La Silfide*[91] by Giuseppe Prospero Galloni (a composer of sacred music but also of dance music), published by the prolific Milanese publisher Luigi Bertuzzi, and the *Raccolta di cinque quadriglie per piano-forte sopra musica del ballo La Silfide*, 'reduced' by Paolo Perelli, ballet master at the Imperial Royal Conservatory in Milan, published by Ricordi in Milan, probably in 1842.[92]

Conclusion

At the conclusion of our investigation of the many *Silfidi* appearing in Italy between the 1830s and the 1860s, it is clear, as one may see in the libretti, that there were many variations in the plot; the differences in the music and choreography were probably no less numerous. Given the characteristics of the Italian choreographic language of the time and the contemporaneous aesthetic, it is possible to hypothesise that at least in the first performances of the ballet, the mimed aspect was emphasised at the expense of the dance segments, in keeping with the practices of the Italian school in those years. In later years, however, probably along with the evolution taking place in choreography, it can be assumed that the dance portion acquired more weight, at the expense of mime. In any case, one can surely say that the Italian *Silfide* – if for the sake of discussion we may still speak of the ballet in the singular – was something quite other than the ballet as created in France by Filippo Taglioni. Any examination of *La Silfide*'s incarnations in Italy, as mentioned at the beginning of this chapter, automatically raises the matter how Italian ballet choreographers re-created – and even reinvented – French ballets in Italy. And this, in turn, brings up the impact on the process of the choreographers' and performers' personalities, the particular body types favoured by the Italian dance school, and the existence of a wholly original Italian dance and mimic style – a style that was the outgrowth of a more general aesthetic in the visual arts, acting and dramatic traditions. The presence of a passionate audience with a highly characteristic taste was a final element that helped to sculpt the character of the Italian dance tradition.

These were all factors that not even Filippo Taglioni could ignore when staging ballets in Italy, where some of his ballets in the fantastic vein found little success (like *La Péri*, which, in 1843 in Milan was received poorly and judged a weak version of *La Silfide*; and *l'Ombra* in 1846, which a complete failure). In fact, some critics claimed that Taglioni's fantastic ballets were saved only by the interpretations of Maria Taglioni. Cortesi's versions of French romantic ballets, on the other hand, were usually met with great acclaim almost everywhere they went in Italy, evidently because they corresponded more closely to the expectations of audiences.

The spread of *La Silfide* in Italy, as we have seen, demonstrates that the ballet was very successful there, notwithstanding the hostility in some quarters decribed above. This success can be explained by several factors. First, the work was based far more on dance than mime, as opposed to the typical *grandi balli drammatici e storici* (grand dramatic and historic ballets) of this period with their extensively long mime scenes and elaborate action. This enabled even smaller theatres to put on a highly attractive show (especially when only the Forest Scene was performed as a self-standing excerpt) while avoiding the high costs involved in staging *grandi balli*. It also allowed *primi ballerini* to take on the challenge of the roles of the Sylphide and James, which were by now canonic.

La *Silfide* was not the only French romantic ballet to appear amongst the numerous *balli drammatici e storici* that continued to be staged throughout this period – this may be readily seen by consulting any chronology of the ballets performed at any of the many theatrical capitals of Italy.[93] But the *balli drammatici e storici* received more attention than French romantic ballets and generally were more popular. And as noted above, criticism of these two types of ballet proved to be neatly divided: one side of the critical spectrum favoured of *La Silfide* in particular and all such ballets of the magic and fantastic type in general. These critics found in *La Silfide* an example of the new poetic taste (albeit with strange and fantastic subject matter) and appreciated its lightness, simplicity, brevity, and finesse, and its poetic qualities (which were in keeping with the new trends), as well as the delight it brought its spectators. Critics in the opposite camp, while generally appreciating the quality of the performers, objected to the thinness of the subject, the feeble dramatic thread and an inconsistency among the characters. (One must ask, however, if this judgment stems from the basic incompatibility between *La Silfide*'s aesthetic and the values of critics still subscribing to classical criteria who favoured conserving the integrity of traditional Italian ballet – or perhaps to something even deeper, namely, the Italian audiences' approach to aesthetics and beauty, which was quite unlike that of the French.) Unfavourable reception of Taglioni's ballet was not limited to Italy, but extended to other European nations, as in Portugal where the Italian dramatic aesthetic was firmly established. As José Sasportes notes of the 1838 Lisbon performances of Bernardo Vestris' *Silfide*, criticism arose from the divergence between the lifeless French taste and the virile and bold Portuguese taste – and this, of course, relates to the matter of differing national preferences.[94]

On the other hand, theatregoers in Italy (and elsewhere) were looking for diversion and novelty, not common sense. And the French qualities of *La Silfide* were actually appreciated as an asset by some because French taste had become popular in Italy, and had come to prevail in many other creative realms, including fashion. (It was no accident that the fashion world soon introduced a light muslin fabric called 'silfide', which appeared immediately in such periodicals as the *Corriere delle Dame*. This was introduced to Italy with as much success as the French hairstyle *à bandeau*, popularised by Maria Taglioni.) Many fashion magazines and artistic/literary magazines (like *La*

8.4. 'Les Sylphides', Figurine Liebig, serie 866, ca. 1895-1905. Collection of Ornella di Tondo.

silfide – Giornaletto politico per le Dame, printed in Naples in 1848), as well as associations, gymnastic clubs, and theatre and performance halls were named after the ethereal silfide or her male counterpart (the 'silfo'). And in Italy, as elsewhere in Europe, the graceful figures of the sylphides, wilis, ondines and péris seem to underscore the romantic period's longing for the infinite.

The introduction of new tastes and sensibilities was kept in check especially by the Catholic Church and by conservatives, who objected to anything exaggeratedly melancholic or angst-filled on the grounds that it could be dangerous to women and youth. But at the same time, Italian audiences seemed to exalt the romantic ballerinas – perhaps even more than the ballets themselves (and male dancers were also well received). Two primary examples were Fanny Cerrito and Maria Taglioni, who became the objects of much discussion and reading. In this regard, it is worth mentioning the ever more frequent use of the term 'silfide' as a synonym for *danzatrice* (female dancer) in the Italian lexicon, starting from the beginning of the 1840s. The term 'silfide' was often accompanied in the press by the adjectives 'gentile' (delicate), 'leggera' (light), 'aerea' (ethereal), 'graziosa' (gracious), 'soave' (soft), 'bella' (beautiful), 'incantatrice' (enchantress), 'seduttrice' (seductress), or else 'Silfide lombarda' in the case of the Milanese Sofia Fuoco, or 'Silfide Piemontese' in the case of Amalia Ferraris. This use of the term could also imply that a woman was *'leggera'*, or nimble and light. This would have signified either the physique of a woman ('taglia da silfide', the slender physique of a sylphide; see Figure 8.4), or her moral character. (This latter meaning of the term is linked either to the figure of the seductive sylphide who was denigrated by some critics, or else to the immoral reputation the ballerinas carried with them, with their many lovers and followers – real or imagined).

One must not forget that this show of enthusiasm for the stars of romantic ballet, which in some cases was quite extravagant, was harshly criticised during this period by many who considered such waste of money and excessive attention towards the dancers to be immoral. Such critics held that this adulation distracted Italians from their moral and civic obligations, namely, the struggle against the foreign oppressors – a struggle that found full expression in the *balli storici* based on the history of the fatherland. Among the many such critical voices was that of Vincenzo Buonsignori, author of the 1854 *Precetti sull'arte mimica*. His words have been chosen as an epigraph to this work. Buonsignori hoped for a renewal of Italian choreographic art, and strongly criticised the introduction of material from the French school and 'dark mythology of the Scandanavians' which, he averred, was extraneous to the Italian sensibility and incompatible with the pleasant Italian climate and landscape. This view is to be understood not only in the naturalistic sense, also as a view shaped by the complex interplay of historical and cultural forces.

France, which was first to develop a taste for dance, did not advance in step with us, and the French school preferred the same lightness of subject matter that impedes any impulse of the imagination. If anyone had attempted to adapt the masterworks of Voltaire and Racine to dance, we would not have been surprised to find that they had found the task futile and soon returned to ballets featuring sylphides, nymphs and Diana the huntress. There have been those who have attempted to introduce the French style to Italy with the result – whether out of boredom or for reasons discussed above – that good taste was compromised by diluting

Italian ballet with a foreign style to placate an insatiable public. However, this French genre is not warmly welcomed among us, either because of differences in taste or differences in conventions as still found in our respective literatures. In fact, the French style has been regarded as so frivolous that many theatres, lamenting now at being unable to bask in those Italian ballets that flowed with the sublime and the grandiose, have preferred to eliminate *ballo mimico* [mimed dance]. These theatres, while retaining French dancers, expressed a general disregard towards their *mimici componimenti* [mimed segments]. It may be that sylphides are more successful in fog-shrouded regions, where one yearns to see a shining ray of sunlight. However, is it any wonder the sylphides could not establish themselves here under the beautiful Italian sky, where nature presents itself in all its splendour and smiles sweetly to man, where everything in sight speaks to the heart, where the monuments left by the Roman people and advanced to glory by the Italian republics inspire great and sublime ideas to the mind? We would be very impoverished indeed if we were forced to beg material from the dark mythology of the Scandinavians.[95]

— Translation from the Italian by Stephen Patrick McCormick and Marian Smith

I wish to thank Professors Francesca Falcone and Flavia Pappacena, *docenti di Teoria della Danza all'Accademia Nazionale di Danza* in Rome, for their careful and thoughtful review of this study. Special thanks to Marian Smith for her help and patient work in translating and clarifying the text.

Banes, Sally, and Noël Carroll. 'Marriage and the Inhuman: La Sylphide's Narratives of Domesticity and Community', in *Rethinking the Sylph: New Perspectives on the Romantic Ballet*, ed. Lynn Garafola. Hanover, NH: Wesleyan University Press, 1997.

Bazzi, Gaetano. *Prima erudimenti dell'arte drammatica per la recitazione e la mimica*. Torino: Giuseppe Fodratti, 1845.

Biancolelli, Pier Francesco, and Jean-Antoine Romagnesi. *Le Nouveau théâtre italien ou recueil général des comédies representées par les Comédiens italiens ordinaires du Roi.* Vol. 8, Paris: n.p., 1753.

Blasis, Carlo. *Code of Terpsichore.* London: Edward Bull, 1828.

———. *Manuel complet de la danse.* Paris: Roret, 1830.

———. *Studi sulle arti imitatrici.* Milan: Giuseppe Chiusi, 1844.

Bottura, Giuseppe Carlo. *Storia aneddotica documentata del Teatro Comunale di Trieste (1801-1881).* Trieste: C. Schmidl, 1885.

Buonsignori, Vincenzo. *Precetti sull'arte mimica applicabili alla coreografia e alla drammatica.* Siena: dell'Ancora di G. Landi e N. Alessandri, 1854.

Cambiasi, Pompeo. *La Scala 1778-1906: Note storiche e statistiche.* Milan: Ricordi, 1906.

Cavendish, Georgiana. *New Sylph, or the Guardian Angel.* London: W. Lane, 1788.

Caylus. *Le Nouveliste Aérien ou Le Sylphe Amoreux.* Amsterdam: n.p., 1734.

Cazotte, Jacques. *Le Diable amoureux.* Naples, 1772.

Celi, Claudia, and Andrea Toschi. 'Lo spartito animato, o delle fortune ballettistiche dell' "Adelaide di Francia", in *Di sì felice innesto: Rossini, la danza, e il ballo teatrale in Italia,* ed. Paolo Fabbri. Pesaro: Fondazione Rossini, 1996, 143-85.

Cervellati, Elena, 'Da *Giselle* (Parigi, 1841) a *Gisella* (Bologna, 1843): Traduzione e ricezione di un capolavoro in una città italiana dell'Ottocento', in Alessandro Pontremoli and Giannandrea Poesio (eds), *L'Italia e la danza* (AIRDanza/EADH, Roma, 15-17 Oct. 2006), Roma, Aracne, 2008, 161-176.

Cesare, Raffaele De. *La fine di un regno: dal 1855 al 6 Settembre 1860.* Città di Castello: Lapi, 1895.

Crébillon fils. *Le Sylphe, ou Songe de Madame De R***.* Paris: Delatour, 1730.

De Angelis, Marcello. *Le carte dell'impresario: Melodramma e costume teatrale nell'Ottocento.* Florence: Sansoni, 1982.

de Bibiena, Jean Galli. *La Poupée.* Paris: n.p., 1744.

De Boigne, Charles. *Petits mémoires de l'opéra.* Paris: Librairie nouvelle, 1857.

de Choisy, Martin. *Le Sylphe ou le Mari Comme il y en a peu, Comédie en vers libres et en trois actes mêlés d'ariettes.* Montpellier: Jean-François Picot, 1778.

De Jorio, Andrea. *La mimica degli antichi investigata nel gestire napoletano.* Naples: Stamperia del Fibreno, 1832. (Tr. with an introduction and notes by Adam Kerdon as *Gesture in Naples and Gesture in Classical Antiquity.* Bloomington: Indiana University Press, 2002.)

de Moncrif, François-Augustin. *Ouevres de Moncrif.* Vol. 2, Paris: Mardan, 1791.

de Saunier, Beaumont. *Le Gnome, ou Songe de Mme La Comtesse de *** Écrit par*

Elle-Même à Mme de ***, Pour Répondre à la Vision du Sylphe... . Paris: Delatour, 1730.

Délon, Michel. *Sylphes et Sylphides: Montfaucon de Villars, Crébillon, Marmontel, Nougaret, Sade, Quelques Poètes.* Paris: Desjonquères, 1999.

Di Tondo, Ornella. 'Balletto aulico e danza teatrale nel Seicento', in *Storia della danza italiana,* ed. José Sasportes. Torino: EDT, 2011, 71-116.

———. *La censura sui balli teatrali nella Roma dell'ottocento.* Torino: Utet, 2008.

Ertz, Matilda Ann Butkas. 'Nineteenth-Century Italian Ballet Music before National Unification: Sources, Style and Context' Ph.D. diss., University of Oregon, 2010.

Gaillard, Aurélia. 'Songe et enchantement à la fin de l'âge classique', in *Songes Et Songeurs (XIIIe-XVIIIe siècle),* eds. Nathalie Dauvois and Jean-Philippe Grosperrin (Québec: les Presses de l'Université Laval, 2003).

Gautier, Théophile. *Gautier on Dance.* Edited by Ivor Guest. London: Dance Books, 1986.

Guest, Ivor. *The Ballet of the Second Empire 1858-1870.* London: Black, 1953.

Hansell, Kathleen Kuzmick, 'Il ballo teatrale e l'opera italiana', in *Storia dell'opera Italiana,* vol. 5, eds Lorenzo Bianconi and Giorgio Pestelli (Torino: EDT, 1988).

———. 'Theatrical Ballet and Italian Opera', in *Opera on Stage,* eds Lorenzo Bianconi and Giorgio Pestelli. Chicago: University of Chicago Press, 1998.

Jürgensen, Knud Arne. 'Sulle tracce della Silfide italiana.' *Rivista illustrata del Museo Teatrale alla Scala* 1, no. 4 (1989): 18-39.

Lecomte, Nathalie. 'Maria Taglioni alla Scala.' *La Danza italiana* 8-9 (Winter 1990): 47-71.

Marmontel, Jean-François. *Le Mari Sylphe.* Paris: n.p., 1761.

Monaldi, Gino. *Le regine della danza nel secolo XIX.* Turin: Fratelli Bocca, 1919.

Montolieu, Isabelle de. *La Sylphide ou l'ange gardien, nouvelle traduit de L'anglaise* Lausanne and Paris: n.p., 1795.

Nodier, Charles Emmanuel. *Trilby ou le Lutin d'Argail.* Paris: Ladvocat, 1822.

———. 'Trilby ou le Lutin d'Argail', in *Oeuvres,* vol. 1 Paris: Renduel, 1832-37.

———. *Trilby il folletto di Argail.* Edited by Elena Grillo. Rome: Lucarini, 1988.

———. 'Trilby ovvero il folletto di Argail', in *I Demoni della Notte e Altri Racconti.* Milan: Garzanti, 2002.

Nougaret, Pierre-Jean-Baptiste. *Le Singulier Sylphe.* 1800.

Noverre, Jean-Georges. *Programmi di Balletti.* Edited by Flavia Pappacena. Rome: Audino, 2009.

Pagliano, Piero. 'Charles Nodier: La vita', in *I demoni della notte e altri racconti.* Milan: Garzanti, 2002.

Pappacena, Flavia. 'Dagli Zefiri alla fanciulle alate del balletto romantico', in

Il Linguaggio della Danza: Guida all'interpretazione delle Fonti Iconografiche della Danza Classica. Rome: Gremese, 2010.

Quétant, François-Antoine. *L'amant Sylphe, ou la féerie de l'amour, comédie en trois actes, en prose, mêlée d'ariettes, représentée devant leurs Majestés à Fontainebleau*. [Paris]: R.C. Ballard, 1783.

Regli, Francesco. 'Della Coreografia in Italia. Alcune Riflessioni - un voto e una profezia.' *Strenna teatrale italiana* 1 (1838): 69-79.

———. *Dizionario biografico dei più celebri poeti ed artisti melodrammatici, tragici e comici, maestri, concertisti, coreografi, mimi, ballerini, scenografi, giornalisti, impresari Ecc. Ecc. che fiorirono in Italia dal 1800 al 1860*. Torino: Dalmazzo, 1860.

Ruffin, Elena. 'Il Ballo Teatrale a Venezia nel secolo XIX', in *La Danza Italiana* (1987): 151-179.

Sasportes, José, and Antonio Pinto Ribeiro. *History of Dance*. Translated by Joan Ennes. Lisbon: Imprensa Nacional-Casa da Moeda, 1991.

Sowell, Debra. '"Virtue (Almost) Triumphant" Revisited. Of Sylphs and Silfidi.' *Dance Chronicle* 18, no. 2 (1995): 293-301.

Stocchi, Alessandro. *Diario del Teatro Ducale di Parma dell'anno 1843, compilato dal Portiere al Palco Scenico Alessandro Stocchi, Giuseppe Rossetti*. Parma: Giuseppe Rossetti, 1844.

Véron, Louis. *Mémoires d'un Bourgeois de Paris*. Paris: Librairie Nouvelle, 1856.

Zambon, Rita. 'Il Gran Teatro La Fenice', in Roberta Albano, Nadia Scafidi and Rita Zambon, *La Danza in Italia: la Scala, la Fenice, il San Carlo dal XVIII Secolo ai Giorni Nostri*, Direzione Flavia Pappacena. Rome: Gremese, 1998, 89-164.

Notes

1. *Gazzetta di Genova*, 27 May 1837.
2. *Gazzetta privilegiata di Venezia*, Spring 1843. Cited by Elena Ruffin, 'Il ballo teatrale a Venezia nel secolo XIX', in *La Danza Italiana* (1987), 39.
3. See in the bibliography the works of Claudia Celi, Ornella Di Tondo, Flavia Pappacena, José Sasportes, Debra H. Sowell, Rita Zambon.
4. See, for example, the works of Alessandro Manzoni (1785-1873) and Giacomo Leopardi (1798-1837).
5. See, for example, Gaetano Bazzi, *Prima erudimenti dell'arte drammatica per la recitazione e la mimica* (Torino: Giuseppe Fodratti, 1845); Carlo Blasis, *Manuel complet de la Danse* (Paris: Roret, 1830); Andrea De Jorio, *La mimica degli antichi investigata nel gestire napoletano* (Naples: Stamperia del Fibreno, 1832).
6. See Ornella Di Tondo, *La censura sui balli teatrali nella Roma dell'Ottocento* (Torino: Utet, 2008).
7. The stage programme, also known as the 'argomento', was a short document summarising the story, and it tended to be simpler and shorter than the libretto.

8. On the *ballet blanc* and the historiography of French ballet, see Chapter 11 of this volume.
9. See the libretto for 'Zara, Romantic Ballet', in Carlo Blasis, *Code of Terpsichore* (London: Edward Bull, 1828), 419-33 and Blasis, *Manuel complet de la Danse*, 328-40.
10. As Blasis wrote, 'According to the definition of a famous writer: "French opera is epic staged as a spectacle. What the epic poet reveals only to our imagination, French composers have undertaken to perform before our eyes." The ballet composer follows the same procedures when sketching the plans for large-scale compositions. Since the marvelous made visible is the soul of French opera, the same is true of mythological, allegorical and fantastical ballets. Italians have preferred historical ballet subjects and have only staged tragedies and comedies. The ballet composer who wishes to depict natural subjects could easily follow the model of the best Italian lyric tragedies, since these two genres have many points in common. The romantic genre, introduced twenty years ago in literature, has blurred the boundaries and has made a mixed genre of these.' Carlo Blasis, *Studi sulle arti imitatrici* (Milan: Giuseppe Chiusi, 1844), 3.
11.The other leads were Lise Noblet (Effie), M. Elie (Gurn), Mme. Elie (Madge); scenery by Pierre L.C. Ciceri and costumes by Eugène Lami.
12. 'Mlle Taglioni danced the Sylphide. That says it all. This ballet opened the door to a whole new era in choreography, and through it Romanticism entered the realm of Terpsichore.' (Review from *La Presse*, 1 July 1844, benefit of Mlle Taglioni, 29 June 1844, cited in Théophile Gautier, *Gautier on Dance*, ed. Ivor Guest (London: Dance Books, 1986), 142.
13. Charles Emmanuel Nodier, *Trilby ou le Lutin d'Argail* (Paris: Ladvocat, 1822). The success of Nodier's first version led to the publication of a new edition in 1832: Charles Emmanuel Nodier, 'Trilby ou le Lutin d'Argail', in *Oeuvres*, Vol. 1 (Paris: Renduel, 1832-37). Among the Italian editions, see especially Charles Emmanuel Nodier, *Trilby il folletto di Argail*, ed. Elena Grillo (Rome: Lucarini, 1988); Charles Emmanuel Nodier, 'Trilby ovvero il folletto di Argail', in *I demoni della notte e altri racconti* (Milan: Garzanti, 2002), 51-100.
14. In Taglioni's *La Sylphide*, the character of the sylphide is a seductive yet fickle being, at times childish and mischievous. James's desire becomes ever more ardent because of the seductive elusiveness of the sylphide and the other winged spirits. The silence of these sylphs nearly drives James mad when he asks them the whereabouts of the Sylphide. James's passion leads him to bind the Sylphide with a scarf and an embrace, which will prove to be fatal. In vain, the Sylphide insists on being let free. As for James, the fruition of his erotic desire coincides with the loss of the object of his passion. It has often been noted that James is the incarnation of the romantic hero who is unable to reconcile his earthly love (Effie) and his aspiration for the ephemeral (the Sylphide). The character of the Sylphide can in fact be interpreted as a projection of James and of his incapacity to make a decision and of his refusal to commit to Effie in marriage.
According to Sally Banes and Noël Carroll, the ballet constitutes an explicit warning regarding the perils every young man may encounter by choosing to marry outside his own community. Furthermore, the Sylphide is dangerously linked to all the openings of the house – chimney, window, door – that provide contact between the interior and the exterior. The Sylphide represents a liminal figure, both ambivalent and ambiguous, and who is linked to the dichotomies of inside/outside, interior/exterior, supernatural/natural. Apart from her benign temperament, the Sylphide is equal to Madge who, in fact, is the only one to know the Sylphide's nature and how to hold her a prisoner permanently. Like Madge the Sylphide is bound both to the forest – a classic setting for tales of fairies and magic and a place where anything can happen and where one can easily lose one's way – and to an exclusively feminine and non-procreative world. There are all elements that became classic *topoi* in French romantic ballet. Sally Banes and Noël Carroll, 'Marriage and the inhuman: La Sylphide's narratives of domesticity and community', in *Rethinking The Sylph: New Perspectives on the Romantic Ballet*, ed. Lynn Garafola (Hanover, NH: Wesleyan University Press, 1997), 91-105.
15. Crébillon fils [Claude-Prosper Jolyot de Crébillon] , *Le Sylphe, ou Songe de Madame de R**** (Paris: Delatour, 1730); Abbé Saunier de Beaumont [pseud. de Crouzenac], *Le Gnome, ou Songe de Mme la comtesse de *** écrit par elle-même à Mme de ***, pour répondre à la vision du sylphe...* (Paris: Delatour, 1730); le compte de Caylus, *Le nouvelliste aérien ou le Sylphe amoureux* (Amsterdam: n.p., 1734); Jean Galli de Bibiena, *La Poupée* (Paris: n.p., 1744); Jean-François Marmontel, *Le mari sylphe* (Paris: n.p., 1761); Jacques Cazotte, *Le Diable amoureux* (Naples, n.p.,1772); Georgiana Cavendish, Duchess of

Devonshire, *New Sylph, or the Guardian Angel* (London: W. Lane, 1788), translated into French by Isabelle de Montolieu as *La Sylphide ou l'ange gardien, nouvelle traduit de l'anglaise* (Lausanne and Paris: n.p., 1795); Pierre-Jean-Baptiste Nougaret, *Le singulier sylphe* (1800). Several of these texts are noted in Michel Délon, *Sylphes et sylphides: Montfaucon de Villars, Crébillon, Marmontel, Nougaret, Sade, quelques poètes* (Paris: Desjonquères, 1999).

16. See Aurélia Gaillard, 'Songe et enchantement à la fin de l'âge classique', in *Songes et songeurs (XIIIe-XVIIIe siècle)*, ed. Nathalie Dauvois and Jean-Philippe Grosperrin (Québec: les Presses de l'Université Laval, 2003), 171-86.

17. Charles Nodier was a noted bibliophile and librarian of the Bibliothèque de l'Arsenal from 1824. It is here, in fact, where a salon was held, the first social circle of the new romantic movement. See Piero Pagliano, 'Charles Nodier. La vita', in *I demoni della notte e altri racconti* (Milan: Garzanti, 2002), vii-xviii.

18. In this comedy we encounter a Sylphide in love with the moral Eraste, while a Gnomide (the former's comic double) is in love with Arlequin, Eraste's servant. The two female spirits, who are at first invisible, are respectively ethereal and earthly. After each in her own way signals her presence and interest in the object of her love (the Sylphide gently and softly; the Gnomide crassly and comically), they finally become visible to their lovers and bring them back to their kingdom. A Divertissement and a final Vaudeville close the piece, performed by a male sylph and a female sylphide, both singing and accompanied by dancing sylphs and sylphides. The comedy was first published by Pier Francesco Biancolelli and Jean-Antoine Romagnesi in volume VIII of the famous *Le Nouveau théâtre Italien ou Recueil général des comédies representées par les Comédiens italiens ordinaires du Roi*, vol. 8 (Paris: n.p., 1753).

19. Martin de Choisy, *Le Sylphe ou le mari comme il y en a peu, comédie en vers libres et en trois actes mêlés d'Ariettes* (Montpellier: Jean-François Picot, 1778); comte de Linières François-Antoine Quétant, *L'Amant sylphe, ou la Féerie de l'amour, comédie en trois actes, en prose, mêlée d'ariettes, représentée devant leurs Majestés à Fontainebleau* ([Paris]: R.C. Ballard, 1783), music by Martini and choreography by Laval, Maître de Ballets du Roy.

20. See *Zélindor, Roi des Sylphes. Ballet représenté devant le Roi, en son Château de Versailles les 17, 24 mars, et 22 décembre 1745* (Paris: Jean-Baptiste Ballard, 1745) and *Zélindor, Roi des Sylphes. Ballet Représenté devant le Roi, en son Château de Versailles, le Lundi 18 Décembre 1752*, in François-Augustin de Moncrif, *Ouevres de Moncrif*, vol. 2 (Paris: Mardan, 1791), 337-48. In 1753 this work was performed in Bellevue, with choreography by Jean-Bapstiste de Hesse (or Dezais), and interpreted by Mme de Pompadour. In addition to Zélindor, Zirphé and Zulim, and the 'Sylphe, confident de Zelindor', characters in the *corps de ballet* include a 'Choeur de Nymphes', a 'Nymphe', a 'Sylphe', a 'Choeur de Génies élémentaires', 'Sylphes, Gnomes, Ondines, Salamandres', and a 'Sylphide'.

21. *Zélindor, Re de' Silfi. Balletto Rappresentato nel real Theatro di Parma nell'Autunno dell'anno 1757, Tradotto dal Franzese dal Signor Abate Frugoni*, in ibid., 349-63.

22. See the libretto (in the Italian translation by Alessandra Alberti) in Jean-Georges Noverre, *Programmi di balletti*, ed. Flavia Pappacena (Rome: Audino, 2009), 18, 23-31. *Le Jugement de Pâris* was performed in Marseille, 1751; Stuttgart, 1760-1766; Vienna, 1771; Esterhazà, 1772; Milan, 1774-75. On the figures of winged spirits in this ballet, and on the transformation of the iconography of the Sylfide character, see Flavia Pappacena, 'Dagli Zefiri alla fanciulle alate del balletto romantico', in *Il linguaggio della danza: Guida all'interpretazione delle fonti iconografiche della danza classica* (Rome: Gremese, 2010), 177-81.

23. 'La Silfide ovvero *Il genio dell'aria*, Ballo Magico Mitologico in tre atti di Luigi Henry, da rappresentarsi nell'I. R. Regio Teatro alla Scala, la primavera del 1828 (Milano: Per Antonio Fontana, 1828).

24. Louis Henry (1784-1836), a *danseur noble* and choreographer of French origin, trained at the Paris Opéra. Except for sojourns in Vienna and Paris, Henry spent almost the entirety of his career in Italy, at the San Carlo in Naples (where he was the promoter and one of the directors of the dance school) and La Scala in Milan. Carlo Ritorni, the biographer of Salvatore Viganò (a choreographer whom Henry was inspired by on more than one occasion), defined Henry as being 'of French nationality, yet entirely Italian in style.'

25. In Henry's version, for example, the scene set in the orient; the test of love imposed upon the two

lovers to be married (which alludes to the myth of Orpheus and Euridice); and the poignant sacrifice of the mortal lover. Unlike in Taglioni's version, too, in Henry's ballet the feminine, seductive and non-procreative world of the sylphides is marginalised. And in Henry's version, even the plot resolution is different; it uses the last-minute intervention of a generic *deus ex machina* to assist the two lovers. (The finale is analogous to several later versions of the Italian *Silfide* that inspired Taglioni.) The similarities are, however, undeniable: elements of magic and fortune telling, imposed silence and the impossibility of fulfilling erotic desire coinciding with the loss of the lover.

26. The *Almanacco dell'Imperial Regio Teatro della Scala* of 1828 speaks, for example, of 'unbridled imagination', and 'oddities without equal'. In *Teatri Arti e Letteratura*, 12 June 1828, the final judgment on the ballet reads: 'we must only add three things: first, that all the actors played their parts well, Signora Heberlè as Ezelda and Signor Guerra as Azilde being especially good; second, that a good performance isn't enough to make a bad composition good; finally, that the ballet was a failure.'

27. As punishment for his indifference to the beautiful Silfide, the queen transforms Nadan into a hideous monster — as in the well-known fable *Beauty and the Beast*, in which only the love of a compassionate young person can break the spell. *Nadan o l'orgoglio punito, Azione fantastica in cinque parti, composta e diretta dal Sig. Salvatore Taglioni, Maestro di perfezionamento della reale Scuola di Ballo, e Compositore de' reali teatri, da rappresentarsi nel real San Carlo, la sera de' 15 ottobre 1839* (Naples: Plautina, 1839). 'The action takes place in Persia.' Principal interpreters De Mattia, Raffaella Santalicante-Prisco, Luisa Taglioni, Pingitore. In the *corpo di ballo*, there are 'followers of Nadan', 'Silfos and silfides' (i.e., male and female sylphs), 'Genies — Winds' and 'Nani'.

28. The libretto stipulates that the ballet was 'reproduced' by Andrea Palladini (or, according the variable spellings of the period, Paladini, Palladino, Paladino), who had filled the role of *primo ballerino di mezzo carattere* (first demi-character dancer) in the dance troops at La Fenice in Venice in 1838 and at La Scala in Milan in 1841. Agostino Panni had interpreted the role of Madge in both the 1843 *Silfide* of Luigi Bretin in Parma and in the 1845 Taglioni version in Venice. Both, therefore, must have been experts in dance.

29. See Francesco Regli, *Dizionario biografico dei più celebri poeti ed artisti melodrammatici, tragici e comici, maestri, concertisti, coreografi, mimi, ballerini, scenografi, giornalisti, impresari ecc. ecc. che fiorirono in Italia dal 1800 al 1860* (Torino: Dalmazzo, 1860), 143-44.

30. The phrase 'in the footsteps of' signifies that the original libretto inspired the new one, not that the original libretto was closely copied.

31. 'Preface. I return full of confidence before an intelligent and courteous audience, to whose judgment I have often presented my choreographic compositions and whose indulgence has so often comforted and supported me. If I return with a subject already performed in France, I have at the very least made an effort to alter it according to the Italian taste. I have expanded it and have sought to render the action more interesting, and I have inserted new dances, all of my own invention. I would be delighted if the success of *Gisella* corresponds to my expectations and if the audience expresses now, as so many times before, its benevolence on my behalf. The Author.' *Gisella ossia le Willi, ballo fantastico in cinque quadri, composto e diretto, da Antonio Cortesi, da rappresentarsi, nell'I. R. Teatro alla Scala, Il Carnevale 1843* (Milano: Gaspare Truffi, 1843), 3.

32. Cervellati, Elena, 'Da *Giselle* (Parigi, 1841) a *Gisella* (Bologna, 1843): Traduzione e ricezione di un capolavoro in una città italiana dell'Ottocento', in A. Potremoli and G. Poesio, eds. *L'Italia e la danza* (Roma, Aracne, 2008) 161-176; Kathleen Kuzmick Hansell, 'Theatrical Ballet and Italian Opera', in *Opera on Stage*, ed. Lorenzo Bianconi and Giorgio Pestelli (Chicago: University of Chicago Press, 1998), 280. Originally published as 'Il ballo teatrale e l'opera italiana', in *Storia dell'opera italiana*, ed. Lorenzo Bianconi and Giorgio Pestelli (Torino: EDT, 1988).

33. This, in fact, occasioned Théophile Gautier's derision more than once. Simplicity is called for, he says in this comment that also jibes at texted drama: 'A ballet scenario is more difficult for a writer to compose than you would think. It is not easy to write for the legs. There can be no proud bombastic tirades, no fine verse, no poetical clichés, no words for effect, no puns, no declamations against the nobles, nothing but one situation after another. So a good ballet is the rarest thing, tragedies, operas and dramas being nothing by comparison.' Gautier, *Gautier on Dance*, 58. See also Charles de Boigne, who mocks the absurdities contained in ballet scenarios. Charles de Boigne, *Petits mémoires de l'Opéra*

(Paris: Librairie nouvelle, 1857), 252-54.

34. For example, Giulio Ferrario, librarian and author of *Costume antico e moderno* (1817-1834) was a consultant to the great choreographers Gaetano Gioia, Giovanni Galzerani, Salvatore Taglioni, and Antonio Monticini.

35. 'Madge has drawn on the help of other witches in order to seek revenge against James. With the help of her companions, Madge plots to cast a spell upon a scarf, which when worn causes the death of the sylphide. This misfortune, which is to darken the days of the man she detests, is the only solution that will satisfy her vengeance. The spell is soon cast and, losing herself to the joy she finds in this infernal plot, Madge leaves to set the plan in action.'

36. 'Amore cedes to James's supplications. The scene changes into the enchanting chamber of the sylphides. Amore gives life back to the beloved sylphide and unites her with James, and in the same setting ends the action.'

37. One might ask why Filippo Taglioni's version of the ballet was performed only three times at that juncture. Filippo Taglioni was guest choreographer, and on the billboard announcing the perform-ances, we read that performances of *La Silfide* and *La Gitana*, Maria Taglioni's two warhorses, were to be performed between May 18 and June 12, including six of *La Gitana* and three of *La Silfide* (*La Silfide* was given after three performances of the *Gypsy*). On June 12 was a special performance consisting of a mixed bill: Act Three of *La Gitana*, Acts Two and Three of *La Silfide* and the *Pas de Diane*; see Nathalie Lecomte, 'Maria Taglioni alla Scala', *La Danza italiana* 8-9 (1990): 54,70-71. Though *La Gitana* was new to Milan, *La Silfide* was no longer a novelty. The Milanese public was more interested in La Taglioni than in what particular ballet she danced in, or in necessarily seeing her in *La Silfide*.

38. Act Two: 'Madge's Lair': 'The old witch Madge is busy preparing a scheme that will soon unfold. Shortly her companions, followed by repulsive animals, join her. They form a circle around a cauldron in which the magical brew is being prepared; Madge pulls a scarf out of the cauldron and then wraps herself in the scarf while contemplating the demise of James. The witches dance fancifully before they go off.'

39. See Lecomte, 'Maria Taglioni alla Scala', 48.

40. Debra Sowell cites this production de *La Silfide*, also by Rugali, given at Vercelli on an unknown date, for which no other performance can be found, and which uses the same finale. See Debra Sowell, '"Virtue (almost) triumphant" Revisited: Of Sylphs and Silfidi', *Dance Chronicle* 18, no. 2 (1995): 293-301.

41. 'Effie and Anna are followed by Gurn to the old witch Madge in her customary dwelling. They meet with her and, after telling her what has happened, beseech her to support their cause. The proud gypsy, motivated more by James's insults than by the tears of the unfortunate women, prom-ises to avenge them and plot against the one responsible for leading the young spouse astray. She quickly finds a mysterious veil and, with it, promises to exact revenge soon. All of Effie's questions are in vain; 'You will be happy and avenged', says the old Gypsy as she departs. Anna and the distraught young Effie retreat fearfully while Gurn, in the hope of a better future for himself, follows after them, hoping the unexpected turn of events could be advantageous to his love for Effie.'

42. The opinion expressed by the critic Giovanni Carlo Doria on the *ballo grande* of the choreographer Emanuele Viotti, entitled *Margherita di Scozia*, is concise but revealing. This ballet in the serious genre was staged at the Teatro Apollo during carnival season of 1854 and featured a romantic-style plot (with two lovers separated by the father) who are accused of malicious plots, and whose impos-sible love costs them their lives. Doria writes: 'According to my own principles, I would not tolerate it, since any performance featuring exaggeration and romanticism is not fitting for the moral educa-tion of a people living under the government of a monarch. Today, however, this kind of perform-ance is in fashion and there is no way to resist such a trend.' See Di Tondo, *La censura sui balli teatrali*, 40-41.

43. See Raffaele De Cesare, *La fine di un regno: dal 1855 al 6 settembre 1860* (Città di Castello: Lapi, 1895), 308.

44. *Una Silfide a Pekino*. Ballo mimo-danzante, del coreografo Giuseppe Rota, da rappresentarsi, al Teatro di Apollo nel Carnevale 1859 in 60 (Rome: G. Olivieri, 1859). See also Rota, *Una Silfide al celeste impero*, 'azione mimico-danzante' rappresentata a Bologna nel 1860.

45. See in particular *Gazzetta Musicale di Firenze* (Florence, 1853-55); *Gazzetta Musicale di Milano* (Milan, 1842-62); *Italia Musicale* (Milan, 1847-59); *La Musica* (Naples, 1855, and 1857-59); *Il Pirata* (Milan, 1835-53, 1856-67); *Strenna Teatrale Europea* (Milan, 1838-48); *Teatri, Arti e letteratura* (Bologna, 1828-62).

46. In regards to ballet performances, there was always at least a summary comment on whether the piece was well received or not: 'it was well liked', 'it was a huge success', 'it was convincing', 'it met with mild success', or, on the contrary, comments if the ballet were not well received. In the more extensive reviews, the ballet was judged on its degree of verisimilitude, its dramatic coherence and the unfolding of its action, which was successful if it was rapid and vivacious and if it conveyed passions and emotions well. The harmony of the scenes and the variety of the dances was the next point to be considered. After this, praise was given to the correct functioning of the machinery (particular to the Italian tradition) and the composition of dance music. Next, reviews considered the artistry of the performers, mentioning their allegiance to a particular stylistic school and praising technical and stylistic characteristics and the expressiveness of movement and mime. Comparisons with other dancers who had already performed on the same stage and perhaps the same roles were often included. This was especially the case with romantic-era dance celebrities. Finally, but not always, there was commentary in regards to the set design, the costumes and (if it had not already been discussed) the music.

47. From amongst many critical voices, I quote that of Francesco Regli: 'Ballets of today, or mimed sequences as some call them, are going from bad to worse: boring, bland, childish plots as if invented by an amateur; historical and factual errors; irrelevant and ill-conceived costumes; modern stage sets when classic ones are appropriate; cheerful music when sullen and melancholy music is called for; besieging of castles; fires in fortresses; horrible, bleak desolation at the city doors, on the ramparts, in the town squares, upon the rooves; sudden destruction of bridges; clamour of trumpets and arms, gunfire when the period and theme would instead require sword and lance; challenges, duels and plots, which fall into ballets willy-nilly and as randomly as a description of a storm in a sermon, and which resolve themselves in a horrible trampling of feet, amongst an infernal and confused crowd of angry commoners throwing punches and kicks. Such are the ballets of today, which are really veiled versions of those mythological monstrosities which keep popping up from time to time.' Francesco Regli, 'Della coreografia in Italia. Alcune riflessioni - Un voto e una profezia', *Strenna teatrale italiana* 1 (1838): 69-79, 71-72.

48. In ballets the lead roles, often mimed, were usually entrusted to dancers of the Italian school while the dancing roles, the solo pieces, and the *passo a due* and *passo a tre* were given to the 'ballerini danzanti' or the dancers of the French rank (who, however, were not necessarily of French nationality).

49. *Glissons n'appuyons pas - Giornale di scienze, lettere, Arti, Teatri, cronache, varietà e mode*, 4, no. 66, 3 June 1837.

50. *Teatri Arti e Letteratura*, 15 June 1837.

51. *Gazzetta di Genova*, 27 May, 1837.

52. 'A fickle Sylphide (Lumelli), whose light and playful nature creates a rift in the affection between two betrothed commoners, destroys the engaged man's love and takes him through the air to an enchanted wood. Gracious groups of sylphides, stricken with grief and holding in the air the mortal body of the dead Sylphide, offer a refined and intensely poetic performance in the final scene. Our dancers have never before made such a great impression. No wonder their faces are white with fear and they cry out: they are not accustomed to flying and they remember the sad end of Psyche's sisters, whom Zephyr allowed to fall into the deep ravines.'

53. In his memoirs the Director of the Opera Louis Véron describes technical problems and mishaps at the première of *La Sylphide*. 'To disappear up the chimney, Taglioni clung to a hidden bar that elevated her; when she went to the window, she stood on a board that lowered her gently to the floor; she also vanished from the armchair where James had hidden her by covering her up with a blanket. In addition, she made her wings open and close with a mechanism which was replaced before the death scene because the first one had caused her to lose her wings – first one and then the other. Some dancers came and went on a sliding trolley that was hidden by bushes in the glade. For the flights, the dancers were secured to strong metal wires descending from above and hooked to har-

nesses. For extra safety, at the premiere the solo dancers were replaced by extras. An accident occurred September 1838 when Fanny Elssler was abruptly pulled up through the chimney, bumping violently against the armature of the scenery.' Louis Véron, *Mémoires d'un bourgeois de Paris* (Paris: Librairie Nouvelle, 1856) vol. 3, 166-67. See also Gautier, who took this opportunity to criticise the old tradition of flights: 'Happily she was not injured, but this gives us an opportunity to protest against the flying that is a tradition of the old Opéra. We find nothing graceful in the sight of five or six unfortunate girls dying of fright, hooked up high in the air on iron wires that can so easily snap. Those poor creatures thrash their arms and legs about with the desperation of frogs out of water, involuntarily reminding one of those stuffed crocodiles hanging from ceilings. At Mlle Taglioni's benefit performance, two syphides became stuck in mid-air, and no one could move them up or down. In the end a stage hand took charge and climbed down a rope from the flies to rescue them. A few minutes later, Mlle Taglioni, who has only spoken once in her life (on the stage, mind you) came up to the footlights and said: "Gentlemen, no one is hurt." The next day the two minor sylphides received a gift from the real Sylphide. Another hitch like this will very probably happen soon.' *La Presse*, 24 September 1838, in Gautier, *Gautier on Dance*, 55. See also De Boigne, *Petits mémoires de l'Opéra*, 53.

54. See Ornella Di Tondo, 'Balletto aulico e danza teatrale nel Seicento', in *Storia della danza italana*, ed. José Sasportes (Torino: EDT, 2011), 71-116.

55. '*La Silfide* was a resounding success. The dance segments were brilliant, though a little long; beautiful groupings, excellent costumes and good music. The dancers Brugnoli and Rosati are laudable; Lumelli, Pecci and Castelli were also well received. Cortesi, the composer of this gracious ballet, was called back to the stage many times together with the dancers to receive the warm applause of the audience.' *Teatri, arti e letteratura*, 2 November 1837.

56. See, for example, the critic of *Glissons n'appuyons pas*: 'Florence. The ballet *La Silfide*, which devoted itself in this city to the stage of the *Pergola*, had the biggest gathering, and every night attracted and extraordinary crowd to the theatre. The *Giornale di Commercio* of Florence, speaking of la Brugnoli, who plays the role of the protagonist, puts it this way: La Brugnoli, who doesn't dance (some say) but is now flying, now describing the notes with her feet, now beating time for the orchestra, . . . is acclaimed in Florence as the best, after Taglioni.' *Glissons n'appuyons pas*, 4, no. 132, 4 November 1837.

57. *Gazzetta Privilegiata di Venezia*, 31 January 1838.

58. See Rita Zambon, 'Il Gran Teatro La Fenice', in *La danza in Italia: La Scala, La Fenice, il San Carlo dal XVIII secolo ai giorni nostri*, ed. Roberta Albano, Nadia Scafidi, and Rita Zambon, Direzione Flavia Pappaceno (Rome: Gremese, 1998), 106.

59. 'The ballet *Nabucco* [by Cortesi] was not well received, and neither was *La Silfide*; Bretin and Groll were only mildly applauded.' *Teatri, arti e letteratura*, 3 January 1839. Even the *Strenna teatrale europea* cited only 'Luigi Bretin, who also in Paris showed just how bright his fame shines, and the beloved Luigia Groll, who deserves to be compared to the sylphide that plays upon the flowers.' *Strenna teatrale europea* 3, 1840.

60. 'As for dancers, the character of the Sylphide took the victory, and Cerrito was the dominant star. Even if Merante, a truly skilled dancer and unanimously one of the best to honor Italian stages, was not inferior to Cerrito, he did at times surpass her in force and form.' *Strenna teatrale europea*, 5, 1842.

61. 'In the ceremonious autumn season Fanny Cerrito and Saint-Léon received enormous quantities of laurel wreaths. The choreography was by Cortesi, who edified the divine art of Viganò and of Gioja! What a shame that Italian choreography is in such a dilapidated state! The French dances, or divertissements, dealt it the last blow... These dances are mere frivolities utterly unworthy of the Teatro Gerolamo of Milan and the Teatro Gianduia of Turin.' *Strenna teatrale europea* 8, 1845.

62. *Teatri, arti e letteratura*, 4 February 1841.

63. 'Cerrito the winged sylphide, with her dear lover, flew now and again across the stage, along with other delightful enchantments. [...] It would be difficult to express the grace and legerity with which the enchanting Cerrito executes her dance; – just as difficult as describing the verve, flight, brilliance, force, the suave ways and the lovely demeanor with which the young dancer Merante was able to garner applause. [...] Nothing was lacking in the sumptuous costumes and the beauty of the scenery and decorations; dance and scenery were in complete harmony; Merante was truly prodi-

gious and praiseworthy; the ballerina Cerrito was a luminous star, who illuminates and embellishes everything around her and who impassions the souls of the indifferent and stirs up an enthusiasm that will never tire applauding her. Her delicate manner and her pleasant and airy dance we have never seen in any dancer before. All of these details are completely true and all were such that Cerrito and her companion were called back to the stage, along with the composer.'

64. *La Corriere delle Dame*, 30 May 1841.

65. 'There are no words fit to describe the enchantment of Mlle Taglioni's steps and of demeanor, the seduction of her glance, and the magic of her gestures. In her we find a softness and an abandon of forms combined with a confidence and agility in movement and, for this, the eyes are left fascinated. We might speak of gliding rather than dancing, since the steps follow one another so quickly and effortlessly; the person merely follows the impulse of the feet. From the first airs to capture the dreams of the young fiancé, up until the point when she lies dying in the arms of the other sylphides, not a step or gesture goes without acclaim.'

66. 'Watch her and say if art can surpass her, say if the fervid mind could ask for anything more, say if her likeness has been seen in her contemporaries, and if there exist for her difficult or impossible-to-execute dance steps... say if those parts of the world in which she has appeared are misleading themselves when they proclaim her to be unique and most excellent. Maria Taglioni takes the form that the ancient Greeks attributed to the Muses. She is agile, swift, elegant, and ethereal, almost to an incomprehensible extent. With the help of art, Taglioni has reached the apex of perfection that few ever reach; yet of art there are no traces since her every move seems natural, spontaneous, true and inspired. Taglioni is the very sylphide imagined by poets, the sylphide who flies and who sweeps through the air and flutters her wings around hedges of roses or in the airy chambers of Olympus. Taglioni demonstrates that she knows what it is to be a sylphide; she knows it so well that she *is* the sylphide.' *Il Pirata*, 4 June 1841.

67. Dates of Marie Taglioni's performances in *La Sylphide* were as follows: in the spring of 1842 la Taglioni performed in the *passo a due* (*pas de deux*) from *La Silfide* only one time (22 June), whereas in Carnival season 1842-43 she performed in the *passo a due* on several occasions, individually (31 January 1843, 2, 4, 25 February 1843), and on the same evening as the Spanish dance from *La Gitana* (4, 5 March), with *il Chiaro di luna* and *La caccia di Diana* (20 March), with a new *passo a due* from la *Luisa Strozzi* (26 March), and in the Silfide-James-Effie *passo a tre* (*pas de trois*), performed with the Spanish dance from *La Gitana* (13 March). See Lecomte, 'Maria Taglioni alla Scala', 70-71.

68. Gino Monaldi, *Le regine della danza nel secolo XIX* (Turin: Fratelli Bocca, 1919), 157.

69. 'In contemplating her, you do not know if you are falling in love with the poised and agile person, with the truth of the action, or with the mystery of that exceptional dance.' The comments of J. Casabianca are also revealing when describing the scene in which 'Madge, the malicious sorceress, calls and gathers her horrible accomplices: the infernal confusion breaks loose, the haughty toads and the noxious cat add to the filthy potion, the cauldron boils and the fateful scarf takes up the vile poison'. *Teatri, arti e letteratura*, 1 September 1842.

70. Giuseppe Carlo Bottura, *Storia aneddotica documentata del Teatro Comunale di Trieste (1801-1881)*, (Trieste: C. Schmidl, 1885), 776-77.

71. See for example the articles in the *Gazzetta privilegiata di Venezia* of Tommaso Locatelli (from whom the present article draws an example in its opening), cited by Ruffin, 'Il ballo teatrale a Venezia nel secolo XIX', 151-80.

72. Here is what Monaldi writes about the not-so-easy Italian debut of Bretin: 'The quartet in this ballet [*Ettore Fieramosca* by Giovanni Galzerani, 1837] was famous for a long time. It consisted of Bretin, the amazing French *danseur*, and La Verrin, La Zambelli and La Frassi, all three students at the ballet school of Milan. Despite the perfect design of its forms, and the grace and panache of his bravura passages, the public demanded something more: a few pirouettes, a few jumps, a few of the forceful flights and a bit of the gymnastic virtuosity so in vogue these days. It took but a few nights for the audience of La Scala to fall in love with Bretin's distinct and beautiful artistry, but fall in love they did, and they made him their idol. This was no easy thing at a time when ballet boasted such dancers as la Pallerini, l'Heberlé, l'Ancelin, la Finart, la Vague- Moulin, la Carrey, la Brugnoli, and male dancers and mimes like il Guerra and il Ronzani. The competition amongst these very able artists was never-ending; it sometimes became harsh and cruel, and was especially bitter when

choreographers showed favour to their own protegés.' Monaldi, *Le regine della danza nel secolo XIX*, 72.

73. For example, according to the tenor Napoleone Morianni (who sent reports from Rome about the theatre season to the famous Florentine impresario Alessandro Lanari) the ballet caused downright pandemonium, especially because of the performance of the two principal dancers. See Marcello De Angelis, *Le carte dell'impresario. Melodramma e costume teatrale nell'Ottocento* (Florence: Sansoni, 1982). See also *Teatri, arti e letteratura*, 23 March 1843.

74. 'They wanted this foolish ballet to please the audience at any cost. The *passo a due* was admirable and well executed. The part played by Dilda went extremely well.' See Alessandro Stocchi, *Diario del Teatro Ducale di Parma dell'anno 1843, compilato dal portiere al palco scenico Alessandro Stocchi, Giuseppe Rossetti* (Parma: Giuseppe Rossetti, 1844), 41.

75. 'The appearance of Maria Taglioni met with lukewarm approval, and what is worse is that it continued on like this, perhaps because of the fact that she was second to Elssler. The dancer Penco garnered much honour.' See *Teatri, arti e letteratura*, 5 March 1846. See also *Il Pirata*, 10 February 1846.

76. 'The *Faust* about which so much has been said and for which so much attention and care was spent, did not survive the first night. *La Silfide* was staged in great haste in order to remedy the situation, and remove from public sight once and for all that *Assedio di Calais*, which threatened to last as long as the siege of Troy. Fortune was not at all averse to this ballet of Cortesi, even if it has been reproduced many times. Miss Maywood played the part of the protagonist to much acclaim. Despite all of this, the theatre was not brimming with enthusiasm.' See *L'Italia Musicale*, 1, no. 34, 23 February 1848.

77. *L'Italia musicale*, 30 April 1851.

78. *L'Italia musicale*, 30 April, 1851.

79. *Teatri, arti e letteratura*, 31 May 1851.

80. Pompeo Cambiasi, *La Scala 1778-1906: Note storiche e statistiche* (Milan: Ricordi, 1906), 392.

81. See Ivor Guest, *The Ballet of the Second Empire 1858-1870* (London: Black, 1953), 61-62.

82. It is possible that some of the ballerinas depicted as the Silfide did not dance the entire ballet, but only the *passo a due*, since after the mid-nineteenth century productions of the entire ballet were rare.

83. The 'first violinist for ballets' is indicated in the 1843 *Silfide* production in Parma, with choreography by Luigi Bretin ('Signor Giuseppe Carlucci primo Violino e Direttore de' Balli al servizio della D.C. ed Accademico Filarmonico di Roma ['Signor Giuseppe Carlucci, first violinist and director of ballets, at the service of the D.C. and the Accademico Filarmonico of Rome']), and also in the 1845-46 Cagliari production with choreography by Giuseppe Lasina ('Primo violino dei balli Sig. Fortunato Cordoni' ['First violinist for ballets, Sig. Fortunato Cordoni']).

84. On musical sources for nineteenth-century Italian ballet housed at the John and Ruth Ward Italian Ballet Collection at the Harvard Theatre Collection, and at the New York Library for the Performing Arts Research Collections, see Matilda Ann Butkas Ertz, 'Nineteenth-century Italian Ballet Music before National Unification: Sources, Style and Context' (Ph.D. diss., University of Oregon, 2010).

85. See Knud Arne Jürgensen, 'Sulle tracce della Silfide Italiana', *Rivista illustrata del Museo Teatrale alla Scala* 1, no. 4 (1989): 27-34.

86. When he was still a student at the Conservatorio in Naples, Mercadante composed the music for the following ballets: in 1818 *Il Servo Balordo*, with choreography by Salvatore Taglioni; and *Il Califfo generoso*, with choreography by Armando Vestris; in 1819 *I Portoghesi nelle Indie*, with choreography by Salvatore Taglioni. Other ballets with music by Mercadante can be found on the website www.sbn.it

87. 'Passo a due / nel Ballo / La Silfide / eseguito nell'I.R. Teatro alla Scala / da Madamigella Fanny Cerrito e dal Sig. F. Merante / Musica del M.° / Antonio Mussi / ridotta per Piano- forte a quattro mani / dal M.° / L. Truzzi / Milano, presso Gio. Ricordi" (Lastra 12519). Passo a due / nel Ballo / La Silfide / danzato all'I. R. Teatro alla Scala / dalla somma Taglioni e dal Sig.r Merante / musica del M.o/ G. Panizza / eseguita col clarinetto dal celebre Sig.r / E. Cavallini / ridotta per clarinetto con accomp.° di Piano-forte dall'Autore / Milano / Giovanni Ricordi' (Lastra 12574).

88. See the 'Atto secondo del ballo *Adelaide di Francia* del Sig.r Henry, Musica del Sig.r M° Cesare

Pugni ridotta per Piano-forte dal M° L. Truzzi', Milan: Ricordi, in Claudia Celi and Andrea Toschi, 'Lo spartito animato, o delle fortune ballettistiche dell' 'Adelaide di Francia',' in *Di sì felice innesto : Rossini, la danza, e il ballo teatrale in Italia*, ed. Paolo Fabbri (Pesaro: Fondazione Rossini, 1996), 143-85.

89. 'Naples. In regards to *La Silfide*, a new ballet by Signor Paladino, we read in the Omnibus: "We sincerely praise two acts of the music by maestro Giaquinto. It is certainly rare to hear refined pieces of music in a ballet, and the *Aurora* and the scene of the witches and evils spirits are two magnificent pieces of music that demonstrate virtuosity and a man of good taste. A very sincere praise to this master already noted not only for ballet music, but also for semi-serious theatre pieces." *L'Italia musicale*, 24 May 1851.

90. 'The music for the *passo a due serio* was expressly written by Signor Luigi Alfano, and the first-act *passo a solo* is by Signor maestro Agostino Auriemma.' *La Silfide* (Palermo: Teatro Carolino), 1856, 2.

91. Giuseppe Prospero Galloni, '*Silfide* / Jouez comme je Danse / Valzer pour le Piano / par G.P. Galloni / Op. 11 / Presso Luigi Bertuzzi - n. 1147.'

92. Paolo Perelli, 'Raccolta di cinque quadriglie per piano-forte sopra musica del ballo *La Silfide* / ridotta da Paolo Perelli / Milano / Giovanni Ricordi' [1842].

93. See for example the chronology of ballets performed in the Argentina and Apollo theatres in Rome between 1815 and 1870 (in Di Tondo, *La censura sui balli teatrali nella Roma dell'Ottocento*, 267-84). Between 1837 and 1861, only around a dozen out of 132 ballets performed were on a fantastic theme, and at least eighty were on historical and dramatic themes.

94. See José Sasportes and Antonio Pinto Ribeiro, *History of Dance*, trans. Joan Ennes (Lisbon: Imprensa Nacional-Casa da Moeda, 1991), 39-40.

95. See Vincenzo Buonsignori, *Precetti sull'arte mimica applicabili alla coreografia e alla drammatica* (Siena: dell'Ancora di G. Landi e N. Alessandri, 1854), 51-54.

Appendix A: Performance Chronology of *La Silfide* in Italy (1837-1861)

A = Stagione di Autunno (Autumn Season)
C = Stagione di Carnevale (Carnival Season)
E = Stagione Estiva (Summer Season)
P = Stagione di Primavera (Spring Season)

Date	City, Theatre	Genre	Number of parts or acts	Choreographer	Composer(s)	Interpreters of the Sylphide/ James
24/05/37	Genova Carlo Felice	'Ballo mitologico'	II P	Antonio Cortesi		Amalia Lumelli Francesco Rosati
08/09/37	Firenze La Pergola	'Ballo mitologico'	II P	Antonio Cortesi		Amalia Lumelli/ Amalia Brugnoli Samengo Francesco Rosati
30/01/38	Venezia La Fenice	'Ballo mitologico'	II P	Antonio Cortesi		Amalia Brugnoli Samengo Domenico Matis
28/09/39	Torino Regio	'Ballo mitologico'	II P	Antonio Cortesi		Luigia Groll Luigi Bretin

226

Date	City, Theatre	Genre	Number of parts or acts	Choreographer	Composer(s)	Interpreters of the Sylphide/James
27/01/41	Milano La Scala	'Ballo di mezzo carattere fantastico'	III A	Antonio Cortesi	Gioachino Rossini Antonio Mussi Saverio Mercadante	Fanny Cerrito Francesco Merante
29/05/41	Milano La Scala	'Ballo fantastico'	III A	Filippo Taglioni (*Passo a due*)	Giuseppe Panizza	Maria Taglioni Francesco Merante
E. 1842	Vicenza Eretenio	'Ballo fantastico'	III A	Filippo Taglioni		Maria Taglioni Domenico Matis
A. 1842	Alessandria Civico	'Ballo fantastico'	IV A	Ferdinando Rugali		Genoveffa Monticelli Domenico Matis
15/01/43	Roma Apollo	'Ballo di mezzo carattere fantastico'	III A	Luigi Bretin		Flora Fabbri Bretin Luigi Bretin
16/05/43	Parma Ducale	'Ballo di mezzo carattere fantastico'	III A	Luigi Bretin		Flora Fabbri Bretin Luigi Bretin
C.1843-44	Trieste Grande	'Ballo fantastico'	III P	Luigi Bretin		Flora Fabbri Bretin Luigi Bretin
A. 1844	Bologna Comunitativo	'Azione fantastico-danzante'	III A	Antonio Cortesi		Fanny Cerrito Arturo Saint-Léon
31/03/45	Trieste Grande			Filippo Taglioni	Giuseppe Alessandro Scaramelli	Maria Taglioni Francesco Merante

Date	City, Theatre	Genre	Number of parts or acts	Choreographer	Composer(s)	Interpreters of the Sylphide/ James
P. 1845	Venezia San Benedetto	'Ballo fantastico'	II P	Antonio Cortesi		Maria Taglioni Francesco Penco
C.1845-46	Cagliari Civico	'Ballo fantastico'	II P	Giuseppe Lasina		
31/03/46	Roma Apollo	'Ballo'	III A	Giovanni Galzerani		Maria Taglioni Francesco Penco
C. 1846	Voghera Sociale			Nicola Libonati (?)		Vincenzina Libonati Lorenzo Vienna
C.1846-47	Perugia Del Pavone			Raffaello Gambardella		Clotilde Gambardella Raffaello Gambardella
19/02/48	Milano La Scala			Andrea Palladino		Augusta Maywood Eraclito Nikitin [?] Jules Perrot [?]
22/04/51	Firenze Borgognissanti			Agostino Panni		Virginia Lamanta Dario Fissi
26/06/51	Napoli San Carlo			Andrea Palladino	Giuseppe Giaquinto	Luigia Zaccaria Francesco Merante
C.1854-55	Cuneo Civico	'Ballo fantastico'	III A	Antonio Giuliani		Carlotta Lazzeri Carlo Bavassano

Date	City, Theatre	Genre	Number of parts or acts	Choreographer	Composer(s)	Interpreters of the Sylphide/James
C. 1856	Modena Comunale [?]			Antonio Cortesi		
1856 [?]	Palermo Regio Carolino		III A	David Costa	Luigi Alfano (*Passo a due*) Agostino Auriemma (*Passo a solo*)	Amina Boschetti David Costa
C.1859-60	Palermo S. Ferdinando		III A	Tommaso Ferranti		
C.1860-61	Torino Regio	'Ballo Mitologico'	II A	Federico Massini		Olimpia Priora Eugenio Durand
C.1860-61	Milano Canobbiana	'Ballo Mitologico'	II A	Federico Massini	Basso, Boro e Carignani	Enrichetta Massini Giovanni Della Croce

Appendix B: Genealogy of *La Silfide* libretti in Italy

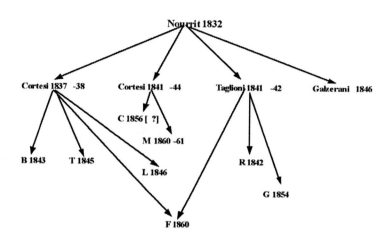

B 1843 = Bretin (1843 Roma, Parma, Trieste)
C 1856 = Costa (1856[?] Palermo)
F 1860 = Ferranti (1860 Palermo)
G 1854 = Giuliani (1854 Cuneo)
L 1846 = Lasina (1846 Cagliari)
M 1860-61 = Massini (1860-61 Milano, Torino)
R 1842 = Rugali (1842 Alessandria)
T 1845 = Taglioni (1845 Venezia)

Appendix C: Bibliography of Primary Sources

a) Libretti of *La Sylphide*, 1832-1834 (in chronological order)

1. 'La Sylphide / Ballet en deux actes / Par M. Taglioni / [...] / Paris / J. N. Barba / 1832'.

2. 'La Sylphide / Ballet en deux actes / Par M. Taglioni / Musique de M. Schneitzhoeffer / représenté pour la première fois, à Paris, / Sur le Théâtre de l'Académie Royale de Musique / Le 12 mars 1832 / Paris / J. N. Barba / 1834'.

b) Libretti of *La Silfide*, 1837-1861 (in chronological order)

1. '*La Silfide* / Ballo mitologico in due parti / composto, e diretto / da Antonio Cortesi / da rappresentarsi nell'I. e R. Teatro / in Via della Pergola / L'Autunno del 1837/ [...] Firenze / presso Giuseppe Galletti'.

2. '*La Silfide* / Ballo mitologico in due parti / composto e diretto / da Antonio Cortesi / da rappresentarsi / al Gran Teatro la Fenice / nel Carnevale e Quadragesima 1837-38 / Venezia / Tipografia Molinari Edit'.

3. '*La Silfide* / Ballo di mezzo-carattere fantastico / in tre atti / composto / da Antonio Cortesi / sul programma del Sig. Nourrit. / Milano / Per Gaspare Truffi'.

4. '*La Silfide*/ Ballo fantastico in tre atti / di / Filippo Taglioni / da rappresentarsi / nel I. R. Teatro alla Scala / La Primavera 1841 / Milano / Per Gaspare Truffi'.

5. '*La Silfide*/ Ballo fantastico in tre atti / di / Filippo Taglioni / da rappresentarsi / nel Teatro Eretenio / L'Estate 1842 / Vicenza / Tip. Teatrale Paroni'.

6. '*La Silfide*/ Ballo fantastico in quattro atti / del Signor / Filippo Taglioni / e messo su queste scene / da Ferdinando Rugali', in '*Corrado d'Altamura* / Dramma lirico / da rappresentarsi / nel Teatro dell'Ill. Città di Alessandria / L'autunno 1842 / Alessandria / Capriolo / 1842'.

7. '*La Silfide* / Ballo di mezzo carattere fantastico / in tre atti / composto dal sig. Filippo Taglioni / messo in scena / dal Sig. Luigi Bretin / Nel nobile Teatro di Apollo / Nel Carnevale dell'anno 1843 / Roma, Tipografia Puccinelli a Torre Sanguigna'.

8. '*La Silfide* / Ballo di mezzo carattere fantastico / in tre atti / composto dal sig. Filippo Taglioni / messo in scena / dal Sig. Luigi Bretin / Nel Ducale Teatro di Parma / La primavera / del 1843 / Parma / Dalla Stamperia Carmignani'.

9. '*La Silfide* / Ballo di mezzo carattere fantastico / in tre atti / composto dal sig. Filippo Taglioni / messo in scena / dal Sig. Luigi Bretin / Nel Teatro Grande di Trieste / Il Carnevale e Quaresima 1843-44 / Tip. Weis'.

10. 'La Silfide / Azione fantastico-danzante in tre atti / composta / da / Antonio Cortesi / sul programma del sig. Nourrit / da rappresentare al Teatro Comunitativo di Bologna / l'Autunno del 1844 / Bologna / Tip. Gov. alla Volpe'.

11. 'La Silfide / Ballo fantastico in tre atti / composto dal signor / Filippo Taglioni / Da rappresentarsi / nel Teatro Gallo a S. Benedetto / la Primavera 1845 / Venezia / Tipografia Rizzi'.

12. 'La Silfide / Ballo fantastico in due parti / riprodotto dal compositore primo ballerino / sig. Giuseppe Lasina / Da rappresentarsi / nel Teatro Civico di Cagliari nel Carnevale 1845-46 / Cagliari, 1845 / Tip. di A. Timon'.

13. 'La Silfide / Ballo / del sig. Filippo Taglioni / posto in scena / da Giovanni Galzerani / da rappresentarsi / Nel Teatro di Apollo / il Carnevale dell'anno 1846 / Roma / Nella Tipografia Oliveri'.

14. 'La Silfide / ballo fantastico / in 3 atti / di Filippo Taglioni / messo in scena / al Teatro Civico di Cuneo / Il Carnovale 1854-55 / da / Antonio Giuliani / Cuneo 1854 / presso Bartolomeo Galimberti / Tipografo del teatro'.

15. 'La Silfide' [Teatro Carolino, Palermo, 1856 ?].

16. 'La Silfide/ Ballo mitologico / in quattro quadri / composto e diretto dal coreografo / Federico Massini / da rappresentarsi / al Regio Teatro di Torino / La stagione di carnevale-quaresima / 1860-61 / Torino / V. Bona Tipografo / 1861'.

17. 'La Silfide/ Ballo mitologico / in quattro quadri / composto e diretto dal coreografo / Federico Massini / da rappresentarsi per la prima volta su le scene / del R. Teatro alla Canobbiana / In Milano / Carnevale 1860-61/ Milano / Reale Stabilimento Tipografico di P. Carpano Ripamonti'.

c) Sheet music of *La Silfide* (in order of the edition number)

1. 'Passo a due / nel Ballo / La Silfide / eseguito nell'I.R. Teatro alla Scala / da Madamigella Fanny Cerrito e dal Sig. F. Merante / Musica del M.° / Antonio Mussi / ridotta per Piano- forte a quattro mani / dal M.° / L. Truzzi / Milano, presso Gio. Ricordi' (Lastra 12519).

2. 'Passo a due / nel Ballo / La Silfide / danzato all'I. R. Teatro alla Scala / dalla somma Taglioni e dal Sig.r Merante / musica del M.o/ G. Panizza / eseguita col clarinetto dal celebre Sig.r / E. Cavallini / ridotta per clarinetto con accomp.° di Piano-forte dall'Autore / Milano / Giovanni Ricordi' (Lastra 12574).

3. 'La Silfide / ballo fantastico / con tanta grazia eseguito / sulle scene dell'I.R. Teatro alla Scala / dalla celebre danzatrice / Madamigella Fanny Cerrito / Musica ridotta per pianoforte solo / dal M.° Gio. Toja / A S.C. la

Contessa / Giulia Samoyloff / dall'editore Ricordi dedicata / Milano, presso Gio. Ricordi' (Lastra 12777).

4. 'Passo a due / nel Ballo / La Silfide / danzato all'I. R. Teatro alla Scala / dalla somma Taglioni e dall'egregio / Sig.r Merante / accompagnato col piccolo clarino dal celebre Sig.r / E. Cavallini / musica del signor maestro G. Panizza ridotta per pianoforte dal M.° / Luigi Truzzi / G. Ricordi in Milano' (Lastra 12970).

d) Instrumental, vocal and dance music inspired by *La Silfide* (in alphabetical order by composer)

Bertelli, Clotilde, '*La Silfide* / dieci melodie per canto e pianoforte /di/ Clotilde Bertelli, Bologna, Gioacch. Stagni' [1865] (Lastre 01151-01160).

Coop, Ernesto Antonio Luigi, '*Silfide* / romanza per pianoforte / op. 103 / composta da Ernesto A. L. Coop / Napoli', Milano / Regio Stabilimento Tito di Gio. Ricordi, 1865' (Lastra 36530).

Felici, Francesco, '*Silfide Tiberina* / Polka / [di] F. Felici, Firenze, A Lapini, 1898'.

Ferraris, Francesco, '*La Silfide* / pensiero grazioso per piano-forte op. 64 / di F. Ferraris, Torino, Giudici e Strada, 1865' (Edition number 7120).

Galloni Giuseppe Prospero, '*Silfide* / Jouez comme je Danse / Valzer pour le Piano / par G.P. Galloni / Op. 11 / Presso Luigi Bertuzzi - n. 1147.'

Maggi, Paolo, '*Sono una Silfide* / di Carlo D'Ormeville / musica di Paolo Maggi', in '*Gabriella di Belle Isle* / Dramma lirico in tre atti / riduzione per canto colle voci di Sop. e Ten. in chiave di sol con accomp. di pianoforte, Milano, F. Lucca' [circa 1882].

Malinconico, Giuseppe, '*Silfide* / polka brillante / composta e ridotta per pianoforte da Giuseppe Malinconico, Firenze, L. Berletti' (Lastra 4175).

Perelli, Paolo, 'Raccolta di cinque quadriglie per piano-forte sopra musica del ballo *La Silfide* / ridotta da Paolo Perelli. 1. Pantalons 2. L' Etè 3. La Poule 4. La Pastorelle 5. La finale grand et figure de l'Etè), Milano Giovanni Ricordi' [1842].

Perullo, Ludovico, '*La Sylphide* / polka-mazurka [per pianoforte] / di Ludovico Perullo, Napoli, Regio Stabilimento Musicale di Teodoro Cottrau' [1859] (Lastra 0000013464)

Chapter 9

Characters, Settings, Machinery

Alexander Bennett

The characters of *La Sylphide*

In Adolphe Nourrit's libretto for *La Sylphide*, he lists the characters: the Sylphide; James Reuben, a Scots peasant; Anna Reuben, his mother; Effie, peasant girl, Anna's niece; Gurn, Scots peasant; Old Madge, the witch. But he offers no specific guidelines for interpreters of these roles. And while staging manuals for operas were beginning to be published around the time of *La Sylphide*'s première in 1832, such manuals for ballets circulated only privately and are difficult to find.[1]

Dancers performing a leading role in classical or Romantic ballet, then, must consider as much as possible the traditional rendering of the character involved. Then, with the aid of an imaginative producer or director, they present their own conceptions of the role within the confines of the mime and choreography. Erik Bruhn, the celebrated Danish premier danseur, puts it thus:

> The role is also what you think it is – your thoughts – your mind. You give life to the role by bringing to it what is true for you at that moment.[2]

There are six main characters in *La Sylphide*: the Sylph, James, Effie, Madge, Gurn, and Mother Anna. Let us consider each of them in turn.

The Sylphide

In *La Sylphide*, as in the subsequent ballets *Giselle*, *Ondine*, *La Péri* and *Swan Lake*, supreme interest is concentrated on the ballerina.[3] The role of the sylphide requires someone with phantom-like airiness and powers of elevation. Her qualities should be waif-like, ethereal, of the other world; she must have thistledown lightness, be poignant in interpretation and wistful in expression and appearance. It has been suggested that the ballerina playing the role of the Sylph should be smaller in stature than those playing leading roles in other ballets, since this evokes more sympathy from both James and the audience, and adds more credulity to her fragile, innocent appearance. Her character, which Jules Janin found both dangerous and enchanting, is subject to various interpretations. In some Danish productions she bears a likeness in character to Madge the witch, creating almost an expression of the demonic – a connection implied by James's words in Nourrit's libretto: 'her love revealed the delights of heaven to me; but she is a demon who takes pleasure in breaking my heart'. In some French productions, notably that by Pierre Lacotte, seductiveness and coquettishness are part of the Sylph's character and this would seem in accordance with contemporary accounts of Marie Taglioni's and Fanny Cerrito's interpretations.

Ghislaine Thesmar, the French ballerina renowned for her interpretation of the Sylph, makes this observation:

> The Sylph is the personification of feminine seduction, with everything the 18th century bequeathed to us of light, tender, frivolous and wicked innocence. Her power is all the more spellbinding for being the fruit of James's imagination. ...[S]he is like an instrument of fate in the guise of enchantress. She knows, and so does the spectator, that she cannot reciprocate the amorous desire of the young man and that these moments of rapture are ephemeral, never to lead to a happy outcome. But she cannot resist the pleasure of being desirable and she plays on it, all the while fleeing endlessly. It is a passion, essentially 'romantic', outside the usual bounds, without sensual contact, platonic and sublime.[4]

Lincoln Kirstein in his *Four Centuries of Ballet* comments, '[t]he Sylph became dominantly feminine, a symbol of lightness, who conquered air and space and gained freedom from the tyranny of the down to earth; she was a metaphor of evanescence, transparency, floating, the essence of ballet as an ideal concept.'[5] However, no matter how the character of the Sylph is interpreted, it is clear that her personality is divided. The Sylph, like the Péri of Gautier's poem '. . . *eût voulu goûter nos plaisirs, nos amours*' (...had wanted to taste our pleasures, our desires).[6] I would contend, too, that her character is connected to the idea of harmony and the malign forces that can destroy it.

The Sylph's death is a symbol of James's inability to find balance between the down-to-earth Effie and the ethereal Sylph; James longs passionately for physical contact with the Sylph. In the French version the element of passion is less apparent ('James holds her in his arms, she repulses him') while in the Danish version it is more so ('James, who had thought to possess her forever and in his outburst of joy gives her a thousand caresses').

Although some historians and balletomanes maintain that this tactile contact is fatal to the Sylph[7] – they believe when touched, she dies and can never become human – I would argue that she dies as a result of the poisoned scarf and not the physical contact.

James

Despite the fact that it is entitled *La Sylphide*, the ballet is really very much about James. James is in love both with the Sylph, who represents ideal love and the unattainable, and with Effie, who represents earthly prosaic love. As Nourrit writes in the libretto, '[d]espite his love for Effie, the image of the sylphide follows him everywhere and he cannot help but love her.'

These two traits in James's nature represent the material and the spiritual side of man, and correspond to Victor Hugo's concept of man's duality:

> On the day when Christianity said to man: 'Thou art twofold, thou art made up of two beings, one perishable, the other immortal, one carnal, the other ethereal, one enslaved by appetites, cravings and passions, the other borne aloft on the wings of enthusiasm and reverie – in a word, the one always stooping toward the earth, its mother, the other always darting up toward heaven, its fatherland' – on that day the drama was created. Is it, in truth, anything other than that contrast of every day, that struggle of every moment, between two opposing principles which are ever face to face in life, and which dispute possession of man from the cradle to the tomb?[8]

In *La Sylphide* this dual aspect of man is undeniably evident in the role of James, torn between reality – his earthly desires – and the ideal – his yearning for his soul. As Thesmar explains, 'James flees from the real world to follow a mirage, to a different world – delightful because it is unknown.'[9] Erik Bruhn, famous for his portrayal of the Romantic James, also points out James's attraction to an illusory world:

> For me James is the youngest in the gallery of Romantic Ballet heroes. He is an idealist; a poet. In the end when he tries to grasp his ideal and tries to make her a real woman, he dies. Without this dream, this illusion, he can no longer exist. All he wants to catch is a dream which exists in his head and which nobody else can see. He is a true escapist...when he is alone with his dream he is quite himself; he is a total being. When the dream is gone he must die with it. He believes only in this dream. And it is sad that he could never grasp reality.[10]

As Bournonville wrote in *My Theatre Life*, the 'ingeniously poetic idea' of *La Sylphide* was that '. . .man, in pursuing an imaginary happiness, neglects the true one and loses everything just when he thinks he is about to attain the object of his desire'.[11]

Erik Aschengreen has remarked that 'in *La Sylphide* our sympathetic pain, our identification with, and understanding of, James's striving are stronger than the moral lesson we can and must obtain.'[12] It is for this reason, says Aschengreen, that we see James closest to the audience in the final moments of the ballet and not Effie and her new bridegroom, Gurn. If there is a moral to the character of James, it is this: Marry your own kind; otherwise, risk destruction.

The interpreter of James needs to be both romantic and virile, graceful but strong in movement with a strong classical technique; a convincing mime with a sensitive appreciation of style and atmosphere.

Effie

The role of Effie is that of a bonnie Scots lass who is very much in love with her cousin James. She is a hard-working, simple, religious girl; she is tenacious, the kind who would make a good wife and mother; a girl who has definite plans for the future and who will not be dominated by her husband. (For instance, when James gets angry she calms him down, and so forth.) The interpreter of the role must be pretty in looks, sweet and innocent in disposition, a strong demi-caractère dancer with a reasonable classical technique but most important be a fine, convincing mime.

It is important to contrast the style of dancing for the aerial sylphide on pointe with that of the earthly bride on demi-pointe.

Madge, the Witch

In his preface to *Cromwell* Victor Hugo declares that

> [The modern muse] will realise that everything in creation is not humanely beautiful, that the ugly exists beside the beautiful, the unshapely beside the graceful, the grotesque on the reverse of the sublime, evil with good, darkness with light. . . . It is the grotesque which impels the ghastly antics of the witches' reels, which gives Satan his horns, his cloven foot, and his bat's wings. . . .As a means of contrast with the sublime, the grotesque is, in our view, the richest source that nature can offer.[13]

Bearing in mind Hugo's words about the 'ghastly antics of the witches' reels', let us consider Madge. In Act One of *La Sylphide*, Madge appears as a helpless old woman, afraid of the storm and wanting only to warm her hands by the fire, and willing to tell fortunes. However, in Act Two her anger, power and control may be seen.

Standing triumphantly over the cauldron she beckons her sister witches to come forth, and with anger and resentment she tells them of the affront she has suffered at the hands of James. She implores their help. With arms waving frantically up and down like one demented, she casts the spell over the scarf. Her sister witches circle the cauldron, their movements jerky, angular and asymmetrical. She wends her way back to the cave.

When James comes upon her to ask forgiveness for the harsh treatment in the farmhouse, she raises her body high as if with the pride of someone insulted but whose anger will not abate until ultimate revenge is achieved. In the final scene her body towers over the prone body of James with arms held high in exultation.

Madge and her grotesque entourage of sister witches are necessary evil forces in contrast to the purity of the Sylphide and her sister sylphs. The role demands a strong mime and forceful personality with a powerful presence and frightening stature. The French interpreters usually have been female, while the tradition in the Danish theatre has been male *en travestie* but with some outstanding female interpreters as well, including Gerda Karstens, Vivi Flindt, and Sorella England.

Gurn

The role of Gurn is rather like that of Hilarion in *Giselle* – he is James's rival and is truly in love with Effie (his 'Giselle'). A simple Scots peasant, rugged and virile, he carries a musket over his shoulder in some versions of Bournonville's Act One and like Hilarion is a man of the forest – a hunter, and a good marksman. (In some versions of the Bournonville production, he offers Effie flowers but should instead offer the plumes of a heron he has killed, as the French libretto calls for.) The original interpreters of Gurn in both versions were known more for their powers of mime than dancing, and so no variation was given. However, in today's productions of Bournonville, Gurn is often given a variation to dance. So today's interpreters of this role must have a strong classical technique with a demi-caractère slant, and possess convincing powers of mime.

Anna Reuben

Anna Reuben, James's mother, is conceivably a woman in her forties, a sturdy Scotswoman, the hardworking widow of a farmer, who loves her son and wishes him to marry her niece, Effie. The interpreter must be a good actress and have a strong sense of mime.

Other Characters

The other characters listed in the original programme are old men and women, a piper, and children of the village. These men, women, and children present a close-knit farming community – a village which comes to the house to celebrate the wedding of two 'locals', James and Effie. In Act Two – aside from James, Madge, and the Sylphide – there are witches, animals and sylphides.

The witches and their grotesque animal companions (described by Sally Banes as 'monstrous inversions of humanity'[14]) are more like a cabalistic pack of demons in a den of iniquity. After flying in on broomsticks, they circle the cauldron three times. Their movements are strong and earthbound; angular and jagged; they cackle as they drink from the boiling cauldron.

The sylphs and (in the French version) their baby counterparts live in nature in the forest in a single-sex community, each one dressed similarly in what could be deemed their 'first communion' white dresses. Unlike the witches, their movements are symmetrical, light and airy as they fly from tree to tree, suspend themselves from tree branches and swing to and fro.

Some sets for *La Sylphide*

The Original French Set, Act One. According to the libretto, 'the stage represents a farmhouse in Scotland', but no mention is made of the period in history or the time of year in which the action takes place. Balanchine, in his *Complete Stories of the Ballet*, says 1830.[15] In a chapter on Romanticism in *Costumes de l'Opéra*, Carlos Fischer, the costume historian, describes the Scotsmen in *La Sylphide* as 'of the 16th century, if I am not mistaken, and come from the best clans – the Clan Royal itself....'[16] As for the time of year, I suggest wintertime, since the witch comes into the farm house for shelter from the storm and to warm her hands by the fire.

What does the libretto say about the farmhouse?

At the back there is a door; a raised window to the right of the door; on the same side, near the front of the stage, a large fireplace; on the opposite side, a small staircase leading to the apartments occupied by the farmer's wife and her family.

This does not fully match Pierre Ciceri's original design, in which – according to period engravings – the fireplace and armchair are placed to the left of the public. (The description in the libretto, however, was matched by both the Bartholomin score and the published text of a play by Ernst Jaime and Jules Seveste, which had the text and dialogue of the Taglioni ballet and was given in Montmartre in 1832.[17]) Putting the available information together and attempting to match Ciceri's design, I believe it is appropriate to arrange the set in the following manner:

Act One

On the Public's Right:
Downstage wing   An ante chamber and Effie's bedroom.

Second wing	A large window, five feet from the ground.
Third wing	A brick pillar.
Back wing	A broad buffet and a door at the back.
On the Public's Left: Downstage wing	A large Gothic fireplace. Downstage, a very big armchair.
Upstage wing	A staircase with a balcony ledge as in *La Fille mal gardée*.

With slight modifications to the size of the fireplace, window and staircase and respective placement on stage, this first act setting has remained constant in its essentials and has served as a model for many subsequent productions around the world.

The Original French Set, Act Two. According to the libretto,

The stage represents a forest. To the left is the mouth of a cave formed by high rocks, along which a path opens. At the rise of the curtain it is still nighttime, and the forest is covered with a thick fog which allows only the nearest trees to be seen. At the front of the stage, slightly to the side, is a large beech tree.

According to the critic Fiorentino, the Ciceri set should have been preserved in a museum.[18] Unfortunately, it wasn't. And after the storehouse fire it was thought that the only tangible evidence left would be in the drawings and lithographs. However, in 1948 Ivor Guest found a model of the set in the archives of the Opéra and pieced it together.[19] The result is depicted in Figure 9.1.

Bearing in mind the model of the Ciceri set as well as the description in Nourrit's libretto, I believe it is appropriate to follow these guidelines for Act Two.

Act Two

| On the Public's Left:
Downstage wing | Entrance to a cave between two gloomy large rocks over which there is a path. |

9.1. Model of the original Act Two set by Ciceri for *La Sylphide*. Photo used by permission of Ivor Guest.

Second wing	A half broken solitary tree. Between the tree trunks are rocking chairs made from branches and leaves.
Upstage wing	A small hill near the loch. In the distance a chapel.[20]

The Original Danish Set. For Bournonville's 1836 production of *La Sylphide* (*Sylphiden*), entirely new scenery was created, which was rare for a ballet at that time.[21] The Act One set, shown in a photograph (likely from 1903), is laid out as follows, and is likely very similar to the original 1836 set, which as Jürgensen says 'was kept almost unchanged for nearly ninety years from the 1836 première to the production on March 13, 1924.'[22]

Centre	A fireplace. To the right of the fireplace a window approximately five feet from the floor.
On the Public's Right Upstage wing	Staircase leading to Effie's bedroom. A buffet table.

On the Public's Left   A door to the left of the fireplace.

Downstage wing   An armchair.

In N. Christensen's set for Act Two, the back half of the stage was a large three dimensional painting with grass carpet floor, a continuation of the backdrop on both sides, and free standing trees with many tree and bush props. The stage plan for the second act, in the words of Erik Aschengreen, shows that 'in this magical forest world [there was]... a powerful apparatus with devices allowing the sylphs to swing and float past each other, swings, seesaws and shrubs with movable arms'.[23]

The Machinery in *La Sylphide*

The most remarkable aspect of *La Sylphide* is the machinery, which is a very important part of the plot and composition, and was used to support the fantastic elements of the action and the illusion of flying.

In Act One, this machinery enabled the Sylph to be lifted vertically up the chimney, to slide down the wall, be lowered from the window, to disappear through the chair, and to fly low across the stage before she exits with James.

In Act Two (Taglioni version) the machinery made it possible for fifteen witches to fly on broomsticks, for the cauldron to emerge from below the stage (Petipa version); for twelve to fifteen sylphs to fly from tree to tree (a smaller number of sylphs flew in the Bournonville version); for them to be lowered from the branches to the ground; for the Sylph to glide on a moving ramp across the back of the stage and down the narrow path between the rocks; for her to swing on a tree branch (Taglioni version), lean forward from a platform raised in the wings and operated like a seesaw as in *Giselle* Act Two and appear from a water lily (Petipa version). Although every effort was made to ensure the safety of the equipment, tension was high. According to Slonimsky, 'during the *pas de deux* the machinery lifted the Sylph onto the rocks, onto the branch of a tree, and sometimes into the arms of her part-ner'.[24]

I can confirm from Von Rosen's version for Rambert that to reach the bird's nest, the Sylph was raised up by the machinery inside the tree operated by a stage hand hidden in the tree. I believe the same thing was done in Taglioni's version. For the final ascent into the sky in Taglioni productions, the machinery lifted the dead Sylph, cradled in the scarf, together with twelve to fifteen sister sylphs and after a vertical lift-off, made a circular flight as seen in drawings in the final scene from *Les Beautés de l'Opéra*. This same flight in Bournonville productions is carried out with the Sylph being air-borne, followed by her sister sylphs on the ground exiting the stage with arms held *à deux bras*. They look heavenwards to the sylph lying prostrate on a swing-like platform with a baby sylph at each and moving diagonally upwards into the sky.

In my opinion, the most effective usage of this machinery and trap doors was made by the Royal Danish Ballet, Ballet Rambert, Scottish Ballet, and Scottish-American Ballet. In all four companies, the appearances and disappearances of the Sylph were simply and effectively carried out. For instance, the disappearance-up-the chimney effect is created, quite simply, by placing two men on a ledge behind the fireplace some four or five feet off the ground, each one taking an arm of the Sylph as she runs and takes a *soubresaut à deux bras* (a jump, keeping both feet crossed together with two outstretched arms either side of her body) and lifting her up bodily onto the ledge.

This same moment in American Ballet Theatre's production (1964) and Pierre Lacotte's film production (1971) does not have nearly as convincing an effect. In their productions, the Sylph runs to the chimney, stands in fifth position and waits (only too obviously) for the wire to be attached and then some seconds later to be whisked up.

Act One

From the Window. On the last page of the Bartholomin score, it states that 'the sylph places her foot on a ledge under the window (which is five feet from the ground) and alights on the ground holding onto a wire . . . *en attitude* as if flying'. This was no doubt effectively carried out in Paris and Brussels, and probably in some early Bournonville productions as well, but in the productions by contemporary companies such as the Scottish Ballet, Paris Opéra Ballet, and Les Grands Ballets Canadiens, the window is only two feet from the ground and the magical effect is not as strong. (Harald Lander replaced much of the old machinery in Copenhagen in the 1930s, and in some contemporary Bournonville productions the Sylph walks down a few steps from the window; this is not nearly as effectively as original Taglioni effect.)

Through the Chair. The Bartholomin rehearsal score states clearly that a large mechanical chair is placed over a trap door which leads under the stage. Therefore, the Sylph would have disappeared through the seat of the chair. This same effect in many Bournonville versions is carried out by placing the chair in front of the fireplace; the back of the chair opens like a garden gate and the Sylph makes her exit that way and up the chimney.

Through the Pillar. The Bartholomin score tells us that 'The sylph crosses over through the *quadrilles*[25] of the *corps de ballet* (in the first reel) and disappears through the pillar on the Public's right, near the window.' This pillar had an English trap door with two battens.[26]

Through the Trap door above the Staircase by the Door. According to the Bartholomin score, 'The sylph crosses over the *quadrilles* of the *corps de*

ballet in the second reel and disappears through the trap door above the staircase.' In some Bournonville productions, the Sylph, during the reel,
disappears through the door leading to Effie's bedroom.

Through the Trap door above the Staircase *(when the Sylph leads
James to the forest)*. At the end of Act One, according to the Bartholomin
score, when the Sylph leads James to the forest, they exit through the trap
door above the staircase. 'It is through the trap door above the staircase that
the sylph disappears with James.' Perhaps in the original this was carried
out. In all of Bournonville's versions, Lacotte's version, and Bennett's version, James and the Sylph leave by the door at the back of the stage.

Act Two

Across the Sky. In the many Bournonville versions, the Sylph sits on a
kind of chair lift suspended from the flies and crosses the back of the stage in
the air. In the old French versions, I believe that the Sylph, in an arabesque,
is pulled across the back on a moving ramp, after which she slides down
another ramp between the rocks. In a drawing by André Roller for an 1835
production in Russia, one can clearly see this ramp. Lacotte uses the original
Taglioni effect (as it is explained in the Bartholomin score).

Her Suspension from the Tree. While the sister sylphs are swinging on
the branches of trees, the Sylph, too, 'swings on the branch of a tree.' This is
described in the Bartholomin score, and was done in the von Rosen/
Bournonville and Bennett/Taglioni versions but is not commonly done today.

Up the Tree to Fetch the Bird's Nest. This action is not indicated in
Bartholomin's score, but seen in Lacotte's version, Bennett's version, and all
of the Bournonville reproductions with which I am acquainted.

Final Crossing Across the Sky. In the original Taglioni, this scene was
carried out with the aid of twelve wires.[27] Lacotte's version has the main
Sylph and twelve others on wires; Bournonville versions have the Sylph on
the chair lift with two baby sylphs, one at each end.

Ashengreen, Erik. 'Mit Egentlige kald – Idéinhold og Iscenesaettelse hos
    Bournonville [My True Calling – the Concepts and Staging of
    Bournonville]', in *Perspektiv på Bournonville*, ed. Erik Aschengreen,
    Marianne Hallar and Jørgen Heiner. Copenhagen: Nyt Nordisk Forlag
    Arnold Busck, 1980.
Balanchine, George, and Francis Mason. *Balanchine's Complete Stories of the
    Great Ballets*. Revised and enlarged ed. Garden City, NY: Doubleday, 1977.

Banes, Sally. *Dancing Women: Female Bodies on Stage.* London and New York: Routledge, 1998.

Bournonville, August. *My Theatre Life.* Translated by Patricia N. McAndrew. Middletown, CT: Wesleyan University Press, 1979.

Bruhn, Erik. 'Beyond Technique.' *Dance Perspectives* 36 (1968).

Clark, Barrett Harper, ed. *European Theories of the Drama: An Anthology of Dramatic Theory.* New York: D. Appleton and Company, 1929.

Cohen, H. Robert, ed. *Douze livrets de mise en scène lyrique datant des créations parisiennes.* Vol. 3, Musical Life in 19th-Century France. Stuyvesant, NY: Pendragon, 1991.

————, ed. *The Original Staging Manuals for Ten Parisian Operatic Premières.* Vol. 6, Musical Life in 19th-Century France. Stuyvesant, NY: Pendragon, 1998.

Fischer, Carlos. *Les Costumes de L'opéra.* Paris: Librarie de France, 1931.

Fitzgerald, Percy Hetherington. *The Art of Acting.* London: Swan Sonnenschein and Company, 1892.

Gautier, Théophile. 'La Péri', in *Poésies Complètes* vol. 1. Paris: Charpentier, 1877.

Guest, Ivor. *Adventures of a Ballet Historian – an Unfinished Memoir.* New York: Dance Horizons, 1982.

————. *The Romantic Ballet in Paris.* London: Dance Books, 1980.

Huckenpahler, Victoria. 'Confessions of an Opera Director: Chapters from the *Mémoires* of Dr. Louis Véron, Part One.' *Dance Chronicle* 7, no. 1 (1983): 50-106.

Jacobshagen, Arnold. 'Analyzing *Mise-En-Scène*: Halévy's *La Juive* at the Salle Le Pelletier', in *Music, Theater, and Cultural Transfer: Paris, 1830-1914,* ed. Annegret Fauser and Mark Everist. Chicago: University of Chicago Press, 2009.

Jaime, Ernst and Jules Séveste. *La Sylphide, drama en deux actes, mêlé de chant, imité du ballet de M. Taglioni.* Paris: Barba, 1832.

Jürgensen, Knud Arne. *The Bournonville Ballets – a Photographic Record 1844-1933.* London: Dance Books, 1987.

Kirstein, Lincoln. *Four Centuries of Ballet: Fifty Masterworks.* New York: Dover, 1984.

Justamant [or Justament], Henri. *Giselle ou les Wilis. Ballet Fantastique en deux actes. Faksimile der Notation von Justamant aus den 1880er Jahren.* ed. Frank-Manuel Peter. Hildesheim: Georg Olms Verlag, 2008.

Slonimsky, Yuri. *'Sil'fida' Balet.* Leningrad: Academia, 1927.

Thesmar, Ghislaine. 'Le Personnage de la Sylphide', in *La Sylphide* Program Book, Paris Opéra (1990).

Véron, Louis. *Mémoires d'un Bourgeois de Paris.* Paris: Librairie Nouvelle, 1856.

Notes

1. On staging manuals for opera, see, for example, H. Robert Cohen, ed. *Douze livrets de mise en scène lyrique datant des créations parisiennes*, vol. 3, Musical Life in 19th-Century France (Stuyvesant, NY: Pendragon, 1991); H. Robert Cohen, ed. *The Original Staging Manuals for Ten Parisian Operatic Premières*, vol. 6, Musical Life in 19th-Century France (Stuyvesant, NY: Pendragon, 1998); and Arnold Jacobshagen, 'Analyzing *mise-en-scène*: Halévy's *La Juive* at the Salle Le Peletier', in *Music, theater, and cultural transfer: Paris, 1830-1914*, ed. Annegret Fauser and Mark Everist (Chicago: University of Chicago Press, 2009), 176-94. See also this manuscript staging manual for ballet, Justamant [or Justament], Henri. *Giselle ou les Wilis. Ballet Fantastique en deux actes. Faksimile der Notation von Justamant aus den 1880er Jahren.* ed. Frank-Manuel Peter (Hildesheim: Georg Olms Verlag, 2008).

2. Erik Bruhn, 'Beyond Technique', *Dance Perspectives* 36 (1968): 15.

3. [Note, however, the importance of James in Bournonville's production. See Chapter 5 of this volume. — Editor's note.]

4. Ghislaine Thesmar, 'Le Personnage de la Sylphide', in *La Sylphide* programme book, Paris Opéra (1990), 32-33.

5. Lincoln Kirstein, *Four Centuries of Ballet: Fifty Masterworks* (New York: Dover, 1984), 146.

6. Théophile Gautier, 'La Péri' (the poem, not the libretto), in *Poésies complètes* (Paris: Charpentier, 1977), 195.

7. See, for example, this volume, Chapter 5.

8. Preface to *Cromwell*, trans. George Burnham Ives, in Barrett Harper Clark, ed. *European theories of the drama: an anthology of dramatic theory* (New York: D. Appleton and Company, 1929), 374.

9. Thesmar, 'Le Personnage de la Sylphide.'

10. Bruhn, 'Beyond Technique', 15.

11. August Bournonville, *My Theatre Life*, trans. Patricia N. McAndrew (Middletown, CT: Wesleyan University Press, 1979), 78.

12. Erik Ashengreen, 'Mit egentlige kald – Idéinhold og iscenesaettelse hos Bournonville [My True Calling – The concepts and staging of Bournonville]', in *Perspektiv på Bournonville*, ed. Erik Aschengreen, Marianne Hallar, and Jørgen Heiner (Copenhagen: Nyt Nordisk Forlag Arnold Busck, 1980), 126.

13. Preface to *Cromwell*, Clark, trans. George Burnham Ives, *European theories of the drama: an anthology of dramatic theory* 368- 70.

14. Sally Banes, *Dancing Women: Female Bodies on Stage* (London and New York: Routledge, 1998), 18.

15. George Balanchine and Francis Mason, *Balanchine's Complete Stories of the Great Ballets*, Revised and enlarged ed. (Garden City, NY: Doubleday, 1977), 645.

16. Carlos Fischer, *Les Costumes de l'Opéra* (Paris: Librarie de France, 1931), 208.

17. Ernst Jaime et Jules Séveste, *La Sylphide, drama en deux actes, mêlé de chant* (Paris: Barba, 1832). First performed 20 September 1832 at the Théâtre Montmartre.

18. Ivor Guest, *The Romantic Ballet in Paris* (London: Dance Books, 1980), 15.

19. Ivor Guest, *Adventures of a Ballet Historian – an unfinished memoir* (New York: Dance Horizons, 1982), 18. There is no mention of the second act layout in either the Bartholomin score or the Jaime/ Seveste play.

20. [There is no mention of a visible chapel in Nourrit's libretto. — Editor's note.]

21. Knud Arne Jürgensen, *The Bournonville Ballets – A photographic record 1844-1933* (London: Dance Books, 1987), 20.

22. Ibid.

23. Ashengreen, 'Mit egentlige kald – Idéinhold og iscenesaettelse hos Bournonville [My True Calling – The concepts and staging of Bournonville]', 234-36.

24. [In this paragraph, the author is relying on the Bartholomin score and Louis Véron, *Mémoires d'un bourgeois de Paris* (Paris: Librairie Nouvelle, 1856) for information about the Taglioni production, and on Slonimsky for information about the Petipa production. Yuri Slonimsky, *'Sil'fida' balet* (Leningrad: Academia, 1927), 40. Translation from the Russian by Alexander Bennett. — Editor's note.]

25. [A quadrille of dancers in this case refers to a group of *corps* dancers. — Editor's note.]

26. 'The *trappe anglaise* is an English invention. . . A spirit or genius will of a sudden disappear through a wall; and this is arranged by an 'English trap', which consists of a number of elastic leaves of steel or twigs, like two combs placed with their teeth together. These are covered with painted canvas like any scenic door. The actor flings himself against it; it lets him pass through, then flies back to its original state. The same principle is carried out on the stage itself, when a pantomimist seems to pass through the boards, which close after him.' Percy Hetherington Fitzgerald, *The Art of Acting* (London: Swan Sonnenschein and Company, 1892), 150.

27. Victoria Huckenpahler, 'Confessions of an Opera Director: Chapters from the *Mémoires* of Dr. Louis Véron, Part One', *Dance Chronicle* 7, no. 1 (1983): 80.

Chapter 10

Simplified Choreographic Script

of *La Sylphide*

Alexander Bennett

Thanks to the careful preservation by generations of Danish dancers and ballet masters, the Bournonville choreography for *La Sylphide* has been kept alive from the original production in 1836 to the present day – albeit with alterations.

Unfortunately, we have no comparable record of Taglioni's version of the ballet. Though some notes and drawings remain, they only suggest an outline of the Taglioni *Sylphide* ballet as a whole, leaving historians and balletomanes frustrated in their search for a record of the actual choreography.

[In order to create this simplified choreographic script, the author has focused on his recollections of the Bournonville versions with which he was acquainted, and 'where possible, gleaned information about Taglioni's choreography from lithographs, paintings, and contemporary reviews'.[1]]

Act One

Scene 1. The opening scene. In both versions the curtain rises on a fireside scene with the Sylph in a cloud of white muslin and kneeling at the feet of the sleeping farmer with her elbow resting on the armchair. Rising onto the tips of her toes, she declares in pantomime her love and slowly circles the armchair with rippling steps tip-toeing (*pas de course*). Joyously she flies around the room with a sequence of aerial steps which alternate between stirring the air, in Bournonville's version with *rond de jambe sauté*, delicately cutting the air with *fouetté cabriole* and balancing in *arabesque* and *attitude* suggesting hovering and fluttering.

This same opening scene in Filippo Taglioni's original has been aptly recorded by Jules Collignan in the woodcut illustrating the essay in *Les Beautés de l'Opéra*, and described by Johanne Luise Heiberg thus: 'There she stood, like a fine transparent marble statue, whose first movement surprised one as much as if a real marble statue had actually begun to stir.'[2] No doubt similar steps (gliding, hopping, and jumping) were used by Taglioni, père, to express the Sylph's joy felt at being near the one she loves.

Before placing a kiss on James' forehead, the Sylph climbs behind the armchair in Taglioni's version and settling above his head, flutters her wings to cool the air over his face. Queen Victoria, when a young Princess, captured this moment in one of her rare watercolors housed in the Royal Library at Windsor Castle.[3] This moment is not recorded by Bournonville. However, in both versions the awakened James bursts forth from his chair and, seeing the object of his desire before him, pursues the vision around the room.

In Bournonville, she eludes his pursuit, strikes delicate poses in *arabesque* position and flits around the room with *grands jetés* (big jumps) and *temps levé en arabesque* (hops in the arabesque position), taking refuge in the chimney over the fireplace and disappearing from sight up the flue. No doubt poses in *arabesque* and steps of elevation were used by Taglioni in his original introductory scene.

Musically, Løvenskjold ends this scene at this point. However, Schneitzhoeffer continues with a whole passage of music, almost like a soliloquy, wherein James interprets his *grand étonnement* (great astonishment) in danced mime. To reassure himself that he has not been dreaming, he awakens Gurn, who is asleep on a bed of straw under the window, and questions him on whether he has seen a sylph fly up the chimney.

In the conversation which appears in both Nourrit's libretto and in Bartholomin's violin score, Gurn tells James that he has been dreaming and that the good fortune of marrying Effie that morning has gone to his head. This conversation between James and Gurn does not take place in Bournonville since his Gurn does not appear until the next scene, marked 'Entrance of Effie.'

Scene 2.   Mother's entrance with Effie. Bournonville's Effie makes her entrance with James' mother (her aunt) from the bedroom door, stage left, on the upper floor. Taglioni's Effie and aunt make *their* entrance from an anteroom downstage on stage left at stage level. This is noted in two sources: Victor Bartholomin's stage notes and play by Messieurs Jaime and Seveste for which the set is clearly described and which corresponds to Pierre Ciceri's ground plan.[4]

This scene in Bournonville is carried out in pure pantomime with Gurn entering carrying a musket over his shoulder and flowers in his hand which he duly presents to Effie. Taglioni's Gurn (as prescribed by Nourrit in the libretto) offers the feathers of a heron which he has just shot.

Scene 3.   Entry of the Villagers.   No one knows exactly how the villagers entered in Taglioni's version – presumably dancing to a typical Écossaise in a demi-character manner. However, Bournonville brings the village girls onstage, choreographically speaking, with dancing steps which include *posé développé devant* and *jeté derrière*.

Scene 4.   Madge's Entrance.   According to the libretto, 'Madge enters behind the villagers and sits down at the fireside.' This scene in both versions is pure mime.

Scene 5. Window Scene. The Window Scene in Taglioni has been immortalised by Alfred Edouard Chalon, the Swiss painter, in the famous Taglioni pose in which she leans on the corner of the window sill with her head resting on the wall, arms crossed in low fifth position, *dans une attitude mélancolique* (Figure 3.1). The Bartholomin score tells us that James imitates her pose and asks her to come down from the window. In the original stagings of both Taglioni and Bournonville, the Sylph placed her foot on a ledge (five feet from the floor) and descended *dans une attitude comme elle volait* holding onto a wire. Since all the scenes in the Taglioni version were likely expressed in dance, it is fair to say that the window scene included 'mimed dance' with some supported *adage* as seen in the Erik Ruth watercolor where Taglioni is in an *arabesque penché* supported by Christian Johannson, the Swedish dancer and pupil of Bournonville (Stockholm, 1841). In complete contrast, Bournonville's window scene is conducted in pure pantomime.

Present-day Sylphs in Bournonville productions sometimes carry out this scene by walking down a small flight of stairs, as noted in the previous chapter.

The solo for the Sylph to express her joy at being loved includes such steps as *jeté battu, chassé coupé ballonné, fouetté sauté* in Bournonville; similar steps were in the Taglioni version.

Scene 6. Removal of Plaid by Gurn. This scene is pure mime in both versions. 'I saw, in that chair over there, a young woman.'

Scene 7. Wedding Divertissements. In the Taglioni original there were four wedding dances: two character dances, a *pas de deux* and a *pas de trois*. During the two character dances the Sylph mingles in the crowed (unseen by all but James) disappearing through the pillar during the former, and through the trap door above the staircase in the latter.

Looking at the Paris Opéra répétiteur, you see that the second Highland Reel was danced by *sujets et enfants* (soloists and children). However, by 1844 Gautier tells us the Reel was danced by supernumeraries, and from his description in his review of *La Sylphide* in 1844, he was not amused. '...The cheering was then followed by titters when the supers went into a hilarious Scottish jig. Such slipshod execution is quite inexcusable in a theatre like the Opéra and indeed is high treason, for there the public is king. The supers dance better than that at the Porte-Saint-Martin and the Cirque.'[5]

Bournonville's Reel is taken from an authentic Scottish Highland dance called 'Gillie Gaescach', whose format was balleticised into a well known nineteenth century dance, 'Highland Laddie', which is still performed today at Highland games around the world. Bournonville's Reel includes: step high kick (step *ballonné devant* to open 4th), repeated three times, travelling in a circle, *arabesque en demi plié* with arms folded, *coupé ballonné derrière* with both right leg and left finishing with a break step.

The *pas de deux* in the Taglioni original was danced by two of the wedding guests, Mlle Julia de Varennes and M. Antoine Coulon (son of the celebrated teacher). The *pas de trois* was danced by two other wedding guests, M. Frémolle, Mme Dupont (née Felicity Noblet) and Effie Lise Noblet, her sister. After a short introduction, the music suggests a variation for the man, followed by variations for Effie and the other wedding guest (Mme Dupont), and finishing with a rousing finale.

Théophile Gautier confirms a solo for Effie in his review of *La Sylphide* in 1852. 'Mlle Luigia Taglioni, who was playing the role of Effie, wanted to live up to her name and displayed great brilliance in her variation in the first act, so much so that several people could not understand why the Scotsman preferred Mlle Priora [the Sylphide]....'[6]   The original Bournonville Effie, Helga Lund, did not have a variation.

Hans Brenaa gives his Effie a short solo which includes a series of *glissades changés*, and *jetés battus derrière*. The choreography for the two male farm worker's variations (danced by Gurn and James in today's productions) contains intricate footwork *assemblé, sissonne en arabesque, brisé volé, cabriole devant*.

Scene 8. Preparation for the Wedding. In this scene Bournonville follows exactly the same format as Taglioni and remains faithful to the Nourrit libretto. Effie is seated downstage left, surrounded by her friends, while James alone is on the opposite side. The male guests form a circle upstage right with their backs towards the audience. The Sylph enters from the fireplace and entreats James to abandon Effie and follow her off to the forest. In the Bartholomin score, specific reference is made to the disappearance of the Sylph and James through the trapdoor above the staircase. All Bournonville productions show the Sylph and James leaving by the door. Both versions end with the same picture group of Effie in the arms of Mother Anna surrounded by villagers.

Act Two
Scene 1. The Witches' Scene where 'the lighting effects entertained and delighted'[7] was carried out in the French original by fifteen sorcerers flying on broomsticks, accompanied by hideous animals (Nourrit text). The libretto had called for twenty witches, but

> ... as M. Duponchel was already very keen on the devilries in *La Tentation* (an opera-ballet by Cavé), then in the course of preparation, he haggled with M. Taglioni over the devils, and the ballet master often came to me

bewailing the meanness of his hell and the paltry number of demons he was allowed.[8]

Bournonville's witches' scene was originally much longer and may have contained some demi-caractère dance but in 1903 Hans Beck cut out three-quarters of the original music, and since then this scene has been pure mime.

Scene 2. The Forest Scene was described in *L'Entr'acte* as 'something ravishing beyond description in which painting, music and dancing vie with one another',[9] while André Levinson, in retrospect, described it thus:

> This rocky landscape seen through the trees was acclaimed a marvel. It was the diorama transported to the Opéra. When the mist rises the stage reveals one of the most picturesque glades in an emerald forest. A misty battalion of sylphs with pink and blue wings appears through the trees. The daughters of the air hover with timed and rhythmic wings about their sister. Some attach scarves to the trees and gently swing themselves; others, taking hold of the ends of the branches, bend them down and receive an impetus which carries them into the air.[10]

In Taglioni's version, as the libretto tells us, 'Above the rocks, the sylph is seen leading James by the hand. They arrive on the stage by a narrow and steep path which the young man descends fearfully while the Sylph guides his steps, gliding over the tops of the rocks; her feet no longer seem to touch the ground.' This appearance of her gliding is achieved by means of a mechanical ramp on which the Sylph places her foot and, with her other leg in an *arabesque penchée*, descends to the stage. In a rare watercolour of the set for the second act in the first Russian production of *La Sylphide* (1835), André Roller, a French designer in St Petersburg, shows the structure of this ramp (now in the Lunacharsky Museum, St Petersburg).

Bournonville's sylph makes her entrance sitting on a chair-like swing which creates the effect of her flying across the sky (suspended on wires from the flies). The Sylph then calls her sister sylphs from the trees. In Taglioni's version, the sylphs descended from the trees suspended on wires from the flies and advanced from the back of the stage in groups of four to form a delightful group in the very front. André Levinson describes it thus: 'The entrance by fours in the quadrilles from the back of the stage to the front has remained celebrated in the annals of choreographic art.'[11]

Bournonville also groups his *corps* in a semi-circle and they, too, extend their arms and legs à la seconde but in *écarté*, as opposed to *en face* in the Taglioni version.

Both choreographers made ingenious use of mechanical inventions with aerial crossings, although Taglioni made more use of them than Bournonville.

After a musical introduction which sounds almost like Adam's music for the entrance of his Wilis, Bournonville placed his *corps de ballet* in horizontal lines facing each other in pairs. They execute *développé devant* to fourth position *à terre*, followed by little runs, up or downstage. Still facing each other, they do *penché* in first arabesque (reminiscent of the face to face coupling of Coralli's *corps de ballet* in *Giselle* Act Two). Their pairings move out into single rows, form a revolving ring (also reminiscent of Coralli's second Act of *Giselle*) and end up forming a diagonal line facing upstage to their leader balanced on the branch of a tree. (Taglioni's choreography was probably similar. We don't know.)

This similarity of Bournonville's choreography here to *Giselle* Act Two is not by chance. The extended section in Bournonville's second act known as 'The Sylph's Scene' is a seven-part divertissement added some years after the première in 1836 (probably around 1842), and stemmed from Bournonville's desire to emulate the new Romantic ballet *Giselle* (staged in 1841) which he had seen. Inspired by Coralli's work (which had grown from the roots of Taglioni's *La Sylphide*), Bournonville strengthened his *Sylphiden* with more choreography and more stage effects.

As a result the main section of the Sylphides' *pas* – the 'ballet blanc' section in which the array of white dresses of the *corps de ballet* signify the beauty of the Romantic era – included an additional solo for the Sylph, two solos for James and a *pas de trois* for his three leading sylphs.

Scene 3. Grand Pas de Deux. In front of this spectacle of mass movement, the main *pas de deux* begins – a poetic game of hide and seek or 'hunt the shadow', which provides the theme for the duet. Once more the arabesque is taken up by the *corps de ballet* during the *Adage* section and throughout the main dancing movement. It is repeated in mass movement, sounding (in a poetic key) in various intonations and strengthened by pronounced action.

During a visit to Moscow in 1992, I witnessed a performance of the Petipa/Taglioni *pas de deux* given by two dancers from the Kirov Ballet, Margaretta Perkun and André Ustinov. Staged by Yevgeny Kocharov, a former partner of Ekaterina Geltzer, the choreography was from the production staged by Vasily Tikhomirov (1925). In it were some interesting lifts. For example, one swept from the 'fish' position to *a développé devant en tournant*, to fourth position supported *en l'air*; while another ended in the Bluebird shoulder lift with the ballerina's feet in *soubresaut*. Two other lifts were executed in supported *temps de flèche* (*en avant* and *en arrière*). At one point, for a fleeting moment, I recognised the *tour en attitude* mentioned by Louis Henry's sister. The lifts, however, could not be from the original Taglioni *pas de deux* and were likely introduced in the twentieth century.

Bournonville, of course, did not include supported *adage* or lifts in his *pas de deux*. He abhorred using his male dancers as *porteurs* and considered them the equal counterpart to the female in the dancing duet.

I can confirm that throughout the entire version of *La Sylphide* set by Elsa Marianne von Rosen for Ballet Rambert (1960), I supported the Sylphide only once, i.e., at the end of the dance of the sylphs *en arabesque penchée*.

However, according to Johanne Luise Heiberg, the early productions of Bournonville's *Sylfiden* included a long *pas de deux* in which the Sylph was repeatedly in the arms of James, who constantly touched her. Heiberg and others from the Royal Theatre complained so vehemently about the illogical dramaturgy that Bournonville changed this in 1842.[12]

During the dance of the Sylphs, the variations for James and the Sylph follow in true canonical form. Although there is no record of James' variations in the Taglioni version, an interesting comment by a leading Bolshoi dancer and ballet master throws light on the original choreography. Piotr Gusev, a graduate of the Kirov Opera, Petrograd (1922) was familiar with the Petipa version (revived by Ponomaryov in 1922). He learned the two variations as class graduation pieces and subsequently danced the role of James (1922). He told Allan Fridericia (who visited the Soviet Union in the 1960s) that after seeing the Bournonville version staged by von Rosen, he perceived that the Taglioni choreography for James was similar to that of Bournonville. So, with this in mind, I speculate that the Taglioni choreography for James's solo contained similar steps to those used by Bournonville, viz: *entrechat quatre royale, échappé sauté à la seconde, fouetté sauté en arabesque, jeté en avant en attitude derrière* with arms in first position, *temps levé chassé, coupé ballonné.* (Some of these steps were included in James's solo in the performance I saw in Moscow in 1992.)

The choreography for the Sylph's solo in Bournonville includes: *relevé piqué en quatrième devant, doubles ronds de jambe en l' air, sissonnes fermées battues.* However, we know very little of the Sylphide's solo in the Taglioni version beyond the valuable account of her steps as recorded by the critic of the *Dublin Journal* (1836).

Nothing can exceed the sweep and flourish of her feet in some of her majestic vaultings. As critics, we mention, technically, her *ronds de jambe avec glissades jetés*, and her *pas de bourre enlevé*, in which she shifts so adroitly the foot expected to descend, and mounts on each alternately into the air, as if striding clouds. Also, her amazing *pas de basque en tournant*, in which she flings herself round without a jerk, as though by mere instinct, with a suppleness almost unimaginable.[13]

There is no record of the choreography for the coda in the Taglioni version but we do have an accurate account of Bournonville's coda (bearing in mind that today's version dates from 1842). (We wonder what kind of choreography was used in Løvenskjold's original coda in 1836.) Bournonville's sylph begins the coda with a *posé temps levé en tournant,* in a diagonal downstage, then proceeds upstage with *glissade posé développé en tournant* followed by *jeté en avant en arabesque.* James reinforces this by picking up the momentum leaping forward, after two spring points to the fourth *devant,* with *glissade jeté en avant,* then darting upstage with *posé fouette sauté.*

The *corps de ballet* joins James and the Sylph in a typical Bournonville ending using *pas de basque en avant, posé fouetté relevé* upstage, ending with *coupé grand rond de jambe* to *quatrième derrière,* and finishing with a *pirouette en dedans,* and making a picture group around the Sylph and James.

After the coda the *corps de ballet* leave the stage. (In the Taglioni version they flew off with the aid of wires, and probably did so in the original Bournonville version. But in Bournonville productions today, they run off stage.) The scene which follows in the Bournonville version has been added to give more meaning to the action and is played in pure pantomime.

Gurn returns on the scene looking for James. He sees James's beret on a tree trunk and is about to call his friends when Madge interrupts. Throwing the beret off into the distance, Madge reminds Gurn of her prediction in Act One and on seeing Effie arrive on the scene, makes him kneel down and plead for Effie's hand in marriage. (Madge involves herself in Gurn's business in Bournonville's libretto, but not in Nourrit's.)

Scene 4. The scene with Madge, James and the Scarf. James enters and is confronted by Madge who shows him the talisman: the scarf. Schneitzhoeffer's music at this point in the Taglioni version suggests a variation for James with the scarf to illustrate joy. It may be that Taglioni's James danced a 'mimed dance' in this scene. No music for a solo exists in the Løvenskjold score.

Scene 5. James and the Sylph and the Scarf. In the Taglioni version, according to the Bartholomin score, 'the Sylph enters, sees a bird's nest in the tree and runs to get hold of it'. The famous Chalon lithograph captures Taglioni in this pose. Her flight is carried out in both versions by simple machinery (she places her foot on a see-saw levered platform and floats gently up the tree) to Schneitzhoeffer's music for *pas de deux Gavotte.* The Bartholomin score tells us,

James calls her and she comes down. She shows James the nest; he tells her to put it back. He shows her the scarf and immediately tries to wrap it around her. They make several crossings. James takes advantage of one of these crossings to attach the scarf under her wings. She wants to get up but she cannot. She falls onto her knee and begs him to detach it [the scarf]. He refuses. She turns pale – totters – her wings fall off. She falls.

According to Gautier, Fanny Elssler gave a poignant rendering of this scene:

> Her miming in the scene where her lover catches her in the folds of the enchanted scarf, expresses sorrow and forgiveness, and the sense of fall and irreparable error, with a rare feeling for poetry, and her last long look at her wings as they lie on the ground is a moment of great tragic beauty.[14]

Her sister sylphs return dancing and stop abruptly. Their dance probably afforded the spectator two examples of how the expressive potentialities of an *enchaînement* (combination of steps) can be varied according to its manner of execution and its timing. The music for the farewell and reproaches of the Sylph is played on the flute and oboe (Schneitzhoeffer). She dies.

The Bournonville version follows more or less the same pattern except that we do have an account of the choreography. James and the Sylph face each other making a *cabriole derrière* preceded by a *glissade* with James teasing the Sylph with the scarf. (This section of crossing over diagonally with steps of *batterie* is also reminiscent of Albrecht's and Giselle's crossings in Act Two.) The wings of Bournonville's Sylph fall off later in the action than in Taglioni's version.

The death of the Sylph in both cases is sad and mournful. Gautier tells us, 'the idea for this very poetic *pas* is no doubt borrowed from the life of insects, from virgin grasshoppers whose wings drop off as soon as they have made love. Nature has foreseen everything – even the endings of ballets.'[15]

Scene 6. Death of the Sylph. A poignant moment in Bournonville is the added action of the Sylph turning blind after losing her wings. This moment is not mentioned in Nourrit and therefore is not in Taglioni's version.

Scene 7. The Final Ascent. The ending in both versions can be seen to advantage by comparing the woodcut from *Les Beautés de l'Opéra* showing the circular flight with Taglioni and her sister sylphs with photographs of any Bournonville production, where the final ascent to the heavens is realised with the aid of a chair lift on which lies the Sylph and a baby sylph at either end.

Had Bournonville, perhaps, recalled more than the melodies of Schneitzhoeffer to Løvenskjold? In any case, both choreographers undoubtedly treated the theme of love for mortal and spirit with refinement and lyricism, and even though we lack a substantial record of the Taglioni production, we can safely conclude that the second acts of both versions were masterpieces of choreographic poetry.

Gautier, Théophile. *Gautier on Dance*. Edited by Ivor Guest. London: Dance Books, 1986.

Guest, Ivor. *The Romantic Ballet in Paris*. London: Dance Books, 1980.

Heiberg, Johanne Luise. *Et Liv Gjenoplevit i Erindringen* [A Life Relived in Memory]. Vol. 1, Copenhagen: Gylendal, 1973.

Heiberg, Johanne Luise, and Patricia McAndrew. 'Memories of Taglioni and Elssler.' *Dance Chronicle* 4, no. 1 (1981): 14-18.

Huckenpahler, Victoria. 'Confessions of an Opera Director: Chapters from the *Mémoires* of Dr. Louis Véron, Part One.' *Dance Chronicle* 7, no. 1 (1984): 50-106.

Jaime, Ernst and Jules Séveste. *La Sylphide, Drame en 2 Actes, mêlé de Chant, imité du Ballet de M. Taglioni*. Paris: Barba, 1832.

Janin, Jules, Philarète Chasles, and Théophile Gautier. *Les beautés de l'opéra, ou chefs-d'œuvre lyriques: illustrés par les premiers artistes de Paris et de Londres sous la direction de Giraldon*. Paris: Soulié, 1845.

Levinson, André. *Marie Taglioni*. Translated by Cyril Beaumont. London: Imperial Society of Teachers of Dancing, 1930.

Warner, Marina, ed. *Queen Victoria's Sketchbook*. New York: Crown Publishers, 1979.

Notes

1. Alexander Bennett, unpublished manuscript.

2. Johanne Luise Heiberg, *Et Liv gjenoplevit I Erindringen* [A Life Relived in Memory], vol. 1 (Copenhagen: Gylendal, 1973), translated by Patricia McAndrew, 'Memories of Taglioni and Elssler', *Dance Chronicle* 4, no. 1 (1981): 15. Jules Janin, Philarète Chasles, and Théophile Gautier, *Les beautés de l'opéra, ou Chefs-d'œuvre lyriques : illustrés par les premiers artistes de Paris et de Londres sous la direction de Giraldon* (Paris: Soulié, 1845).

3. One of Victoria's paintings, representing the Sylph kneeling by James's side, is reproduced in Marina Warner, ed. *Queen Victoria's Sketchbook* (New York: Crown Publishers, 1979), 46. [Alex Bennett viewed these watercolours at Windsor Castle. — Editor's Note.]

4. Ernst Jaime et Jules Séveste, *La Sylphide, drame en 2 actes, mêlé de chant, imité du ballet de M. Taglioni* (Paris: Théâtre Montmartre, 20 September 1832).

5. *La Presse*, 3 June 1844, in Théophile Gautier, *Gautier on Dance*, ed. Ivor Guest (London: Dance Books, 1986), 132.

6. *La Presse*, 5 March 1852, in ibid., 235.

7. André Levinson, *Marie Taglioni*, trans. Cyril Beaumont (London, 1929), 48.

8. Victoria Huckenpahler, 'Confessions of an Opera Director: Chapters from the *Mémoires* of Dr. Louis Véron, Part One', *Dance Chronicle* 7, no. 1 (1984): 80. Translation modified by Alexander Bennett.

9. *L'Entr'acte*, 13 March 1832, tr. and quoted in Ivor Guest, *The Romantic Ballet in Paris* (London: Dance Books, 1980), 115.

10. Levinson, *Marie Taglioni*, 46.

11. Ibid.

12. 'At our theater [in Copenhagen] the Sylph, at least during the early years, danced a long pas de deux with her lover in which they touched one another and continually rested in each other's arms. This took place before the catastrophe, which was, as a result, rendered incomprehensible and totally meaningless. Indeed, the whole idea of the composition was thereby obliterated, for since he had touched the Sylph many times before, why, in the end, did she disintegrate simply because he touched her?' See Heiberg and McAndrew, 'Memories of Taglioni and Elssler', 16.

13. Newspaper clipping marked '*Dublin [illegible] and Morning Post, 23 July*' in a section labelled 'Dublin 1833.' Marie Taglioni scrapbook, fonds Taglioni [R2, Bibliothèque de l'Opéra, 75.

14. *La Presse*, 24 September 1838, in Gautier, *Gautier on Dance*, 54.

15. *La Presse*, 3 June 1844, in ibid., 132.

Chapter 11

Levinson's *Sylphide*

and the danseur's bad reputation

Marian Smith

Jules Janin did not care much for the art of Jules Perrot, who danced at the Paris Opéra in the 1830s:

> Monsieur Perrot is a man of great lightness, it is true; but that is all ... A man has no right to dance, no right to round a leg or an arm, or smile while doing an entrechat. The male animal is too ... ugly. His habits are too disgusting, his neck too thick, skin too tough, hands too red, legs too lanky, and feet too flat to practice the same trade as the likes of Mlle Taglioni, Mlle Dupont, Mlle Noblet, Mlle Julia, and so many others who have a pretty face, a charming neck, flawless white hands, a very fine leg, a bosom that thrills, an eye that shines, a warm pink mouth, and a white dress that floats in the breeze. This must be said again and again to all the gentlemen who dance, light or not.[1]

In this passage Janin forcefully expresses a binary opposition familiar to readers of dance history: danseuses of the period, particularly those in ethereal white tutus, were appealing; danseurs were not.

Janin's unkind generalisations are typical of a significant strain of French newspaper criticism during what is widely recognised today as ballet's 'golden age' in Paris, the years roughly coinciding with the July Monarchy (1830-1848). Janin's illustrious counterpart at *La Presse*, Théophile Gautier, for example, was of the same mind. Neither of these critics could resist ridiculing the entire male sex even when admitting to a particular danseur's merits. Here are some samples of their invective, which in its mildest form still damns with faint praise:

> Under no conditions do I recognise a man's right to dance in public.[2]

> As for M. Petipa, he did not worry the audience at all, being not too repulsive for a man.[3]

> ... a man, a frightful man, as ugly as you and I, a wretched fellow who leaps

about without knowing why, a creature specially made to carry a musket and a sword and to wear a uniform. That this fellow should dance as a woman does – impossible![4]

Perrot ... has nothing of that feeble and inane manner that usually makes male dancers so unbearable.[5]

I do not like male dancing at all. A male dancer performing anything other than *pas de caractère* or pantomime has always seemed to me something of a monstrosity. Until now [on seeing Jules Perrot in *Zingaro*] I have only been able to bear men in *mazurkas*, *saltarellos*, and *cachuchas*. With the exception of Mabille and Petipa, the male dancers of the Opéra only reinforce my view that women alone should be admitted into the ballet company.[6]

Just as damning as these critics' frequent insults was their even more frequent silence on the subject of men, for they lavished far more attention on the danseuse. Under the customary format for reviews of premières – which constituted the majority of ballet reviews – most of the column inches were expended recounting the plot, a form of popular literature akin to the serial novels that also appeared in the feuilletons.[7]   Only in the preamble, in asides during the course of the narrative, or at the very end of the column, was the reader likely to find any eyewitness descriptions. And it was the danseuse and not the danseur who attracted the critic's attention if performers were discussed at all.

In this chapter I discuss some reasons for these critics' harsh treatment of the male dancer, arguing that their insults, together with their glowing assessment of *La Sylphide*, lit the path for the extremely influential critic André Levinson (1887-1933), who promulgated the false notion that men had disappeared from nineteenth-century ballet. (He did so, I contend, as part of a zero-sum historiographical manoeuvre that denigrated the danseur and at the same time elevated *La Syphide* and Marie Taglioni to celestial heights.) I then attempt a brief but sympathetic portrait of the danseur at the Opéra during that 'golden age', pointing out what he was doing and why it mattered. In particular, I compare *La Sylphide* to another successful ballet of the time, *La Jolie Fille de Gand*, which offered a wider array of roles for male dancers than *La Sylphide* did.   My overall aim is to provide insight into Levinson's canonisation of *La Sylphide* and undo some of the damage he has done to the nineteenth-century danseur's reputation, while at the same time offering contextualising details about ballet in Paris during that celebrated age.

Why the derision?

What set of circumstances made it permissible for Janin and Gautier, among others, to declare open season on the male? Since it is rarely the merit of the danseur's actual performance but more often his maleness, his style, and his very presence that so offended, one must look beyond any genuine male repulsiveness or technical ineptitude to discover why they treated him so roughly.

First, Gautier and Janin were radical proponents of a new, ethereal style of dancing first made famous by Marie Taglioni. They deemed men unsuited for it, and were quick to associate the danseur more than the danseuse with the old *noble* style, a style originating in the court of Louis XIV and known for its precision, multiple leg-beats, slow deliberate preparations, solemn elegance, graceful *arabesques* and majestic unfoldings of the arms and legs. As Gautier wore the Romantic *gilet rouge* in the battle of *Hernani* in 1830, so did he fight passionately for the cause of the new aesthetic in ballet. Janin, for his part, was the first to apply explicitly the aesthetic of *l'art pour l'art* to ballet. Both critics looked askance at the old style: 'Abandon ... once and for all', Janin pleaded in one of his many diatribes against it, 'the *danse noble*, the *ballet d'action*, the role of *grands danseurs*, the great desperate passions, the choreographic tragedies, the little Corneilles of the ballet'.[8] They championed ballet as a medium ideally suited for stimulating the imagination by presenting evocative images: 'Why deprive ballet of its most glorious prerogatives – disorder, dream, and the absence of common sense?'[9] For them, it was only the female body in motion that could serve as the instrument of poetic expression. Thus, as these critics promoted with great zeal and skill the feminised and poetic possibilities of dance, they mercilessly derided the long-established *danse noble* and its male exponents. These gendered opposites are sometimes presented rather unsubtly to say the least:

> Taglioni is the dance of antiquity, modest and gentle, a dance that causes all other poetry to be forgotten and eliminates the need for all other poetry. ... Before her no one danced in France. Dance in France was a continual torture, a never-ending struggle to overcome perpetual difficulties, a ceaseless whirling of legs and faces. ... The *danseur noble*, when he is about to dance, usually rushes from the wing. He is hidden there, under a flowering apple tree when it is a country scene; behind Nero's column ... if it is a heroic scene. ... He progresses to the front of the stage. As soon as he arrives, in order to puff up his veins, he stiffens his leg and thigh, and his calf, if he has one, and his two little arms; he sucks in his chest as much as possible, and pants; his face is very red; then he aimlessly beats his legs; he goes to the right, and to the left; to the front with one leg; to the front with the other. He jumps! He jumps! He turns! He turns! Then, after several

minutes of this, he returns to the back of the stage, lifts his arms to the right, and poses with his leg to the left; or by a refinement of good taste, he lifts his arms to the left and poses with his legs to the right. The aim of all this is to say to the audience 'applaud me'. The audience does not disappoint him. It applauds with enthusiasm. This is the full secret of the *danse noble*! People say, 'He is so noble! He is so noble! What deportment! What looks! What deportment!' It is truer to say, 'He is so stiff!'[10]

In a recent study Ramsay Burt has forcefully brought up 'the trouble with the male dancer' of the nineteenth century, suggesting several reasons for it, including squeamishness about sexuality (although, as he points out, ballet's overt association with male homosexuality is not known to have been made before the twentieth century). As the Opéra became famous for the pleasurable viewing of females by males – the exploits of the Jockey Club are well known in this regard – the very presence of males onstage may have caused heterosexual male viewers, a significant constituency of the Opéra, to wonder anxiously if enjoying the spectacle meant enjoying men.[11]

Burt also suggests that Gautier, Janin and others like them may have been rankled by what appeared to be a grossly miscalculated attempt at representing class on the ballet stage, at least so far as men were concerned. He cites Janin's complaints about the failure of *danse noble* to represent the new bourgeois man:

That this bewhiskered individual who is a pillar of the community, an elector, a municipal councilor, a man whose business is to make and above all unmake laws, should come before us in a tunic of sky blue satin, his head covered with a hat with a waving plume amorously caressing his cheek, a frightful danseuse of the male sex, come to pirouette in the best place while the pretty ballet girls stand respectfully at a distance — this was surely impossible and intolerable, and we have done well to remove such great artists from our pleasures.[12]

When Janin wrote these words it had been less than fifty years since the demise of the Versailles court and its choreographic approach to daily life, where male courtiers had learned to fence, bow, promenade and dance ballet, and had deployed these skills equally as a means of gaining prestige.[13] But if the male dancing body and its carefully wrought gestures and movements had once been signs of political potency, for some observers they were now too reminiscent of the old aristocracy.

Burt notes further that the overt virtuosity that had entered male dancing during the Napoleonic era – mostly notably in the person of Auguste Vestris – was coming under suspicion, perhaps for reasons of class, since vigorous activity was now more obviously associated with the lower classes.[14] Certainly our two critics did from time to time describe the physicality of the male disgustedly. For example, Gautier disliked the sight of 'a man showing off his red neck, great muscular arms, and parish beadle legs, and the whole of his heavy frame shuddering with leaps and pirouettes'.[15] In any case, as male refinement offended, so did vigour and physicality. The danseur's supposed sexuality and class seemed all wrong and made his detractors terribly uncomfortable, particularly when he danced in the old *noble* style.

Continuing disrespect

Many ballerinas rose to fame in this era, but the one who originated the new ethereal dancing, Marie Taglioni, and the first full-length ballet created to showcase this style, *La Sylphide*, occupy a special place in the gendered binary construct in which males were linked with outworn classicism and females with Romanticism. Thus, as the ballet most celebrated in pro-female, pro-Romanticism diatribes, *La Sylphide* deserves a central place in the present consideration of the anti-male criticism of that era.

The centrepiece of *Sylphide* reception is Gautier's now-famous 1844 review of Taglioni's revival of her role as the sylph after a long sojourn in Russia. In this review, twelve years after *La Sylphide's* première, Gautier declares the ballet revolutionary. Cast in feminine terms (note his mention of pink tights and transparent skirts), his words exaggerate, quite poetically, *La Sylphide's* impact on the history of ballet:

> This ballet opened the door to a whole new era in choreography, and through it Romanticism entered the realm of Terpsichore. After *La Sylphide*, *Les Filets de Vulcain* and *Flore et Zéphyre* [the old mythological ballets] were no longer possible. The Opéra was given over to gnomes, undines, salamanders, elfs, nixes, wilis, péris, all those strange, mysterious creatures who lend themselves so wonderfully to the fantasies of the ballet master. The twelve mansions of marble and gold of the Olympians were relegated to the dust of the scenery shop, and artists were commissioned to produce only romantic forests and valleys lit by that pretty German moon of Heinrich Heine's ballads. Pink tights remained pink, for there can be no choreography without tights, and all that was changed was the satin ballet slipper for the Greek corthurna. This new style brought in its wake a great abuse of white gauze, tulle and tarlatan, and colours that dissolved into mist by means of transparent skirts. White became almost the only colour used.[16]

That *La Sylphide* wrought profound changes in choreography, plot and even costume is beyond doubt. Nor could anyone deny that Marie Taglioni, as the sylph, truly revolutionised dance technique. By developing her upper-body strength and pointe dancing, she became able to elevate herself in a fashion that made her seem truly lighter than air, spiritual, ethereal. But Gautier never meant all of his words about the sudden takeover of ballet by Romantic ballerinas in filmy costumes to be taken literally. He knew full well, like the readers of *La Presse*, that the mythological *Les Filets de Vulcain* had remained in the Opéra's repertoire for several years after *La Sylphide*'s première, and that brightly-lit scenes involving mortal characters in colourful costumes – both men and women – far outnumbered the moonlit ethereal scenes in ballets at the Opéra. Indeed, he created some such scenes in his own ballet libretti, and created parts for male dancers.

If the regular readers of his passionate writings in *La Presse* were able to take this concept of a Romantic feminisation of ballet with a grain of salt, many subsequent readers of this passage, as it has been extracted from its context, have not. This impassioned bit of on-the-spot history writing comes up often, explicitly or implicitly, in twentieth-century accounts of Parisian ballet of the 1830s and 1840s, usually without any acknowledgement of the strong anti-classical sentiment behind it, nor of Gautier's sometime habit of using gendered opposites to make his case. To name one example of many, an article of 1964 by Lillian Moore, written on the occasion of *La Sylphide*'s introduction into the repertoire of American Ballet Theatre, echoes Gautier's famous paragraph and leaves a distinctly feminine impression of the whole era: '*La Sylphide* changed the course of ballet. It introduced a whole new world of sylphs, dryads, water nymphs, wood sprites, swan maidens and other mysterious, ethereal creatures in diaphanous veils and filmy white skirts – the world which is still, to most people, the true realm of the ballet.'[17]

A few historians actually exceed Janin's and Gautier's claims. Among them is Alexander Bland, who in *The Dancer's World* (1963) reproduces their ideas about the exclusive appropriateness of the danseuse for Romantic ballet but implies, further, that men were little involved in ballet during the period in question:

Men are by nature more active than women, and from earliest time dancing was a male prerogative. Even today popular dancing, from the Congo to the Cotswolds, from the Trepack to the Twist, is a man's affair. It is due to historical chance that in ballet women have been more prominent. Ballet grew up with a rush at the height of the nineteenth century Romantic movement, with its emphasis on unearthly mystery, sentiment and moonlit unreality – qualities most fit for female expression. In this century the balance has slowly been righted.[18]

In an important study of travesty dancers Lynn Garafola also suggests that men receded from the stage:

> Beginning with Romanticism, a twenty-year golden age stretching from the July Revolution to about 1850, the *danseuse en travesti* usurped the position of the male *danseur* in the *corps de ballet* and as a partner to the ballerina ... the disappearance of the male dancer coincided with the triumph of romanticism and marketplace economics.[19]

She does add that 'the ban on male talent was not, strictly speaking, absolute', pointing out that men continued to play character parts even after mid-century, like Coppélius in *Coppélia* (1870). Nonetheless, this passage and the phrase 'disappearance of the male dancer' could give the impression that the danseur left the stage during the period under scrutiny here. But he did not. He continued to dance, sometimes playing title roles (as in *Le Corsaire*, 1856).

Such misleading accounts have led to the formation of a familiar narrative about nineteenth-century ballet which goes as follows: after *La Sylphide*'s première in 1832 the typical ballet featured moonlight and white diaphanous costumes; such ballets, feminine as they were, pushed the male dancer virtually out of the picture for the rest of the century, except in Denmark.[20] The implicit corollary to this tale is that the danseur need not be reclaimed from the shadows into which he receded as the ballerina took over the limelight. Thus there exists a wide lacuna in present-day knowledge about the danseur in the age of Taglioni, and a set of built-in reasons to keep ignoring him: he was incompetent, ridiculous, unsettling to watch, and on his way out anyway.

Yet even though the danseur's visibility, numbers and prestige sank below the danseuse's during this era, he still warrants our scrutiny and analysis. Like his female counterparts, he laboured, rehearsed, performed, perspired and contributed to the success of 'golden-era' ballet. He did not disappear from the stage, even though Gautier, Janin and other critics seem sometimes to have wished he had. He was still there; he was still acting and dancing. A fuller portrait of him could surely deepen our understanding of the stage in the nineteenth century. Simply put, there is much more to say about him than that he was eclipsed.

He has not been overlooked by everyone, of course. Most notably, Ivor Guest's detailed and scrupulously researched histories of ballet in London and Paris, his dancer biographies (of Fanny Cerrito, Carlotta Grisi, Fanny Elssler, Jules Perrot), and his compilations (of Gautier's ballet reviews and Arthur Saint-Léon's letters) offer the reader a fuller and richer sense of the year-to-year unfolding of ballet history and the danseur's part in it than the above-cited simple storyline offers. Sandra Noll Hammond's studies of ballet pedagogy reveal specific information about his technique, and provide insight into the passing down of traditions and styles. John Chapman lists the types of non-sylph roles that existed and devotes attention to male roles. Giannandrea Poesio protests the heavy Franco-centrism of ballet historiography and points out that, despite reports to the contrary, the Italian male remained vital throughout the period in question, along with his Danish counterparts. Studies of Polish, Roman and English ballet – while not specifically focused on the male dancer – confirm that he was alive and well outside the French capital. Ramsay Burt, the first to undertake a full-length critical study of representations of masculinity in twentieth-century dance, notes the prejudice that arose against male dancers in the nineteenth century, and seeks its origins, as I have indicated above.[21]

Despite all this, however, the danseur's place in the historiography of the nineteenth-century stage remains far paltrier than his reduced role and dwindling prestige warrant. Further evidence of this neglect are the gaps in much traditional historiography, in which, as noted above, Gautier's ideas seem to prevail over the source-based scholarship of Guest and others, and the fact that most late twentieth-century specialised scholarship on the 1830s and 1840s focuses far more on the female than the male.[22] Such studies are valuable, and when written were long overdue. Indeed, there remains plenty of work to do on the subject of the danseuse. However, the scholar bent on exploring in depth the danseur of 'golden-era' ballet has yet to appear. Nor has the chilling effect on the danseur of his early detractors in the press, nor the gendered *Sylphide*-centrism of twentieth-century scholarship, been fully taken into account or redressed in writings about men.[23] In the present study I hope to reveal the potent effects of these nineteenth-century ideas, and to clear a space for a fuller and less charged approach to the danseur's place in nineteenth-century ballet.

Levinson's *Sylphide*

After *La Sylphide* fell from the Opéra's repertory in the second half of the nineteenth century, it receded from historical accounts as well, and for many decades the 1832 première of *La Sylphide* was not considered a seminal event. Nor did the diaphanous white tutus, moonlight and fantastic creatures of Gautier's famous declaration hold a sure place in the record. Indeed, neither *La Sylphide* nor Marie Taglioni were fixtures of the narrative at all.

The usual practice was to name dancers and ballets and offer brief descriptions; men were nearly always left out of accounts, with the occasional exception of Jules Perrot, Antonio Guerra and a few others. Although Taglioni and *La Sylphide* did come up, their mention was by no means obligatory. In Albert Czerwinski's 1879 *Brevier der Tanzkunst*, for example, *La*

Sylphide goes unmentioned, although Taglioni does appear.[24] She is omitted, however, from a list of important ballerinas which includes Elssler, Cerrito, Grisi and Grahn in Henri de Soria's *Histoire pittoresque de la Danse* (1897).[25] In Félicien de Ménil's *Histoire de la Danse* (1905) *La Sylphide* is cited as the ballet for which the short skirt was adopted, and Taglioni's natural dancing is attested to, but far heavier emphasis is placed on Fanny Elssler (who is depicted dancing the cachucha) and Carlotta Grisi.[26] Raoul Charbonnel in *La Danse* (1899) lists *L'Orgie*, the nuns' ballet in *Robert le diable*, and *La Tentation* as typical ballets of the era; neither *La Sylphide* nor Marie Taglioni is mentioned.

No wonder Yuri Slonimsky could complain in his 1927 monograph on *La Sylphide* that the ballet had not attracted its due share of attention.[27] However, it was the eloquent, erudite, and unequivocal writings of his countryman Andrei Yakovlevich Levinson (1887-1933), known after his emigration to Paris during the Revolution as André Levinson, that assured this ballet and the creator of its title role their canonic status. Slonimsky had deemed *La Sylphide* worthy of recognition as the first truly Romantic ballet, but found it in the final analysis inferior to *Giselle*, which he considered a more mature and effective rendering of the same ideas.[28] Levinson, on the other hand, exalted *La Sylphide* above all other ballets of its era, according it a place of heroism in the struggle between realism and abstraction, which for him constituted the fundamental dialectic of ballet history.

In the now-famous essay 'The Idea of the Dance: from Aristotle to Mallarmé' (1927), Levinson situated *La Sylphide* at the epicentre of this struggle and cast Taglioni as 'the supreme incarnation ... of the great romantic renaissance of 1830 ... in which dance came into its own again' after being long subsumed to Aristotelian sophistry in the form of the eighteenth-century *danse noble*:

In *La Sylphide*, the dance, instead of being subservient to expressive gestures, itself became the interpreter of the emotions and their symbolic equivalent. The classical step, which even Noverre had called the mechanical and material part of the dance, the severe discipline of stylized movement, which he termed 'sterile academic routine', in short the dancer's technique came to express the highest things of the soul. In a constant approach to geometric purity of design, making a pattern in space of straight lines and sweeping perfect curves, idealizing the dancer's body and dematerializing her costume, the *ballet blanc* is able to transmute the formal poses of the slow dance movement – the *Arabesques* of the *Adagio* – as well as those aerial parabolas outlined by seemingly imponderable bodies (technically known as the *grands temps d'élévation*) into a mysterious and poetic language. Those words from *Faust*, 'Alles Vergängliche ist nur ein Gleichnis' seem particularly applicable to this highly spiritualized art... [29]

Just as Gautier and Janin, early in their careers in Paris, had found themselves at the cusp of a new type of ballet, so Levinson found swirling about him a spirited argument about 'old ballet' and 'new ballet' as he came of age in Russia nearly a century later.[30] In the two separate debates these three critics took the same side: they favoured the Platonising view, opposing ballets in which – as they saw it – the dance existed only to recount stories necessitating excessive pantomime, to serve the other arts in an ancillary way.

If in the 1830s supporters of ballets like *La Sylphide* were considered classicism's radical opponents, however, by Levinson's day they were its conservative defenders. For in the early twentieth century the 'old' ballet of the nineteenth century was coming under attack by reformers both outside the Imperial ballet, including adherents of Isadora Duncan and of Emile Jaques-Dalcroze's Eurythmics, and in it, like Michel Fokine. Fokine made no secret of his conviction that 'the older ballet turned its back on life and on all the other arts and shut itself up in a narrow circle of traditions'.[31] Thus many of his radical choreographies for the Ballets Russes in Europe were deeply offensive to Levinson.[32]

From his earliest days as a critic, and without any hesitation, Levinson aligned himself firmly with opponents of the 'new ballet', defending classicism against the reformers' antidotes to it, dryly calling them 'cures by antiquity, painting, music, rationalism, psychology, naturalness'.[33] His determination to defend ballet against realism – against, for example, 'Fokine's unnecessary, superficial, and jejune attempt to dramatize ballet'[34] – was part of his larger belief in the primacy of 'pure' over 'expressive dance' (terms comparable to 'absolute' and 'program music'), and of the autonomous value of dance and its capacity to reach an audience without being called on to depict particular emotions, subjects or characters.

It is worth examining in some detail Levinson's powerful arguments, since it was he who elevated Marie Taglioni above all other performers of her era, both male and female, and cast her in the role of Platonic saviour and feminiser of ballet. Thus did she and *La Sylphide* re-emerge from obscurity in retrospect, and a ballerina and a ballet not even necessarily mentioned in previous accounts of nineteenth-century French ballet came to occupy the most hallowed place in the canon. Levinson's very influential position has skewed our view of the period in question, obscuring among other things the history of the danseur.

Why, and how, did Levinson do what he did?

In their introduction to a volume of Levinson's essays, Joan Acocella and

Lynn Garafola have posited that the critic's nostalgia and esteem for the Maryinsky ballet of his youth, deepened by his own sense of personal loss on being driven out of Russia and his terrible fear that its great ballets would be lost forever, led him to take up as a personal crusade the rescue of what he saw as the Platonic ideals of Marius Petipa, the Maryinsky's longtime choreographer. This same deep drive, I would submit, led him to perceive Marie Taglioni and *La Sylphide* as he did. In any case, *La Sylphide* and its epoch-changing redemptive effects – which Levinson feared would be squandered and despoiled by the 'new ballet' – tower above everything in his *Marie Taglioni*, the remarkable biography (published two years after 'The Idea of the Dance' and soon translated into English by Cyril Beaumont) in which Levinson articulates several basic concepts which have since become axiomatic, including the notion that the male dancer was eclipsed by the female dancer in the nineteenth century. A *tour de force* of advocacy, steeped in erudition and spoken in the voice of a poet, this volume beatifies the ballerina (if not the human being) who created the role of the sylph. It does so largely by deeming her transcendently pure and eliminating all competitors: not only Taglioni's rival danseuses and danseurs, but the other *characters* she created and played. Three of his nine chapters even include the term 'sylph' in the title: 'The Sylphide', 'Sylphidiana' and 'The Anatomy of the Sylphide'. None of her other celebrated roles are so honoured.

Let us examine precisely how Levinson made his case. First, hinting that Taglioni bore a lifelong dedication to Platonic ideals, he asserts that even in her early days at the Opéra she '[o]bstinately ... keeps to pure dancing; she appears only in impersonal and, so to speak, abstract parts, independent of the dramatic action', for example, a naiad in *La Belle au Bois Dormant*.[35] Next he declares Taglioni inseparable from the role of the sylph, her own identity abolished: 'She is mingled with the image of the Sylphide which becomes her 'astral body'. Further, he dismisses Taglioni's other major roles: 'She will create many other parts. But none of these successive characters will supplant that supreme incarnation of her being'. And, after devoting an entire chapter to elevating Taglioni above Fanny Elssler (whose popularity was as great as his heroine's, and whose dancing was often characterised as sensual, colourful, and of the earth), he dispatches Taglioni's female peers in a single sentence:

Nothing in the years which followed detracted from the recognized supremacy of Taglioni, neither Fanny Elssler's abortive attack, nor the 'Cerritomania' with which the second Fanny inflamed the dandies of 'Fop's alley' ... nor the welcome accorded to the Dane, Lucile Grahn, who like Adèle Dumilâtre, belonged to the same 'ideal school' as Taglioni's.

Levinson also deftly dismisses Gautier's criticisms of Taglioni in 1838, deeming them the symptom of a personal weakness – although he retains his affection for 'good Théo', 'old Théo', 'the poet of *Albertus*', upon whose pro-Sylphide writings Levinson depends, and whose presence hovers throughout the book almost like an avuncular character:

> From 1838, Théophile Gautier declares that Mlle. Taglioni, exhausted by endless travel, is no longer what she was; she has lost much of her lightness and elevation. 'The princes and kings of the north', slyly insinuates old Théo, 'in their imprudent and pitiless admiration have over-applauded her … they have made so many showers of flowers and diamonds fall upon her that they have weighed down her tireless feet…' And he emphasizes this theme and compares Marie of the graces to a bird with wet wings. Why does the critic set upon the Sylphide? We already know the reason for it. He sacrifices her to Fanny Elssler. … Undoubtedly, Gautier was the most honest man in the world; but his change of opinion in regard to Taglioni are the outcome of the sentimental weaknesses of a great and fickle heart.[36]

Levinson's dependence upon Gautier is perhaps nowhere more evident than in this famous passage, in which he sums up his arguments about Taglioni, recalling the elder writer's 'moonlight/sylphs/pink tights/white gauze' paragraph, and retaining its feminine tilt and its idea of Sylphide as revolutionary:

> This part is the apex of her career; it obliterates the trial sketches which were only preludes to this high attainment. Henceforth, dancer and character are indivisible. To speak of the Sylphide is to name Taglioni. At the Opéra she had been a sublime intruder, foreign to the atmosphere of the place; a gothic madonna set on an Empire style pedestal. With *La Sylphide* a new spirit invades the scene, glides over the stage, soars towards the 'flies'. No revolution in the order of ideas could have been more complete. Fairy-tale takes the place of mythology, and the *ballet blanc* supplants the anacreontic interlude. Dancing becomes a transcendental language, charged with spirituality and mystery: a celestial calligraphy, it admits nothing profane.[37]

At the same time, though, Levinson strips out the material objects that Gautier had brought up (tights, shoes, gauze, skirts), and adds the notion of dance as transcendental language, surely influenced by Stéphane Mallarmé's late-nineteenth-century Symbolist writings on dance.[38]

Crucially, Levinson also brings in the term '*ballet blanc*', a fixture in today's vocabulary but one that did not come into use until late in the century, long after the creation of *La Sylphide*.[39] Thus, his sleight of hand in this paragraph relies not only on dismissing other roles and other ballerinas, and purging Gautier's references to materiality, but also on using a simple term for the sort of spiritual, mysterious, feminine ballet Levinson so values, a term (though not specifically defined) for something where none existed in Gautier's approach to the matter. Levinson offers no such all-encompassing or evocative name for the sorts of scenes (which might be called *ballets de couleur*) intended to show contrast to the *blanc* world and likely to include character dance, local colour, and performers – both male and female – in coloured costumes.[40] Ballets of *La Sylphide*'s type, of course, were intended to show the contrast between the earth and the spirit world, and it was in that contrast that so much of their fascination lay.[41] One type of scene would be pointless without the other. Giving a precise name to one side but not its countervailing opposite, however, has misleadingly privileged the *ballet blanc* over its unnamed counterpart. This, in turn, has led to a widespread but erroneous belief in the existence of numerous self-standing nineteenth-century *ballet blancs*, and in some cases to the assumption that entire acts (like *Giselle* Act Two) were *blanc* when this was simply not the case.[42] In fact, the idea of creating ballets that were white in their entirety did not take hold until the early twentieth century, famous exemplars including *Les Sylphides* (1907) and *La Mort du Cygne* (*The Dying Swan*) (1907), both of which pointedly recall famous nineteenth-century ballets but refrain from making any reference to the *ballets de couleur* that appeared alongside the *ballets blancs* therein.[43] Levinson surely did not mean to create false impressions about the pervasiveness of the *ballet blanc*, but his staunch partisan stance and his minimisation of Taglioni's roles other than the Sylph do make other elements of nineteenth century ballet easy to forget. Gautier's 'white gauze' declaration, combined with Levinson's writings on *La Sylphide* and his use of the term *ballet blanc*, have left a strong and powerful impression – so strong and powerful perhaps especially because it is such a *visual* one – that affords little room for a wider view of ballet.

Although by the late twentieth century some dance historians, most notably Lynn Garafola, had begun to object to the disproportionate attention paid to the Sylph, Levinson's paternity of pro-Sylphide historiography has never been acknowledged, nor has the appropriateness of *La Sylphide*'s high place in the canon been questioned since Levinson established it. His powerful advocacy of Taglioni as the Sylph not only ensured the unshakeable historical prestige of both the ballerina and the role but, I would argue, also made for the general ignorance today of Taglioni's other important roles and the breadth of her capabilities. More germane to the present study of men in ballet, however, is the fact that the danseur fares very badly in Levinson's masterful and influential biography *Marie Taglioni* – worse, even, than Taglioni's female competitors and the sylph's rival roles.

In a short but devastating epilogue to *Marie Taglioni*, one finds a blunt expression of the notion underlying much subsequent twentieth-century dance scholarship. In Levinson's words, Taglioni, 'in causing the *eternal feminine* to triumph, evicted male dancing. The eclipse was complete.'[44] Levinson's case for the 'eviction' of men consists of three observations and three quotations, all presented in a single paragraph, the penultimate one of the book. The observations are that the number of male dancers in the *corps de ballet* was reduced in 1832; that the danseur Antonio Guerra was hissed at the Opéra because audiences were so unaccustomed to men; and that male characters were portrayed by women in the *Grand Pas des Gitanes* in *Paquita* in 1846. Here are the quotations:

Arthur Saint-Léon: 'The *danseur* has fallen into decline.'

Charles de Boigne: 'It may be said that today [1856] the male dancer no longer exists. A few years have sufficed to turn them into fossils ... male dancers fill the posts of teachers, mimes or *maîtres de ballet*.'[45]

Jules Janin: 'We have suppressed male dancers.'

Levinson's paragraph provides convincing evidence of the danseur's occultation. However, it hardly constitutes a detailed and nuanced study of the male's varying fortunes throughout Taglioni's day and beyond. Nor does it attempt to illuminate the place of the male at the Opéra during Taglioni's time, nor compare the degraded conditions of both male and female dancers after mid century. Nor was it intended to do any of these things. On the contrary, it was meant to dismiss males from the reader's picture of nineteenth-century ballet as far as possible, without probing any more deeply than one paragraph's worth of tendentious observations could do.

To sum up: the danseur of the 1830s and 1840s, the 'golden age' of ballet, is caught up in a complicated historiographical mess. During his own day he was regularly derided for various reasons by, among others, two rhetorically brilliant, highly partisan writers who openly insulted males on a fairly regular basis. In the early twentieth century he was dealt another blow by Levinson who, for reasons of his own, championed Taglioni above her peers, both male and female. Finally, Levinson's reputation and powerful prose compelled many twentieth-century ballet historians to follow his lead.

The scope of this study prevents me from extricating the danseur single-handedly from his predicament, but in the remaining part of this chapter I can at least sketch a picture of danseurs' activities in what many still call the age of Taglioni. Since the Opéra is a house thought to have been evacuated by danseurs, or at best a house whose danseurs are now remembered in large part for their shortcomings, it is a suitable starting place for reconsidering the male's role in ballet of this period. Relying on the evidence of libretti, as well as favourable reviews less often quoted than the derisive ones, I shall first offer a discussion of the sorts of roles men played, and then compare *La Syphide* to *La Jolie Fille de Gand*, a ballet popular in the 1840s that featured many male roles. Although these sources have not been consulted by the dance historians sold on the Levinsonian Sylphide-as-heroine idea, they demonstrate plainly that men played a crucial part in ballet in 1830s and 1840s France, and, moreover, that much of the danseurs' activities consisted of things other than *noble* dancing. In particular, these sources show the breadth of male dancers' capabilities, suggesting that if we examined *only* their *noble* roles, their place on the stage would indeed look much smaller than it was.

The danseur: Stories, characters, styles

No study of the danseur in Parisian ballet in the era of *La Sylphide* is possible without the clear-eyed recognition that ballets told stories. These stories usually centred around the fortunes of a young couple. They involved many characters, including parental figures, rivals in love, servants and superiors, and a host of minor figures, such as members of royal courts and shipmates. In a few cases, ballet characters had supernatural powers. Conveying these stories to audiences required many danseurs of varying ranks and possessed of a wide range of skills.

Breadth of range was indeed a fact of life for the highest-ranking danseurs who played leading roles in these dramas. Like their female counterparts, all of them were not only ballet dancers, but also mimes and character dancers. Joseph Mazilier (1797-1868), for instance, first made a name for himself at the Théâtre de la Porte-Saint-Martin in the late 1820s, where he imitated the great comic dancer Charles Mazurier 'like a monkey', performed male heroic leads in ballet-pantomimes (including Armand the choreographer in *Les Artistes*), and brought the house down with his mazurka in the melodrama *Les Prisonniers de guerre*.[46] He was engaged by the Opéra in 1830, and over the course of a long career there deployed his broad range of skills, appearing in opera divertissements (for instance, *Gustave III* and *Les Huguenots*) and creating major roles in ballets, including all the male Romantic leads between 1831 and 1841. The vastly different characters he played give some insight into the extent of his range. These include the dreamy Scottish farmer James in *La Sylphide* (who chooses the Sylph over his mortal fiancée but then falls prey to a witch who brings about his woodland lover's demise); the fugitive Roundhead Stenio in *La Gipsy* (who joins a band of gypsies, falls in love with a young Scottish woman whom they had kidnapped years earlier, and is ultimately stabbed to death by the jealous gypsy queen); the adventurous Sicilian naval officer Octavio in *L'Ile des pirates* (who infiltrates a pirate gang on an island to do battle with its chief for the hand of a woman whom they both desire); and the young Calabrian villager Luidgi [sic] in *La Tarentule* (who impresses his future in-laws by rescuing a lady from brigands but is then bitten by a tarantula on the eve of his wedding and is nearly compelled to forfeit his fiancée to the doctor who saves his life). One of Mazilier's last roles, the tippling Polish basketmaker Mazourki in *Le Diable à quatre*, 1845 (one of the twenty-one works that the danseur choreographed for the Opéra between 1839 and 1858[47]), finds himself at the mercy of an overbearing Countess who, through magical body-switching, suddenly replaces his more docile wife.

Lucien Petipa (1815-1898), like Mazilier, danced a wide variety of roles during his many years as a leading danseur. The elder brother of Marius Petipa (whose illustrious career as a choreographer in Russia is well known), Lucien was trained by his father Jean-Antoine Petipa, the ballet master at the Théâtre de la Monnaie in Brussels. As a child, he appeared onstage at the Monnaie, and then as principal dancer in The Hague and Bordeaux before arriving at the Opéra in 1839. Among the many male Romantic leads he created there were the Silesian nobleman Albrecht in *Giselle*; the sultan of a seraglio Achmet (who in an opium dream falls in love with the Péri queen); Telemachus, the son of Ulysses in *Eucharis* (who is shipwrecked off the shore of Calypso's island and falls in love with her handmaiden); the French officer Lucien in *Paquita* (who is engaged to the Governor's daughter but is nearly killed by hired gypsy assassins and is ultimately saved by the title character); and the English Prince Charles in *Betty* (whose taste for entertainment in low haunts is cured through a series of connivances and misadventures). He was known as a 'very intelligent mime [who] always holds the stage and never overlooks the smallest detail' as well as a passionate and warm dancer, who had 'an ardent and chivalrous grace'. And he was called by Gautier – never mind his better-known anti-male writings – the tenor of the dance.[48]

Indeed, if one were to place the 'tenor' Petipa on the continuum of the old genres (*noble*, *demi-caractère*, and *comique*, officially abolished at the Opéra by 1830 but far from forgotten during the period under study) he would appear closer to the *noble* end than Mazilier. Horst Koegler has referred to him as one of the best *danseurs nobles* of his time.[49] Yet at the same time Petipa was an excellent character dancer whose skill at the polka, a complex and technically challenging dance, for example, was demonstrated in both *Le Diable à Quatre*, in which he played one of the top male roles, and a celebrated polka competition in which a contingent of Opéra danseurs was challenged by highly skilled members of the social-dance elite and beat them handily.[50]

The two danseurs most frequently seen in Romantic leads, then, played the same kinds of roles – indeed some of the *same* roles – and were capable of miming, and of dancing in both the classical and the character style (i.e. balleticised folk-dance style), yet at the same time earned reputations as specialists.[51] In the middle ranks of the Opéra, too, *danseurs* upheld these different styles and traditions, all of which found a place on the stage. Jean-Baptiste Barrez (1795-1868) and Georges Elie (1800-1883), for example, 'those two excellent comic mimes',[52] according to Gautier, played a variety of character roles over the years, some of them broadly comic and grotesque, many of them calling for substantial stage time. Elie, for instance, played Zug in *Nathalie, ou la Laitière suisse* (1832), where the main action was 'interspersed with the comical despair of that excellent mime [Elie] whose mournfully skinny legs repel all the girls to whom he pays court with inexhaustible patience';[53] and Jonathas the dancing master in *Les Mohicans* (1837), on whose cowardice rested the 'whole of the comic effect of the piece ... Elie, who is cast in this role, played it with a witty feeling for the fantastic.'[54] A testament to Elie's strong character acting may be found in the fact that he was sometimes cast in roles requiring a change of identity, such as Mentor in *Eucharis*, who in the end reveals himself as Minerva, and the blind fiddler in *Le Diable à quatre*, who turns into a magician and causes a countess to switch places with a peasant woman.

Gautier describes two performances given by Barrez: first, his rendering, with Elie, of Cervantes' two most famous characters in a short-lived revival of the forty-year old ballet *Les Noces de Gamache* in 1841:

> Could you wish for a more delightful Don Quixote than Elie? What a tall, thin, emaciated fellow he is! How gaunt his features, burned by the double tan of insanity and the sun of the Sierra Morena! What a heroic nose, what a knightly moustache! ... This perfect Don Quixote is followed by a no less perfect Sancho Panza. No doubt you have seen the engraving of Decamps' drawing showing the hero of La Mancha preceded by his faithful squire. Barrez, the Asmodeus of *Le Diable boiteux*, the Dr. Oméopatico of *La Tarentule* and the Governor of *Le Diable amoureux*, has brought that engraving to life. ... Barrez conveys the character's naive greediness, voracious impudence and skill at robbing foodstores in a manner that would have aroused the envy of Duburau [the great mime of the Boulevard theatres], that tall white ghost who is always so half-starved. How well he mimicked, *non passibus aequis*, the great strides of his master, and what a majestic figure he cut on his donkey! ... We ought to have begun by mentioning the ladies – Maria, who plays the role of Quitterie, Mlle

Blangy and the beautiful Dumilâtre – but the fantastic figures of Elie and Barrez caught our eye first of all.[55]

In bringing to life Barrez's lovestruck performance in *Manon Lescaut* – in a *pas* he describes as 'a perfect evocation of rococo, Watteau and Pompadour ... a fireplace top in action, a living fan' – Gautier gives us insight into Barrez's use of facial expression and dance steps:

> Imagine amusing old Barrez dressed as a pilgrim embarking for Cythera with crook and haversack, all the trappings of a shepherd of the Lignon, and holding in his hand ... a posy that he has not the courage to place in the bodice of his shepherdess... He starts forward, then draws back, expressing his passion by tremendous *entrechats*, rolling his eyes and breathing deep sighs as he offers his posy, but all to no avail... Luckily love comes to his aid in the form of the god Cupid himself – in pink silk breeches with diamond-studded garters, ... a golden quiver, and a little three-cornered hat... From his quiver he daintily draws a very sharp arrow and pierces the heart of the shepherdess through and through, permitting the lovelorn Thyrsis to place the posy in her corsage and steal a kiss. This scene is acted by Barrez with infinite wit and an excellent sense of comedy.[56]

These strong character roles were not strictly limited to ballets. Minor character roles for ballet soloists were occasionally called for in operas, like the emperor Sigismond in Act One of *La Juive*, played enthusiastically by Germain Quériau (1815-?), and described in Charles de Boigne's memoir:

> Have you seen a figurant, the coryphée charged with the silent role of the emperor Sigismond? ... In his modest sphere, Quériau has been the most conscientious and fanatical servant ever to work at the Opéra. So sincere is Quériau's identification with the role of the Emperor that he seems to truly believe himself to *be* the emperor.[57]

Among Quériau's many other roles were an officer in *La Fille du Danube*, Mohamet in *La Révolte des femmes*, Albrecht's father in *Giselle*, and a sailor in *Ozaï*. These were far less prominent roles than those usually given to Elie and Barrez and others of their rank, but were still necessary for the unfolding of the drama.

These character parts, it must be emphasised, were often given a great deal of stage time, and in many cases were vital to the imparting of the plot (the original Hilarion, Albrecht's rival in *Giselle*, comes to mind as an example, though his part has been reduced in scope in the past century). Excellent portrayals of such roles were praised by even the most cynical critics and appreciated by audiences. Today such roles are often minimised or deleted altogether and are allocated to performers considered past their prime, or of lesser ability. However, this current-day attitude should not be applied to the 1830s and 1840s, a time when these roles were more highly regarded and regularly written into ballet libretti.[58]

Men of the *corps de ballet* also remained an active force at the Opéra throughout the period, although more in opera than in ballet.[59] Table 1 gives a list of parts for male and female *corps* dancers and of travesty roles.[60] Because of the taste for foreign settings at the Opéra, *corps* dancers were fully expected to perform character dance – like the *tyrolienne* in *Guillaume Tell* and the tarantella in *La Tarentule* – which was as crucial for localising effect as the scenery, props and costumes so painstakingly wrought. Although their numbers waned with the years and travesty parts for *corps* women increased, men of the *corps* were still busy and versatile. One Monsieur Scio, for example – to name a *corps* danseur at random – was given a wide variety of roles, and often played more than one part in a given evening (for instance, a peasant in *Le Freyschutz* and a vine-gatherer in *Giselle* on Wednesday, June 28, 1843, and a reveller in ball scene and a cross-bowman in *La Jolie Fille de Gand* two nights later).[61] Table 2 gives a partial list of his roles.[62]

La Jolie Fille de Gand and *La Sylphide*

La Jolie Fille de Gand, a popular ballet created in 1842 (ten years after *La Sylphide*) and remaining in the repertoire until 1848, deserves brief scrutiny here as a ballet that exploited the full range of the danseur at the Opéra. Its libretto was fashioned by Vernoy de Saint-Georges after a successful melodrama at the Théâtre de la Porte Saint-Martin, and its choreography devised by François Decombe, known as 'Albert' (1787-1865), the last man at the Opéra to have held the official designation of *danseur noble*. Albert's celebrated performing career there spanned the years 1808-1831, and entailed such title roles as the king in *Alfred le grand* and the god of war in *Mars et Vénus ou les Filets de Vulcain*. Well after leaving the stage, he remained a highly respected teacher, who, along with Mazilier, Barrez and Jean Coralli (1779-1854), taught the Opéra's company classes in the 1840s, and, after the old manner, provided the violin accompaniment himself. (Georges Elie also taught at the Opéra in the 1840s.)

For *La Jolie Fille de Gand* Albert came out of retirement to play the arrogant Marquis de San Lucar, a role first intended for the young Lucien Petipa, but one played with great success by the choreographer himself, whose well-cultivated capacity to impart *hauteur* surely enabled him to appear 'elegant, noble, with a haughty and refined allure, and [to ruin] himself like a true nobleman'.[63] Petipa instead played Benedict, the frustrated fiancé of Beatrix

(Carlotta Grisi), who finds herself unready to marry and spends the second and nearly all of the third act as the Marquis's mistress, living in his Venetian palace but eventually losing him to the prima ballerina of La Fenice (Louise Fitzjames). Georges Elie, known for his comic roles, 'showed that he is equally suited to serious parts', by playing Bustamente, a friend of the Marquis who wins Beatrix in a wager and dies in a furious swordfight shortly after attempting to claim his prize.[64]

Barrez played the comical dancing master Zéphyros, who in the second act has become the manager of La Fenice and in the third returns to Ghent in rags. Louis Montjoie (1790-1865), a longtime soloist at the Opéra who ceded many of his roles to Quériau upon his retirement later in 1842, played Beatrix's father Césarius, a wealthy goldsmith of Ghent, who travels with Benedict to Venice and publicly humiliates his wayward daughter immediately after her coronation as queen of the ball. Minor *personnages* were played by Eugène Coralli (Count Léonardo), François Simon (a farmer and a gypsy), L. Petit (a notary) and Bégrand (a provost). Unnamed solo roles were also accorded to (among others) Léopold Adice and Hippolyte Barrez (Jean-Baptiste's son), who performed a three-legged *pas comique* to entertain the revellers at the Venetian ball, and the high-ranking soloist Auguste Mabille, who with Sophie Dumilâtre danced a Cracovienne and mazurka for the pleasure of the same crowd, both attired in costumes of blue velvet edged with swansdown. (Most of the action, it turns out, is only a dream; Beatrix is properly chastened for her reluctance to marry Bénédict and happily submits to him in the end.)

In *La Jolie Fille de Gand*, then, are five major male roles, covering a broad spectrum of types – a villan, a young lover, two serious and one comic supporting characters – and four minor ones, not including a major *pas de deux* in the Polish style, calling for one top-ranking male soloist. The men playing the major roles at the première varied considerably in age (Albert was about 55 years old, Petipa 27, Elie 42, Barrez 47, Montjoie 52, and Mabille, who performed the Polish dances, 27), and brought to the stage a vast range of experience and tradition.[65] These nine male *personnages* exceeded by far the mere two of *La Sylphide*: a lovestruck Scottish farmer and his hayseed rival Gurn. Indeed, the average for the era was about five women and five men. In its sheer numbers and types of men in dramatic roles, then, *La Jolie Fille de Gand* can be taken as a good counterbalancing example to *La Sylphide*.[66] Although it did not survive into the next century, it did flourish. The mere fact that the Opéra's administrators invested so heavily in such a *ballet d'action* – a term still used in those days to describe ballets emphasising dramatic action – with its colourful bright displays, constitutes strong proof that *La Sylphide*, as popular as it was in its own day and as enduring as it has been, was not the only sort of ballet that succeeded.[67]

Let us not think of these two ballets as existing in two utterly different worlds, though, for this would only further promote the dichotomy, proposed by Gautier and elaborated upon by Levinson, which depicts the *ballet d'action* as the vanquished and the Romantic, ethereal ballet as the victor – a dichotomy that, as a historiographical construct, has not done justice to the ballet culture of the nineteenth century. It is better to note that these ballets actually had much in common. For instance, the title role in both was created by a female star renowned for lightness and ethereality. (In *Jolie Fille*, it was Carlotta Grisi, who had created the title role in *Giselle*, and had even been compared favourably to Taglioni.) Ballerinas with the capability of dancing in the new style, then, could and did perform important mortal roles. Both ballets also relied on mime scenes, character dance, and men. And both called for many characters, drawn from the same set of traditions and types.

This chapter has, I hope, offered worthwhile insight into how *La Sylphide* was seized upon by certain influential critics – critics whose polemical salvos still affect the way ballet history is told. To sum up: Janin and Gautier, overwhelmed by the beauty of *La Sylphide* and Taglioni's performance in it, deployed this ballet and its new ethereal style as weapons in their take-no-prisoners verbal warfare over old classical tastes and new romantic ones, identifying males with the unbearably old fusty style and females with the wonderful new ethereal one. Levinson, nearly one hundred years later, retold nineteenth-century ballet history by reviving the memory of *La Sylphide* and Taglioni (by then largely forgotten), canonising them, and demoting male dancers to the lowest status possible. He did all of this while engaged in a war of words in the early 1900s with the heartfelt belief that the very survival of ballet was at stake.

These great writers succeeded in conveying the powerful effect wrought by this ballet and by Marie Taglioni (though Levinson, of course, never saw her dance the role) but their potent advocacy has done an injustice, in my view, to the danseur of Taglioni's era, and left us with too sketchy a sense of the rest of the repertory at the Paris Opéra. In this chapter I hope to have ameliorated these shortcomings.

Acocella, Joan, and Lynn Garafola, eds. *André Levinson on Dance: Writings from Paris in the Twenties*. Hanover, NH: Wesleyan University Press, 1991.
Arkin, Lisa C., and Marian Smith. 'National Dance in the Romantic Ballet', in

Rethinking the Sylph: New Perspectives on the Romantic Ballet, ed. Lynn Garafola. Hanover, NH: Wesleyan University Press, 1997.

Aschengreen, Erik. 'Bournonville and Male Dancing: An Inheritance and a Challenge', in *The Royal Danish Ballet and Bournonville*. Copenhagen: Ministry of Foreign Affairs of Denmark, 1979.

Balanchine, George, and Francis Mason. *Balanchine's Complete Stories of the Great Ballets*. Revised and enlarged ed. Garden City, NY: Doubleday, 1977.

Bland, Alexander. *The Dancer's World*. London: Collins, 1963.

Bryson, Norman. 'Dance History and Cultural Studies.' Paper presented at the conference 'Choreographing History', University of California, Riverside, February 1992.

Burt, Ramsay. 'The Trouble with the Male Dancer', in *Moving History/Dancing Cultures*, ed. Ann Dils and Ann Cooper Albright. Hanover, NH: Wesleyan University Press, 2001.

Celi, Claudia. 'The Arrival of the Great Wonder of Ballet', in *Rethinking the Sylph: New Perspectives on the Romantic Ballet*, ed. Lynn Garafola. Hanover, NH: Wesleyan University Press, 1997.

Chapman, John. 'Jules Janin: Romantic Critic', in *Rethinking the Sylph: New Perspectives on the Romantic Ballet*, ed. Lynn Garafola. Hanover, NH: Wesleyan University Press, 1997.

―――. 'An Unromantic View of Nineteenth-Century Romanticism.' *York Dance Review* 7 (1978): 28-40.

Clark, Maribeth. 'Bodies at the Opéra: Art and the Hermaphrodite in the Dance Criticism of Théophile Gautier', in *Reading Critics Reading: Opera and Ballet Criticism in France from the Revolution to 1848*, ed. Roger Parker and Mary Ann Smart. Oxford: Oxford University Press, 2001.

Copeland, Roger, and Marshall Cohen. *What Is Dance? Readings in Theory and Criticism*. New York: Oxford University Press, 1983.

Corbin, Alain. *The Fragrant and the Foul: Odour and the French Social Imagination*. Cambridge, MA: Harvard University Press, 1986.

Czerwinski, Albert. *Brevier der Tanzkunst: Die Tänze bei den Kulturvölkern von den Ältesten Zeiten bis zur Gegenwart*. Leipzig: Spamer, 1879.

Daly, Ann. 'The Balanchine Woman: Of Hummingbirds and Channel Swimmers', *Drama Review* 31 (1987): 8-21.

de Boigne, Charles. *Petits mémoires de l'Opéra*. Paris: Librairie nouvelle, 1857.

de Géréon, Léonard (a.k.a. Eugene Ronteix). *La Rampe et les Coulisses: Esquisses biographiques des directeurs, acteurs et actrices de tous les théâtres*. Paris: Les marchands de nouveautés, 1832.

de Ménil, Félicien. *Histoire de la Danse à travers les Ages*. Paris: A. Picard & Kaan, 1905.

de Soria, Henri. *Histoire pittoresque de la Danse*. Paris: H. Noble, 1897.

Foster, Susan Leigh. 'The Ballerina's Phallic Pointe', in *Corporealities: Dancing*

Knowledge, Culture and Power, ed. Susan Leigh Foster. London: Routledge, 1996.

———. *Choreography and Narrative: Ballet's Staging of Story and Desire.* Bloomington: Indiana University Press, 1996.

Garafola, Lynn, ed. *Rethinking the Sylph: New Perspectives on the Romantic Ballet.* Hanover, NH: Wesleyan University Press, 1997.

———. 'The Travesty Dancer in Nineteenth-Century Ballet.' *Dance Research* 17/18 (1985-1986): 35-40.

Gautier, Théophile. *Gautier on Dance.* Edited by Ivor Guest London: Dance Books, 1986.

Guest, Ivor. *The Romantic Ballet in Paris.* London: Dance Books, 1980.

Gutsche-Miller, Sarah. 'Pantomime-Ballet on the Music-Hall Stage: The Popularisation of Classical Ballet in Fin-de -Siècle Paris.' Ph.D. diss., McGill University, 2010.

Hammond, Sandra Noll. 'Ballet's Technical Heritage: The Grammaire of Léopold Adice.' *Dance Research* 13 (1995): 35-58.

———. 'Clues to Ballet's Technical History from an Early Nineteenth-Century Ballet Lesson.' *Dance Research* 3 (1984): 53-66.

———. 'A Nineteenth-Century Dancing Master at the Court of Württemberg: The Dance Notebooks of Michel St. Léon.' *Dance Chronicle* 15, no. 3 (1992): 291-315.

Janin, Jules. *Le Journal des débats*, 29 April 1833.

———. *Le Journal des débats*, 27 June 1832.

———. *Le Journal des débats* 2 March 1840.

Koegler, Horst. *The Concise Oxford Dictionary of Ballet.* 2nd ed. London: Oxford University Press, 1982.

Levinson, André. *Ballet Old and New*, Translated by Susan Cook Summer. New York: Dance Horizons, 1982.

———. 'The Idea of the Dance: From Aristotle to Mallarmé.' *Theatre Arts Monthly*, 1927.

———. *Marie Taglioni*. Paris: F. Alcan, 1929.

———. *Marie Taglioni*, Translated by Cyril Beaumont. London: Imperial Society of Teachers of Dancing, 1930.

Mallarmé, Stéphane. 'Mallarmé: Selected Prose Poems, Essays, and Letters.' Baltimore: Johns Hopkins Press, 1956.

Manning, Susan. 'Borrowing from Feminist Theory', in *Proceedings of the Society of Dance History Scholars: Retooling the Discipline: Research and Teaching Strategies for the 21st Century*, ed. Linda Tomko. Riverside, CA: Society of Dance History Scholars, 1994.

———. *Ecstasy and the Demon*. Berkeley and Los Angeles: University of California Press, 1993.

McCarren, Felicia. *Dance Pathologies: Performance, Poetics, Medicine.* Stanford: Stanford University Press, 1998.

Moore, Lillian. 'La Sylphide, Epitome of the Romantic Ballet.' *Dance Magazine* 39 (1965): 42-47.

Novack, Cythia. *Sharing the Dance: Contact Improvisation and American Culture.* Madison: University of Wisconsin Press, 1990.

Noverre, Jean-Georges. *Lettres sur la danse, et sur les ballets.* Stuttgart and Lyon: Aimé Delaroche, 1760.

Poesio, Giannandrea. 'Blasis, the Italian Ballo, and the Male Sylph', in *Rethinking the Sylph: New Perspectives on the Romantic Ballet,* ed. Lynn Garafola. Hanover, NH: Wesleyan University Press, 1997.

Pritchard, Jane. 'Collaborative Creations for the Alhambra and the Empire.' *Dance Chronicle* 24 (2001): 55-82.

Pudelek, Janina. 'Ballet Dancers at Warsaw's Wielki Theater', in *Rethinking the Sylph: New Perspectives on the Romantic Ballet,* ed. Lynn Garafola. Hanover, NH: Wesleyan University Press, 1997.

Richardson, Philip J. S. *The Social Dances of the Nineteenth Century in England.* London: H. Jenkins, 1960.

Robin-Challan, Louise. 'Danse et danseuses à l'Opéra de Paris, 1830-1850.' Thèse de 3ème Cycle, Université de Paris VII, 1988.

———. 'Social Conditions of Ballet Dancers at the Paris Opera in the 19th Century.' *Choreography and Dance* 2 (1992): 17-28.

Scholl, Tim. *'Sleeping Beauty': A Legend in Progress.* New Haven: Yale University Press, 2004.

Slonimsky, Yuri. *'Sil'fida' Balet.* Leningrad: Academia, 1927.

Smart, Mary Ann. 'Redefining Italian Romanticism: Rossini vs. Salvatore Viganò.' Paper presented at the National Meeting of the American Musicological Society, Houston, November 2003.

Smith, Marian. *Ballet and Opera in the Age of 'Giselle'.* Princeton: Princeton University Press, 2000.

Sowell, Debra. 'A Plurality of Romanticisms: Italian Ballet and the Repertory of Antonio Cortesi and Giovanni Casati.' Paper presented at the National Meeting of the Society of Dance History Scholars, Limerick, June 2003.

Stravinsky, Igor. *Autobiography.* New York: Norton, 1936.

Vaillat, Léandre. *Histoire de la Danse.* Paris: Plon, 1942.

An earlier version of this study was published as 'The Disappearing Danseur', *Cambridge Opera Journal* 19 (2007), 33-57, and appears here by gracious permission of Cambridge University Press.

Notes

1. Jules Janin, *Le Journal des débats*, 29 April 1833. Translated and cited in John Chapman, 'Jules Janin: Romantic Critic', in *Rethinking the Sylph: New Perspectives on the Romantic Ballet*, ed. Lynn Garafola (Hanover, NH: Wesleyan University Press, 1997), 218-19.

2. Jules Janin, *Le Journal des débats*, 27 June 1832.

3. *La Presse*, 1 July 1839, in Théophile Gautier, *Gautier on Dance*, ed. Ivor Guest (London: Dance Books, 1986), 70-71.

4. Jules Janin, *Le Journal des débats* 2 March 1840; cited in Ivor Guest, *The Romantic Ballet in Paris* (London: Dance Books, 1980), 21.

5. *La Presse*, 2 March 1840, in Gautier, *Gautier on Dance*, 89.

6. Ibid.

7. Gautier recounts particularly well the plots he conceived himself for the ballets *Giselle* and *La Péri* (see *La Presse*, 28 June 1841 and 25 July 1843, in ibid., 94-102 and 112-121). For sarcastic takes on the practice, see Hector Berlioz, review of *La Chatte Metamorphosée en femme*, in *La Revue et gazette musicale* (Paris), 22 October 1837, quoted in Marian Smith, *Ballet and opera in the Age of 'Giselle'* (Princeton: Princeton University Press, 2000), 117-18 and Janin, review of *Les Mohicans*, in *Le Journal des débats*, 10 July 1837, quoted in Chapman, 'Jules Janin: Romantic Critic', 227-29.

8. Janin, *Le Journal des débats*, 14 December 1835, cited in Chapman, 'Jules Janin: Romantic Critic', 222. For a discussion of the old and new ballet, and Janin's position in the debate, see Chapman, 'Jules Janin: Romantic Critic'. The *ballet d'action* presented a dramatic action or story through dance and mime, and was intended to be morally uplifting, according to Jean-Georges Noverre's famous *Lettres sur la danse, et sur les ballets* (Stuttgart and Lyon: Aimé Delaroche, 1760).

9. Janin, *Le Journal des débats*, 27 June 1832, trans. in Chapman, 'Jules Janin: Romantic Critic', 204.

10. Janin, *Le Journal des débats*, 24 August 1832, trans. in ibid., 213 slightly altered by the present editor.

11. Ramsay Burt, *The Male Dancer: Bodies, Spectacle, Sexualities* (London: Routledge, 1995), 24-28. See also Ramsay Burt, 'The Trouble with the Male Dancer', in *Moving History/Dancing Cultures*, ed. Ann Dils and Ann Cooper Albright (Hanover, NH: Wesleyan University Press, 2001), 44-55.

12. Janin, *Le Journal des débats*, 2 March 1840, trans. Guest, *The Romantic Ballet in Paris*, 21. Also quoted in Burt, *The Male Dancer*, 25. Susan Leigh Foster reads this description as one that casts the male dancer as 'embarrassingly effeminate'; see Susan Leigh Foster, *Choreography and Narrative: Ballet's Staging of Story and Desire* (Bloomington: Indiana University Press, 1996), 219-20.

13. Norman Bryson, 'Dance History and Cultural Studies' (paper presented at the conference 'Choreographing History', University of California, Riverside, February 1992).

14. Burt cites J. S. Bratton's idea that the hornpipe, when performed as a potentially threatening British working-class entertainment, offended the middle class by displaying physical prowess. Burt also mentions that critics' almost prudish revulsion at the *danseur*'s physicality may be likened to a middle-class distaste for the strong-smelling animal-based perfumes used by the older aristocracy and regarded as 'a sign of their decadence, degeneracy and lack of hygiene'; Burt, *The Male Dancer*, 26-27. For more, see Alain Corbin, *The Fragrant and the Foul: Odour and the French Social Imagination* (Cambridge, MA: Harvard University Press, 1986).

15. *La Presse*, 7 May 1838, in Gautier, *Gautier on Dance*, 35. A month after publishing these words, Gautier made a point of restricting his target to *danseurs nobles*.

16. *La Presse*, 1 July 1844, in ibid., 142.

17. Lillian Moore, 'La Sylphide, Epitome of the Romantic Ballet', *Dance Magazine* 39 (1965): 42. See also Léandre Vaillat, *Histoire de la Danse* (Paris: Plon, 1942), 63. Guest, in *The Romantic Ballet in Paris*, 10, and Yuri Slonimsky, in *'Sil'fida' balet* (Leningrad: Academia, 1927), 42-43 have pointed out that this statement is an exaggeration. George Balanchine and Francis Mason read it as a complaint on Gautier's part (and wrongly state that the term 'ballet blanc' was first used by Gautier); see George Balanchine and Francis Mason, *Balanchine's Complete Stories of the Great Ballets*, revised and enlarged ed. (Garden City, NY: Doubleday, 1977), 654.

18. Alexander Bland, *The Dancer's World* (London: Collins, 1963), unpaginated.

19. Lynn Garafola, 'The Travesty Dancer in Nineteenth-Century Ballet', *Dance Research* 17/18 (1985-1986): 35-40.

20. On the strong presence of males in Danish ballet of this period, under the guidance of August Bournonville, see, for example, Erik Aschengreen, 'Bournonville and Male Dancing: An Inheritance and a Challenge', in *The Royal Danish Ballet and Bournonville* (Copenhagen: Ministry of Foreign Affairs of Denmark, 1979), 24-27.

21. See Sandra Noll Hammond, 'Clues to Ballet's Technical History from an Early Nineteenth-Century Ballet Lesson', *Dance Research* 3 (1984): 53-66; Sandra Noll Hammond, 'A Nineteenth-Century Dancing Master at the Court of Württemberg: the Dance Notebooks of Michel St. Léon', *Dance Chronicle* 15, no. 3 (1992): 291-315; Sandra Noll Hammond, 'Ballet's Technical Heritage: The Grammaire of Léopold Adice', *Dance Research* 13 (1995): 33-58; John Chapman, 'An Unromantic View of Nineteenth-Century Romanticism', *York Dance Review* 7 (1978): 28-40; Giannandrea Poesio, 'Blasis, the Italian Ballo, and the Male Sylph', in *Rethinking the Sylph: New Perspectives on the Romantic Ballet*, ed. Lynn Garafola (Hanover, NH: Wesleyan University Press, 1997), 131-42; Janina Pudelek, 'Ballet Dancers at Warsaw's Wielki Theater', in *Rethinking the Sylph: New Perspectives on the Romantic Ballet*, ed. Lynn Garafola (Hanover, NH: Wesleyan University Press, 1997), 143-64; Claudia Celi, 'The Arrival of the Great Wonder of Ballet', in *Rethinking the Sylph: New Perspectives on the Romantic Ballet*, ed. Lynn Garafola (Hanover, NH: Wesleyan University Press, 1997), 165-80; and Jane Pritchard, 'Collaborative Creations for the Alhambra and the Empire', *Dance Chronicle* 24 (2001): 55-82. Debra Sowell's and Mary Ann Smart's reconsiderations of Italian Romanticism also shed new light on ballet in nineteenth-century Europe; see Debra Sowell, 'A Plurality of Romanticisms: Italian Ballet and the Repertory of Antonio Cortesi and Giovanni Casati' (paper presented at the National Meeting of the Society of Dance History Scholars, Limerick, June 2003); Mary Ann Smart, 'Redefining Italian Romanticism: Rossini vs. Salvatore Viganò' (paper presented at the National Meeting of the American Musicological Society, Houston, November 2003). See also Chapter 8 of the present volume.

22. To name a few such studies: Louise Robin-Challan's on the social conditions of the danseuse at the Opéra in the 1830s and 1840s, Susan Manning's on the carryover between backstage fact and onstage fiction in female roles at the Opéra, Lynn Garafola's on the rise of the female travesty dancer, Felicia McCarren's on the pathologising of the emerging agency of female performers, Susan Leigh Foster's on the ballerina as phallus. See Louise Robin-Challan, 'Danse et Danseuses à l'Opéra de Paris, 1830-1850' (Thèse de 3ème Cycle, Université de Paris VII, 1988); Louise Robin-Challan, 'Social Conditions of Ballet Dancers at the Paris Opera in the 19th Century', *Choreography and Dance* 2 (1992): 17-28; Susan Manning, *Ecstasy and the Demon* (Berkeley and Los Angeles: University of California Press, 1993), 33-34; Susan Manning, 'Borrowing from Feminist Theory', in *Proceedings of the Society of Dance History Scholars: Retooling the Discipline: Research and Teaching Strategies for the 21st Century*, ed. Linda Tomko (Riverside, CA: Society of Dance History Scholars, 1994), 331-34; Garafola, 'The Travesty Dancer in Nineteenth-Century Ballet'; Lynn Garafola, ed. *Rethinking the Sylph: New Perspectives on the Romantic Ballet* (Hanover, NH: Wesleyan University Press, 1997); Felicia McCarren, *Dance Pathologies: Performance, Poetics, Medicine* (Stanford: Stanford University Press, 1998); Susan Leigh Foster, 'The Ballerina's Phallic Pointe', in *Corporealities: Dancing Knowledge, Culture and Power*, ed. Susan Leigh Foster (London: Routledge, 1996), 1-24. The latter study is not restricted to ballets of the 1830s and 1840s, but offers a critique of classical ballet choreography in general. On gendered roles in dance, see Ann Daly, 'The Balanchine Woman: Of Hummingbirds and Channel Swimmers', *Drama Review* 31 (1987): 8-21; Cythia Novack, *Sharing the Dance: Contact Improvisation and American Culture* (Madison: University of Wisconsin Press, 1990).

23. The need for an antidote to the disproportionate dominance of *La Sylphide* was expressed plainly in the title of Lynn Garafola's edited volume *Rethinking the Sylph: New Perspectives on the Romantic Ballet*.

24. Albert Czerwinski, *Brevier der Tanzkunst: Die Tänze bei den Kulturvölkern von den ältesten Zeiten bis zur Gegenwart* (Leipzig: Spamer, 1879), 204-08.

25. Henri de Soria, *Histoire pittoresque de la Danse* (Paris: H. Noble, 1897), 242.

26. Félicien de Ménil, *Histoire de la danse à travers les ages* (Paris: A. Picard & Kaan, 1905), 312-15, 18.

27. Slonimsky, *'Sil'fida' balet*, 3.

28. Ibid., 56.

29. André Levinson, 'The Idea of the Dance: from Artistotle to Mallarmé', *Theatre Arts Monthly*, 1927, originally published in English and reprinted in Joan Acocella and Lynn Garafola, eds., *André Levinson on Dance: Writings from Paris in the Twenties* (Hanover, NH: Wesleyan University Press, 1991), 80.

30. On the debate in the Russian press beginning in 1928, see Tim Scholl, *'Sleeping Beauty': A Legend in Progress* (New Haven: Yale University Press, 2004), 74-76.

31. Michel Fokine, letter to *The Times*, 6 July 1914, reprinted in Roger Copeland and Marshall Cohen, *What Is Dance? Readings in Theory and Criticism* (New York: Oxford University Press, 1983), 257-61.

32. In this paragraph and the next I rely on the illuminating introductory essay by Joan Acocella and Lynn Garafola to *André Levinson on Dance: Writings from Paris in the Twenties*, 1-26.

33. André Levinson, *Ballet Old and New*, trans. Susan Cook Summer (New York: Dance Horizons, 1982), 77-78.

34. Ibid., 45.

35. André Levinson, *Marie Taglioni* (Paris: F. Alcan, 1929), 26. See also the English translation with the same title, André Levinson, *Marie Taglioni*, trans. Cyril Beaumont (London: Imperial Society of Teachers of Dancing, 1930), 32. He overlooks the usual contractual requirements of débutantes to fill such peripheral parts before taking on the more challenging requirements of a principal role.

36. Respectively Levinson, *Marie Taglioni*, 52, 52, 97, 90; trans. Beaumont, 51, 51, 81, 77. As Acocella and Garafola have pointed out (*Levinson on Dance*, 20), his extensive quotations of Gautier in *Marie Taglioni*, along with an essay on Gautier in *La Revue Musicale*, 'Théophile Gautier et la ballet romantique', proved influential both for ballet and its historiography in the twentieth century.

37. Levinson, *Marie Taglioni*, 39-40 ; trans. Beaumont, 42. See also Slonimsky, 'Sil'fida' balet, 45.

38. See in particular Stéphane Mallarmé, 'Mallarmé: Selected Prose Poems, Essays, and Letters', (Baltimore: Johns Hopkins Press, 1956), reprinted in Copeland and Cohen, *What Is Dance? Readings in Theory and Criticism*, 111-15.

39. I have not encountered any uses of the term 'ballet blanc' before the twentieth century, but I am indebted to Sarah Gutsche-Miller for pointing out to me that it indeed appears in late-nineteenth-century Parisian newspapers. Examples include Pédrille's comment about the closing ballet in *La Prétentaine* (vaudeville-operetta in 4 acts by Paul Ferrier and R. Bénédite with music by Léon Vasseur) in 'Foyers et Coulisses', *Le Petit Journal*, 14 Oct, 1893. ('Quant au ballet blanc, c'est une véritable merveille.' [As for the *ballet blanc*, it is a veritable marvel.]) This ballet was described thus by Frimousse, in 'Les Premières', *Le Gaulois*, 11 Oct 1893: 'In an all-white palace, maskers all dressed up in white circulate amongst themselves: white harlequins, white hussars, white roosters, white hens, white bears and white poodles. From the many pillars there hang long white garlands' from which red and green lights shine when the ballet starts. The play of lights came into favor after the rise of Loie Fuller's popularity. See also Sarah Gutsche-Miller, 'Pantomime-Ballet on the Music-Hall Stage: The Popularisation of Classical Ballet in Fin-de Siècle Paris' (Ph.D. diss., McGill University, 2010).

Stravinsky also uses the term, in a Levinsonian way, in his discussion of the ballet *Apollo*: 'When, in my admiration for the beauty of line in classical dancing, I dreamed of a ballet of this kind, I had specially in my thoughts what is known as the "white ballet", in which to my mind the very essence of this art reveals itself in all its purity. I found that the absence of many-colored effects and of all superfluities produced a wonderful freshness. This inspired me to write music of an analogous character'. Igor Stravinsky, *Autobiography* (New York: Norton, 1936), 211-12.

40. Character dance, often called 'national dance' during the period under scrutiny, is balleticised folk dance, and was immensely popular and an integral part of ballet in the nineteenth century. With Lisa C. Arkin I make a case for character dance, and for Taglioni's non-sylph roles, in Lisa C. Arkin and Marian Smith, 'National Dance in the Romantic Ballet', in *Rethinking the Sylph: New Perspectives on the Romantic Ballet*, 11-68 and 245-52. On more refined definitions of the term, and on character-dance training for top dancers, see 14-15 and 34-35.

41. I owe this insight to Ivor Guest.

42. The Concise Oxford Dictionary of Ballet defines *ballet blanc* as 'a ballet in the classical style in which the danseuses wear the white tulle skirts introduced by Taglioni in *La Sylphide* in 1832. Typical examples are the second act of *Giselle* and *Les Sylphides*'; Horst Koegler, *The Concise Oxford*

Dictionary of Ballet, 2nd ed. (London: Oxford University Press, 1982), 33.

43. One could even argue that the earliest version of *Les Sylphides* (called 'Chopiniana', the title still used by the Kirov Ballet) does honour its model by including character dance.

44. Levinson, *Marie Taglioni*, 136; trans. Beaumont, 110.

45. 1856 was the year of the première of *Le Corsaire*, a ballet in which a male played the title role.

46. See Léonard de Géréon (a.k.a. Eugene Ronteix), *La Rampe et les Coulisses: Esquisses biographiques des directeurs, acteurs et actrices de tous les théâtres* (Paris: Les marchands de nouveautés, 1832), 32. This analogy also calls to mind Mazurier's portrayal of the monkey hero in *Jocko, ou Le Singe du Brézil*.

47. These included both ballets and divertissements in operas.

48. Note that Gautier wrote the libretti for *Giselle* and *La Péri*. *La Presse*, 25 July 1843, in Gautier, *Gautier on Dance*, 121 and *La Presse*, 15 October 1849, in ibid., 219. Perrot, Gautier points out, was reduced to the status of a comic opera bass in *La Filleule des fées*, the ballet in which Petipa as the 'tenor' won his bride at the end.

49. Koegler, *The Concise Oxford Dictionary of Ballet*, 323.

50. See Philip J. S. Richardson, *The Social Dances of the Nineteenth Century in England* (London: H. Jenkins, 1960), 83.

51. Jules Perrot, the greatest *danseur* of the age, had hoped for a long career at the Opéra, but his spectacular talents as both dancer and choreographer were for the most part exploited at other houses than the Opéra.

52. *La Presse*, 27 August 1839, trans. Guest, *Gautier on Dance*, 77.

53. *La Presse*, 16 October 1837, in ibid., 21.

54. *La Presse*, 11 July 1837, in ibid., 13.

55. *La Presse*, 23 January 1841, in ibid., 91-92. Guest points out that '*non passibus aequis*' ('with ill-matched steps') comes from Virgil's *Aeneid*, II.724, describing a small boy walking beside his father.

56. *La Presse*, 30 January 1840, in ibid., 82-83.

57. Charles de Boigne, *Petits mémoires de l'Opéra* (Paris: Librairie nouvelle, 1857), 81-83. In a few instances silent mime roles were assumed by dancers of the highest rank; see Smith, *Ballet and opera in the Age of 'Giselle'*, chapter 5.

58. The Ugly Sister as Frederick Ashton portrayed her in his production of *Cinderella* (1948), a major role crucial to the plot and beloved of audiences and critics, is perhaps a more appropriate analogue to the leading character roles in Parisian ballets of the 1830s and 1840s.

59. On the stronger male presence in opera, see Smith, *Ballet and opera in the Age of 'Giselle'*, chapter 3.

60. This is based on libretti published at the time of the ballets' and operas' premières.

61. It must also be pointed out that, while solo female travesty dancers came to be featured in some *divertissements*, and their number increased in the *corps* (particularly those in the roles of male pages, of whom four seems to have been a standard number for many years), no leading male roles at the Opéra were taken by women during this period. Thérèse Elssler, Fanny Elssler's taller sister, whose appearances at the Opéra were guaranteed as a condition of Fanny's contract there, achieved popularity in *pas de deux* with her sister in *divertissements* and played female dramatic roles as well (for instance, she portrayed the gypsy queen Mab in *La Gipsy*, and the sister of characters played by Fanny in *L'Ile des Pirates* and *La Volière*). On the female travesty dancer, see Garafola, 'The Travesty Dancer in Nineteenth-Century Ballet'; and Maribeth Clark, 'Bodies at the Opéra: Art and the Hermaphrodite in the Dance Criticism of Théophile Gautier', in *Reading Critics Reading: Opera and Ballet Criticism in France from the Revolution to 1848*, ed. Roger Parker and Mary Ann Smart (Oxford: Oxford University Press, 2001), 244-47.

62. This is based on libretti published at the time of the ballets' and operas' premières.

63. *La Presse*, 2 July 1842, in Gautier, *Gautier on Dance*, 110-11. Petipa took over the part successfully when Albert retired again the following year.

64. Gautier particularly liked this scene: 'This duel is one of the best produced and most energetic ever to have been seen on the stage. The duellists rush upon one another with indescribable fury, in spite of the efforts of the terrified Beatrix to separate them. Finally, with a skillful thrust, San Lucar [Albert] strikes Bustamente's [Elie's] sword from his hand. Bustamente retreats toward the window, and from there into the Grand Canal'; *La Presse*, 2 July 1842, in ibid.

65. I have calculated these ages by subtracting the birth year of each man from the première year of *La Jolie Fille de Gand*, 1842.

66. *La Sylphide* featured eight women and two men in named roles; *La Jolie Fille de Gand* featured six women and nine men in named roles.

67. *La Jolie Fille de Gand* was the most expensive ballet produced at the Opéra up to that date, requiring 562 costumes and seven different sets, including a goldsmith shop, a lush floral park at night lit with coloured lamps, and a sumptuous Venetian ballroom ablaze with light. For information on costumes, see the documents in the *Archives nationales*, Paris, AJ 13 183 and 215.

Table 11.1

Parts for corps de ballet dancers in selected operas and ballet-pantomimes
(Paris Opéra, 1830-50)

This table is intended to show the relative abundance and types of *corps de ballet* parts for men and women 1830-50, and the fact that travesty roles for women were rather few in number, despite widespread belief to the contrary.

N.B. *Corps* dancers sometimes played multiple roles within a single work; therefore the number of parts might exceed the number of dancers in any given work. This table does not include the extras and students who frequently appeared in these productions, nor the solo parts taken by high-ranking dancers in entertainments falling within the action.

* children

Title, date of première, examples of characters	Parts for males	Parts for females
Le Dieu et la Bayadère, 1830 2-act opera males: soldiers, musicians females: bayadères	16	28
La Sylphide, 1832 2-act ballet males: Scottish villagers females: Scottish villagers, witches, sylphides travesty roles: 4 men play female witches	22	56
Don Juan, 1834 5-act opera Corps and chorus parts included Spanish ladies and knights, Moorish knights, female slaves, blacks, pages, people, villagers, monks, policemen, servants, young women and children in Don Juan's household, and women in white who appear after the Don is dragged to hell	30	53
Brézilia, 1835 1-act ballet-pantomime women: entourages of the queen, of Brézilia	0	36
Le Diable boiteux, 1836 3-act ballet-pantomime men: revellers at a ball, scullions, tradesmen, lords, domestics, goblins, call-boy, hair stylist, ballet master, répétiteur, inspector, musicians, players, gypsies, Basques,	128 21*	120 21*

Title, date of première, examples of characters	Parts for males	Parts for females

nobles, boléro-dancers, Galicians, Castillians, Catalans,
Andalusians, smugglers, merchants
women: revelers at a ball, bacchantes, sylphides, ballerinas
in class, players, gypsies, Basques, noblewomen, boléro-dancers,
Galicians, Castillians, Catalans, Andalusians, smugglers
travesty roles: 4 women play pages with heads of roosters

La Esmeralda, 1836	41	50
opera	13*	14*

men: beggars, black people, maskers, confessor
beadle, clerks
women: beggars, unspecified corps parts

La Chatte Metamorphosée en Femme, 1837	40	59

3-act ballet
men: men of the people, warriors, lance carriers,
standard-bearers, officers of the court
women: women of the people, ladies in waiting,
Chinese ladies
travesty roles: 18 women play male pages
(some of these may be children)

Benvenuto Cellini, 1838	36	44
2-act opera (Berlioz, no choreographer listed)	10*	24*

men: parade, acrobats, minions, lords, swordsmen
women: parade, women of the people
travesty roles: 4 women play male pages

Le Diable Amoureux, 1840	125	140

3-act ballet-pantomime (Benoist/Réber, Mazilier)
men: fishermen, peasants, demons, eunuchs, pirates,
merchants
women: peasants, demons, bayadères, odalisques

Giselle, 1841	35	73
2-act ballet-pantomime (Adam, Coralli)	6*	18*

men: vinegatherers, musicans, lords, hunters
women: vinegatherers, ladies, wilis
travesty roles: 4 women play male pages

La Jolie Fille de Gand, 1842	106	130
3-act ballet-pantomime (Saint-Georges, Albert)	18*	38*

men: bourgeois men, farmers, lads of the inn,
a charlatan, a trumpeter, charlatan's valet,
crossbowmen, lords, revellers at a travesty ball, a dwarf,
lords, gypsies, peasants
women: female merchants, shop assistants, fiancées,
bourgeois women, a servant, peasants, revelers
at a travesty ball, a dwarf, nymphs, bacchantes, Venetian
ladies, gypsies, peasants
travesty roles: 7 woman play male pages;
4 women play black men

Title, date of première, examples of characters	Parts for males	Parts for females
Dom Sébastien, 1843	52	51
5-act opera (Donizetti, Albert)	6*	0
men: Portuguese nobles, king's officers,		
sailors, Arabs, inquisitors		
women: Arabs, Algerians, Portuguese slaves		
travesty roles: 11 women play male pages		
Eucharis, 1844	12	58
2-act ballet-pantomime	6*	0
men: fauns, boys, satyrs		
women: graces, dryads, bacchantes		
L'Etoile de Séville, 1845	46	76
4-act opera (Balfe, Coralli)	6*	6*
men: chevaliers, alcades, domestiques		
women: ladies		
travesty roles: 18 women play male pages		
Betty, 1846	27	60
2-act ballet-pantomime	5*	0
men: sailors, deckhands (mousses)		
women: women of the people		
travesty roles: 10 women play male sailors		
David, 1846	0	11
3-act opera (Mermet, Coralli)		
no characters described; pas de deux, pas de cinq		
Jérusalem, 1847	38	43
4-act opera (Verdi, Mabille)		
men: knights, followers of the legat, pilgrims,		
Arabs, guards, executioner		
women: Arabs		
travesty roles: 4 women play male pages		

This table is based on libretti published at the time of the ballets' and operas' premières.

Table 11. 2

Some corps de ballet parts danced by Monsieur Scio

1831	*L'Orgie* (ballet), drinker and dancer
1832	*La Tentation* (ballet-opera), shepherd, member of the third squadron of demons
1833	*Ali-Baba* (opera), slave
1833	*La Révolte des femmes* (ballet), man of the people
1834	*Don Juan* (opera), *3eme corps de ballet*
1836	*Le Diable boiteux* (ballet), smuggler
1837	*La Chatte metamorphosée en femme* (ballet), standard-bearer
1837	*Les Mohicans* (ballet), English soldier
1838	*Guido et Ginevra* (opera), soldier of fortune
1838	*Benvenuto Cellini* (opera), *corps de ballet*
1839	*Le Lac des fées* (opera), faun
1841	*Giselle* (ballet), vine-gatherer
1841	*Le Freyschutz* (opera), peasant
1841	*La Reine de Chypre* (opera), vassal
1842	*La Jolie Fille de Gand* (ballet), reveler in ball scene, bowsman
1844	*Lady Henriette* (ballet), soldier, inmate at Bedlam
1844	*Le Lazzarone* (opera), *corps de ballet*
1844	*Marie Stuart* (opera), Levite
1846	*L'Ame en peine* (opera), peasant
1846	*Robert Bruce* (opera), highland chief
1847	*Ozaï* (ballet), sailor

This table is based on libretti published at the time of the ballets' and operas' premières.

Chapter 12

Les Sylphides (Plural)

Marian Smith

The two ballets *La Sylphide* (1832) and *Les Sylphides* (1909) have much in common. Both were set some time in the hazy Romantic past, and both involved white-clad sylphs dancing ethereally. Both featured a ballerina whose portrayal of a sylph caused a great sensation: Marie Taglioni in the nineteenth century and Anna Pavlova in the twentieth. And – perhaps since the second ballet was deliberately created to look like the first – the two 'are often mistaken for one another'. [1]

Despite these two ballets' similarities in appearance, they came out of entirely unlike circumstances, and they differ from one another in crucial ways. Though of course the present volume has focused entirely on *La Sylphide* (albeit it in many manifestations), I believe it fitting to close with this short chapter describing *Les Sylphides* and its genesis in order to remind readers of the modernity of the newer ballet, and to point out that by borrowing only the ethereal, otherworldly aspect of its predecessor and then becoming terribly famous, *Les Sylphides* has created a misleading impression of *La Sylphide*, which of course is a story ballet with many mortal characters and witches, too. A further complicating factor is that *Les Sylphides* looked so old-fashioned in comparison to the other anti-establishment ballets its choreographer was creating around the same time ('a pale anemone blooming delicately amid the colorful violence of *Scheherezade*, *Cléopâtre* and *Prince Igor*'[2]) that it passed – from the very beginning – for a reasonable facsimile of a ballet from the 1830s, even though it was not.

Let us now turn our attention to *Les Sylphides*, a set of relatively short dances which took shape incrementally over the course of three years in the hands of Michel Fokine (1880-1942), a *premier danseur* in the Imperial Ballet and a choreographer bent on reform. This ballet began in 1907 in Russia as a series of tableaux, most of them programmatic, under the name *Chopiniana* (for it was choreographed to Glazunov's suite of the same name, consisting of orchestrated piano works of Chopin) and wound up as an abstract piece, inspired in part by the 1832 *La Sylphide*, and danced in Diaghilev's first

Saison Russe in Paris in 1909 at the Théâtre du Châtelet under the name *Les Sylphides.*

In the ballet itself, and in Fokine's peppery comments in his memoirs about its genesis, we may see a refraction of the passionate struggle taking place in the Maryinsky company between two factions: Fokine and his followers (known variously as the 'Fokintsy' and 'the innovators'), and the 'Imperialitsy', led by Nikolai Legat and the prima ballerina Matilde Kschessinska, celebrated for her stunning technique (and likely the subject of a satirical portrait in the character of the mechanical-doll ballerina of Fokine's *Petroushka*, 1911). The Fokintsy, who counted among their number Bronislava Nijinska and Vaslav Nijinsky, believed that ballet had come to emphasise empty virtuosity without dramatic expressiveness.[3] Fokine laid out the polarisation as he saw it in a famous letter to the *Times* of London in 1914, drawing a distinction between 'the new ballet' and 'the older ballet', and declaring five principles of reform:

1) Movement must be appropriate to the 'period and character of the nation represented' instead of based on ready-made and established dance steps.

2) Dance and gesture must serve the dramatic action, instead of being used as 'mere divertissement or entertainment'.

3) Performers should be expressive from head to foot, 'replacing gestures of the hands by mimetic of the whole body', and employing conventional gesture 'only where it is required by the style of the ballet'.

4) The group, or *corps de ballet*, should express the appropriate sentiment of the ballet instead of, as in the old ballet, being 'ranged in groups only for the purpose of ornament'.

5) Dancing is equal in stature to music and scenic decoration in ballet. It does not serve as a slave to either. Nor, 'in contradistinction to the older ballet' does the new ballet 'demand "ballet music" of the composer as an accompaniment to dancing; it accepts music of every kind, provided only that it is good and expressive. It does not demand of the scenic artist that he should array the ballerinas in short skirts and pink slippers. It does not impose any specific "ballet" conditions on the composer or the decorative artist, but gives complete liberty to their creative powers.'[4]

Fokine also wrote at some length in his *Memoirs* about his frustration with the establishment at the Maryinsky, arguing (not for the first time in the history of the theatre) that expressiveness and portrayal of emotion and character should take precedence over vacuous virtuosity. He wrote of truth and naturalness, embracing the idea of barefoot dancing, finding it less artificial than 'toe dancing'. In this regard he was no doubt influenced by Isadora Duncan, whose performances in Russia, the first of which took place in 1904, sent shock waves through the ballet establishment there. Also,

Duncan sometimes performed to the music of Chopin played on the piano, a practice not lost on the eager young Fokine.[5]

In any case, lest there be any doubt about *Chopiniana* as a reform ballet – for it has nothing of the pointedly modern look of some of Fokine's other early works – Fokine himself averred that in *Chopiniana* he expressed his notions about reform even more plainly than in his prose writings:

> From the outset I myself pictured the ballet as most varied in content and form, expressive of life. I recognised the dramatic, the abstract, the character, and the classic dance; and I believe that, in this ballet, I expressed my sentiments more clearly than in any other, more clearly even than in my own program of reforms.[6]

The first version (February 1907). Indeed, the first *Chopiniana* (created for a charity event at the Maryinsky) did cover a broad span, consisting of five separate tableaux danced to piano pieces of Chopin. Fokine's own description of its five scenes is worth quoting in its entirety, for it gives a clear sense both of the ballet's variety of content and form (so 'expressive of life' as the choreographer saw it), and of the importance he placed on the lack of spectacular feats in the *pas de deux* (no. 4), a genre then expected to feature virtuosic display.[7]

1) Polonaise in A Major, op. 40 no. 1. [Polish ball in a luxurious palace] '... in gorgeous costumes, a large ensemble performed Polish ballroom dances. (Whenever I endeavor to prove the connection existing between a national dance and the life which created it, I always think of the Polonaise as the best example. It was created in the period of the fullest bloom of the Polish nation; it reflects and exemplifies its majesty, luxury, pride, and at the same time its chivalrous homage to the fair sex.)'

2) Nocturne in F Major, op. 15 no. 1. [Chopin in Majorca] '...the curtain opens disclosing Chopin sitting at the piano in a monastery on the island of Majorca, where, during the night, the ill composer suffers nightmarish hallucinations. He sees dead monks rising from their graves and slowly approaching him to the accompaniment of a monotonously beating rain. Frightened, he rushes away from the piano, trying to seek safety from the horrible visions. He finds salvation in his Muse. Again he sits at the piano and finds calm in the sounds of the Nocturne.

Chopin was portrayed by an excellent pantomimist, Alexis Bulgakov, who was made up to resemble the composer. The Muse was portrayed by a beautiful dancer, Anna Ourakova, who specialised in Good Fairy roles. The male dancers played the roles of the monks. The female dancers, in light, transparent gauze costumes, interpreted the music of the Nocturne ...'

3) Mazurka in c-sharp minor op. 50 no. 3. [Wedding in a Polish Village] 'An unfortunate young girl is being married to an elderly man whom she does not love. In the course of the general dancing, her beloved finds his way to her. As a result of his passionate pleas, she throws the wedding ring at the unwanted suitor and flees with her beloved. The part of the bride was danced by Julie Sedova.'

4) Waltz in c-sharp minor op. 64 no. 2. [Plotless *pas de deux*] 'The Waltz was danced by Anna Pavlova and Michael Oboukhov. Pavlova appeared in a Taglioni costume from the sketch by Léon Bakst. It was a simple repro-duction of the etchings of the 1840 period. Oboukhov was attired in a very romantic black velvet costume from the ballet 'Fairy Doll', also from a sketch by Bakst.

The choreography differed from all other *pas de deux* in its total absence of spectacular feats. There was not a single *entrechat*, turn in the air, or pirouette. There was a slow turn of the ballerina, holding her partner's hand, but this could not be classified as a pirouette because the movement was not confined to the turn but was used for a change of position and grouping.

When composing, I placed no restrictions on myself; I simply could not conceive of any spectacular stunts to the accompaniment of the poetic, lyrical Waltz of Chopin. I was totally unconcerned whether this romantic duet would bring applause or satisfy the audience or the ballerina, for I did not think of methods for guaranteeing success.'

5) Tarantella in A-flat Major, op. 43. [Public festival with the Bay of Naples and Vesuvius in the background.] 'This was performed by Vera Fokina assisted by a large ensemble. I tried to project the authentic character of the national dances which Vera and I had observed on our trip to Italy, when we studied them in detail on the island of Capri.'

Fokine was also intent on proving a few points in regard to toe dancing: he had not renounced it, he did understand it, and moreover its proper use eschewed needless display:

Before I created *Chopiniana* it had already been pointed out to me that . . .I had renounced toe dance and had devoted myself exclusively to barefoot dancing. I wished to demonstrate, therefore, that I loved not only the dramatic, but the dance in its pure form; that I recognized the toe dance, and the ballet skirts – but only in their proper place, and not in the place they then occupied in the ballet.

It was in the Waltz *pas de deux* in particular that he meant to establish that even though toe dancing was not natural or realistic, it could still be deployed in a tasteful and expressive manner:

> Toe work I recognized as one of the means of the dance, a more poetic form, removed from the realistic life of some dancing. However, when a dancer jumps and performs feats on her toes, unrelated to and unconnected with the subject of the moment, for the sole purpose of demonstrating that she is the possessor of 'steel' toes, I fail to see any poetry in such an exhibition. . . .With the production of the 'Chopiniana' Waltz I wanted to show how I understood the unique beauty of the classic dance.[8]

So keen on creating one non-characteristic choreography was Fokine that he had commissioned Glazunov to orchestrate another Chopin piece for the purpose, to be added to the four numbers the composer had already orchestrated. Not incidentally, he chose the Waltz in c-sharp minor op. 64 no. 2 that Isadora Duncan had famously danced to. ('I needed *that* waltz', wrote Fokine, 'because most of the other waltzes suggested character dancing. . .'[9])

The second version ('Danses sur la Musique de Chopin', March 1908). Fokine's next version of the ballet (performed at a charity evening at the Maryinsky under the title 'Danses sur la musique de Chopin') was, he said, 'in substance an elaborate evolution of the same waltz and a repetition of the earlier experiment on a much greater scale'. He erased the ballet's characteristic qualities, putting all of the ballerinas throughout the whole piece in long white diaphanous tutus instead of character costumes; he re-choreographed the Nocturne as an abstract ensemble dance instead of a depiction of Chopin in Majorca; he jettisoned the Tarantella scene altogether; he stripped the Polanaise of its characteristic dancing, moving the music to the beginning to serve as an overture. The effect of the new overture, according to Nijinska, was breathtaking, for it drew attention to the ballet's dreaminess:

> The overture: the pompous 'Polonaise' attunes the Theatre. In the audience there is an air of festivity in the anticipation of a brilliant performance. But there is a long pause... and then, to the soft sounds of Chopin's dreamy 'Nocturne', the mood in the Theatre changes ... as the curtain is slowly raised an eerie enchantment descends over the Theatre and envelops the spectators and the dancers onstage.[10]

In this new version of *Chopiniana*, Fokine left intact only the choreography of the plotless Waltz *pas de deux*, which had been conceived as an abstract number to begin with, and now added four new Chopin pieces (orchestrated by one Maurice Keller): the Waltz in G-flat (op. 70 no. 1), the Mazurka in D (Op. 32 no. 2), the Mazurka in C (Op. 67 no. 3), and the Prelude in A (Op. 28 no. 7). The choreography for each of these was a solo, plotless dance. As Fokine put it proudly, '[t]his ballet contains no plot whatsoever. It was the first abstract ballet.'[11] It featured Ninijsky in the only male role, and twenty-three female dancers in white costumes ('twenty-three Taglionis', as Fokine described them[12]).

By narrowing the focus of the ballet, he explains, he could show up his critics – again – by proving his mettle as a choreographer of classical and *pointe* dancing; he could

> ... repudiate the accusation that I was rejecting the toe dance, that either I did not understand it or I did not love it, and that I was destroying the old ballet. I did understand the toe dance, but I understood it differently from my contemporaries. . . .[13]

Another incentive for altering the ballet thus, said Fokine, was his wish to present two ballets widely separated in style in the course of one evening, and this 'reverie Romantique' appeared with *Egyptian Nights* (later called *Cléopâtre*), a strikingly modern piece calling for profile positions, flat palms and angular lines, and a snake dance for Pavlova (featuring a live snake which, after curling up around Pavlova's arm and remaining motionless during the première, was returned to the zoo and replaced with a better-behaved prop snake made of oilcloth[14]).

But he was particularly compelled by this approach because of his desire to restore ballet to its former greatness – that is, to the heights of the Taglioni era, a time he compared very favourably to his own decadent, empty, era:

> ... I had come to the conclusion that, in the pursuit of acrobatic feats, ballet and the toe dance had lost the very important purpose for which they were created.
>   When I looked at the etchings and lithographs of ballerinas of the romantic period – Taglioni, Grisi, Cerrito, and others – I clearly saw that their dancing and goals were entirely different from those of the present. For theirs was not the demonstration of physical strength but of pure poetry.
>   It is easy to understand the colossal difference between the romantic and the modern periods of the ballet if we compare their pictorial representations. Following the poetic romantic ballet, there was a period of decline. In my 'reverie Romantique', as I called my new 'Chopiniana', I tried to return to the ballet the conditions of its period of highest development.[15]

The third version (Les Sylphides, June 1909). The ballet remained largely unchanged in its third and now best-known incarnation, which became a part of the Imperial Ballet repertoire and made its western debut in Paris at the Théâtre du Châtelet in Paris during the first Saison Russe in June 1909. The company director Serge Diaghilev had altered the ballet a little, discarding the Polonaise overture and replacing it with the mysterious, hushed Prelude op. 28 no. 7, which set the mood for a peaceful, dreamy atmosphere in an entirely different way than the jauntier Polonaise had done in St. Petersburg. Diaghilev also commissioned new orchestrations for all but the C-sharp minor Waltz − for which he kept the Glazunov version − including two from Stravinsky[16] (Figure 12.1.) And he also changed the title

PROGRAMME

Soirée du Samedi 19 Juin 1909

Boris Godounow
Opéra de Modeste Moussorgsky
2e Acte — 3e Acte : 2e Tableau

Boris
M. Chaliapine

Le Tsarevitch Fédor	*La Nourrice*	*Xenia*
Mme Pétrenko	Mme Karénine	Mme Pavlova

Chouisky	*Pimène*
M. Davidow	M. Zaporojetz

LES SYLPHIDES
Rêverie Romantique en un acte
Musique de Chopin

Groupes et danses de M. Fokine
Décor peint par M. Yarémitsch d'après la maquette de M. A. Benois
Costumes de M. A. Benois

Nocturne, op. 32   Instrumenté par M. *J Stravinsky*
  Mlles Anna Pavlova, Karsavina, Baldina, Alexandra Fédorova, Smirnova.
  M. Koslow.
  Mmes Barasch, Constantinova, Dobrolubova, Anna Fédorova, Fokina,
  Goloubéva, Léonova, Léontiéva, Loukachévitch, Nijinska, Olkhina,
  Sadonova, Scholar, Soboleva, Sprichinska, Tchernicheva, A. Vassilièva,
  Vlassova.
Valse, op. 70   Instrumentée par M. *A. Tanéiew*
  Mme Karsavina.
Mazurka, op. 33   Instrumentée par M. *N. Sokolow*
  Mlle Anna Pavlova.
Prélude, op. 28   Instrumenté par M. *A. Tanéiew*
  Mlle Baldina.
Valse, op. 64   Instrumenté[e] par M. *A. Glazounow*
  Mlle Pavlova et M. Koslow.
Grande Valse Brillante, op. 18   Instrumenté[e] par M. *I. Stravinsky*

Bibliothèque de l'Opéra, Carton 2238

12.1. Information given in a programme from the first Russian Season, 1909.

to *Les Sylphides*, surely to draw his Parisian audience's attention to the ballet's similarities to *La Sylphide*.[17]

This number-by-number description, below, of *Les Sylphides*, paraphrasing and quoting the words of George Balanchine and Francis Mason, offers a good sense of what the ballet looked and sounded like at its Parisian première:[18]

Overture (Prelude Op. 28, no. 7). The mood of the music is quiet and contemplative. The curtain rises (before the overture ends) on a secluded wood near an ancient ruin; sylphs are grouped about the scene in a still tableau. The light is soft and bluish white. (One observer in 1909 reported that 'when the curtain went up... the whole house gasped with admiration and surprise ... the dancers were like blue pearls'.[19])

Nocturne Op. 32, no. 2 – Some of the danseuses begin to dance, and are joined by the principal dancers, who stand in a cluster at the back.

Waltz Op. 70 no. 1 – One danseuse dances a solo to 'music suggestive of beautiful and controlled happiness'.

Mazurka Op. 33 no. 3 – The music is 'not as soft; it is bolder, more open and free' and so is the choreography, in which 'the ballerina bounds diagonally across the stage' in great forward leaps.

Mazurka Op. 67 no. 3 – The danseuses form a decorative tableau around the stage, and then the danseur performs a solo.

Prelude op. 28 no. 7 (the piece used for the overture) – the 'sylphs form picturesque groups, the girls kneeling about central figures'. A ballerina enters softly, pauses, and seems to listen to a distant call. She moves among the groups 'adroitly and sweetly, but completely removed from them in her rapt attention to what she might hear'.

Waltz op. 64 no. 2 – Now the danseur carries the ballerina across the stage; she appears to be lighter than air. After she is released, the *pas de deux* begins. As the momentum of the music increases, the ballerina responds with 'unhesitating swiftness and flight to the inspiration from the music and the night'.

Waltz Op. 18 no. 1 – After a moment of silence and an empty stage, the dancers return to this buoyant waltz; they fill the stage with movement 'like the swift fluttering of butterfly wings'. The principal dancers appear and dance short solos. At the end, all are standing still in the same tableau with which the ballet begins.[20]

This choreographic manifesto, delivered sweetly to the strains of Chopin, broke convention after convention. It ensured that no solo ended in the same fashion as any other; it avoided specific hand gestures; it erased obvious distinctions between *corps* and solo dancers, integrating them choreographically and even calling for them to wear the same costumes. It removed all formal positions from the flowing *port de bras*, eliminated applause breaks, and made defiant use of *pointe* dancing, eschewing obvious displays of virtuosity, though the poses and flowing steps required great control and strength.[21] Moreover, aside from being the first abstract ballet of the twentieth century (according to Fokine), it was, as Balanchine and Mason asserted decades later, the first 'ballet as a whole (with precedents from Ivanov and Gorsky) in which movement itself projected from important music was a prime factor rather than a propulsive accompaniment.'[22]

Yet Fokine's concerns as a reformer were not communicated to the French audience in the programme book essay by Martial Teneo.[23] Instead, Teneo's essay, like Diaghilev's new title for the ballet, emphasised *Les Sylphides*'s connectedness to France. It explained to the audience that Fokine's choreography was meant to represent Chopin's music in bodily form:

[He] has succeeded in his enterprise: presented on a Romantic set, his *reverie* is charming, and makes visible the hazy sense of amorousness that Chopin instilled in his works. . .

Teneo stated, further, that *Les Sylphides* constituted a continuation of the great traditions of French ballet of the past, oddly positing a connection between Vestris and Nijinsky, and invoking the long tenure of Petipa in Russia (never mind that Fokine wished to erase some of the hallmark features of Petipa's choreography):

. . [this work]... evokes, through the talent of the dancers, the character of our late-eighteenth century *école de danse*, so admirably carried on for fifty-five years in Russia by the illustrious ballet master Marius Petipa. Seeing Nijinsky, incomparable in his flexibility and lightness, brings to mind [Auguste] Vestris, 'the god of the dance', as he was called by his father, so proud of the jumps and entrechats made stylish by his son. . .[24]

So what we find in *Les Sylphides* is a work by a reform-minded choreographer that began as a demonstration of the breadth of ballet's possibilities, in its next phase focused on the poetic qualities of Romantic ballet as Fokine perceived them, and in its final tweaking by Diaghilev and under a name reminiscent of *La Sylphide* was presented to Parisians – with the help of Teneo's essay – in a fashion pointedly aimed at awakening pride in their ballet history, and invoking family ties that connected the Ballets Russes to Paris.

Let us conclude by noticing how little of her original surroundings the sylph brought back with her to Paris in 1909. In the first ballet she was the instigator of a conflict that helped reveal both an unreal world and a real one. Such otherworldly or exotic figures – usually in the form of unattainable females, longed for by mortal, unexotic men of the sort the Opéra's male clientele could identify with – never kept the stage to themselves for an entire ballet. Their role was to interact and attract; to play against beings of another sort. Fokine's sylphs, on the other hand, occupied a world without witches or Scottish villagers or any other sort of opposing groups. It was simply a coterie of sylphs in long white dresses, and a sole male, forming beautiful pictures in a moonlit setting but whose story, if there was one, was known only to themselves. That is, *La Sylphide* had all the components of a typical story ballet of the 1830s: characters with well-defined personalities, an identifiable geographical setting, and obvious conflicts. *Les Sylphides* had none of these things, but instead explored the pure and mysterious world of the 'white' scene, and in its modern way, self-consciously occupied a world of ballet itself. Moreover, the music for the first sylph was conceived after the story had been written, and was custom-made to help impart her story to the audience. Fokine's sylphs, on the other hand, as dancers in one of the first of the type identified by Fokine as a 'new ballet', were animated by music that had come into existence on its own, and not for the sake of ballet. Since narrative itself was missing from *Les Sylphides*, so was the sort of narrative music that had in the 1830s been intended to explain it.

The figure of the sylph, as she appears both in *La Sylphide* and *Les Sylphides* occupies a place of signal importance both in ballet historiography and in the popular imagination. She is a symbol of the Opéra of the 1830s and beyond; she is a character everlastingly linked with the careers of both Marie Taglioni and Anna Pavlova; she is, by Théophile Gautier's proclamation in the nineteenth century the usherer-in of Romanticism to the realm of Terpsichore, and by André Levinson's in the twentieth the saviour of ballet itself. Her pervasiveness as a symbol has been closely examined by scholars (for instance, in *Rethinking the Sylph*[25]) and the white ballet, or *ballet blanc*, with which she is associated was rebelled against by a whole generation of modern-dance choreographers. Becoming more closely acquainted with this figure, as she came to grace the stage in both of these ballets, allows us to enter more fully into her beautiful, complicated, and mysterious world.

Balanchine, George, and Francis Mason. *Balanchine's Complete Stories of the Great Ballets*. Revised and enlarged ed. Garden City, NY: Doubleday, 1977.
Buckle, Richard. *Diaghilev*. New York: Atheneum, 1979.

Carbonneau, Suzanne. 'Michel Fokine', in *International Encyclopedia of Dance*, edited by Elizabeth Aldrich and Selma Jeanne Cohen, New York: Oxford University Press, 1998, vol. III, 14-28.

Copeland, Roger, and Marshall Cohen. *What Is Dance? Readings in Theory and Criticism.* New York: Oxford University Press, 1983.

David, André. 'Histoire de deux ballets "La Sylphide" et "Les Sylphides",' *Le combat*, 19 December 1957.

Drummond, John. *Speaking of Diaghilev*. London: Faber and Faber, 1997.

Fokine, Michel. *Memoirs of a Ballet Master*. Translated by Vitale Fokine. Edited by Anatole Chujoy Boston: Little, Brown, 1961.

Garafola, Lynn, ed. *Rethinking the Sylph: New Perspectives on the Romantic Ballet.* Hanover, NH: Wesleyan University Press, 1997.

Goodwin, Noël. 'Sight and Sound: Fokine and Chopin.' *Dance and Dancers* (November 1991): 15-17.

Lomax, Sondra. 'Fokine's Manifesto and *Les Sylphides*', in *New Directions in Dance*, ed. D. T. Taplin. Toronto: Pergamon Press, 1979.

Nijinska, Bronislava. *Early Memoirs*. Translated by Irina Nijinska and Jean Rawlinson. Durham, NC: Duke University Press, 1992.

Robert, Grace. *The Borzoi Book of Ballets*. New York: A. A. Knopf, 1946.

Smith, Marian. '*La Sylphide* and *Les Sylphides*', in *Music, Theater, and Cultural Transfer: Paris, 1830-1914*, ed. Annegret Fauser and Mark Everist. Chicago: University of Chicago Press, 2009.

Svetlov, Valerien. *Le Ballet Contemporain*. Translated by Michel Calvocaressi. Paris: M. de Brunoff, 1912.

Notes

1. '*La Sylphide* et *Les Syphides* sont deux ballets complètement différents que l'on confond souvent.' André David, 'Histoire de deux ballets "La Sylphide" et "Les Sylphides",' *Le combat*, 19 December 1957.

2. Grace Robert, *The Borzoi Book of Ballets* (New York: A. A. Knopf, 1946), 217.

3. See Suzanne Carbonneau, 'Michel Fokine', in *International Encyclopedia of Dance*, ed. Elizabeth Aldrich and Selma Jeanne Cohen (New York: Oxford University Press, 1998), vol. III, 14-28.

4. Fokine, Letter to the *Times*, 6 July 1914, reprinted in Roger Copeland and Marshall Cohen, *What Is Dance? Readings in Theory and Criticism* (New York: Oxford University Press, 1983), 260.

5. Fokine chose Glazunov's existing suite of orchestrated Chopin pieces, as well as its title,

Chopiniana, for his new work, asking the composer to orchestrate one more number, the Waltz in C Sharp minor op. 64 no. 2 (a waltz that Duncan had used in her performance as well). See Noël Goodwin, 'Sight and Sound: Fokine and Chopin', *Dance and Dancers* (1991): 15-17.

6. Michel Fokine, *Memoirs of a Ballet Master*, ed. Anatole Chujoy, trans. Vitale Fokine (Boston: Little, Brown, 1961), 105.

7. Ibid., 100-05.

8. Ibid., 105.

9. Ibid., 99. My emphasis.

10. Bronislava Nijinska, *Early Memoirs*, trans. Irina Nijinska and Jean Rawlinson (Durham, NC: Duke University Press, 1992), 251.

11. Fokine, *Memoirs of a Ballet Master*, 102-05.

12. Ibid., 129.

13. Ibid., 128.

14. Ibid., 127-28.

15. Ibid., 128-29.

16. He did so, perhaps, because he had no access to the Keller arrangements, or because as Richard Buckle has put it he 'could not leave a score alone.' Richard Buckle, *Diaghilev* (New York: Atheneum, 1979), 148. As Goodwin points out, the arrangements commissioned by Diaghilev were never published, so subsequent productions have necessitated the creation of new arrangements. 'This subtly alters the look of the ballet according to treatment of the music, from the richly swooping Glazunov-Keller arrangements in the Soviet *Chopiniana* to the sharp instrumental clarity of Britten's reduced version in 1940 for Ballet Theatre and, somewhere in between, the partly brighter colouring of the Roy Douglas arrangement long used by the Royal Ballet companies and many others.' Goodwin, 'Sight and Sound: Fokine and Chopin', 17.

17. The title *Chopiniana* is retained in some Russian productions of this ballet, as is the Polonaise overture.

18. George Balanchine and Francis Mason, *Balanchine's Complete Stories of the Great Ballets*, revised and enlarged ed. (Garden City, NY: Doubleday, 1977), 653-58.

19. Valerien Svetlov, *Le ballet contemporain*, trans. Michel Calvocaressi (Paris: M. de Brunoff, 1912), 98-99. Translated and quoted in Buckle, *Diaghilev*, 148. Svetlov was reporting on the dress rehearsal, for which the house was full.

20. On Nijinsky and his performance in *Les Sylphides*, Cyril Beaumont said Nijinsky 'was a very great artist, and every role that he created was quite different from the other ones. You see some dancers who have very considerable talents technically, perhaps even mimetically, but on the other hand you can see it's just the same dancer wearing a different costume. But with Nijinsky that wasn't the case at all. In *Schéhérazade* he was rather gross and seemed to broaden his body, and when you saw him in *Carnaval* as Harlequin, he was very slim and mercurial and something quite different. Again when you saw him in *Sylphides*, there he was a wonderful romantic person. He seemed to epitomise the romantic movement.' John Drummond, *Speaking of Diaghilev* (London: Faber and Faber, 1997), 126.

21. See Buckle, *Diaghilev*, 149 and Sondra Lomax, 'Fokine's Manifesto and *Les sylphides*', in *New Directions in Dance*, ed. D. T. Taplin (Toronto: Pergamon Press, 1979), 113-20, in which she shows specifically how the ballet enacts Fokine's five principles of anti-Imperial Ballet reform.

22. Balanchine and Mason, *Balanchine's Complete Stories of the Great Ballets*, 656.

23. Teneo, *bibliothécaire* of the Opéra from 1912 till 1922, was a composer, librettist, and music critic. Nor did it look particularly radical to the audience, though some critics remarked on its plotlessness, and its use of pre-existing music. See, for example, the review by one Nozière in *Le Théâtre - Revue bimensuelle illustrée*, 12 (1909): 12-15. Richard Buckle points out that a critic in *L'Intransigeant* (in an undated press clipping) noted that the visiting company had had the 'Russian impudence' to orchestrate Chopin. Buckle, *Diaghilev*, 151.

24. Programme book, 19 June 1909, Bibliothèque de l'Opéra, Paris, Carton 2238. Nijinska, however, writes: 'The advance publicity for the Saison Russe had hailed Nijinsky as a new Vestris, but once the public saw Nijinsky "lifted to heaven, weightless, above a group of sylphs", all comparison with Auguste Vestris vanished.' Nijinska, *Early Memoirs*, 275, no citation given for the quotation.

25. Lynn Garafola, ed. *Rethinking the Sylph: New Perspectives on the Romantic Ballet* (Hanover, NH: Wesleyan University Press, 1997).

Appendix 1

Some Productions of *La Sylphide*

is table does not offer a complete list of productions of *La Sylphide*, but rather is
ended to give some sense of the ballet's history and continuing presence in today's
•ertory.

In some cases it is difficult to differentiate a production from a performance, e.g.
igi Bretini's three *Silfides* of 1843-44 may not have varied enough to be listed as a
•arate productions, but I have listed them as such here. Also, declaring a work to
ve been staged 'after' or 'in the tradition of' is a complicated matter in many cases,
d the correctness of my decisions may be debated.

e of first ɔrmance	Place	Staging	Composer	Other
Mar. 1832	Paris Opéra	F. Taglioni	Schneitzhoeffer	Nourrit, uncredited librettist S: M. Taglioni; J: Mazilier; E: Noblet
uly 1832	Covent Garden, London	F. Taglioni	Attributed on the poster to Schneitzhoeffer and Adam[1]	S: M. Taglioni; J: Paul Taglioni; E: Amalia Galster Taglioni; Madge; Mr. Laporte; scenery: Grieve[2]
⸱2	Königliche Theater? Berlin[3]	F. Taglioni	Schneitzhoeffer	
⸱3	Theatre Royal, Dublin	F. Taglioni	?Schneitzhoeffer	S: M. Taglioni; J: Silvain; E: Garbois[4]
ɔril 1835 S. 28 May)	Bolshoi Theatre, St. Petersburg	Antoine Titus after Taglioni	?Schneitzhoeffer	
⸱5	London			S: Mlle Varin+
⸱pt. 1835	Théâtre de la Monnaie, Brussels	Victor Bartholomin (?after Taglioni)	Schneitzhoeffer	
Nov. 1836	Royal Danish Ballet, Royal Theater, Copenhagen	Bournonville; choreography by Bournonville	Løvenskiold	S: Grahn; J: Bournonville; Madge: Carl Fredstrup; Bournonville restaged it in Copenhagen in 1849, 1856, 1865, and 1867.
⸱. 1836	Bordeaux			S: Elssler; Elssler danced an interpolated pas de deux with her sister Thérèse in Act Two.[5]

Date of first performance	Place	Staging	Composer	Other
Dec. 1836	Marseilles			S: Mlle. Fourcisy[6]
1837	London			S: Pauline Duvernay+
5 May 1837	Carlo Felice, Genova	Cortesi		S: Lumelli J: Rosati***
8 Sept. 1837	La Pergola, Florence	Cortesi		S: Lumelli, Brugnoli; J: Rosati***
18 Sept. 1837 (O.S. 6 Sept.)	Bolshoi Theatre, St. Petersburg	F. Taglioni	?Schneitzhoeffer	S: M. Taglioni
30 Jan.1838	La Fenice, Venice	Cortesi		S: Brugnoli J: Matis***
1838	Brussels[7]			
Dec. 1838	Royal Theatre of São Carlos, Lisbon	Bernardo Vestris after Taglioni		Scenography: Giuseppe Cinatti & Achille Rambois[8]
22 May 1839	Park Theater, NY	Paul Taglioni	?Schneitzhoeffer	S: Amalia Galster Taglioni; J: Paul Taglioni
28 Sept. 1839	Regio, Turin	Cortesi		S: Groll J: Bretin
August 1840	Park Theater, NY		?Schneitzhoeffer	S: Fanny Elssler
1840	Munich[9]	unknown; choreography of F. Taglioni	Schneitzhoeffer	
27 Jan. 1841	La Scala, Milan	Cortesi after Taglioni	Gioachino Rossini, Antonio Mussi, Saverio Mercadante	S: Cerrito; J: F. Merante; design by B. Cavolotti and D. Menozzi 3 acts***[10]
29 May 1841	La Scala, Milan	Taglioni	*Passo a due* by Giuseppe Panizza	S: Taglioni J: F. Merante 3 acts***
1841	London			S: Cerrito[11]
Summer 1842	Eretenio, Vicenza	Taglioni		S: Taglioni; J: Matis 3 acts***
Autumn 1842	Civico, Alessandria	Ferdinando Rugali		S: Monticelli; J: Matis 4 acts***
15 Jan. 1843	Apollo, Rome	Luigi Bretin		S: Flora Fabbri Bretin; J: Luigi Br[etin] 3 acts***

f first nance	Place	Staging	Composer	Other
y 1843	Ducale, Parma	Luigi Bretin		S: Flora Fabbri Bretin; J: Luigi Bretin 3 acts***
val 44	Grande, Trieste	Luigi Bretin		S: Flora Fabbri Bretin; J: Luigi Bretin 3 parts***
	Bolshoi Theatre, Moscow	Théodore Guérinau ?after Taglioni	?Schneitzhoeffer	S: Aleksandra Veroniva Ivanova
n 1844	Comunitativo, Bologna	Cortesi		S: Taglioni; J: F. Merante***
	Melbourne	Charles Young		S: Eliza Young J: Charles Young[12]
rch 1845	Grande, Trieste	Taglioni	Giuseppe Alessandro Scaramelli	S: Taglioni; J: F. Merante***
1845	San Benedetto, Venice	Cortesi		S: Taglioni; J: Penco***
	London			S: Miss Ballin+
845	Her Majesty's, London			S: Taglioni+
val 46	Civico, Cagliari	Giuseppe Lasina***		
rch 1846		Giovanni Galzerani		S: Taglioni; J: Penco 3 acts***
val 1846	Sociale, Vogherea	Nicola Libonati?		S: Vencenzina Libonati; J: Vienna***
val 7 ia	Del Pavone, Gambardella	Raffaello		S: Clotilde Gambardella; J: Raffaello Gambardella***
. 1848	La Scala, Milan	Andrea Palladino		S: Maywood; J: Nikitin? Perrot?***
ril 1851	Borgognissanti, Florence	Agosto Panni		S: Lamanta; J: Fissi***
ne 1851	San Carlo, Naples	Andrea Palladino	Giuseppe Giaquinto	S: Zaccaria; J: F. Merante***
	London			S: Marie Taglioni (the younger)+
	London			S: Regina Forli+
val 55	Civico, Cuneo	Antonio Giuliani		S: Lazzeri; J: Bavassino 3 acts***

Date of first performance	Place	Staging	Composer	Other
Carnival 1856	Comuale?, Modena	Cortesi***		
1856?	Regio Carolino, Palermo	David Costa	Luigi Alfano (*passo a due*), Agostino Auriemma (*passo a solo*)	S: Boschetti; J: David Costa***
Carnival 1859-60	S. Ferdinando, Palermo	Tommaso Ferranti		3 acts***
Carnival 1860-61	Regio, Turin	Federico Massini		S: Priora; J: Durand***
Carnival 1860-61	Canobbiana, Milan	Federico Massini	Basso, Boro, and Carignani	S: Enrichetta Massini; J: Giovann Della Croce***
1 April 1862	Kungliga Teatern, Sweden	August Bournonville		Design: F. Ahlgrensson; 11 performances*
1891	Royal Danish Ballet	Hans Beck, after Bournonville[13]		
19 Jan. 1892 (O.S. 7 Jan.)	Maryinsky Theatre, St. Petersburg	Petipa, after Taglioni	additional music by Drigo	S: Vavara Nikitina; scenery Henrykh Levot and M. I. Bochar cos. E..P. Ponomoryov
9 April 1922	State Academic Theater for Opera and Ballet, Petrograd	Vladimir Ponomoryov after Petipa		
2 Feb. 1925	Bolshoi Ballet, Moscow	Vasily Tikhomirov after Petipa		S: Ekaterina Geltser; J: Tikhomir
1939	Royal Danish Ballet	Valborg Borschsenius and Harald Lander		
Dec. 1946	Ballet des Champs-Elysées, Théâtre des Champs-Elysées	Victor Gsovsky in the tradition of Taglioni[14]	Schneitzhoeffer, re-orchestrated by Grégoire Krettly[15]	S: Nina Vyroubova; J: Roland Pet costumes: Christian Bérard; scenery: A. Serebriakov; books a MSS were consulted by Roland Petit and Boris Kochno in the cre tion of the choreography; fp London, Winter Garden Theatre 1947.[16]
9 Dec. 1953	Grand Ballet du Marquis de Cuevas, Théâtre de l'Empire, Paris	Harald Lander after Bournonville	Løvenskiold	scen and cos: Barnard Daydé. fp La Scala Ballet, Milan, 18 Jan. 1962 with scenery and cos: Nicolas Benois; fp American Ballet Theatre,

of first rmance	Place	Staging	Composer	Other
				San Antonio Municipal Auditorium, 11 Nov. 1964 with additional music by Edgar Cosma[17]; scenery and cos: Robert O'Hearn; fp in NY at NY State Theater, 13 March 1965 by American Ballet Theatre.
eb. 1958	Royal New Zealand Ballet, New Zealand	Poul Gnatt	Løvenskiold	Design: Rigmore Gnatt; 101 performances*
b. 1960	Scandinavian Ballet, Vaxjö, Sweden; Vaxjö Theater	Elsa Marianne von Rosen after Bournonville (including dance and mime sequences reconstructed by Ellen Price)	Løvenskiold	S: Margrethe Schanne; von Rosen; J: Stanley Williams, Flemming Flindt; Design: Elvin Gay; 250 performances; fp Ballet Rambert, Sadler's Wells Theatre 20 July 1960; Alexander Bennett was among those dancing the role of James; scenery and cost: Robin and Christopher Ironside. 134 performances; fp by National Ballet of Washington, Washington D.C. Lisner Auditorium, 26 March 1969, scenery and cos: Robin and Christopher Ironside (Dame Margot Fonteyn appeared as guest); fp 1 Nov. 1974, Stora Teatern, Göteborg Sweden, design: Anna Gisle; 56 performances[18]
uly 1960	Ballet Rambert (Rambert Dance Company)	Elsa Marianne von Rosen after Bournonville	Løvenskiold	Design: Robert and Christopher Ironside; 134 performances*
an. 1962	Teatro Alla Scala, Milan	Harald Lander after Bournonville	Løvenskiold	Design: Nicolas Benois*
une 1963	Teatro Municipal Santiago, Chile	Elsa Marianne von Rosen	Løvenskiold	Design: Emilio Hermansen*
Nov. 1964	American Ballet Theatre	Harald Lander after Bournonville	Løvenskiold	Design: Robert O'Hearn
Dec. 1964	Bremen Ballet, Theater der Freien Hansestadt	Richard Adama in the tradition of Taglioni	Schneitzhoeffer	Scenery and cos: Karm-Ernst Hermann
Dec. 1964	National Ballet of Canada	Erik Bruhn after Bournonville	Løvenskiold	Scenery and cos: Robert Prévost; fp Royal Swedish Ballet, Stockholm, Kungliga Teatern 3 June 1968; design: Yngve Gamlin, 16 perform-

Date of first performance	Place	Staging	Composer	Other
				ances; fp American Ballet The NY State Theater, July 1971; Nureyev as guest artist with National Ballet of Canada at N Opera House, Spring 1973; fp Teatro dell'Opera di Roma, 22 1973, design: Enrico D'Assia, performances[19]
15 Aug. 1967	Royal Danish Ballet, Royal Theatre, Copenhagen	Hans Brenaa and Flemming Flindt after Bournonville	Løvenskiold	fp Covent Garden, London, 29 1968
19 Nov. 1967	Opéra de Monte Carlo	Elsa Marianne von Rosen after Bournonville	Løvenskiold	Design: Reinhardt after R. and Ironside*
1968	Glasgow	Alexander Bennett after Taglioni and Petipa	Schneitzhoeffer	S: Noreen Sopwith; J: Alexand Bennett
1968	Ballet de Monte Carlo	Elsa Marianne von Rosen after Bournonville	Løvenskiold	S: Fracci; J: Nureyev; M: von Ro
1 June 1968	Kungliga Theatern	Erik Bruhn, John Price	Løvenskiold	Design: Yngve Gamlin; 16 per ances*
22 Jan. 1969	Norwegian National Ballet	Terry Westmoreland after Bournonville	Løvenskiold	Design: Alistair Powell*
26 March 1969	Washington Ballet	Elsa Marianne von Rosen after Bournonville	Løvenskiold	Design: Robert and Christophe Ironside*
23 April 1971	Miami Ballet	Frederick Franklin after Bournonville	Løvenskiold	Design: Robert and Christophe Ironside; 2 performances*
7 July 1971	American Ballet Theatre	Erik Bruhn after Bournonville	Løvenskiold	See above, Erik Bruhn's produ for the National Ballet of Cana
1 Jan. 1972 (French television) 7 June 1972	French Television; Paris Opéra	Pierre Lacotte in the tradition of Taglioni	Schneitzhoeffer; music for *pas de trios* Act One from *L'ombre* by Ludwig	French television: S: G.Thesm M. Denard Paris Opéra: S: N. Pontois; J: C

te of first formance	Place	Staging	Composer	Other
ris Opéra)			Maurer	Atanasoff; scenery: Marie Claire Musson after Ciceri; costumes. Michel Fresnay after Lami
Feb. 1973	Teatro dell' Opera di Roma	Erik Bruhn after Bournonville	Løvenskiold	Design: Enrico D'Assia; 6 performances*
ov. 1974	Stora Teatern, Göteborg	Elsa Marianne von Rosen after Bournonville	Løvenskiold	Design: Anna Gisle; 56 performances*
an. 1975	Capab Ballet, South Africa	Hans Brenaa after Bournonville	Løvenskiold	Design: Peter Cazalet; 56 performances*
June 1975	Kirov Opera and Ballet	Elsa Marianne von Rosen after Bournonville	Løvenskiold	Design: Oleg Vinogradov; 210 performances*
July 1975	Companie Rosella Hightower	Ingrid Glindemann, Rosella Hightower	Løvenskiold	2 performances*
75	Maly Ballet (now Mikhailovsky Ballet), Leningrad (now St. Petersburg)	Elsa Marianne von Rosen after Bournonville	Løvenskiold	
77-78 season	Pittsburgh Ballet Theater	Frederick Franklin		
April 1979	Bayerische Staatsoper	Kirsten Ralov after Løvenskiold	Løvenskiold	Design: Andrej Mayewski*
gust, 1979	London Festival Ballet (now called English National Ballet)	Peter Schaufuss after Bournonville	Løvenskiold, with restorations from the original score[22]	Scenery: David Walker[23] ; 117 performances Niels Bjorn Larsen, guest artist, in the role of Madge; this production later entered the repertories of several other companies, including the Stuttgart Ballet, the Deutsche Oper Berlin and Roland Petit's Ballet National de Marseilles[24] ; it replaced Henning Kronstam's version when Schaufuss was named head of the Royal Danish Ballet in 1994[25]

Date of first performance	Place	Staging	Composer	Other
26 Sept. 1979	The Royal New Zealand Ballet	Patricia Rianne after Hans Brenaa	Løvenskiold	Design: Raymond Boyce; 38 performances*
3 Oct. 1980	Pittsburgh Ballet Theatre	Kirsten Ralov, Lizzie Rode	Løvenskiold	Design: Robert and Christophe Ironside*
30 April 1981	Kiev Opera- and Balletteater	Oleg Vinogradov after Elsa Marianne von Rosen	Løvenskiold	Design: Vjacheslav Okunev; 105 performances*
6 April 1982	Stuttgart Ballet	Peter Schaufuss, Mona Vangsaae	Løvenskiold	Design: David Walker; 19 performances*
14 May 1982	Deutsche Oper Berlin	Peter Schaufuss, Mona Vangsaae	Løvenskiold	Design: David Walker; 41 performances*
14 Oct. 1982	The Royal New Zealand Ballet	Harry Haythorne after Patricia Rianne	Løvenskiold	Design: Raymond Boyce; 35 performances*
25 Dec. 1982	Estonia Teater	Oleg Vinogradov	Løvenskiold	Design: Igor Svanov; 60 performances*
3 Feb. 1983	American Ballet Theatre	Erik Bruhn	Løvenskiold	
16 Feb. 1983	Louisville Ballet Company	Erik Bruhn	Løvenskiold	Design: Paul Owen; 12 performances*
19 March 1983	Bolsjoj, Minsk	Oleg Vinogradov after Elsa Marianne von Rosen	Løvenskiold	Design: I. Ivanon; 54 performa
22 April 1983	BalletMet (Ballet Metropolitan)	Paol Gnatt after Bournonville	Løvenskiold	6 performances*
14 Dec. 1983	Teatro Communale Firenze	Peter Schaufuss after Bournonville	Løvenskiold	Design: David Walker; 7 performa
3 March 1984	Teatr Wielki Warsaw	Kirsten Ralov	Løvenskiold	Design: Jadwiga Jarosiewicz*
Oct. 1984	Ballet de Santiago	Ivan Nagy	Løvenskiold	Design: Sergio Zapata; 12 performances*

e of first ormance	Place	Staging	Composer	Other
34	Milwaukee Ballet Company	Toni Lander after Bournonville	Løvenskiold*	
Dec. 1984	Kazan Opera- and Ballet	Xenia Ter- Stepanova	Løvenskiold	Design: Anna Kazhdan; 63 performances*
March 1985	Dallas Ballet	Flemming Flindt	Løvenskiold	Design: Robert O'Hearn; 4 performances*
rch 1985	Pennsylvania Ballet, Philadelphia Academy of Music	Peter Martins, Robert Weiss, Solveig Østergaard, after Bournonville	Løvenskiold	S: Melissa Podcasy; J: Marin Boieru; G: Jeffrey Gribler; Madge: Edward Myers
il 1985	Lithuania Opera and Ballet	Oleg Vinogradov	Løvenskiold	Design: Irina Sokolova; 72 performances*
Oct. 1985	The Australian Ballet	Erik Bruhn	Løvenskiold	Design: Anne Fraser; 76 performances*
ruary 1986	San Francisco Ballet	Peter Martins after August Bournonville, staged by Solveig Ostergaard	Løvenskiold	S: Lupukhova, Cowden, Van Dyck; J: Gil; Sohm, Dow; Madge: Courtney, Caniporoli; sets borrowed from Pennsylvania Ballet[26]
Feb. 1987	Hong Kong Ballet	Patricia Rianne after Hans Brenaa	Løvenskiold	Design: Brian Tilbrook and Kim Baker*
Sept. 1987	London City Ballet	Solveig Østergaard	Løvenskiold	Design: Peter Farmer; 110 performances*
t. 1987	Dallas Ballet; Majestic Theater	Flemming Flindt after Bournonville	added pas de tois, with music of Løvenskiold arranged by Chuck Mandernach	S: Evelyne Desutter; J: Jacob Sparso; G: Kevin Sparso; E: Krista Welch; Madge: Vivi Flindt[27]
Oct. 1987	San Francisco Ballet	Helgi Tomasson	Løvenskiold	Design: Jose Varona; 12 performances*
May 1988	Teatro alla Scala	Flemming Flindt	Løvenskiold	Design: Luisa Spinatelli*
ct. 1988	Boston Ballet Company	Dinna Bjørn	Løvenskiold	Design: Jose Varona; 11 performances*
88	Royal Danish Ballet	Henning Kronstam and	Løvenskiold	

Date of first performance	Place	Staging	Composer	Other
		Anne Marie Vessel after Hans Brenaa[28]		
9 March 1989	The Royal Ballet of Flandern	Vivi Flindt after Flemming Flindt	Løvenskiold	Design: Roger Bernard*
1989	Bayerische Staatsballett	Dinna Bjørn	Løvenskiold*	
1990s	Twin Cities Ballet Bloomington Illinois	Alexander Bennett after Bournonville & Taglioni	Schneitzhoeffer	
16 Feb. 1990	Ballett der Wiener Staatsoper	Peter Schaufuss	Løvenskiold	Design: David Walker; 16 performances*
3 April 1990	The Norwegian National Ballet	Dinna Bjørn	Løvenskiold	Design: Alistair Powell; 12 performances*
28 Aug. 1990	The Royal New Zealand Ballet	Poul Gnatt	Løvenskiold	Philip Markham; 29 performance
30 Dec. 1990	Odessa Opera and Ballet	K. M. Ter-Stepanova	Løvenskiold	Design: I. I. Press*
26 March 1991	Teatro dell' Opera di Roma	Peter Schaufuss after Bournonville	Løvenskiold	Design: David Walker; 9 performan
21 Oct. 1991	Ballet Iowa	Kennet Oberly	Løvenskiold*	
24 Nov. 1991	Tbilisi Opera and Ballet, Georgia	Nikita Dongushin	Løvenskiold*	
1994	Bolshoi Ballet	Oleg Vinogradov after von Rosen after Bournonville	Løvenskiold	S: Nadezhda Gracheva; J: Sergei Fi
1994	Royal Danish Ballet	Peter Schaufuss after Bournonville	Løvenskiold	
1997	Royal Danish Ballet	Dinna Bjørn after Bournonville	Løvenskiold++	

e of first formance	Place	Staging	Composer	Other
‣9	National Ballet of China	Frank Andersen after Bournonville	Løvenskiold++	
‣9	Inoue Ballet	Frank Andersen after Bournonville	Løvenskiold++	
‣9	Royal Swedish Ballet	Frank Andersen after Bournonville	Løvenskiold++	
‣ch 2001	Dutch National Ballet	Dinna Bjørn after Bournonville	Løvenskiold	
‣3	Royal Danish Ballet	Nikolaj Hübbe after Bournonville	Løvenskiold	
‣3/4	Arizona Ballet	Nikolaj Hübbe		
‣5	National Ballet of Canada, Toronto	Nikolaj Hübbe	Løvenskiold*	
‣5	Royal Ballet, Covent Garden	Johan Kobborg, Sorella Englund after Bournonville	Løvenskiold**	
‣7	National Ballet of Estonia	Frank Andersen after Bournonville	Løvenskiold[30]	
Feb. 2008	Bolshoi Ballet, Bolshoi Theatre, New Stage	Johan Kobberg after Bournonville	Løvenskiold	S: Osipova; J: Vyacheslav Lopatin; Madge: Irina Zibrova (in other casts male Madges, Gennady Yanin, Johan Kobberg[31])
‣ 2009	Eisenhower Theatre, Washington Ballet, Washington D.C.	Thomas Lund, Sorella Englund after Bournonville	Løvenskiold	
‣0	Teatr Wielki Warsaw			
‣. 2011	Guangzhou Ballet	Pierre Lacotte in the tradition of Taglioni	Schneitzhoeffer	
‣ 2012	Wiener Staatsopera Ballet	Pierre Lacotte in the tradition of Taglioni	Schneitzhoeffer	

Unless otherwise noted, information in this table comes from the *Dictionary catalog of the Dance Collection: a list of authors, titles, and subjects of multi-media materials in the Dance Collection of the Performing Arts Research Center of the New York Public Library* (New York: New York Public Library, Astor, Lenox, and Tilden Foundations; Boston: distributed by G. K. Hall, 1974) and supplements to the *Dictionary catalog,* published as *New York Public Library Dance Collection: Bibliographic Guide to Dance* (Boston: G. K. Hall, 1975-2003).

* Karen Vedel, 'Survey of Bournonville Ballets Worldwide', in *Bournonvilleana,* ed. Marianne Hallar and Allette Scavenius (Copenhagen: Rhodos, 1992), 255-57.

** Erik Aschengreen, Chapter 5 of the present volume.

*** Ornella di Tondo, Chapter 8 of the present volume.

\+ Ivor Guest, '"La Sylphide" in London', *Ballet* 6, no. 3 (1948): 41.

++Anne Middelboe Christensen, 'Deadly sylphs and decent mermaids: the women in the Danish romantic world of August Bournonville', in *The Cambridge Companion to Ballet,* ed. Marion Kant (Cambridge: Cambridge University Press, 2007), 126-27.

1. Guest, '"La Sylphide" in London', 41.
2. Beaumont, *Complete Book of Ballets,* 85-86 and Guest, '"La Sylphide" in London', 39-43, 45.
3. Jean-Madeleine Schneitzhoeffer, *Filippo Taglioni, Die Sylphide, Ballet in 2 Abtheilungen [libretto]* (Berlin, 1832)., posted on line by the Bayerische Staatsbibliothek at http://daten.digitale-sammlungen.de/~db/0005/bsb00058359/images/index.html?id=00058359&fip=xsfsdreay aeayawxdsydsdassdasxdsydsdasewq&no=7&seite=5 [accessed 29 August 2011]
4. Dublin newspaper clippings (titles difficult to discern) in Marie Taglioni's scrapbook, pp. 71-79, fonds Taglioni [R2, Bibliothèque de l'Opéra.
5. *Revue et Gazette Musicale,* 11 Sept. 1836, p. 320.   Fanny Elssler danced a *pas* with her sister Thérèse in *La Sylphide* in Paris as well. See Gautier, *La Presse,* 24 Sept. 1838, in *Gautier on Dance,* ed. Ivor Guest (London: Dance Books, 1986), 142.
6. *Revue et Gazette Musicale,* 11 Dec. 1836 (mistakenly dated 41 Dec.), 439.
7. *Revue et Gazette Musicale,* 28 January 1838, 40.
8. Almanacco di Gherardo Casaglia, on Amadeus online, http://www.amadeusonline.net/ almanacco.php?Start=450&Giorno=&Mese=12&Anno=&Giornata=Domenica&Testo=&Parola=Stringa [accessed 6 September 2011]
9. Schneitzhoeffer, Jean-Madeleine. *Filippo Taglioni, Die Sylphide, Ballet in 2 Abtheilungen* [libretto], Munich, 1840[?], posted on line by the Bayerische Staatsbibliothek at http://daten.digitale-sammlungen.de/~db/0005/bsb00058361/images/ [accessed 29 August 2011]
10. *Dictionary catalog of the Dance Collection* and Ornella Di Tondo, Ch. 8 of the present volume.
11. Guest, '"La Sylphide" in London', 42 and 'Fanny Cerrito,' in *Waldie's select circulating library* Vol. 16 ([Philadelphia]: A. Waldie, 1841), 15.
12. Blazanka Brysha,'Ballet', eMelbourne, http://www.emelbourne.net.au/biogs/EM00147b.htm, [accessed August 30, 2011]
13. This volume, Chapter 7.
14. Léandre Vaillat, noting the claim 'Chorégraphie d'après Ph. Taglioni' in the programme, wondered if M. Roland Petit had found the transcription of the choreography. 'I would be very surprised if he had.' Léandre Vaillat, 'Danse – *La Sylphide*', *Le Carrefour,* 9 January 1947 in *La Sylphide,* dossier d'oeuvre, Bibliothèque de l'Opéra.
15. René Dumesnil, 'Ballet des Champs-Elysées – *La Sylphide*', *Le Monde,* 7 January 1847 in *La Sylphide,* dossier d'oeuvre, Bibliothèque de l'Opéra.
16. Royal Opera House Collections Online, http://www.rohcollections.org.uk/record.aspx?ref =110002587&collection=Frank%20Sharman%20Photographic%20Collection&row=

8&searchtype=collection&company=Les%20Ballets%20des%20Champs-Elysées, [accessed 29 September 2011]

17. Jack Anderson, in a review of a 1984 revival of Lander's production by the Milwaukee Ballet, writes that 'Musically, [Lander's version] was unconventional because Lander had the original score by Herman Lovenskjold reorchestrated by Edgar Cosma, a contemporary composer who lives in Paris. Mr. Cosma also added new music of his own. What resulted was a peculiar mixture. Much of the time, fortunately, the music proceeded in a fashion that sounded quite acceptably Romantic in atmosphere. However, Mr. Cosma occasionally seemed to feel an urge to add piquant 'moderne' harmonies to the old tunes. It was as if Lovenskjold in 1836 had sent his score via time machine to be touched up by Les Six.' *New York Times*, 3 June 1984.

18. *Dictionary catalog of the Dance Collection:* Marianne Hallar and Alette Scavenius, *Bournonvilleana*, trans. Gaye Kynoch (Copenhagen: Rhodos, 1992), 255-57; and this volume, Chapter 6.

19. *Dictionary catalog of the Dance Collection* and Hallar and Scavenius, *Bournonvilleana*, 255.

20. Alexander Bennett, unpublished manuscript.

21. Erik Aschengreen, Chapter 5 of the present volume.

22. See Erik Aschengreen, 'Bournonville Style and Tradition', *Dance Research* 4, no. 1 (1986): 61.

23. Anna Kisselgoff, 'A New and Longer 'Sylphide' from London', *New York Times*, 5 July 1989.

24. Octavio Roca, 'Timeless "Sylphide" From Danish Ballet - Revamped version in Orange County,' *San Francisco Chronicle*, 27 May 1995.

25. Lewis Segal, 'Out of Step? Peter Schaufuss' staging of 'La Sylphide' has been criticized on questions of taste, style and tone – so has his reign as artistic director of the Royal Danish Ballet.' *Los Angeles Times*, 21 May 1995.

26. Martin Bernheimer, 'S.F. "Sylphide": Borrowed Bournonville', *Los Angeles Times*, 23 February 1986.

27. Jack Anderson, 'Dallas Ballet in Lengthened Sylphide,' *New York Times*, 29 September 1987.

28. Christensen, 'Deadly sylphs and decent mermaids: the women in the Danish romantic world of August Bournonville,' 126-27; Martin Bernheimer, 'A Royal 'Sylphide' for All Seasons,' *Los Angeles Times*, 12 June 1992.

29. Ismene Brown, 'Made of Air,' *Dance Now* (2008), http://web.me.com/cijc/ismeneb.com/A-K_files/Made%20of%20Air.pdf [accessed 4 September 2011].

30. Frank Anderson home page, http://www.frank-andersen.com/default.asp?ID=232 [accessed 22 September 2011]

31. Brown, 'Made of Air'.

Appendix 2

French libretto of *La Sylphide*, English Translation

The Sylphide,
Ballet

Characters
La Sylphide
James Reuben, Scots peasant
Anne Reuben, his mother
Effie, peasant, Anne's niece
Gurn, Scots peasant
Old Madge, witch
Sylphides
Witch
Sylphides
Scots peasants and old people
Witches
The scene takes place in Scotland.

FIRST ACT

The stage represents a Scottish farmhouse. At the back there is a door; a raised window to the right of the door; on the same side, near the front of the stage, a large fireplace; on the opposite side, a small staircase leading to the apartments occupied by the farmer's wife and her family. Daybreak.

Scene i

James and Gurn are sleeping, James in a big armchair near the front of the stage, Gurn further away on bundles of straw. At the rise of the curtain, a sylphide is kneeling at James's feet; she contemplates him lovingly, and expresses her joy at being so near to the one she loves. She flies around him, and places herself above his head, beating her blue wings to refresh the air he breathes. James's sleep is disturbed, and he seems to follow the sylphide's movements. Spurred on by her desire, which she tries in vain to restrain, she approaches him gently and kisses his forehead. He suddenly awakens, and throws himself at the feet of the sylphide, who eludes his pursuits and disappears up the chimney. He is troubled by this mysterious apparition, which more than once has charmed his sleep. He searches in vain to persuade himself that it is a dream. No, his senses do not betray him; he was truly awake, and his forehead is still warm from the kiss he received. But Gurn was there

— perhaps he saw the sylphide. He must be questioned. James awakens him and plies him with questions. Gurn was sleeping deeply, and all he saw, in a dream, was the lovely Effie, with whom he is desperately in love, despite her preference for James. This recollection soothes James's mind. He must forget this fantastic being who follows him everywhere, and think only of his love for Effie. In a few hours they will be married, and a happy future lies ahead of them.

Scene ii

Effie enters, arm-in-arm with Mother Anne Reuben. Gurn rushes eagerly to the young Scots girl's side, greets her timidly, and offers as a decoration for her straw hat the feathers of a heron he has killed. Effie thanks him graciously, and approaches James, who, ever pre-occupied, didn't see his fiancée drawing near. — What are you thinking about?— James comes back to her: I was thinking... I was thinking of you, my pretty cousin. — You're deceiving me. —No, I assure you. — You are sad, James, yet it is today that we will be betrothed! — Oh! I am happy, my dear Effie, because I love you and wish never to love anyone but you. — Very good. She gives him her hand to kiss; Gurn steps forward and he, too, wishes to take the young girl's hand; she withdraws it, and James rushes up, placing himself between her and his rival, whom he threatens and ridicules. Gurn leaves in shame, hiding his tears, which he cannot hold back. His chagrin doubles when he sees Mother Anne placing Effie's hand in that of her cousin. The young couple kneel and receive Mother Anne's blessing.

Scene iii

Effie's friends arrive, each of them carrying her wedding gift: a plaid, a belt, a crown, wedding veil, bouquet, etc. The young girls congratulate James on his marriage, and laugh at the chagrin of Gurn, who would like to enlist them to speak in his favor. Effie kisses her companions and thanks them, and while she joyously adorns herself with the gifts she has received, James, ever distracted, drifts involuntarily toward the chimney. The image of the sylphide remains before his eyes, and his glances turn toward the place where she disappeared. What does he see? A hideous figure: it is Madge the witch, who has come in behind the young girls. — What are you doing there?— I am afraid of the storm and I am looking for shelter. — Leave this place at once, you daughter of hell; your presence is a bad omen. Leave, and keep your wretched face out of our sight! The young girls intercede in favor of the old woman. Madge knows all, and she is going to predict when it shall be their turn to marry. The witch examines each girl's palm.— Soon you will find happiness, she says to the first one. — And me? — Alas! never! — And me? — You're just a child; I have nothing to say to you. — And me? asks a fourth girl. Madge looks at her malevolently. You know that nothing is hidden from me! — Well, speak up.... — The old woman whispers into her ear; the young girl blushes, and dashes away, her eyes lowered. Effie, for her turn, asks if she will be happy in her domestic life. — Yes, responds the gypsy. — My fiancé loves me as much as I love him? — She examines James' hand. No. — James, irritated, begs Effie to ignore the old woman's predictions. Gurn then presents his hand to Madge. — Oh! This one loves you truly, Effie, and perhaps before long you shall regret rejecting his love. James's anger is redoubled; he chases the witch furiously while Gurn makes a last effort to stop Effie's marriage to her cousin. — The witch told you I'm the one who deserves preference. — The young girls make fun of him, and Effie tries to calm James and assure him that she doesn't believe the gypsy's words.

Mother Anne puts an end to this scene by reminding her niece that she must prepare herself for the wedding ceremony, and that little time remains for her to do so. Anne, Effie and the young girls leave by a staircase which leads to the interior of the farmhouse. Gurn goes to the other side while sadly looking at Effie. James wants to follow his intended, but the young girls stop him, and before leaving, Effie sends him a farewell kiss from afar.

Scene iv

James, now left alone, can at first can think of nothing but the joy of marrying his pretty cousin. But soon, the memory of the sylphide returns to his thoughts. — What can this delicious vision possibly be, this vision which comes every night to bewitch my sleep? Could it be my good angel? Could it be a benevolent fairy who watches over my destiny? Never mind; I shall put it out of my thoughts. All of a sudden, the window opens as if blown by a gust of wind. James turns around and sees the sylphide nestled in a corner of the window. She is sad, and hides her face in her hands. James invites her to come forward, and she descends by gliding down the wall. James asks her what is the matter; she refuses to answer him, but gazes at him tenderly. He asks her again to confide her chagrin. — Oh! Can't you tell what is the matter with me? You are going to marry Effie! — What does it matter? — Alas, you can't understand my love. — What! You love me? That's not possible! You wish to play on my credulity.— The first day when I saw you, my destiny was attached to yours. Visible or not, I am always near you. This foyer is my sanctuary; in the daytime, I accompany you to the depths of the forest, to the steep crags of our mountains. At night, I drive away the evil spirits from your cottage, and keep watch at your bedside, and your dreams of love: it is I who sends them to you.— James is deeply moved, and his heart is touched by the sylphide's love. She wishes to know if he is responding to her tenderness. — Duty prevents me; I have pledged myself to Effie, and I love no one but her. — The sylphide is in despair; she wants nothing any more than death, for he does not love her. She moves away from him; he will see her no more.

James is touched by her appeal; he seeks in vain to hide his agitation; that which has transpired in his heart is incomprehensible. Despite his love for Effie, the image of the sylphide follows him everywhere and he cannot help but love her.

The sylphide evinces the greatest joy, and takes flight anew, flying around the young man while beating her wings. Then making the most of his confusion, she seeks to lead him away. — What is your wish? — Come, come with me! — Abandon Effie? No, I would sooner die. Go away! You are only a vain shadow who seeks to fool my senses. — He disengages himself from her arms and pushes her away with contempt. The sylphide wraps herself in the plaid Effie had left on the armchair as she left, and when James comes back, he finds at his feet the sylphide, recalling the image of his beloved. At this sight James' reason fails him, he bids the sylphide rise; he presses her to his heart, and gives her a kiss.

Scene v
Gurn, who has entered at the end of the previous scene, rushes to alert Effie that she is being betrayed by her fiancé; he has crept furtively down the staircase leading to the farmhouse. When he returns, he enters first and sees James in the arms of the young woman, and signals to Effie and her companions to approach. At the first sound, James hides the sylphide in the armchair and covers her with the plaid. But Gurn had already seen everything and advances, leading Effie. James wishes first to keep her from coming forward, but Effie looks at him worriedly. He lowers his eyes and remains immobile. Gurn and Effie raise the plaid; the sylphide has disappeared...... The young girls burst out laughing; Effie is vexed with Gurn, who in order to excite her jealousy, has now unjustly accused poor James, who is yet more agitated; Gurn is confused.

Scene vi
The entire village has come to celebrate the betrothal of James and Effie. The old people sit down at the table and drink from jugs of ale; the young people dance. — Divertissement.

During the dancing, James is continually preoccupied, and seems to be looking for his aerial beloved. He is so distracted that he forgets to invite his fiancée to dance; it is she who must ask him. In the middle of the groups formed by the dancers, the sylphide appears several times, visible only to James, who disrupts the contredanse by running after her. But she disappears at the moment when he believes he has caught her. No one knows what to make of his distractedness; doubtless the love he feels for his cousin has turned his head; they must hasten to marry, before he loses his senses altogether. The dancing ceases and they prepare for the betrothal ceremony; Effie's friends surround her. They place the bridal crown on her head, and hand her the bouquet, and she receives her engagement ring from old Mother Anne. All eyes are on Effie, and everyone congratulates her. Only James is not occupied by his fiancée; he is sad, and he leaves the group that encircles Effie; from his finger he removes the ring which he is to exchange with his cousin; he turns his head toward her and seems to wonder why he has met with such painful feelings at the moment when he is to be united with someone he has loved for so long. At that moment, the sylphide appears at the hearth and snatches up the ring that he holds in his hand; surprise and embarrassment of James. The sylphide will die if he marries Effie; she expresses the most violent despair. The young man tries to calm her; his efforts are in vain; she will die if he abandons her. James's reason is entirely confused: he no longer sees anything but the danger of losing his sylphide, and she profits from his agitation by leading him away; they disappear behind the crowd gathered around Effie.

The young girl is ready; she has received the farewell kiss from her friends. They call the bridegroom; he does not reply. Where is he? They search for him in vain. General surprise. Gurn has seen him flee with a woman toward the mountains. Sorrow of Effie, anger of Mother Anne, indignation of everyone. Gurn is triumphant, and reminds Effie of the witch's prediction. He tells her again of his love, and the young girls take his side. Effie cannot respond; she is in despair, indifferent to her friends' consolations. Mother Anne holds Effie in her arms and Gurn kneels before them.
Tableau.
End of the first act.

SECOND ACT
The stage represents a forest. To the left is the mouth of a cave formed by high rocks, along which a path opens. At the rise of the curtain it is still nighttime, and the forest is covered with a thick fog which allows only the nearest trees to be seen. At the front of the stage, slightly to the side, is a large beech tree.

Scene i
Old Madge is occupied with preparing for the Sabbath. She traces a circle and places at its center a cauldron, which she turns upside down on a tripod; she arranges the utensils around it: bellows, a pan, the skimmer, two spheres, a skull, animal craniums, a transparent vase containing writhing reptiles, a bag filled with dried herbs, etc. She circles the cauldron three times, striking it with a ladle. At this signal, there arrive twenty witches, riding broomsticks

and each holding a glowing lantern. They ride in a circle three times; each witch is accompanied by a hideous animal: an ape, a tiger cat, a long-tailed monkey, a pig, an enormous owl, a crocodile, etc. At Madge's gesture, the animals place themselves around the cauldron; they turn it rightside up and poke at the fire while jumping grotesquely. The witches leave their broomsticks and gather poisonous things to throw into the cauldron for the magic spell.   One brings toads, the other a snake, this one brings lizards, that one brings an old howling cat, wolf's teeth, hemlock, the feet of a goat and the ears of a cat. Madge pours out some liquid; thick smoke rises from the cauldron. The long-tailed she-monkey is charged with skimming the brew; the other animals blow air onto the fire with the bellows. Fantastic dance of the witches, which Madge brings to a halt after a short while. The cauldron is boiling; it overflows with foam. To work! To work! The witches mount their broomsticks and line up once again around the circle, each holding a glass. The animals crouch in front of the cauldron, forming a pulpit upon which Madge opens the large book of cabalistic signs. She casts the spell, and soaks various objects in the cauldron; these will become talismans. She distributes them to the witches, keeping a scarf for herself; she wraps herself up in it. After this procedure she again stirs the pot — a red flame leaps out, and with the ladle she fills the glasses, which the witches clink together while howling sharply; the animals answer. Glasses are emptied, the spell is cast; a new round. The witches set forth again on their broomsticks, just as they had arrived; the animals carry the utensils of the Sabbath, and all of them re-enter in the cave, in a chain formation. Towards the end of this scene the fog begins to dissipate, and one can see, little by little, a landscape which takes shape through the trees.

Scene ii
Above the rocks, the sylph is seen leading James by the hand. They arrive on the stage by a narrow and steep path which the young man descends fearfully while the Sylph guides his steps, gliding over the tops of the rocks; her feet no longer seem to touch the ground. — Where are you leading me? — To the place where I live. This is my kingdom; here that I want to hide you from all eyes and to make you forget your earthly home.

In spite of his love for the sylphide, James cannot help thinking of Effie, whom he has abandoned. In vain, in order to erase these painful memories from his mind, the sylphide tries to distract him with her airy dancing; always before his eyes is the image of his fiancée in tears. The sylphide then calls her sisters, and from all sides young sylphides with blue and pink wings are seen, brushing aside the branches of the trees and emerging from the groves of hawthorne and wild roses. James is astounded by this delightful sight, and the dance by the daughters of air soon dissolves his sadness. Some attach scarves to the trees and swing gently; others bend the tree branches down and then spring upward into the air.

James is in ecstasy; these graceful pictures exalt his imagination; he is more charmed than ever with the Sylph. Continually he wants to hold her, but she always escapes him; he follows her without ever being able to reach her, and at the moment when he thinks he has caught her, she eludes him. His excited desire becomes still more intense, and when he no longer sees the Sylph, who has disappeared among her friends, he seeks her worriedly and asks each one of them about her. The sylphs do not reply, and one by one they escape into the forest.

Scene iii
Alone, James is without hope; he has allowed himself to be fooled by a vain chimera; the Sylph does not love him, and in order to chase after this imaginary happiness, he has broken his promises and visited despair upon the one to whom he had promised joy. All is lost to him.

Scene iv
Old Madge has come out of the cave; she observes James's despair, and maliciously comes to ask him the cause of his grief. — I am very unhappy! I love a mysterious creature whom I cannot catch. She has deceived me with false tenderness, and just as I think I am about to attain happiness, she eludes me and leaves only remorse and despair in my soul; her love revealed the delights of heaven to me; but she is a demon who takes pleasure in breaking my heart. However, I love her more than ever, and I would give my life to keep her near me for a single moment. — I know the object of your passion; you love a sylphide. To catch her is not an easy thing; however, I have a solution.— Give, give it to me quickly, and all that I possess is yours. — Madge: But, this morning you refused to believe me; you threw me out unjustly.— Forget my mistake; you see me at your feet; forgive me in my repentance; restore my life to me by assuring me possession of the one I love. — I should punish you, but I am too kind-hearted, and I yield.... You see this scarf? Trust in its magic power and you will be happy. Wrap this gauze around the Sylph, and her wings will fall off; once deprived of her freedom, she will be beside you forever.

James throws himself at the witch's feet. Nothing is equal to his gratitude; a hundred times he kisses this marvelous talisman which will bring him good luck. The old woman leaves him, reminding him once again of the power of the scarf; he thanks her once again and leads her up to the entrance of the cave.
Scene v
On returning to the scene, he notices the Sylph among the branches of a tree,

playing with a nest of little birds; in order to attract her attention he lets the scarf fly up. The Sylph comes down and comes to offer him the nest which she holds in her hands in exchange for the scarf. — No, I do not want it; the poor little birds would die if they lost their freedom; you must give them back to their mother. —You are right. She goes and puts the nest back in the trunk of the tree and, coming back to James, she tries to get hold of the scarf, which he refuses to give up. He is angry with her; she is always flying off and never lets herself get caught. The Sylph insists on having the scarf and promises never to fly away again. James pretends to refuse again. She approaches him to take it away; then he wraps around her so she cannot draw up her arms. The Sylph is captured and she falls to her knees to ask for mercy; but James does not take the scarf away until he has seen her wings fall off. At the same moment, the sylphide has put her hand over her heart, as if struck by a fatal blow. James holds her in his arms, she repulses him; he throws himself at her feet ... mortal pallor covers the sylph's brow.

What have you done? — I have attached you to me, and from now on you belong to me and we will never be apart. — You have made a mistake! All is finished for me.... in taking away my freedom you have robbed me of my life. — What are you saying? —You see the pallor of my brow: soon I shall be forever deprived your love. — Woe is me. — Don't weep, you whom I have loved so dearly! I could not belong to you.... I was blessed by your love; but I could not bring you happiness.... Adieu, I shall die.... Here, take your betrothal ring.... hasten away, you can marry the one you loved before you knew me.... Adieu, I die content, because I carry the hope that you will be happy. —No, if I must lose you, I wish to die too.

At this moment the witch appears; she has come to rejoice at James' despair. — Monster, see your handiwork; you are the one who betrayed me. For such a light offense, did you really have to take such a strong revenge? Ah! May the heavens curse you, just as I do!

The strength of the sylphide is ebbing imperceptibly: her sisters arrive to surround her in her last moments, and she dies in their arms. James is at her knees, which he embraces, in tears. The sylphides cover their sister's face with a scarf, and carry her away through the air; some little sylphs hold her up while kissing her feet.

The witch laughs at James's sorrow, and points out his fiancée, who, acceding to Gurn's wishes, is on her way to be married at the chapel in the neighboring village. Through the trees of the forest the wedding procession can be seen, and the sound of wedding bells is heard in the distance.

All at once, everything overwhelms poor James, who casts a last glance at the sylphide and falls to the ground in a faint.

End of last act.

—Translated from the French by Marian Smith

Appendix 3

Danish libretto of *Sylphiden*, English translation

La Sylphide. A Romantic Ballet in Two Acts

The Characters
The Sylphide.
ANNA, a tenant farmer's widow.
JAMES, her son.
EFFY, her niece, James's bride.
GURN, a peasant lad.
MADGE, a fortune-teller.
Scottish Peasant Folk. Sylphides and Witches.

The scene is laid in Scotland.

Act One
A spacious room in a farmhouse. In the background, a door and a staircase leading to the sleeping chamber. To the right, a window. To the left, a high fireplace. Dawn.

James is asleep in a large armchair. A feminine being in airy raiment and with transparent wings is kneeling at his feet. Her arm is resting on the seat of the chair. With her hand beneath her chin, she fixes her loving gaze on the sleeping youth. She expresses the joy she feels in being near the one she loves. She hovers round him and flutters her wings in order to cool the air he breathes.

James slumbers restlessly. In his dreams he follows every one of the airy creature's movements and when, carried away with tenderness, she approaches him and lightly kisses his brow, he suddenly wakens, reaches out to grasp the lovely image and pursues it about the room as far as the fireplace, into which the Sylphide vanishes.

Beside himself at the sight of this vision, which has already enchanted him several times in dreams but now stood alive before his eyes, James awakens and questions the farmhands, who are sleeping in the same room. Confused and sleepy, they do not know what he is saying and do not understand his questions. He rushes out the door in order to see whether the Sylphide might still be outside; but he does not notice that in his haste he has run into Gurn, who has already been out hunting. Gurn and the farmhands regard one another with astonishment, but when James immediately returns to overwhelm them with questions about the airy figure who knelt by his couch, kissed his brow, fluttered about the room, and flew up through the chimney, their wonder dissolves into laughter and they strive to convince James that the whole thing has been a dream. James comes to himself again and remembers that this very day he is to be betrothed to his cousin, the amiable Effy. Vexed, Gurn leaves him, bemoaning the injustice he must suffer because of the superiority that Effy bestows upon this daydreamer.

James sends the farmhands away to prepare everything for the celebration and quickly finishes dressing in order to please his lovely bride. But as he draws closer to the fireplace, he falls ever deeper in thought. Effy is brought in by her aunt. Her first glance is directed at James, who takes no notice of her. Gurn, on the other hand, is immediately at her service. He begs her not to reject the spoils of the hunt and gives her a bouquet of fresh wild flowers. Effy rather absent-mindedly accepts his compliment and goes over to the thoughtful James in order to ask him what he is brooding about, whether he is distressed, and why. He begs her to forgive him for being so distracted and assures her that he is really very happy, especially today, when he shall be united to the one he loves and will live for eternally. Tender and happy, Effy gives him her hand to kiss. Gurn also tries to take one of her hands, but she quickly withdraws it. James threateningly steps between her and Gurn, who, ashamed and distraught, goes away in order to hide the tears he can no longer hold back. His sorrow is further augmented by seeing Anna unite the young couple who, kneeling, receive her blessing.

Some young girls, friends of Effy, come to congratulate the loving couple. They bring presents for the bride; a plaid, a scarf, a wreath, a veil, a bouquet; in short, everything that can delight her. Gurn begs them to put in a good word for him but they make fun of him and offer him their love amid laughter and teasing. Weeping, he tears himself loose and goes over to sit down in a corner.

Effy thanks and embraces her childhood playmates while James once more becomes lost in thought. He approaches the fireplace — but what does he see! A loathsome figure! Old Madge, the fortune-teller, who has stolen in among the young girls. 'What are you doing here?' 'I am warming myself by the fire!' 'Get away from here, witch! Your presence is an evil omen.' James is about to drive her away but the girls plead for her. Gurn bids her be seated and offers her a glass of spirits, which she greedily swallows.

Madge knows hidden things and the girls cannot resist their desire to know what lies in store for them. They surround the witch and hold out their hands in order to have her predict their fortunes. To one she promises happiness in marriage, while she tells the other she will never be wed. This one is but a child and gets no prediction at all, but another has her fate whispered in her ear, and walks away blushing. Finally, Effy asks if she will be happy in marriage? 'Yes!' is the answer. 'Does my bridegroom love me sincerely?' 'No!' James begs her not to believe this hateful old woman. Gurn also gets the desire to question Madge. 'AH!' she says, 'this man loves you with his heart and you will soon come to regret the fact that you have spurned his love.' James now becomes furious, seizes the fortune-teller, and hurls her to the door. Gurn quotes her statement and makes yet another effort to hinder the wedding he detests so much, but everyone laughs him to scorn and calms James by reassuring him that they do not believe at all in the prophecy.

Anna and the young girls follow Effy to her room to array her in festive dress. Gurn goes sadly away, looking back at Effy all the while. James wishes to accompany his beloved but the girls hold him back and Effy blows him a parting kiss. James is delighted with this amiable bride but the memory of the Sylphide soon returns to his soul. He cannot account for the nature of this being. Perhaps she is his good angel, a powerful fairy who watches over his destiny! With this, as if by a gust of wind, the casement opens. The Sylphide is seated in the corner, melancholy and hiding her face in her hands.

James bids her approach, and she glides down from the wall. He asks the cause of her grief, but she refuses to answer. When he continues to demand her confidence she finally confesses that his union with Effy constitutes her misfortune; from the first moment she saw him her fate was joined to his and this hearth is her favourite place of refuge. She hovers about him, visibly and invisibly, night and day, follows him on the hunt, among the wild mountains, watches over his sleep, wards off the evil spirits from his bed, and sends him gentle dreams. James has listened to her with mounting agitation. He is touched by the Sylphide's love, but does not dare to return it. Effy has received his vow: his heart belongs to her alone. The Sylphide rushes desperately away. She has nothing to hope for, only death to desire. James calls her back. He cannot hide his confusion; he does not understand what magic is controlling him; but despite his love for Effy he is enraptured by the Sylphide.

She expresses the liveliest joy, regains her airy lilt, and hovers about the youth as she flutters her transparent wings. She tries to use his agitated state of mind in order to lure him away with her, but he shudders at the thought of deserting Effy, tears himself loose from the Sylphide, and spurns her. But the Sylphide has wrapped herself in Effy's plaid, and when he turns around he finds her at his feet, reminding him of the beloved object. James is intoxicated at this sight. He raises the Sylphide, presses her to his heart, and enthusiastically kisses her.

Gurn, who has witnessed part of the foregoing scene, hastens to acquaint Effy with everything that has happened, but when James hears a noise he hides the Sylphide in the armchair and covers her with the plaid. Gurn has summoned Effy and her friends in order to take the unfaithful bridegroom by surprise. At first, they see nothing at all. However suspicion soon falls on the covered armchair. James is bewildered; Effy turns pale with jealousy and, together with Gurn, lifts the plaid aside. The Sylphide has vanished. The girls laugh. Effy becomes angry at Gurn, who stands ashamed and startled.

All of the villagers arrive to celebrate the betrothal of James and Effy. The old folk sit down at table while the young ones enjoy merry dancing. James is so distracted that he forgets to ask his bride to dance. It is she who invites him. But in the midst of the dance he perceives the Sylphide, who is visible only to him and then disappears once more. He forgets everything in trying to reach her, but she always eludes him and the guests think it is high time James was married since he stands in danger of losing his reason from sheer affectionate longing.

The dancing ceases and the bride is adorned for the ceremony. Anna gives her the ring which she shall exchange for that of her bridegroom, and everyone surrounds her with congratulations and expressions of sympathy. James alone is melancholy. He stands apart from the others with the betrothal ring in his hand. The Sylphide emerges from the fireplace, snatches the ring from him, and signifies with an expression of utter despair that she must die if he marries Effy.

The bride is ready. She has given her girlhood friends a parting embrace. They summon the bridegroom, but he is nowhere to be found. General astonishment. Gurn has seen him flee to the hills with a woman. Effy is plunged in grief. Anna expresses indignation; everyone, anger and disapproval.

Gurn triumphantly mentions what Madge had predicted for him. He still talks of love and now finds support among the young girls. Effy is overwhelmed with grief and despair. She is indifferent to all consolation and leans helplessly on Anna's breast. Gurn kneels at her feet and all express the liveliest sympathy.

Act Two

The forest and night. A dense fog permits only a glimpse of the foremost trees and cliffs. To the left, the entrance to a cave.

Madge prepares for a meeting with the other witches. They come from all quarters, each with lamp and broomstick, each with her familiar spirit. They dance about the fire in a circle, hail Madge, and by way of welcome empty a cup of the glowing brew she has prepared for them. Madge calls them to work. Some spin, wind, and weave a rose-coloured drapery, while others dance and fence with the broomsticks. The spell is complete. They drink a farewell and the flock of witches disappear into the cave.

The fog disperses. Dawn gives way to sunrise and the landscape presents a charming blend of woods and mountains. The Sylphide leads James down from a steep mountain path, which he fearfully treads while she scarcely seems to touch the cliff with her foot. This is her kingdom. Here she will live for the one she loves, hide him from the eyes of the world, and allow him to share the joys that she prizes most highly. James is enraptured with delight and admiration. The Sylphide seems to explore each one of his wishes, brings him the loveliest flowers, and refreshes him with fruits and spring water. James regards her with rapture. He forgets everything for the one he loves and lives only to possess her. But she is more retiring than usual. She will not sit with him, easily disengages herself from his arms, and eludes him every time he ardently tries to embrace her. James is on the verge of becoming annoyed, but then she hovers about him in the most delightful attitudes. Without knowing it, James's movements take on a more airy lilt. He follows the Sylphide in her easy flight, and their dancing blends together in harmony.

Despite his love for the Sylphide and the magical power that irresistibly sweeps him away with her, the memory of Effy still returns and points out to him the injustice he has inflicted upon her. He becomes melancholy once more and he feels as drained as if he had been intoxicated.

The Sylphide perceives his state of mind and by her innocent gaiety seeks to dispel his dark thoughts. She knows a way: her sisters shall help her to cheer her beloved. At a signal they all come into view through the bushes, on the boughs, and over the cliffs. The young sylphides with wings of blue and rose colour soon chase away the youth's distress. Some of them swing in airy draperies which they hang between the trees, while others stand on the tip of a bough and bend it to the ground with their weight, to have it raised into the air again by a puff of wind. Their dancing and delightful groupings arouse James's enthusiasm. He is more than ever taken with the Sylphide but she eludes his embraces and, after having disappointed him several times, she disappears at the very moment he thought to grasp her. In vain he questions the remaining sylphides. They do not answer him but fly away one after another. Anxious and grief-stricken, James cannot remain alone but rushes after the enchanting creature.

James's friends come into view on the hill. Gurn is with them. They seek and question one another about the runaway, but until now their search has been fruitless. They spread out, but Gurn discovers a hat. It belongs to James. He is about to call the others, but Madge steps out of the cave, seizes the hat, and flings it away. Gurn is frightened by the witch's sudden appearance, but she calms him, orders him to be silent and clever, as she points to the hill, from whence Effy is coming with some of her friends.

Nobody has found James and Madge now tells them of his unfaithfulness. He is lost to Effy but her prophecy will be fulfilled, for Gurn, the fine, good-hearted young fellow, is destined by fate to be Effy's husband. All the others, outraged at James's behaviour, support Gurn's pleas. Effy, although deeply distressed, is nevertheless moved by the slighted Gurn's affection, and she allows him to escort her home. Madge remains alone.

James returns without having overtaken the Sylphide. His heart is a prey to regret and despair. He feels how deeply he has violated his responsibilities towards his bride, but he does not have the strength to tear himself loose from this being, who, like a dream-image, charms and confuses his senses and captures his thoughts. Old Madge has been watching him secretly and approaches him with feigned compassion. He readily tells her everything and says that he would gladly give his life to capture the celestial maiden if only for a single moment. 'But the one you love is a *sylphide*! Naught but a talisman can bind her to you.' 'Give it me! In return I will bestow upon you all that I possess.' 'But this morning you mocked me, cast me away!' Kneeling, James begs her to forgive him for his hardness and to give him life by the possession of the Sylphide. Madge suffers herself to be moved and meaning-fully hands him the rose-coloured scarf: 'Believe in its strength and you shall succeed! Entwine her with this blossom. Then her wings will fall and she is yours forever.' Beside himself with joy and gratitude, James kisses the scarf and follows the witch to her cave with a thousand expressions of thanks.

He espies the Sylphide, sitting on a bough with a bird's nest in her hand. He waves the scarf; she climbs down and offers him her catch, but James reproaches her for her hardness towards innocent creatures. Deeply moved, she regrets what she has done and hastens to replace the nest. She now pleads for the pretty scarf, which he purposely refuses her. She begs him for it and promises never more to flee from him. Greedily, she reaches for the scarf but at the same instant he twists it about her so tightly that she cannot move her arms. The Sylphide is captured and, kneeling, asks for mercy; but James does not release the scarf before her wings have fallen off. The Sylphide puts her hand to her heart as if she felt mortally wounded. James presses her to him but she pushes him away from her. He throws himself at her feet...the pallor of death covers the Sylphide's brow.

James, who had thought to possess her forever and in his outburst of joy gives her a thousand caresses, suddenly stops: what has he done! The un-happy creature! By taking away her freedom has he robbed her of life? 'Do not weep! You, whom I have so dearly loved! I was blessed by your tender-ness but I could not belong to you, could not bestow upon you the happiness you longed for. I must die! Take your betrothal ring. Make haste, return it.

You can still marry her whom you loved before me...Farewell! I die with the hope of your future happiness.' ...

At this moment the fortune-teller enters to rejoice at James's despair, and counters his reproaches with the icy laughter of revenge. She points to the background, where Gurn is leading Effy to the altar. The Sylphide's strength is decreasing little by little. James lies at her feet. Her sisters surround her and in their arms she breathes forth her spirit. Sylphs and sylphides veil the beloved body and carry it away through the air. Overwhelmed with grief, the unfortunate James casts yet another look at his airy mistress and falls to the ground in a swoon.

— Translated from the Danish by Patricia N. McAndrew

Appendix 4

Plot summary of *La Sylphide* in *Le Courrier des Théâtres*, 13 March 1832

(Note: In keeping with custom, the story of *La Sylphide* was summarised in newspaper reviews. This one clearly borrows copiously from the libretto.)

Act I: A farm in Scotland. James and Gurn, two young highlanders, are sleeping. A Sylphide is at James' knee, gazing admiringly at him and covering him with kisses. James wakes up. Now he sees nothing, but this mysterious apparition has been haunting his dreams. He asks Gurn if he saw anyone. Gurn saw nothing. Then Effie the farm girl, James's fiancée, enters on the arm of his mother, Anne Reuben. Gurn hastens to her side, but Effie can think only of James; she sees that he is preoccupied. I was only thinking of you, says James. They kneel and receive the blessing of their mother. Gurn, in despair, draws away.

Effie's friends arrive, offering wedding gifts and scoffing at Gurn's sorrow. James is pre-occupied by thoughts of the Sylphide, and looks around for her everywhere. Behind the groups of girls he finds a hideous figure: it is old Madge, the witch. Madge tells Effie's fortune, examining her hand and telling her that James does not love her as much as Effie would wish. Mother Anna then leads Effie away to prepare for the betrothal ceremony. James is now alone again, still thinking of his mysterious dream.

At this time a strong gust of wind opens the window; the Sylphide appears, huddled in a corner. She tells James of her love for him; she will die if he rejects her love. Effie's fiancé turns his eyes away; then he sees her at his feet, wrapped up in the cloak of his beloved; his wits abandon him; he lifts her up, presses her to his heart and gives her a kiss. Gurn, who has been spying, goes to find Effie, so he can show her this proof of James' infidelity.

At the very moment they arrive, James hides the Sylphide in an armchair and covers her up in a plaid. Gurn saw everything, but when he pulls the plaid away, the Sylphide has disappeared. The highlander is confounded. Everyone celebrates the engagement of James and of Effie; the dances begin. James forgets to invite his fiancée to dance.

Then comes the hour for the ceremony. James removes his ring, which he is going to exchange with his cousin [Effie]. The Sylphide, emerging from the hearth, snatches it away from him. James's mind is disturbed; he fears losing his Sylphide, and escapes with her behind the throng that surrounds Effie.

General surprise when they realise he is gone. Despair of Effie, who sees that the witch's prediction has come true.

Act II: A forest. On the left is the mouth of a cave. The old witch Madge and her companions celebrate a Sabbath; each one departs, carrying a talisman. Madge reserves a scarf for herself. Then, above the rocks, the Sylphide appears, guiding James' steps. She stops in the middle of the forest, the depth of which is just becoming apparent as the fog dissipates. In vain James seeks to embrace the Sylphide, but she keeps eluding him. Then, from the foliage there appears a bevy of sylphides with pink and blue wings. James is intoxicated by this delicious spectacle.

But, imperceptibly, the Sylphides move away, and, one by one, disappear amongst the wild roses. James then contemplates his past faults. He would like to find a way to keep the Sylphide forever by his side, this Sylphide who rendered him a faithless lover.

Now, Madge emerges from the mouth of the cave and gives him the scarf, which will cause the wings of the Sylphide to fall off. James then retraces his footsteps, and finds the Sylphide playing with a bird's nest. She runs up to him, hoping to have the scarf for herself. James benefits from this moment, wrapping her up in the magic fabric, which he loosens only when the wings fall. The Sylphide fades; her life force grows dim, she dies. Madge arrives, so she can exult in her triumph. The Sylphs and the Sylphides descend from above, hovering in the air, and carry away their luckless companion. This forms a charming *tableau*. Overwhelmed, James takes one last look at the Sylphide, and sees, through the trees, a nuptial party filing by as wedding bells ring: they are celebrating the marriage of Gurn and Effie. Finally, exhausted by so many blows, he falls unconscious.

Acte Ier. C'est dans une ferme de l'Ecosse. James et Gurn, deux jeunes montagnards, sont endormis. Une Sylphide est aux genoux de James, caressant son sommeil et le couvrant de baisers. James se reveille. Il ne voit rien. Cependant ces apparitions mystérieuses se sont souvent renouvelées dans ses rêves. Il demande à Gurn s'il n'a vu personne. Gurn n'a rien aperçu. Alors entre dans la ferme Effie, la fiancée de James, appuyée sur le bras de sa mere, Anne Beuden [sic]. Gurn court au-devant d'elle, mais Effie ne songe qu'à James; elle le voit préoccupé. Je pensais à toi, lui répond James. Ils se mettent à genoux et reçoivent la bénédiction de leur mère. Gurn s'éloigne au désespoir. Les compagnes d'Effie viennent lui offrir les présens de noces et rient du chagrin de Gurn. James toujours occupée de la Sylphide la cherche partout des yeux; il aperçoit derrière les groupes de jeunes filles une figure hideuse, c'est la vieille sorcière Madge. Elle examine la main d'Effie et lui prédit qu'elle n'est point aimée de James autant qu'elle l'aime. La mere Anne enmène ensuite sa fille pour le preparer à la cérémonie des fiançialles. James resté seul pense encore à son apparition mystérieuse. A ce moment un coup de vent ouvre la fenêtre; la Sylphide paraît blottie dans un coin. Elle apprend à James l'amour qu'elle a pour lui; elle n'a plus qu'à mourir s'il la repousse. Le fiancée d'Effie détourne les yeux; puis la voyant à ses pieds envelopée dans le manteau de son amante, l'esprit l'abandonne, il la relève, la presse sur son Coeur et lui donne un baiser. Gurn qui l'épiait a été chercher Effie pour lui prouver l'infidélité de James. A l'instant où ils entrent, James fait cacher la Sylphide dans un fauteuil et la recouvre de son plaid. Gurn a tout vu; il va le relever, mais la Sylphide a disparu; le montagnard demeure confondu. On célèbre les fiançailles de James et d'Effie, les danses commencent, James oublie d'inviter son amante; puis viens l'heure de la cérémonie. James alors ôte de son doigt l'anneau qu'il va echanger avec sa cousine. La Sylphide, sortie de l'âtre, lui arrache l'anneau. La raison de James se trouble, il craint de perdre sa Sylphide, et s'échappe avec elle derrière la foule pressée autour d'Effie. Surprise generale lorsqu'on vient à l'appeler; désespoir d'Effie, qui voit s'accomplir a prediction de la sorcière.

Acte II: Le theatre représente un forêt. A gauche est l'entrée d'une caverne. La vieille sorcière Madge célèbre un sabbat avec toutes ses compagnes, et chacune se retire en emportant un talisman; Madge s'est réservé une écharpe. Alors, paraît au-dessus des rochers la Sylphlide guidant les pas de James. Elle s'arrête au milieu de la forêt, dont les brouillards dissipés laissent voir le profondeur. En vain James veut l'entourer de caresses, elle lui échappe toujours. Puis du sein du feuillage sortent une foule de sylphides au ailes bleues et roses. James est enivrée de ce délicieux spectacle; mais insensiblement les Sylphides s'éloignent, et, une à une, se perdent dans les églantiers. James alors songe à ses fautes passées; il voudrait trouver un moyen de retenir pour jamais auprès de lui la Sylphide qui l'a rendu infidèle. Madge sort de la caverne et lui donne son écharpe, à l'aide de laquelle les ailes de la Sylphide tomberont d'elles-mêmes. En revenant sur ses pas James aperçoit la Sylphide jouant avec un nid d'oiseau. Elle court à lui pour lui ravir l'écharpe. James profite d'un instant pour l'envelopper dans le tissu magique, qu'il ne desserre que lorsque les ailes sont tombées. La Sylphide pâlit, les forces l'abandonnent, elle meurt. Madge vient jouir de son triomphe. Les Sylphes et les Sylphides descendent et enlèvent leur malheureuse compagne, ce qui forme un tableau ravissant. James accablé jette un dernier regard sur la Sylphide, voit à travers les arbres de la foret la noce qui défile au son des cloches, pour célébrer le marriage de Gurn et d'Effie, et enfin, épuisé par tant de coups, tombe sans connaissance.

— Translated from the French by Marian Smith

Appendix 5

Regarding the 1835 Brussels Manuscript of *La Sylphide* (the 'Bartholomin score')

Draft written by Alexander Bennett (October 2000)

Following on the heels of the article 'The earliest *Giselle*', in which the author states that 'a good many such [annotated violin rehearsal scores] have survived and are awaiting discovery in archives and private collections,'[1] I have pleasure in confirming that I have in my private collection a copy of one of the earliest *violon répétiteurs* (violin rehearsal scores) of *La Sylphide*, the Romantic ballet.

I had the good fortune of receiving this score, a photocopy of Victor Bartholomin's 1835 répétiteur from the Théâtre de la Monnaie in Brussels, from my ballet teacher Marjory Middleton, the pioneer of Scottish ballet. The original had been passed down through Bartholomin's daughter, Adèle Bartholomin Monplaisir. (Ironically, after being preserved for over a century, this manuscript has disappeared and my photocopy of it is the only one extant.[2]) Annotated répétiteurs were frequently exported in the nineteenth century to Belgium where they were used to mount the Parisian ballets in vogue at the time. *[Editor's note: such scores were also exported to Russia, and likely to many other places as well.]* According to David A. Day there is extant at the Archives de la Ville in Brussels a violon répétiteur for *La Sylphide* (sent from the Paris Opéra for use at the Théâtre de la Monnaie) but it is not much annotated.[3] Fortunately, my copy of Bartholomin's manuscript *is* — most profusely.

Full of information and directions pertaining to the actions and gestures made during the dramatic scenes, it spells out, measure by measure, the details of the *mis en scène*; the dialogue between the characters; the exact placement of the Ciceri décor of the first act, with particular emphasis on the location of trapdoors and mechanical effects, flying equipment and the 'when' and 'where' of the Sylphide's appearances and disappearances.

Who was the annotator? Was it Barthlomin himself or a professional copyist? We cannot be certain until further studies are carried out, but we can speculate: it is likely that this score describes the original Filippo Taglioni production of 1832.

Similar in length to the *Giselle* répétiteur found in St. Petersburg, the Bartholomin score has one hundred and fifty-eight pages, and is scored for two violins. Every page has twelve staves and on nearly every page the copyist has divided them into six two-staff systems. The tempo markings (e.g., *poco agitato*) are in Italian while the ballet instructions are in French, and are situated between the upper and lower stave in most cases, but sometimes above the staff.

Synchronised to the exact moment musically when certain action takes place, these annotations, long forgotten, recall vital information about the staging of the ballet but, more importantly, indicate how close was the working liaison between choreographer and composer, giving us a fuller picture of the connection of mime, music and dance in the Romantic ballet.

If this matching up of music with action had not been so important, nineteenth century ballet masters and choreographers would simply have used the libretto, which, although offering effective information on the action, would not suffice for the matching of the mimed gestures to the music.

The balance of performance is greatly affected if this synchronisation of gesture and music is not properly adhered to and if the original intention of composer and choreographer is misconstrued and falsely interpreted. For example, in the first act of Lacotte's version, he uses the music for James' awakening as a vehicle for an additional solo for the sylph, thus placing the kiss twenty-four bars later on music intended for the sylph to disappear up the chimney (as is clearly marked in both the Bartholomin and the Parisian orchestral score). Similarly in Act Two when the sylph's wings fall off (clearly indicated in the Bartholomin and the Parisian orchestral score) 'she falls to the ground' and 'she totters, her wings become detatched, she falls', Lacotte's Sylphide is still gaily dancing and loses her wings on music intended to signify her farewell.

Like the score of the early *Giselle* showing that nearly half of the ballet was devoted to plot-propelling mime and action, the score of *La Sylphide* also indicates a large proportion of mime. The following breakdown of the musical structure gives one some idea the important place occupied by mime in the ballet.

Act One
1. Fireside scene with James and the Sylphide (mime and dance)
2. Dialogue between James and Gurn (mime)
3. Effie's entrance with Mother Anne (mime)
4. Effie and James (mime and danced mime)
5. Madge's entrance and fortune-telling (mime)
6. Villagers' entrance (dance)
7. Window Scene (mime and danced mime)
8. Removal of the plaid by Gurn (mime)
9. Wedding Divertissement (dance)
10. Wedding preparation (mime)

Act Two
1. Witches' scene (mime and dance)
2. The Forest, dance of the sylphides (dance)
3. Pas de deux (dance)
4. James and the Witch (mime and dance)
5. Scarf dance with James and the Sylphide (dance)
6. Death of the Sylph (mimed dance)
7. Finale (ascent of sylphs in the sky)

Another important feature of the annotations is the insight they offer into the secondary characters; it is clear from these mime scenes that Effie, Gurn, Madge and Mother Anne had very definite profiles of their own. Such performers at the Paris Opéra of the caliber of Lise Noblet (Effie), M. Élie (Gurn), Madame Élie (Madge) and Caroline Brocard (Mother Anna) were well known and lauded for their powers of acting.

To go to the Paris Opéra to see *La Sylphide* in 1832 was first and foremost to see a dramatic story ballet – which included all the excitement and spectacle of flying witches and sylphs, plus the magic of disappearances through trap doors in the chimney piece, pillar and staircase.

Day, David A. 'The Annotated Violon Repetiteur and Early Romantic Ballet at the Theatre Royal De Bruxelles (1815-1830)' Ph.D. diss., New York University, 2008.
Smith, Marian. 'The Earliest Giselle? A Preliminary Report on a St Petersburg Manuscript', *Dance Chronicle* 23, no. 1 (2000): 29-48.

1. Marian Smith, 'The earliest Giselle? A preliminary report on a St. Petersburg Manuscript', *Dance Chronicle* 23, no. 1 (2000): 29-48.
2. Mr. Bennett sent a copy of his copy to me, and I have deposited a copy of it in the New York Public Library, Dance Collection.
3. See also David A. Day, 'The Annotated Violon Repetiteur and Early Romantic Ballet at the Theatre Royal de Bruxelles (1815-1830)' (Ph.D. diss., New York University, 2008).

Appendix 6

Comparison of three manuscript scores for Schneitzhoeffer's *La Sylphide (1832)*

This table was completed by Matilda Ann Butkas Ertz from a draft by Alexander Bennett and compares the general contents of the scores (whole musical numbers) and produces annotations therein. It does not account for small cuts, nor (in most cases) musical variants from score to score. Some spellings are phonetic or otherwise idiosyncratic.

Bartholomin Répétiteur (1835)[1]	*Paris Opéra Répétiteur (1832)[2]*	*Paris Opéra Full Score (1832)[3]*
ACT I	**ACT I**	**ACT I**
[Overture missing]	[Overture missing; a miscellaneous timpani part appears in the beginning, entitled *Final*, before the start of scene 1]	Overture: **Introduction, Presto** **Andante poco Allegro Agitato** *à la paganini* **Vivace**
Scene 1 **Andante poco Adagio** *James est endormi dans un fauteil. La Sylphide à genoux près de lui le contemple. Elle passe plusieurs fois devant lui*	**Scene 1** **Adagio Moderato**	**Scene 1** **Act 1, No. 1** *lever du Rideau* *les ailes battent plus vite* *Tom est agité*
Même mouvement **tutti** *elle mouvant derrière de fauteuil et agite ses ailes sur la [missing] James Elle redescen de place devant lui et ne peut resister au desir au lui donne un baiser*	**Allegretto** **Tempo 1°**	**même mouvement** **Tutti**
Allegro Agitato *James s'éveille apperçoit la Sylphide veut [missing] Elle lui échappe il la conjure de rester près de lui elle refuse s'échappe une seconde fois il court après elle* *elle disparait par la cheminée à gauche du public*	**Allegro Agitato** *agitato con moto*	*le baiser* **Allegro** *Tom cherche à s'emparer de la Sylphide*
Lento *il reste seul dans le plus grand étonnement*	**Lento Moderato**	**Lento**

Bartholomin Répétiteur (1835)	Paris Opéra Répétiteur (1832)	Paris Opéra Full Score (1832)
Allegro agitato **Adagio** *James s'approche de Burle qui est endormi sous la grande fenêtre à droite du public il parvient a l'éveiller* **Allegretto** *il lui demande qu'il n'a pas vu la sylphide... [indistinct] ...qu'il perd la tête ... cela vaut du bonheur qu'il a d'épouser la jeune Effie*	**Allegro Agitato** **Adagio**	**Allegro agitato** **Adagio**
	Allegretto *Scène de James et Gurn Gurn James ensemble*	**Allegretto** Duo entre Tom et Garn Tom Garne Tom Garne
Scene 2 **Allegretto Grazioso** *Ici parait Effie et sa mère devant ... porte au droite du public...Effie reproche à son amant la preoccup [missing] on à parait être... il s'excuse...*	**Scene 2** **Allegretto Grazioso/Andante** *No. 2 [top left] Gurne parle à Anne et aux jeunes filles, Effie va à James. Il regarde du coté de la cheminée [indistinct]*	**Scene 2** **Allegretto Grazioso, Nos. 2, 3**
Allegro Agitato poco Andante *la mère s'approche les deux*	**Allegro Agitato** [indistinct – plaid, Gurn] **petit silence**	**Allegro Agitato poco Andante**
Lento **Vivace** *La mère bénit le amans*	**un peu plus lent** **Allegro poco presto**	**Lento** **Vivace même mouvement**
Scene 3 **Ecossaise Allegretto** *Entrée du corps de ballet qui appr [missing] de la cheminée et va se chauffer James apperçoit la sorcière et veut qu'elle s'éloigne elle implore pour rester mais [indistinct] ce n'est qu'a la prière d'Effie qui causent a la laisser* **Andante** *Les jeunes filles demandent à la sorcière leur disent lu bonne aventure elle se place au mileu d'elles*	**Scene 3** **Allegro poco presto** *Arrive de jeunes filles, il pense à la sylphide, il voit Madge, il parle à la sorcière les petites filles vont à la sorcière* **Andante Grave**	**Scene 3** *à la Paganini*
	Vivace *1ˢᵗ paysanne 2ⁿᵈ paysanne 3ʳᵈ paysanne 4ᵗʰ paysanne Effie s'approche de la sorcière*	**Vivace**
Moderato *... dit à l'une qu'elle sera bientôt mariée l'autre qu'elle est ... [indistinct] amant" Effie veut que la sorcière dise la bonne aventure à James il [indistinct] refuse d'abord et finit par consentir la sorcière après*	**No. 3** *La sorcière prend la main d'Effie* **Tempo 1°** *Effie [indistinct]James d'aller chez la sorcière, La main de James, Colère de James, Gurn va à la sorcière James ... la sorcière*	**Poco ritard** *La sorcière prend la main d'Effie Colère de Tom*

Bartholomin Répétiteur (1835)	Paris Opéra Répétiteur (1832)	Paris Opéra Full Score (1832)
quelque [indistinct] *lui prend la main et lui dit qu'il n'aime point Effie Indignation de James il veut frapper la Sorcière il la poursuit on cherche* [indistinct] *on fait sortir la sorcière*		
Andante sostenuto *Effie console James de ce* [missing] *de lui dire la Sorcière*	**Andante** *Effie cherche à calmer Tom les jeunes filles se moquent de Gurne Gurne se désespére et se fâche comme Tom de ce qu'on se moque de lui*	**Andante sostenuto** *Effie cherche à calmer Tom les jeunes filles se moquent de Gurne Gurne se désespére et se fâche comme Tom de ce qu'on se moque de lui*
Allegro *il lui jure la sincerité de son amour*	**Allegro mosso**	
Allegretto poco Andante *on emmène Effie dons le cabinet afin de la parer ses ornemens de mariée*	**Allegretto poco Andante** [much of this section is annotated but also crossed out] *Les jeunes filles apportent les habits de noce et les font examiner à Effie* [indistinct] *Tom est agité*	**Allegro** *Le jeunes filles apportent les habits de noce et les font examiner à Effie*
Presto *James veut l'y suivre, quelques jeunes filles l'en empêche, lui disant qu'il s'est encore que son fiancé*	**Presto** [written in later]	**Presto**
Andantino *James reste seul tout en exprimant* [indistinct] *il aime Effie ne peut s'empêcher de songer a la Sylphide*	**Lento, Andante, Silence** **Scene 4** [mostly crossed out, not present in full score]	**Andantino**
[missing pages 39-41]		
Scene 4 **Andantino** *Il se promène lentement, laissant les yeux à la fenêtre*	**Scene 4** **Andante** **No. 4, Orage più mosso** [more crossed out measures]	**Scene 4** **La Silphy No. 4, Orage,** **Andantino**
Cantabile poco Adagio	**Duetto** *La Sylphide exprime son amour à James Il ... James,*	**Duetto, Cantabile poco adagio** *La Sylphide exprime son amour à Toms,* **Retenu**
Largo	**Adagio** *James pense à Effie et la Sylphide, La Silph frissonne apprenant que Toms aime beaucoup Effie*	**Largo** *La Silph frissonne apprenant que Toms aime beaucoup Effie, Tom dit qu' Effie a reçu ses serments*
Agitato *Elle veut l'emmener avec elle il regarde du coté du*	**Allegro Agitato, No. 5** *La Silph se désespére, Elle lui dit qu'elle*	**No. 5, Agitato** *La Silph se désespére Elle lui dit qu'elle*

Bartholomin Répétiteur (1835)	Paris Opéra Répétiteur (1832)	Paris Opéra Full Score (1832)
cabinet et refuse de la suivre elle pleure et s'assied sur le grand fauteuil	n'a plus qu'à mourir **très lent**	n'a plus qu'à mourir **très lent** Il la rappelle
Adagio James s'attendrit, il va près d' elle	**Adagio**	**Adagio** pour Toms, pour la Silphy, il cherche à cacher ce qui se passe dans son coeur Elle temoignue son contentment elle bondit au tour de tom
même mouvement des tems Il lui fait serment de toujours	**Allegro marque** l'aimer Elle bondit au tour de Tom	
Elle reprend sa joie Elle danse	**Retenu** la sylphide danse	**Retenu** La Sylphy danse
Allegro poco Presto Elle veut de nouveau l'emmener il s'y refuse encore elle lui demande si elle [missing] par aussi jolie qu'effie et pour le convaincre du m[issing] elle se couvre du plaid en manteau qui est sur le grand fauteuil Silence	**Allegro** Tom pense d'Effie non il dit qu'il ne peut s'abandonner il envoie la Silphy la Silphy est aux pieds de Tom surprise de Tom Silence	**[same music]** Tom pense à Effie Non il dit qu'il ne peut s'abandonner il renvoie la Silphy la Silphy est aux pieds de Tom surprise de Tom Silence
Allegro agitato il ne peut plus resister il s'approche doucement de la Sylphide	**Allegro agitato (No. 5)**	**Allegro agitato**
Largo au même instant Burle parait sur l'escalier du tout et voit le baiser que James donne à la Sylphide	**Largo** James embrasse la sylphide	**Largo**
Scene 5 **Allegretto** Burle court au cabinet pour tout compter à Effie et à sa mère, James cache la Sylphide et couvre avec plaid, James qui a vu Burle inquiet le ce qu'il va [missing] cache la Sylphide sur le fauteuil en la couvrant entièrement avec le m[missing] **Plus vite** Burle revient avec Effie et la mère...on cherche la Sylphide... ne la voyant pas on traite Burle de [missing] ... il s'indigne ... s'approche de fauteuil lève le [missing] la Sylphide a disparu et [indistinct] papillon	**Scene 5** **Allegretto** Gurn rachercher Effie la Sylphide s'enveloppe du plaid	**Scene 5** **Allegretto**
		Moins vite

Bartholomin Répétiteur (1835)	Paris Opéra Répétiteur (1832)	Paris Opéra Full Score (1832)
Presto on se moque de lui	**Presto** *Gurn se met à genoux d'Effie*	**En pressant le mouvement** **Presto**
Divertissement	**Divertissement**	**Divertissement**
Divertissement, No. 1, **Allegretto poco andante,** **Anglaise**	**Divertissement, No. 1**	**Allegretto poco andante,** **Anglaise**
Allegretto	**Divertissement, Ecossaise**	
[not present]	**Un peu plus lent** **Pas de quatre nouveau** [Both of the above pieces are crossed out] [missing pages 76-80]	[not present]
Prestissimo Anglaise *la Sylphide parait traverse* *les quadrilles du corps de ballet* *James s'appercois la suit qu'esques* [missing] *elle lui échappe ... la trappe* *anglaise qui est a* [unclear] *de la fenêtre la danse continue*	**Anglaise Prestissimo** *Lui* *Le Dames* **Coda,** *1ˢᵗ Danseur*	**Presto** **Coda**
Pas de deux **Adagio**	**Divertissement Pas de deux,** **No. 2** **Adagio**	**Pas de deux**
Allegretto [Dame, homme, etc. same as middle Opéra rép. column, according to Alex Bennett's notes; this page is now missing]	**Allegretto** *Dame, homme, La Dame, etc.*	
Andante Allegretto	**Andante, con espressione** *Dame, l'homme, etc.* **Plus vite** *Dame, homme etc.* *Tout les 2*	**Andante**
Pas de trois **Andante Lento** **Allegro**	**Pas de trois** [much crossed-out material] **Andante** **Allegro** *homme, Dame, homme, Dame,* **Coda**	**Pas de Trois** **Introduction** **Allegro**
Anglaise, Presto	**Final** [crossed out *Introduction du ballet*] *Sujet et enfants* *Le Sujet* [crossed out at end: *à l'introduction du pas de 3*]	**Anglaise**

Bartholomin Répétiteur (1835)	Paris Opéra Répétiteur (1832)	Paris Opéra Full Score (1832)
Après la Danse, Andante poco allegro *on conduit Effie à gauche de l'acteur pour lui placer la couronne et le bouquet virginal*	**No 6, Après le Divertissement, Allegro poco**	**Final du 1e acte, Andante poco allegro**
toutes les jeunes filles s'entoure James reste seul de l'autre côté la sylphide parait et decide James a la suivre par la porte	*l'anneau elle emmène Toms*	
[confusion] ... générale de ne pas le trouver		
Presto *Inquietude d'Effie Elle prie Burle d'aller de chercher dans sa chambre Arrivez il obeit avec repugnance Burle revient dire qu'il ne la pas le trouvé... [indistinct]* **Vivace** *Elle tombe dans les bras de sa mère Tableaux général... Rideau*	**piu mosso – Allegro** *on cherche Toms ... Gurn renouvelle sa declaration d'amour Effie pense toujours à Toms Elle repousse Gurn* **Vivace**	**Presto** **Retenu** **Vivace**
	[More pieces appear here, only in this score: **Moderato, Adagio, Moderato,** M. Mazillier, **Majeur, Coda** [many cross-outs throughout]	
ACT II, scene 1	**ACT II, scene 1**	**ACT II, scene 1**
Act 2e, Nuit, Moderato Sostenuto *Lever du rideau La toile lève Medje la sorcière fait une conjuration* **Allegretto** *[Bach Prelude in F] Elle appelle ses compagnes elles sortent de la grotte l'une après l'autre*	**Adagio** *Elle frappe trois coups* **[not present]**	**Allegro** *Elle frappe trois coups* **[Bach Prelude in F]** *Les Sorcières arrivent par grouppes Premier groupe Cf. J.S. Bach – Clavecin Bientemperé 2nd groupe 3rd groupe 4th groupe*
Grave *Elle raconte aux sorcières l'affront que [indistinct] par James et l'intention [indistinct] elle est de se venger elle s'implore leur aide les sorcières promettent de l'aider et rentrent dans la grotte*	**[not present]**	**Grave**

Bartholomin Répétiteur (1835)	Paris Opéra Répétiteur (1832)	Paris Opéra Full Score (1832)
Allegro *Elles resortent de la grotte portant tout* [missing] *faut pour opérer les charmes*	[The Witches' Dance is present in this score, albeit shortened]	**Danse des Sorcières,** **Ralentisser un peu** **Allegro moderato**
Medje prend tout ce qu'elles ont apposé et le jette dans la chaudière *les sorcières dansent en rond autour de la chaudière* **Allegro** *Medje exprime que le charme a opéré* *Chaque sorcière prend un verre et boit du bouillon de la grande marmite* *Medje retire de la marmite l'écharpe qu'elle* [missing] *le charme etant terminé dit aux sorcières de s'éloigner* *les sorcières rentrant toutes dans la grotte*		
Scene 2	**Scene 2**	**Scene 2**
Andante Sostenuto, plus lent de moitié, **Jour** *le jour commence* *Medje après s'être réjouit du mal qu'elle se promet de f* [missing] *rentre dans la grotte*	**Andante sostenuto**	**Andante sostenuto, plus lent de moitié**
Andante poco agitato *La Sylphide parait seul Elle va chercher son amant James lui demande en quel lieu il se trouve. Elle lui répond qu'elle est dans son empire*	[present, unlabelled]	**Andante poco agitato**
Adagio [2 harps, again here] *La sylphide appelle ses compagnes Groupes voluptueux de different côtés groupes*	**Adagio sostenuto**	**Adagio**
	Fine	
Allegretto *La Sylphide se balance à une branche d'arbre* *D'autres traversent la scène dans les airs* *corps de ballet*	**Les Balances du Corps de Ballet** *traversés* *Mm. Dominique et James* *Les 3 Sylphides* *James et la Sylphide* *James seul* *Les trois sylphides* *Corps de ballet et Choriphées* *Caroline*	[same music]

Bartholomin Répétiteur (1835)	*Paris Opéra Répétiteur (1832)*	*Paris Opéra Full Score (1832)*
Pas de deux, maestoso **Adagio [unique]**	[no pas de deux] **[slow piece in D major, triple meter, unique]**	[not present] **[Extensive danced number, unique at first]**
[matches other 2 scores beginning roughly mid-way through]	[briefly matches other scores, many cuts after]	[Extensive danced number, unique at first]
Allegretto, plus lent **Coda** **Allegro, Après le pas de deux** **Andante** **Même mouvement** **Allegro** **Tempo 1°** *danse general de toutes les sylphides* *Elles sortent petit à petit et laissent James tout seul*	*après le pas de 2* *Le dame du ballet* *Le Cavalier* *Le Danseur Lente* *Ballet*	*après le pas de deux*
Scenes 3 and 4	**Scenes 3 and 4**	**Scenes 3 and 4**
Allegro Agitato *Inquietude de James de ne plus voir la sylphide* *il la cherche vainement de tout côté*	**Allegro Agitato** *la sorcière sort de la caverne*	**Allegro Agitato** *Les sylphides s'envolent* *Pour le vol des Sylphides* *la sorcière sort de sa caverne*
Andante *ici parait Medje la sorcière tout de la grotte elle interroge James sur le motif de son inquietude* *à la Paganini* *il lui fait connaître sa peine* *elle lui dit que si elle n'avoir pas tant de sujet de se plaindre de lui lui indiquerait le moyen de fixer sa maîtresse* *à la Paganini*	**Andante** *à la Paganini*	**Andante** *à la Paganini*
		à la Paganini
Presto *il la conjure de lui apprendre ce moyen.* *elle se fait prier pour y consentir elle lui donne l'écharpe et lui dit qui doit servir pour* [missing] *les ailes de la* [missing]	**Presto** *La Sor[cière] reproche a Toms qui l'a chassée de la Ferme* *Toms prie la sorcière* *La Sorcière feint d'avoir pitié de lui*	**Presto** *La Sorcière reproche a Toms qui l'a chassée de la Ferme* *Toms prie la sorcière* *Il se jette à ses pieds* **Retenu** *La Sorcière feint d'avoir pitié de lui* *Elle lui montre l'ècharpe et lui dit de se confier a son pouvoir*
Andantino *James remercie et exprime sa joie*	**Andante** *Te seras heureux tâche s'envelopper dans cette gaze*	**Andante** *Te seras heureux tâche s'envelopper dans celle gaze*

Bartholomin Répétiteur (1835)	Paris Opéra Répétiteur (1832)	Paris Opéra Full Score (1832)
	Tom couvre de baisers l'écharpe et remercie la Sorcière	Tom couvre de baisers l'écharpe et remercie la Sorcière
Andante sostenuto à la Paganini La sorcière s'éloigne	à la Paganini	**Andante sostenuto** à la Paganini
Scene 5	**Scene 5**	**Scene 5**
	[same music, unlabelled]	**Andante**
Andante La sylphide reparaît Elle voit un nid son un arbre et cours s'en emparer **Gavotte, Andantino, Sourdines** James l'appelle elle descend de l'arbre et vient a [missing] et lui montre le nid ils forment plusieurs passes ensembles James profite d'une passé pour lui attacher le [missing] avec l'écharpe [indistinct] elle veut s'élever mais elle ne peut plus elle tombe à genoux et elle conjure de la détaché il s'y refuse Silence elle pâlit chancelle ses ailes se détachent elle tombe	**[same music, unlabelled]**	**Gavotte Pas de deux avec Sourdine** Il... l'enveloppe Les ailes se préparent
Ses compagnes reparaissent en dansant ... Elle s'apperç [indistinct], s'arrête [indistinct] **Adagio** Reproches et adieu de la sylphide à James Elle meurt	**[present]** **Adagio [crossed out]** **Adagio** *"même mouvement"*	**Adagio, point de contre balle** **[present]**
Allegro Ses compagnes l'emportent dans les coulisses Désespoir de James La sorcière reparaît et se moque de lui **Allegretto** la noce d'Effie avec Burle traverse au fond du théâtre les sylphide portant la morte	**Agitato**	**Allegro** La Sylphide expire Désespoir de James J'ai perdu mon Euridice Il écoute la cloche Cloche sur le théâtre

Bartholomin Répétiteur (1835)	*Paris Opéra Répétiteur (1832)*	*Paris Opéra Full Score (1832)*

*dans l'écharpe paraissent en
milieu du théâtre et s'envolent
tableau général*

*Acte 1er
Au 1er plan a droite du public
un cabinet et la chamber d'effie
Au 2e plan une large fenêtre
qui ouvrent deux battants et
qui est à cinq pieds de terre
au dessous de la fenêtre un
patiner coulisse sur le que la
sylphide pose un pied et
descend à terre placé en
attitude comme si elle volait
une poignée qu'elle* [indistinct]
*Au 3e plan – a droite aussi un
pillier ou* [indistinct] *de mar
avec une trappe anglaise à deux
battants avec des ressords qui
la fait fermer de la même acte*
[missing] *beaucoup de
promptitude
4eme plan un escalier avec un
praticable comme dans la fille
mal gardée
une autre trappe a l'anglaise
est placée en haut de l'éscalier
a côté de la por* [missing]
*c'est par la que la sylphide
disparait avec James
Au 1er plan a gauche une
grande cheminée Gothique au
fond de laquelle il y a encore
une trappe à l'anglaise ces 3
trappes doivent être placé
droite
Sur l'avant scène une trappe
qui s'enforce dessous le théâtre
lorsque la Sylphide s'y est
placée couverte d'un manteau
de James*

**Additional pieces at the
end of this score:**
• 2nd violin part for an
Allegro from Act II
• a third manuscript (Mat.
19 [302 (27) entitled *Pas de
deux*, music by
Schneitzhoeffer, with the
annotation "La Sylphide":
Maestoso, Allegro Moderato,
Andante Cantabile, Allegro
Moderato, 1er Echo-Alle-
gretto, 2er Echo-Allegro
Moderato, 3e Echo-Moderato,
Final-Mouvement de Galop.

Notes

[1] Violin répétiteur (private collection of Alexander Bennett), once owned by Victor Bartholomin, used for an 1835 performance at the Théâtre de la Monnaie in Brussels. See Appendix 5.
[2] Paris Opéra Mat. 19 [302 (25-27)
[3] Paris Opéra (A.501) (1832)
[4] This is in a different hand than the rest of the manuscript, and is probably a later addition to the ballet. It shows little evidence of use. Pierre Lacotte employs this music in his productions.

Bibliography

Aasted, Elsebeth. *Sylfide Og Heks: Den Romantiske Balletdanserinde Lucile Grahn.* Danmarks Købstadsmuseums Skriftrække. Århus: Den Gamle By, 1996.

Abrahamson, Werner H., Rasmus Nyerup, and Knud Lyne Rahbek. *Udvalgte Danske Viser Fra Middelalderen* [Selected Danish Ballads from the Middle Ages]. 5 vols. Copenhagen: J.F. Schultz, 1812–14.

Acocella, Joan, and Lynn Garafola, eds. *André Levinson on Dance: Writings from Paris in the Twenties.* Hanover, NH: Wesleyan University Press, 1991.

Adice, G. Léopold. *Théorie de la gymnastique de la danse Théâtrale.* Paris: Chais, 1859.

Afzelius, Erik Gustaf Geijer and Arvid August. *Svenska Folk-Visor från Forntiden* [Swedish Folk Ballads from Ancient Times]. 3 vols. Stockholm: Strinnholm and Häggström, 1814–16.

Albano, Roberta, Nadia Scafidi, and Rita Zambon. *La danza in Italia: la Scala, la Fenice, il San Carlo dal XVIII Secolo ai Giorni Nostri.* Direzione Flavia Pappacena. Rome: Gremese, 1998.

Albertieri, Luigi. *The Art of Terpsichore/an Elementary, Theoretical, Physical, and Practical Treatise of Dancing.* New York: G. Ricordi, 1923.

Andersen, Hans Christian. *O.T.* Borgen: Det danske Sprog- og Litteraturselskab, 1987.

Anderson, Jack. 'Dallas Ballet in Lengthened Sylphide.' *New York Times,* 29 September 1987.

Anon. [Un vieil abonné]. *Ces Demoiselles de l'Opéra.* Paris: Tresse & Stock, 1887.

Antolini, Bianca Maria, ed. *Dizionario degli Editori Musicali Italiani 1750-1930.* Rome: Società Italiana di Musicologia, 2000.

Aragona, Livio. *Catalogo dei Libretti del Conservatorio "Benedetto Marcello" di Venezia.* Florence: Olschki, 1995.

Arkin, Lisa C., and Marian Smith. 'National Dance in the Romantic Ballet', in *Rethinking the Sylph,* ed. Lynn Garafola. Hanover, NH: Wesleyan University Press, 1997.

Arrigoni, Paolo, and Achille Bertarelli. *Ritratti di musicisti ed artisti di teatro.* Milan: del Popolo d'Italia, 1934.

Arwidsson, Adolph Ivar. *Svenska Fornsånger* [Ancient Swedish Songs]. 3 vols. Stockholm: P.A. Norstedt, 1834–42.

Aschengreen, Erik. *The Beautiful Danger: Facets of the Romantic Ballet.* Translated by Patricia N. McAndrew. *Dance Perspectives* Vol. 58. New York: Dance Perspectives Foundation, 1974.

———. 'Bournonville and Male Dancing: An Inheritance and a Challenge', in *The Royal Danish Ballet and Bournonville,* 1979.

———. 'Bournonville Style and Tradition.' *Dance Research* 4, no. 1 (1986): 45-62.

———. *Harald Lander: His Life and Ballets*. Translated by Patricia N. McAndrew. Alton, Hampshire, UK: Dance Books, 2009.

———. 'Mit egentlige kald – Idéinhold og iscenesaettelse hos Bournonville [My True Calling – the Concepts and Staging of Bournonville]', in *Perspektiv På Bournonville*, ed. Erik Aschengreen, Marianne Hallar and Jørgen Heiner. Copenhagen: Nyt Nordisk Forlag Arnold Busck, 1980.

Auber, D. F. E. *Le Dieu et la Bayadère*. Paris: Bezou, 1830. [libretto]

Augustyn, Frank. 'Footnotes: The Classics of Ballet', vol. 1. West Long Branch, NJ: Kultur International Films, 1995.

Balanchine, George, and Francis Mason. *Balanchine's Complete Stories of the Great Ballets*. Revised and enlarged ed. Garden City, NY: Doubleday, 1977.

Balduino, Armando. 'Significato delle polemiche romantiche sulla mitologia.' *Lettere italiane* 15, no. 1 (1963): 28-40.

Banes, Sally. *Dancing Women: Female Bodies on Stage*. London and New York: Routledge, 1998.

Banes, Sally, and Noël Carroll. 'Marriage and the Inhuman: La Sylphide's Narratives of Domesticity and Community', in *Rethinking the Sylph: New Perspectives on the Romantic Ballet*, ed. Lynn Garafola. Hanover, NH: Wesleyan University Press, 1997.

Basso, Alberto, ed. *Dizionario della musica e dei musicisti*. Torino: Utet, 1988.

———, ed. *Storia del Teatro Regio di Torino*. Vol. 5. Torino: Cassa di Risparmio di Torino, 1988.

Bazzi, Gaetano. *Primi erudimenti dell'arte drammatica per la recitazione e la mimica*. Torino: Giuseppe Fodratti, 1845.

Beaumont, Cyril. *Complete Book of Ballets: A Guide to the Principal Ballets of the Nineteenth and Twentieth Centuries*. New York: Grosset and Dunlap, 1938.

———. *Complete Book of Ballets*. Garden City: Garden City Publishing Co., 1941.

Beaumont, Cyril W., and Stanislas Idzikowski. *A Manual of the Theory & Practice of Classical Theatrical Dancing (Méthode Cecchetti)*. New York: Dover, 1975.

Bellina, Anna Laura. 'Balli scaligeri e polemiche romantiche nella Milano del "Conciliatore".' *Lettere italiane* 33, no. 3 (1981): 350-84.

Bellorini, Egidio. *Discussioni e polemiche sul Romanticismo*. Rome and Bari: Laterza, 1943.

Bennett, Alexander. Alexander Bennett papers, ca. 1953-1990. Newberry Library. Dance MS Bennett, A.

Bergmüller, Friedrich. *La Péri: Ballet in Two Acts*. London: R. Cocks, 1843. [libretto]

Berlioz, Hector. *Mozart, Weber and Wagner*. Translated by Edwin Evans. The Critical Writings of Hector Berlioz. London: W. Reeves, n.d.

Bernay, Berthe. *La Danse au Théâtre*. Paris: Librairie de la Societé des Gens de Lettres, 1890.

Bernheimer, Martin. 'A Royal 'Sylphide' for All Seasons.' *Los Angeles Times*, 12 June 1992.

———. 'S.F. "Sylphide": Borrowed Bournonville.' *Los Angeles Times*, 23 February 1986.

Biancolelli, Pier Francesco, and Jean-Antoine Romagnesi. *Le Nouveau theater Italien ou recueil general des comedies representées par les comédiens Italians Ordinaires du Roi.* Vol. 8. Paris: n.p., 1753.

Bidera, Giovanni Emanuele. *L'arte di declamare ridotta a principii per l'uso del foro, del pergamo e del teatro.* Milan: Giuseppe Cattaneo, 1856.

Bignami, Luigi. *Cronologia di tutti gli spettacoli rappresentati al Teatro Comunale di Bologna dalla sua apertura 14 Maggio 1763 a tutto l'autunno del 1881.* Bologna: Giuseppe Mattiuzzi, 1882.

Binney, Edwin. *Glories of the Romantic Ballet.* London: Dance Books, 1985.

———. 'Sixty Years of Italian Dance Prints 1815-1875.' *Dance Perspectives* 53 (1973).

Bland, Alexander. *The Dancer's World.* London: Collins, 1963.

Blasis, Carlo. *Code of Terpsichore.* London: Edward Bull, 1828.

———. *L'uomo fisico, intellettuale e morale.* Milan: Guglielmini, 1857; facsimile, eds. Ornella Di Tondo and Flavia Pappacena Chorégraphie, Lucca: LIM, 2007.

———. *Manuel complet de la Danse.* Paris: Roret, 1830; facsimile Paris, Laget, 1980.

———. *Notes Upon Dancing.* London: Delaporte, 1847.

———. *Saggi e Prospetto delle materie del trattato generale di pantomima naturale, e di pantomima teatrale.* Milan: Guglielmini e Redaelli, 1841.

———. *Studi sulle arti imitatrici.* Milan: Giuseppe Chiusi, 1844; facsimile Bologna, Forni, 1971.

———. *Traité élémentaire théorique et pratique de l'art de la danse.* Miland: Beati et Teneti, 1820; facsimile Bologna, Forni, 1969.

Blessington, Marguerite. *The Idler in France.* 2 vols. London: H. Colburn, 1841.

Bon, Francesco Augusto. *Principi d'arte drammatica rappresentativa.* Milan: Sancito, 1857.

Borrow, George. *Romantic Ballads.* London: J. Taylor, 1826.

Bottura, Giuseppe Carlo. *Storia aneddotica documentata del Teatro Comunale di Trieste (1801-1881).* Trieste: C. Schmidl, 1885.

Bournonville, August. *Efterladte Skrifter* [Posthumous Writings]. Edited by Charlotte Bournonville. Copenhagen: Andr. Schous Forlag, 1891.

———. *My Dearly Beloved Wife! Letters from France and Italy, 1841.* Translated by Patricia McAndrew. Alton, Hampshire: Dance Books, 2005.

———. *My Theatre Life.* Translated by Patricia N. McAndrew. Middletown, Conn.: Wesleyan University Press, 1979.

———. *Sylphiden: Romantisk Ballet in to Akter.* Copenhagen: J.H. Schubothe, 1836.

Brittan, Francesca. 'Miniaturism, Nostalgia, and Musical Microscopy: The Fairy Fantastic in Nineteenth-Century France.' Paper presented at the American Musicological Society Annual Meeting, Nashville, November 2008.

———. 'On Microscopic Hearing: Fairy Magic, Natural Science, and the *Scherzo Fantastique*.' *Journal of the American Musicological Society* 64, no. 3 (2011): 527-600.

Brocca, Ambrogio. *Il teatro Carlo Felice - Cronistoria del 7 aprile 1828 al 27 febbraio 1898*. Genova: Montorfano, 1898.

Brooks, Peter. *The Melodramatic Imagination - Balzac, Henry James, Melodrama, and the Mode of Excess*. New Haven, CT: Yale University Press, 1976.

Brown, Ismene. 'Made of Air', in *Dance Now* (2008). http://web.me.com/cijc/ismeneb.com/A-K_files/Made%20of%20Air.pdf. Accessed 4 September 2011.

Bruhn, Erik. 'Beyond Technique.' *Dance Perspectives* 36 (1968).

Bruzelius, Margaret, 'Women - Wild and Otherwise', in *Romancing the Novel: Adventure from Scott to Sebald*. Lewisburg, PA: Bucknell University Press, 2007.

Bryson, Norman. 'Dance History and Cultural Studies.' Paper presented at *Choreographing History*, University of California, Riverside, 1992.

Buchan, David. 'Ballads of Otherworld Beings', in *The Good People: New Fairylore Essays*, ed. Peter Narváez. New York: Garland, 1991.

———. 'Talerole Analysis and Child's Supernatural Ballads', in *The Ballad and Oral Literature*, ed. Joseph Harris. Cambridge, MA: Harvard University Press, 1991.

Buckle, Richard. *Diaghilev*. New York: Atheneum, 1979.

Buffelli, Domenico. *Elementi di mimica*. Milan: Visaj, 1829.

Buonsignori, Vincenzo. *Precetti sull'arte mimica applicabili alla coreografia e alla drammatica*. Siena: dell'Ancora di G. Landi e N. Alessandri, 1854.

Burt, Ramsay. *The Male Dancer: Bodies, Spectacle, Sexualities*. London: Routledge, 1995.

———. 'The Trouble with the Male Dancer', in *Moving History/Dancing Cultures*, ed. Ann Dils and Ann Cooper Albright. Hanover, New Hampshire: 2001.

Burwick, Frederick. *The Journal of John Waldie Theatre Commentaries*. University of California Los Angeles: Charles E. Young Research Library, Department of Special Collections, 2008.

Cafiero, Rosa, 'Musica per gli occhi, ovvero ballo teatrale e musica coreutica sulle scene napoletane', in *Donizetti e i Teatri Napoletani dell'Ottocento*, ed. Franco Mancini and Sergio Ragni. Napoli: Electa, 1997.

Cambiasi, Pompeo. *Il Teatro di Varese (1776-1891)*. Milan: G. Ricordi, 1891.

———. *La Scala 1778-1906. Note storiche e statistiche*. Milan: Ricordi, 1906.

Cametti, Alberto. *Il Teatro di Tordinona poi di Apollo*. Tivoli: Arti Grafiche Chicca, 1938.

Camilli, Lorenzo. *Istituzioni sulla rappresentativa, fondate ne' classici autori antichi e moderni e ridotte a sistema teorico-pratico universale*. Aquila: Atermina, 1835.

Canova, Angelo. *Lettere sopra l'arte di imitazione*. Torino: Mussano, 1839.

Carbonneau, Suzanne. 'Michel Fokine', in *International Encyclopedia of Dance*, edited by Elizabeth Aldrich and Selma Jeanne Cohen, New York: Oxford University Press, 1998, vol. 3, 14-28.

Castil-Blaze, *Dictionnaire de musique moderne*. Bruxelles: Academie de Musique, 1828, 2 vols.

———. *L'académie impérial de musique*. Paris: Castil-Blaze, 1855.

————. *La Danse et les Ballets depuis Bacchus jusqu'à Mlle Taglioni.* Paris: Paulin, 1832.

Catalogo generale delle Edizioni G. Ricordi. 3 vols. Milan: G. Ricordi, n.d.

Cavendish, Georgiana. *New Sylph, or the Guardian Angel.* London: W. Lane, 1788.

Caylus. *Le nouveliste aérien ou le Sylphe amoreux.* Amsterdam: n.p., 1734.

Cazotte, Jacques. *Le Diable amoureux.* Paris: Le Jay, 1772.

————. *Le Diable amoureux.* Naples, n.p., 1772.

Celenza, Anna Harwell. *The Early Works of Niels Gade: In Search of the Poetic.* Burlington, VT: Ashgate, 2001.

————. 'Efterklange af Ossian': The Reception of James Macpherson's *Poems of Ossian* in Denmark's Literature, Art, and Music.' *Scandinavian Studies* 70, no. 3 (1998): 359–96.

————. *Hans Christian Andersen and Music: The Nightingale Revealed.* Burlington, VT: Ashgate, 2005.

Celi, Claudia. 'The Arrival of the Great Wonder of Ballet', in *Rethinking the Sylph*, ed. Lynn Garafola. Hanover, NH: Wesleyan University Press, 1997.

————. 'L'epoca del coreodramma (1800-1830),' in *L'arte della danza e del ballet.* Vol. 5, Musica in scena: Storia dello spettacolo musicale, ed. Alberto Basso. Torino: Utet, 1995.

————. 'Percorsi romantici nell'Ottocento Italiano,' in *L'arte della danza e del balletto.* Vol. 5, Musica in scena: Storia dello spettacolo musicale, ed. Alberto Basso. Torino: Utet, 1995.

Celi, Claudia, and Andrea Toschi. 'Lo spartito animato, o delle fortune ballettistiche dell' "Adelaide Di Francia", in *Di sì felice innesto: Rossini, la danza, e il ballo teatrale in Italia*, ed. Paolo Fabbri. Pesaro: Fondazione Rossini, 1996.

Cervellati, Elena, 'Da *Giselle* (Parigi, 1841) a *Gisella* (Bologna, 1843): Traduzione e ricezione di un capolavoro in una città italiana dell'Ottocento', in Alessandro Pontremoli and Giannandrea Poesio (eds), *L'Italia e la danza* (AIRDanza/EADH, Roma, 15-17 Oct. 2006), Roma, Aracne, 2008, 161-176.

Cervetti, Valerio, Claudio Del Monte, and Vincenzo Segreto. *Cronologia degli spettacoli lirici del Teatro Regio di Parma. Indici 1829-1979.* Parma: Grafiche Step, 1982.

Cesare, Raffaele De. *La fine di un regno: dal 1855 al 6 settembre 1860.* Città di Castello: Lapi, 1895.

Chapman, John. 'Auguste Vestris and the Expansion of Technique.' *Dance Research Journal* 19, no. 1 (Summer 1987): 11-18.

————. 'Jules Janin: Romantic Critic', in *Rethinking the Sylph*, ed. Lynn Garafola. Hanover, NH: Wesleyan University Press, 1997.

————. 'An Unromantic View of Nineteenth-Century Romanticism.' *York Dance Review* 7 (1978): 28-40.

Chazin-Bennahum, Judith. *The Lure of Perfection: Fashion and Ballet, 1780-1830.* New York: Routledge, 2005.

Child, Francis James. *English and Scottish Ballads.* 8 vols. Boston: Little, Brown, & Co., 1857–59.

Chiti, Rossana, and Federico Marri. *Testi drammatici per musica della Biblioteca Labronica di Livorno*. Livorno: Quaderni della Labronica, 1993.

Christensen, Anne Middelboe. 'Deadly Sylphs and Decent Mermaids: The Women in the Danish Romantic World of August Bournonville', in *The Cambridge Companion to Ballet*, ed. Marion Kant. Cambridge: Cambridge University Press, 2007.

———. *Sylfiden Findes: en svævebog* [The Sylphide Exists: a Soaring Book]. Copenhagen: Schønberg, 2008.

Christensen, Charlotte. 'Temaer fra Shakespeare og Ossian', in *Maleren Nicolai Abilgaard*. Copenhagen: Gyldendal, 1999.

Cinelli, Carlo. *Memorie cronistoriche del teatro di Pesaro dall'anno 1637 al 1897*. Pesaro: A. Nobili, 1898.

Clark, Barrett Harper, ed. *European Theories of the Drama: An Anthology of Dramatic Theory*. New York: D. Appleton and Company, 1929.

Clark, Maribeth. 'Bodies at the Opéra: Art and the Hermaphrodite in the Dance Criticism of Théophile Gautier', in *Reading Critics Reading: Opera and Ballet Criticism in France from the Revolution to 1848*, ed. Roger Parker and Mary Ann Smart. New York: Oxford University Press, 2001.

Clarke, Mary, and Clement Crisp. *Ballet Art from the Renaissance to the Present*. New York: Clarkson N. Potter, 1978.

Cohen, H. Robert, ed. *Douze livrets de mise en scène lyrique datant des créations parisiennes*. Vol. 3, Musical Life in 19th-Century France. Stuyvesant, NY: Pendragon, 1991.

———, ed. *The Original Staging Manuals for Ten Parisian Operatic Premières*. Vol. 6, Musical Life in 19th-Century France Stuyvesant, NY: Pendragon, 1998.

Collins, Willa. 'Adolphe Adam's Ballet Le Corsaire at the Paris Opéra, 1856-1868: A Source Study.' Ph.D. diss., Cornell University, 2008.

Columbo, Marta. *La Raccolta di Libretti d'opera del Teatro S. Carlo di Napoli*. Lucca: LIM, 1992.

Cooper, Suzanne Fagence. 'The Liquefaction of Desire: Music, Water and Femininity in Victorian Aestheticism.' *Women: A Cultural Review* 20, no. 2 (2009): 186–201.

Copeland, Roger, and Marshall Cohen, eds. *What Is Dance? Readings in Theory and Criticism*. New York: Oxford University Press, 1983.

Coralli, Eugéne. *La Péri*. 2nd ed. Paris: Mme Vve Jonas, 1843.

Corbin, Alain. *The Fragrant and the Foul: Odour and the French Social Imagination*. Cambridge, MA: Harvard University Press, 1986.

Cordova, Sarah Davies. *Paris Dances: Textual Choreographies in the Nineteenth-Century French Novel*. Bethesda, MD: International Scholars Publications, 1999.

Crébillon fils [Claude-Prosper Jolyot de Crébillon]. *Le Sylphe, ou songe de Madame De R****. Paris: Delatour, 1730.

Crosten, William F. *French Grand Opera: An Art and a Business*. New York: King's Crown Press, 1948.

Crowe, David M. 'The Roma Holocaust', in *The Holocaust's Ghost: Writings on Art,*

Politics, Law and Education, ed. F.C. DeCoste and Bernard Schwartz. Edmonton: University of Alberta Press, 2000.

Cunningham, Allan. *The Songs of Scotland*. 4 vols. London: J. Taylor, 1825.

Czerwinski, Albert. *Brevier der Tanzkunst: Die Tänze bei den Kulturvölkern von den ältesten Zeiten bis zur Gegenwart*. Leipzig: O. Spamer, 1879.

Dal, Erik, ed. *H.C. Andersens Nye Eventyr og Historier*. H.C. Andersens Eventyr, vol. II. Copenhagen: Hans Reitzel, 1964.

Daly, Ann. 'The Balanchine Woman: Of Hummingbirds and Channel Swimmers.' *Drama Review* 31 (1987): 8-21.

Danziger, Filippo. *Memorie del Teatro Comunale di Trieste dal 1801 al 1876-raccolte da un vecchio teatrofilo*. Trieste: B. Appolonio, n.d.

David, André. 'Histoire de deux ballets "La Sylphide" et "Le Sylphides".' *Le combat*, 19 December 1957.

Day, David A. 'The Annotated Violon Repetiteur and Early Romantic Ballet at the Théâtre Royal de Bruxelles (1815-1830).' Ph.D. diss., New York University, 2008.

De Angelis, Alberto. *Il Teatro d'Alibert o delle Dame (1717-1863)*. Tivoli: Chicca, 1951.

De Angelis, Marcello. *Le carte dell'impresario: melodramma e costume teatrale nell'Ottocento*. Florence: Sansoni, 1982.

————. *Le cifre del melodramma: L'Archivio inedito dell'impresario teatrale Alessandro Lanari (1815-1870) nella Biblioteca Nazionale Centrale di Firenze*. Florence: La Nuova Italia, 1982.

De Beaumont, Saunier (l'abbé) [pseud. de Crouzenac]. *Le Gnome, ou Songe de Mme la Comtesse de *** écrit par elle-même à Mme de ***, pour répondre à la vision du sylphe...* . Paris: Delatour, 1730.

de Bibiena, Jean Galli. *La Poupée*. Paris: n.p., 1744.

De Boigne, Charles. *Petits mémoires de l'Opéra*. Paris: Librairie nouvelle, 1857.

De Cahusac, Louis. *La Danse ancienne et moderne ou Traité historique de la danse*. La Haye: Chez J. Neaulme, 1754.

De Cesare, Raffaele. *La fine di un regno*. Lapi: Città di Castello, 1895.

De Choisy, Martin. *Le Sylphe ou le mari comme il y en a peu, comédie en vers libres et en trois actes mêlés d'ariettes*. Montpellier: Jean-François Picot, 1778.

de Géréon, Léonard [a.k.a. Eugene Ronteix]. *La Rampe et les Coulisses: Esquisses biographiques des directeurs, acteurs et actrices de tous les Théâtres*. Paris: Les marchands de nouveautés, 1832.

De Jorio, Andrea. *La mimica degli antichi investigata nel gestire napoletano*. Naples: Stamperia del Fibreno, 1832. (Tr. with an introduction and notes by Adam Kerdon as *Gesture in Naples and Gesture in Classical Antiquity*. Bloomington: Indiana University Press, 2002.)

De Moncrif, François-Augustin. *Oeuvres de Moncrif*. Vol. 2, Paris: Mardan, 1791.

de Soria, Henri. *Histoire pittoresque de la danse*. Paris: H. Noble, 1897.

Delaforest, A. *Cours de littérature dramatique*. Paris: Allardin, 1836.

Delle Sedie, Enrico. *Estetica del canto e dell'arte melodrammatica*. Livorno: self-published, 1885.

————. *L'art Lyrique - Traité complet de chant et de déclamation lyrique*. Paris: Léon Escudier, 1874; facsimile Bologna, Forni, 1979.

Délon, Michel. *Sylphes et Sylphides: Montfaucon de Villars, Crébillon, Marmontel, Nougaret, Sade, quelques poètes*. Paris: Desjonquères, 1999.

Di Tondo, Ornella. 'Balletto aulico e danza teatrale nel Seicento', in *Storia Della Danza Italana*, ed. José Sasportes. Torino: EDT, 2011.

————. 'I balli negli allestimenti rossiniani a Milano', in *Di sì felice innesto: Rossini, la danza e il ballo teatrale in Italia*, ed. Paolo Fabbri. Pesaro: Fondazione Rossini, 1996.

————. 'Italian Operas Staging Manuals (Disposizioni Sceniche) and Ballet - An Example: Arrigo Boito's *Mefistofele* (1877)', in *Die Beziehung Von Musik und Choreographie im Ballet, Bericht vom Internationalen Symposium (Hochschule für Musik und Theater, Leipzig, 23-25 marzo 2006)*, ed. Michael Malkiewicz and Jörg Rothkamm. Berlin: Berlin, Vorwerk, 2007.

————. *La Censura sui balli teatrali nella Roma dell'Ottocento*. Torino: Utet, 2008.

————. 'Madamigella de La Vallière, Appunti Coreografici di Gioacchino Coluzzi (1878): La Distribuzione della scena e le indicazioni drammaturgiche, mimiche e scenotecniche del ballo.' *Chorégraphie* 1, no. 2 (2004): 43-92.

Dictionary Catalog of the Dance Collection: A List of Authors, Titles, and Subjects of Multi-Media Materials in the Dance Collection of the Performing Arts Research Center of the New York Public Library. New York: New York Public Library, Astor, Lenox, and Tilden Foundations; Boston: distributed by G. K. Hall, 1974.

Drummond, John. *Speaking of Diaghilev*. London: Faber and Faber, 1997.

Ducrey, Guy. *Corps et Graphies: Poétique de la danse et de la danseuse à la fin du XIXe Siècle*. Paris: Honoré Champion, 1996.

Duelund, Peter. 'Denmark: Cultural Policy Profile.' In *Compendium: Cultural Policies and Trends in Europe* (2011). http://www.culturalpolicies.net/web/denmark.php. Accessed 23 August 2011.

Dugulin, Adriano. *Quarant'anni di balletto al Teatro Verdi di Trieste (1845-1885)*. Catalogo Della Mostra, Civico Museo Teatrale Carl Schmidl, Trieste, 14 Aprile - 30 Settembre 1981. Trieste: Acelum, 1981.

Dumesnil, René. 'Ballet Des Champs-Elysées - "*La Sylphide*".' *Le Monde*, 7 January 1947.

Edgecombe, Rodney Stenning. 'On the Limits of Genre: Some Nineteenth-Century Barcaroles.' *Nineteenth-Century Music* 24, no. 3 (2001): 252-67.

Ertz, Matilda Ann Butkas. 'Nineteenth-Century Italian Ballet Music before National Unification: Sources, Style and Context.' Ph.D. diss., University of Oregon, 2010.

Fabbri, Paolo. *Tre secoli di musica a Ravenna*. Ravenna: Longo, 1983.

Fabbri, Paolo, and Roberto Verti. *Due secoli di teatro per musica a Reggio Emilia. Repertorio cronologico delle opere e dei balli 1645-1857*. Reggio Emilia: Edizioni del Teatro Municipale Valli di Reggio Emilia, 1987.

Ferrari, Paolo Emilio. *Spettacoli drammatico-musicali e coreografici in Parma (1628-1883)*. Parma, 1884.

Fétis, François-Joseph. 'Jean-Madeleine Schneitzhoeffer' in *Biographie universelle de musiciens*, 2nd edition. Paris: Firmin-Didot Frères, 1875, vol. 7, 495.

Finlay, John. *Scottish Historical and Romantic Ballads*. 2 vols. Edinburgh: J. Ballantyne, 1808.

Fischer, Carlos. *Les Costumes de L'Opéra*. Paris: Librarie de France, 1931.

Fitzgerald, Percy Hetherington. *The Art of Acting*. London: Swan Sonnenschein and Company, 1892.

Fléche, Alfred, L. W. Webb, and George Willig. *The Sylvia Waltz*. Baltimore: G. Willig Jr., 1840.

Flom, George Tobias. *Scandinavian Influence on Southern Lowland Scotch: A Contribution to the Study of the Linguistic Relations of English and Scandinavian*. Columbia University Germanic Studies. New York: Columbia University Press, 1900.

Fog, Dan. *Musikhandel og nodetryk i Danmark efter 1750*. 2 vols. Copenhagen: Dan Fog, 1984.

Fokine, Michel. *Memoirs of a Ballet Master*. Translated by Vitale Fokine. Edited by Anatole Chujoy. Boston: Little, Brown, 1961.

Forlani, Maria. *Il Teatro Municipale di Piacenza (1804-1984)*. Piacenza: Cassa di Risparmio di Piacenza, Comune di Piacenza, 1985.

Foster, Susan Leigh. 'The Ballerina's Phallic Pointe', in *Corporealities: Dancing Knowledge, Culture and Power*, ed. Susan Leigh Foster. London: Routledge, 1996.

———. *Choreography and Narrative: Ballet's Staging of Story and Desire*. Bloomington: Indiana University Press, 1996.

Franceschi, Enrico Luigi. *Studi teorico-pratici sull'arte di recitare e di declamare nelle sue corrispondenze coll'oratoria, colla drammatica e colla musica*. Milan: Giovanni Silvestri, 1857.

Gaillard, Aurélia. 'Songe et enchantement à la fin de l'âge classique', in *Songes et songeurs (XIIIe-XVIIIe Siècle)*, ed. Nathalie Dauvois and Jean-Philippe Grosperrin. Québec: les Presses de l'Université Laval, 2003.

Gaioni, Berti Alberto. *Cronistoria del Filarmonico (1732-1938)*. Verona: Bettinelli, 1963.

Gandini, Alessandro. *Cronistoria dei Teatri di Modena dal 1539 al 1871*. Modena: Sociale, 1873.

Garafola, Lynn, ed. *Rethinking the Sylph*. Hanover, NH: Wesleyan University Press, 1997.

———. 'The Travesty Dancer in Nineteenth-Century Ballet.' *Dance Research* 17/18 (1985-1986): 35-40.

Gatti, Carlo. *Il Teatro alla Scala di Milano. Cronologie opere-balletti-concerti 1778-1977*. 2 vols. Gorle: Grafica Gutemberg, 1977.

Gattinelli, Gaetano. *Dell'arte rappresentativa in Italia - Studi riformativi onde richiamare il teatro drammatico al primitivo suo scopo di educare il popolo*. Torino: Gianini e Fiore, 1850.

———. *Dell'arte rappresentativa. Manuale ad uso degli studiosi della drammatica e del canto*. Rome: F. Capaccini, 1877.

Gautier, Théophile. *Gautier on Dance*. Edited by Ivor Guest. London: Dance Books, 1986.

———. 'La Péri', in *Poésies complètes* vol. 1. Paris: Charpentier, 1977.

———. *The Péri*. London: W. S. Johnson, 1843.

Gialdroni, Giuliana, and Maria Teresa Gialdroni. *Libretti per musica del fondo Ferrajoli della Biblioteca Apostolica Vaticana*. Lucca: LIM, 1993.

Girardi, Michele, and Franco Rossi. *Il Teatro La Fenice: Cronologia degli Spettacoli 1792-1936*. Venice: Albrizzi, 1989.

Goethe, Johann Wolfgang von. *Italian Journey*. Translated by Robert R. Heitner. Edited by Thomas P. Saine. New York: Suhrkamp Publishers, 1989.

Goodwin, Noël. 'Sight and Sound: Fokine and Chopin.' *Dance and Dancers* (1991): 15-17.

Gottlieb, Robert, ed. *Reading Dance - a Gathering of Memoirs, Reportage, Criticism, Profiles, Interviews, and Some Uncategorizable Extras*. New York: Pantheon Books, 2008.

Granberg, Gunnar. *Skogsrået i yngre nordisk folktradition*. Skrifter Utgivna av Gustav Adolfs Akademien för Folklivsforskning. Uppsala: Lundequistska bokhandeln, 1935.

Greiling, R.O., and A.G. Smith. 'The Dalradian of Scotland: Missing Link between the Vendian of Northern and Southern Scandinavia?'. *Physics and Chemistry of the Earth, Part A: Solid Earth and Geodesy* 25, no. 5 (2000): 495–98.

Greskovic, Robert. *Ballet 101: A Complete Guide to Learning and Loving the Ballet*. Pompton Plains, NJ: Limelight Editions, 2005. New York: Hyperion, 1998.

Grundtvig, Svend. *Engelske og Skotske Folkeviser* [English and Scottish Folk Ballads]. 4 vols. Copenhagen: Wahlske Boghandling, 1842–46.

Grundtvig, Svend, Axel Olrik, Hakon Grüner-Nielsen, Hjalmar Thuren, and Sven H. Rossel, eds. *Danmarks gamle Folkeviser*. 12 vols. Copenhagen: Samfundet til den danske Literaturs Fremme, 1853–1976.

Guest, Ann Hutchinson. 'Is Authenticity to be had?' in *Preservation Politics: Dance Revived, Reconstructed, Remade*, ed. Stephanie Jordan. London: Dance Books, 2000.

Guest, Ivor. *Adventures of a Ballet Historian – an Unfinished Memoir*. New York: Dance Horizons, 1982.

———. *The Ballet of the Second Empire 1858-1870*. London: Black, 1953.

———. *Fanny Cerrito. The Life of a Romantic Ballerina*. London: Phoenix, 1956.

———. *Fanny Ellsler*. London: Black, 1970.

———. ed. *Gautier on Dance*. London: Dance Books, 1986.

———. *Jules Perrot, Master of the Romantic Ballet*. New York: Dance Horizons, 1984.

———. 'L'Italia e il balletto romantico.' *La Danza italiana* 8-9 (1990): 7-15.

———. ''La Sylphide' in London.' *Ballet* 6, no. 3 (1948): 39-43, 45.

———. *Letters from a Ballet Master. The Correspondence of Arthur Saint-Léon*. London: Dance Books, 1981.

———. *The Romantic Ballet in Paris*. 2nd ed. London: Dance Books, 1980.

————. *The Romantic Ballet in Paris.* 3rd ed. Alton, Hampshire, UK: Dance Books, 2008.

Guest, Ivor, and John Lanchberry. 'The Scores of *La Fille mal gardée.' Theatre Research* 3, no. 1 (1961): 32-42.

————. 'The Scores of *La Fille mal gardée.' Theatre Research* 3, no. 2 (1961): 121-34.

Gutsche-Miller, Sarah. 'Pantomime-Ballet on the Music-Hall Stage: The Popularisation of Classical Ballet in *Fin-de-Siècle* Paris.' Ph.D. diss., McGill University, 2010.

Hall, Alaric. 'Getting Shot of Elves: Healing, Witchcraft and Fairies in the Scottish Witchcraft Trials.' *Folklore* 116 (2005): 19–36.

Hallar, Marianne, and Alette Scavenius. *Bournonvilleana.* Translated by Gaye Kynoch. Copenhagen: Rhodos, 1992.

Hammond, Sandra Noll. 'Ballet's Technical Heritage: The Grammaire of Léopold Adice.' *Dance Research* 13 (1995): 35-58.

————. 'Clues to Ballet's Technical History from an Early Nineteenth-Century Ballet Lesson.' *Dance Research* 3 (1984): 53-66.

————. 'In the Dance Classroom with Edgar Degas: Historical Perspectives on Ballet Technique', in *Imaging Dance - Visual Representations of Dancers and Dancing*, Sparti, Barbara, and Judy Van Zile, eds., with E. Ivancich Dunan, N. G. Heller, and A. L. Kaeppler.. Hildesheim: Georg Olms Verlag, 2011.

————. 'A Nineteenth-Century Dancing Master at the Court of Württemberg: The Dance Notebooks of Michel St. Léon.' *Dance Chronicle* 15, no. 3 (1992): 291-315.

————. 'Searching for the Sylph: Documentation of Early Developments in Pointe Technique.' *Dance Research Journal* 19, no. 2 (1987-8): 27-31.

————. 'Steps through Time: Selected Dance Vocabulary of the Eighteenth and Nineteenth Centuries.' *Dance Research* 10, no. 2 (1992): 93-108.

————. 'Windows into Romantic Ballet, Part 2: Content and Structure of Solo Entrées from the Early Nineteenth Century', in *Proceedings, Dance History Scholars.* Riverside, CA: Society of Dance History Scholars, 1998.

————. 'Windows into Romantic Ballet: Content and Structure of Four Early Nineteenth-Century Pas De Deux', in *Proceedings, Dance History Scholars* Riverside, CA: Society of Dance History Scholars, 1997.

Hammond, Sandra Noll, and Phillip E. Hammond. 'Technique and Autonomy in the Development of Art: A Case Study in Ballet.' *Dance Research Journal* 21, no. 2 (1989): 15-24.

Hansell, Kathleen Kuzmick. 'Il ballo teatrale e l'opera italiana', in *Storia dell'opera italiana*, vol. 5, ed. Lorenzo Bianconi and Giorgio Pestelli. Torino: EDT, 1988.

————. 'Theatrical Ballet and Italian Opera', in *Opera on Stage*, ed. Lorenzo Bianconi and Giorgio Pestelli. Chicago: University of Chicago Press, 1998.

Heiberg, Johanne Luise. *Et Liv gjenoplevit i Erindringen* [A Life Relived in Memory], Vol. 1, Copenhagen: Gylendal, 1973.

Heiberg, Johanne Luise, and Patricia McAndrew. 'Memories of Taglioni and Elssler.' *Dance Chronicle* 4, no. 1 (1981): 14-18.

Hertel, Hans. 'P.L. Møller and Romanticism in Danish Literature.' *Scandinavica* 8 (1969): 35–48.

Holmstrom, Kirsten Gram. 'Attitude and Shawl Dance' in *International Encyclopedia of Dance*, edited by Elizabeth Aldrich and Selma Jeanne Cohen. New York: Oxford University Press, 1998, vol. 1, 198-199.

Howitt, William and Mary. *Literature and Romance of Northern Europe*. 2 vols. London: Colburn, 1852.

Hubbard, Tom. 'European Reception of Scott's Poetry: Translation as the Front Line', in *The Reception of Sir Walter Scott in Europe*, ed. Murray Pittock. London, New York: Continuum, 2006.

Huckenpahler, Victoria. 'Confessions of an Opera Director: Chapters from the *Mémoires* of Dr. Louis Véron, Part One.' *Dance Chronicle* 7, no. 1 (1984): 50-106.

Hugo, Victor. *The Works of Victor Hugo*. Translated by George Burnham Ives. Vol. 3: Dramas, Boston: Little, Brown, & Company, 1909.

Hunt, David. 'Ballet Music from Denmark.' *Dance and Dancers* (October 1953): 9.

Hustvedt, Sigurd Bernhard. *Ballad Criticism in Scandinavia and Great Britain During the Eighteenth Century*. New York: American-Scandinavian Foundation, 1916.

Iacono, Concetta Lo. 'Forse s'avess'io l'ale', in *La Silfide, Programma di sala, Teatro dell'opera di Roma, Stagione 1990-91*. Rome: Edizioni del Teatro dell'Opera di Roma, 1990.

———. 'Minima Choreutica: Fasti e dissesti del ballo italiano sul declino dell'Ottocento', in *Musica Senza Aggettivi, Rivista Musicale Italiana*, vol. 2. Florence: Olschki, 1991.

Ireland, Joseph Norton. *Records of the New York Stage, from 1750 to 1860*, 2 vols. New York: Morrell, 1866.

Isaacson, Lanae H. 'Dramatic Discourse in the Scandinavian Ballad.' *Scandinavian Studies* 64, no. 1 (1992): 68–95.

Ivaldi, Fabio. '"Divas de la danse" al Teatro Carlo Felice di Genova (1828-1860).' *Chorégraphie: Rivista di ricerca sulla danza* 3 (2003): 31-125.

Jacobshagen, Arnold, 'Analyzing *mise-en-scène*: Halévy's *La Juive* at the Salle Le Peletier', in *Music, Theater, and Cultural Transfer: Paris, 1830-1914*, ed. Annegret Fauser and Mark Everist. Chicago: University of Chicago Press, 2009.

Jamieson, Robert. *Popular Ballads and Songs*. 2 vols. Edinburgh: A. Constable, 1806.

Janin, Jules, Philarète Chasles, and Théophile Gautier. *Les Beautés de l'Opéra, ou Chefs-d'œuvre lyriques: illustrés par les premiers artistes de Paris et de Londres sous la direction de Giraldon*. Paris: Soulié, 1845.

Jarvis, Charles, Fanny Elssler, and Peter S. Duval. *Melle. Fanny Elssler's Quadrilles: Arranged for the Piano Forte*. Keffer Collection of Sheet Music. Philadelphia: A. Fiot, 1840.

Jensen, Lisbeth Ahlgren. *Det Kvindelige Spillerum: Fem Kvindelige Komponister i Danmark i 1800-tallet*. Copenhagen: Multivers, 2007.

Jeschke, Claudia, and Robert Atwood. 'Expanding Horizons: Techniques of Choreo-Graphy in Nineteenth-Century Dance.' *Dance Chronicle* 29, no. 2 (2006): 195-214.

Jordan, Stephanie. 'The Role of the Ballet Composer at the Paris Opera: 1820-1850.' *Dance Chronicle* 4, no. 4 (1982): 374-88.

Jürgensen, Knud Arne. *The Bournonville Ballets - a Photographic Record 1844-1933*. London: Dance Books, 1987.

———. *The Bournonville Heritage: A Choreographic Record 1829-1875*. London: Dance Books, 1990.

———. 'Bournonville Composers' in *International Encyclopedia of Dance*, ed. Elizabeth Aldrich and Selma Jeanne Cohen. New York: Oxford University Press, 1998, vol. I, 514-516.

———. *The Bournonville Tradition: The First Fifty Years, 1829–1879*. 2 vols. London: Dance Books, 1997.

———. 'Sulle tracce della Silfide italiana.' *Rivista illustrata del Museo Teatrale alla Scala* 1, no. 4 (1989): 18-39.

Jürgensen, Knud Arne, and Francesca Falcone, eds. *Études Chorégraphiques (1848, 1855, 1861)*. Lucca: LIM, 2005.

Jürgensen, Knud Arne, and Vivi Flindt. *Bournonville Ballet Technique-Fifty Enchaînements*. London: Dance Books, 1992.

Justamant [or Justament], Henri. *Giselle ou Les Wilis: Ballet Fantastique en deux actes. Faksimile der Notation von Henri Justamant aus den 1860er Jahren*. Ed. Frank-Manuel Peter. Hildesheim: Georg Olms Verlag, 2008.

Kawabata, Maiko. 'Virtuosity, the Violin, the Devil...What Really Made Paganini "Demonic"?'. *Current Musicology* 83 (2007): 85–108.

Kirstein, Lincoln. 'Ballet and Music', in *The International Cyclopedia of Music and Musicians*, ed. Oscar Thompson and Bruce Bohle. 10th ed. New York: Dodd, Mead, 1975.

———. *Dance: A Short History of Classic Theatrical Dancing*. New York: G. P. Putnam's Sons, 1935.

———. *Four Centuries of Ballet: Fifty Masterworks*. New York: Dover, 1984.

Kisselgoff, Anna. 'A New and Longer 'Sylphide' from London.' *New York Times*, 5 July 1989.

Koegler, Horst. 'Ballet Blanc.' In *The Concise Oxford Dictionary of Ballet*. London, 1982.

———. *The Concise Oxford Dictionary of Ballet*. London: Oxford University Press, 1977.

Kramer, Lawrence. 'Musical Form and *Fin-de-Siècle* Sexuality', in *Music as Cultural Practice, 1800–1900*. Los Angeles: University of California Press, 1990.

Kuhlau, Friedrich. *Elverhøj: Skuespil i Fem Acter, Op. 100*. Copenhagen: C. C. Lose, 1829; repr., Dan Fog Musikforlag, 1978.

Kværndrup, Sigurd. *Den Østnordiske Ballade - Oral Teori og Tekstanalyse: Studier i Danmarks Gamle Folkeviser*. Copenhagen: Museum Tusculanum, 2006.

Kvideland, Reimund, and Henning K. Sehmsdorf, eds. *Scandinavian Folk Belief and Legend*. Minneapolis: University of Minnesota Press, 1988.

Landstad, Magnus Brostrup. *Norske Folkeviser* [Norwegian Folk Ballads]. Christiania: Tönsberg, 1853.

LaPointe-Crump, Janice D. 'Birth of a Ballet: August Bournonville's *a Folk Tale*, 1854.' Ph.D. diss., Texas Woman's University, 1980.

Lecomte, Nathalie. 'Maria Taglioni alla Scala.' *La Danza italiana* 8-9 (1990): 47-71.

Leeder, Paul Robert. 'Scott and Scandinavian Literature: The Influence of Bartholin and Others.' *Smith College Studies in Modern Languages* 2 (1920): 8–57.

Levinson, André. *Ballet Old and New*. Translated by Susan Cook Summer. New York: Dance Horizons, 1982.

———. 'The Idea of the Dance: From Aristotle to Mallarmé.' *Theatre Arts Monthly*, 1927.

———. *Marie Taglioni*. Translated by Cyril Beaumont. London: Imperial Society of Teachers of Dancing, 1930.

Lichtenthal, Pietro. *Dizionario e bibliografia della musica*. Milan: Fontana, 1836.

Lindow, John. 'Supernatural Others and Ethnic Others: A Millennium of World View.' *Scandinavian Studies* 67, no. 1 (1995): 8–31.

Lomax, Sondra. 'Fokine's Manifesto and *Les sylphides*', in *New Directions in Dance*, ed. D. T. Taplin. Toronto: Pergamon Press, 1979, 113-120.

Lombardi, Carmela. *La Ballerina immaginaria: Una Donna nella letteratura e sulla scena nell'età dell'industrialismo 1822-1908*. Naples: Liguori, 2007.

Løvenskiold, Herman Severin. *Contredanses françaises sur des motifs de La Sylphide* [French Contradances on the Motives of *La Sylphide*]. Copenhagen: Lose & Olsen, 1837.

———. *Introduction af Første Act af Balletten Sylphiden arr. af Componisten* [Introduction to Act One of the Ballet *Sylphiden*]. *Musikalsk Trilogie* [Musical Trilogy]. Copenhagen: Wilhelm Hansen, 1859.

———. *La Sylphide, Ouverture et morceaux choisis* [*La Sylphide*, Overture and Selected Pieces]. Copenhagen: Lose & Olsen, 1837.

Løvenskiold, Herman Severin, and August Bournonville. *Les Sylphides: contredances françaises pour le pianoforte sur des motifs de la composition de Mr H. de Løvenskjold*. Copenhagen: C.C. Lose and Olsen, 1837.

———. cond. David Garforth. *Music for the Bournonville Ballet La Sylphide*. Colchester, Essex, England: Chandos Records, 1986, reissued 1991, 2001, 2004.

Lui, Ernesto, and Aldo Ottolenghi. *I cento anni del Teatro Sociale di Mantova (1822-1922)*. Mantova: G. Mondovì, 1923.

Macauley, Alastair, 'The author of *La Sylphide*, Adolphe Nourrit,' *Dancing Times* (1989): 140-143.

Mackrell, Alice. *Shawls, Stoles, and Scarves*. The Costume Accessories Series. Edited by Aileen Ribeiro. London: B. T. Batsford, Ltd., 1986.

Magri, Gennaro. *Trattato teorico-prattico di ballo*. Naples: Orsino, 1779.

Maione, Paologiovanni, and Francesca Seller. *Teatro di San Carlo di Napoli. Cronologia degli spettacoli (1851-1900)*. Avagliano: Cava de' Tirreni, 1999.

Mallarmé, Stéphane. 'Ballets' in *Mallarmé: Selected Prose Poems, Essays, and Letters*, trans. Bradford Cook. Baltimore: Johns Hopkins Press, 1956.

Manning, Susan. 'Borrowing from Feminist Theory.' Paper presented at the National Meeting of the Society of Dance History Scholar. Riverside, CA, 1992.

———. *Ecstasy and the Demon: feminism and nationalism in the dance of Mary Wigman*. Berkeley: University of California Press, 1993.

Maragliano, Alessandro. *I teatri di Voghera*. Cronistoria, Casteggio: Cerri, 1901.

Marinelli, Roscioni Carlo. *Il Teatro San Carlo: Cronologia 1737-1987*. Naples: Guida, 1987.

Marmontel, Jean-François. *Le mari sylphe*. Paris: n.p., 1761.

Martuscelli, Francesco. *Saggio sulla scienza dell'espressione nelle sue relazioni coll'arte rappresentativa*. Naples: Sautto, 1861.

Marx, Wolfgang. 'The Ballet as a 'Genre': Initial Thoughts on the Genetic Identity of a Multimedia Art Form', in *Die Beziehung von Musik und Choreographie im Ballett*, ed. Michael Malkiewicz and Jörg Rothkamm. Berlin: Vorwerk 8, 2007.

Massa, Maria Rosaria. *Libretti di melodrammi e balli nella Biblioteca Palatina di Caserta*. Lucca: LIM, 1992.

Mayseder, Joseph. *Souvenir de La Sylphide; Air de Mayseder arr. pour le piano seul par A. Thys*. Philadelphia: George Willig, 1840.

———. *La Sylphide as danced by Fanny Elssler*. New York: Atwill, 184?

Mazilier, Joseph. *Marco Spada, ou, La Fille du Bandit.* Paris: Jonas, 1857.

McAndrew, Patricia. 'Bournonville', in *International Encyclopedia of Dance*, ed. Elizabeth Aldrich and Selma Jeanne Cohen. New York: Oxford University Press, 1998, vol. 1, 502-514.

McCarren, Felicia. *Dance Pathologies: Performance, Poetics, Medicine*. Stanford: Stanford University Press, 1998.

Meisner, Nadine. 'Pierre Lacotte and the Romantic Ballet', in *Preservation Politics: Dance Revived, Reconstructed, Remade*, ed. Stephanie Jordan. London: Dance Books, 1997.

Melisi, Francesco. *Catalogo dei libretti per musica dell'Ottocento della Biblioteca del Conservatorio 'San Pietro a Majella' di Napoli*. Lucca: LIM, 1990.

Ménil, Félicien de. *Histoire de la danse à travers les ages*. Paris: A. Picard & Kaan, 1905.

Meyerbeer, Giacomo. *Robert le diable*. Paris: Schlesinger, 183-, reprinted New York: Garland Publishing, 1980, 2 vols.

Mitchell, Jerome. *The Walter Scott Operas: An Analysis of Operas Based on the Works of Sir Walter Scott*. Birmingham: University of Alabama Press, 1977.

Monaldi, Gino. *Le regine della danza nel secolo XIX*. Turin: Fratelli Bocca, 1919.

Montolieu, Isabelle de. *La Sylphide ou L'ange gardien, nouvelle traduit de L'anglaise*. Lausanne and Paris: n.p., 1795.

Moore, Lillian. *Images of the Dance: Historical Treasures of the Dance Collection 1581-1861*. New York: The New York Library, 1965.

———. '*La Sylphide*, Epitome of the Romantic Ballet.' *Dance Magazine*, March 1965, 42-47.

Moreira, James H. 'Narrative Expectations and Domestic Space in the Telemark Ballads.' *Scandinavian Studies* 73, no. 3 (2001): 317–48.

Morelli, Alamanno. *Prontuario delle pose sceniche.* Milan: Borroni e Scotti, 1854.

Morici, Ottaviano. *I cento anni del teatro delle Muse di Ancona 1827-1927.* Ancona: Nacci, 1927.

Morini, Ugo. *La R. Accademia degli Immobili e il suo Teatro 'La Pergola'.* Pisa: Simoncini, 1926.

Mørk, Ebbe. 'A Friendship: Andersen and Bournonville', in *The Royal Danish Ballet and Bournonville.* Copenhagen: Ministry of Foreign Affairs of Denmark, 1979.

Morrocchesi, Antonio. *Lezioni di Declamazione e d'arte Teatrale.* Florence: all'Insegna di Dante, 1832.

Motherwell, William. *Minstrelsy, Ancient and Modern.* Glasgow: J. Wylie, 1827.

Music to the Bournonville Ballets. Performed by the Aaloborg Symphony orchestra, directed by Ernst Lassen. Copenhagen: Danacord, 2005. CD.

Napoli-Signorelli, Pietro. *Elementi di poesia drammatica.* Milan: n. p., 1801.

Nectoux, Jean-Michel. 'Trois Orchestres Parisiens en 1830: L'académie Royal de Musique, Le Théâtre-Italien et la Société Des Concerts du Conservatoire', in *Music in Paris in the Eighteen-Thirties,* ed. Peter Bloom. Stuyvesant, NY: Pendragon, 1987.

New York Public Library Dance Collection: Bibliographic Guide to Dance. Boston: G. K. Hall, 1975-2003.

Nielsen, Jørgen Erik. ' "His Pirates Had Foray'd on Scottish Hill": Scott in Denmark with an Overview of His Reception in Norway and Sweden', in *The Reception of Sir Walter Scott in Europe,* ed. Murray Pittock. New York, London: Continuum, 2006.

Nijinska, Bronislava. *Early Memoirs.* Edited by Irina Nijinska and Jean Rawlinson. Durham, NC: Duke University Press, 1992.

Nodier, Charles Emmanuel. *Trilby Il Folletto Di Argail.* Edited by Elena Grillo. Rome: Lucarini, 1988.

———. *Trilby ou le Lutin d'argail.* Paris: Ladvocat, 1822.

———. 'Trilby ou le Lutin d'argail', in *Oeuvres,* vol. 1. Paris: Renduel, 1832-37.

———. 'Trilby ovvero il folletto di Argail', in *I demoni della notte e altri racconti.* Milan: Garzanti, 2002.

Nørlyng, Ole. 'Bournonville og hans musikalske medarbejdere' [Bournonville and his musical collaborators], in *Perspektiv på Bournonville,* ed. Marianne Hallar, Erik Aschengreen, and Jørgen Heiner. Copenhagen: Nyt nordisk forlag, 1980.

———. 'The Composer Herman Severin Løvenskiold'. Liner notes in *Music for the Bournonville ballet La Sylphide.* Eng. Trans. Gaye Kynoch, Colchester, Essex, England: Chandos, 1986. LP.; 1991. CD.

———. 'Drøm eller virkelighed: om de musikalske kilders betydning i forbindelse med en idag forsvunden mimsk scene i *Sylphiden*', in *Bournonville: Tradition, Rekonstruktion,* ed. Ole Nørlyng and Henning Urup. Copenhagen: C.A. Reitzel, 1989.

————. 'The Music for La Sylphide'. Liner notes in in *Music for the Bournonville ballet La Sylphide*. Eng. Trans. Gaye Kynoch, Colchester, Essex, England: Chandos, 1986. LP.; 1991. CD.

————. 'Musikken er phantasiens skjønneste Organ', in *Salut for Bournonville*, ed. Ebbe Mørk. Copenhagen: Statens Museum for Kunst, 1979.

Nougaret, Pierre-Jean-Bapstiste. *Le singulier sylphe*. 1800.

Novack, Cythia. *Sharing the Dance: Contact Improvisation and American Culture*. Madison, WI: University of Wisconsin Press, 1990.

Noverre, Jean-Georges. *Lettres sur la danse, et sur les ballets*. Stuttgart and Lyon: Aimé Delaroche, 1760.

————. *Programmi di balletti*. Edited by Flavia Pappacena. Rome: Audino, 2009.

Nozière [pseud. of Fernand Weyl]. *Le théâtre: Revue bimensuelle illustrée*, 1909, 12-15.

Oberzaucher-Schüller, Gunhild. 'La Sylphide, Oder Verschleierte Phantasmagorien', in *Meyerbeer-Studien* 4. Paderborn: University Press, 2002.

Olwig, Kenneth. 'Place, Society, and the Individual in the Authorship of St. St. Blicher', in *Omkring Blicher 1974*, ed. Felix Nørgaard. Copenhagen: Gyldendal, 1974.

Overskou, Thomas. *Den danske Skueplads i dens Historie fra de første Spor af danske Skuespil indtil vor Tid*. 7 vols. Copenhagen: Thieles, 1864.

Ovid. *Metamorphoses*. Translated by Charles Martin. New York: W. W. Norton and Company, 2004.

Oxfeldt, Elisabeth. *Nordic Orientalism: Paris and the Cosmopolitan Imagination 1800–1900*. Copenhagen: Museum Tusculanum Press, 2005.

Paganini, Nicolò, and Ricardo Tagliorozzo, *Le Streghe: variazioni per violino e pianoforte, op.8* (no. 3 delle opere postume). Milan: G. Ricardi, 1918.

Pagliano, Piero. 'Charles Nodier: La Vita', in *I demoni della notte e altri racconti*. Milan: Garzanti, 2002.

Pandolfo, Patrizia, and Valentina Rinaldo, eds. *Il real Teatro Bellini di Palermo: un teatro da riscoprire*. Palermo: Nuova graphicadue, 2000.

Paoli, Catelani Bice. *Il Teatro Comunale del "Giglio" di Lucca*. Pescia: Benedetti, 1941.

Pappacena, Flavia. 'Dagli Zefìri alla fanciulle alate del balletto romantico', in *Il linguaggio della danza: Guida all'interpretazione delle fonti iconografiche della danza classica*. Rome: Gremese, 2010.

————. *Il linguaggio della danza: guida all'interpretazione delle fonti iconografiche della danza classica*. Rome: Gremese, 2010.

————. *Il Trattato di Danza di Carlo Blasis 1820-1830*. Lucca: LIM, 2005.

————. ed. *Jean-Georges Noverre. Programmi di balletti*. Rome: Dino Audino, 2009.

————. 'L'eredità Classica e l'ispirazione alle arti ne L'Uomo fisico, intellettuale e morale di Carlo Blasis', in *Carlo Blasis, L'uomo fisico, intellettuale e morale*, ed. Flavia Pappacena and Ornella Di Tondo. Lucca: LIM, 2007.

————. *La Danza classica: Le Origini*. Rome: Laterza, 2009.

————. ed. *Recupero, ricostruzione, conservazione del patrimonio coreutico italiano del XIX Secolo: Atti Del Convegno Di Studi Roma, 10 Dicembre 1999*. Rome: Consiglio nazionale delle ricerche, 2000.

———. *Ricostruzione della linea stilistica di Carlo Blasis*. Vol. 1, Rome: Meltemi, 2002.

Pappalardo, Paolo. *L'arte della parola - Precetti di pronunziazione, espressione e declamazione*. Palermo: Mirto, 1888.

Pasi, Mario. 'La Silfide. Il personaggio e il balletto', in *La Silfide, Programma di sala, Teatro dell'opera di Roma, stagione 1990-91*. Rome: Edizioni del Teatro dell'Opera di Roma.

Pastori, Jean-Pierre. *Pierre Lacotte: Tradition*. Eng. trans. Jacqueline Gartmann. Paris: Favre, 1987.

Pellegrini, Almachide. *Spettacoli Lucchesi nei Secoli XVII-XIX*. Lucca: Giusti, 1914.

Perrot, Jules. *Lalla Rookh*. London: G. Stuart, 1846.

Pittock, Murray. 'Scott and the European Nationalities Question', in *The Reception of Sir Walter Scott in Europe*, ed. Murray Pittock. New York, London: Continuum, 2006.

Poesio, Giannandrea. 'Balletic Mime.' *Dancing Times* (June 1990): 895-99.

———. 'Blasis, the Italian Ballo, and the Male Sylph', in *Rethinking the Sylph*, ed. Lynn Garafola. Hanover, NH: Wesleyan University Press, 1997.

———. 'Carabosse Revisited. Enrico Cecchetti and the Lost Language of Mime', in Society of Dance paper presented at the National Meeting of the History Scholars, Eugene, OR, 1998.

Prior, R.C. Alexander. *Ancient Danish Ballads*. 3 vols. London, Edinburgh: Williams and Norgate, 1860.

Pritchard, Jane. 'Collaborative Creations for the Alhambra and the Empire.' *Dance Chronicle* 24 (2001): 55-82.

Pudelek, Janina. 'Ballet Dancers at Warsaw's Wielki Theater', in *Rethinking the Sylph*, ed. Lynn Garafola. Hanover, NH: Wesleyan University Press, 1997.

Quétant, François-Antoine. *L'amant Sylphe, ou La Féerie de l'amour, comédie en trois actes, en prose, mêlée d'ariettes, représentée devant leurs majestés à Fontainebleau*. [Paris]: R.C. Ballard, 1783.

Racinet, A. *Le Costume Historique*. 6 vols. Paris: Firmin-Didot, 1888.

Radiciotti, Giuseppe. *Teatro, musica e musicisti in Recanati*. Recanati: Simboli, 1904.

———. *Teatro, musica e musicisti in Senigallia*. Milan: Ricordi, 1893.

Raggi, Alessandro e Luigi. *Il Teatro Comunale di Cesena (1500-1905)*. Cesena: Vignunzi, 1906.

Raimondi, Ezio, ed. *Il Sogno del coreodramma: Salvatore Viganò, Poeta Muto*. Bologna: Il Mulino, 1984.

———. *Romanticismo italiano e romanticismo europeo*. Milan: Mondatori, 1997.

Rameau, Pierre. *Abbregé de la nouvelle methode dans l'art d'écrire ou de traçer toutes sortes de danses de ville*. Paris: self-published, 1725.

Regli, Francesco. 'Della coreografia in Italia. Alcune riflessioni - un voto e una profezia.' *Strenna teatrale italiana* 1 (1838): 69-79.

————. *Dizionario biografico dei più celebri poeti ed artisti melodrammatici, tragici e comici, maestri, concertisti, coreografi, mimi, ballerini, scenografi, giornalisti, impresari ecc. ecc . che fiorirono in Italia dal 1800 al 1860.* Torino: Dalmazzo, 1860.

Richardson, Philip J. S. *The Social Dances of the Nineteenth Century in England.* London: H. Jenkins, 1960.

Rinaldi, Mario. *Due secoli di musica al teatro Argentina.* Florence: L. S. Olschki, 1978.

Ristori, Cesare. *Manuale pratico di declamazione ad uso degli studiosi l'arte rappresentativa applicata al puro canto.* Torino: G. Tarino, 1888.

————. *Studio della declamazione applicata al canto.* Milan: Emilio Civelli, 1880.

Ritorni, Carlo. *Commentarii della vita e delle opere coreodrammatiche di Salvatore Viganò e della coreografia e dei corepei.* Milan: Guglielmini e Redaelli, 1838.

Robert, Grace. *The Borzoi Book of Ballets.* New York: A. A. Knopf, 1946.

Robin-Challan, Louise. 'Danse et Danseuses à l'Opéra de Paris, 1830-1850.' Université de Paris VII, 1988.

————. 'Social Conditions of Ballet Dancers at the Paris Opera in the 19th Century.' *Choreography and Dance* 2 (1992): 17-28.

Roca, Octavio. 'Timeless "Sylphide" from Danish Ballet - Revamped Version in Orange County.' *San Francisco Chronicle,* 27 May 1995.

Roller, Franz Anton. *Systematisches Lehrbuch der bildenden Tanzkunst und körperlichen Ausbildung.* Vienna: Bernh. Fr. Voigt, 1843.

Romani, Luigi. *Teatro alla Scala: cronologia di tutti gli spettacoli rappresentati in questo teatro dal giorno del solenne suo aprimento sino ad oggi.* Milan: Luigi di Giacomo Pirola, 1862.

Rossel, Sven H. 'From Romanticism to Realism', in *A History of Danish Literature,* ed. Sven H. Rossel. *A History of Scandinavian Literatures.* Lincoln: University of Nebraska Press, 1992.

Rossi, Franco. *La Fondazione Levi di Venezia, Catalogo del Fondo Musicale.* Venice: Fondazione Levi, 1862.

Rothkamm, Jörg. *Balletmusik im 19. und 20. Jahrhundert: Dramaturgie einer Gattung.* Mainz: Schott Music, 2011.

————. 'Dialogähnliche und Acktionsbezogene Musik im Ballett *Sylphiden* Von Herman Løvenskjold und August Bournonville (1836).' *Die Tonkunst* 2 (2008): 20–33.

Ruffin, Elena. 'Il Ballo Teatrale a Venezia nel secolo XIX', *La Danza Italiana* 5-6, (1987), 151-179.

Russell, Peter. *The Themes of the German Lied from Mozart to Strauss.* Studies in the History and Interpretation of Music. Vol. 84, Lewiston: Edwin Mellen, 2002.

Rygg, Kristin. 'Mystification through Musicalization and Demystification through Music: The Case of *Haugtussa*', in *Cultural Functions of Intermedial Exploration,* ed. Erik Hedling. New York: Rodopi, 2002.

Said, Edward W. *Orientalism.* 25th Anniversary Edition. 1994 New York: Random House Vintage Books, 1978.

Saint-Léon, Arthur. *De l'état actuel de la danse*. Lisbon: Typographie du Progresso, 1856.

———. *La Sténochorégraphie ou art d'écrire promptement la danse*. Paris: Chez l'Auteur et chez Brandus, 1852.

Salfi, Francesco Saverio. *Della Declamazione*. Naples: di Androsio, 1878.

Santoro, Elia. *Il Teatro di Cremona*. Cremona: Pizzorni, 1969.

Sasportes, José, 'Invito allo studio di due secoli di danze teatrali a Venezia (1746-1859)', in *Balli Teatrali a Venezia*, vol. 1, ed. Elena Ruffin and Giovanna Trentin. Drammaturgia Musicale Veneta. Milan: Ricordi, 1994.

———. 'La parola contro il corpo ovvero il melodramma nemico del ballo.' *La Danza italiana* 1 (1984): 21-41.

———. 'Vincenzo Buonsignori.' *La Danza italiana* 7 (1989): 150-51.

———. 'Virtuosismo e spettacolarità: le risposte italiane alla decadenza del balletto romantico', in *Tornando a Stiffelio: Quaderni della Rivista Italiana di Musicologia*, ed. Giovanni Morelli. Florence: Olschki, 1987.

Sasportes, José, and Antonio Pinto Ribeiro. *History of Dance*. Translated by Joan Ennes. Lisbon: Imprensa Nacional-Casa da Moeda, 1991.

Scafidi, Nadia. 'Il Teatro alla Scala', in *La Danza in Italia: La Scala, La Fenice, Il San Carlo. dal XVIII secolo ai giorni nostri*, ed. Nadia Scafidi, Rita Zambon and Roberta Albano, Direzione Flavia Pappacena. Rome: Gremese, 1998.

———. 'La Scuola di ballo del Teatro alla Scala: L'ordinamento legislativo e didattico nel XIX secolo.' *Chorégraphie* 7-8 (1996): 51-72.

———. *Ricerche di storia della danza 1994-2000*. Rome: Ass. Culturale Chorégraphie, 2009.

———. ed. *Studi sulla scuola italiana*. Rome: Melterni. *Chorégraphie*, nuova serie, 2. (2002).

Scavenius, Bente, ed. *The Golden Age in Denmark: Art and Culture 1800–1850*. Copenhagen: Gyldendal, 1994.

Schlüter, Anne Marie Vessel, ed. *The Bournonville School - the Dance Programme*. Copenhagen: the Royal Danish Theatre, 2005.

Schmidl, Carlo. *Dizionario Universale dei Musicisti*. Milan: Sanzogno, 1937.

Schneitzhoeffer, Jean Madeleine, and A. Aulagnier. *Rondino pour le piano, sur des motifs de La Sylphide, op. 13*. Paris: Aulagnier, 1832.

Schneitzhoeffer, J. M., and J. Tolbèque. *Trois Quatrilles sur les motifs de La Sylphide [for Flute and Piano]*. Paris: Aulagnier, 1832.

Scholl, Tim. *'Sleeping Beauty': A Legend in Progress*. New Haven: Yale University Press, 2004.

Schueneman, Bruce R., and William E. Studwell. *Minor Ballet Composers: Biographical Sketches of Sixty-Six Underappreciated yet Significant Contributors to the Body of Western Ballet Music*. New York: Haworth Press, 1997.

Scott, Sir Walter. 'The Fairies of Popular Superstition', in *Minstrelsy of the Scottish Border*, vol. 2 Kelso: J. Ballantyne, 1802.

———. *Minstrelsy of the Scottish Border*. 2 vols. Kelso: J. Ballantyne, 1802.

Séchan, Charles. *Souvenirs d'un homme de Théâtre, 1831-1855*. Paris: Calmann Levy, 1883.

Second, Albéric. *Les Petits Mystères de L'opéra*. Paris: G. Kugelmann, 1844.

Segal, Lewis. 'Out of Step? Peter Schaufuss' Staging of "La Sylphide" Has Been Criticized on Questions of Taste, Style and Tone—So Has His Reign as Artistic Director of the Royal Danish Ballet.' *Los Angeles Times*, 21 May 1995.

Séveste, Jules and Ernst Jaime. *La Sylphide, drame en 2 actes, mêlé de chant, imité du ballet de M. Taglioni*. Paris: Théâtre Montmartre, 20 September 1832.

Shore, Dan. 'The Emergence of Danish National Opera, 1779-1846.' Ph.D. diss., CUNY, 2008.

Silvestri, Lodovico. *R.R. Teatri Scala e Canobbiana - Indice Generale, a spese del compilatore ed editore*. Milan, n. d. (but after 1869).

Slonimsky, Yuri. *'Sil'fida' Balet*. Leningrad: Academia, 1927.

Smart, Mary Ann. 'Redefining Italian Romanticism: Rossini vs. Salvatore Viganò.' Paper presented at the National Meeting of the American Musicological Society. Houston, 2003.

Smith, Marian. *Ballet and Opera in the Age of 'Giselle'*. Princeton: Princeton University Press, 2000.

———. 'Ballet, Opera and Staging Practices at the Paris Opéra', in *La realizzazione scenica dello spettacolo verdiano: Atti del Congreso internazionale di studi. (Parma, 28-30 settembre 1994)*, ed. Pierluigi Petrobelli and Fabrizio Della Seta. Parma: Istituto Nazionale di Studi Verdiani, 1996.

———. 'Borrowings and Original Music: A Dilemma for the Ballet-Pantomime Composer.' *Dance Research* 6, no. 2 (1988): 3-29.

———. 'The Disappearing Danseur.' *Cambridge Opera Journal* 19, no. 1 (2007): 33-57.

———. 'The Earliest Giselle? A Preliminary Report on a St. Petersburg Manuscript.' *Dance Chronicle* 23, no. 1 (2000): 29-48.

———. '*La Sylphide* and *Les Sylphides*', in *Music, Theater, and Cultural Transfer: Paris, 1830-1914*, ed. Annegret Fauser and Mark Everist. Chicago: University of Chicago Press, 2009.

———. 'Music for the Ballet-Pantomime at the Paris Opéra, 1825-1850.' Ph.D. diss., Yale University, 1988.

Soldà, A. *Maria Taglioni: episodi vicentini*. Vicenza: di Gaetano Longo, 1875.

Sowell, Debra. 'A Plurality of Romanticisms: Italian Ballet and the Repertory of Antonio Cortesi and Giovanni Casati.' Paper presented at the National Meeting of the Society of Dance History Scholars. Limerick, 2003.

———. 'Rethinking the Repertory: Genre Descriptors in 19th Century Ballet Libretti', in *L'italia e la danza - Storie e rappresentazioni, stili e tecniche tra teatro, tradizioni popolari e società: Atti del Convegno Internazionale, Accademia Nazionale di Danza, Roma, 13-15 Ottobre 2006*, ed. Alessandro Pontremoli and Giannandrea Poesio. Rome: Aracne, 2008.

———. "Virtue (Almost) Triumphant' Revisited: Of Sylphs and Silfidi.' *Dance Chronicle* 18, no. 2 (1995): 293-301.

Sowell, Madison. 'Poesia e Litografia: Immagini Liriche e Visive del Balletto Romantico in Italia', in *L'italia e la danza. Storie e rappresentazioni, stili e tecniche tra teatro, tradizioni popolari e società: Atti del Convegno Internazionale, Accademia*

Nazionale di Danza, Roma, 13-15 Ottobre 2006, ed. Giannandrea Poesio and Alessandro Pontremoli. Rome: Aracne, 2008.

Sowell, Madison, Debra Sowell, Francesca Falcone, and Patrizia Veroli. Il Balletto Romantico: Tesori Della Collezione Sowell. Palermo: L'Epos, 2007.

Sparti, Barbara, and Judy Van Zile, eds., with E. Ivancich Dunan, N. G. Heller, and A. L. Kaeppler. Imaging Dance - Visual Representations of Dancers and Dancing. Hildesheim: Georg Olms Verlag, 2011.

Stahly, Franz Joseph Arthur. Elementi di un sistema di drammaturgia, ossia di un edificio teorico delle arti drammatiche. Rome: F.lli Bocca, 1881.

———. La mimica e la recitazione drammatica nel riflesso della R. Scuola di Declamazione di Firenze. Rome: Bodoniana, 1881.

Stocchi, Alessandro. Diario del Teatro Ducale di Parma dell'anno 1843, compilato dal portiere al palco scenico Alessandro Stocchi, Giuseppe Rossetti. Parma: Giuseppe Rossetti, 1844.

Strakosch, Maurice. La Sylphide, Fantasie Romantique. New York: W. M. Hall and Son, 1849.

Stravinsky, Igor. Autobiography. New York: Norton, 1936.

Süssmayr, Franz Xaver, Salvatore Viganò, and Giulio Viganò. Il Noce Di Benevento: Ballo Al[l]egorico. Biblioteca Di Musica, Anno 3, Classe 2. Milan: Ricordi, 1822.

Svetlov, Valerien. Le ballet contemporain. Translated by Michel Calvocaressi. Paris: M. de Brunoff, 1912.

Swanston, Roderick. 'Highland Fling by Matthew Bourne, Sadler's Wells 1-5 March 2005.' In Online Review London. http://www.onlinereviewlondon. com/matthew-bourne. Accessed 29 August 2011.

La Sylphide. Directed by René Mathelin, music by J.M. Schneitzhoeffer, performed by the Paris Opéra Ballet. Le Service de la Musique. Sea Bright, NJ: Kultur Inc., 1971. Videocassette.

La Sylphide. Music by J.M. Schneitzhoeffer, Filmed live at the Opéra National de Paris, Palais Garnier in July 2004. Ratingen: TDK, 2005. DVD.

La Sylphide: Ballet in Two Acts. Production after Hans Brenaa, music by H. Løvenskiold, Royal Danish Ballet. West Long Branch, NJ: Kultur, 1988. DVD.

Taglioni, Filippo [and Adolphe Nourrit, unnamed]. La Sylphide. Paris: J.-N. Barba, 1832.

———. Die Sylphide, Ballet in 2 Abtheilungen. Berlin, 1832.

———. The Sylphid: A Ballet in Two Acts by M. Taglioni; the Music by M. Schneitzhoeffer. London: W. Glindon, 183-?

———. Filippo Taglioni, Die Sylphide, Ballet in 2 Abtheilungen. Munich, 1840?

Tangherlini, Timothy R. 'From Trolls to Turks: Change and Continuity in Danish Legend Tradition.' Scandinavian Studies 67, no. 1 (1995): 32–62.

Taruskin, Richard, and Piero Weiss, eds. 'The "Music of the Future" Controversy', in Music in the Western World: A History in Documents. 2nd ed, Belmont, CA: Thomson/Schirmer, 2008.

Testa, Alberto. 'Cronologia dei balli 1740-1936', in Cronologie, vol. 5, ed. Marie-

Thérése Bouquet, Valeria Gualerzi, Alberto Testa and Alberto Basso. Storia Del Teatro Regio Di Torino. Torino: Cassa di Risparmio di Torino, 1988.

———. 'Duecentocinquanta anni di balletto al teatro San Carlo', in *Il Teatro San Carlo*, vol. 3, ed. Bruno Cagli and Agostino Ziino. Naples: Electa, 1987.

———. *I grandi balletti. Repertorio di quattro secoli del teatro di danza*. Rome: Gremese, 1991.

———. 'La Silfide una e due', in *La Silfide, Programma di sala, Teatro dell'opera di Roma, Stagione 1990-91*. Rome: Edizioni del Teatro dell'Opera di Roma.

Théleur, E. A. *Letters on Dancing Reducing This Elegant and Healthful Exercise to Easy Scientific Principles*. London: Sherwood, 1831.

Théleur, E. A., and Sandra Noll Hammond. *Letters on Dancing*. Studies in Dance History. Vol. 2, Pennington, NJ: Society of Dance History Scholars, 1990.

Thesmar, Ghislaine. 'Le Personnage de la Sylphide', in *La Sylphide* Program Book, Paris Opéra. 1990.

Thiele, J.M. *Danmarks Folkesagn*. 2 vols. Vol. 2, Copenhagen: Reitzel, 1843.

Thomas, Helen. 'Reconstruction and dance as embodied textual practice', in *Rethinking Dance History: A Reader*, ed. Alexandra Carter. New York: Routledge, 2004.

Tintori, Giampiero. 'Cronologia completa degli spettacoli e dei concerti', in *Il Teatro alla Scala nella storia e nell'arte (1778-1963)*, ed. Carlo Gatti. Milan: Ricordi, 1964.

Tobias, Tobi. 'An Oral History of the Royal Danish Ballet and Its Bournonville Tradition. ' Archival Materials, Houghton Library, Harvard University.

———. 'The Royal Danish Ballet in New York.' In *Seeing Things*. http://www.artsjournal.com/tobias/2011/06/the_royal_danish_ballet_in_new.html. Accessed 8 September 2011.

Torelli, Serafino. *Analisi generale della mimica*. Milan: Truffi, 1843.

———. *Trattato dell'arte scenica*. Milan: Francesco Albertazzi, 1866.

Trezzini, Lamberto. *Due secoli di vita musicale: Storia del Teatro Comunale di Bologna*. Bologna: Alfa, 1966.

Vaillat, Léandre. 'Danse – *La Sylphide*.' *Le Carrefour*, 9 January 1947.

———. *Histoire de la danse*. Paris: Plon, 1942.

———. *La Taglioni ou la vie d'une danseuse*. Paris: Albin Michel, 1942.

Vedel, Karen. 'Survey of Bournonville Ballets Worldwide', in *Bournonvilleana*, ed. Marianne Hallar and Allette Scavenius. Copenhagen: Rhodos, 1992.

Veroli, Patrizia. *Baccanti e dive dell'aria: donne, danza e società in Italia 1900-1945*. Edimond: Città di Castello, 2001.

Véron, Louis. *Mémoires d'un bourgeois de Paris*. Paris: Librairie Nouvelle, 1856.

Waldie, John. 'Fanny Cerrito', in *Waldie's Select Circulating Library*, vol. 16 [Philadelphia]: A. Waldie, 1841.

Warner, Marina, ed. *Queen Victoria's Sketchbook*. New York: Crown Publishers, 1979.

Weber, Henry, Robert Jamieson, and Sir Walter Scott. *Illustrations of Northern Antiquities*. Edinburgh: J. Ballantyne, 1814.

Wiley, Roland John. *Tchaikovsky's Ballets: Swan Lake, Sleeping Beauty, Nutcracker*. Oxford: Oxford University Press, 1985.

Winter, Marian Hannah. *The Pre-Romantic Ballet*. London: Pitman Publishing, 1974.

Worsaae, Jens Jakob Asmussen. *An Account of the Danes and Norwegians in England, Scotland, and Ireland*. London: J. Murray, 1852.

Zambon, Rita. 'Alla Riscoperta Di Giovanni Galzerani. 1° Parte - L'interprete.' *Chorégraphie* 3, no. 5 (1995): 35-45.

———. 'Alla Riscoperta Di Giovanni Galzerani. 2° Parte - Il Coreografo.' *Chorégraphie* 3, no. 6 (1995): 67-90.

———. 'Quando Il Ballo Anticipa L'opera: 'Il Corsaro' Di Giovanni Galzerani', in *Creature Di Prometeo: Il Ballo Teatrale dal Divertimento al Dramma. Studi Offerti a Aurel M. Milloss*, ed. Giovanni Morelli. Florence: Olschki, 1996.

———. 'Il Gran Teatro la Fenice', in Roberta Albano, Nadia Scafidi, and Rita Zambon. *La danza in Italia: la Scala, la Fenice, il San Carlo dal XVIII Secolo ai Giorni Nostri*. Direzione Flavia Pappacena. Rome: Gremese, 1998, 89-164.

Zecca, Laterza Agostina. *Il Catalogo Numerico Ricordi 1857*. Rome: Nuovo Istituto Editoriale Italiano, 1984.

19th-century periodicals quoted

Italy:
Gazzetta di Genova
Gazzetta musicale di Milano
Gazzetta musicale di Firenze
Gazzetta privilegiata di Venezia
Glissons n'appuyons pas - giornale critico-letterario d'arti, teatri e varietà [Milan]
Italia Musicale [Milan]
La Musica [Naples]
Il Pirata [Milan]
Strenna Teatrale Europea [Milan]
Teatri, arti e letteratura [Bologna]

Paris:
Le Journal des débats
Le Petit Journal
La Presse
La Revue et gazette musicale
La Revue musicale

Index

CPSIA information can be obtained at www.ICGtesting.com
Printed in the USA
LVOW10s1905260114

371006LV00004B/50/P